KU-263-891

Politics in the European Union

ACC. No: 02563288

Politics in the
EUROPEAN UNION

SECOND EDITION

Ian Bache

Stephen George

OXFORD

UNIVERSITY PRESS

341/2422
/BAC

320.94

OXFORD
UNIVERSITY PRESS

Great Clarendon Street, Oxford OX2 6DP

Oxford University Press is a department of the University of Oxford.
It furthers the University's objective of excellence in research, scholarship,
and education by publishing worldwide in

Oxford New York

Auckland Cape Town Dar es Salaam Hong Kong Karachi
Kuala Lumpur Madrid Melbourne Mexico City Nairobi
New Delhi Shanghai Taipei Toronto

With offices in

Argentina Austria Brazil Chile Czech Republic France Greece
Guatemala Hungary Italy Japan Poland Portugal Singapore
South Korea Switzerland Thailand Turkey Ukraine Vietnam

Oxford is a registered trademark of Oxford University Press
in the UK and in certain other countries

Published in the United States
by Oxford University Press Inc., New York

© Ian Bache & Stephen George, 2006

The moral rights of the authors have been asserted
Database right Oxford University Press (maker)

First published 2006

All rights reserved. No part of this publication may be reproduced,
stored in a retrieval system, or transmitted, in any form or by any means,
without the prior permission in writing of Oxford University Press,
or as expressly permitted by law, or under terms agreed with the appropriate
reprographics rights organizations. Enquiries concerning reproduction
outside the scope of the above should be sent to the Rights Department,
Oxford University Press, at the address above

You must not circulate this book in any other binding or cover
and you must impose this same condition on any acquirer

British Library Cataloguing in Publication Data

Data available

Library of Congress Cataloging in Publication Data

Data available

Typeset by Laserwords Private Limited, Chennai, India
Printed in Great Britain
on acid-free paper by
Ashford Colour Press Limited, Gosport, Hampshire

ISBN 0-19-927658-7   978-0-19-927658-5

10 9 8 7 6 5 4 3 2 1

Dedicated to our families:

Pamela, Thomas, and Anna;

Linda, Margaret, and Alan.

GREENLAND
(Denmark)

Jan Mayen
(Norway)

ICELAND

Arctic Circle

Norwegian Sea

ATLANTIC
OCEAN

Faroe Islands
(Denmark)

Shetland
Islands
(U. K.)

Orkney Islands
(U. K.)

*North
Sea*

SWEDEN

FINLAND

NORWAY

DENMARK

ESTONIA

LATVIA

LITHUANIA

RUSSIA

BELARUS

Baltic Sea

RUSSIA

UNITED
KINGDOM

IRELAND

English Channel

NETHERLANDS

BELGIUM

GERMANY

POLAND

UKRAINE

LUXEMBURG

CZECH REP.

SLOVAKIA

MOLDOVA

AUSTRIA

HUNGARY

ROMANIA

FRANCE

SWITZERLAND

LIECHTENSTEIN

SLOVENIA

CROATIA

BOSNIA &
HERZEGOVINA

Serbia and
Montenegro

BULGARIA

Black Sea

TURKEY

*Bay
of
Biscay*

SAN
MARINO

MONACO

ANDORRA

Corsica
(France)

Adriatic Sea

MACEDONIA

ALBANIA

*Bosporus
Strait*

PORTUGAL

SPAIN

*Balearic Islands
(Spain)*

Sardinia
(Italy)

ITALY

GREECE

*Aegean
Sea*

CYPRUS

Mediterranean Sea

Sicily
(Italy)

A F R I C A

MALTA

Crete
(Greece)

The Original Six
(Belgium, France, Germany, Italy
Luxemburg, Netherlands)

The First Enlargement
(Britain, Denmark, Ireland, 1973)

The Mediterranean Enlargement
(Greece, 1981; Portugal,
Spain, 1986)

The EFTA Enlargement
(Austria, Finland, Sweden, 1995)

The Eastern Enlargement
(Czech Republic, Estonia, Hungary,
Latria,Lithuania, Poland, Slovakia, Sloven
Cyprus, Malta, 2004)

Brief Contents

Detailed Contents

Part One Theory   1

Part Three Institutions   227

About the Authors

Ian Bache is Senior Lecturer in Politics at the University of Sheffield. He took his first degree in Politics and Parliamentary Studies at the University of Leeds and worked as a researcher in the House of Commons, the US Congress, and for a UK/EU public sector interest group, before completing an MA in International Studies and PhD at the University of Sheffield. Most recently he completed an MEd in Teaching and Learning for University Lecturers at the University of Sheffield.

He has published widely on the European Union and related issues, including: *The Politics of European Union Regional Policy* UACES/Sheffield Academic Press, 1998; *Politics in the European Union*, 1st edition (with Stephen George), Oxford University Press, 2001; *Multi-Level Governance* (with Matthew Flinders), Oxford University Press, 2004; and *The Europeanization of British Politics?* (with Andrew Jordan), Palgrave Macmillan, 2006. He is currently writing a book on *Europeanization and Multi-Level Governance* for Rowman and Littlefield, due for publication in 2007.

He has published scholarly articles in a range of academic journals, including the *British Journal of Politics and International Relations*; *Current Politics and Economics of Europe*; *Journal of Common Market Studies*; *Journal of European Public Policy*; *Journal of Public Policy*; *Local Government Studies*; *Political Studies*; *Public Administration*; *Public Policy and Administration*; *Regional and Federal Studies*; and *Scandinavian Political Studies*.

Between 2003 and 2005, Dr Bache convened the UACES Study Group and ESRC Seminar Series on The Europeanization of British Politics and Policy-Making, and is currently Reviews Editor of the *Journal of European Integration*. He is an experienced teacher, having taught numerous undergraduate and postgraduate courses, and has supervised a number of PhD students to completion.

Stephen George taught in the Department of Politics at the University of Sheffield for thirty years, the last ten as Professor. During that time he authored or co-authored four major books on the European Community/European Union, two of which—*Politics and Policy in the European Union* and *An Awkward Partner: Britain in the European Union*—went into multiple editions. He also edited books on Europe, contributed some two dozen chapters to edited books, and articles to several academic journals, including *The Annals of the American Academy of Political and Social Science, The British Journal of International Studies, Contemporary Record, Current Politics and Economics of Europe, European Access, International Affairs, Journal of European Integration, Journal of European Public Policy, Millennium: Journal of International Studies, Modern History Review, West European Politics*, and *The World Today*. He has given innumerable talks, guest lectures, and conference papers throughout the world, mostly on aspects of the European Union. Between 1997 and 2000 he was Chair of the University Association for

Contemporary European Studies (UACES). As a teacher he successfully supervised eight PhD students, and for undergraduate students devised innovative teaching materials on the European Union, including a simulation exercise in European decision making. Since 2003 he has been Emeritus Professor of Politics, retired from active teaching and administration, but still involved in research and writing.

About the Book

This is a textbook on the study of the European Union (EU) within the cognate disciplines of political science and international relations. It reflects both the most significant contributions to the study of the EU within these disciplines and the gaps in existing research. It is designed to be used by students as part of a university course or module, although we hope it works well for the independent reader also.

While we would argue that there is no easy separation between economics and politics, or between law and politics, this book is explicitly concerned with politics in the EU. Thus we address some of the standard issues of the disciplines of political science and international relations. Is the EU developing into a super-state of some sort? If so, of what sort? Have national governments voluntarily surrendered sovereignty to European institutions, or are there forces at work dragging member states towards ever closer union against the will of the governments? Is the process driven by vested interests that stand to benefit from it, or by ideas that place a positive value on international integration? Does the process have legitimacy in the eyes of the people who are being brought into an ever closer union? If so, why? If not, why not?

These questions are relevant not because of their practical importance—although they do have a great deal of practical importance; nor because they figure in the coverage of the EU in the media—although because of their practical importance they do so figure. Rather, they are relevant because they are questions generated by the theories of political scientists and students of international relations about the nature of European integration and of the EU. Academic disciplines are formed when scholars are brought together by shared concerns, and they are forged by academic debates, which are fiercest when they are between advocates of different theories. That is why the textbook begins with theory. It is theory that provides our criteria of relevance. Many eclectic textbooks do exist in politics and international relations, books that never mention theory—and we are not thinking here exclusively of books on the EU. Our view is that theory is very important. It shapes what is studied and what is not, what is included and what is excluded. We see it as central to the study of the EU and not as an optional extra. However, for those who wish to know something of the EU before approaching theoretical issues, it is possible to read the History section of the book first without having read the Theory section: it is primarily the conclusions to the history chapters that refer back to the theories in Part 1.

The History section in this edition contains an expanded treatment of the Treaty of Amsterdam, and three new chapters covering subsequent developments. Of course, it is difficult to know where to draw the line when writing a history. In the Introduction to the first edition of this book we said: 'the European Union is a dynamic entity, a "moving target"'. The truth of both these statements came home to us forcefully when the first drafts of this edition were completed, and we were sitting waiting for the referees' comments to come back, and the French and Dutch rejections of the Constitutional Treaty threatened to plunge the EU into crisis. At the time of writing, the significance of these votes was still unravelling. Because of this, we have ended the History section (Part II) at the referendums. Information on what the Constitution would have meant for the institutions has been included in Part III (Institutions) because it is likely that some at least of these reforms will be implemented in some form in the future, but also because the terms of the Constitution that was rejected remain of considerable interest despite its apparent demise.

As the comments above illustrate, there is always a problem about keeping up with events in a subject such as ours. This book was as contemporary as we could make it when it left our hands. It will have been overtaken by new developments by the time it reaches yours. But it will lead you to the point where you can understand the background to contemporary developments in the EU as reported in the media.

Change happens not only in the field of study, but also in the study of the field. Since the first edition of the book, the study of the EU has expanded tremendously. The volume of academic literature that has appeared in the intervening four years surprised even us when we came to bring the text up to date, and we had both been teaching the subject, so we were already familiar with much of it. In the area of theory the developments have been particularly rich and varied. We have added two completely new chapters to this section. Obviously the output did not just stop when we finished writing, so there will be more for the student to explore, but we think that this edition is as up-to-date on the academic literature as it could be. The strong rooting of the text in the research literature is one of the distinctive features of this book.

We have also made changes in response to the comments made to us about the first edition. In consultation with Jane Clayton and the production team at Oxford University Press we have worked to make the pedagogical features more useful. In the updated Policies section we have added a new introductory chapter on policy making in the EU, and the previous chapter on External Relations has been split into two separate chapters on External Economic Relations and the Common Foreign and Security Policy (respectively).

Those familiar with the first edition of this book cannot fail to notice that the old Part III, on the member states, has disappeared from this edition. We apologize to those colleagues who valued that part of the book and used it in their teaching. It was a tremendous challenge to write that part when there were fifteen member states; with twenty-five it was beyond us. We have sought to address issues relating to the member states thematically, not least through the addition of a new section on Europeanization in Part 1. In addition, some material on the member states will be available via the book's Online Resource Centre.

Guided Tour of Textbook Features

This text is enriched with a range of pedagogic tools to help you navigate the text material and reinforce your knowledge of Politics in the European Union. This guided tour shows you how to get the most out of your textbook package and do better in your politics studies.

CHAPTER O

The period bega
Union of 25 sta
leaving the EU

OVERVIEW

d began with the 2004 enlargement, an ambi
f 25 states. However, it closed with perhaps the
awn up at the Paris Peace Conference in the Com
and the Netherlands created uncertainty about the legi
of the European project. Butthe problem sratifying the t
nificant problems in this period. This chapter looks at th
for the new member states, which raised issues that cha
asm for membership in some states, but also illustrated
then turns to the EU elections and the diffcult approval
mission. It reflects on the progress towards the objectiv
considering the ratification crisis.

Chapter overviews

Brief overviews at the beginning of every chapter set the scene for themes and issues to be discussed, and indicate the scope of coverage within each chapter topic.

INSIGHT 5.1

The League of

ns was inspired by the vision of US Pres
awn up at the Paris Peace Conference in 19
refused to ratify the Treaty so the United States never becar
League.

· The League Covenant committed the states that signed to r
territorial integrity of other states, and not to resort to force
submit them to arbitration by the League

· The League's institutional structure consisted of a General A
states were represented, and a Council. The Council had fou
members—Britain France Italy Japan; then Germany from

'Insight' boxes

A number of topics benefit from further explanation or exploration in a manner that does not disrupt the flow of the main text. Throughout the book, 'Insight' boxes provide you with extra information on particular topics that complement your understanding of the main chapter text.

France and Germany's smaller neighbours it was still a
-emergence of a threat to their sovereign independence

rs tried to pr   as cru   ugh a traditional mil-
participati   d France in N   This approach pro-
etween B   the Benelux sta   ch 1947, and the
itain, Frar   German aggressi   s in March 1948.
ore at fore   n than they were at

tried to pre   e of any Germanstate.
ce would have liked to have kept Germany underallied
ted the former German state to be divided into a large
By1949 it had become apparent that this was not going

Glossary terms

The field of politics has its own language. To help you learn this language, key terms are bold-faced in the text and defined in a glossary at the end of the text, to aid you in exam revision.

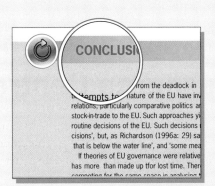

Conclusions

Conclusions at the end of each chapter reflect on the significance of conceptual and theoretical themes developed in Part I of the book, and relate these back to the material you have just read.

Key Points

Following each Conclusion is a set of Key Points that summarize the most important arguments developed within each chapter topic, and that are organized under the headings used in each chapter to facilitate revision and cross-checking with the main text.

Further Reading

To take your learning further, reading lists have been provided as a guide to find out more about the issues raised within each chapter topic and to help you locate the key academic literature in the field. At the end of each Further Reading section is an indication of what further helpful material might be accessed on the Online Resource Centre that accompanies this book.

Online Resource Centre

To take your learning further, reading lists have been provided as a guide to find out more about the issues raised within each chapter topic and to help you locate the key academic literature in the field. At the end of each Further Reading section is an indication of what further helpful material might be accessed on the Online Resource Centre that accompanies this book.

Guided Tour of Online Resource Centre

 online resource centre

www.oxfordtextbooks.co.uk/orc
bache_george2e/

The Online Resource Centre that accompanies this book provides students and instructors with ready-to-use teaching and learning materials. These resources are free of charge and designed to maximise the learning experience.

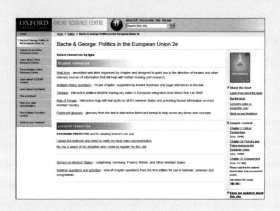

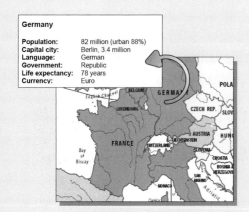

Interactive map of Europe

To better visualise the process of EU integration, an interactive map of Europe has been provided with 'hot-spots' on each of the member countries. Simply click on the member state you are interested in knowing more about, and read the pop-up window containing vital social and political facts about that state and its role in EU politics.

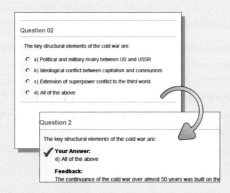

Multiple-choice questions

The best way to reinforce your understanding of EU politics is through frequent and cumulative revision. As such, a bank of self-marking multiple-choice questions have been provided for each chapter of the text, and include instant feedback on your answers and cross-references back to the main textbook to assist with independent self-study.

Web links

A series of annotated web links organised by chapter have been provided to point you in the direction of important treaties, working papers, articles and other relevant sources of political information, and to keep you informed of the latest developments in European integration.

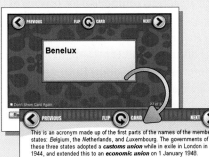

Flashcard glossary

A series of interactive flashcards containing key terms and concepts have been provided to test your understanding of EU terminology and help you master the language of politics before exams.

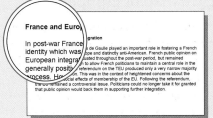

Dedicated chapters on the 'Big Three' member states

In-depth material on Germany, France and Britain has been taken from the previous edition of this textbook and provided in electronic format for those interested in a more thorough examination of the 'Big Three' member states.

Seminar questions and activities (instructors only)

A suite of challenging revision questions and activities that encourage class debate and reinforce understanding of key chapter themes have been provided for use by instructors in tutorials, seminars and assignments.

Acknowledgements

This is the second edition of a textbook that first appeared in 2001. In revising it we have been helped enormously by the comments of colleagues and students who used the first edition. We are particularly grateful to those academic colleagues who acted as anonymous referees for the drafts of the second edition (they are identified and credited by the publisher elsewhere in this volume) and also to Linda McAvan MEP, who commented on sections of Part 3 (Institutions). We have tried to incorporate as many of these comments as possible, but some we have not been able to accommodate for reasons of time, space, and the limits of our own competence.

We would like to thank all the production staff at Oxford University Press—the Production Editor, Nicola Bateman, the Copy-Editor, Susan Beer, Designers Tim Branch and Charlotte Dobbs; and especially our Commissioning Editor, Ruth Anderson, and Development Editor, Jane Clayton for their advice, assistance and patience, in what has been a long and demanding process. Especial thanks also to our respective partners, Pamela and Linda, for their continued support.

We have been tremendously encouraged by the positive feedback that we have received both on the first edition and, from the referees, on the drafts of this edition. We hope that it will prove a stimulating textbook for teachers and students alike, and will lead to interesting and critical debates in seminars.

Ian Bache
Stephen George
November 2005

Reviewers

This text has benefited from the thoughtful criticisms and valuable insights of a range of politics experts across Britain, and Oxford University Press would like to acknowledge all of the reviewers for their contribution to the book, which include but are not limited to:

ALISTAIR SHEPHERD, University of Wales (Aberystwyth)
SUE MILNER, University of Bath
ALISON STATHAM, De Montfort University
ANGELA BOURNE, University of Dundee
ANDREW MACMULLEN, Durham University
VASSILIKI KOUTRAKOU, University of East Anglia
DAVID HOWARTH, University of Edinburgh
MICHAEL BURGESS, University of Hull
ROBERT LADRECH, Keele University
THOMAS LUNDBERG, Keele University
NICK ROBINSON, University of Leeds
HELEN DRAKE, Loughborough University
DIMITRIS PAPADIMITRIOU, University of Manchester
STEPHEN DAY, University of Newcastle
ANDREAS BIELER, University of Nottingham
LORI THORLAKSON, University of Nottingham
LEE MCGOWAN, Queen's University Belfast
CHRISTOS KASSIMERIS, University of Reading
ALAN REID, Robert Gordon University
FRANK GREGORY, University of Southampton
FRANCIS MCGOWAN, University of Sussex
PHILIPPA SHERRINGTON, University of Warwick

This part of the book consists of four chapters. Its purpose is two-fold: first, to review the main theories used in the study of the European Union; and second, to identify themes that will inform our analysis of subsequent chapters. We do not see this exercise as being an optional extra for a textbook: it is fundamental to understanding the academic study of the European integration and the European Union (EU).

Our understanding of the world is guided by our particular conceptual lenses or theoretical frameworks, whether we are aware of them or not. The theoretical frameworks we adopt determine the questions we ask, and so the answers that we find. Thus, as Rosamond (2003: 110) suggests, understanding theory is not a self-indulgent exercise that is optional to students of the EU: 'Rather, being conscious about the theoretical propositions chosen by authors is vital because alternative "readings" of the EU and European integration follow from alternative theoretical premises.'

There has been no shortage of theoretical models and frameworks applied to understanding the European Union and we provide an overview of what to us appear to be the most important. While doing this inevitably requires a degree of choice, there is considerable consensus among scholars about particular phases in the study of the EU, which our selection reflects.

The first phase of study, during the early stages of co-operation between west European states, was dominated by approaches from the study of international relations. As the EU became more established and institutionalized, international relations approaches were increasingly accompanied by insights from the study of domestic governance, public policy, and comparative politics. The most straightforward way of understanding this theoretical shift is to see it as a move away from treating the EU as an international organization similar to others (such as the North Atlantic Treaty Organization—NATO) to seeing it as something unique among international bodies. The uniqueness here relates both to the nature and to the extent of its development, which means that at least in some areas of activity the EU displays properties more akin to national political systems than to those of international organizations.

While the traditional international relations theories set out in Chapter 1, 'Theories of European Integration', and the later theoretical developments set out in Chapter 2, 'Theories of EU Governance', continue to provide important contributions to the study of the EU, they have been joined by more critical perspectives that question many of the assumptions on which established theories of the EU were based. Questions about the nature of knowledge and how we should study the world are central to the rationalist–reflectivist debate, which has become a key component of EU studies in recent times. The contributions covered in Chapter 3, 'Critical Perspectives', are organized under the themes of *social constructivism* and *critical political economy*. In our final chapter in this section, we turn to attempts to theorize some of the most important implications of European integration. Specifically, Chapter 4, 'Theorizing Consequences', looks at the contribution of *Europeanization* to understanding the consequences of European integration for domestic politics and governance, while the second part of the chapter is devoted to approaches to understanding the challenges for *democracy*.

CHAPTER 1

Theories of European Integration

CHAPTER OVERVIEW

The dominant approaches to understanding the early phase of European integration came from international relations (IR). In particular, the study of integration was dominated by the competing approaches of neofunctionalism and intergovernmentalism. Although neofunctionalist theory neatly fitted events in the 1950s and early 1960s, subsequent events led to its demise and the rise of intergovernmentalist explanations. While theorizing European integration has moved on significantly from these early approaches, much of what followed was either framed by this debate or developed as a rejection of it. The debate about whether the EU is characterized by intergovernmentalism or supranationalism still informs much of the academic work on the subject.

> 'international theory' has been too readily written off by contemporary writers seeking to offer theoretical treatments of the EU
> (Rosamond 1999: 19)

The signing of the Treaty of Paris in April 1951 by the governments of Belgium, France, Germany, Italy, Luxemburg, and the Netherlands (Chapter 6, p. 94) began the process commonly referred to as European integration (see Insight 1.1). This process has meant that the economies of participating states, and subsequently other policy areas, have been increasingly managed in common. Decisions previously taken by national governments alone are now taken together with other governments, and specially created European institutions. Governments have relinquished the sole right to make legislation over a range of matters (national sovereignty), in favour of joint decision making with other governments (pooled sovereignty). Other tasks have been delegated to European institutions.

It was something of a surprise to academic theorists of IR when governments in western Europe began to surrender their national sovereignty in some policy areas. For the first half of the twentieth century the nation state seemed assured of its place as the most important unit of political life in the western world, especially in Europe. As such, the process of European integration constituted a major challenge to existing theories and

INSIGHT 1.1

European Integration

European integration has a number of aspects, but the main focus of Chapter 1 is on *political* integration. E. B. Haas (1968: 16) provided a definition of European political integration as a *process*, whereby:

political actors in several distinct national settings are persuaded to shift their loyalties, expectations and political activities toward a new center, whose institutions possess or demand jurisdiction over the pre-existing national states. The end result of a process of political integration is a new political community, superimposed over the pre-existing ones.

Implicit in Haas's definition was the development of a European federal state. More cautiously, Lindberg (1963: 149), provided a definition of political integration as a process, but without reference to an end point:

political integration is (1) the process whereby nations forego the desire and ability to conduct foreign and key domestic policies independently of each other, seeking instead to make joint decisions or to delegate the decision-making process to new central organs; and (2) the process whereby political actors in several distinct national settings are persuaded to shift their expectations and political activities to a new center.

The first part of this definition refers to two 'intimately related' modes of decision making: sharing and delegating. The second part of the definition refers to 'the patterns of behaviour shown by high policy makers, civil servants, parliamentarians, interest group leaders and other élites' (Lindberg 1963: 149), who respond to the new reality of a shift in political authority to the centre by reorientating their political activities to the European level.

generated an academic debate about the role of the state in the process. The two competing theories that emerged from IR to dominate the debate over early developments in European integration were neofunctionalism (E. B. Haas 1958; Lindberg 1963) and intergovernmentalism (Hoffmann 1964; 1966).

Before discussing these two main positions in the debate, it is necessary to consider the intellectual context from which the idea of European integration emerged. Below we look first at the functionalist ideas of David Mitrany on how to avoid war between nations, then at the ideas of the European federalists, and finally at the 'federal-functionalism' of Jean Monnet. We then turn to look first at neofunctionalism and then at intergovernmentalism before looking at two later contributions to this debate, liberal intergovernmentalism and supranational governance.

The Intellectual Background

To understand the ideas that fed into the first attempts to theorize European integration, it is useful to start with one of the approaches that was influential after the Second World War about how to avoid another war. This 'functionalist' idea, which was particularly associated with the writings of David Mitrany, informed the United Nations movement. It was a theory of how to achieve world peace, rather than a theory of regional integration, and it took a very different approach to the question from the European federalists, who wanted to subordinate national governments to an overarching federal authority. The ideas of both the functionalists and the federalists were brought together in the 'functional-federalism' of Jean Monnet, which in turn provided one important source of intellectual inspiration for the neofunctionalist theory of European integration.

Mitrany and Functionalism

David Mitrany (1888–1974) was born in Romania, but spent most of his adult life in Britain and the United States. He was not a theorist of European integration. His concern was with building a *Working Peace System*, the title of his Fabian pamphlet (Mitrany 1966; first published 1943). For Mitrany, the root cause of war was nationalism. The failure of the League of Nations to prevent aggression prompted debate even before the outbreak of the Second World War about a new type of international system. For those who blamed the failure of the League on its limited powers, the response was the development of an international federation. In other words, the League had not gone far enough and the same mistake should not be repeated: henceforth, nations should be tied more closely together.

Mitrany did not agree with the idea of federation as the means of tying states together. He opposed the idea of a single world government because he believed that it would pose a threat to individual freedom. He also opposed the creation of regional federations, believing this would simply reproduce national rivalries on a larger scale. Any political reorganization into separate units must sooner or later produce the same effects; any international system that is to usher in a new world must produce the opposite effect of subduing political division.

Instead of either of these possibilities—a world federation or regional federations—Mitrany proposed the creation of a whole series of separate international functional agencies, each having authority over one specific area of human life. His scheme was to take individual technical tasks out of the control of governments and to hand them over to these functional agencies. He believed that governments would be prepared to surrender control because they would not feel threatened by the loss of sovereignty over, say, health care or the co-ordination of railway timetables, and they would be able to appreciate the advantages of such tasks being performed at the regional or world level. As more and more areas of control were surrendered, states would become less capable of independent action. One day the national governments would discover that they were enmeshed in a 'spreading web of international activities and agencies' (Mitrany 1966: 35)

These international agencies would operate at different levels depending on the function that they were performing. Mitrany gave the example of systems of communication. Railways would be organized on a continental basis; shipping would be organized on an intercontinental basis; aviation would be organized on a universal basis. Not only would the dependence of states on these agencies for their day-to-day functioning make it difficult for governments to break with them, the experience of the operation of the agencies would also socialize politicians, civil servants, and the general public into adopting less nationalistic attitudes and outlook.

Spinelli and Federalism

A completely different approach to guaranteeing peace was devised during the war in the ranks of the various Resistance movements. It was a specifically European movement, and whereas Mitrany aimed explicitly to depoliticize the process of the transfer of power away from national governments, federalists sought a clear transfer of political authority.

The European Union of Federalists (EUF) was formed in December 1946 from the war-time Resistance movements. It was particularly strong in Italy, where the leading figure was Altiero Spinelli. Federalism appealed to the Resistance groups because it proposed superseding nationalism. It is important to bear in mind that whereas in Britain (and Russia) the Second World War was a nationalist war (in the former Soviet Union it was 'the great patriotic war'), in countries such as France and Italy it was an ideological war. Resistance fighters drawn from Communist, Socialist, and Christian democratic groups were in many cases fighting their own countrymen—Vichy supporters in unoccupied France, Italian Fascists in Italy.

While being held as political prisoners of the Fascists on the island of Ventotene, Spinelli and Ernesto Rossi (1897–1967) produced the Ventotene Manifesto (1941), calling for a 'European Federation'. It argued that, left alone, the classes 'most privileged under old national systems' would seek to reconstruct the order of nation states at the end of the war. While these states might appear democratic, it would only be a matter of time before power returned to the hands of the privileged classes. This would prompt the return of national jealousies and ultimately, to renewed war between states. To prevent this development, the Manifesto called for the abolition of the division of Europe into national, sovereign states. It urged propaganda and action to bring together the separate national Resistance movements across Europe to push for the creation of a federal European state.

The EUF adopted the Ventotene Manifesto, and began agitating for an international conference to be called that would draw up a federal constitution for Europe. This ambitious proposal was designed to build on what Milward called 'the wave of hope for a better world and a changed future for the human race which had swept across Europe' and which included an 'extraordinary wave of enthusiasm for European federation' (Milward 1984: 55).

The strategy of the EUF was to exploit the disruption caused by the war to existing political structures in order to make a new start on a radically different basis from the Europe of national states. They aimed to achieve a complete break from the old order of nation states, and to create a federal constitution for Europe. Their Congress took time to organize, though. It eventually took place in The Hague in May 1948 (see Ch. 5, p. 84). By that time the national political systems had been re-established, and what emerged from the Congress was an intergovernmental organization, the Council of Europe, not the new federal constitutional order that the federalists had hoped for. Many federalists then turned to the gradualist approach that was successfully embodied in the European Coal and Steel Community (ECSC).

Monnet and Functional–Federalism

The plan for the ECSC was known as the Schuman Plan because it was made public by the French Foreign Minister Robert Schuman, but it is generally accepted that it was drawn up within the French Economic Planning Commission (*Commissariat du Plan*), which was headed by the technocrat Jean Monnet. It was the task of the Planning Commission to guide the post-war reconstruction and modernization of the French economy, and it was through his experiences in this task that Monnet came to appreciate the economic inadequacy of the European nation state in the modern world. He saw the need to create a 'large and dynamic common market', 'a huge continental market on the European scale' (Monnet 1962: 205). He aimed, though, to create more than just a common market.

Monnet was a planner: he showed no great confidence in the free-market system, which had served France rather badly in the past. He placed his faith in the development of **supranational institutions** as the basis for building a genuine economic community that would adopt common economic policies and rational planning procedures. Coal and steel were only intended as starting points. The aim was to extend integration to all aspects of the west European economy; but such a scheme would have been too ambitious to gain acceptance all at once. There had been a clear indication of this in the failure of previous efforts to integrate the economies of France, Italy, the Netherlands, Belgium, and Luxemburg.

There was also a new factor in the equation, the key factor prompting Monnet's plan: the emergence in 1949 of a sovereign West German state. For Monnet, the existence of the Federal Republic of Germany posed two problems in addition to that of how to create an integrated western European economy. The first problem was how to organize Franco-German relations in such a way that another war between the two states would become impossible. To a French mind this meant how to control Germany. The pooling of coal and steel production would provide the basis for economic development as a first step towards a 'federation of Europe', and by stimulating the expansion of those industries for peaceful purposes would provide an economic alternative to producing war materials for those regions of Europe that had been largely dependent on providing military material. The second problem facing Monnet was the very practical one of how to ensure adequate supplies of coking coal from the Ruhr for the French steel industry. The idea of pooling Franco-German supplies of coal and steel would tie the two states into a mutual economic dependency, in addition to taking out of the immediate control of the national governments the most basic raw materials for waging another war.

Mitrany (1966) described Monnet's strategy as 'federal-functionalism'. It is not clear, though, how far Monnet was a federalist at all. He might be seen as a supreme pragmatist who proposed the ECSC as a solution to the very practical problems described above. To solve these problems Monnet adopted a solution similar to that of Mitrany: remove control of the strategically crucial industries—coal and steel—from the governments and put it in the hands of a free-standing agency. This was the High Authority of the ECSC, and in Monnet's original plan it was the only institution proposed. The development of other supranational institutions came from other pressures (see Ch. 7). The High Authority was the prototype for the later Commission of the EEC, which became central to the neofunctionalist theory of European integration.

International Relations Theories of European Integration

Realism was the dominant approach in IR in the 1950s. It assumed that sovereign states formed the fundamental units of analysis for understanding international relations. The appearance of the EC therefore provided fertile ground for those who wished to develop a critique of this dominant approach. Neofunctionalism was the name given to the first theoretical attempt to understand European integration. Its implied critique of realism led to a counter-theory from within a broadly state-centred perspective, which became known as intergovernmentalism. The debate between these two broad positions has evolved over time, but the central issues of dispute remain much the same today as they were in the 1950s.

Neofunctionalism

Starting with the analysis of the ECSC by Ernst Haas (1958), a body of theorizing about European integration known as neofunctionalism was built up in the writings of a group of US academics (see Insight 1.1, p. 4). These theorists drew on the work of Mitrany and Monnet in particular. In addition to Haas, the main figures in this school of analysis were Leon Lindberg (1963, 1966), and Philippe Schmitter (1970).

Neofunctionalism was a pluralist theory of international politics. In contrast to the more traditional realist theories, it did not assume that a state was a single unified actor; nor did it assume that states were the only actors on the international stage. In the concepts that it used it anticipated later writings on global interdependence (Keohane and Nye 1977).

In the first period of European integration, neofunctionalism appeared to be winning the theoretical debate. Neofunctionalism sought to explain 'how and why they (states) voluntarily mingle, merge and mix with their neighbours so as to lose the factual attributes of sovereignty while acquiring new techniques for resolving conflict between themselves' (Haas 1970: 610). There were four key parts to the neofunctionalist argument:

(1) The concept of the 'state' is more complex than realists suggested.

(2) The activities of interest groups and bureaucratic actors are not confined to the domestic political arena.

(3) Non-state actors are important in international politics.

(4) European integration is advanced through 'spillover' pressures.

In contrast to realists, neofunctionalists argued that the international activities of states were the outcome of a pluralistic political process in which government decisions were influenced by pressures from various interest groups and bureaucratic actors. In common with the general tenor of US political science at the time, it was often assumed that these pressures constituted the complete explanation for government decisions. So, if the analyst could identify the strength and direction of the various pressures accurately, it would be possible to make predictions about government behaviour in international relations.

Using the concepts that were later called 'transnationalism' and 'transgovernmentalism' (Keohane and Nye 1977: 129–30), neofunctionalists expected nationally based interest groups to make contact with similar groups in other countries (transnationalism), and departments of state to forge links with their counterparts in other states, unregulated by their respective foreign offices (transgovernmentalism).

Neofunctionalists pointed to the activities of multinational corporations to illustrate their argument that non-state actors are important in international politics. However, for neofunctionalists, the European Commission was the most important non-state international actor. The Commission was believed to be in a unique position to manipulate both domestic and international pressures on national governments to advance the process of European integration, even where governments might be reluctant. This contrasted with realist explanations of international relations that focused exclusively on the international role of states.

Neofunctionalists used the concept of spillover to explain how once national governments took the initial steps towards integration, the process took on a life of its own, and swept governments along further than they anticipated going. As Lindberg (1963: 10) put it:

In its most general formulation, 'spillover' refers to a situation in which a given action, related to a specific goal, creates a situation in which the original goal can be assured only by taking further actions, which in turn create a further condition and a need for more action, and so forth.

Two types of spillover were important to early neofunctionalist writers: functional and political. A third type, cultivated spillover, was added by later theorists to explain the part played by the Commission in fostering integration.

Functional spillover argued that modern industrial economies were made up of interconnected parts. As such, it was not possible to isolate one sector from others. Following this understanding, neofunctionalists argued that if member states integrated one functional sector of their economies, the interconnectedness between this sector and others would lead to a 'spillover' into other sectors. Technical pressures would prompt integration in those related sectors, and the integration of one sector would only work if other functionally related sectors were also integrated. For example, if a joint attempt were made to increase coal production across member states, it would prove necessary to bring other forms of energy into the scheme. Otherwise, a switch by one member state away from coal towards a reliance on oil or nuclear fuels would throw out all of the calculations for coal production. In addition, any effective planning of the total energy supply would involve gathering data about future total demand, implying the development of overall plans for industrial output across member states. (For other examples see Insight 1.2.)

To this technical logic of functional spillover, the neofunctionalists added the idea of political spillover, and set perhaps more store by this than by functional spillover in explaining the process of integration. Political spillover involved the build-up of political pressures in favour of further integration within the states involved. Once one sector of the economy was integrated, the interest groups operating in that sector would have to exert pressure at the supranational level, on the organization charged with running their sector. So the creation of the ECSC would lead to the representatives of the coal and steel industries in all the member states switching at least a part of their political lobbying from national governments to the new supranational agency the High Authority. Relevant trade unions and consumer groups would follow suit.

It was argued that once these interest groups had switched the focus of their activity to the European level, they would rapidly come to appreciate the benefits available to them as a result of the integration of their sector. Further, they would also come to understand the barriers that prevented these benefits from being fully realized. As the main barrier would be that integration in one sector could not be effective without the integration of other sectors, these interest groups would become advocates of further integration and would lobby their governments to this end. At the same time they would form a barrier themselves against governments retreating from the level of integration that had already been achieved. This was important because such a retreat would be the one alternative way in which pressures caused by functional spillover could be resolved. In addition, governments would come under pressure from other interest groups who would see the advantages accruing to their counterparts in the integrated sector and realize that they could profit similarly if their sectors of the economy were also integrated.

INSIGHT 1.2

Three Illustrations of Functional Spillover

(1) From removing tariff barriers to a common monetary policy

If tariff barriers (i.e. import taxes) were removed on trade between member states, this would not in itself create a common market. So long as the rates of exchange between national currencies were allowed to fluctuate, prices would be unpredictable and no genuinely unified market would develop. At the same time, national governments would find it much more difficult to control their economies' performance once they could no longer turn to tariffs to regulate imports. They would be forced to use their individual powers over monetary policy to change the exchange rate more often, thereby increasing monetary instability and making a genuine common market even less likely. The removal of tariffs would therefore increase the pressure for governments to surrender control over their national exchange rates as well: it would prove necessary to move towards a common monetary policy in order to make a reality of the common market.

(2) From a common monetary policy, to a common economic policy, to a common regional policy

A common monetary policy would make it almost impossible for governments to control their domestic economies, because it would deprive them of their last instrument for regulating imports and exports. Thus monetary union would imply full economic union, with economic policy being regulated centrally for the whole area of the common market. Without the adoption of a common economic policy, it would be doubtful whether the monetary union would hold anyway, because economic policy is one of the key determinants of currency stability. If some governments adopted more inflationary policies than others did, the value of the currency used in countries that were trying to avoid inflation would be undermined. So macro-economic policy would have to be centrally controlled; but this would prevent governments from helping the weaker regions of their own national economies, and this responsibility would also have to be assumed at the centre, implying a common regional policy.

(3) From a common agricultural policy to a common monetary policy

A different line of progress to the same conclusion as example 2 could be traced by starting from an attempt to construct a common agricultural policy, aimed at the equalization of food prices throughout six states. This policy would run into severe difficulties if national currencies were allowed to fluctuate relative to one another. What would start out as a common level of prices, expressed in a neutral accounting unit, would become several price levels if all the exchange rates were to change. So pressure would build up for agricultural policy to be complemented by the tying together of exchange rates, thus restricting fluctuations. From this point the logic of functional spillover proceeds just the same way as in example 2, from monetary union to economic union to a common regional policy.

For Haas, the driving force of political integration was the calculated self-interest of political élites:

The 'good Europeans' are not the main creators of the regional community that is growing up; the process of community formation is dominated by nationally constituted groups with specific interests and aims, willing and able to adjust their aspirations by turning to supranational means when this course appears profitable.

(**Haas 1966: p. xxxiv**)

Neofunctionalists looked for spillover pressures to be encouraged and manipulated by the Commission. It was expected both to foster the emergence of EC-wide pressure groups and to cultivate contacts behind the scenes with national interest groups and with bureaucrats in the civil services of the member states, who were another group of potential allies against national governments (Tranholm–Mikkelsen 1991). This was the third type of spillover, which was known as cultivated spillover because it involved the Commission cultivating the contacts and the pressure on governments.

In the 1950s, neofunctionalist theory neatly fitted events, particularly in explaining the transition from the ECSC to the European Community (EC). Events in the 1960s were less supportive. The beginning of the end for neofunctionalist theory in its original manifestation came in the early 1960s and in particular the use of the veto by de Gaulle, leading to the 'empty chair' crisis of 1965–6 (see Ch. 10, pp. 133–4). National governments had power and were clearly prepared to use it to determine the nature and pace of integration:

> By 1967 Haas was already attempting to cope with the possibility that De Gaulle had 'killed the Common Market' by revising his theory to account for the prospect of 'disintegration', and by 1975 he was announcing the 'obsolescence of regional integration theory'.
>
> (**Caporaso and Keeler 1995: 36–7**).

Intergovernmentalism

In response to the neofunctionalist analysis of European integration, a counter-argument was put forward by Stanley Hoffmann (1964; 1966). This argument drew heavily on realist assumptions about the role of states, or more accurately, the governments of states in international relations. Essentially there were three parts to Hoffmann's criticism of neofunctionalism.

(1) European integration had to be viewed in a global context. Regional integration was only one aspect of the development of the global international system. The neofunctionalists predicted an inexorable progress to further integration; but this was all predicated on an internal dynamic, and implicitly assumed that the international background conditions would remain fixed. This criticism became particularly relevant in the light of changes in the global economic situation in the early 1970s.

(2) National governments were uniquely powerful actors in the process of European integration: they controlled the nature and pace of integration guided by their concern to protect and promote the 'national interest'.

(3) Although, where 'national interests' coincided governments might accept closer integration in the technical functional sectors, the integration process would not spread to areas of 'high politics' such as national security and defence.

Hoffmann rejected the neofunctionalist view that governments would ultimately be overwhelmed by pressures from élite interest groups to integrate. However, his argument departed from classical realism, in which states were treated as unified rational actors, with little importance attached to domestic politics. Hoffmann's intergovernmentalist position was more sophisticated than that of realists in this respect, and his political awareness was also greater than that of the neofunctionalist writers who tended to adopt a rather simplified pluralist view of political processes.

Hoffmann claimed the neofunctionalist argument was based on 'false arithmetic' that assumed that the power of each élite group (including national governments) was approximately equal, so that if the governments were outnumbered they would lose. In addition, he argued that government decisions could not be understood simply as a response to pressure from organized interests, but that, often, political calculations led governments to take positions to which powerful groups were hostile (Hoffmann 1964: 93). These political calculations were driven by domestic concerns, particularly in relation to the impact of integrative decisions on the national economy and on the electoral implications for the governing party.

Hoffmann acknowledged that actors other than national governments played a role in the process of integration. He recognized that in the 'low-politics' sectors (e.g. social and regional policy) interest groups did influence the actions of governments: but, as he pointed out, they were not the only influence. Other influences included government officials (particularly on economic matters) and also the electoral considerations of the party or parties in office (Hoffmann 1964: 89). However, he considered national governments to be the ultimate arbiters of key decisions. The governments of states were said to be uniquely powerful for two reasons: first, because they possessed legal sovereignty; and second because they had political legitimacy as the only democratically elected actors in the integration process. In this view, where the power of supranational institutions increased it did so because governments believed it to be in their national interest.

In Hoffmann's picture of the process of European integration, governments had much more autonomy than in the neofunctionalist view. The integration process therefore remained essentially intergovernmental: it would only go as far as the governments were prepared to allow it to go. However, Hoffmann also pointed to the fact that European integration was only one aspect of the development of international politics. That insight led to a more restrictive view of government autonomy. In this respect Hoffmann, like the realists, stressed the external limitations on autonomy: states were seen as independent actors, but their governments were constrained by the position of the state in the world system.

Liberal Intergovernmentalism

Andrew Moravcsik (1993) provided a later and more rigorous version of the intergovernmental explanation of the EC. Like Hoffmann, Moravcsik started from a critique of neofunctionalism. He restated the argument that neofunctionalism failed to explain developments in the EC itself, but he put more weight on a theoretical critique. In particular, he argued that the self-criticisms of the neofunctionalists themselves had to be taken seriously. He identified three such self-criticisms (Moravcsik 1993: 478–80):

(1) theories of European integration had to be supplemented (or even be supplanted) by more general theories of national responses to international interdependence;

(2) the development of common policy responses needed to be looked at as much as did institutional transfers of competence; the emphasis on formal transfers of authority to the EC often concealed a failure to effect a real surrender of sovereignty;

(3) unicausal theories were inadequate to deal with the phenomenon under consideration; more than one theory was needed to grasp the complexity of EC policy making.

Instead of reviving neofunctionalism, Moravcsik argued that these criticisms should be taken seriously, and a theory constructed that took account of them. He believed that all of the points could be accounted for if the analysis of the EC was rolled into what he called 'current theories of international political economy' (Moravcsik 1993: 480).

Moravcsik's approach, like that of Hoffmann, assumed that states were rational actors, but departed from traditional realism in not treating the state as a **black box**. Instead it was assumed that the governments of states were playing what Putnam (1988) called 'two-level games'. A domestic political process determined their definition of the national interest. This constituted the first part of the analysis and determined the position that governments took with them into the international negotiation.

This approach built on the undeveloped argument of Hoffmann about the role of domestic politics, but in some ways it was less sophisticated in its account of domestic politics than Hoffmann's. Moravcsik's view of domestic politics, which he called a liberal view, was essentially the same as that of the neofunctionalists, which we have called above a pluralist view. The primary determinant of the preferences of a government was the balance between economic interests within the domestic arena. He was frequently criticized for this rather restricted view of the domestic political process (Wincott 1995: 601; Forster 1998: 357–9; Caporaso 1999: 162; Wallace 1999: 156–7).

The second part of the analysis was to see how conflicting national interests were reconciled in the negotiating forum of the Council of Ministers. This process was divided into two logically sequential stages. The first stage was to reach agreement on the common policy response to the problem that governments were trying to solve. The second stage was to reach agreement on the appropriate institutional arrangements. Moravcsik (1999: 21–2) gave the example of monetary union: it would be impractical to try to understand the negotiations over the constitution of a European Central Bank without first understanding the objectives that the bank was being set up to achieve.

The analytical framework of liberal intergovernmentalism was applied by Moravcsik (1999) to five key episodes in the construction of the EU:

• the negotiation of the Treaties of Rome (1955–8)

• the consolidation of the common market and the Common Agricultural Policy (CAP) (1958–83)

• the setting up of the first experiment in monetary co-operation and of the European Monetary System (EMS) (1969–83)

- the negotiation of the Single European Act (SEA) (1984–8)
- and the negotiation of the Treaty on European Union (TEU) (1988–91).

On the basis of these case studies Moravcsik came to the following conclusions:

(1) The major choices in favour of Europe were a reflection of the preferences of national governments, not of the preferences of supranational organizations.

(2) These national preferences reflected the balance of economic interests, rather than the political biases of politicians or national strategic security concerns.

(3) The outcomes of negotiations reflected the relative bargaining power of the states; the delegation of decision-making authority to supranational institutions reflected the wish of governments to ensure that the commitments of all parties to the agreement would be carried through rather than federalist ideology or a belief in the inherent efficiency of international organizations.

However, he was criticized for his choice of case studies. As Scharpf (1999*a*: 165) put it:

Since only intergovernmental negotiations are being considered, why shouldn't the preferences of national governments have shaped the outcomes? Since all case studies have issues of economic integration as their focus, why shouldn't economic concerns have shaped the negotiating positions of governments? And since only decisions requiring unanimous agreement are being analysed, why shouldn't the outcomes be affected by the relative bargaining powers of the governments involved?

The alternative would have been to look at the smaller-scale day-to-day decisions that constitute the bulk of the decisions made within the EU. Here the picture might be very different. Supranational actors might have more influence, and national preferences might be less clearly defined and less vigorously defended. We look at some of these arguments later in the book (Chs. 19 to 21).

Supranational Governance

Starting from the intergovernmentalism versus supranationalism debate, a team of scholars led by Wayne Sandholtz and Alec Stone Sweet (1998) claimed to offer an alternative that cut through the dichotomy. It was an approach that drew on the transactionalism of Karl Deutsch (1953, 1957) and on new institutionalism as applied to the EU (Ch. 2, pp. 23–8), although the authors themselves located the origins of their approach in neofunctionalism.

Fundamental to the approach was the argument that if the EU was to be analysed as an international regime, as Moravcsik insisted it could be, then it had to be seen not as a single regime but as a series of regimes for different policy sectors. The authors therefore sought to explain the different levels of supranationalism that existed in different policy sectors. The three key elements in their approach were the development of transnational society, the role of supranational organizations with meaningful autonomous capacity to pursue integrative agendas, and a focus on European rule-making to resolve what they

INSIGHT 1.3

Supranational Governance 1 The Emergence of Supranational Society—Merger Control

Two companies in the same sector operating across national borders might decide to merge so as to rationalize their operations and reduce their costs. To do so they might have to get the approval not just of national monopoly and merger authorities in their two states of origin, but also in all those states where either company or both combined had a significant proportion of the relevant market. To avoid this situation of 'multiple jeopardy' we would expect to see considerable support from large companies for the transfer of merger approval to the supranational level, giving them a one-stop approval procedure to negotiate, and this is what has actually happened (Cini and McGowan 1998).

called 'international policy externalities'. By this last phrase the authors meant the unintended effects on one country of policies being followed in another country, such as the pollution of the air in one country by smoke from factories in a neighbouring country.

Following Deutsch, Stone Sweet and Sandholtz (1997) argued that transactions across national boundaries were increasing. As they increased, so a supranational society of relevant actors would emerge. These actors would favour the construction of rules to govern their interactions at the supranational level because nationally based rules would be a hindrance to them. If companies that operated across national boundaries had to comply with different rules in every member state, this would impose additional costs on their activity. A good example here is merger control (Insight 1.3). Another example of what the authors call the emergence of supranational society is provided by the case of the emergence of a supranational telecommunications regime (Insight 1.4).

INSIGHT 1.4

Supranational Governance 2 The Emergence of Supranational Society—Telecommunications

In the 1980s the sector was dominated by national monopoly suppliers, the nationalized Postal, Telegraph, and Telephone companies (PTTs). These national suppliers formed parts of policy communities consisting of the PTTs, the officials in the relevant national ministries, and the suppliers of switching equipment, who were also nationally based and who had a guaranteed market from the PTTs. Sandholtz (1998) showed how the domination of the sector by these national policy communities came to be challenged by a coalition of users of telecommunications who demanded cheaper and more technically advanced services than were provided by the PTTs. These users formed a supranational coalition for change, allying with the Commission and with the British government, which had liberalized its own telecommunications market and wished to extend liberalization to the other national EC markets. Gradually the pressure from this coalition eroded the hold of the PTTs on the policy preferences of national governments and opened a window of opportunity for the Commission to get proposals through the Council of Ministers for opening up national markets to competition.

The construction of rules at the supranational level would result in the 'Europeaniz-ation' of a sector: that is the regulation of the sector would be at the EU level. Once the initial step is taken in the Europeanization of a policy sector, Stone Sweet and Sandholtz argued that the consolidation of the supranational regime would proceed through the emergence of European rules. Actors working within the new framework of European rules would start to test the limits of those rules. They would seek clarification from the adjudicators—administrators and courts. These clarifications would not only establish the precise meaning of rules, but would also and at the same time modify them. The act-ors would then face a different set of constraints, which would be tighter than the previ-ous constraints, because more precise, and the actors would adjust their behaviour accordingly. As rules became more precise, so they would tend to develop away from the original intentions of the member states, and would simultaneously become more difficult to modify in any different direction. This pointed to the same process as in the historical institutionalist concept of path dependence (see Ch. 2).

Branch and Øhrgaard (1999) argued that Stone Sweet and Sandholtz had not suc-ceeded in escaping the intergovernmental–supranational dichotomy, but had instead offered a mirror-image of Moravcsik's liberal intergovernmentalism. In particular they argued that both theories privileged certain types of actors, and therefore certain types of decisions; and that both theories classified actors as either intergovernmental or supra-national in a way that ensured that they would oversimplify the complexity of the nature of the EU. According to Branch and Øhrgaard, Moravcsik gave a privileged role in his theoretical framework to national actors and intergovernmental bargains. He therefore concentrated on episodes, the grand bargains, which were highly likely to demonstrate the value of these concepts. On the other side of the mirror, Stone Sweet and Sand-holtz gave a privileged role to transnational business actors and supranational actors, and to the operation of supranational rules of governance. They therefore concentrated on routine decision making in policy sectors that were concerned with economics and trade, which were highly likely to demonstrate the value of these concepts.

Branch and Øhrgaard also argued that both Moravcsik and Stone Sweet and Sandholtz equally made the mistake of treating evidence of influence on policy decisions by supra-national actors as necessary and sufficient evidence of supranational integration, and evidence of decisions remaining in the hands of national governments as necessary and sufficient evidence of intergovernmentalism. In contrast, Branch and Øhrgaard argued that not all European integration was driven forward by transnational and supranational actors. In fields such as social policy, the process had been driven by national govern-ments anxious to correct for the effects of the economic integration that *had* been driven by transnational and supranational actors. They further argued that European integra-tion could not simply be equated with the influence of supranational actors. In the field of the Common Foreign and Security Policy (CFSP) (see Ch. 30), although the mech-anisms remained intergovernmental and the formal power of the supranational institu-tions remained limited, academic experts agreed that the process involved much more than just diplomatic consultation. CFSP was a form of European integration that did not involve supranational governance.

A further criticism of Stone Sweet and Sandholtz's approach is that the framework of analysis ignored the wider context within which the process of 'Europeanization' takes place. This criticism points to an omission that is curious given the association of one of the authors, Sandholtz, with a seminal analysis of the emergence of the single market (Sandholtz and Zysman 1989) which put particular stress on the wider context of global capitalism in explaining the emergence of the policy. This study is examined in Chapter 26 (see pp. 411–12). In the empirical studies contained in the book that they edited (Sandholtz and Stone Sweet 1998), the influence of the wider capitalist system did not emerge very clearly. For example, Sandholtz (1998) explained the emergence of the supranational European society in the telecommunications sector without referring to the deregulation of US telecommunications, which both put European-based companies who were consumers of telecommunications at a disadvantage in comparison with their US competitors, and led to intense pressure from the US government for the European market to be opened to entry by US telecommunication providers (Dang–Nguyen *et al.* 1993; Fuchs 1994). This inadequacy in the analysis reflected the inadequacy in the theory.

 ## CONCLUSION

Essentially the same academic debate about the process of European integration has been going on for over four decades. Related concepts like federalism linked to this debate have been present throughout and emerged again prominently in debates on the proposed Constitutional Treaty (Ch. 16 and Ch. 17). Central to this continuing debate is the nature and role of the state executives in the development of the EU. In intergovernmental perspectives, European integration is a process whereby the governments of states voluntarily enter into agreements to work together to solve common problems. Some constraints operate on the autonomy of national governments, but they remain in control of the process. The alternative perspective suggests that although governments started the process, it soon took on a life of its own which went beyond the control of the governments. This 'intergovernmental–supranational debate' forms the first of the themes that recur throughout this book.

These questions are of more than just academic interest. The nature of the EU, and where the process is going, are fundamental issues of political debate in the member states of the EU today. However, there is some irony in how explanations of the process of integration have been used. In the 1950s and 1960s, neofunctionalist ideas were eagerly embraced by members of the Commission as a blueprint for constructing a united Europe. Today, opponents of further integration implicitly invoke the neofunctionalist idea that the process is no longer under control and threatens national identity. Conversely, intergovernmentalist arguments are more likely to be voiced by the advocates of further steps, who echo Hoffmann and Moravcsik in reassuring hesitant European public opinion that the governments of states remain in charge: that sovereignty is only 'pooled', not lost.

While, as will be discussed in subsequent chapters, theorizing about the EU has in many ways moved beyond the intergovernmental–supranational dichotomy, this debate continues to inform research (for example, on 'Eastern' enlargement see Moravcsik and Vachudova 2002: 2003). Moreover, a number of the debate's key themes—state power, the role of organized interests, the influence of supranational institutions—remain prominent in other approaches to the EU.

The Intellectual Background

☐ David Mitrany was not a theorist of European integration, but influenced later integration theorists. He sought to prevent war between states by taking routine functional tasks out of the hands of national governments and giving them over to international agencies.

☐ Mitrany argued that world government would limit freedom, and that regional federations would reproduce on a larger scale the conditions that produced wars between states.

☐ European federalism attracted strong support among Resistance groups in war-time Europe. The leading intellectual figure was Altiero Spinelli, who advocated a 'constitutional break' at the end of the war to supersede the system of sovereign states with a federal constitution for Europe.

☐ By the time the Congress called to adopt this new constitution had been arranged, national political élites were re-established in European states. While the (Hague) Congress did produce the Council of Europe, this was an intergovernmental body that fell far short of federalist aspirations.

☐ The Schuman plan for the ECSC was devised by Jean Monnet, the head of the French economic planning commission, who believed the European nation state was inadequate as an economic unit in the modern world and argued for a Europe-wide economy.

☐ The pooling of coal and steel resources was the first step towards a Europe-wide economic zone. It also removed strategic industries from German control and ensured adequate supplies of coal for the French steel industry: both were concerns for Monnet.

International Relations Theories of European Integration

☐ IR theory in the 1950s was dominated by realism. This theory treated nation states as the fundamental units of international relations. It did not lead to any expectation that the governments of states would voluntarily surrender their sovereign control over policy. As such, the first European integration theorists posed a direct challenge to realist assumptions.

☐ *Neofunctionalism* suggested that European integration was a process that, once started, would undermine the sovereignty of states beyond the expectations of governments.

☐ Neofunctionalism argued that states are not unified actors, but that national interests were determined through a pluralistic process in which states interact with organized interests. Organized interests were also seen to be important transnational actors.

☐ The concept of spillover was central to the neofunctionalist theory. Functional spillover, political spillover, and cultivated spillover would lead the process of European integration to run out of the control of national governments.

☐ Hoffmann's *intergovernmentalism* argued that neofunctionalists had made three mistakes: regional integration was not a self-contained process, but was influenced by a wider international context; states were uniquely powerful actors because they possessed formal sovereignty and democratic legitimacy; and integration in low politics sectors would not necessarily spill-over into high politics sectors.

- Moravcsik's *liberal intergovernmentalism* incorporated the neofunctionalist insight that national interests are defined as part of a domestic pluralist political process; but he denied the importance of supranational actors and insisted that governments remained in control of the process of European integration.

- Moravcsik proposed a two-level analysis of EU bargaining, in which governments' preferences were determined at the domestic level, and then used as the basis for intergovernmental negotiations at the European level.

- For Moravcsik, the primary determinant of a government's preferences was balance between economic interests within the state.

- Moravcsik divided intergovernmental negotiations into the reaching of agreement on a common policy response to a problem, and the reaching of agreement on the appropriate institutional arrangements.

- The approach of *supranational governance* was located in neofunctionalism, but also drew on transactionalism and new institutionalism. Stone Sweet and Sandholtz argued that the EU should be studied not as one international regime, but as a series of regimes for different policy sectors, and that increased transactions across national boundaries would create a supranational society that favoured the creation of supranational rules to govern its behaviour.

- Branch and Øhrgaard argued that this approach did not escape the intergovernmental–supranational dichotomy. Rather, it privileged certain types of actors and also classified actors as either intergovernmental or supranational in a way that oversimplified the complexity of the EU. The approach was further criticized for not placing the analysis in a global context.

 FURTHER READING

The key texts on the early development of neofunctionalist theory are: E. B. Haas, *The Uniting of Europe: Political, Social and Economic Forces 1950–57* (London: Library of World Affairs, 1958); E. B. Haas, *The Uniting of Europe: Political, Social and Economic Forces, 1950–1957* (2nd edn) (Stanford, Calif.: Stanford University Press, 1968); and L. Lindberg, *The Political Dynamics of European Economic Integration* (Stanford: Stanford University Press; London: Oxford University Press, 1963). On intergovernmentalism, the main early contributions are: S. Hoffmann, 'The European Process at Atlantic Crosspurposes', *Journal of Common Market Studies*, 3 (1964): 85–101, and S. Hoffmann, 'Obstinate or Obsolete? The Fate of the Nation State and the Case of Western Europe', *Daedalus*, 95 (1966): 862–915.

Neofunctionalism is elaborated, expanded, and defended in J. Tranholm-Mikkelsen, 'Neofunctionalism: Obstinate or Obsolete? A Reappraisal in the Light of the New Dynamism of the European Community', *Millennium*, 20 (1991): 1–22. The earliest statement of liberal intergovernmentalism is in A. Moravcsik, 'Preferences and Power in the European Community: A Liberal Intergovernmentalist Approach', *Journal of Common Market Studies*, 31 (1993): 473–524. A later statement of the theory, which differs subtly, is given in A. Moravcsik, *The Choice for Europe: Social Purpose and State Power from Messina to Maastricht* (London: UCL Press, 1998).

Supranational governance is outlined in Stone Sweet and W. Sandholtz, 'European Integration and Supranational Governance', *Journal of European Public Policy*, 4 (1997): 297–317. It is developed in W. Sandholtz and A. Stone Sweet (eds.), *European Integration and Supranational Governance* (Oxford: Oxford University Press, 1998); and contested in A. P. Branch and J. C. Øhrgaard, 'Trapped in the Supranational–Intergovernmental Dichotomy: A Response to Stone Sweet and Sandholtz', *Journal of European Public Policy*, 6 (1999): 123–43.

online resource centre

Visit the Online Resource Centre that accompanies this book for links to more information on theories of European integration.

CHAPTER 2

Theories of EU Governance

CHAPTER OVERVIEW

As European integration progressed, the academic focus began to shift from explaining the integration process to understanding the EU as a political system. As such, EU scholars increasingly drew on approaches from the study of domestic and comparative politics. While some attempts to escape the supranational—intergovernmental dichotomy have proved more successful than others, these contributions undoubtedly broadened the study of the EU considerably beyond the traditional IR debate. This chapter surveys a number of approaches that focus on the EU as a political system. These approaches fall within the broad categories of 'new institutionalism' and 'governance and networks'. While they diverge in some important ways, there is also considerable overlap between the approaches.

a newer generation of scholars, uninspired by debates between intergovernmentalism and neofunctionalism ... struck out on their own (Caporaso 1998: 341)

The theoretical stand-off between intergovernmental and supranational interpretations remains significant in the study of the EU. However, alongside this debate other voices have emerged that move beyond the supranational-intergovernmental dichotomy. Approaches from the study of domestic and comparative politics turn away from the focus of IR theories on the process of European integration, and instead treat the EU as a political system that is already in existence, and try to explore 'the nature of the beast'.

This chapter looks at attempts to study the EU using concepts and theories drawn from domestic and comparative politics. In a seminal article, Simon Hix (1994) issued a call to scholars within the discipline of comparative politics to wake up to the existence of the EU as a suitable subject for study using their established concepts. He heeded his own call a few years later, producing a textbook on the EU that took a radically different approach to the subject.

Instead of asking questions such as how far the EU was dominated by the member states and how far it operated as an autonomous entity, Hix (1999: 1) asked questions that derived from the study of comparative politics:

How is governmental power exercised? Under what conditions can the Parliament influence legislation? Is the Court of Justice beyond political control? Why do some citizens support the central institutions while others oppose them? How important are political parties and elections in shaping political choices? Why are some social groups able to influence the political agenda more than others?

The approach succeeded in shifting the focus away from the study of European integration as a process to '*how the EU works today*' (Hix 1999: 1; emphasis in original).

An increasing number of concepts are applied to the EU that originated from the study of comparative and domestic politics. Here we look at two influential sets of approaches that come under the headings of 'new institutionalism' and 'governance and networks'. While we identify these as separate approaches, and there are variants within each approach, there is also a significant overlap between the two categories and a close relationship between these approaches and other concepts increasingly applied to the study of the EU.

New Institutionalism

One adaptation of an approach that was originally applied to the study of domestic and comparative politics that Hix drew upon was new institutionalism (March and Olsen 1984, 1989, 1996). This was a reaction to the behavioural approaches that had come to dominate political science in the 1960s and 1970s. Behaviouralism had been a reaction against formal institutional analyses of government and politics that had lost sight of the real political processes that lay behind the formal structures of government; in particular, the influence of societal groups. New institutionalism argued that the reaction against the old, formal institutional analyses had gone too far; that the importance of institutions in structuring political action had been lost. It reasserted the view that *institutions matter*.

One thing that was new about this reassertion of institutionalism was that institutions were not just defined as the formal organizations that the old institutionalism had recognized—such as parliaments, executives, and judicial courts—but extended to categorize informal patterns of structured interaction between groups as institutions themselves. These structured interactions were institutions in the sense that they constrained or shaped group behaviour.

At the same time, new institutionalism argued that formal institutions were more important than behaviouralists had suggested. Behaviouralists treated formal institutions as neutral arenas within which the struggle for influence between the different societal actors was carried out. New institutionalists disagreed with this perspective in two ways. First, they argued that formal institutions were not neutral arenas, since formal institutional structures and rules biased access to the political process in favour of some societal groups over others. Second, they argued that institutions could be autonomous political actors in their own right.

While collectively, this reassertion of institutionalist perspectives is known as new institutionalism, it is now common to distinguish between three varieties: rational choice institutionalism, historical institutionalism and sociological institutionalism (Hall and Taylor 1996). These approaches emerged at around the same time, but in relative isolation from each other.

Rational Choice Institutionalism

Rational choice institutionalism focuses on the constraints that formal institutional structures impose on actors. It suggests that in trying to understand the behaviour of political actors it is important to identify the parameters that are set by the fact that they are acting within a specific framework of rules. So, for example, the activities of interest groups reflect the procedures that prevailed for the passage of the legislation that affected them, the access points that were available to them in that process, and the previous relationships that they had established with key decision makers. Thus, in the case of the EU, whether interest groups chose to try to influence legislation through national governments or through the Commission and the European Parliament (EP) would reflect:

- the relative openness to those groups of the national government actors compared with the supranational actors;
- the extent to which the process was intergovernmental (e.g. what decision rules applied within the Council of Ministers);
- what role the EP had in the final decision.

If national decision making was dominated by other interest groups, then 'outsider' groups trying to influence EU policy might turn to the supranational institutions because they would be more likely to get their voices heard there. In competition policy decisions, for example, national monopoly suppliers, which had a close working relationship with national government officials, would tend to work through national channels. In contrast, potential competitors, who wanted to see the dismantling of the advantages that the national monopoly suppliers enjoyed at the national level, would be more likely to turn to the Commission because it was difficult for them to obtain access to the national decision makers and easier for them to obtain access to the supranational institutions.

Where unanimity applied in the Council of Ministers, it would be more important to lobby at the national level because one vote against a proposal could block it; but where Qualified Majority Voting (QMV) applied the potential influence of the Commission would be greater, making it a more attractive target for lobbying. In areas where the powers of the EP were extended under the Single European Act (SEA), the Treaty on European Union (TEU), and the Treaty of Amsterdam (see Ch. 21), interest groups began to lobby the EP more extensively than they had previously, and to do so more than did interest groups in policy sectors where the powers of the EP remained restricted to the consultation procedure.

Rational choice institutionalists also made a significant contribution to understanding the ways in which supranational actors could obtain a degree of autonomy from national governments, allowing them to make their own input to the policy process (Pollack 1997). Applying what is known as **principal-agent theory**, rational choice institutionalists pointed to the difficulties of principals (the national governments) in keeping a check on the activities of their agents (the central institutions).

- As the range of delegated tasks increased, so the difficulties of monitoring what the agents were doing would increase.
- As the number of principals increased with successive enlargements of membership, so the agents could play off the preferences of different coalitions of principals against the attempts of other principals to restrain them.
- As QMV expanded, so the constraints on the Commission in constructing a winning coalition in support of its proposals were reduced.

In a recent study, Mark Pollack (2003) applied rational choice theory to test hypotheses about the delegation of power by the member states to the EU's supranational organizations (mainly the Commission, the Court of Justice and the Parliament) and the efforts of these organizations to shape the process of European integration. Pollack's first concern was with the types of functions that governments delegate to supranational organizations and the conditions under which greater or less discretion is allocated to these agents. Here, principal-agent theory suggested that governments would delegate to supranational agents to reduce the transaction costs of EU policy making. The evidence suggested that this was the case with the Commission and Court of Justice, but delegation to the EP was motivated more by governments' attempts to reduce the EU's democratic deficit (Ch. 4, p. 67–70) and was thus more effectively explained in terms of the logic of appropriate behaviour identified by sociological institutionalists (below), rather than rational choice explanations.

Historical Institutionalism

Historical institutionalists place emphasis on the argument that political relationships have to be viewed over time. Their approach argues that decisions are not made according to an abstract rationality, but according to perceptions and within constraints that are structured by pre-existing institutional relationships. While rational choice institutionalism focuses its analysis primarily on formal institutions, historical institutionalism takes a broader definition of institutions to incorporate also informal constraints on behaviour such as values and behavioural norms.

They can range from the rules of a constitutional order or the standard operating procedures of a bureaucracy to the conventions governing trade union behaviour or bank-firm relations. In general, historical institutionalists associate institutions with organizations and the rules or conventions promulgated by formal organization.

(Hall and Taylor 1996: 938)

Central to historical institutionalism is the concept of 'path dependence'. This is the argument that once one decision is made it tends to close down some potential avenues for development of policy and make it more likely that policy continues to develop in the same direction. Or, as Hall and Taylor (1996: 941) put it 'forces will be mediated by the contextual features of a given situation often inherited from the past'. In extreme cases, path dependence can turn into 'lock-in' (Pierson 1996) where other avenues of policy are entirely blocked off by the bias towards the existing route that is built into the system. This could be one explanation of why policies such as the CAP proved so resistant to reform even after their negative effects had become obvious.

Applying historical institutionalism to the EU led to a further critique of intergovernmental analyses, and revealed further reasons for thinking that national governments might not be entirely in control of the process of integration. Intergovernmental analyses tended to focus on the historic decisions, represented mainly by revisions to the treaties (see Ch 1, p. 15). Intergovernmentalists treated what happened between these historic decisions as simply the working through of the decisions. Historical institutionalists argued that after the decision had been taken it would be likely to produce unanticipated and unintended outcomes. This might be because of a simple failure to think through the implications; but it might be for one or both of two other reasons (Pierson 1998: 41). First, the preferences of governments might change over time. For example, the preference for a common agricultural policy based on price support might have been a rational response to conditions in the 1960s in Europe, when security of food supplies was a paramount concern, but no longer appropriate in the changed circumstances of the 1990s, when technological advances had removed this concern. Second, national governments might change. For example, the EC directives on social policy to which a British Labour government had agreed were not to the liking of the Conservative governments between 1979 and 1997.

Even where preferences changed, governments would find it extremely difficult to change the decision. One reason for this was the institutionalization of the policy sector. Initial policy choices tended to structure subsequent patterns of behaviour, thus creating path dependence. Once the CAP was in place, structured relationships

developed between European farmers' representatives, the relevant Commission officials, and national agricultural policy officials that crystallized into a European-level
policy community (see below, and Ch. 25) that was very resistant to change.

A second reason why governments found it difficult to change a decision was because
the voting rules in the Council of Ministers made it very difficult to get agreement to
move back from a policy once it was agreed. Where, as with agriculture, the rule was
unanimity, it was impossible to retreat so long as one member state benefited from the
status quo and refused to move from it. This was sometimes referred to as 'the ratchet effect'. Even where QMV applied, in order to effect change it was necessary to construct a
coalition representing more than a simple majority of states (the exact number depending on the weighting of the votes of the members of the coalition, and therefore on the
identity of the states involved). It was impossible where the changed preference involved
only a few states or, as in the case of social policy quoted above, only one state.

The insights of new institutionalism fed into a number of studies of specific EU
policies, such as the single market programme (Armstrong and Bulmer 1998). They also
informed more elaborated frameworks of analysis such as the multi-level governance
approach, which is dealt with later in this chapter. Most recently, historical institutionalism has made a significant contribution to the burgeoning literature on Europeanization (see Chapter 4), in particular by providing sensitivity to how domestic institutions
(formal and informal) mediate EU pressures (see Bulmer and Burch 2000; Bulmer and
Radaelli 2004).

Sociological Institutionalism

The emergence of sociological institutionalism is closely linked with the 'constructivist
turn' in the study of the EU and international politics, which is dealt with in the next
chapter (pp. 43–7), so the discussion here is relatively brief. Like constructivism, sociological institutionalism takes as its starting point a rejection of the rationalist approach
to the study of politics that characterizes rational choice institutionalism and some contributions to historical institutionalism and places more emphasis on broadly 'cultural'
practices (see Chapter 3 for more on this debate).

Hall and Taylor (1996: 947) identified three features of sociological institutionalism
that distinguished it from the other new institutionalisms. First, the definition of what
constitutes 'institutions' is considerably broader than in the other approaches, so that
it includes not just formal rules, but 'symbol systems, cognitive scripts, and moral tem-
plates that provide the "frames of meaning" guiding human action'. This definition
blurred the lines traditionally separating the notions of 'institutions' and 'culture'.

Second, sociological institutionalism takes a distinct approach to the relationship
between institutions and individual action that flows from the 'cultural' approach. In
particular, it suggests that institutions do not simply influence the 'strategic calculation'
of actors, but have a deeper effect on their preferences and very identity. As Hall and
Taylor (1996: 948) put it:

*The self images and identities of social actors are said to be constituted from the institu-
tional forms, images and signs provided by social life.*

This does not mean that actors are not 'rational' in the pursuit of the goals and object-ives; rather, that these goals and objectives are constituted differently (i.e. socially) and are more broadly defined than rationalist theory would suggest.

Finally, sociological institutionalism contrasts with rationalist explanations on how institutions are formed and developed. For rational choice institutionalists, institutions are developed by rational actors to meet particular ends efficiently, such as reducing transaction costs (see above). For sociological institutionalists, institutions are often cre-ated and developed because they contribute to social legitimacy rather than efficiency. In some cases, this may mean that the formal goals of an organization are overrid-den by these broader social goals. Here a distinction is made between the rational-ist 'logic of instrumentality' with the sociological 'logic of appropriateness'. Thus, in the case of delegation to supranational institutions discussed above, it may not be in the instrumental interests of national governments to enhance the EP's powers, but the need to enhance the democratic legitimacy of the EU provided a powerful logic of appropriateness.

Rosamond (2003: 117) suggested that the application of sociological institutionalism may be particularly useful in the EU in contributing to understanding of why the Com-mission's directorates-general operate in very distinct ways. It may also provide insights into whether 'formally intergovernmental processes . . . conform to established patterns of interstate interaction, or whether they bring about new norms of exchange between the envoys of member states' (See Ch. 20, pp. 284–6, on socialization of national officials in COREPER). As with historical institutionalism, this variant of new institutionalism is making an important contribution to explaining the domestic mediation of European-ization (Börzel 1999; Marshall 2005), discussed in Chapter 4.

New Institutionalism Assessed

For Hall and Taylor (1996: 95), none of the new institutionalisms is particularly 'wrong headed' or 'substantially untrue': rather, 'each seems to be providing a partial account of the forces at work in a given situation or capturing different dimensions of the hu-man action and institutional impact present there'. The three approaches rest on dif-ferent assumptions about the world that led them to focus on different questions. This is illustrated in relation to EU enlargement, where sociological institutionalists have placed more emphasis on why the EU decided to enlarge and how we can account for the subsequent negotiations, while rational choice institutionalists have devoted greater attention to the impact of enlargement on the EU's institutional arrangements and historical institutionalists on the process of reform in Central and Eastern Europe (Pollack 2004: 151).

The various strands of new institutionalism are increasingly being refined, through both empirical research and through engagement with the other strands and with other conceptual approaches to the EU. The new institutionalisms link closely to research on constructivism (Chapter 3), Europeanization (Chapter 4), and theories on governance and networks, to which we now turn.

Governance and Networks

Sharing a number of features with aspects of new institutionalism, governance and networks approaches are equally prominent in the study of the EU. Moreover, while we distinguish between 'governance' and 'network' approaches to reflect labels assigned by particular scholars, these two concepts are very closely linked.

Definitions of governance abound (for different perspectives, see Pierre 2000). Jachtenfuchs and Kohler-Koch (2004: 99) gave a broad definition of governance as 'the continuous political process of setting explicit goals for society and intervening in it in order to achieve these goals', and suggested that 'networking is the most characteristic feature of EU governance' (Jachtenfuchs and Kohler-Koch 2004: 100). Common to more specific definitions of governance is the view that policy making is increasingly characterized by wide participation of public, private, and voluntary actors. In the context of the EU, the multi-level governance framework (below) brings together this increased 'horizontal' mix of actors with increased 'vertical' interactions between actors organized at different territorial levels (supranational, national, and subnational).

Policy Networks and Epistemic Communities

Richardson (1996a) took up Hix's call to approach the EU from different disciplinary directions, but instead of organizing the study around the concepts of comparative politics, he advocated organizing it around the concepts that he and others had been using for some time to study the policy-making process within member states. He argued in particular for the application of two concepts: policy networks and epistemic communities. The first of these concepts was originally developed in studies of public policy making in the United States and later became prominent in Britain, particularly through the work of Rhodes (1981; 1988). It was subsequently applied to the study of the EU by Peterson (1992), Bache, George, and Rhodes (1996) and others. Ironically, the second concept originally arose from the study of international relations and then fed back into domestic policy analysis before being applied to the EU. Both concepts are mid-range or 'meso-level', aimed at explanations of particular policy sectors or issues.

According to the 'Rhodes model', a policy network is a set of resource-dependent organizations, meaning that each of the groups that makes up the policy network needs something that the others have in order to fulfil its own objectives (Rhodes 1988). The types of resources that organizations bring to a policy network to exchange in the process of bargaining include constitutional-legal, organizational, financial, political, and informational resources. These 'resource dependencies'—the extent to which organizations depend on each other for resources—are the key variable in shaping policy outcomes. As Peterson and Bomberg (1993: 28) put it, 'They set the "chessboard" where private and public interests manoeuvre for advantage'. However, interdependence between network participants is 'almost always asymmetrical' and in some cases it is possible to talk of 'unilateral leadership' within networks (Rhodes 1986: 5).

The policy networks approach does not constitute a predictive theory of policy making, but is seen to contribute to explaining policy outputs. For Peterson and Bomberg (1993: 31):

Policy networks are essentially descriptive theoretical tools which simply help order facts and evidence in novel ways. However, policy networks can be used to anticipate and explain policy outputs by providing insights into how and why decisions were taken which produced them.

One way in which the approach contributes to anticipating and explaining outputs is by outlining the importance of different structural characteristics of different types of networks. Rhodes (1988) distinguished between different types of networks, ranging from highly integrated policy communities to loosely integrated issue networks (Insight 2.1). These different 'structural characteristics' of networks have different effects on both the internal dynamics of the networks and on the ability of networks to resist external pressures for change. However, policy outputs are generally not just a function of internal network characteristics, but are shaped also by changes in the broader political and economic environment (Rhodes, Bache, and George 1996). As such, the approach is often at its strongest when used in conjunction with a macro-level theory of politics or policy making that seeks to explain broader changes in the environment within which the network is situated.

A particular strength of the policy-networks approach is its emphasis on policy implementation as an important phase in policy making: a phase in which policy 'is actually made in the course of negotiations between the (ostensible) implementers' (Rhodes 1986: 14). This aspect of the approach is particularly important in the context of the EU,

---

INSIGHT 2.1

Policy Communities and Issue Networks

A policy community is marked by:

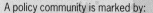

- limited membership;
- stable membership over long periods of time;
- a high level of interaction between the members;
- shared values between members;
- some degree of equality in the distribution of resources;
- a relative balance of power and influence between members.

An issue network, in contrast, is marked by:

- large and diffuse membership;
- frequent shifts in the membership;
- fluctuating frequency of contact between members;
- lack of shared values;
- marked inequality in the distribution of resources;
- marked inequality in power and influence within the network.

in which the Commission is heavily dependent upon domestic actors for effective policy implementation.

Policy Networks and the Study of the EU

The applicability of the policy networks framework to the analysis of the EU was questioned by Kassim (1994). He argued that EU processes were not settled enough to allow policy networks to emerge. Interest groups used different channels to influence decisions; sometimes national, sometimes EU-level. The multinational character and institutional complexity of the EU made it difficult to delimit policy networks, and particularly to identify the relevant public sector actor. Sometimes national agencies would be key, sometimes the Commission, sometimes other EU-level institutions. The institutions themselves often acted as lobbyists in the EU in pursuit of their own objectives.

One of the scholars who had advocated the use of policy networks replied to Kassim (Peterson 1995a). He questioned Kassim's insistence on the fluidity of EU policy-making procedures, arguing that while some sectors remained fluid, others were settling into more stable patterns. Indeed, he argued that the Commission was so under-resourced that it had to try to enter into stable relationships with partners whom it could trust, who had information that it could use. While he accepted Kassim's points about the complexity of the role of institutions in the EU in comparison with national institutional arrangements, he argued that the policy-networks approach was perfectly compatible with new-institutionalist analyses of the EU, which allowed theorization of the working of institutional relations. While he accepted that the delineation of policy networks at the EU level was a difficult task, Peterson insisted that this did not make it a less important one.

Peterson's most interesting observation, though, was the need to be clear about the level of the policy-making process that was being analysed. He argued that the policy networks model was best able to explain what he called 'the policy-shaping decisions', when proposals were being formulated and before a political decision was taken which 'set' the policy (Peterson 1995a: 400). In a subsequent article, the same author expanded on this argument (Peterson 1995b). He here identified three 'levels' of analysis in EU decision making. The highest level he termed the 'super-systemic' or 'history-making' decisions. These were mainly decisions taken by national governments in the European Council or at IGCs, and were most fruitfully analysed using intergovernmental ideas. The second level he termed the 'systemic' or 'policy-setting' stage. At this level a combination of intergovernmental and inter-institutional analysis was needed to understand outcomes. The third level he called the 'sub-systemic' or 'policy-shaping' stage. At this level policy networks were a useful concept for understanding how policy options were formulated in bargaining between the Commission Directorates-General, national civil servants, and private actors (see Table 2.1).

More recently, Peterson (2004: 119) put his case more strongly, suggesting that 'policy network analysis is never more powerful than when it is deployed at EU level'. He set out a three-pronged argument for the applicability of the policy-networks approach to the study of the EU: first, that there is considerable variation in how different EU policy sectors operate; second, that much of the EU's policy making is highly technical; and, third, that EU policy making is 'underpinned by an extraordinarily complex labyrinth

TABLE 2.1			
Levels of Analysis in EU Decision Making			
Level	Type of decision	Dominant actors	Rationality
super-systemic	history making	European Council, National governments in IGCs Court of Justice	political, legalistic
systemic	policy setting	Council of Ministers, Committee of Permanent Representatives (COREPER)	political, technocratic administrative
sub-systemic/ meso-level	policy shaping	Commission, committees, Council groups	technocratic consensual administrative

Source: Reproduced from *Journal of European Public Policy*, 2 (1995): 71.

of committees that shape policy options before policies are 'set' by overtly political decision makers such as the college of Commissioners, Council of Ministers, or European Parliament' (Peterson 2004: 117).

Jachtenfuchs (2001: 254) made a complementary case for the advantages of network analysis:

It appears that, on the whole, the fragmented and fluid institutional structure of the EU and the lack of a strong power centre leads to an increase of channels of access and a larger variation of participants in the policy-making process as compared to governance systems in territorial states.

Epistemic Communities

Whereas policy networks are held together by resource interdependence, epistemic communities are knowledge-based groups. An epistemic community was defined by Haas (1992: 3) as:

a network of professionals with recognised expertise and competence in a particular domain and an authoritative claim to policy-relevant knowledge within that domain or issue-area.

The members of an epistemic community share both normative beliefs and causal beliefs, i.e. they hold a common set of values about what is right and desirable, and a common set of assumptions about how to achieve those goals. They also agree on notions of validity, so they have a common basis for settling differences of opinion between themselves, and they share a common policy enterprise, so that they are all involved in efforts to solve the same problems.

Epistemic communities are likely to exercise particular influence over policy when policy makers face conditions of uncertainty about the likely consequences of policy choice. Such uncertainty is thought to be particularly high where international co-ordination of policy is concerned. Success in such situations is heavily dependent on the actions of other states. There is also a high degree of uncertainty about the possible unforeseen consequences. In these circumstances state actors are highly likely to turn to epistemic communities because they are not sure how to define the national interest.

Members of transnational epistemic communities can influence state interests either by directly identifying them for decision makers or by illuminating the salient dimensions of an issue from which the decision makers may then deduce their interests. The decision makers in one state may, in turn, influence the interests and behavior of other states, thereby increasing the likelihood of convergent state behavior and international policy co-ordination, informed by the causal beliefs and policy preferences of the epistemic community.

(Haas 1992: 4)

Haas's perspective suggested that epistemic communities are useful as a means of helping governments to think their way through situations of uncertainty, and to provide a common framework of analysis that could act as a guarantee that states that try to co-ordinate policy will all work along the same lines. However, going beyond Haas's arguments, epistemic communities might also be used by supranational actors such as the European Commission as a means of furthering the Europeanization of policy. The expert analysis that they provide, and the policy prescriptions that they advocate, if they point in the desired direction, could form a powerful lever for supranational actors to move states in the direction of common European solutions to problems that confronted them.

While developed separately from the Rhodes model of policy networks, the notion of epistemic communities is a compatible approach that provides a way of understanding how professionals can come to dominate policy making. Sabatier's advocacy coalition framework, which offers an explanation for how policy change is brought about by coalitions within networks bound together by a shared belief system, has similar potential (Sabatier 1988; 1998). Moreover, Peterson (2004: 121) suggested that alliances of epistemic communities and advocacy coalitions may form to influence policy making and provides the example of the EU's 'quite radical liberalization of its agricultural sector during the Uruguay Round which gave birth to the WTO in the early 1990s'.

Multi-Level Governance (MLG)

Multi-level governance has strong antecedents in neofunctionalism, but is less concerned with explaining the process of European integration and more with explaining the nature of the EU that has emerged from that process. In that respect it is entirely in line with the approach advocated by Hix (1999).

Multi-level governance was first developed from a study of EU structural policy (Ch. 28) and was later developed and applied more widely. An early definition by Gary Marks (1993: 392) spoke of:

the emergence of multi-level governance, *a system of continuous negotiation among nested governments at several territorial tiers—supranational, national, regional and local.*

In this context, Marks was referring particularly to the way in which EU structural funds were administered: to the implementation stage of policy (see Ch. 28, pp. 472–4). However, in conjunction with other writers, he subsequently extended the concept to cover the policy-making phase as well (Marks, Hooghe, and Blank 1996). While accepting that integration involved intergovernmental bargains, multi-level governance theorists reasserted the neofunctionalist critique of realism, that individual governments were not in control of the process.

Marks, Hooghe, and Blank made three key points against the intergovernmental view, some of which echoed the arguments of new institutionalists:

(1) Collective decision making involves loss of control for the governments of individual states.

(2) Decision-making competencies in the EU are shared by actors at different levels, not monopolized by the governments of states.

(3) The political systems of member states are not separate from each other, as Moravcsik (Chapter 1, pp. 13–15) assumed, but are connected in various ways.

While Marks, Hooghe, and Blank accepted the central role of the Council of Ministers in EU decision making, they pointed to a number of constraints on the ability of individual governments to control the outcomes of such collective decision making. The use of qualified majority voting in the Council was an obvious constraint: any individual government might be outvoted. The Luxemburg Compromise (see Ch. 9, p. 134) did allow a government to exercise a veto if it felt that its vital national interests were threatened, but the prevailing culture in the Council worked against frequent use of this option, making it a rather blunt instrument for maintaining national sovereignty. So, while it was true that governments might be able to attain desired objectives by pooling their sovereignty, this was not the same as arguing that their control of the process remained intact.

Supranational institutions might be created by member governments to assist them, as Moravcsik argued, but these did not remain under close national government control. For intergovernmentalists, national governments could ultimately choose to rein in the power of these institutions. For multi-level governance theorists this was difficult in practice because changes to the role of supranational institutions required unanimous agreement, which was difficult to secure with so many member states.

Another reason why Marks, Hooghe, and Blank believed governments had difficulty in controlling supranational institutions was because the state itself was not a unified actor. Moravcsik accepted this in his liberal intergovernmentalist position in suggesting that national interests were defined via a pluralistic domestic process. Marks, Hooghe, and Blank went further by arguing that the determining of the national interest was not purely a domestic matter. Sections of the government, and non-state actors, could form alliances with their counterparts in other member states, which influenced national governments' negotiating positions on EU matters. These alliances would not be under the control of the core institutions of the central government, such as the Foreign Office or the Prime Minister's Office; and the Commission in particular would be able to exploit the existence of these 'transgovernmental' and 'transnational' networks of actors to promote their policy preferences within the 'domestic' politics of member states.

Rather than a coherent theory, multi-level governance was initially an amalgamation of perspectives that were primarily directed at what its advocates saw as the misrepresentation of the nature of the EU by the intergovernmental theorists. It did contain some elements of an explanation for the development of the EU, but it was primarily concerned with the analysis of the *nature* of the EU. As such, it lacked the basis for the analysis of political dynamics that was present in neofunctionalism.

Andrew Jordan (2001) identified seven key criticisms of MLG:

- MLG was nothing new, but an amalgam of existing theories
- it provided a description of the European Union, but not a theory
- it overstated the autonomy of subnational actors (SNAs)
- it adopted a 'top–down' view of SNAs
- it focused on SNAs to the exclusion of other subnational actors
- it mistook evidence of SNA mobilization at European level as evidence of SNA influence
- it ignored the international level of interaction.

Stephen George (2004) argued that Jordan's criticisms were of 'variable validity'. He agreed with the first claim, but suggested that it was 'scarcely a criticism'. More significantly, George (2004: 125) suggested that MLG went beyond description to offer a theory of what sort of organization the EU is: 'It is hypothesized to be an organization in which the central executives of states do not do all the governing but share and contest responsibility and authority with other actors, both supranational and subnational.' Of course, the validity of this theory was contested, but MLG offered counter-hypotheses to those of (liberal) intergovernmentalism.

George agreed that work adopting the MLG perspective had tended to focus on SNAs to the exclusion of other actors, but had not sufficiently addressed the question of whether the mobilization of SNAs had made a real difference to outcomes in the policy process. It had also not been applied sufficiently to the international level, where the European Union itself stands in the role of potential gatekeeper between different arenas.

In a development of the approach, Hooghe and Marks (2003; 2004) developed a two-fold typology of MLG (see Table 2.2). This typology addressed both analytical and normative concerns: that is, it aimed to capture not only how governance is organized, but also how it should be organized. Type 1 MLG has echoes of federalism, suggesting a system-wide arrangement in which the dispersion of authority is restricted to a limited number of clearly defined, non-overlapping jurisdictions at a limited number of territorial levels, each of which has responsibility for a 'bundle' of functions. By contrast, Type 2 MLG is one in which the jurisdiction of authority is task-specific, where jurisdictions operate at numerous territorial levels and may be overlapping. In Type 1, authority is relatively stable, but in Type 2 it is more flexible to deal with the changing demands of governance.

TABLE 2.2

Types of Multi-Level Governance

Type I	Type II
General-purpose jurisdictions	Task-specific jurisdictions
Non-intersecting memberships	Intersecting memberships
Jurisdictions at a limited number of levels	No limit to the number of jurisdictional levels
System-wide architecture	Flexible design

Source: Hooghe and Marks 2004: 17.

Other recent contributions have focused on the normative dimension of MLG. Peters and Pierre (2004) suggested that the flexible and informal modes of co-ordination of MLG might bring dangers. In particular, they argued that MLG could be a type of 'Faustian bargain' in which the purported advantages of MLG in terms of functional efficiency are traded for core democratic values as authority seeps away from the formal institutions where democratic accountability is exercised. or where political actors use these informal and opaque processes to escape accountability for their decisions (see also Ch. 4).

In a similar vein, Jan Olsson (2003) considered the 'democracy paradoxes' in MLG in relation to structural policy, the policy area from which the concept first emerged. He suggested that one way to address the democratic challenges inherent in the partnership arrangements established to deliver structural policy (see Ch. 28, p. 467) would be to allocate a greater role to the formal institutions in the region, which were directly elected. This could be done by both abolishing the institutions of MLG (multi-level and cross-sectoral partnerships) and allocating their functions to elected institutions; or, more realistically, by allowing elected institutions to play a greater role in regulating partnerships.

In summarizing the state of the debate, Bache and Flinders (2004: 197) identified four common strands in the literature on multi-level governance that raised hypotheses for future research:

(1) that decision making at various territorial levels is characterized by the increased participation of non-state actors;

(2) that the identification of discrete or nested territorial levels of decision making is becoming more difficult in the context of complex overlapping networks;

(3) that in this changing context the role of the state is being transformed as state actors develop new strategies of co-ordination, steering, and networking to protect, and in some cases to enhance state autonomy;

(4) that in this changing context the nature of democratic accountability has been challenged.

CONCLUSION

Attempts to get away from the deadlock in the debate between intergovernmentalists and supranationalists over the nature of the EU have involved scholars from disciplines other than international relations, particularly comparative politics and policy analysis, applying the concepts that are their stock-in-trade to the EU. Such approaches yield a number of insights, especially concerning the more routine decisions of the EU. Such decisions may not be as monumental as the 'history-making decisions', but, as Richardson (1996a: 29) said, they constitute 'the nine-tenths of the policy iceberg that is below the water line', and 'some means has to be found of analysing it'.

If theories of EU governance were relative latecomers to the study of the EU, their proliferation has more than made up for lost time. There are a number of overlapping and related approaches competing for the same space in analysing the operation of the EU system. For organizational purposes, we have made a distinction between the categories of 'new institutionalism' and 'governance and networks'. However, the reality is less clear-cut, not only between these categories, but also within them. A key theme that cuts through these categories is the emphasis on interests v. ideas, alternatively viewed as the 'rationalist v. reflectivist' dichotomy, which for some has replaced the intergovernmental–supranational dichotomy as the dominant debate within EU studies. However, as a cursory examination of the approaches covered here suggests, this dichotomy has a long lineage in theorizing on the EU and provides a strong thread running through 'newer' theories of EU governance and the long-standing theories of integration covered in the previous chapter.

The governance and networks category of approaches raises again the theme that was prominent in Chapter 1: that of the role of interest groups. In the policy networks approach the emphasis is squarely on the links between interest groups and policy makers and the motive force of policy making is conceived to be vested interest. This approach reproduces at the sectoral level the insight of neofunctionalists that European integration would be driven forward more by interests responding in a rational, self-serving manner to the changed circumstances produced by the existence of the EC than by an idealistic commitment such as that shown by the federalists. Liberal intergovernmentalism also emphasizes interests rather than ideas as the key to analysing the EU. However, the concept of an epistemic community (and also the advocacy coalition framework) modifies this emphasis on interest, and brings knowledge and ideas back into the analysis. Here, the key actors in networks coalesce and bring about change through shared values, ideas and knowledge.

Sociological and historical institutionalists also bring ideas back in. The other type of new institutionalists, rational choice institutionalists, analyse the logical responses of actors to the institutional rules that they face, and so are working on the same lines as neofunctionalists and liberal intergovernmentalists. Sociological and historical institutionalists put a great deal of emphasis on the values and norms that actors develop within institutionalized relationships over time. These values and norms can be interpreted as ideas that actors hold, perhaps not fully consciously, which affect and at least partially explain their behaviour. While rational choice theorists, neofunctionalists, and liberal intergovernmentalists would all tend to argue that the existence of the EU structures the responses of actors because it provides a new set of rules within which they pursue their interests, sociological and historical institutionalists would tend to argue that the existence of the EU affects the way in which the actors perceive their interests, their aims, and their objectives. The theme of the role of interests in the EU is therefore also about the role of ideas.

Moving beyond the rationalist–reflectivist dichotomy, one problem with the application to the EU of concepts that were originally derived from the study of domestic political systems is that they tend to underemphasize the influence of the wider international system. An appreciation of the impact of the wider international system is the strength of some approaches derived from international relations. The absence of such a dimension was one of the most telling criticisms made by Hoffmann of neofunctionalism, although Hoffman may himself be criticized for having under-theorized this aspect. So, approaches originating in the study of domestic politics are not alone in this failing; the point remains important though, as the effects of globalization show no signs of abating (Ch. 3, pp. 48–9). Of the theories discussed here, MLG perhaps has the greatest potential for effectively conceptualizing the relationship between developments 'internal' and 'external' to the EU. There is nothing inherent in the framework that would exclude its propositions being applied to governance beyond the EU; indeed Type 2 MLG (see Table 2.2, p. 36) appears partly designed to meet that challenge.

Finally, we should keep in mind that, MLG apart, the approaches and theories discussed in this section are primarily mid-range: they seek to explain developments at a sub-system or sectoral level and are not attempts at theorizing the EU system more broadly. Moreover, as the EU becomes more complex, there may be greater application of mid-range theories. The possibilities for applying the policy network approach to the EU are borne out by an increasing number of sectoral studies highlighted by Peterson (2004: 129–30), particularly in the domains of cohesion policy, research policy, and the common agricultural policy. Governance theories more broadly defined may become more prominent with the increased use of more informal modes of governance in the EU, such as the Open Method of Coordination (see Ch. 24, pp. 357–8).

KEY POINTS

☐ Approaches from the study of domestic and comparative politics turn away from the focus of IR theories on the process of European integration, and instead treat the EU as a political system that is already in existence, and try to explore 'the nature of the beast'.

New Institutionalism

☐ New institutionalism argued that analysts had lost sight of the importance of institutions in structuring political action.

☐ Three varieties of new institutionalism can be distinguished: *rational choice institutionalism, historical institutionalism, and sociological institutionalism.*

☐ Rational choice institutionalism emphasizes the argument that the behaviour of political actors is shaped by the specific framework of rules within which they operate.

☐ Historical institutionalism emphasizes the argument that political relationships have to be viewed over time and that decisions are shaped by the nature of pre-existing institutional relationships.

☐ Sociological institutionalism emphasizes the argument that the behaviour of political actors is shaped by informal norms and values.

Governance and Networks

☐ Definitions of governance commonly emphasize the proliferation of non-state actors in the policy process.

☐ Richardson advocated the application of two concepts from the study of domestic politics: policy networks and epistemic communities.

☐ A *policy network* is a set of resource-dependent organizations. The approach advocates analysis of sectoral policy networks that range from tightly knit policy communities to loosely-bound issue networks.

☐ As a 'meso-level' approach, policy network analysis is often most effectively used in conjunction with broader theories. It places emphasis on policy implementation, which is particularly relevant in the context of the EU.

☐ Kassim argued that EU processes were not settled enough for policy networks to emerge. Against this, Peterson argued that while some EU policy sectors remained fluid, others had developed into policy networks. He later argued that the networks approach was particularly relevant to studying the EU.

☐ *Epistemic communities* are knowledge-based groups that are most likely to be influential when policy makers face uncertainty over policy choices. This approach is complementary to the policy networks approach.

Multi-Level Governance

☐ MLG has strong antecedents in neofunctionalism, but is a theory of the nature of the EU rather than a theory of the process of European integration.

☐ While accepting that integration involved intergovernmental bargains, MLG theorists argued that individual governments were not in control of the process. Actors at supranational and subnational levels played a key role also.

☐ While initially established by national governments, supranational EU institutions develop a degree of autonomy from the control of governments.

☐ Transnational and transgovernmental alliances mean that states are open to external influences. The Commission is able to exploit this situation to promote its own agenda.

☐ MLG has been criticized on a number of counts, not least for its analysis of the role and significance of subnational actors.

☐ Hooghe and Marks have developed a two-fold typology of MLG that addresses both analytical and normative concerns.

☐ Peters and Pierre have warned of a 'Faustian bargain' in which the purported gains in efficiency from MLG are suggested that the gains brought by MLG in terms of efficiency may be traded for core democratic values.

☐ Bache and Flinders identified four common strands in the literature on multi-level governance that raised hypotheses for future research.

FURTHER READING

The clearest statement of dissatisfaction with approaches to the EU based on theories of international relations is S. Hix, 'The Study of the European Community: The Challenge to Comparative Politics', *West European Politics*, 17 (1994): 1–30. Significant applications of the new institutionalist approach to the EU are to be found in P. Pierson, 'The Path to European Integration: A Historical and Institutionalist Analysis', *Comparative Political Studies*, 29 (1996): 123–63; S. Bulmer, 'New Institutionalism and the Governance of the Single European Market', *Journal of European Public Policy*, 5 (1998): 365–86; and M. Pollack, *The Engines of European Integration: Delegation, Agency and Agenda Setting in the EU* (Oxford: Oxford University Press, 2003).

Epistemic communities are explained in P. Haas, 'Introduction: Epistemic Communities and International Policy Coordination', *International Organization*, 46 (1992): 1–35. The application of policy networks and policy communities is debated in H. Kassim, 'Policy Networks, Networks and European Policy Making: A Sceptical View', *West European Politics*, 17 (1994): 15–27, and J. Peterson, 'Policy Networks and European Policy Making: A Reply to Kassim', *West European Politics*, 18 (1995): 389–407. On multi-level governance, arguably the classic statement is G. Marks, L. Hooghe, and K. Blank, 'European Integration from the 1980s: State-Centric v. Multi-Level Governance', *Journal of Common Market Studies*, 34 (1996): 341–78; the most complete statement of the approach is contained in L. Hooghe and G. Marks, *Multi-Level Governance and European Integration* (London: Rowman and Littlefield, 2004); the collection by I. Bache and M. Flinders (eds.), *Multi-Level Governance* (Oxford: Oxford University Press, 2004) undertakes a critical assessment of both the potentialities and limitations of MLG, drawing both on theoretical contributions scholars from different academic traditions and fields, and on different policy studies.

 **online resource centre**

Visit the Online Resource Centre that accompanies this book for links to more information on theories of EU Governance.

CHAPTER 3

Critical Perspectives

CHAPTER OVERVIEW

This chapter focuses on approaches to understanding the EU that are critical of some of the 'rationalist' assumptions that underpin the main debates covered in Chapters 1 and 2, and particularly of the dominant intergovernmental–supranational dichotomy. These approaches share a critique of rationalism and an emphasis on the role of ideas in political action. Beyond this, there are important differences between social constructivism and political economy and also significant variations within each approach.

> In place of the old neofunctionalist/intergovernmentalist dichotomy, the last half of the 1990s has witnessed the emergence of a new dichotomy in both IR theory and EU studies, pitting rationalist scholars, who generally depict European institutions as the products of conscious Member State design, against constructivist scholars who posit a more profound role for EU institutions and socializing and constituting the actors within them.
>
> **(Pollack 2001: 237)**

While the critical perspectives covered here have recently become more prominent in EU studies, there have been critical perspectives offered in previous periods. A notable contribution was made by Stuart Holland (1980), whose interdisciplinary approach is discussed below. More recently, the rise of critical perspectives in EU studies has ignited a rationalist–reflectivist debate, which for some has superseded the traditionally dominant intergovernmental-supranational dichotomy.

The Rationalist–Reflectivist Debate

This debate came to prominence in EU studies in the late 1990s. On the one side are rationalist scholars who argue that the EU is the result of conscious action by national governments; on the other are reflectivist scholars, who highlight the extent to which national actors redefine their positions on integration through their socialization with other European actors involved in the process.

This debate overlaps significantly with the literature on the new institutionalisms (Chapter 2). In summary, rationalists on the one hand,

*tend to operate within a view of the world (an **ontology**) that sees interests as materially given. They also adhere to a positivistic conception of how knowledge should be gathered. This involves a commitment to 'scientific' method, the neutrality of facts and the existence of observable realities.*

(Rosamond 2003: 121)

On the other hand, reflectivists:

see interests as socially constructed rather than pre-given... [and] ... are interested in how collective understandings emerge and how institutions constitute the interests and identities of actors.

(Rosamond 2003: 121)

Thus, rationalists and reflectivists make different assumptions both about what should be studied in relation to the EU and about how it should be studied. While there are important differences in the approaches outlined in this chapter, which will be discussed below, the common link between them is a critique of rationalism.

Social Constructivism

Social constructivism is not a theory of European integration. It is 'an ontological approach to social inquiry' (Cowles 2003: 110). As such, it does not necessarily reject an interpretation of Europe that is intergovernmental or supranational; rather, it rejects the assumptions, or rationalist **ontology**, on which the dominant contributions to that debate have been built.

Some constructivists are closer to the reflectivist end of the rationalist–reflectivist continuum than others, and many would see their approach as an attempt to bridge the two. Others prefer not to present these contrasting approaches as a continuum, but as two points of a triangle with constructivism providing the third. The argument here is that this image is more adequate since, 'in general, theorists tend to position their work in-between the corners' (Christiansen, Jørgensen, and Wiener 1999: 531) (see Figure 3.1).

The social constructivist approach is closely related to sociological institutionalism (Chapter 2). Both approaches emphasize that actors' behaviour is influenced by the 'logic of appropriate behaviour' or norms, which Katzenstein (1996: 5) defined as 'collective expectations for the proper behaviour of actors with a given identity'. In this view, political actors internalize social norms, which shape their identities and thus their interests. This is what constructivists refer to as the 'constitutive effects' of norms.

The constructivist view that the actions of individuals cannot be understood in isolation from their social environment contrasts with the rationalists' emphasis on 'methodological individualism', in which the central focus is on 'individual human action' (Risse 2004: 160). However, while constructivists emphasize that individuals' interests and identities are shaped by the social environment in which they exist, equally, they argue that the social environment is shaped over time by the actions of individuals. The relationship is one of two-way interaction and thus, in the words of constructivists, 'mutually constitutive'.

The essential constructivist critique of rationalist approaches is that a focus on material interests (such as economic interests or security) alone offers an inadequate explanation of key developments in European integration. Such an explanation ignores the role played by deeply embedded cultures that shape national positions, and the role of ideas and values that connect political leaders or other actors one with another.

Specifically, constructivists point to the importance of reflecting on how interaction with the EU over

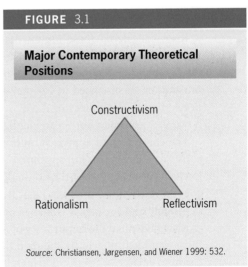

FIGURE 3.1

Major Contemporary Theoretical Positions

Constructivism

Rationalism   Reflectivism

Source: Christiansen, Jørgensen, and Wiener 1999: 532.

time may shape and redefine national positions, which places it in conflict with the 'domestic politics' assumptions of liberal intergovernmentalism (Chapter 1). As such, a constructivist history of the EU would,

focus on the ongoing struggles, contestations, and discourses on how 'to build Europe' over the years and, thus, reject an imagery of actors including governments as calculating machines who also know what they want and are never uncertain about the future and even their own stakes and interests.

(Risse 2004: 162)

However, while the distinctions between constructivism and liberal intergovernmentalism are clear, it is less clear how neofunctionalism relates to constructivism. On the one hand, there are rationalist assumptions in neofunctionalism: for example, interest groups are seen to act rationally in shifting their political activities to a new political centre at European level to maximize their gains. On the other hand, key neofunctionalist texts also refer to interest groups' 'loyalties' moving to the new centre, which is very much the language of constructivism.

European Identity

Risse (2004: 165–6) set out three main ways in which social constructivism contributes to our understanding of the EU:

- highlighting the mutually constitutive nature of agency and structure allows for a deeper understanding of the impact of the EU on its member states and particularly on statehood;
- emphasizing the constitutive effects of EU rules and policies facilitates study of the ways in which EU membership shapes interests and identities of actors;
- focusing on communicative practices highlights both how the EU is constructed discursively and how actors come to understand the meaning of European integration.

Risse considered these arguments in relation to the development of a common European identity. For constructivists, this is a relatively neglected aspect of the study of the EU, but one that their approach places as central to an understanding of European integration. As discussed in Chapter 4, identity is seen by many as a key component to developing the legitimacy of the EU, and thus to further political integration. To date, however, a common European identity has been slow to emerge.

The constructivist approach on this suggests that there is no fixed meaning of what constitutes Europe or 'Europeanness', but different constructions that emerge from different contexts, (e.g. over time or in different places). This does not mean that 'anything goes' in relation to European identity, but that its meaning is not fixed and is context-dependent and, as such, it is shaped or 'constructed' over time.

Risse illustrated the importance of identity construction by arguing that the common European identity held by the then fifteen member states partly explains the EU's decision to enlarge to twenty-five members in 2004. Commission officials acted as 'norm entrepreneurs' to promote a sense of shared community values (democracy, human rights, and market economics) between the fifteen, which generated a normative obligation towards the applicant states who shared these values. In this way, 'Rhetorical commitment to community values entrapped EU member states to offer accession negotiations to the CEE [Central and Eastern Europe] and other Eastern European countries despite the initial preferences against enlargement' (Risse 2004: 172). It was noted, however, that once negotiations began, rationalist accounts provided a more fitting explanation of the strategic bargaining by national governments that took place. This acceptance of the differential appropriateness of forms of explanation is evidence that constructivism does not seek to displace rationalist theories entirely, but to contribute to a more complete picture of how the EU works.

The EU as a Discursive Construct

Hay and Rosamond (2002) used constructivism to highlight how the process of globalization and European integration can be understood as 'discursive constructs'. Here, the *idea* of either European integration or globalization (or both) as external constraints on domestic action may be accepted as true by political actors (with or without evidence of the material reality) and thus influence their actions. In other words, 'it is the ideas that actors hold about the context in which they find themselves rather than the context itself which informs the way in which actors behave' (Hay and Rosamond 2002: 148).

They illustrated this argument by identifying four alternative discourses of globalization found in contemporary Europe: as external economic constraint; as the threat of homogenization; as a desirable yet contingent outcome; as a contingent and undesirable outcome. In the latter discourse, globalization is viewed as a fragile and malleable process, but not a favourable one. This discourse is used by some pro-integrationists to construct a view of the EU as a 'bulwark' against the negative consequences of globalization, in particular against the threats to the notion of a European social model that places greater emphasis on welfare provision than the neo-liberal imperatives of globalization would allow (Hay and Rosamond 2002: 152–57).

While globalization discourses can be used to advance arguments for European integration, discourses of European integration are sometimes used by domestic actors to justify particular courses of domestic action or inaction. Hay and Rosamond (2002: 157) argued that:

In a number of contemporary European contexts, it is the process of European integration (often in the immediate form of the Maastricht convergence criteria) which is (or has been) invoked as the proximate cause of often painful social and economic reforms elsewhere legitimated in terms of globalization.

The increased focus on the real or perceived constraints placed by European integration on domestic choice, and constructive arguments more generally, has been central to an upsurge in interest in the notion of Europeanization as transformation of domestic politics (Ch. 4).

Liberal and Critical Constructivism

Van Apeldoorn, Overbeek, and Ryner (2003) argued there is an important distinction between what they termed 'critical constructivism' and 'liberal constructivism'. The former, their preferred approach, suggests that an understanding of the development of ideas should be grounded in material circumstance, particularly economic interests (below). By contrast, liberal constructivism 'tends towards idealism' in that it highlights constraints, such as discourses, that are not grounded in material reality.

Thus, each of these variants of constructivism emphasizes the role of structures in shaping actor behaviour: the key point of difference between them is the nature and origins of the structures. This was illustrated in relation to a constructivist study by Risse and Wiener, who argued that it was difficult to explain agreement on EMU through economics-based explanations because very different views existed within the EU and within member states on the best way forward in terms of material economic interests. Instead, at a 'critical juncture', a trajectory was determined, influenced by ideas that had their origins in 'historical, religious, communal heritage (which includes liberal democracies and social markets)' (van Apeldoorn, Overbeek, and Ryner 2003: 32). Once this trajectory was taken, it was subsequently followed irrespective of how perceived material interests changed subsequently.

Van Apeldoorn, Overbeek, and Ryner (2003: 32) criticized this argument on two counts. First, on the separation between the ideas and material (economic) interests; and second, on the grounds that when material interests are discussed, they refer to the interests of national economies without any particular justification for doing this. In contrast, they argued that there can be no easy separation between ideas and material interests (below); and the material interests that matter are best understood in relation to social classes, or perhaps particular sectors of the economy, rather than the notion of national economic interest. Thus, while van Apeldoorn, Overbeek, and Ryner (2003) agreed with the constructivist emphasis on ideas, they argued that these needed to be firmly ground in material circumstances (below).

Constructivism Assessed

Cowles (2003: 110–11) identified three criticisms of constructivism:

- it lacks a theory of agency and shows a tendency to over-emphasize the role of structures rather than the actors who help to shape those structures;
- that much of the early constructivist literature tended to focus its analysis on public actors to the relative neglect of important non-state actors;
- that there is tendency of some constructivists to identify the good things that have been socially constructed rather than the bad.

On the positive side, constructivism has played an important role in highlighting the importance of ideas in shaping both European integration and the more routine operation of the EU. Constructivists acknowledge that interests-based explanations continue to have validity, but that the role of ideas has been much neglected in studies of the EU to date. The source of ideas in shaping actor behaviour in the EU is now itself an important debate, which leads us neatly into the more material-based conceptions of ideas rooted in political economy.

Critical Political Economy

While the focus of this chapter is on 'critical' perspectives, it is important to note that not all approaches to political economy are critical of dominant approaches to the study of the EU; indeed some traditionally dominant approaches covered in the previous chapters of this book are themselves informed by a political economy perspective. Verdun (2003) categorized the various political economy approaches as neo-realism, neo-liberal institutionalism, social constructivism, and critical approaches.

Neo-realism emphasizes the actions of states, who have given interests and seek to maximize these interests in an 'anarchic' international arena. This approach informed the work of intergovernmentalists, such as Hoffmann and Moravcsik (Chapter 1). Moravcsik in particular highlighted the relationship between domestic economic interests and state behaviour in international relations.

Neo-liberal institutionalism accepts that states are key actors, but places greater faith in the ability of international institutions to regulate the behaviour of states on the world stage. Here, there is an emphasis on path dependence and socialization, which is highlighted in the new-institutionalist literature on the EU (Chapter 2).

Social constructivism is discussed at length above. For Verdun (2003: 92), it has three essential features: that the individual is a social creation who gains knowledge and finds identity through interaction with social processes; that an understanding of 'reality' is coloured by whoever observes or interprets it; and that social scientists studying social action are involved in the process and this involvement colours their findings.

Critical approaches to political economy are subdivided into various groups, such as the Amsterdam school, the British school, and the neo-Gramscians. They have in common the view that dominant approaches to international relations (IR) and international political economy (IPE) focus on the state and other élite actors without situating their behaviour in the context of underlying power structures (below).

These approaches all focus on issues relating to the role of the state and its relationship with the broader international economic system, but are otherwise quite distinct. The purpose in identifying these contrasting approaches is to situate what we term 'critical political economy' perspectives, which is the focus of our discussion below.

Globalization and European Integration

In critical political economy, European integration cannot be separated from the phenomenon of globalization. In this perspective, the former is often viewed as a particular regional expression of the changing nature of global capitalism.

Globalization is variously defined. On some definitions, it is no more than a contemporary term to describe a set of processes that have a long history; but more commonly globalization is taken to refer to a new phenomenon of linkages transcending territorial boundaries. Although globalization has cultural and social aspects, the view of globalization as an observable economic phenomenon is an influential one.

This economic explanation is characterized by the growth of multinational companies that operate in a number of states, and which own especial loyalty to no one state. It also highlights the emergence of global flows of capital, which increased dramatically in the last part of the twentieth century. These flows are both of **investment capital** and **liquid capital**. The rise of multinationals and the increased flows of investment capital intensify competition between states to provide the most attractive conditions for investment. If they try to impose higher taxes or more restrictive regulatory rules than their competitor states, they will lose investment to those other states.

The question of the degree of control that states have over this process is the subject of academic dispute. The term 'globalization' is often used as though it is a process beyond the control of governments, which constrains them in the policies that they can follow (see the quotation from Hay and Rosamond above). Some scholars suggest that globalization is a myth (Hirst and Thompson 1996): that it is just a new term to describe the internationalization of capitalist activity, which has been ongoing for a long time. In fact, the present 'global' economy is less open than was the international economy between 1870 and 1914. Most so-called multinational corporations are actually large national companies that trade internationally. The myth of globalization is used as an argument to prevent national governments from trying to control the forces of capitalism; but if governments co-ordinated their efforts they could regulate global markets.

A third view (Amoore *et al.* 1997; Payne 2000) is that globalization has two aspects. On the one hand, developments that are largely independent of governments, such as technological advances, have changed the scale of operation of capitalist enterprises and made it more difficult for governments to regulate their activities. On the other hand, the responses of states to these developments have themselves fed the process. Technology makes it possible to move funds across international exchanges at speeds never envisaged in earlier periods, and this poses problems for governments in regulating the process. They could respond by investigating new, perhaps collaborative ways of regulating the exchanges; but they have mostly responded by capitulating to 'the inevitable' and lifting capital controls. This response makes a reality of the globalization of capital markets; but it could have been otherwise.

It is important in this context to see that globalization is a process, not a fixed condition. It is not the case that globalization started on a particular date; it is a name given to changes in the capitalist system that have developed in the post-war period. At each stage in this development, governments and other actors have played a role in shaping the nature of the process. Not only is the process itself fed by the actions of states and other actors; it also affects their outlooks and arguably the institutional arrangements that govern them. Here, the EU is a case in point.

The EU and Globalization

At first sight, the emergence of the EU as a regional grouping seems to be in contradiction to the direction and thrust of globalization. It is true that to some extent the project of European integration, which started as a response to the problems of post-war reconstruction, became a process of responding to the evolution of the international system. However, the European project has always been one of 'open regionalism'.

Open regionalism means that policy is directed towards the elimination of obstacles to trade within a region, while at the same time doing nothing to raise external tariff barriers to the rest of the world (Gamble and Payne 1996: 251). There has been no significant voice in the debate about the nature of the EU that has advocated closing western Europe off from the global system. The central debate has been between the British position and the French position on this issue.

The British position has favoured global free trade and free movement of capital. It has seen the freeing of trade within the EU as a stepping stone to this end. The French position has seen the EU as a means of organizing European capitalism to compete more effectively on world markets. It has been a 'strategic trade' view rather than a 'free trade' view. But it has never advocated the EU being a closed trading bloc. Instead it has argued the case for the liberalization of national markets to be accompanied by the introduction of European-level industrial and technology policies to build up and promote European champions, companies that could compete effectively with US and Japanese companies on world markets.

These debates reflect differences in national approaches to the management of capitalism within Europe. French governments have generally been less willing than British to accept that the free market should determine the shape of the national economy, and have favoured a larger role for the state (George 1989). However, the belief that there has been a quantitative and qualitative change in the extent and nature of global economic transactions has affected the policies of individual states, and the nature of the process of European integration. This insight is central to modern critical political economy perspectives.

Neo-Marxism

Recent neo-Marxist scholarship on European integration and the EU was prefigured in the work of Stuart Holland (1980), which offered a neo-Marxist explanation of European integration that focused on the close relationship between economics and politics and would now be placed in the category of 'critical political economy'.

Holland (1980: 89) took issue with the explanations of and justifications for integration offered by then contemporary economists, arguing that 'the conventional theory of economic integration largely neglects issues of social and economic class' and that this theory played a role in 'mystifying or obscuring the real power relations in capitalist society'. This argument that the dominant theories of integration serve to obscure deeper underlying explanations and purposes of the EU is echoed by more recent contributors to the debate (below). Holland's argument was explicitly class-based. Thus, while then contemporary 'economic' integration theorists justified their position by arguing that broader social and political issues were not the concern of economists, Holland (1980: 89) suggested that there were other reasons for their failure to incorporate social class and political power into their analysis:

Class analysis has Marxist connotations which raise issues of exploitation and power which are inconveniently disturbing to many of the élites engaged in integration itself. Lifting the lid on class relations opens a Pandora's box of the kind which key exponents and advocates of international integration have been trying to close and bury for some time.

From this perspective, the dominant neofunctionalist theory had similar flaws to the approaches of conventional economists. It rested on pluralist assumptions regarding the wide dispersal of power within society, which meant that no single group would be able to dominate the integration process. Neofunctionalism identified the role of élites and interest groups in advancing integration, but did not link the role of these actors to the class structure that distributed power unevenly between them. Thus, while neofunctionalists emphasized the role of business interests in promoting integration, this would not be conceptualized in terms of 'class power'. For neofunctionalists, the main reason why business interests were more prominent in advancing integration than were labour interests was that business was better organized than labour. Holland accepted that capitalist interests were more effectively organized than labour, but suggested that this argument obscured a more important explanation for capitalist influence over the process. What was important was not an observable process of business leaders influencing state actors, but a shared world view; or, as Holland (1980: 91–2) put it: 'the combination of governmental élites and the self-electing élites of private capital, bound on a common venture in fulfilment of a common ideology'.

A generation of scholars later, the starting point of the argument by van Apeldoorn, Overbeek, and Ryner (2003: 17) was essentially the same as that of Holland, that the dominant theories of integration have basic flaws that obscure understanding of the nature of power in the EU:

by their very design they are unable to conceptualize adequately power relations that are constitutive of capitalist market structures. In other words, these mainstream theories fail to account for the structural power that determines the particular trajectory of European integration.

In particular, 'mainstream theories' make assumptions about the inherent rationality of market forces that leave no room for alternative organizing principles. Specifically, they 'assume either explicitly or implicitly that market forces are expressions of an inner rationality of universal human nature that is held to be the essence of the realm of freedom in political affairs' (van Apeldoorn, Overbeek, and Ryner 2003: 18). Critical political economists dispute the assumption that the market is a reflection of human nature and that its operation equates with freedom in political affairs, and suggest instead that this starting point obscures the uneven distribution of power inherent in the operation of markets. The consequence is that mainstream theories define power narrowly in relation to control by political authorities and thus the empirical focus is on how this power is organized. In the critical political economy perspective, this view needs to be supplemented with a view of power derived from social forces (generally, class relations) that underpin market relations and shape formal political authority.

To understand the true nature of power in the EU, van Apeldoorn, Overbeek, and Ryner (2003) proposed a neo-Marxist approach, drawing on the work of Antonio Gramsci. This is where the 'constructivist' strand of their approach is prominent in critical political economy, with the role of ideas being central to the understanding of Gramsci's concept of 'hegemony'. Unlike liberal constructivists, though, ideas here are firmly embedded in social relations. Gramsci argued that the capitalist class does not rule by force, either exclusively or primarily, but through consent generated by the diffusion of its ideas (via state institutions and organizations in civil society). In this way, the specific interests of the capitalist class become internalized by all as the general interest and thus states only need to use force to govern as a last resort. Thus, mainstream theories of the EU not only fail to expose the underlying nature of class power that shapes its emergent political structures, but in doing so serve to reproduce the consent that legitimizes and thus sustains this state of affairs.

Competing Models of Capitalism

A distinctive feature of the neo-Gramscian approach to the EU is its focus on the question of what model of capitalism is likely to emerge from the current struggle between competing interests and ideas at the EU level. Rhodes and van Apeldoorn (1997: 171) argued that, while there was still considerable diversity among the national 'capitalisms' in western Europe in the late 1990s, both globalization and European integration were 'eroding national particularities'. Distinctive national systems were being replaced by systems that embodied the ideas of liberalization, balanced budgets, and primary emphasis on anti-inflationary monetary policies.

The acceptance of these policies implied the dismantling of the different national systems that were set up after the war. These varied in the emphasis that they put on different elements in the mix, hence the diversity noted above; but they typically involved some or all of the following: extensive welfare provision, paid for out of taxation; a steering role for the state in the economy; significant state ownership in some sectors of industry; a role for the representatives of organized labour in economic policy making; an implicit guarantee that wages would increase to allow workers to share in the benefits of economic growth; some degree of job security for the workforce. These variations on a 'European model' of capitalism can be contrasted with the 'American' model that prevailed in the United States, which gave a much smaller role to state regulation of the economy, and a much bigger role to market forces than did the European models.

Globalization has placed the distinctive features of the European models under strain. High taxes to support a high level of welfare provision provide a disincentive to investment, which under conditions of globalization is more likely to be redirected to states with lower tax burdens. State interference in the working of the market economy is another incentive for potential investment to go elsewhere, to find bases for production that are regulated with a lighter touch, leaving management more flexibility to respond to changing market conditions. State ownership of industry acts as a barrier to penetration of national markets from outside, and so has come under sustained attack from multinational producers; while selling off state shares in industry ('privatization') has proved to be a useful source of revenue for governments trying to keep their budget deficits within acceptable margins. The reaction of organized labour to privatization and to attempts to reduce welfare commitments has obstructed marketization, encouraging governments to minimize the involvement of the representatives of organized labour in policy making. Maintaining wage increases, especially in the public sector, is dependent on maintaining rates of economic growth, and at certain periods has proved difficult without increasing budget deficits. Job security translates into inflexibility in labour markets, and was identified as the biggest problem preventing Europe from benefiting to the same extent as the United States from the advent of new, potentially labour-saving technologies.

Within the EU, leading states have embraced policies of liberalization with varying degrees of enthusiasm. From the 1970s, and particularly under Margaret Thatcher, Britain moved closest to the American model. It promoted liberal policies of removing capital controls, privatizing publicly-owned enterprises, and deregulating labour markets. Essentially the same policies continued under the Labour government from 1997, albeit with stronger compensatory redistributive policies, and Prime Minister Blair tried to convert the rest of the EU to support them.

Rhodes and van Apeldoorn (1997: 171) argued that, beyond the changes occurring in national 'capitalisms', there was also a question of what kind of socio-economic order, or 'model of capitalism' was emerging within the supranational regime of the EU. Debate over the future economic, social, and political structure of the EU in the light of the impact of globalization became central to the history of European integration during the period when Jacques Delors was President of the Commission (see Chs. 12 and 13), and has remained so since. Hooghe (1998) characterized the key distinction in this debate as one between *regulated capitalism* and *neo-liberalism*.

Some of the voices that resisted neo-liberal market-oriented policies in this debate may have been genuinely rejecting the alleged logic of globalization for economic and social policies. However, the extent to which the market-oriented policies have prevailed suggests another explanation. Governments faced with the prospect of having to dismantle their post-war national systems because of the impact of globalization, might protest in public so that they could avoid having to accept responsibility for unpopular measures at home. As Mitchell Smith (1997) explained, the claim that 'the Commission made me do it' can provide governments with a strategic advantage in domestic politics, allowing them to achieve their real objectives while allowing the Commission to take the blame. At the same time this can have a negative effect on the image of the Commission, and of the EU as a whole, in the state concerned. It can contribute to the EU being seen as a negative, even malign influence, and so undermine its popularity and legitimacy (see Chapter 4).

The New Regionalism

While the formation of regional blocs such as the EU, particularly for trading purposes, is not particularly new, there has been a proliferation of such blocs from the mid-1980s, which is explicitly linked to globalization. They include the North American

Free Trade Association (NAFTA), Asia Pacific Economic Co-operation (APEC), and Mercusor (a Spanish acronym for the common market of countries in South America: Argentina, Bolivia, Brazil, Chile, Paraguay, and Uruguay). This proliferation of regional groupings in the context of globalization gave rise to a new group of scholars studying the phenomenon under the label of the 'new regionalism' (see Breslin *et al.* 2002).

The essential argument here is that in the context of globalization, and particularly a globalized economy, states in a particular 'region' pool resources to survive and compete in a more demanding economic environment. Of course, as with the EU, there is debate over the extent to which states voluntarily pool resources, and how far the state-élites are responding to other actors or forces shaping integration. There is a further debate about how far these regional formations are a response to globalization and how far they promote and accelerate it.

This issue relates to an academic divide between those who see the EU as *sui generis* and those who see it as a particular example of a wider phenomenon. In the latter view, there is greater emphasis on comparing examples of regional integration, an emphasis that has revived in recent times under the heading of the 'new regionalism'. On this question, Rosamond (2003: 124) argued that in comparative terms, the EU is at most a 'deviant case' of regional integration:

Its longevity rules out any claim that the EU was created as a response to global economic upheavals in the 1970s and early 1980s. Moreover, compared to other cases of regionalism the EU is considerably more institutionalized and much more deeply integrated. Yet at the same time the acceleration of economic integration through the single market programme and progress towards monetary union has coincided with the growth of regional projects elsewhere.

Critical Political Economy Assessed

Contributions from this perspective raise important questions for 'mainstream' theorists, in particular about the assumptions that underpin dominant theories both of European integration and of the operation of the EU as a political system. In addition to highlighting the role of ideas, neo-Marxist contributions raise questions about the nature of power in the EU that have often been ignored entirely by mainstream theorists or dealt with in a cursory manner. The argument that academics should widen their lenses beyond what is most observable to reveal the hidden sources of power and authority is a powerful one.

One obvious criticism of this perspective is that a number of scholars are explicitly working with mid-range theories and are not concerned with underlying processes that shape the broad contours of political power, but with how the political system works on a day-to-day basis. It is highly unlikely that scholars focusing on such matters are unaware of neo-Marxist arguments. It may be that they simply reject the neo-Marxist analysis based on class power; or it maybe that they accept the essential analysis but feel this is inevitable and so time should be spent on understanding (and thus improving) political processes within this context.

THEORY

CONCLUSION

This chapter has summarized contributions that can be broadly categorized as 'critical perspectives'. As the discussion shows, these perspectives are not only critical of mainstream theories, but also of each other. Importantly, though, they share a critique of reflectivist assumptions that lead to a study of observable phenomena. Instead, critical approaches emphasize the 'hidden' sources of power in the realms of ideas and social forces.

Critical perspectives have a long history in other disciplines (e.g. sociology) and other subdisciplines of political studies (e.g. international relations). But while there has been a recent groundswell of interest in critical perspectives in the study of the EU, we should not view the applications of critical perspectives as entirely new. Some of the contributions discussed above have a longer lineage in the study of the EC/EU than is at first obvious. Most notably, there are constructivist elements in neofunctionalism and the neo-Marxist contributions from critical political economy of recent years closely resemble the arguments of Holland a generation earlier. Why these aspects should have been evident in earlier debates but absent for so long is an interesting question.

It is clearly the case that, particularly with the collapse of the communist regimes in the Soviet bloc in the late 1980s and early 1990s, neo-Marxist approaches fell from grace in some areas of study at least. Their revival and application to the study of the EU may be evidence of rescuing the 'baby' from the bathwater that was discarded, to highlight previously obscured aspects of European integration and the nature of political authority in the EU. Alternatively, this may be a cyclical phenomenon: there is a tendency in the academic world—and the study of the EU is no different—for theories and concepts to drift out of scholarly debate only to be revived at some later point in a revised form.

A further possible explanation is the relative isolation of academic networks. Communities of scholars, like policy communities, are often 'nested' and relatively disconnected from others. The growing application of critical perspectives to the EU suggests a greater cross-fertilization of ideas between scholarly communities than may have been the case for some time. Empirical developments, and particularly globalization—if it is accepted as an empirical fact—have undoubtedly stimulated this cross-fertilization of ideas, not least between EU and IR scholars.

KEY POINTS

The Rationalist–Reflectivist Debate

☐ Critical perspectives on the EU have a long history, but have recently become prominent in the context of the rationalist–reflectivist debate.

☐ Rationalists and reflectivists make different assumptions about both what should be studied in relation to the EU and how it should be studied.

Social Constructivism

☐ Social constructivism is not a theory of European integration, but 'an ontological approach to social inquiry'.

☐ It relates closely to sociological institutionalism in emphasizing the influence on actors of norms and the 'logic of appropriate behaviour'.

☐ In relation to the EU, it puts particular emphasis on how national positions and perceived national interests are shaped through the engagement of national actors with EU actors.

☐ Constructivists emphasize the role of identity and its fluidity.

☐ How constructions of Europe shape domestic politics has been important in increasing interest in the study of 'Europeanization'.

☐ A distinction has been made between liberal constructivism and critical constructivism, in which the latter places greater emphasis on the material context from which ideas originate.

Critical Political Economy

☐ Verdun identified four varieties of political economy: neo-realism, neo-liberal institutionalism, social constructivism and critical approaches.

☐ Holland (1980) argued that then contemporary theories of integration obscured the underlying power relations in the EC.

☐ A generation later, van Apeldoorn, Overbeek and Ryner (2003) picked up and developed the same theme, drawing more explicitly on the analysis of Antonio Gramsci.

Globalization and European Integration

☐ In critical political economy, European integration and globalization are inextricably linked, with the former generally viewed as a particular regional expression of the changing nature of global capitalism.

☐ While on first sight, the EU as a regional grouping may appear in conflict with globalization, the EU's free-trade approach to the rest of the world has been characterized as 'open regionalism'.

☐ While globalization has been seen as a threat to distinct models of capitalism, a broad distinction remains between variations on a 'European model' and an 'American model' that gives a smaller role to state regulation of the economy and a bigger role to market forces. Competition between these models continues both within states and within the EU system as a whole.

☐ The proliferation of regional groupings in the context of globalization has given rise to a new group of scholars studying this phenomenon under the label of the 'new regionalism'.

FURTHER READING

On constructivism, see the influential collection in the Special Issue of the *Journal of European Public Policy* (1999: Vol. 6, No. 4), edited by T. Christiansen, K. Jorgensen, and A. Wiener. Other helpful contributions: J. Checkel and A. Moravcsik, 'A Constructivist Research Programme in EU Studies?', *European Union Politics*, 2 (2001): 652–68; B. Rosamond, 'New Theories of European Integration' in M. Cini, *European Union Politics* (2003): 109–27; and T. Risse, 'Social Constructivism and European Integration' in Wiener and Diez (eds.) (2004): 159–76.

On critical political economy, the key contributions are A. Bieler, and A. Morton (eds.), *Social Forces in the Making of the New Europe: The Restructuring of European Social Relations in the Global Political Economy* (London: Palgrave, 2001); B. van Apeldoorn, *Transnational Capitalism and the Struggle over European Integration* (London: Routledge, 2002); and A. Cafruny and M. Ryner (eds.), *A Ruined Fortress? Neoliberal Hegemony and Transformation in Europe* (Lanham: Rowman and Littlefield, 2003).

online resource centre   Visit the Online Resource Centre that accompanies this book for links to more information on 'critical perspectives'.

CHAPTER 4

Theorizing Consequences

CHAPTER OVERVIEW

As the EU has increasingly been understood as a political system in its own right, so academic attention has shifted to understanding the implications of this development. This chapter focuses on two sets of consequences that have prompted much scholarly interest and look set to remain at the forefront of academic debates for some time to come. The first is 'Europeanization', which is understood here as a process in which domestic politics, policies, and polities are changed through engagement with the EU system. The second concerns the consequences of the EU for democracy.

> Having spent intellectual energy in seeking to understand the 'nature of the beast', that is, the nature of European integration, political scientists have now realised that a EU political system is in place, produces decisions, and impacts on domestic policies in various guises. Hence the focus has shifted to studying those impacts
>
> **(Bulmer and Radaelli 2004: 3)**

This chapter brings together what have usually been presented as separate 'consequences' of European integration: Europeanization effects, and challenges to democracy. However, there are clear links between the two, particularly when Europeanization is understood as a process through which domestic politics and polities are changed by their engagement with the EU. Most obviously, the process of Europeanization can challenge domestic democratic structures and processes by transferring responsibilities and obscuring lines of accountability. More positively, Europeanization may add to what is termed 'output democracy' by increasing the policy-making capacities of governments through collective action.

Europeanization

Europeanization has recently emerged as a key theme in studies of the European Union, and has become 'a staple component of European integration courses in political science and public policy degrees' (Radaelli 2004: 1). However, as is often the case with emerging concepts, its meaning is contested and leaves the field of study looking somewhat disorderly, casting doubt on the extent to which it has added value to those approaches that already existed for studying Europe. For example, some scholars refer to Europeanization as an EU-related phenomenon, while others see it as a phenomenon broader than, or largely separate from the EU. Beyond this distinction, other definitions and usages abound. Increasingly though, the main value of the concept appears to be in highlighting the changing nature of relations between the EU and its member (and accession) states, and this has become the primary focus of empirical studies of Europeanization. Here, we outline the range of uses before focusing on the development of Europeanization studies that relate specifically to the EU.

Meanings of 'Europeanization'

While Europeanization has become a key theme in studies of the EU in recent years, it is not a new term. Rather, its importance has grown as scholars have sought to give more precise meaning to a term that has been used loosely to indicate a range of issues and processes. In the debates over the meaning and relevance of the term, the extent to which it has been applied in different contexts with different purposes has become evident. Buller and Gamble (2002), Olsen (2002), and Bache and Jordan (2004) have each identified five uses of Europeanization, some of which overlap while others do not (see Insights 4.1,

INSIGHT 4.1

Uses of Europeanization 1

Olsen (2002) distinguished between five possible uses of the term Europeanization:

- as changes in external territorial boundaries;
- as the development of institutions of governance at the European level;
- as central penetration of national and sub-national systems of governance;
- as exporting forms of political organization and governance that are typical and distinct for Europe beyond the European territory;
- as a political project aiming at a unified and politically stronger Europe.

INSIGHT 4.2

Uses of Europeanization 2

Buller and Gamble (2002) identified five different ways in which Europeanization has been used by academics

- to refer to the development of institutions of governance at the European level;
- to refer to examples where distinct European forms of organization and governance have been exported outside Europe's territorial boundaries;
- to denote the achievement of the political unification of Europe;
- as a process whereby domestic politics becomes increasingly subject to European policy-making;
- as a smokescreen for domestic political manoeuvres.

4.2, and 4.3). Drawing on these contributions, we summarize the ways in which various scholars have used the term 'Europeanization', and distinguish between those uses that relate specifically to the EU and those that are not EU-specific.

Our concern here is with notions of Europeanization that relate specifically to the EU (Tables 4.1 and 4.2). In particular, we focus on uses of the term Europeanization that highlight the changing relationship between the EU and its member (and accession) states. Definitions that refer to the creation of new powers for the EU are largely synonymous with conceptions of European integration, which are discussed elsewhere in this volume (Ch. 1, p. 4). Yet even in relation to this narrower focus, there is a considerable theoretical and empirical literature, which we survey below.

The Development of the Field

Attempts to give a more precise meaning to Europeanization span just over a decade. An early and influential contribution was Robert Ladrech's study of the EU and France, in which Europeanization was defined as, 'an incremental process reorienting the direction

THEORY

Uses of Europeanization 3

Bache and Jordan (2004) suggested that Europeanization is most commonly used in one of five ways. As either:

- **A top down** process of domestic change deriving from the EU
- the creation of **new EU powers**
- the creation of **a new, European lodestar of domestic politics**
- **horizontal transfer** or 'crossloading' of concepts and policies between states
- an increasingly **two-way interaction between states and the EU.**

TABLE 4.1

Uses of Europeanization: EU-Specific

Usage	Focus on
A top-down process of change deriving from the EU	The effects of EU membership on domestic politics, policies, and polities (Héritier *et al.* 2001; Buller and Gamble 2002). Later research highlighted issues of culture, discourse, identity, and norms (Bulmer and Radaelli 2004).
The creation of new EU powers	The development of EU structures of governance and the accumulation of EU competences (Cowles *et al.* 2001). This usage is similar to the notion of European integration.
The creation of a European lodestar of domestic politics	The idea of the EU as an increasingly important reference point for the political activities of domestic actors, such as subnational governments and interest groups (Hanf and So-etendorp 1998; Fairbrass 2003).
An increasingly two-way interaction between states and the EU	States seeking to anticipate and ameliorate the effects of top-down Europeanization pressures by 'uploading' their preferences to the EU level. As such, the EU both affects and is affected by domestic processes (Bomberg and Peterson 2000; Börzel 2002).
Changes in external boundaries	The expansion of Europe as a political space, particularly through the process of enlargement (Olsen 2002; 2003).
A 'smokescreen' for domestic manoeuvres	A process in which domestic actors 'hide behind' the EU to legitimize domestic action (or inaction) that may be unpopular (Buller 2000; Buller and Gamble 2002; Dyson and Featherstone 1999; Radaelli 2004).

and shape of politics to the degree that EC political and economic dynamics become part of the organizational logic of national politics and policy-making' (Ladrech 1994: 69). In other words, domestic politics was being changed by the response of domestic organizations to the changing context brought about by EU membership.

TABLE 4.2	
Uses of Europeanization: Non EU-Specific	
Usage	Focus on
Horizontal transfer or 'crossloading' between states	The movement of ideas and practices between European states (whether EU members or not). The EU may or may not play a role in facilitating these movements. This usage is linked to ideas of policy transfer (Bomberg and Peterson 2000) and is also referred to as 'crossloading' (Burch and Gomez 2003; Howell, 2003).
Exporting forms of political organization	The transfer of European political ideas and practices beyond Europe (Olsen 2002; 2003).

Yet while Ladrech observed Europeanization effects in France, he did not suggest that the effects of the EU would be the same across all member states. Thus, fears of harmonization or homogenization were unfounded. Instead, domestic factors played an important role in shaping the nature of the Europeanization effects in France, and would do so elsewhere. There would be 'national-specific adaptation to cross national inputs' (Ladrech 1994: 84). Ladrech's arguments about the importance of domestic mediating factors were borne out in subsequent studies.

In their study of Britain, Bulmer and Burch (1998) looked at the effects of EU membership on the machinery of central government and argued that 'while change has been substantial, it has been more or less wholly in keeping with British traditions' (1998: 603). At key points in Britain's relationship with the EU, the administrative response had been shaped by the way in which important political actors had perceived the integration process. So, 'the construction of the issue of integration interacts with the prevailing characteristics of national governmental machinery to explain the different starting points for national adaptation' (Bulmer and Burch 1998: 606). A related study by James Smith (2001: 160) on the Scottish Office came to a similar conclusion that 'while the culture has undergone subtle realignment in adapting to "European" administrative practice, the *overall* ethos and parameters of the culture have not been altered to any great extent'.

Uploading and Downloading

While early studies focused on the downward flow of pressures from the EU to the national level, later studies increasingly highlighted the interactive two-way relationship between member states and the EU. As well as being 'downloaded' by the member states from the EU level, ideas and practices are also 'uploaded' from member states to the EU level. The incentive to upload is that if states can get their existing policy preferences accepted as the preferences of the EU, they will have less trouble adapting to the EU policy when it comes into force. As Mény, Muller, and Quermonne (1996: 5) noted, 'Often, the most effective results are achieved through controlling the initial stages of the development of a policy . . . The advantages accrue to those leading countries which succeed in convincing the Community institutions and public opinion that their options or solutions are the best.'

A study of environmental policy by Börzel (2002) emphasized how national executives tried to minimize the domestic implementation costs of EU environmental initiatives by seeking to upload their own preferred policy models to the EU level. Different states' executives had different uploading strategies, according to both their policy preferences and their capacity to participate at the EU level. A distinction was made between the *pace-setting* strategies of those state executives actively seeking to promote their preferences at EU level, and the *foot-dragging* strategies of those seeking to delay or block EU action so as to avoid heavy implementation costs. A third strategy of *fence-sitting* described those states that did not seek to advance or block policies, but worked opportunistically with both 'pace setters' and 'foot draggers' to trade their support on environmental policy for reciprocal support in other policy areas.

While this interactive dynamic of Europeanization was widely recognized, much empirical research continued to focus on downward pressures. Of particular note was a multi-state study by Cowles, Caporaso, and Risse (2001), which focused on the downward pressure from the EU level on 'domestic structures'. The study looked at two categories of domestic structure: *policy structures*, a concern extending beyond policy content to changes in the political, legal and administrative structures of policy; and *system-wide domestic structures*, relating to changes in the nation state, its society, and economy. The findings of this study echoed those of Ladrech (1994) on the importance of national factors in shaping outcomes. In particular, they emphasized the importance of the degree of 'fit' between EU-level changes and existing domestic structures, policies and practices. Poor fit implies strong pressure to adapt: good fit implies weak pressure. The extent to which adaptational pressure leads to domestic change depends on five intervening factors: multiple veto points in the domestic structure; facilitating institutions; domestic organizational and policy-making cultures; the differential empowerment of domestic actors; and learning (Cowles *et al.* 2001: 2).

This theme of domestic adaptation was developed further by Olsen (2002: 932), who, drawing on the new-institutionalist arguments of March and Olsen (1989), argued that:

> the most standard institutional response to novelty is to find a routine in the existing repertoire of routines that can be used. External changes are interpreted and responded to through existing institutional frameworks, including existing causal and normative beliefs about legitimate institutions and the appropriate distribution, exercise and control of power.

Olsen provided two broad explanations for different patterns of Europeanization across member states. The first related to the nature of the pressures 'coming down' from the EU, specifically, that EU pressures are more likely to have an impact in the domestic arena under the following circumstances: 'the more precise their legal foundation; when they are based on hard law rather than soft law; when the affected parties (constituent units) have been involved in developing the arrangement; the greater the independence of their secretariat; if the secretariat is single-headed rather than multiple-headed; and the greater the financial autonomy of the institution or regime' (2002: 933). The second explanation pointed to different responses to adaptive pressures across member states because 'the (West) European political order is characterized by long, strong and varied institutional histories, with different trajectories of state- and nation-building, resources and capabilities' (Olsen 2002: 934).

The studies summarized above employed different definitions of Europeanization, but common findings emerged. Most obviously, these studies illustrated divergence in the domestic effects of EU membership across different dimensions (e.g. institutions, policies). This was explained by variations in the nature of the EU initiative or decision, and the degree of fit between this and domestic preferences and practices. Despite the focus on downward causation, there was agreement that Europeanization is a two-way process in which states also seek to upload their preferences to the EU level.

'Second Generation' Studies

Dyson and Goetz (2002) distinguished between first-generation and second-generation Europeanization studies to illustrate differences between those studies that emphasized the more formal, observable consequences of EU membership and those that focused on less formal and less observable changes. While first-generation Europeanization studies can be traced back to the early 1970s, the second generation emerged in the 1990s and was consistent with a broader sociological turn in EU studies around that time (see Chs. 2 and 3). In the perspective of second-generation studies, Europeanization is not limited to changes in political–administrative structures and policy content, but also focuses on the effects on ideas, discourses, and identities.

Anderson (2002: 9) captured the broader concerns of second-generation analyses through the categories of interests, institutions, and ideas (Insight 4.4). These categories are often separated for analytical purposes, but the point is to understand their relationship. That is, for example, how the motivations and values of political actors are shaped by the institutional context in which they operate; or how the ideas held by political actors shape what they perceive their interests to be. This is significant in 'isolated' domestic contexts, but in the context of EU membership such isolation is not possible. As such, the EU 'matters' because it 'automatically entails mutilayered interactions of interests, institutions, and ideas at and across the national and supranational levels' (Anderson 2002: 10).

The key features of first-generation and second-generation Europeanization research are summarized in Table 4.3.

It should be noted that while this generational division provides a useful way of distinguishing between the differing emphases of different Europeanization studies, many cover aspects contained in both categories.

Europeanization Assessed

Interest in the concept of Europeanization remains central to the study of the EU. Indeed, it has increasingly been applied to shed light on the dynamics of the process of enlargement, both in terms of the acceptance and assimilation of the formal *acquis communautaire* by accession states, and in terms of the pressures on accession states to conform to less formal, but nonetheless important norms of democratic behaviour—that is,

INSIGHT 4.4

Interests, Institutions, and Ideas

- *Interests* are causally important because they directly shape policy responses by establishing a distribution of societal preferences that national officials take into account as they seek to build electoral coalitions capable of winning and then holding political power.

- *Institutions* influence what actors do or do not do by allocating power to some actors but not others, structuring the content and sequence of policy making, and providing opportunities for and constraints on the state as its officials seek societal support for their policy choices.

- *Ideas* matter because they enable actors to manage uncertainty about the expected consequences of alternative choices, and they provide actors with a symbolic and conceptual language to advance their causes. In the context of strategic interaction among numerous actors, shared ideas can bring about the convergence of expectations and strategies facilitating agreement and co-operative outcomes.

Source: Anderson 2002; 2003.

acceptance of both the 'regulatory pillar' and the 'normative pillar' (Bulmer and Radaelli 2004: 2).

Yet given the diversity of Europeanization research to date, it is valid to ask whether the concept has been stretched too far to remain useful. In response to this question, Olsen (2003: 334) suggested that the field was still relatively new and, rather than risk abandoning a potentially useful term prematurely, the challenge was 'to explore the ways in which (or indeed whether) the term might be useful for understanding the dynamics of the evolving European polity'. Peter Mair (2004: 346) offered a more robust justification for continuing to use the term to stimulate research, and suggested that 'some of the very best and most innovative and challenging work in political science is now being carried out by scholars working in the field of European integration and Europeanization'.

Radaelli (2004) suggested that, while it was difficult to map and summarize the diverse range of empirical studies to date, a number of results stood out. In particular, the evidence for the Europeanization of public policies was more robust than the evidence for the effect of Europeanization on political competition, state structures, or the polity. Moreover, while Radaelli was clear that Europeanization did not lead to uniform convergence across Europe, there was evidence of 'clustered convergence' as states with similar characteristics or preferences in a given domain responded in similar ways to particular pressures or opportunities.

Mair (2004: 342) argued that there had been significant 'informal' Europeanization in terms of cross-cultural convergence, although this might not be directly the result of the EU. While this argument is slightly beyond our EU focus here, it is important in drawing attention to notions of 'Europeanization as convergence' that are long established in the study of comparative politics and that may have implications for the study of the EU. In this academic tradition, Europeanization is equated with the older historical process of 'nationalization': a polity-building process. The logic of this process is that:

TABLE 4.3

Summary of Dyson and Goetz on the 'Two Generations of Europeanization Research'

First generation	Second generation
• Generally top-down approaches, seeking to explain domestic change from EU 'pressures'	• Emphasizes more complex interactions (top-down, bottom-up and horizontal)
• Assumed 'misfit' between European and domestic levels—particularly formal institutional	• Greater emphasis on the 'political' dynamics of fit: interests, beliefs, values and ideas
• Emphasis on reactive and involuntary nature of adaptation	• Greater emphasis on voluntary adaptation through policy transfer and learning
• Focus on policy and polity dimensions	• Greater emphasis on politics, e.g. identities, electoral behaviour, parties, and party systems
• Expected increasing cross-national convergence	• Emphasizes differential impact of Europe
• Defined Europeanization in substantive terms—focus on the 'end state' effects	• Emphasizes impact of Europeanization on domestic political, institutional and policy dynamics

Note: Earlier versions of this table appeared in Bache (2003) and Bache and Marshall (2004).

Through 'coercion' or through 'authoritative allocation' in the case of more formal processes, and through education, communication, and sheer imitation and diffusion in the more informal cases, certain rules, practices and forms of behaviour become increasingly standardized throughout a given political and social system. And where this once applied and led to the more or less wholesale 'nationalization' of state territories, we now appear to witness it being applied and leading to the—admittedly far more uneven—'Europeanization' of a spreading transnational territory.

(Mair 2004: 342)

Thus, debates on Europeanization look set to remain prominent for some time. Europeanization research remains a complex but important field of inquiry, the potential of which has probably not yet been fully realized. At this stage of its development it is probably best understood in terms used by Radaelli (2004: 25), as a challenging and exciting 'problem' rather than a conceptual solution that provides 'off-the-shelf' explanations.

Democracy

For a long time, European integration proceeded with relatively little public or political debate on the implications for democracy and legitimacy. Decisions were taken by élites in the context of a 'permissive consensus'—the absence of public debate and protest on developments was taken as evidence of consent. European integration appeared to have low salience for most people. Economic integration was relatively uncontroversial in the context of a globalizing marketplace, and unanimous voting procedures were in place to protect perceived national interests.

However, as the EU's reach extended into a wider range of activities, and decision-making procedures changed, reducing the use of unanimous voting, European publics increasingly signalled their objections to further integration, most obviously through negative votes in referenda on treaty reforms. The contentious ratification of the Maastricht Treaty was a particularly significant moment (see Ch. 13, pp. 171–5). In this changing context, debates about popular control over the integration process and the accountability of EU élites have grown. Most recently, these debates intensified with the impending accession of ten, mostly small, new member states, and they were a prominent feature of the deliberations of the Constitutional Convention (see Ch. 16, pp. 204–7).

While public debate on democracy in the EU has until recently been limited, there has been a long-standing academic debate over the EU's perceived 'democratic deficit'. This debate has taken a significant twist in recent years, with an increasing number of academics arguing that the democratic deficit has been overstated and, indeed, that it may not actually exist. Alongside the debate on the democratic deficit has been a related interest in the concept of legitimacy. In some cases, democracy and legitimacy are used somewhat interchangeably, although it is more usual to view legitimacy as a broader concept (see below).

Democracy and Legitimacy

Birch (2001: 72) argued that 'the term "democracy", in its modern sense, came into use during the course of the nineteenth century to describe a system of representative government in which representatives are chosen by free competitive elections and most male citizens are entitled to vote'. However, the term has been used in various ways by political theorists, leaving the concept somewhat contested. The same is true for the concept of legitimacy. In simple terms, democracy is concerned with the public control over their leaders exercised by citizens with broadly equal rights (Insight 4.5), while legitimacy is a broader concept that can be understood as the public acceptability of the exercise of power (Lord 2001: 187). Democracy is an important source of legitimacy, but not the only source.

Beetham and Lord (1998) pointed to three liberal-democratic criteria of legitimacy that are relevant to the authority of the EU. These are performance, democracy, and identity. The concept of a legitimacy deficit relates to all three, not simply the democratic dimension. *Performance,* defined as 'effectiveness in the attainment of agreed ends or purposes of government', is considered 'an important component of legitimacy' rather than as something separate from it (Beetham and Lord 1998: 25). In terms of *democracy,* EU institutions are seen to be deficient in each of the three aspects of direct democratic legitimacy: authorization, accountability, and representation. However, extending direct democratic legitimacy in the EU depends on the development of a more robust common European *identity* among the EU electorate, which is generally considered, at best, to be embryonic (Smith 1992).

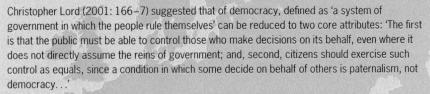

Democracy

Christopher Lord (2001: 166–7) suggested that of democracy, defined as 'a system of government in which the people rule themselves' can be reduced to two core attributes: 'The first is that the public must be able to control those who make decisions on its behalf, even where it does not directly assume the reins of government; and, second, citizens should exercise such control as equals, since a condition in which some decide on behalf of others is paternalism, not democracy. . .'

Albert Weale (1999: 14) defined democracy as a condition in which 'important public decisions on questions of law and policy depend, directly or indirectly, upon public opinion formally expressed by citizens of the community, the vast bulk of whom have equal political rights'.

The notion of a 'democratic deficit' has been the focus of much scholarly work in this area. The key concern here has been the lack of public accountability of the EU's institutions. More broadly, the concept of a 'legitimacy deficit' is used to describe the gap between the principles and practice of decision making. It is concerned with the difference between 'the moral authority or normative standing *required* by a public authority engaged in the production of binding rules and allocations, and that which it is *actually able* to command' (Beetham and Lord 1998: 126). For Beetham and Lord (1998: 3), legitimacy in the EU system 'has to be understood as a process of interaction between the EU and member state levels'. For traditional international organizations, legitimacy is secured through the recognition of their authority by other legitimate authorities (member states): an indirect rather than direct form of legitimacy, which is dependent on the pre-existing legitimacy of the member states. However, the nature of the EU is increasingly seen as different from traditional international organizations and in some respects to resemble domestic systems of governance (see Ch. 2). As such, the EU requires a legitimacy that is wider than the indirect legitimacy provided by the consent of national élites.

As will be seen below, the relationship between notions of democracy and legitimacy, and how and why they are in 'deficit' in the EU, is not always clear in the academic literature. Most particularly, the performance dimension of legitimacy outlined by Beetham and Lord is similar to the notions of *output democracy*, while their democratic accountability dimension is echoed by the notion of *input democracy*. Thus, for Scharpf (1997: 2) democracy is a 'two-dimensional concept relating to the inputs and outputs of the political system at the same time' (Insight 4.6).

The Democratic Deficit

The notion of the democratic deficit has been defined in a number of ways, but is essentially concerned with the degree to which the EU adequately represents and is accountable to European citizens (Box 4.7).

THEORY

INSIGHT 4.6

Input–Output Democracy

Sharpf (1997: 19) argued that: 'On the **input side**, self-determination requires that political choices should be derived, directly or indirectly, from the *authentic preferences* of citizens and that, for that reason, governments must be held accountable to the governed…

'On the **output side**, however, self-determination implies *effective fate control*. Democracy would be an empty ritual if the political choices of governments were not able to achieve a high degree of effectiveness in achieving the goals, and avoiding the dangers, that citizens collectively care about. Thus, input-oriented authenticity and output-oriented effectiveness are equally essential elements of democratic self-determination'.

INSIGHT 4.7

The Democratic Deficit

- The idea that EU decisions are 'in some ways insufficiently representative of, or accountable to, the nations and the people of Europe' (Lord 2001: 165).
- That the EU suffers from 'deficiencies in representation, representativeness, accountability and support' (Eriksen and Fossum 2002: 401).

Lord (1998: 11) referred to a number of features contributing to the perceived democratic deficit:

the unelected character of the European Commission, the alleged weakness of the European Parliament, the withdrawal of powers from national parliaments, lack of a European political identity or 'demos', low voter participation in European elections, the absence of strong democratic intermediaries such as political parties, the remoteness and obscurity of the Union's decision making procedures, and doubtless much else besides…

A lot of the early literature on the democratic deficit focused on the relative weakness of the European Parliament (EP) within the EU's institutional balance. Strengthening the EP, the only directly elected EU body, has been widely viewed as an appropriate means through which to close the democratic deficit. To some extent, this particular deficit has been addressed, as the EP's powers have increased dramatically since direct elections were introduced in 1979 (Ch. 21, pp. 299–300). However, it remains only one of four influential organizations and, by most accounts, it is still not the most powerful. Moreover, the contribution of the EP to correcting the democratic deficit remains limited because elections tend to be fought on national rather than European issues and turnout is generally low (Ch. 21, pp. 304–5). This is because European electorates do not perceive themselves as being part of an EU-wide democratic community in the same way as they do see themselves being part of a national democratic community. So, the EU still lacks the popular authority of national assemblies. The absence of a strong common

European identity or 'demos' remains a central challenge for those seeking to address the problem of the democratic deficit by strengthening further the powers of the EP. As van der Eijk and Franklin (1996: 7), put it: 'It is true that the European Parliament lacks certain powers in comparison with modern-day national parliaments; but what it lacks most is not power but a mandate to use that power in any particular way.'

However, some scholars have suggested that the notion of the democratic deficit is something of a 'non-problem'. Andrew Moravcsik (2002) argued that the EU has been unfairly judged in democratic terms. Specifically, it has been judged either against ideal standards of democracy or compared with national standards and practices, neither of which is appropriate:

Comparisons are drawn between the EU and an ancient, Westminster-style, or frankly utopian form of deliberative democracy. While perhaps useful for philosophical purposes, the use of idealistic standards no modern government can meet obscures the social context of contemporary European policy-making—the real-world practices of existing governments and the multi-level political system in which they act.

(Moravcsik 2002: 605)

Moravcsik (2002: 603) argued that, rather than acting unfettered, as much of the democratic-deficit argument suggests that they do, the EU's institutions are 'tightly constrained by constitutional checks and balances: narrow mandates, fiscal limits, supermajoritarian and concurrent voting requirements and separation of powers'. Moreover, the EU's appearance of being relatively insulated from democratic accountability reflects the nature of its main functions, such as central banking, constitutional adjudication, and economic diplomacy, which are generally low-key affairs in national systems, and are often delegated to non-governmental or quasi-governmental actors. So, the EU's system should not be singled out for criticism on these grounds.

Concerns over the institutional balance, and the EU's procedures for ensuring accountability, are heightened by the perception of some scholars that the EU fails to deliver on the 'output' side of the equation. Scharpf (1999) argued that the economic focus of the European integration project, and the relative underdevelopment of effective European social and welfare policies, provide an output imbalance that favours business and economic actors. In the context of intensified market competition, states could face a 'race to the bottom' in terms of welfare spending, which would be accelerated by the neo-liberal bias within the EU. The consequence of this is the alienation of those social groups that benefit least from the EU's system—the poor, women, and recipients of welfare benefits. Moravcsik (2002: 617) recognized Scharpf's argument as 'the most empirically and theoretically nuanced criticism of the EU's democratic deficit that currently exists', but suggested that it should be qualified on a number of grounds, in particular, that there 'is little evidence of a race to the bottom'; that 'the level of social welfare provision remains relatively stable'; and that there is 'little evidence that the EU is driving social protection downward' (Moravcsik 2002: 618).

Moravcsik's position on the democratic deficit flows logically from his argument that the EU is largely characterized by liberal intergovernmentalism (Ch. 2, pp. 13–15). In this view, national governments dominate the policy process, so the outputs of the system are legitimized primarily by the democratic accountability of those governments. Only rarely does delegation to supranational institutions lead to unintended consequences for national governments, and only in relatively few areas does the EU depart from national practices (the degree of independence given to the European Central Bank being the most important example). Thus, concerns arising from the lack of direct accountability of the EU's main institutions are misplaced.

Simon Hix (2006: 6) took a different view from Moravcsik, suggesting that input democracy, based on competitive elections so as to provide for the direct accountability of policy makers, brings a number of advantages. First, competitive elections ensure that decision makers respond to citizens' preferences. Second, party-political competition stimulates public debate, which forms public opinion on the EU and, in so doing, provides political élites with a mandate to undertake reform. Third, competitive elections play a role in identity formation, so rather than waiting for the emergence of a common European identity before democratizing the EU's institutions further, introducing electoral competition now could assist in the development of this identity.

Vectors of Legitimation

Lord and Magnette (2004) considered whether the existence of very different views on how the EU ought to be legitimated might in itself add to its overall legitimacy. In doing so, they identified four 'vectors of legitimation' in the EU: indirect, parliamentary, technocratic, and procedural legitimacy.

- *Indirect legitimacy* depends on the existing legitimacy of the EU's member states, on the EU's respect for the sovereignty of the member states, and on the ability of the EU to serve the purposes of the member states.

- *Parliamentary legitimacy* depends on both an elected European Parliament and the representation of the member states via the Council system. This dual legitimation reflects the co-existence of both a single people that relates to and is affected by the EU in broadly the same way, and a series of peoples with separate identities.

- *Technocratic legitimacy* depends on the ability of the EU to meet the demands and improve the quality of life of its citizens, that is, that it has problem-solving efficiency.

- *Procedural legitimacy* rests on the observance of particular procedures—such as transparency, balance of interests, proportionality and consultation. Beyond the observance of 'due process', procedural legitimacy is also derived from the observance of given rights, and the capacity to generate new rights (Lord and Magnette 2004: 184–7).

Lord and Magnette (2004) then drew on the distinction between *input legitimacy* and *output legitimacy* to illustrate the different vectors of legitimacy evident at two broad stages of policy making (Table 4.4).

The authors pointed out that these vectors were 'ideal types', which did not exist in pure form in the EU context, but provided the basis for analysing and understanding

TABLE 4.4

Input and Output Legitimacy under the Four Vectors of Legitimation

	Input	Output
	EU policies are legitimate to the extent that they are based on the following:	EU policies are legitimate to the extent that they deliver the following:
Indirect	Authorization by states	State preferences
Parliamentary	Elections	Voters' preferences
Technocratic	Expertise	Efficiency
Procedural	Due process and observance of given rights	Expanded rights

Source: Lord and Magnette 2004: 188.

the nature of legitimacy and how institutions had developed to combine or manage conflicts between the different vectors. They insisted that arguments about different types of legitimacy need not be divisive, but that 'conflict about legitimacy may even stimulate acceptance' (Lord and Magnette, 2004: 197) in the way that conflict between government and opposition in classic parliamentary systems has played a role in enhancing the overall acceptance of a regime.

Recent Debates

Democracy and legitimacy remain high on the agenda of EU studies, reflected in a published exchange on the issues by leading scholars in 2004. Amitai Etzioni (2004) suggested that what he described as 'halfway integration' was a central problem for the development of democracy at the level of the EU. This position is characterized by advanced integration in the economic sphere, but a relative lack of political integration and weak EU institutions, in comparison to the power of national institutions within their own territories. Etzioni suggested that one solution to the democratic challenge was to increase economic integration further so that more national interest groups would shift their focus to the EU level, which would in turn 'pressure the EU to develop more EU-wide political powers to work out these differences, which in turn would build the legitimacy of an EU government' (Etzioni 2004: 3). This argument reflects early neofunctionalist thinking, as outlined in Chapter 1 (pp. 8–12), although Etzioni (2004: 3) called it 'a syndicalist integration leading to a fully-fledged supranational one', leading to political integration by stealth:

the idea is, instead of a frontal attack and a bold attempt to jump from many nations into a United States of Europe, allow processes to unfold gradually, according people time to adjust to the new supranational realities and for their new loyalties to evolve.

(**Etzioni 2004: 3**)

Some would argue that this is what is already happening: others would argue that it will never happen. Either way, Etzioni did not set out what a democracy in a supranational Europe would look like. His main point was that halfway integration is not politically sustainable and the EU needs either to move forwards or to step back.

Philippe Schmitter (2004) argued that there was little evidence that European citizens were unduly concerned about EU democracy, but that the 'democratic deficit' was largely a concern and construct of academics and intellectuals. He illustrated this with reference to the Constitutional Convention: 'We have just seen during the "Convention on the Future of Europe" that ordinary citizens did not seem to be willing to devote much attention to the prospect of constitutionalizing, much less of democratizing EU institutions' (Schmitter 2004: 3).

On the surface, this is a far from persuasive argument: that a problem can only exist if it is perceived as such by mass publics. What Schmitter saw as a sign that there was no problem could just as easily be seen as a symptom of the problem for European democracy—that citizens do not engage with EU issues. This interpretation was supported by the rejection of the Constitutional Treaty in referendums in France and the Netherlands in the early summer of 2005.

However, Schmitter's argument was that the main challenges to democracy brought by European integration are challenges for national democracy rather than for the EU system. The shift of authority away from the nation state to the EU, which Schmitter suggested was 'not a practicing democracy', was 'gradually diminishing the accountability of rulers to citizens acting indirectly through the competition and co-operation of their representatives' (Schmitter 2004: 3). He suggested 'two good reasons why it may be timely to begin experimenting with continental democracy sooner rather than later': the evidence that democracy in the national arena is increasingly contested (greater electoral abstention, decline of party identification, lower prestige for politicians etc.); and evidence that EU citizens increasingly find the remoteness of the EU unsatisfactory (Schmitter 2004: 3).

Vivien Schmidt (2004) argued that the starting point for discussing EU democracy was to be clear about what the EU *is*. Like Moravcsik, she suggested that comparing it to nation states is a false point of departure. Instead, the EU should be conceived as a *regional state*, in which:

the creative tension between the Union and its member-states ensures both ever-increasing regional integration and ever-continuing national differentiation. As a result, the EU will continue to be characterized by shared sovereignty, variable boundaries, a composite identity, compound governance institutions, and fragmented democracy.
(Schmidt 2004: 4)

Comparisons with democracy in member states is misleading for a number of reasons, not least that partisan politics is very weak at the level of the EU and is generally submerged by an emphasis on consensus and compromise. Thus, while member states have 'government *by*, *of* and *for* the people—through political participation, electoral representation, and governing effectiveness', as well as what can be called 'government *with* the people', through interest consultation—'the EU level emphasizes governance *for* and *with* the people while leaving to the national level government *by* and *of* the people' (Schmidt 2004: 4).

Like Moravcsik, Schmidt identified a number of factors that protect democracy in the EU, but also noted that the very checks and balances that can protect democracy can also prevent changes to policies and practices that are ineffective or unpopular (i.e. lacking output legitimacy). Reform of the common agricultural policy is a prominent example (see Ch. 25). Moreover, this complex system of checks and balances presents other problems: not least that national politicians are often held to account over decisions they no longer control—although it is also not unknown for national politicians to blame decisions on the EU inappropriately. However, Schmidt also took the view that the real democratic deficit is at the national level. National governing practices have changed, but national ideas have not responded accordingly. The same argument was made by Sharpf (1997, 2004), who suggested that domestic control had been lost over issues that were once central to national party-political competition, such as economic management. While this might have output benefits in terms of more effective economic management, Scharpf's outstanding concern was that the viability of national welfare states was being challenged by European economic integration, thus reducing the effectiveness of democratic self-determination at the national level.

Ways Forward?

While there is disagreement over the nature and extent of the democratic challenges facing the EU, there is continued debate over how the EU's democracy and legitimacy might be enhanced. Chryssochoou (2003) identified four models that might aid democratization of the EU: the parliamentary, the confederal, the federal, and the consociational.

- *The parliamentary model*, as the name suggests, emphasizes the role of the elected assembly as legislator within a political system, and would democratize the EU through the enhanced role of elected representatives. However, this model would imply the extension of majority rule to all policy areas, which would be highly unlikely, and also rests on a degree of European social unity that is not yet present.

- *The confederal model* brings states together into a form of union that does not compromise their national identity or political sovereignty. It is a model that does not rest on the development of a new polity or demos, but is based on a *unity of states* rather than a *unity of peoples*. This model would democratize through national channels by 'renationalizing' some issues to provide a greater role for national parliaments, which would be unpalatable to many European and domestic actors involved in the integration process.

- *The federal model* rests on the creation of a unity of people rather than simply a union of states. This model seeks to reconcile the requirement of greater political union with the demands of the component states. In doing so, it aims to 'establish a co-operative democratic ethos in relations between the centre and the subunits' (Chryssochoou 2003: 376). The model has been criticized for its emphasis on the need for clearly demarcated competencies in an age where more flexible forms of governance are required (on types of multi-level governance see Ch. 2, pp. 33–6).

- *The consociational model* has generally been attempted where there are conflicting demands from different societal groups and, in particular, to prevent the abuse of minority rights. It has four features: a grand coalition (such as a council containing élites from the different group); proportionality (representation of societal groups reflects their size); segmental autonomy (some group control in specific areas); and mutual vetoes (on important decisions). Chryssochoou (2003: 377) suggested that each of these features is evident within the EU. Its main limitation is that it is essentially an elitist approach to seeking compromise and, as it reflects much of the present EU system, it would not appear the likeliest candidate for enhancing democracy.

While none of the models outlined is without limitations or inherent problems, Chryssochoou (2003) concluded that the adoption of a parliamentary and/or federal approach would promise most in terms of EU democratization.

Warleigh (2003: 125) argued that any approach to reform of EU democracy should recognize that it is as an ongoing process rather than assuming that there might be a 'once and for all' solution:

popular preferences will legitimately differ over time, according to policy issue and in each of the member states. In turn, this points towards a difficult quadruple balancing act: between various (national élite) views of the purpose of the Union; between different levels of governance (European-national-regional-local); between output and input legitimacy; and between different normative views of democracy.

CONCLUSION

This chapter has brought together what have usually been presented as separate 'consequences' of European integration: Europeanization effects and challenges to democracy. However, as noted at the outset, there are clear links between the two, particularly when Europeanization is understood as a process through which domestic politics and polities are changed by their engagement with the EU. Most obviously, the process of Europeanization may obscure lines of political accountability, so that citizens are unsure whom to hold to account on particular issues. Alternatively, political élites may use 'Europeanization' as a smokescreen that conceals their own activities and deliberately mislead voters if it is expedient for them to do so. Equally, political élites may themselves be unclear about where responsibility, and thus accountability, should lie.

On a more positive note, Europeanization effects may enhance output democracy. Common action at the level of the EU may bring 'performance' benefits to citizens, for example through more efficient management of macro-economic policy. However, for this to enhance legitimacy it is necessary that the increased efficiency is recognized and that it is recognized as an effect of membership of the EU. It is perhaps a problem for Europhiles that some of the main benefits of European integration are relatively intangible, while some of its failings are not. Moreover, the EU's supporters have the problem of proving the counterfactual: how do we know that member states and their citizens would not have fared as well, if not better, without EU membership?

According to most commentators, the outstanding problem facing democratic development in the EU is the absence of a shared identity that would produce a genuine demos. Eurosceptics often argue that democracy cannot be established at the European level because there is no such thing as a European people. Democracy can only operate within national cultures. If an attempt is made to force the diverse peoples of Europe into an artificial union, nationalism will be stirred up rather than be abolished. Here also, Europeanization processes may be crucial. However, this may be less to do with changes in formal institutions and policy through membership of the EU, and more to do with the diffusion of informal norms and values—the cultural dimension, as described by Peter Mair (2004). However, while this remains an important possibility, there is clearly still a long way to go.

KEY POINTS

Europeanization

- ☐ Europeanization has emerged as a key concept in EU studies and has been used and defined in a variety of ways. For some, Europeanization is a phenomenon that is broader than or separate from the EU. However, it is predominantly used to conceptualize the changing relationship between the EU and its member states.

- ☐ Ladrech provided an influential early conceptualization of Europeanization. He highlighted the importance of domestic factors in mediating Europeanization effects and argued that fears of harmonization or homogenization were thus unfounded.

- ☐ While research remained focused on the effects of EU membership on states, the Europeanization process became increasingly understood as one characterized by a two-way exchange between states and the EU level: i.e. both *uploading* and *downloading* of ideas and practices by domestic actors.

- ☐ *First generation* studies tended to focus on observable changes through Europeanization and explained variations in relation to the degree of fit or misfit between EU decisions and domestic practices and preferences.

- ☐ *Second generation* studies placed greater emphasis on the changes in ideas, values, and identities rather than more immediately observable effects of Europeanization. Europeanization remains prominent in debates on the EU and has recently been applied to studies of the enlargement process.

Democracy

- ☐ For a long time, European integration proceeded with little public debate about the democratic dimension. This changed as the EU's competencies expanded.

- ☐ Democracy and legitimacy are contested concepts and their relationship is not always clear in the EU literature. In essence, democracy is concerned with public control over the exercise of power, while legitimacy is understood as public acceptability of the exercise of power.

- ☐ Much attention on the democratic deficit has focused on the lack of accountability of the EU's institutions and, in particular, on the relatively weak position of the EP as the only directly elected body. However, increasing attention has been paid to the 'output' dimension of EU democracy.

☐ Moravcsik (2002), among others, has argued that when judged against reasonable criteria, concerns over the EU's democratic deficit are misplaced. However, Hix (2005) identified a number of advantages for the EU of competitive elections.

☐ Lord and Magnette (2004) identified four vectors of legitimation in the EU: indirect, parliamentary, technocratic and procedural legitimacy. They also distinguished between input and output legitimacy to illustrate how the four vectors are evident at different policy-making stages.

☐ Democracy and legitimacy in Europe remain high on the academic agenda. Etzioni (2004) has characterized the present EU as 'halfway integration' that requires further integration as a precondition to democratization. Schmitter (2004); Schmidt (2004); and Scharpf (1997, 1999) all emphasized the challenges to national democracy in the context of European integration.

☐ Chryssochoou (2003) identified four models that might aid democratization of the EU: the parliamentary, the confederal, the federal, and the consociational. Of these, he believed that the parliamentary and/or federal model offered the most promise. Warleigh (2003) argued against 'once and for all' solutions to the challenges facing EU democracy.

FURTHER READING

Europeanization

For an overview of the main conceptual contributions to the debate, see: J. Buller and A. Gamble, 'Conceptualising Europeanization', *Public Policy and Administration*, 17, 2 (2002): 4–24; J. Olsen 'The Many Faces of Europeanization', *Journal of Common Market Studies*, 40, 5 (2002): 921–52 (a revised version of this article can also be found in M. Cini (ed.), *European Union Politics* (Oxford: Oxford University Press, 2003): 333–46; and C. Radaelli, 'Europeanisation: Solution or Problem?', in M. Cini and A. Bourne (eds.) *The Palgrave Guide to European Studies* (Basingstoke: Palgrave, 2005).

For studies of Europeanization effects in individual member states see K. Dyson and K. Goetz, K. (eds.), *Germany, Europe and the Politics of Constraint* (Oxford: Oxford University Press, 2003), and I. Bache, and A. Jordan (eds.), *The Europeanization of British Politics?* (Basingstoke: Palgrave, 2006). Cross-national studies include: M. Cowles, J. Caporaso and T. Risse (eds.), *Transforming Europe: Europeanization and Domestic Change* (Ithaca and London: Cornell University Press, 2001); K. Featherstone and C. Radaelli (eds.), *The Politics of Europeanization* (Oxford: Oxford University Press, 2003); A. Héritier, D. Kerwer, C. Knill, D. Lehmkuhl, M. Teutsch, and A-C. Douillet, *Differential Europe: The European Union Impact on National Policymaking* (Lanham, MD: Rowman and Littlefield, 2001). C. Knill, *The Europeanization of National Administrations: Patterns of Institutional Change and Persistence* (Cambridge: Cambridge University Press, 2001).

Democracy

For an introduction to EU democracy and the notion of the democratic deficit see: D. Chryssochoou, 'EU Democracy and the Democratic Deficit', in M. Cini (ed.), *European Union Politics* (2003): 365–382; R. Katz, 'Models of Democracy: Élite Attitudes and the Democratic Deficit in the European

Union' *European Union Politics*, 2, 1 (2001): 53–79; C. Lord, 'Democracy and Democratization in the European Union' in S. Bromley (ed.), *Governing the European Union* (London: Sage, 2001), 165–190. On the argument that the democratic deficit is a non-problem, see: A. Moravcsik, 'In Defence of the "Democratic Deficit": Reassessing Legitimacy in the European Union', *Journal of Common Market Studies*, 40, 4 (2002): 603–24.

An analysis of key debates and suggested ways forward can be found in A. Warleigh, *Democracy in the European Union* (London: Sage, 2003). On legitimacy, see D. Beetham and C. Lord, *Legitimacy and the European Union* (London and New York: Longman, 1998), and C. Lord and P. Magnette, 'E Pluribus Unum? Creative Disagreement about Legitimacy in the EU', *Journal of Common Market Studies*, 42, 1 (2004): 183–202. On new forms of democratic control in the EU, see the special issue of the *Journal of European Public Policy*, 'The Diffusion of Democracy—Emerging Forms and Norms of Democratic Control in the European Union', 10, 5 (2003).

 **online resource centre**

Visit the Online Resource Centre that accompanies this book for links to more information on theorizing consequences, including papers on Europeanization.

PART TWO

History

Deciding where to begin a history is often difficult, but not really in this case. While there were attempts to integrate Europe before the twentieth century, the end of the Second World War in 1945 provided the catalyst for the phase of European integration with which we are familiar today. There is little dispute among historians that 1945 is the most appropriate starting point for discussing the events leading to the creation of what is today the European Union. Thus, while we reflect briefly on previous attempts to integrate Europe, our point of departure here is the end of the Second World War.

The history we present is largely a familiar account of developments in European integration in the second half of the twentieth century. The history of European integration often told is one that emphasizes individuals, perhaps at the expense of broader social, economic, and political forces that shape events. Our account here generally reflects this dominant approach, not least because it is the function of a textbook to cover the most recognized contributions on the field of study. However, we have sought to add to the dominant narrative in the conclusions to the chapters in this section by drawing on the many themes and perspectives discussed in Part I of the book.

As with all histories, we have had to make choices about how our history is organized. Here, we follow a conventional path. In our opening chapters we focus on the history of 'important' decisions, in particular those leading to the Treaties establishing the European Communities. Later in the section we identify phases in the process of European integration that are distinguished by the pace of events: for example, the 'dark ages' of European integration. Towards the end we return again to a focus on events leading to key decisions.

As time passes, it is likely that events and developments in post-war integration that seem important to observers now may seem less important to future generations. Conversely, matters less obvious at the beginning of the twenty-first century will grow in importance. Similarly, the distinct eras in the process of integration that we identify will demand redefinition at some future date. In this sense, all histories are inevitably transient and imperfect. Thus, the basis on which we organize our history is simply an informed choice in the light of current understanding and should be read as such.

CHAPTER 5

Europe after the War

CHAPTER OVERVIEW

Attempts at European integration have a long history; but most have taken the form of conquest. While the outbreak of the Second World War illustrated the force of nationalism in Europe, its aftermath provided conditions for moves towards a consensual approach to European unity. This chapter documents the moves towards European integration in the early post-war period, explaining why federalist ideas were not put into practice and how both internal and external pressures were crucial to shaping the Europe that emerged after the war.

> " If Europe were once united in the sharing of its common inheritance, there would be no limit to the happiness, to the prosperity and the glory which its three or four hundred million people would enjoy.
>
> (Winston Churchill, Zurich 1946) "

Our starting point for this discussion of European integration is the end of the Second World War: but the idea of European integration is not unique to this era. Politicians and intellectuals alike aspired to European unity over two centuries. Plans for achieving perpetual peace in Europe by overcoming the division into nation states can be traced back at least to the early eighteenth century, and the *Project for Perpetual Peace* of the Abbé de Saint Pierre (Forsyth *et al.* 1970: 128). At a practical level, though, moves for European unity took the form of attempts by one nation or another to dominate Europe through conquest. Both France under Napoleon and Germany under Hitler could be accused of trying to forge European unity in this way.

Whereas attempts at enforced European *political* integration foundered, the potential benefits of *economic* integration proved attractive to European political élites. Yet nineteenth-century experiments with **free-trade areas** across nation states were short-lived, while early **customs unions** were specific to regions within nation states. Ultimately these experiments in economic integration suffered the same fate as attempts at political unity.

Movements in favour of peaceful integration emerged in Europe after the First World War, but the political settlement after the war was based on the peaceful co-existence of nation states rather than integration. The failure of the League of Nations (Insight 5.1) to sustain peace was rapid and complete, with the resurgence of nationalism in the 1920s and 1930s. The pro-integration groups emerging in Europe after 1918 were unable to offer any practical solutions to this. The outbreak of the Second World War destroyed hopes of European unity. The aftermath of the war, though, provided the origins for the modern movement for European integration.

Emerging from the war physically devastated, Europe began a process of both economic and political reconstruction. The idea of European unity was present in this process from the outset, as the ideology of federalism had attracted a great deal of support during the war. However, the story cannot be told simply in terms of ideals. Although influential figures showed some degree of attachment to the concept of federalism, the steps that were taken were informed by hard-headed realism about what was necessary for reconstruction to succeed. They were also taken in the context of an emerging Cold War that divided the continent on ideological lines.

The End of the War, Federalism, and The Hague Congress

The war in Europe had extensively destroyed physical infrastructure, disrupted economic production, and caused severe social dislocation. Roads, railways, and bridges

INSIGHT 5.1

The League of Nations

- The League of Nations was inspired by the vision of US President Woodrow Wilson. Its Covenant was drawn up at the Paris Peace Conference in 1919, but the US Congress refused to ratify the Treaty so the United States never became a member of the League.

- The League Covenant committed the states that signed to respect the sovereignty and territorial integrity of other states, and not to resort to force to resolve disputes, but to submit them to arbitration by the League

- The League's institutional structure consisted of a General Assembly, in which all member states were represented, and a Council. The Council had four, then later six permanent members—Britain, France, Italy, Japan; then Germany from 1926, and the USSR from 1934.

- Between 1931 and 1939 the League failed to deal effectively with aggression by Japan, Italy, Germany, and the USSR. In 1935 Japan and Germany withdrew from membership.

- Although it failed to prevent war, the League did successfully establish a number of special agencies working at a functional level to deal with matters such as health and the protection of labour. The success of these bodies may have influenced the thinking of David Mitrany (see Ch. 1, pp. 5–6).

had been destroyed by allied bombing or by the retreating German army in its attempt to slow the advance of the allied forces. According to Laqueur (1972: 17–18) coal production at the end of the war was only 42 per cent of its pre-war level; pig iron output in 1946 was less than one-third of that in 1938; and crude steel output was about one-third of what it had been before the war. There were millions of refugees wandering around Europe trying to return to their homes, or without any homes to return to.

Accompanying the economic and social dislocation, there was political dislocation as governments that had collaborated with the Nazis were displaced. Germany and Austria remained occupied and divided between the occupation zones of the allies. Elsewhere, there was a mood in favour of change; a feeling that there should be no return to the pre-war élites and the pre-war ways.

This mood particularly benefited parties of the left. In Britain a Labour government was elected in 1945 with a massive majority, despite the Conservatives being led by the war-time hero Winston Churchill. In France, the provisional government that was set up in 1945 was presided over by General de Gaulle, the conservative leader of the Free French forces, which had fought on outside of the occupied country; but the first elections favoured the parties of the internal Resistance, particularly the communists but also the Socialists and the centre-left Christian party, the *Mouvement Républicain Populaire* (MRP). In Italy, although the Catholic south ensured the emergence of a large conservative Christian Democratic Party, the communists dominated in the industrial north.

The mood for change also fed a strong popular sentiment in the countries that had suffered from Fascism, in favour of a decisive move away from nationalism in the post-war reconstruction. Ideas favouring European federalism gained support, particularly in Italy, but also in France, Germany, and elsewhere in continental Europe, although not in Britain or the Scandinavian countries.

The European Union of Federalists (EUF) was formed in 1946 from the war-time Resistance movements. It attempted to exploit the disruption caused to existing political structures by the war to make a new start on a basis radically different from the Europe of nation-states, and to create a federal constitution for Europe, as part of a more distant plan for global unity. However, it took until 1947 to organize the conference that was supposed to pave the way to the new constitution, by which time national governments had already been restored to office everywhere. The conference, the European Congress, eventually took place in The Hague in May 1948.

The Congress attracted considerable attention at the time. It was attended by representatives of most of the political parties of the non-communist states of Europe, and its Honorary President was Winston Churchill, who had used a speech in Zurich in 1946 to call for a united Europe. Churchill had implied in the Zurich speech that Britain, with its Commonwealth of Nations, would remain separate from the 'United States of Europe' to which he referred. Britain, along with the United States and possibly the USSR, would be 'friends and sponsors of the new Europe'. The vital development in this project would be a 'partnership' between France and Germany. Beyond this, and the 'first step' of forming a Council of Europe (Insight 5.2), Churchill did not detail how the process towards European unity should proceed.

The Hague Congress was an occasion for fine speeches, but it gradually became apparent that the British were not interested in being part of a supranational organization that would compromise their national sovereignty. While the Congress did lead to the creation of the Council of Europe, this was so dominated by national governments that there was little realistic prospect of it developing in the federal direction that the EUF hoped.

The Council of Europe still exists today, and it has many solid achievements to its credit. In particular, it was responsible for adopting the European Convention on Human Rights in 1950, and it maintained both a Commission on Human Rights (replaced by a Commissioner in 1999) and a Court of Human Rights; the former to investigate alleged breaches of such rights by governments, and the latter to rule definitively on whether a violation of rights has occurred. It also serves useful functions as a meeting place for parliamentarians from the diverse member states and promotes Europe-wide cultural activities. This all falls far short of the hopes of the EUF.

European integration was not to be achieved in one great act of political will, because the will was not there. Some blamed the failure of the Council of Europe to develop in a federal direction on the attitude of the British; but the truth is that no national government, once installed, was willing to surrender much of its power. In 1947 the attention of governments was still focused on national economic reconstruction, not on superseding the nation state. Yet there were soon more insistent pressures on the governments to move away from national sovereignty than those that the federalists could muster.

INSIGHT 5.2

The Council of Europe

Founded in 1949 as a result of the 1948 Congress of Europe in The Hague, the Council of Europe is not connected to the EU and should not be confused with the European Council, which is the name of the institutionalized summit meetings of the EU Heads of State and Government.

The Council of Europe is an intergovernmental organization based in the French city of Strasburg. It originally had ten members, and by 2005 had 46, including 21 countries from central and eastern Europe. Its main institutions are:

- the Committee of (Foreign) Ministers
- the Parliamentary Assembly, consisting of 245 members of national parliaments, with 245 substitutes
- the Congress of Local and Regional Authorities of Europe
- the Secretariat
- the European Commissioner for Human Rights
- the European Court of Human Rights.

The Council was set up to:

- defend human rights, parliamentary democracy and the rule of law,
- develop continent-wide agreements to standardize member countries' social and legal practices,
- promote awareness of a European identity based on shared values and cutting across different cultures.

Since 1989, its main job has become:

- acting as a political anchor and human rights watchdog for Europe's post-communist democracies,
- assisting the countries of central and eastern Europe in carrying out and consolidating political, legal and constitutional reform in parallel with economic reform,
- providing know-how in areas such as human rights, local democracy, education, culture and the environment.

Source: http://www.coe.int/T/e/Com/about_coe/

The Cold War

To understand the origins of the EU it is essential to see them in the context of the emerging Cold War between the capitalist West and the communist Soviet Union. Before the Second World War, advocates of a European union had assumed it would stretch to the borders of the USSR. But as relations between the former allies deteriorated throughout 1946 and into 1947, it became clear this would be a project confined to the western part of the continent.

Agreement was reached at an Allied summit meeting in Yalta in 1945 to divide Europe at the end of the war into 'spheres of influence'. This was intended by the western Allies to be only a temporary arrangement, but the Soviet Union soon started to make it permanent. Regimes friendly to the USSR were installed in those countries of central and eastern Europe that at Yalta had been assigned to the Soviet sphere. This led Churchill to make a speech in Fulton, Missouri in March 1946 in which he talked about an 'iron curtain' descending across Europe. The speech did not receive a sympathetic hearing in Washington, where the prevailing mood was still in favour of co-operation with the USSR; but this mood changed in the course of 1946.

In September 1946 communist insurgents restarted a civil war in Greece. This was a decision that could not have been taken without the agreement of the Soviet Union. In 1945 Stalin had ordered the Greek communists, who controlled large areas of the country, not to continue with an armed insurrection against the government that the British had installed in Athens. Greece was in the British sphere of influence according to the Yalta agreement, and it seemed that whatever unwelcome moves Stalin might be making in the Soviet sphere, he was at least intent on respecting the limits set at Yalta. The recommencement of hostilities in Greece threw that interpretation into doubt. During 1946, too, the Soviet Union refused to withdraw its troops from Persia, which was also outside its sphere, and made territorial demands on Turkey.

The weather in the European winter of 1946–7 was particularly severe, and put considerable strain on the economic recovery that was underway. This had direct consequences for the emergence of the Cold War. In February 1947, London informed Washington that it could not afford to continue economic and military aid to Greece and Turkey. In response, President Truman asked Congress in March 1947 for $400 million of economic and military aid for Greece and Turkey. To dramatize the situation, he spoke of the duty of the United States to assist 'free peoples who are resisting attempted subjugation by armed minorities or by outside pressures'. This became known as the Truman doctrine, and it marked a clear statement of intent by the US Administration to remain involved in the affairs of Europe and the wider world, and not to allow isolationist sentiments within the country and within Congress to force a withdrawal from an international role.

Perhaps even more significant in converting the US Administration to Churchill's view, was the collapse of the Four-Power Council of Foreign Ministers, a standing conference to discuss the administration and future of Germany. Soviet intransigence in that forum, and the eventual walk-out of the Soviet representative in April 1947, convinced those who were trying to negotiate on behalf of Washington that it was not possible to work with the USSR. From that point on the emergence of separate West and East German states became gradually inevitable.

A second direct consequence of the bad winter and economic setback of early 1947 was that waves of strikes spread across France and Italy. In both cases the strikes were supported by communists, who engaged in revolutionary anti-capitalist rhetoric. In the light of events in Greece, this was interpreted as further evidence of the Soviet Union attempting to undermine stability outside its sphere of influence, although in both cases it may have been an incorrect interpretation. Certainly in France, where the Communist Party was part of the coalition government, the strikes appeared to take them by surprise. However, it was very difficult for the French communists not to support their core electorate, and indeed not to interpret the strikes as evidence of the imminent collapse of capitalism.

The other parties in the French coalition responded by expelling the communists from the government: the Truman Administration responded with the Marshall Plan.

The Marshall Plan and the OEEC

On 5 June 1947 George Marshall, the US Secretary of State, announced that the United States Administration proposed to offer financial and food aid to Europe to assist in its economic recovery (Insight 5.3). Suspicious of US motives, the USSR and its allies rejected the offer. There were some grounds for this suspicion: the American gesture went far beyond simple altruism to a concern with economic self-interest.

Marshall presented the American people with a vision of Europe in crisis in 1947. People were starving. The economy had broken down. Milward (1984: 3–4) contested this orthodox view. He denied there was a crisis, although he accepted that there was a serious problem about the ability of the west European states to build and sustain international trade because of a lack of convertible currencies to finance it. In his view the Marshall Plan was entirely political in its conception and objectives, although its means were entirely economic. The misleading representation of the economic position in Europe was designed to get the agreement of the US Congress to the reconstruction programme.

Marshall Aid offered an injection of dollars into the European economy, which would finance trade between the European states and the United States, and trade between the European states themselves. This was a policy much favoured by those sections of US industry that were involved in exporting. It was less favoured by those sections of US industry that were oriented towards the domestic market, and that suspected that they would pay the bill for European reconstruction without gaining the benefits. This section of domestic opinion was strongly represented within Congress, and so it was by no means a foregone conclusion that the Administration would get its plans through Congress. Following the Soviet Union's rejection of aid, Truman and Marshall were able to justify the Plan as part of the same response to the threat of communism as was the Truman Doctrine. Marshall argued that economic conditions in western Europe in 1947

INSIGHT 5.3

The Marshall Plan

- The European Recovery Programme (ERP) was announced by US Secretary of State George C. Marshall in a speech at Harvard University on 5 June 1947.

- It involved the United States giving a total of $13bn in financial aid to the states of western Europe. The assistance was offered to the states of eastern Europe, but they declined under pressure from the Soviet Union.

- The European states that accepted held a conference in July 1947 in Paris, and set up the Organization for European Economic Co-operation (OEEC) to facilitate the unified response that the United States required.

were so serious that they provided a breeding ground for communism. The struggle had to be waged by economic as well as military means.

Whether it was motivated by genuine concern for the condition of western Europe, or by economic considerations that had more to do with lobbying by the larger US corporations, Marshall Aid came with strings attached. The US Administration was committed to the idea of free trade. It was concerned to see what it described as 'European integration', meaning that national economic barriers to trade should be broken down. Both of the motives discussed above would support this position. Given that the Administration genuinely believed that free trade would strengthen the west European economies, integration was compatible with the stated aim of strengthening western Europe against communist expansion. However, it was also compatible with the aim of creating a large and exploitable market for US exports and for investments by US multinational corporations.

The United States insisted that decisions on the distribution and use of Marshall Aid be taken by the European states jointly. To implement this, a body known as the Committee for European Economic Co-operation (CEEC) was set up. Despite the professed aim of allowing the Europeans to make their own decisions on the use of the aid, the United States was represented on this committee, and because it was contributing all the funds, it clearly had some economic and political leverage. The CEEC was transformed in April 1948 into a more permanent body, the Organization for European Economic Co-operation (OEEC). The OEEC initially had 15 members, but was soon joined by the newly independent Federal Republic of Germany (1949), while the United States and Canada became associate members in 1950.

For Marshall and other members of the US Administration, the OEEC was to be the basis for the future supranational economic management of Europe. Nobody was quite clear what 'supranational' meant in this context, but it certainly meant breaking down national sovereignty in economic affairs. In particular, the US view was that western Europe should become a free-trade area as the first step towards global free trade.

This was not a vision that particularly appealed to the governments of the European states involved. The British did not particularly want to be tied into any arrangement with the Continental states. The French had already embarked on their own recovery programme, which was based on a much more restrictive view of the role of free trade and the free market. Other governments shared some of the French concern to keep as much control as possible over their own economies, giving away sovereignty neither to a supranational organization nor to the workings of the international free market.

Crucial to the economic and political stance of the European states was the position of Germany. Whether the German economy and state would be reconstituted was still an open question when the CEEC began operations. The US wanted the decisions to be made by the OEEC. Germany's neighbours were simply not prepared to see that happen. In particular, they were nervous about the extent of political leverage the United States was able to exercise within the OEEC because of its economic influence as the sole contributor to the reconstruction funds. However, despite its economic leverage, the United States simply did not have sufficient political weight to overcome the combined opposition of Britain, France, and the smaller European states to allowing the OEEC to develop as a powerful supranational organization (Milward 1984: 168–211).

The body within the OEEC controlling policy and administration was the Council of Ministers, which consisted of one representative from each member state. Decisions taken by the Council were binding on members but each member state retained the right of veto. While effective within its limited remit, the OEEC promised little in terms of further integration.

Despite its limitations, the OEEC continued its work for twelve years and, according to Urwin (1995: 22) 'played a major role in driving home the realization that European economies were mutually dependent, and that they prospered or failed together'. In 1961, the OEEC was superseded by the Organization for Economic Co-operation and Development (OECD), which had a broader remit, concerned with issues of economic development both in Europe and globally, and included the USA and Canada as full members.

Germany

The German problem came increasingly to dominate the debate about the future of Europe. For the United States and Britain the future of Germany was inevitably linked to the emerging Cold War. For France and Germany's smaller neighbours it was still a question of how to prevent the re-emergence of a threat to their sovereign independence from Germany itself.

Initially Germany's neighbours tried to protect themselves through a traditional military alliance, in which British participation was seen as crucial. This approach produced the Treaty of Dunkirk between Britain and France in March 1947, and the Treaty of Brussels between Britain, France, and the **Benelux** states in March 1948. Both alliances were directed more at forestalling German aggression than they were at the Soviet Union.

The French government also tried to prevent the emergence of any German state. Ideally the French Foreign Office would have liked to have kept Germany under allied occupation. Failing that, it wanted the former German state to be divided into a large number of small separate states. By 1949 it had become apparent that this was not going to happen. Again the crucial dynamic was the rapidly emerging Cold War. In 1948 the Soviet Union walked out of Allied talks on the future of Germany. The United States and Britain responded by starting to prepare the Anglo-American zones for independence. The French were left in no doubt that they were expected to merge their occupation zone into the new West German state, which would be created under the plans for independence. Once the Federal Republic of Germany came into existence in 1949, the French policy had to be rethought.

CONCLUSION

Several of the themes raised in the opening chapters are already apparent in this chapter: the importance of legitimacy and identity; the conflict between different models of capitalism; and the importance of 'external' actors and issues in shaping the emerging contours of post-war Europe.

The governments that took office in post-war western Europe faced a series of challenges. They faced a demand from their electorates for security both from the economic problems that had afflicted pre-war Europe, and from further war. They faced a lack of popular confidence in the ability of the sovereign national state to meet these demands. They faced a challenge from federalism, which offered an alternative way of organizing Europe politically, but one that would have removed the levers of power from the hands of national governments. They faced an even more serious challenge from communism: an ideology that promised to deliver the economic security that people doubted capitalism could deliver. They faced demands from the United States that they reconstruct their economies in a way that would open them to foreign competition, which if met would have reduced the ability of national governments to control the impact of the market on their electorates.

The success of socialist governments in many west European states in the first post-war elections indicated the extent of the desire among the people of western Europe for a fairer and more managed economic system. It was in response to this demand that the first steps were soon taken in the construction of the welfare state systems, and an active role for the state in economic management began to be mapped out. The distinctive 'European model' of regulated capitalism began to emerge. Before these systems could work, though, there had to be economic recovery from the war. This proved elusive in the early years.

The United States showed itself to be willing to finance recovery through the Marshall Plan, in return for reconstruction being on the basis of liberal market economies that were open to competition. To ensure this openness, the United States insisted that recovery plans be constructed on a European basis, not a national basis. West European governments had to cope with a demand that they surrender some of their ability to control their national economies as the price for US financial assistance.

So the first tentative steps towards some form of west European economic integration were taken in response to a combination of internal and external pressures on governments. The decisions were undoubtedly intergovernmental: there were no supranational institutions to push the process forward at this stage. They were taken by governments whose legitimacy had to be established. Recourse to nationalism was not an option for gaining legitimacy because of the popular lack of confidence in the nation-state following the war. On the other hand, embracing federalism implied a surrender of authority and control that most national governments were unwilling to undertake. The most efficacious way of gaining legitimacy was to provide economic growth, but this required the support of the dominant economic power in the post-war world, the United States. Support was offered on condition that the economic recovery plan would go beyond the nation-state. This was not a demand for a surrender of political sovereignty, and was therefore easier for the west European states to accept than a full-blown move to a federal constitution. At the same time the governments were able to adopt federalist rhetoric. They could appear to be moving in a popular direction while not losing control of the process.

At the same time, the insistence by the United States that the reconstruction be based on open market systems did threaten the post-war models of regulated capitalism. The implication of opening national economies to external competition was that jobs would be lost in some sectors. The European model of capitalism could only be reconciled with open markets if there were high rates of economic growth, so that any jobs lost to competition were replaced by new jobs generated by this growth. This was a gamble, but it was a gamble that the national governments had no choice but to make. Unless the post-war economic recovery could be got underway, there would be no jobs to be lost. In the end the influence of the United States, exercised through the conditions attached to the Marshall Plan, was decisive.

KEY POINTS

The End of the War, Federalism, and The Hague Congress

- ☐ The Second World War caused great economic and social dislocation and created a mood for political change.

- ☐ In general, this mood favoured the left, and federalist ideas also gained support in much of continental Europe, leading to the formation of the European Union of Federalists (EUF) in 1946.

- ☐ The Hague Congress of 1948 promised much in terms of integration, but in the end delivered little beyond the Council of Europe, which was dominated by national governments.

The Cold War

- ☐ The post-war process of European integration has to be understood in the context of emerging tension between the capitalist West and the communist Soviet Union.

- ☐ As the Soviet Union began to install friendly regimes in the countries of central and eastern Europe, Churchill spoke of an 'iron curtain' descending across Europe.

- ☐ As economic and political tensions in Europe grew, the 'Truman doctrine' of 1947 declared the United States' intention to maintain an active role in world affairs.

- ☐ Following the principles of the Truman doctrine, the 1947 Marshall Plan provided US aid to assist the recovery of European economies and the CEEC was established to administer this.

- ☐ The issue of how to deal with Germany came to dominate the European agenda. When the Soviet Union walked out of talks on the future of Germany in 1948, Britain and the US advanced plans for an independent West German state.

FURTHER READING

The early post-war period is not particularly well written-up, except as part of wider histories. For the whole history of European integration D.W. Urwin, *The Community of Europe: A History of European Integration since 1945* (London and New York: Longman, 2nd edn, 1995) and Urwin, *Western Europe since 1945: A Short Political History* (London and New York: Longman, 4th edn, 1985) should be treated as standard reference sources.

A particularly controversial account of the early post-war origins of European integration is given by A.S. Milward, *The Reconstruction of Western Europe, 1945–51* (London: Routledge, 1984).

For more information on European federalism, see M. Burgess (ed.), *Federalism and Federation in Western Europe* (London: Croom Helm, 1986), and *Federalism in the European Union: Political Ideas, Influences and Strategies* (London and New York: Routledge, 1989).

online resource centre   Visit the Online Resource Centre that accompanies this book for links to more information on Europe after the War.

CHAPTER 6

The Schuman Plan
for Coal and Steel

CHAPTER OVERVIEW

The Schuman Plan to pool coal and steel production, announced in 1950, involved a considerable surrender of sovereign control over these industries for the six participating states. It would be a decisive first step towards European unity. It would make war between France and Germany not only unthinkable, but also materially impossible. It would lay the foundation for the economic unification of the participating states. This chapter examines the reasons for the participation of the six states in this Plan, and for the non-participation of Britain. It also looks at the negotiations that led from the Schuman Plan to the European Coal and Steel Community (ECSC).

> **By pooling basic production and by instituting a new High Authority, whose decisions will bind France, Germany and other member countries, this proposal will lead to the realization of the first concrete foundation of a European federation indispensable to the preservation of peace.**
>
> **(Schuman Declaration)**

In May 1950 the French Foreign Minister, Robert Schuman, proposed a scheme for pooling the coal and steel supplies of France and Germany, and invited other European states who wished to participate to express an interest. The idea involved a surrender of sovereignty over the coal and steel industries. It was devised by Jean Monnet, a French civil servant (Insight 6.1), and addressed practical problems for France that arose from the establishment of the Federal Republic of Germany. The first problem was how to avert the threat of future conflict between France and Germany; the second was how to ensure continuing supplies of coal for the French steel industry once the Ruhr region reverted to German sovereign control. The plan was welcomed by the German Chancellor, Konrad Adenauer, and the Benelux states and Italy indicated that they would wish to participate. The British government declined an invitation to take part. The negotiations between the six states that did wish to participate were marked by hard bargaining in defence of national interests, but eventually agreement was reached on what became the European Coal and Steel Community (ECSC). The Six signed the Treaty of Paris in April 1952, and the ECSC came into operation in July 1952 (see Ch. 8).

INSIGHT 6.1

Jean Monnet

Jean Monnet (1888–1979) was born into a small brandy-producing family in Cognac. He left school at 16, and after a period gaining experience of financial affairs in London, he worked for the family business, travelling widely.

In 1915 he was declared unfit for military service, and spent the war instead in the civil service. He rose rapidly to the position of representative of the French government in London.

After the war he was appointed deputy secretary-general of the League of Nations, but he returned to private life when the family firm got into difficulties in 1922. He subsequently became an investment banker and financier.

In the Second World War he worked first for the British government in Washington, then for de Gaulle in Algiers. He was instrumental in preventing the British and Americans from replacing de Gaulle, who in 1946 appointed him as head of the CdP.

He devised both the Schuman Plan and the Pleven Plan for a European Defence Community (EDC).

He was the first President of the High Authority of the ECSC between 1952 and 1955. Following the defeat of the proposed EDC in the French National Assembly, he resigned from the High Authority to be free to promote further schemes for European integration, setting up the Action Committee for the United States of Europe.

In the following analysis the positions of the six founder states are examined, and then that of Britain. The analysis starts with France, the country that proposed the scheme, then looks at Germany, without whose participation the scheme would never have got off the ground. The Benelux states are considered together because their reasons for participation were extremely similar. Italy's reasons for joining the negotiations require a little more explanation. Britain's reasons for not joining are important for the future relationship between Britain and the EC.

France

The plan for the ECSC was known as the Schuman Plan because it was made public by the French Foreign Minister, Robert Schuman. He was born in Luxemburg, lived in Lorraine when it was part of the German empire, was conscripted into the German army in the First World War, and only became a French citizen after the war when Alsace and Lorraine reverted to French sovereignty. Thus he had a particular reason for wanting to reconcile the historic conflict between the two countries.

Milward (1984: 395–6) argued that the Foreign Ministry must have played a role in devising the plan, but the more generally accepted view is that it was drawn up within the French Economic Planning Commission (Commissariat du Plan—CdP), which was headed by Jean Monnet. It was the task of the CdP to guide the post-war reconstruction and modernization of the French economy, and it was through his experiences in this task that Monnet came to appreciate the economic inadequacy of the European nation state in the modern world. As he himself put it:

For five years the whole French nation had been making efforts to recreate the bases of production, but it became evident that to go beyond recovery towards steady expansion and higher standards of life for all, the resources of a single nation were not sufficient. It was necessary to transcend the national framework.
(Monnet 1962: 205)

The wider framework that Monnet had in mind was an economically united western Europe. He saw the need to create a 'large and dynamic common market', 'a huge continental market on the European scale' (Monnet 1962: 205). But he aimed to create more than just a common market. Monnet was a planner: he showed no great confidence in the free-market system, which had served France badly in the past. He placed his faith in the development of supranational institutions as the basis for building a genuine economic community that would adopt common economic policies and rational planning procedures.

Coal and steel were only intended as starting points. The aim was to extend integration to all aspects of the west European economy; but such a scheme would have been too ambitious to gain acceptance all at once.

Europe will not be made all at once, or according to a single plan. It will be built through concrete achievements which first create a de facto *solidarity.*

(Schuman Declaration 1950)

There had been a clear indication of this need for incrementalism in the failure of various post-war efforts to integrate the economies of France, Italy, The Netherlands, Belgium, and Luxemburg. Although negotiations for an organization to be known as 'Finebel' had proceeded for some time, they were on the verge of collapse in 1950. Besides, the new factor in the equation, and the key factor prompting Monnet's plan, was the emergence in April 1949 of a sovereign West German state.

For Monnet the existence of the Federal Republic of Germany posed two problems in addition to that of how to create an integrated west European economy. The first was how to organize Franco-German relations in such a way that another war between the two states would become impossible. To a French mind this meant how to control Germany. The pooling of coal and steel production would provide the basis for economic development as a first step towards a 'federation of Europe', and would change the future of those regions devoted to producing munitions, which had also been 'the most constant victims' of war.

The solidarity in production thus established will make it plain that any war between France and Germany becomes not merely unthinkable, but materially impossible.

(Schuman Declaration 1950)

The problem of how to control Germany remained at the heart of the process of European integration throughout the early post-war period.

The second problem facing Monnet was the very practical one of how to ensure continuing adequate supplies of coking coal from the Ruhr for the French steel industry. The idea of pooling Franco-German supplies of coal and steel was not new: similar schemes had been proposed on many occasions previously (Gillingham 1991b: 135; Duchêne 1994: 202). In fact the idea of pooling coal and steel supplies had featured in two recent publications, one from the Assembly of the Council of Europe and the other from the UN Economic Commission for Europe (Urwin 1995: 44). These reports were concerned with the very practical problems affecting the coal and steel industries of Europe. There was excess capacity in steel, and a shortage of coal. This combination was of particular concern to Monnet, whose recovery plan for France involved expanding steel-producing capacity. The French steel industry was heavily dependent on supplies of coking coal from the Ruhr.

At the end of the war, the Ruhr region of Germany had been placed under joint Allied control. Its supplies of coal had been allocated between the various competing users by the International Authority for the Ruhr (IAR), which had been established in April 1945. It seemed unlikely that this arrangement could be long continued once the Federal Republic was constituted, which raised the question of how France could ensure that it continued to get access to the supply of scarce Ruhr coal that its steel industry needed. The coal and steel pool had the potential to achieve this.

In summary, Monnet's reasons for proposing the plan to pool Franco-German supplies of coal and steel were a combination of taking a first step on the road to complete integration of the west European economy, finding a way to organize Franco-German relations which would eliminate the prospect of a further war between the two states, and solving the problem of how to ensure continued access for the French steel industry to supplies of coking coal from the Ruhr. That Schuman essentially accepted this thinking, informs the standard explanation for France's participation in the Schuman Plan.

Germany

Chancellor Adenauer accepted the Schuman Plan with alacrity. Yet if the proposal had been made to serve French interests, why was the German Chancellor so keen on it?

As with Schuman, one of the factors was a commitment on the part of Adenauer to the ideal of European integration. Like Schuman, Adenauer came from a border region, in his case the Rhineland. Like Schuman, he was a Roman Catholic and a Christian Democrat. In accepting the Schuman Plan, Adenauer committed himself to Franco-German reconciliation and to European integration. This does not mean, though, that he acted only for idealistic reasons. There were also very practical reasons for Adenauer's acceptance of the Schuman Plan. The Federal Republic needed to gain international acceptance; Adenauer wanted to make a strong commitment to the capitalist West; and the new German government was looking for a way of getting rid of the IAR.

The legacy of the Nazi era and of the war had left Germany a pariah nation. It had also left it divided into two separate states, the Federal Republic in the west and the Democratic Republic in the east. Adenauer wanted to establish the Federal Republic as the legitimate successor to the pre-war German state, but also as a peace-loving state that would be accepted as a full participant in European and international affairs. Adenauer also wanted to establish the western and capitalist orientation of the Federal Republic beyond question or reversal. This was important to Adenauer because the Social Democratic Party (*Sozialdemokratische Partei Deutschlands*—SPD) was arguing for the Federal Republic to declare itself neutral in the emerging Cold War, in the hope that this would facilitate re-unification of the country. As well as being strongly anti-communist, Adenauer believed that the Democratic Republic was dominated by the Soviet Union, and he feared the cultural influence of Russia would be damaging to the vitality of German culture and to the process of moral renewal in the aftermath of Nazism, which, as a devout Catholic, he believed to be essential. (Milward 1992: 329–30).

The importance for Adenauer of getting rid of the IAR was both political and economic. Politically it was important to him that the region be integrated into the Federal Republic. Economically, the Ruhr had always been one of the powerhouses of the German industrial economy, so it was important to the prospects of economic recovery that it be unchained from the restrictions that the IAR placed on its industrialists. There was a risk that in accepting the Schuman Plan, Adenauer would commit his country to a relationship from which French industry would gain at the expense of German industry. However, Adenauer was confident that German industrialists could stand up for their interests within a coal and steel pool (Gillingham 1991a: 233).

The Benelux States

The reason why the Benelux states agreed to enter the negotiations for the ECSC was the same in each case: they could not afford to stay out of any agreement between France and Germany on coal and steel. These commodities were essential to the economies of the three states, and there was a high degree of interdependence between the industries in the border regions of France and Germany, and those in Belgium and Luxemburg particularly. There was also support in all three states for any moves that promised to reduce the risk of war between their two larger neighbours.

Italy

Italian reasons for joining in the negotiations require a little more explanation than the reasons for Benelux participation. Italy is not geographically part of the same industrial region as the other participants, so there was not the same inevitability about its involvement. In many ways the reasons for Italian participation in the negotiations resembled those of Germany more closely than those of the Benelux states.

Like Germany, Italy was governed by Christian Democrats; and as in the case of Adenauer (and of Schuman) the individual who dominated the government was a Roman Catholic and someone who originated in a border region. Alcide di Gasperi came from the Alto Adige region of Italy, which had been part of the Austro-Hungarian empire before the First World War. Like Germany, Italy had to rebuild its international reputation after the war. Mussolini had been Hitler's ally and had ended up as his puppet. Like Germany, Italy was on the front line in the emerging Cold War. Geographically, it had a land frontier with the Communist state of Yugoslavia, and only the Adriatic Sea separated it from Albania. At the end of the war there had been a serious risk that the Italian Communist Party would take over the country in democratic elections, and it remained the largest single party in terms of support. Di Gasperi therefore had a similar need to that of Adenauer in Germany to enmesh his country in a complex of institutional interdependencies with the capitalist west, to establish its western and capitalist identity politically, economically, and in the minds of its own people.

Britain

The other state that was invited to participate in the conference that followed the Schuman Plan was Britain. The negative attitude of the British government has been extensively analysed (Dell 1995; George 1998: 19–22; J. W. Young 1993: 28–35; H. Young 1998).

All accounts accept that there were certain peculiarities of the British position that made it highly unlikely that its government would welcome the proposal. Whereas in continental Europe, nationalism had been discredited through its association with Fascism, in Britain Fascism had never succeeded, and the war had been fought as a national war. Unlike the other states, Britain had neither been defeated nor occupied in the war. There was not the same sense in Britain of discontinuity with the past. The attitude of the British governing élite was that Britain was not just another European state. It was a world power with global responsibilities. Although this attitude has been described as a 'delusion of grandeur' (Porter 1987) it had some basis in reality. Britain still had a considerable empire; British companies had interests in all parts of the world; and British armed forces were globally deployed in keeping the peace, or acting as a bulwark against communist encroachment.

The perception at the time was that Britain was economically far stronger than the other western European states, and that tying the future of the British economy to that of the German and French economies was dangerous. Britain had adequate indigenous supplies of coal, and the Labour government had just completed the nationalization of the coal and steel industries. Having campaigned over many years for nationalization, the Labour Party was unlikely to surrender control once it had been achieved. Also, European integration was at this time particularly associated with the leader of the Conservative Party, Winston Churchill. Although there were some Labour Party members who participated in the Hague Congress and remained supporters of a united Europe, the idea was associated with the opposition, not the government.

To add to these general factors, Ernest Bevin, the Foreign Secretary, was personally upset that he had no forewarning of Schuman's announcement. Dean Acheson, the US Secretary of State, was told about the Plan in advance by the French Prime Minister, Georges Bidault; and Acheson subsequently met Bevin, but did not mention the Plan. As Acheson had been given the information in confidence, this was reasonable enough; but it led Bevin to see a Franco-American plot to seize the initiative away from Britain in the formulation of plans for western Europe (Young 1998: 52). Bevin's annoyance was increased when the French government insisted that all those who wished to participate in the scheme must accept the principle of supranationalism. This condition was pressed by Monnet, who was concerned that otherwise the outcome would be another intergovernmental organization. He must have known that it would be an impossible condition for the British government to accept, given the strong attachment of the Labour Party to national sovereignty, and perhaps he did not really want British participation at the outset. It was, after all, the British who had been primarily responsible for the watering down of the commitment to supranational institutions in the Council of Europe.

The British government did not immediately reject the demand for a commitment to supranationalism. Instead, the French were asked to specify exactly what they meant by the phrase, to spell out the full extent of the surrender of sovereignty that was envisaged and its effects. After some three weeks of inconclusive discussions of the implications of supranationalism, Schuman announced on 1 June 1950 that the principle was non-negotiable, and that any state that wanted to be involved in the negotiations must accept it by 8.00 p.m. on 2 June. The British Cabinet immediately rejected this condition.

From the Schuman Plan to the Treaty of Paris

Negotiations between the six began on 20 June, with all delegations supposedly committed to the principle of supranationalism. However, both the Belgians and the Dutch had

HISTORY

INSIGHT 6.2

Bargaining Concessions in the ECSC Negotiations

- At the insistence of the Dutch, supported by the Germans, a Council of Ministers, consisting of representatives of national governments, was added to the institutional structure to curtail the supranationalism of the High Authority.
- At the insistence of the Belgians, a special 'equalization tax' on efficient coal producers was agreed, which would be used to subsidize the modernization of inefficient mines. In practice this amounted to a subsidy from Germany to Belgium.
- At the insistence of the Italians, the Italian steel industry was allowed to maintain tariffs against the rest of the participants for five years, and to continue to import cheap coking coal and scrap metal from outside the ECSC. As with the Belgian coal mines, there was to be an equalization fund to finance the modernization of inefficient Italian steel plant, although this was much smaller than the coal equalization tax.

reservations, as became apparent once the opening session was completed and the substantive negotiations began on 22 June (Duchêne 1994: 209).

Monnet insisted that the French delegation should be hand-picked by himself, and he rigorously excluded representatives of the French coal and steel industries from influence in the process. This was not the case with the other delegations, which consisted of diplomats and officials from the national energy ministries, who were open to influence from the affected industries.

There followed months of hard bargaining during which various departures were made from the original principles set out in Monnet's working document (Insight 6.2). These concessions were necessary to make a success of the negotiations. That they had to be made reinforces the view that most participants were concerned to use the ECSC to further their own national interests. The biggest concessions were made by the German government, for whom the main potential advantage of the Schuman Plan was the opportunity it offered to get the removal of the constraints imposed by the IAR.

At the end of the war, the Allies had forced the deconcentration of the coal and steel industries in Germany, and the break-up of the cartels that had restricted competition. From the German point of view this only served to give an artificial advantage to their French competitors. The IAR acted to prevent reconcentration and re-emergence of cartels, so the German industrialists wanted to get rid of it. But they did not want the High Authority of the ECSC to take over those functions from the IAR, whereas Monnet was determined that the High Authority would do exactly that.

From the French point of view, concentration was dangerous because it gave too much political influence to the large industrial concerns. The support of the Ruhr industrialists for Hitler had contributed to the Nazis coming to power. Cartelization was a device that, in Monnet's eyes, acted as a restraint on competition. In this view he was strongly supported by the United States.

The role of the United States Administration in the negotiations was vital. Not officially represented at the talks, the United States nevertheless exerted a tremendous influence behind the scenes. A special committee was set up in the US Embassy in Paris to monitor progress, and it acted as a sort of additional secretariat for Monnet. For the United States the cartel arrangements were an outrageous interference with the operation of market forces, and could not be tolerated. There was initially less concern about the concentration issue because the size of the units involved would still be much smaller than those in the United States. However, after the outbreak of the Korean War in June 1950, the US Administration came to the reluctant conclusion that Germany would have to be rearmed. In this context, the issue of not allowing the emergence of the industrial conglomerates that had supported the previous militaristic German regime became more significant in US minds.

After months of hard negotiation, the United States cut through the arguments and forced a settlement. On 3 March 1951 Adenauer was summoned to see John J. McCloy, the United States High Commissioner in Bonn, who told him that the delays caused by the Germans were unacceptable, and that 'France and the United States had no choice but to impose their own decartelization scheme' (Gillingham 1991a: 280). Despite vigorous protests from the Ruhr producers, Adenauer accepted the ultimatum because for him the political gains of the ECSC were paramount, and he could not afford to allow the process to collapse.

It appeared, then, that although Monnet's concept had been severely modified, the essential purpose had been achieved of creating a supranational body that could exercise some control over the coal and steel producers in the interests of promoting efficiency and competition (see Insight 6.3).

INSIGHT 6.3

Extracts from the Treaty Establishing the European Coal and Steel Community

Article 2

The European Coal and Steel Community shall have as its task to contribute, in harmony with the general economy of the Member States and through the establishment of a common market as provided in Article 4, to economic expansion, growth of employment and a rising standard of living in the Member States.

The Community shall progressively bring about conditions which will of themselves ensure the most rational distribution of production at the highest possible level of productivity, while safeguarding continuity of employment and taking care not to provoke fundamental and persistent disturbances in the economies of Member States.

Article 3

The institutions of the Community shall, within the limits of their respective powers, in the common interest:

(a) ensure an orderly supply to the common market, taking into account the needs of third countries;

(b) ensure that all comparably placed consumers in the common market have equal access to the sources of production;

(c) ensure the establishment of the lowest prices under such conditions that these prices do not result in higher prices charged by the same undertakings in other transactions or in a higher general price level at another time, while allowing necessary amortization and normal return on invested capital;

(d) ensure the maintenance of conditions which will encourage undertakings to expand and improve their production potential and to promote a policy of using natural resources rationally and avoiding their unconsidered exhaustion;

(e) promote improved working conditions and an improved standard of living for the workers in each of the industries for which it is responsible, so as to make possible their harmonization while the improvement is being maintained;

(f) promote the growth of international trade and ensure that equitable limits are observed in export pricing;

(g) promote the orderly expansion and modernization of production, and the improvement of quality, with no protection against competing industries that is not justified by improper action on their part or in their favour.

Article 4

The following are recognized as incompatible with the common market for coal and steel and shall accordingly be abolished and prohibited within the Community, as provided in this Treaty:

(a) import and export duties, or charges having equivalent effect, and quantitative restrictions on the movement of products;

(b) measures or practices which discriminate between producers, between purchasers or between consumers, especially in prices and delivery terms or transport rates and conditions, and measures or practices which interfere with the purchaser's free choice of supplier;

(c) subsidies or aids granted by States, or special charges imposed by States, in any form whatsoever;

(d) restrictive practices which tend towards the sharing or exploiting of markets.

Article 5

The Community shall carry out its task in accordance with this Treaty, with a limited measure of intervention.

To this end the Community shall:

- provide guidance and assistance for the parties concerned, by obtaining information, organizing consultations and laying down general objectives;

- place financial resources at the disposal of undertakings for their investment and bear part of the cost of readaptation;

- ensure the establishment, maintenance and observance of normal competitive conditions and exert direct influence upon production or upon the market only when circumstances so require;

- publish the reasons for its actions and take the necessary measures to ensure the observance of the rules laid down in this Treaty.

The institutions of the Community shall carry out these activities with a minimum of administrative machinery and in close cooperation with the parties concerned.

The High Authority was funded through a direct levy on Europe's coal and steel firms and had a wide brief on taxes, production, and restrictive practices. Alongside it were established a Council of Ministers consisting of national government representatives, and a Common Assembly. In addition, a Consultative Committee to the High Authority was established to represent producers, employers and consumers. More significantly in terms of future integration, a Court of Justice was set up with judges drawn from the national judiciaries to rule on the legality of the High Authority's actions.

CONCLUSION

The first steps in the process of European integration were taken not primarily because of any commitment to the ideas of the federalists, but in response to practical problems. Schuman, Adenauer, and de Gasperi may have had personal reasons for wanting to see a move away from nationalism, but the architect of the ECSC, Jean Monnet, was concerned with solving immediate and longer-term problems. The two immediate problems were, first the reconstruction of the two industries that were central to the European economies of the day, coal and steel, and second how to accommodate West Germany within the system of capitalist European states without reviving the risk of war, and without serious damage to the French steel industry. In the longer term, he was looking at how to ensure that Europe would be competitive in comparison with the United States. The way in which solutions to practical problems became the basis for advances in European integration recurs throughout the story of the founding and evolution of the European communities.

Another consistent theme of the story of European integration is the tension between free-market capitalism and planned capitalism. The system of planned capitalism, or managed markets, is sometimes known by the French word *dirigisme*. Monnet saw very clearly the economic necessity for western Europe to move away from the fragmentation of national markets to form a single large market. He did not consider that the way to achieve this was through the immediate creation of a free market. He wanted the process to be controlled by planners, such as himself, and to proceed economic sector by economic sector. The end result, though, would be a managed European market rather than managed national markets. This theme is returned to in the conclusion to Chapter 8 (p. 125).

The importance of the background of the Cold War was again evident in the launch of the ECSC. The breakdown of cooperation between the Soviet Union and the western Allies led to the creation of a West German state, posing the problems of how to handle Germany and how to ensure adequate coking coal for French steel manufacturers. It coloured the reaction of the governments to the Schuman Plan, particularly in Germany and Italy where the theme of the search for a new national identity was particularly prominent. In both states the governments wanted to find a way of consolidating their position in the western capitalist camp. The ECSC offered a way of embedding their states into the capitalist west, and they could appeal to the idea of European federalism as a way of convincing their electorates that the move was a good one.

This did not mean that the governments of any of the states that agreed to take part in ECSC were prepared to sell short their national interests as they perceived them. A consistent theme of the history of European integration is that advances are made only after hard bargaining between governments. This bargaining tends to produce package deals that give something to everyone. E. B. Haas (1968: 155) said of the Treaty of Paris that set up the ECSC:

The very ambiguity of the Treaty ... made this pattern of convergence possible. Something seemed to be 'in it' for everybody and a large enough body of otherwise quarrelling politicians was persuaded to launch the first experiment in deliberate integration.

In this process of bargaining, the United States was a central actor. Although not having a formal seat at the negotiating table, the US Administration exerted influence on the negotiations and imposed its position on the maintenance of the cartels. Many episodes in the process of European integration can only be fully understood with reference to the position of the United States, which was often either directly involved, or was a factor in the reckoning of the participants.

Finally, the analysis that has been presented here focuses on the interests of states as interpreted by their governments, not on the activities of interest groups. In Chapter 1 (pp. 8–13) a distinction was drawn between realist and pluralist theories of international relations. For realists, states are the only significant actors in the international arena. For pluralists, other actors such as interest groups are also significant. In the case of neofunctionalism, a key role was allocated to organized interests. However, even Haas, the founding father of neofunctionalism, could not tell the story of the foundation of the ECSC in terms of interest group pressures. He examined the positions of all the key interest groups in the various states, and was able to show that they affected the detail of the positions taken up by national governments; but in the end the agreement to the ECSC was based on an independent interpretation of the national interests of the participating states taken by the governments of those states. However, this should not be so surprising, because neofunctionalism was essentially a theory about how the interests would react to the first steps in the process of European integration. ECSC *was* the first step. The time for neofunctionalist analysis had not yet arrived.

KEY POINTS

National Positions and the Origins of the ECSC

☐ The reactions to the proposal for coal and steel known as the Schuman Plan, and the reasons for accepting it, varied from state to state.

☐ The French government saw the coal and steel pool as a way to solve its problem with the emergence of a West German state, and as a way to guarantee supplies of coal from the Ruhr.

☐ The German government saw participation in the scheme as a route back to international respectability, and Adenauer saw in it a means of consolidating West Germany's capitalist identity.

☐ For the governments of the Benelux states there was no choice but to participate in a coal and steel pool that involved France and Germany, so interdependent were their economies.

☐ The Italian government saw the scheme as a potential protection against a Communist takeover.

☐ The British Labour government was unsympathetic to involvement in any economic union with other European states, and coal and steel had just been nationalized, so the sectors could not have been less well chosen to encourage British participation.

- ☐ Negotiations over the Schuman Plan led to significant changes to reflect national interests.

- ☐ Ultimately, however, the US played an important 'behind the scenes' role in shaping an agreement that angered German steel producers but which Adenauer accepted because for him the political gains from the ECSC were paramount.

- ☐ While Monnet's initial concept was modified, the agreement still created a supranational body, the High Authority, with some control over domestic coal and steel producers.

- ☐ Established alongside the High Authority was a Council of Ministers, a Common Assembly and a Court of Justice to rule on the legality of the High Authority's actions.

FURTHER READING

There is a considerable literature on the Schuman Plan. The outline of the negotiations is ably recounted by D.W. Urwin, *The Community of Europe: A History of European Integration since 1945* (London and New York: Longman, 2nd edn, 1995), but for a detailed insight into the process the account given by F. Duchêne, *Jean Monnet: The First Statesman of Interdependence* (New York and London: W. W. Norton and Co., 1994) is indispensable. Most of J. Gillingham, *Coal, Steel, and the Rebirth of Europe, 1945–1955* (Cambridge: Cambridge University Press, 1991) is devoted to the build-up to the negotiations and the negotiations themselves, and E.B. Haas, *The Uniting of Europe: Political, Social and Economic Forces, 1950–1957* (Stanford, Calif.: Stanford University Press, 1968) contains information on the positions of all the main actors, scattered through a book that is organized thematically rather than chronologically.

For the revisionist view that the ECSC was not a move away from state autonomy but a means of protecting it, the reader should turn to A. Milward, *The European Rescue of the Nation State* (London: Routledge, 1992).

The British failure to take seriously the Schuman Plan is recounted in E. Dell, *The Schuman Plan and the British Abdication of Leadership in Europe* (Oxford: Clarendon Press, 1995).

online resource centre — **Visit the Online Resource Centre that accompanies this book for links to more information on the Schuman Plan.**

CHAPTER 7

The European Defence Community, the European Political Community, and the Road to the Rome Treaties

CHAPTER OVERVIEW

Negotiations over a plan for a European Defence Community (EDC) ran parallel to those over the ECSC, which were discussed in the previous chapter. Connected with the EDC was a proposal to create a European Political Community (EPC) to provide democratic European structures for co-ordinating foreign policies. This provided federalists with another opportunity to pursue their strategy of 'the constitutional break', moving directly from a Europe of nation-states to a federal constitution for Europe. However, the feasibility of doing this was no greater in 1953 than it had been in 1948, and for the same reason: governments were not prepared to surrender their sovereignty. With the collapse of the EDC and EPC, the radical federalist strategy of a direct attack on the system of nation-states disappeared from this story. This chapter looks at the development of the EDC/EPC plan and the ultimate failure to reach agreement on this in 1954, before looking at the relaunch of the integration project in 1955, leading in 1957 to the Treaties of Rome that established the European Economic Community (EEC) and the European Atomic Energy Community (Euratom).

> In the autumn of 1952, there were not one but three prospective Communities, two pillars and the roof of a potential European union. Covering coal, steel, defence, arms production and perhaps elements of foreign policy—that is, economic and political functions close to the core of the state—they provided the outline of a federation in the classic style. To achieve so much would be extraordinary three or four years from a standing start and less than a decade after the war. On the other hand, there were disturbing signs that all this might be a house of cards resting on the fate of the European Army.
>
> **(Duchêne 1994: 234–5)**

While the development of the ECSC (Ch. 6) set much of the tone and framework for future developments in European integration, it was largely overshadowed at the time by parallel negotiations on another plan devised by Monnet, the Pleven Plan for a European Defence Community (EDC). The failure of this proposal was perhaps as much responsible as the successes and failures of the ECSC in explaining the initiatives that led to the Treaties of Rome.

The Pleven Plan

Following the collapse of the four-power administration of Germany (Ch. 5, p. 86), the Cold War developed rapidly. In April 1949 a mutual defence pact, the North Atlantic Treaty, was signed in Washington between the United States, Canada, and ten west European states (Britain, France, the Benelux states, Iceland, Italy, Norway, and Portugal). This set up the North Atlantic Treaty Organization (NATO). In the same month the Federal Republic of Germany came into existence. In June 1950 Communist North Korea invaded capitalist South Korea. The ensuing civil war involved the United States, acting under the auspices of the United Nations, on the side of the South, and the Soviet Union and Communist China on the side of the North. It had a profound impact on western thinking about security.

Like Korea, Germany was divided into capitalist and Communist states. While Korea was at that time geographically peripheral to the main global balance of power, Germany was not. The fear in the West was that the Korean invasion was a precursor to an invasion of West Germany from East Germany. In this context, and because the United States was committing troops to the Korean conflict, the US administration decided that the Europeans had to make a bigger contribution to their own defence. In particular, they reluctantly decided that there was no alternative to reconstituting a German army.

This idea alarmed the French. For them it was unthinkable that a German army should come back into existence. Monnet tried to solve the problem with a proposal based on the same principles as his plan for ECSC. Under his scheme for a European Defence Community, instead of having a German army, he proposed to pool the military resources of France and Germany into a European army. There would be German soldiers, but they would not wear German uniforms, and they would not be under German command. The corollary, of course, was that the French army would at least partially disappear into the same European force. Monnet's proposal did however allow France and the other participants, except Germany, to have their own national armies alongside the European army.

The plan proposed the creation of a European army consisting of fourteen French divisions, twelve German, eleven Italian, and three from the Benelux states. The command of the army would be integrated, but there would be no divisions of mixed nationality. The EDC would have had a similar institutional structure to the ECSC: a Council representing the member states, with votes weighted according to each state's contribution to the European army, alongside a Commission and an Assembly.

As with the pooling of coal and steel, a European army was not a new idea. A similar proposal had been made by the French representatives in the Consultative Assembly of the Council of Europe in August 1950, and had received the support of the Assembly, but had been blocked in the Council of Ministers. Monnet now formalized the idea, making an explicit link to the ECSC. The plan was publicly launched by the French Prime Minister, René Pleven, an old collaborator of Monnet, on 24 October 1950.

Despite the election in Britain in October 1951 of a Conservative government under Churchill, who professed to be a supporter of European integration, the British were unwilling to become involved in plans for the EDC. The US administration was initially cautious, but Monnet talked round the new NATO Supreme Allied Commander in Europe, Dwight D. Eisenhower, and his support swung the administration behind the scheme (Duchêne 1994: 231). Adenauer welcomed the idea, seeing in it a way of finally ending the Allied occupation of West Germany. The other four states that had joined in the Schuman Plan signed up to talks for essentially the same reasons as they had joined ECSC: the Benelux states did not feel that they could stand aside from such an initiative between their two larger neighbours, and Italy continued to seek acceptance into the European states system.

EDC, ECSC, and EPC

At Monnet's prompting, Pleven made it a condition of progress on the EDC that the ECSC Treaty be signed first. This was particularly resented in Germany, because Monnet had accompanied preparation of the Pleven plan with a hardening of his attitude towards the position of the German steel cartels in the talks on the Schuman Plan. This had stalled the talks: Adenauer and the German negotiator, Hallstein, felt that they were being railroaded into accepting an unfavourable agreement on the ECSC in order to secure negotiations on the EDC. They were not mistaken. Gillingham (1991b: 146) was clear that these two developments were linked in Monnet's mind. Indeed, the same author (1991a: 264) went so far as to suggest that the Pleven Plan 'saved the Schuman Plan'. This sort of cross-bargaining worked both ways, however. Duchêne (1994: 250) believed that one explanation for Monnet's failure to press home the Treaty provisions against the Ruhr cartels when he became President of the ECSC High Authority was that Adenauer warned him that any premature action on this front would jeopardize the ratification of the EDC Treaty in the German parliament.

A problem with the proposed EDC was the plan for a common European army without a common foreign policy. The proposed institutions of the EDC would not be able to provide this. At the insistence of Italy, a clause was inserted into the draft treaty linking the EDC with the creation of a European Political Community to provide a democratic dimension to the project. Plans were to be drawn up by the Common Assembly of the EDC, but as delays in ratifying the treaty stretched out the process, Paul-Henri Spaak, the Belgian Premier, suggested that the Common Assembly of the ECSC, enlarged in membership so as to resemble the proposed EDC Assembly, should prepare the EPC proposal.

The opportunity to draft a Treaty for a European Political Community was seized on by federalists within the Assembly. In the course of its work the ECSC Assembly was supplemented by members of the Parliamentary Assembly of the Council of Europe (see Ch. 5, Insight 5.2). The draft Treaty was adopted by this *ad hoc* Assembly on 10 March 1953. It proposed: a two-chamber European Parliament consisting of a People's Chamber that would be directly elected every five years, and a Senate of indirectly elected members from national parliaments; a European Executive Council that would have to be approved by both chambers of the parliament, but once in office would have the power to dissolve the People's Chamber and call new elections; a Council of National Ministers; a Court of Justice. The EPC would not be just a third community, 'but nothing less than the beginning of a comprehensive federation to which the ECSC and EDC would be subordinated' (Urwin 1995: 64).

The Fate of the EDC and EPC

The fate of the EPC was inevitably linked to the fate of the EDC. The EDC treaty had been signed in May 1952, but it had not been ratified by any of the signatories when the EPC proposals emerged. In fact, the EDC treaty was 'rotting before the ink was dry' (Duchêne 1994: 233). Its prospects were crucially dependent on French support, but the French government only signed it on the 'tacit condition that no immediate attempt should be made to ratify it' (Duchêne 1994: 233). German rearmament, even as part of a European army, was unpopular in France. Pleven only managed to get approval for his proposal from the National Assembly by 343 votes to 220. By the time that the intergovernmental negotiations were completed, there had been elections in France and the parliamentary arithmetic did not indicate a clear majority for ratification. In consequence, successive prime ministers refused to bring the treaty to the Assembly for ratification, fearing that its failure would bring down their government.

This prevarication, which went on for almost two years, caused exasperation in the United States, and led Secretary of State John Foster Dulles in December 1953 to threaten an 'agonizing reappraisal' of policy. Eventually the Treaty was submitted to the National Assembly by the government of Pierre Mendès-France at the end of August 1954, but the government gave it no support, and indicated that it would not resign if the Assembly voted against ratification. The EDC treaty was not ratified and the demise of the EDC was accompanied by the collapse of the EPC.

The Aftermath of EDC and EPC

The issue of European defence was eventually solved according to a formula proposed by the British government. The Brussels Treaty of 1948 was extended to Germany and Italy; a loose organization called the Western European Union (WEU) was set up to co-ordinate the alliance; an organic link was made with NATO, to which Germany and Italy were admitted. Adenauer achieved his aim of securing an Allied withdrawal from the whole of West Germany (although not Berlin), and a German army was formed, although it was hedged around with legal restrictions on operating beyond the borders of the Federal Republic. The WEU appeared to contemporary observers to be an organization of no particular importance because it was overshadowed by NATO. However, like other organizations that were set up in the post-war period, it was later to acquire functions that had not been envisaged at the time when it was formed (Insight 7.1).

The other practical significance of the EDC episode, or rather of the related EPC initiative, was that it kept the federalist idea alive. As Gillingham (1991a: 349) put it, it 'kept the cadres in being, dialogue moving, and served as a learning experience'. The importance of this became clear with the 'relaunching of Europe' that followed the collapse of EDC.

Defence was not an obvious next step after coal and steel in the process of building mutual trust through practical co-operation. It was not an issue with a low political profile, but a sensitive issue that struck to the heart of national sovereignty. Had it not been for the international crisis of the Korean War, it would surely not have surfaced at this

INSIGHT 7.1

The Western European Union

Following the collapse of the EDC, the British government proposed an alternative security structure for western Europe. This involved Italy and Germany becoming signatories to the Brussels Treaty of 1948, by which Britain, France, and the Benelux states had committed themselves to treat any act of aggression against one as an act of aggression against all.

The Western European Union (WEU), which resulted, began work on 6 May 1955. Its headquarters were in London. Its institutions consisted of:

- a Council of Foreign and Defence Ministers;
- a Secretariat, headed by a Secretary-General;
- an Assembly (based in Paris), made up of the member states' representatives in the Parliamentary Assembly of the Council of Europe

From the outset WEU was overshadowed by NATO. It was only in the 1980s that it began to assume any significance beyond its original purpose as a means of giving a British security guarantee to Germany's neighbours so that they would agree to German rearmament.

In the 1980s the WEU took on a new role as a bridge between the EC and NATO in the context of efforts to forge a European security and defence identity. The Treaty on European Union (signed February 1992) contained as an annex a Declaration on WEU which said: 'WEU will be developed as the defence component of the European Union and as a means to strengthen the European pillar of the Atlantic Alliance.' The EU's operational activities were transferred to the EU in 2000.

stage. Monnet himself may have been of this view. Duchêne (1994: 229) reports that several people who were working close to Monnet at the time had the impression that he regarded the EDC scheme as premature. After winning over Eisenhower, Monnet took no further part in the negotiations on the plan, suggesting a lack of further commitment to the project.

Messina

In November 1954, Monnet announced that when his first term as President of the High Authority of the ECSC ended in February 1955, he would not seek a second term. Citing the collapse of the EDC, he said that he wanted to free his hands to work for European unity. He then formed an organization called the Action Committee for the United States of Europe, consisting of leading political and trade union figures from the member states of the ECSC, but also from Britain and other states.

The main proposal to come from the Action Committee was for a European Atomic Energy Community (Euratom). It was accompanied by a plan to extend the sectoral responsibilities of the ECSC to cover all forms of energy, and transport. Nothing came of these latter proposals, although transport was given a special place in the Treaty of Rome (EEC). The member governments were simply not interested in extending the remit of the ECSC.

Also accompanying the proposals from the Action Committee was a proposal from Beyen, the Dutch Foreign Minister, for a general common market. Richard Mayne (1991: 115) maintained that this scheme also originated with Monnet, but he offered no evidence for this, and it is a view that is flatly rejected by other writers. Duchêne (1994: 269–72) provided evidence that Monnet actually rejected the idea of a general common market, believing that it was too ambitious, and might produce another EDC débâcle.

There was no great enthusiasm for further sectoral integration. In so far as business interests expressed support for further integration, it was for an extension of the market aspect of the ECSC, not for the centralized regulatory functions of the High Authority. The lesson that was learned from ECSC was the limitations of sectoral integration. As *The Economist* (11 Aug. 1956) reported:

In the last four years the Coal and Steel Community has proved that the common market is not only feasible but, on balance, advantageous for all concerned. But it has also shown that 'integration by sector' raises its own problems of distortion and discrimination. The Six have therefore chosen to create a common market for all products rather than continuing to experiment with the sector approach.

On 4 April 1955, Spaak circulated a memorandum to the governments of the six states of the ECSC proposing that negotiations begin on the extension of sectoral integration to other forms of energy than coal, particularly nuclear energy, and to transport. The proposal met with a cool response; only the French government supported it. Beyen then pressed the case for a relaunch based on the idea of a general common market.

The Federal German government reacted very positively to Beyen's proposal, but in France the idea of a general common market was strongly rejected by industry, which argued that it would not be able to compete with German industry. French politicians had generally accepted this argument, but there was a growing belief that the excuse could not be used forever, and that French industry would never be competitive until it had to compete. At this stage, though, the mood in France was not conducive to taking such a step, which may explain why Monnet was reluctant to advocate it.

Spaak subsequently met with the Dutch Prime Minister, Joseph Bech, and as a result of that meeting, a formal Benelux initiative was launched combining Monnet's ideas for further sectoral integration with Beyen's idea of a general common market. This proposal was circulated in late April 1955, and was discussed at the beginning of June in Messina in Italy at a meeting of the heads of government of the six, which had originally been called to decide on a successor to Monnet as President of the High Authority of the ECSC.

Agreement was reached at Messina to set up a committee under the chairmanship of Spaak to study the ideas in the Benelux memorandum. The French government was not enthusiastic, and appeared not to expect anything to come of the talks, but it was difficult for France to block them so soon after its rejection of the EDC. Because the agreement to hold talks was reached in Messina, the negotiations took that name. In fact most of the meetings were held in Brussels. Their success was unexpected, except perhaps by optimistic partisans of integration like Spaak. In fact, the success of the Spaak Committee, which met in Brussels between July 1955 and March 1956, owed a great deal to his energetic and skilful chairing of the proceedings. Also very important, though, were the changed circumstances between the original Messina meeting and the actual negotiations.

France and the Suez Crisis

One very important change was in the government of France: Guy Mollet, the leader of the Socialist Party, became Prime Minister in 1956. Having originally been sceptical about European integration, Mollet had become convinced that French industry needed to be opened up to competition if it was ever to achieve the sort of productivity gains that lay behind the remarkable German economic recovery. He had also become a member of Monnet's Action Committee, and Duchêne (1994: 287) maintained that a relationship developed between Monnet and Mollet similar to the earlier relationship between Monnet and Schuman.

Mollet was brought to office by the deteriorating situation in Algeria, where French settlers were under attack by the National Liberation Front (FLN) of Algeria. The war that developed there was traumatic for the French, and dominated the nation's attention so that the negotiations in Brussels were able to proceed without attracting much notice from critics. But Algeria was only one of the international events of 1956 that had an effect on the outcome of the Messina negotiations. In October the Soviet Union invaded Hungary to suppress an anti-communist national movement that had the sympathy of the Hungarian army. Hungary brought home to western Europeans once again the reality of the Cold War that divided their continent. More directly, the Suez Canal crisis also blew up in October.

The nationalization of the Suez canal by Egyptian President Gamal Abdel Nasser not only caused outrage in France, as it did in Britain; it also offered the French a possible excuse to topple Nasser, whose pan-Arab rhetoric inflamed the situation in Algeria, and whose regime was suspected of sheltering and arming the Algerian rebels. However, once the nationalization had been effected, Nasser gave no further cause for outside intervention. The canal was kept open to international shipping; it was business as usual under new ownership. To foment an excuse to invade, the French government colluded with the Israeli government and hatched a scheme that was subsequently sold to the British government of Anthony Eden. Israel would invade the canal zone; the French and British governments would demand an immediate withdrawal from the canal by the armed forces of both sides. Egypt would certainly refuse, and the combined Franco-British force would then move in to occupy the canal zone and reclaim the canal. The fall of Nasser was confidently expected to follow.

However, the invasion failed because in the face of opposition from the Soviet Union and, more significantly, from the United States, the British government decided to pull out. France could not carry through the operation alone. The episode was perceived in France as a national humiliation at the hands of the Americans, but also as a betrayal by the British who were believed to be too subservient to US wishes. It fed support for the nationalist position of Charles de Gaulle, who subsequently came to office as first president of the new Fifth Republic in May 1958. It also fed into the Messina negotiations, helping them to reach a speedy and successful conclusion.

Directly, Suez underlined much more than events in Hungary the impotence of France in the post-war world of superpowers. It gave support to the concept of France acting together with other European states. Indirectly, the clear signs that this episode marked the beginning of the end for the government of Mollet, and the strong indications that he would be succeeded by de Gaulle, who had always opposed European integration, accelerated the efforts to reach agreement. A 'rush to Rome' began in an effort to get the Treaties signed before de Gaulle came to office and aborted the whole experiment.

The Road to the Rome Treaties

The agreements reached in the Spaak Committee were a series of compromises between different national positions, particularly those of France and Germany. Central to the agreement detailed in the Spaak Report of March 1956 was the creation of the general common market favoured by the German government. Although Mollet believed that this step would be good for France as well as for Germany, he had to negotiate concessions that would allow him to get the Treaty ratified in the French National Assembly. There were three main areas where the French government extracted concessions: Euratom, agriculture, and relations with France's overseas territories and dependencies.

Euratom was attractive for many French politicians because they saw it as a means of obtaining a subsidy from Germany for the expensive process of developing nuclear energy, which in turn was linked to the development of nuclear weapons. Although Mollet personally believed that France should confine itself to the peaceful use of nuclear energy, the sentiment in the National Assembly in the aftermath of Hungary and Suez was very much in favour of an independent French nuclear deterrent. Euratom offered the opportunity to devote more national resources to the weapons programme, while depriving Germany of a national nuclear capability, and guaranteeing French access to uranium from the Belgian Congo.

Agriculture was given a separate chapter in the EEC Treaty. Its inclusion, not as part of the general common market, but as in effect a further extension of sectoral integration was another factor that was important in ensuring French ratification of the Treaty.

INSIGHT 7.2

Extracts from the Treaty establishing the European Atomic Energy Community

Article 1

By this Treaty the HIGH CONTRACTING PARTIES establish among themselves a EUROPEAN ATOMIC ENERGY COMMUNITY (EURATOM).

It shall be the task of the Community to contribute to the raising of the standard of living in the Member States and to the development of relations with the other countries by creating the conditions necessary for the speedy establishment and growth of nuclear industries.

Article 2

In order to perform its task, the Community shall, as provided in this Treaty:

(a) promote research and ensure the dissemination of technical information;

(b) establish uniform safety standards to protect the health of workers and of the general public and ensure that they are applied;

(c) facilitate investment and ensure, particularly by encouraging ventures on the part of undertakings, the establishment of the basic installations necessary for the development of nuclear energy in the Community;

(d) ensure that all users in the Community receive a regular and equitable supply of ores and nuclear fuels;

(e) make certain, by appropriate supervision, that nuclear materials are not diverted to purposes other than those for which they are intended;

(f) exercise the right of ownership conferred upon it with respect to special fissile materials;

(g) ensure wide commercial outlets and access to the best technical facilities by the creation of a common market in specialized materials and equipment, by the free movement of capital for investment in the field of nuclear energy and by freedom of employment for specialists within the Community;

(h) establish with other countries and international organizations such relations as will foster progress in the peaceful uses of nuclear energy.

For the French governments of the Fourth Republic, agriculture was both politically and economically important. Politically, small farmers had a disproportionate electoral importance under the voting system that was used in the Fourth Republic. The small farmers were inefficient producers, but were determined to retain their independence, which in effect meant that they had to be subsidized by the state through a national system of price-support. By transferring this cost to the common EEC budget, the French state again obtained a subsidy from the more prosperous Germans. Economically, France also had an efficient agricultural sector, and actually produced a considerable surplus of

INSIGHT 7.3

Extracts from the Treaty Establishing the European Economic Community

Article 2

The Community shall have as its task, by establishing a common market and progressively approximating the economic policies of Member States, to promote through the Community a harmonious development of economic activities, a continuous and balanced expansion, an increase in stability, an accelerated raising of the standard of living and closer relations between the States belonging to it.

Article 3

For the purposes set out in Article 2, the activities of the Community shall include, as provided in this Treaty and in accordance with the timetable set out therein:

(a) the elimination, as between Member States, of customs duties and quantitative restrictions on the import and export of goods, and of all other measures having equivalent effect;

(b) the establishment of a common customs tariff and of common commercial policy towards third countries;

(c) the abolition, as between Member States, of obstacles to the free movement of goods, persons, services and capital;

(d) the adoption of a common policy in the sphere of agriculture;

(e) the adoption of a common policy in the sphere of transport;

(f) the institution of a system ensuring that competition in the common market is not distorted;

(g) the application of procedures by which the economic policies of Member States can be co-ordinated and disequilibria in their balances of payments remedied;

(h) the approximation of the laws of Member States to the extent required for the proper functioning of the common market;

(i) the creation of a European Social Fund in order to improve employment opportunities for workers and to contribute to the raising of their standard of living;

(j) the establishment of a European Investment Bank to facilitate the economic expansion of the Community by opening fresh resources;

(k) the association of the overseas countries and territories in order to increase trade and to promote jointly economic and social development.

food, so the guarantee of a protected market for French agricultural exports was another concession that helped to sell the EEC Treaty within France.

In the context of decolonization and the war in Algeria, it was very important for all French governments to ensure that the special links with the former colonies were maintained. There were considerable French economic interests that were dependent on trade with these overseas dependencies and territories, and there was a general sentiment in France in favour of the link. The continuation of this special relationship, by guaranteeing preferential access to the common market for the products of the former colonies, was the third important factor to allow the Treaty to obtain ratification in France.

On each of these points the German government made considerable concessions. There was no sympathy for Euratom in German industrial or government circles; the Germans would have preferred to leave agriculture to national management, and to continue to allow food to be imported as cheaply as possible from the rest of the world; and there was no enthusiasm for supporting the last vestiges of French colonialism. However, in order to obtain the considerable prize of the common market in industrial goods, the German government was prepared to make these concessions to France.

The other major bargaining concession was made to Italy in the form of the inclusion in the Treaty of a commitment to reducing the differences between prosperous and poor regions. This was the Italian government's attempt to claim a subsidy from Germany, given that the problems of the south of Italy represented the main regional disparity within the original six member states.

The Spaak Report was agreed by the governments of the six member states in May 1956. The Spaak Committee was transformed into a conference with responsibility for drafting the necessary treaties. In March 1957, two treaties emerged: one for the EEC; the other for Euratom. The treaties were signed by national governments in Rome in the same month, prior to being passed on for domestic ratification. If the failure of the EDC had meant several steps backwards in the process of integration, the Treaties of Rome promised a major leap forward (Insights 7.2 and 7.3).

CONCLUSION

Several of the persistent themes of this story emerge once more in this chapter. The influence of the Cold War on the whole EDC episode is clear, as is the role of the United States in the affairs of western Europe during this period of its hegemony of the capitalist world. However, the fate of the EDC is vindication of the functionalist analysis that a head-on attack on sovereignty would be resisted, whereas gradual steps to tie states together might succeed.

It is contestable whether the opening of negotiations on the EEC is vindication of the neofunctionalist argument that spillover would operate to move integration forward once the first steps had been taken. The line of spillover from ECSC to Euratom is clearer, and was the line of progression favoured by Monnet. However, the proposal for Euratom was countered, rather than complemented, by the proposal from the Benelux states for a general common market. In this can be seen the tension between *dirigisme* and free-market approaches to integration. The general common market was designed to open national markets by removing tariffs, at that time the main barrier to free trade. It stood in marked distinction to the Euratom proposal to extend the system of planning of the 'commanding heights' of the economy from coal and steel to what was expected to be the new main source of energy.

Monnet's scheme also reflected the need to gain the acceptance of the French political élite. France was developing nuclear energy as a priority project, so it could be expected to support Euratom, which offered France the prospect of a subsidy from the other member states for its research and development costs. A free market in industrial goods was less likely to find favour in a country where there was less industrial efficiency than in West Germany. However, things were changing in France. There was a growing awareness among the political élite that if France were to keep up with its German neighbour it had to modernize its economy. Euratom, and concessions on agriculture and overseas territories, were necessary sweeteners to sell the package to the French National Assembly; but the assertion, often made, that the EEC was a deal between German industry and French agriculture hides the truth, that for certain sections of the French political élite the common market was a useful tool to sweep away the protectionism that was stifling French economic growth. Another theme that reappears later in the story emerges here: this is the argument that 'Europe' is used as a smokescreen by governments to hide behind when pursuing domestically unpopular measures (see Ch. 4).

There is no strong evidence that a commitment to maintaining the momentum of integration was a motive for the acceptance of the EEC by the political élite in any of the member states. Events in Algeria, Suez, and Hungary did, though, bring home to them the weakness of European states in an era of superpowers, and made clinging together more attractive. These dramatic incidents also impacted on public opinion, and reinforced a general sentiment in favour of federalist ideas. Suez and Algeria in particular caused a crisis of identity among the French public that allowed their government to push through the Treaties of Rome behind a rhetoric of maintaining the momentum of integration. At the same time, the account given here shows that the Messina negotiations were no exception to the rule that national interests will be strongly defended in all moves in the direction of integration.

KEY POINTS

The Pleven Plan

☐ While the ECSC is often seen as the first step on the road to the EU, negotiations over the Pleven Plan for a European Defence Community were considered more important at the time.

☐ The EDC would place German troops under European command, thus heading off US demands for German rearmament following the outbreak of the Korean War. Adenauer reacted positively because it offered a means of ending the Allied occupation of West Germany.

☐ The Pleven Plan became linked with a proposal for a European Political Community.

☐ Both projects collapsed when the French National Assembly refused to ratify the EDC Treaty.

Messina

☐ Following the collapse of EDC/EPC, Monnet launched initiatives based on extending the ECSC model to other forms of energy, especially atomic energy, and to transport.

☐ The Benelux states supported a general common market for industrial goods.

☐ The two sets of proposals were discussed together in the Messina negotiations.

☐ The negotiations were given impetus by international events in 1956: the war in Algeria; the invasion of Hungary by the USSR; and the Suez crisis.

The Road to the Rome Treaties

☐ The Treaties of Rome involved compromises between France and Germany.

☐ The French price for accepting the general common market in industrial goods was German agreement on Euratom, the common agricultural policy, and a preferential relationship with the EEC for the former French colonies.

☐ Italy was allowed to have a commitment in the EEC Treaty to create a regional policy.

FURTHER READING

The Pleven Plan and the abortive attempt to create a European Defence Community is less written about than the Schuman Plan, but it is the subject of E. Fursdon, *The European Defence Community: A History* (London: Macmillan, 1980). As with the Schuman Plan, F. Duchêne, *Jean Monnet: The First Statesman of Interdependence* (New York and London: W. W. Norton and Co., 1994), 229–32, provides an insider account.

online resource centre

Visit the Online Resource Centre that accompanies this book for links to more information on the European Defence Community.

CHAPTER 8

The European Coal and Steel Community and Euratom

CHAPTER OVERVIEW

This chapter examines the independent existence of both the European Coal and Steel Community (ECSC) and Euratom up to the merger of the High Authority and Euratom Commission with the Commission of the European Economic Community (EEC) in July 1967. In this period, both the High Authority and the Euratom Commission ran into conflicts with the governments of member states who were reluctant to relinquish actual control over the two key industries, particularly with the French government after de Gaulle became President of France in 1958. Their difficulties had several parallels, and could lead to the conclusion that they were failed experiments. However, Monnet himself claimed that the ECSC at least contributed to changing perceptions of what was necessary to make European integration work. This chapter asks what lessons can be learned from the experience of these two 'failed' attempts at supranational regulation, and identifies issues that can be later applied to the EEC.

> In itself, this was a technical step, but its new procedures, under common institutions, created a silent revolution in men's minds.
>
> (Jean Monnet 1962: 208)

The European Coal and Steel Community

The ECSC survived the EDC débâcle and began operation in July 1952 under the presidency of Jean Monnet. Although it had considerable powers at its disposal (see Insight 8.1, p. 121), it proceeded cautiously in using them, but still found itself in conflict with national governments.

In the original plan for the ECSC there was only one central institution, the High Authority. During the negotiations a Council of Ministers and a European Parliamentary Assembly (EPA) were added to the institutional structure. This reflected concern about the power and possible *dirigiste* nature of the High Authority, but did not allay that concern.

While coal producers were ambiguous about supranational *dirigisme*, most of them hoping for some degree of support for their troubled industry, steel producers were generally hostile to this aspect of the Schuman Plan. German industrialists in particular opposed the *dirigiste* element to the Plan, and the Federal German government supported them. The governments of the Benelux countries also had severe doubts about the role of the High Authority. It was at the insistence of these governments that a Council of Ministers was included in the institutional structure of the ECSC, alongside the High Authority.

Although its independence was reduced from Monnet's original proposal, the High Authority was still given considerable formal powers. Diebold (1959: 78–9) considered that:

It was truly to be an imperium in imperio, wielding powers previously held by national governments and having some functions not previously exercised by governments.

Despite these powers, in practice the High Authority proceeded very cautiously. It was in a constant state of tension with member state governments, who did not take easily to having their sovereignty circumscribed by a supranational body. The Council regularly rejected proposals of the High Authority that conflicted with national interests. For this reason the High Authority needed a strong president who could impose his authority. In their comprehensive history of the ECSC, Spierenburg and Poidevin (1994: 649) argued that the first two presidents, Monnet and René Mayer, fitted this description, as did the last president, Del Bo, although by the time he took office in 1963 the High Authority was already in its twilight years. The two intervening presidents, Finet and Malvestiti, did not carry the same weight (Insight 8.1).

Even taking account of this difficult relationship with the Council, Haas (1968: 459) considered that, 'in all matters relating to the routine regulation of the Common Market, the High Authority is independent of member governments'. Because of this independence, those governments that were concerned about the possible *dirigisme* of the High

INSIGHT 8.1

The High Authority

The High Authority of the ECSC had nine members, two each from France and Germany and one from each of the other member states, the ninth member to be co-opted by the other eight; its seat was in Luxemburg. It had five Presidents:

- Jean Monnet (1952–5)
- Rene Mayer (1955–7)
- Paul Finet (1958–9)
- Piero Malvestiti (1959–63)
- Rinaldo Del Bo (1963–7).

It had the power under the Treaty of Paris to obtain from firms in the coal and steel sectors the information that it required to oversee the industries, and to fine firms that would not provide the information or evaded their obligations (Article 47).

It could impose levies on production, and contract loans to raise finance to back investment projects of which it approved (Articles 49–51), and it could guarantee loans to coal and steel concerns from independent sources of finance (Article 54). It could also require undertakings to inform it in advance of investment programmes, and if it disapproved of the plans could prevent the concern from using resources other than its own funds to carry out the programme (Article 54).

Authority took care to nominate as their members people who were not themselves committed to this outlook. For Milward (1992: 105) the most notable feature of the members of the High Authority was that they never liberated themselves from their national governments. Monnet became the first president of the High Authority, but found himself at the head of a group of people who were not in sympathy with his own view on its role. Haas (1968: 459) argued that in 'the ideology of the High Authority, the free enterprise and anti-*dirigiste* viewpoint . . . definitely carried the day'.

This way of presenting the issue is perhaps a little misleading. It suggests that Monnet was in favour of intrusive public-sector intervention and was opposed by other members who favoured free competition. In fact, one of the things that Monnet wanted the High Authority to do was prevent the reformation of the coal and steel cartels: organizations of producers that regulated the industries through their collaboration on prices and output. Monnet wanted such regulation as there was to be carried out by the High Authority; but he was also committed to preserving competition between producers. The other members of the High Authority were committed to preventing it from interfering with self-regulation of the markets, not to competition. Perhaps this is what Haas meant by a 'free-enterprise' viewpoint, but the terminology tends to suggest that less regulated markets were the objective. In any case, Monnet was frustrated in his policy objectives for the High Authority.

He was also frustrated in his organizational objectives. Mazey (1992: 40–1) argued that Monnet wanted a small, supranational, non-hierarchical, and informal organization; but that internal divisions, bureaucratization, and pressures from corporatist and national interests foiled him in this. Internal divisions between members of the High Authority itself were reproduced within the administration, and when combined with the non-hierarchical structure that Monnet adopted, this led to increasing problems of administrative co-ordination, delays, and duplication of effort because of overlapping competencies.

However, as the demands for administering the common market for coal and steel grew, so did the bureaucratic nature of the High Authority. Problems of co-ordination increased as the different Directorates of the ECSC developed different links with interests and producers in the member states. The consequence was that in the first three years of its operation, 'the administrative services of the High Authority were . . . transformed from an informal grouping of sympathetic individuals into a professional bureaucracy which, in terms of its structure and 'technocratic' character, resembled the French administration' (Mazey 1992: 43).

When the ECSC was proposed, coal was in short supply; but by 1959 the increasing use of oil had led to over-capacity in the industry. This became a crisis in 1958 when a mild winter and an economic downturn produced a serious fall in demand. Although economic growth picked up in the second quarter of 1959, stocks of coal at the pit-head continued to accumulate because of a second mild winter, low transatlantic freight costs which allowed cheap imports of US coal, and an acceleration of the switch from coal to oil. The High Authority diagnosed a manifest crisis, and in March 1959 asked the Council of Ministers for emergency powers under Article 58 of the Treaty. However, this request failed to achieve the qualified majority necessary, primarily because neither France nor Germany was prepared to grant the extra powers to the High Authority that it requested.

This was one of a series of crises in the history of the European Communities that shook the collective morale of the central bureaucratic actors. The immediate effect was to make it very difficult for the High Authority to respond to the crisis. It had to resort to palliative measures such as social assistance, and a restructuring plan for the Belgian industry, which was hardest hit by the crisis. More fundamentally:

The High Authority's powerlessness revealed the inadequacy of sectoral integration for which it was responsible and which did not cover competing energy sources—oil and nuclear energy.

(Spierenburg and Poidevin 1994: 652)

The realization that the attempt to integrate in one sector could not be successful unless integration were extended to other sectors might have led to an increase in the competencies of the High Authority. The Council of Ministers did ask the High Authority to undertake the co-ordination of energy supplies and to draw up plans for a common energy policy; but by this time the Treaties of Rome had come into effect, creating the two new communities, the EEC and Euratom, each with its own Commission.

The decision to make a new start with new institutions, rather than extending the competencies of the High Authority, inevitably produced a conflict between the established bureaucratic actor and the newcomers. Although the High Authority helped the two Commissions to get started by seconding many of its experienced staff, 'there were undeniable jealousies that precluded closer union between the three executive bodies' (Spierenburg and Poidevin 1994: 652).

Finet complained about the 'poaching' of High Authority staff by the Commissions of Euratom and the EEC (Spierenburg and Poidevin 1994: 381) and there were tensions both over issues of responsibility and budgetary matters. The Commissions, one headed by a Frenchman and the other by a German, had the support of the French and German Governments on these matters. More generally, governments were content to see responsibilities of the High Authority transferred to the less supranational new Commissions.

Yet the ECSC could claim partial success for its activities, for example in limiting restrictive practices in the coal and steel sectors. More importantly, for Monnet, the creation of the ECSC laid vital foundations for further European integration:

It proved decisive in persuading businessmen, civil servants, politicians and trade unionists that such an approach could work and that the economic and political advantages of unity over division were immense. Once they were convinced, they were ready to take further steps forward.
(Monnet 1962: 208)

While the supranational instincts of the High Authority were kept under control by national governments, it was significant for future developments in European integration that both the Assembly and the Court of Justice were supportive of its supranational efforts. The Court in particular 'stamped its imprint on the ECSC, and in doing so built up a body of case law, an authority, and legitimacy that could serve as foundations for the future' (Urwin 1995: 56).

Six years after signing the Treaty of Paris establishing the ECSC, the six parliaments ratified the Treaty of Rome establishing the Economic Community, taking the major step towards the creation of a Common Market for all goods and services. Monnet (1962: 211) spoke of a 'new method of action' in Europe, replacing the efforts at domination by the nation-states 'by a constant process of collective adaptation to new conditions, a chain reaction, a ferment where one change induces another'.

Euratom

The Euratom Commission had similar powers and responsibilities to those of its sister institution, the EEC Commission (Insight 8.2). While the EEC Commission made skilful use of these powers during its first decade to push forward the process of integration, the Euratom Commission failed to make any significant progress. Illness forced the resignation of its first president, Louis Armand, in the first year. Armand was replaced in February 1959 by Etienne Hirsch, a former colleague of Monnet's at the CdP (Ch. 6, p. 95). Delays over recruitment and establishing priorities meant that by the time the Euratom Commission really began work in 1960, the context in which it had been created had changed. In particular, the easing of the coal shortage and reduced concern about

INSIGHT 8.2

The Euratom Commission

The Euratom Commission consisted of five members, one from each member state except Luxemburg, which had no national nuclear-power programme. During its time it had three presidents:

- Louis Armand (1958–9),
- Etienne Hirsch (1959–62),
- Michel Chatenet (1963–7).

It was charged to ensure that the member states fulfilled the terms of the Treaty:

- it had the sole right to propose measures to this end to the Council of Ministers;
- it had a duty to oversee the implementation of agreements;
- it represented the Community in the negotiation of agreements with the outside world;
- it was answerable to the European Parliamentary Assembly (EPA) for the proceedings of the Community.

dependence on oil from the Middle East in the post-Suez period removed some of the urgency on the development of nuclear energy.

The delay in the start of Euratom operations also allowed national rivalries to become embedded. France, with the largest nuclear research programme had expected the bulk of the subsidies available, but Italy and West Germany rapidly developed their programmes following agreement on Euratom. After 1959, France, which was then under the leadership of de Gaulle, was less enthusiastic about Euratom than it had been. The Hirsch Euratom Commission clashed with the French government over both the right of the Commission to inspect French plutonium facilities and the Commission's decision to divert funds to a joint programme of reactor development with the United States. On the first, Hirsch found no support in the Council of Ministers. On the second, however, the Commission won a majority vote in the Council. Yet even this victory was hollow, as the French government subsequently insisted that budgetary decisions be taken on the basis of unanimity. Thus in both instances of conflict with the French government, the Commission's position was ultimately weakened. Further, de Gaulle refused to renominate Hirsch as president and his successor, Michel Chatenet, was less assertive in his leadership of the Commission.

From 1962 onwards Euratom drifted into deeper crisis. In 1964 there was deadlock over the size of the budget, which was eventually resolved only at the cost of the Commission having to make massive cut-backs in the already modest remaining research programme. A second crisis in 1966 meant that Euratom went into the merger year of 1967 having to survive on the system of 'provisional twelfths' which allowed no more than one-twelfth of the previous year's budget to be spent each month until agreement was reached on the new budget.

A number of explanations have been offered for the failure of Euratom (Scheinmann 1967). First, because it dealt with a single functional sector, the Commission was unable to offer national governments trade-offs in other policy areas to secure deals on nuclear power. Second, the external environment that favoured the creation of Euratom had changed by the time it became operative. Moreover, internal rivalry between member states increased and was consolidated with the election of de Gaulle. France was particularly important here because the matter of nuclear power development was a key issue for the French government that was closely linked to the high politics issue of nuclear weapons. Perhaps the key weakness of the Euratom Commission was that it failed to develop a transnational network of interests around the nuclear energy issue which could create a momentum that would overcome national rivalries. In sum, while the Euratom Commission faced inevitable constraints, it also failed to deploy tactics that were important to the relative success of the EEC commission.

 CONCLUSION

In the history of the ECSC and Euratom we can see the struggle between *dirigisme* and free-market economics; the fragmentation of the supranational executives that was later to afflict the EC Commission; and the assertion of national control over supranational institutions, but also the first stirrings of independence among the supranational institutions.

The story of *dirigisme* versus free-market economics that is told here offers a warning against a simple assumption that the first is about unwarranted interference in the beneficent workings of the market, while the second is about competition from which the consumer will benefit. In fact it was Monnet, the champion of a *dirigiste* approach, who wanted to create genuine competition in the market for steel by breaking up the German cartels, which were clearly organizations in restraint of trade. The advocates of free-market economics were in reality defenders of monopolistic practices. Capitalism is a system that tends towards monopoly and monopolistic practices, and to avert that, constant regulation and monitoring is necessary. This is one of the functions that the state can perform for national economies. Among business élites, advocates of market economics are often motivated more by a desire to avoid state regulation so as to leave them free to adopt monopolistic practices than they are by an abstract commitment to the public good. In the EC/EU, competition policy has proved to be an important supranational power (see Ch. 24).

The bureaucratization of the High Authority prefigured the bureaucratization of the EC Commission, which was to prove one of its weaknesses in the 1970s. Bureaucratization involved among other things the fragmentation of the High Authority into directorates that operated in relative isolation from each other and formed tightly integrated 'policy communities' with key interest groups. This phenomenon is central to understanding the later history of the EC, and especially the operation of the Common Agricultural Policy (see Ch. 25).

Finally, the assertion of national control over the supranationalism of the High Authority and the Euratom Commission is clear. If we were to focus only on these forerunners of the EC Commission, the lesson to be drawn would have to be that the member states were suspicious of supranational tendencies in the institutions they had created, and were capable of restraining them. But the first stirrings of the supranational ECJ offered a different lesson for the future. The body of case law that the ECJ began to build up was not particularly controversial, and was not widely noted at the time: it was, however, laying the basis for an independent supranational institution of the future (see Ch. 22).

KEY POINTS

The European Coal and Steel Community

☐ The High Authority was not as powerful as originally planned, but still had considerable formal independence.

☐ There was considerable suspicion of Monnet's *dirigiste* tendencies among national governments, who consequently nominated members to the High Authority who were mostly not sympathetic to Monnet's aims.

☐ Monnet tried to run the High Authority on informal lines, but it became internally divided and increasingly bureaucratized.

☐ The hostility of de Gaulle to supranationalism exacerbated matters after 1958; Adenauer preferred the Commission of the EEC, which was headed by his associate Hallstein.

☐ Excess supply of coal led to a crisis in 1959. The Council of Ministers refused the High Authority emergency powers to deal with the crisis. This precipitated a collapse of morale in the High Authority.

☐ Despite its shortcomings, Monnet believed that the ECSC pioneered the development of a community method of working.

Euratom

☐ By the time that Euratom began operation the energy crisis that existed when it was negotiated had disappeared. Instead of a shortage of coal there was a glut.

☐ Whereas France had the only developed programme of research on nuclear energy in the mid-1950s, by the end of the decade Germany and Italy also had independent programmes in competition with that of France.

☐ The French government refused to co-operate with the Euratom Commission and the Commission never managed to build a supportive network of industry groups or technical experts to help it counter French obstructionism.

FURTHER READING

Several books are devoted to, or contain extensive sections on the experience of the early communities: W. Diebold Jr, *The Schuman Plan: A Study in Economic Cooperation: 1950–1959* (New York: Praeger, 1962); J. Gillingham, *Coal, Steel, and the Rebirth of Europe, 1945–1955* (Cambridge: Cambridge University Press, 1991); E.B. Haas, *The Uniting of Europe: Political, Social and Economic Forces, 1950–1957* (Stanford, Calif.: Stanford University Press, 1968).

There is one indispensable work on the ECSC: D. Spierenburg and R. Poidevin, *The History of the High Authority of the European Coal and Steel Community: Supranationality in Action* (London: Weidenfeld, 1994).

On the Euratom there is less. The most revealing piece is a short monograph, L. Scheinmann, 'Euratom: Nuclear Integration in Europe', *International Conciliation*, 563 (1967). There is also a discussion of the adoption of Euratom in A. Milward, *The European Rescue of the Nation State* (London: Routledge, 1992), 200–11.

 **online resource centre** Visit the Online Resource Centre that accompanies this book for links to more information on the European Coal and Steel Community and Euratom.

CHAPTER 9

The European Economic Community: 1958–1967

CHAPTER OVERVIEW

Soon after its creation, the European Economic Community (EEC) emerged as the most important of the three Communities. This chapter takes the story to the 1967 merger of the three Communities, which was effectively a takeover of Euratom and the ECSC by the EEC. In this time, the EEC's successful start in creating a customs union between the six member states was followed by setbacks in 1963 and 1965; the first when de Gaulle unilaterally rejected the British application for membership, and the second and more serious setback was when he withdraw his ministers from Council of Ministers meetings. The eventual compromise on the second crisis damaged the morale of the Commission and undermined the prospects for further integration. The destiny of the project remained firmly in the hands of individual governments and not with supranational institutions, which was what de Gaulle had wanted.

> **...to lay the foundations for an ever closer union among the peoples of Europe**
>
> **(Preamble to the Treaty of Rome establishing the European Economic Community)**

It was not obvious in 1957 which of the two new communities, the EEC or Euratom, would become the more important. Within a few years, though, Euratom had lost all momentum. Driven by the vigorous leadership of Commission President Walter Hallstein, the EEC made a successful start and achieved most of its objectives over most of the first decade of its existence. If attempts to create a European Political Community had been ambitious, the development of EEC was no less so, although the political implications were less obvious. The explicit task was to create a common market within fifteen years. Nonetheless, the Treaty of Rome establishing the EEC implied political integration.

The institutional arrangements of the EEC followed those of the ECSC, with a supranational Commission as the equivalent of the High Authority, a Council of Ministers and a Parliamentary Assembly. In addition, an Economic and Social Committee played an advisory role. Finally, the European Court of Justice (ECJ) was established to interpret the provisions of the Treaty of Rome and to act as arbiter in disputes on Community decisions (Insight 9.1).

INSIGHT 9.1

The Institutional Arrangements of the EEC

The Commission consisted of nine Commissioners appointed by national governments: two each from France, Germany, and Italy, one each for Belgium, Luxemburg, and the Netherlands. While national appointees, Commissioners were not supposed to advocate national interests but to protect the European ideal. The Commission's primary tasks were to make proposals to the Council of Ministers and to implement the Treaty of Rome. (On the Commission see Ch. 19.)

The Council of Ministers consisted of one representative from each member state. Provision was made for it to vote on proposals from the Commission by qualified majority vote (QMV). For these purposes, seventeen votes were allocated among the six member states: four each to France, Germany and Italy; two each for Belgium and the Netherlands; and one vote for Luxemburg; a qualified majority required twelve votes, ensuring that a decision required the support of at least four states. However, in the first stage, prior to the completion of the common market, it was agreed that all decisions would be taken by unanimity. (On the Council see Ch. 20.)

The European Parliamentary Assembly (EPA) of 142 members was a purely consultative body. Although provision was made in the Treaty for direct election, initially the members were nominated by national parliaments from among their own members. (On the European Parliament see Ch. 21.)

The ECJ was made up of seven judges: one from each member state, plus one appointed by the Council. (On the ECJ see Ch. 22.)

The Early Years: 1958–1963

For the whole of its separate existence, the Commission of the EEC had only one President. Walter Hallstein had been the State Secretary in the Foreign Office of the Federal Republic of Germany, and had been in charge of the German team during the negotiation of the EEC. Hallstein's appointment was accepted unanimously, a remarkable development only twelve years after the war.

The very lack of a sense of drama in the choice of a German for the most important of the new posts was not only a tribute to Hallstein's achievements and reputation but proof of giant progress since the Schuman plan.

(Duchêne 1994: 309)

Close to Chancellor Adenauer in his views on west European integration, Hallstein was in no doubt about the political nature of the Commission. In a book published in 1962 he made clear that in his view the logic of economic integration not only leads on toward political unity, it involves political action itself.

We are not integrating economics, we are integrating policies . . . 'Political integration' is not too bold and too grandiose a term to describe this process.

(Hallstein 1962: 66–7)

Hallstein was backed in this view of the role of the Commission by the energetic Dutch Vice-President and Commissioner for Agriculture, Sicco Mansholt. Between them Hallstein and Mansholt gave vigorous leadership to the Commission, which according to one observer constituted 'a relatively united, committed partisan organisation' (Coombes 1970: 259).

The morale of the Commission was increased by its success in getting the Council of Ministers to agree to an acceleration of the timetable for the achievement of a customs union in 1962. It went on to broker agreement on the level of the common external tariff (CET), and at the same time to negotiate acceptance of a Common Agricultural Policy (CAP).

The EEC Treaty (Article 14; now removed) specified a precise timetable for the progressive reduction of internal tariffs. On the original schedule it would have taken at least eight years to get rid of all such tariffs. This rather leisurely rate of progress reflected the concerns of specific industrial groups about the problems of adjustment involved in the ending of national protection. However, once the treaty was signed and it became obvious that the common market was to become a reality, those same industrial interests responded to the changed situation facing them. Even before the treaty came into operation on 1 January 1958, companies had begun to conclude cross-border agreements on co-operation, or to acquire franchised retail outlets for their products in other member states. Just as the neofunctionalists had predicted, changing circumstances led to changed behaviour.

So rapid was the adjustment of corporate behaviour to the prospect of the common market that impatience to see the benefits of the deals that were being concluded and of the new investments that were being made soon led to pressure on national governments to accelerate the timetable. Remarkably, the strongest pressure came from French industrial interests, which had opposed the original scheme for a common market.

On 12 May 1960 the Council of Ministers agreed to a proposal from the Commission to accelerate progress on the removal of internal barriers to trade and the erection of a common external tariff, and on the creation of the CAP. Pressure had come only for the first of these to be accelerated. Progress was slow on agriculture, the negotiations having been dogged by disagreements over the level of support that ought to be given to farmers for different commodities. But the issues were clearly linked: progress on the CAP to accompany progress on the industrial common market had been part of the original deal embodied in the EEC treaty.

It seemed that in keeping the linkage between the two issues in the forefront of all their proposals to the Council of Ministers, the Commission had played a manipulative role that coincided with the view of neofunctionalism about the importance of central leadership. Indeed, it is possibly from the performance of the Commission in this period that the importance of leadership from the centre was first theorized and added to the emerging corpus of neofunctionalist concepts. As described by Lindberg (1963: 167–205), the progress of the EEC between 1958 and 1965 involved the Commission utilizing a favourable situation to promote integration. Governments found themselves trapped between the growing demand from national interest groups that they carry through as rapidly as possible their commitment to create a common market, and the insistence of the Commission that this could only happen if the governments were prepared to reach agreement on the setting of common minimum prices for agricultural products.

These agreements were engineered by the skilful use of the 'package deal': linking the two issues together, and not allowing progress on one without commensurate progress on the other. In that way, each member state would agree to things in which it was less interested in order to get those things in which it was more interested. It was just such a package deal that the French president Charles de Gaulle was to reject in spectacular fashion in 1965, plunging the EEC into crisis. However, before that, in 1963, there was a warning of the problems that lay ahead.

The 1963 Crisis

As Urwin (1995: 103) noted,

To some extent, the Commission could be so active because the national governments, through the Council of Ministers had been content to allow it to be so. Even President de Gaulle had on the whole been quite circumspect about the Commission.

However, the Commission's influence and the apparent smooth progress of the EEC received a setback in January 1963 when President de Gaulle unilaterally vetoed the British government's application for membership. The most comprehensive history of this episode is Ludlow (1997), on which the following account is largely based.

Having declined the invitation to be present at the creation, Harold Macmillan announced in the House of Commons in July 1961 that the British government had decided to apply for membership of the EEC. The development was not welcomed by Walter Hallstein, who saw it as potentially disruptive to the smooth progress of integration among the six. It was also unwelcome to de Gaulle, who had ambitions to use the EEC as a platform for the reassertion of French greatness in international affairs.

To this end de Gaulle tried to get agreement between the Six on co-operation in foreign policy, which he believed that France would be able to dominate. From 1960 it was agreed that the foreign ministers of the member states would meet four times yearly. De Gaulle also developed a special relationship with the German Chancellor, Konrad Adenauer. This relationship was important in securing support for de Gaulle's plans to extend political co-operation between the six. The matter was subsequently considered by a committee chaired by the French official, Christian Fouchet (Insight 9.2). The Fouchet negotiations on political co-operation were taking place in 1961 when the British application was lodged, but they had already run into some difficulties over proposals for foreign and defence policy.

British entry did not fit de Gaulle's plans: it would have provided an alternative leadership for the four other member states, whose governments were suspicious of him and wished to resist French domination. Technically, de Gaulle could have vetoed the application, but politically he was in no position to do so. In addition to Fouchet, there were negotiations proceeding in 1961 on two issues that were of crucial importance to France: the common agricultural policy, and new association terms for Africa. Also, de Gaulle did not want to make it more difficult for the pro-French position of his ally Adenauer to prevail in Bonn.

The approach that de Gaulle chose to adopt was to allow negotiations on enlargement to open, but to instruct the French delegation to set the price high in the hope that the terms would prove unacceptable to the British government. The French position was presented as defending the Treaty of Rome and the **acquis communautaire**. Both had

---

INSIGHT 9.2

The Fouchet Plan

In 1961 President de Gaulle proposed to the other members of the Communities that they consider forming what he called a Union of States. This would be an intergovernmental organization in which the institutions of the existing three Communities would play no role. It would involve the member states in pursuing closer co-operation on cultural, scientific, and educational matters, and, most significantly, in the co-ordination of their foreign and defence policies.

At summit meetings in 1961 it was agreed to set up a committee under the chairmanship of the French Ambassador to Denmark, Christian Fouchet, and subsequently to ask the committee to prepare a detailed plan for such co-operation.

This 'Fouchet Plan' proposed a confederation of states with a Council of Ministers, a Consultative Assembly of seconded national parliamentarians, and a Commission. However, unlike the Commissions of the EEC and Euratom, this Commission would not be a supranational body with independent powers, but would consist of officials from national Foreign Ministries.

been so strongly influenced by French demands that their defence was almost the same as the defence of the French national interest. Because the French demands were couched in *communautaire* language, it was very difficult for the other member states to resist them. They were torn between support for British membership and a desire not to dilute the achievements of the EEC to date.

The negotiations did not collapse, but they went on so long that de Gaulle was eventually presented with the excuse that he needed to issue his unilateral veto: the deal on nuclear weapons that was reached between Macmillan and US President John Kennedy at Nassau in December 1962. Macmillan persuaded Kennedy to sell Britain Polaris missiles to carry Britain's independent nuclear weapons. This was presented by de Gaulle as clear evidence that the British were not yet ready to accept a European vocation, and used as justification for ending negotiations that had stalled in late 1962 anyway.

The other member states reacted angrily to the veto. Given that the negotiations had run into difficulties, the anger was directed less at their enforced ending than at the way in which de Gaulle had undermined the system of collaborative working that had emerged in the Six, and within which the others had operated throughout the negotiations.

The 1965 Crisis

A more fundamental and considerably more serious crisis began in July 1965, when de Gaulle withdrew France from participation in the work of the Council of Ministers in protest at a proposal from the Commission concerning the financing of the Community's budget.

Once agreement had been reached on the details of the CAP, the question arose of how the policy would be funded. For the first time the EEC would have a budget that went beyond the salaries and administrative costs of the central institutions. The Commission proposed that instead of the cumbersome method of annual contributions negotiated between the member states, the Community should have its 'own resources'. These would be the revenue from the CET on industrial goods and the levies on agricultural goods entering the Community from outside, which would be collected by national customs officials at their point of entry into the EEC, and then handed over to Brussels, after the deduction of 10 per cent as a service charge. The justification was that the goods might be intended for consumption in any part of the Community, and it was therefore unreasonable that the revenue should accrue to the state through which the goods happened to enter the common market.

However, the French President questioned another aspect of the proposal. Using the method of the package deal, the Commission linked the idea of having its own resources with a proposal for an increase in the powers of the European Parliamentary Assembly (EPA), giving it the right to approve the budget. The argument for this was that if the revenues passed directly to the EEC without having to be approved by national parliaments, there would be a lack of democratic scrutiny, which could only be corrected by giving that right to the EPA.

President de Gaulle objected to this increase in the powers of a supranational institution, and when discussion became deadlocked he showed how important he held the issue to be by imposing a French boycott of all Council of Ministers meetings from June 1965. This action was subsequently termed the 'empty chair crisis'. In essence, the dispute was about the very nature of the Europe that the Six were hoping to build. For de Gaulle, primacy had to be given to the interests of national governments.

The Luxemburg Compromise

After six months an agreement was reached between France and the other five member states in Luxemburg. The so-called 'Luxemburg Compromise' of January 1966 represented a considerable blow to the process of European integration. First, there was agreement not to proceed with the Commission's proposals: funding of the budget would continue to be by national contributions. Second, France demanded that there be no transition to majority voting in the Council of Ministers. This move had been envisaged in the original treaties once the customs union was complete, and completion was on schedule for January 1966. Under the terms of the Luxemburg Compromise, governments would retain their right to veto proposals where they deemed a vital national interest to be at stake. This agreement was a serious blow to the hope of the Commission that brokering agreement on further integrative moves would be easier in the future.

Third, France made four other demands: that the President of the Commission should no longer receive the credentials of ambassadors to the EEC; that the information services be taken out of the hands of the Commission; that members of the Commission should be debarred from making political attacks on the attitudes of member states; that the Commission should not reveal its proposals to the EPA before they were presented to the Council of Ministers, as it had with the controversial package on the budget.

The terms of the deal precipitated a collapse of morale in the Commission. In particular, the authority of Hallstein and Mansholt was undermined by the episode. Some Commissioners had warned against a confrontation with de Gaulle on supranationality, but Hallstein and Mansholt had overruled them (Camps 1967: 47). Neither was to regain the air of invincibility that he had acquired in the past. Hallstein withdrew his name from the list of nominations for the presidency of the new combined Commission of the ECSC, EEC, and Euratom that was due to take office on 1 July 1967, and simply served out the remainder of his term. Mansholt stayed on as a Commissioner, but did not put his name forward for the presidency.

CONCLUSION

The struggle between supranationalism and intergovernmentalism is the clear theme of this chapter. The neofunctionalist interpretation of the history of European integration seems to get both its strongest support and its greatest challenge from the period under consideration. The support comes from the story of the acceleration agreement as told by neofunctionalists (Ch. 1). Lindberg

(1963) took the role of the Commission in the success of the EEC in the 1960s as clear evidence of its centrality to the process. The setback came from the actions of de Gaulle in vetoing British entry in 1963 and in boycotting the Council of Ministers in 1965.

The acceleration agreement resulted from pressure from business interests for an acceleration of the original timetable for the creation of the common market. This vindicates the neofunctionalist argument that changed circumstances change attitudes and behaviour. The exploitation of this demand by the Commission to lever the member states into accepting a general acceleration of their timetable, for the agricultural negotiations as well as for the reduction of industrial tariffs, vindicates the argument that the central supranational actor can act in conjunction with interest groups to push governments into taking further integrative steps.

However, it should be noted that this interpretation has been strongly contradicted in the inter-governmentalist tradition, notably by Andrew Moravcsik (1999: 159–237; see Ch. 1). It is also incontestable that the pressure came not from transnational interest groups, as neofunctionalist theory predicted that it would, but from national groups, especially French business interests. The linkage to agriculture was hardly a surprise given that the two issues had been linked in the original package, and the French government itself could not simply bow to the wishes of French business and ignore the wishes of French farmers.

Moravcsik's research indicated that the deals were not cut by the Commission but by the governments of other member states. He argued that 'the Commission was ineffective and repeatedly sidelined' (Moravcsik 1998: 233). Its proposals were often ignored, and were only successful when they paralleled proposals made by key member states. Although the Commission made the final proposal on which agreement was reached (as it had to under the rules of the EEC), this was often the opposite of what the Commission had originally proposed.

The 1965 dispute over the funding of the budget certainly illustrated the continued ability of national governments, even of a single national government, to stop the process of European integration in its tracks. It also prefigures, though, another theme that becomes more prominent later in the story. The Dutch government insisted that, if the budget was to be funded from the EC's own resources, the EPA must be given some control over the budget. The Dutch argument was that national parliaments would lose their ability to exercise democratic scrutiny and control of the budget once the own-resources system of financing was introduced, so to ensure that there was some democratic oversight the EPA would have to be given some control. There is an aspect of spillover here. If the success of a policy is defined not just as the instrumental 'does it work', but also in terms of the extent to which it can be seen as an example of democratic decision-making, there is spillover from the removal of decisions from national parliamentary control to the increase in the powers of the EPA or later the European Parliament (EP). When this did not take place, there emerged a democratic deficit within the EC. Governments did not worry too much about the democratic deficit until it began to undermine the legitimacy of the EC in the eyes of their electorates. This was an early example of the Dutch parliament pointing to the potential for such a democratic deficit to open up.

KEY POINTS

The Early Years: 1958–1963

☐ The EEC Commission under the presidency of Walter Hallstein was very proactive in promoting integration.

- ☐ Its apparent successes included getting agreement from the member states to accelerate progress on creating the common market and the CAP.

The 1963 Crisis

- ☐ In 1961 President de Gaulle proposed intergovernmental political co-operation. Negotiations on the 'Fouchet Plan' were ongoing on when Britain applied for EC membership.
- ☐ De Gaulle did not want to see Britain become a member, but rather than risk collapsing the Fouchet negotiations he allowed negotiations on membership to begin while trying to ensure that French demands would make the terms of entry unacceptable to Britain.
- ☐ When the Fouchet negotiations came near to collapse, and the entry negotiations did not, de Gaulle unilaterally vetoed British entry.

The 1965 Crisis

- ☐ In 1965 the Commission proposed a system of financing the CAP that would have given the EEC its own financial resources. This was linked to a proposal to increase the budgetary powers of the EPA.
- ☐ De Gaulle rejected the increase in the powers of the EPA, and when agreement could not be reached he withdrew France from participation in the work of the Council of Ministers.
- ☐ In January 1966 France resumed its place in the Council in exchange for the planned move to QMV be abandoned. This was accepted in the so-called 'Luxemburg Compromise'.
- ☐ The 'empty chair' crisis caused a crisis in the Commission.

FURTHER READING

When we get to the establishment of the EEC the range of reading extends considerably. A. Milward, *The European Rescue of the Nation State* (London: Routledge, 1992) is still relevant, and a similar but subtly different perspective is taken by A. Moravcsik, *The Choice for Europe: Social Purpose and State Power from Messina to Maastricht* (London: UCL Press, 1998), 86–158.

The standard account of the early years of the EEC is L. Lindberg, *The Political Dynamics of European Economic Integration* (Stanford, Calif.: Stanford University Press; London: Oxford University Press, 1963); but this is rejected by Moravcsik (1998: 158–237).

On the British application in 1961, see P. Ludlow, *Dealing with Britain: The Six and the First UK Application to the EEC* (Cambridge: Cambridge University Press, 1997).

online resource centre

Visit the Online Resource Centre that accompanies this book for links to more information on the European Economic Community.

CHAPTER 10

After Luxemburg: The 'Dark Ages' of European Integration?

CHAPTER OVERVIEW

If the period up to the 'empty chair' crisis was characterized by steady progress on integration, the decade following the Luxemburg Compromise began with limited expectations. Signs of a revival began with the Hague Conference in 1969, but the revival was limited by a downturn in economic circumstances. In addition, the accession of three new member states, two of which were opposed to supranationalism, made the prospects for further integration bleak. Although there were some achievements, scholars generally saw this period as a low point for European integration.

> The period from the early 1970s to the early 1980s has often been characterized as the doldrums era or the 'Dark Ages' for the Community
>
> **(Caporaso and Keeler 1995: 37)**

Whereas the 1960s had been an era of high rates of economic growth within a reasonably stable (if militarily threatening) international environment, the 1970s were times of turbulence and flux in the international economic system. Three factors were particularly important: the collapse of the international monetary system in 1971 (Insight 10.1); the oil crisis in 1973; and the concurrence of low growth and high inflation (**stagflation**) producing economic divergence in the EC.

The economic recession that started in 1971 really began to bite after the December 1973 decision of the **Organization of the Petroleum Exporting Countries (OPEC)** to force a quadrupling in the price of oil. This context made governments more defensive and less inclined to agree to integrative measures that would weaken their ability to preserve domestic markets for domestic producers. As the economic context changed, the pace of European economic integration slowed and there was no advance towards political union. Uncertainty within member states restricted the scope for Commission activism. The Hallstein Commission was initially given tremendous credit for promoting integration in the period following the signing of the Treaties of Rome. However, subsequent reassessments suggested that in fact it had done little beyond fill out the details of agreements that had been made between the member states in the Treaty of Rome.

If this view is correct, then for the Commission to play an active role required a new mandate from the member states. During this period the Commission had four presidents (Table 10.1). Neither Jean Rey nor Franco Malfatti had that mandate, and besides they were both preoccupied with the difficult issues involved in combining the three executive bodies of the ECSC, EEC, and Euratom into a single Commission.

When a new mandate was given, at a summit meeting in The Hague in December 1969, it involved completion of the financing arrangements for the EC budget, enlargement to take in Britain and the other applicant states, progress to economic and

INSIGHT 10.1

The Collapse of the International Monetary System

The key aspects of the international monetary system were agreed at a conference at Bretton Woods in New Hampshire in 1944. These were the **International Monetary Fund** (IMF) and the International Bank for Reconstruction and Development (the 'World Bank'). The **General Agreement on Tariffs and Trade** (GATT) was added later. The system worked with the United States playing a leading and directive role and provided a stability that was central to the prosperity of west European economies. However, the gradual erosion of US economic dominance in this period, culminating with the ending of the convertibility of US dollars to gold in 1971, marked the collapse of the Bretton Woods international system and a less secure international economic context.

monetary union, and trying to develop a common foreign policy. The first of these was easily accomplished. The second was successfully carried through for three of the four applicants, but at considerable cost in terms of time and resources for the Commission. Economic and monetary union might have been the mandate that the Commission needed to produce a new impetus to integration, but as Tsoukalis (1977a) argued, this decision was more akin to the decision to negotiate on the EEC than it was to the Treaty of Rome itself. As we shall see, this proved to be an intractable issue. Progress on co-ordination of foreign policy was made in a purely intergovernmental framework.

TABLE 10.1	
Presidents of the Commission, 1967–1977	
1967–70	Jean Rey (Belgium)
1970–72	Franco Maria Malfatti (Italy)
1972	Sicco Mansholt (the Netherlands)
1973–77	François-Xavier Ortoli (France)

Not only were these issues more difficult in themselves: the overall context of the period was unfavourable to further integration. The Luxemburg agreement that ended the French boycott in January 1966 (Ch. 9, p. 134) effectively meant that the national veto was retained on all matters that came before the Council of Ministers. Although the Commission had operated with a veto system in the 1960s, the further integration progressed, the more likely it was that particular vested interests would come under challenge, and that individual states would try to block measures. The problem was exacerbated by enlargement, which brought into membership two more states, Britain and Denmark, that were opposed to supranationalism. The cumulative effect of these developments was to ensure that the second decade of the EEC was not marked by the rapid progress on integration that had marked the first decade.

This chapter examines in more detail the Hague summit and its attempt to relaunch the European project; it assesses the degree of success achieved in each of the four main objectives. It also looks briefly at the origins of one of the major institutional innovations of the period, the formalization of the periodic summit meetings of heads of government as the European Council.

The Hague Summit

The resignation of President de Gaulle in April 1969 appeared to free the way to further integration. De Gaulle was succeeded by his former Prime Minister, Georges Pompidou, who soon let it be known that he did not object in principle to British membership.

Also in 1969 there was a change of government in Germany. The SPD, which had been the junior coalition partner to the Christian Democrats for the previous three years, became the larger partner in a coalition with the Free Democrat Party (FDP). Willy Brandt, the new Chancellor, intended to pursue an active policy of improving relations with the Communist bloc, but was anxious to demonstrate that this *Ostpolitik* did not imply any weakening of German commitment to the EC.

As a result of these two changes, a summit meeting of heads of government was convened in The Hague in December 1969 with the explicit aim of relaunching European integration. This Hague Summit declared the objectives of completion, widening, and deepening. Completion meant tidying up the outstanding business from the 1965 crisis: moving the EC budget from dependence on national contributions to a system of financing from its own resources. Widening meant opening accession negotiations with Britain and other likely applicants. Deepening meant taking the next steps in the process of European integration, specifically in the direction of economic and monetary union and closer political co-operation. The objectives of completion and widening were successfully met; less so the objective of deepening.

Completion

Completion was achieved relatively easily. A system was agreed for the EC to have as its own resources the levies on agricultural products entering the EC under the CAP, and the revenues from the common customs tariff on imports of non-agricultural products from outside of the EC.

There were the usual compromises, but France did accept some budgetary role for the EP, giving it the right to propose amendments to those parts of the budget that were not classified as 'compulsory expenditure' under the treaties, and to propose modifications to the items of 'compulsory' expenditure. The Council of Ministers, acting by qualified majority, could amend the amendments, and could refuse to agree to the modifications, so in effect it retained the final say on the budget. The distinction between compulsory and non-compulsory expenditure defined expenditure under the CAP as compulsory, so making the bulk of the budget difficult for the EP to amend. Nevertheless, there was an acknowledgement that the EP should have some role in scrutinizing the budget, and there was the prospect that deepening would lead to a larger budget in which agriculture was not so dominant, so there would be more areas of non-compulsory expenditure.

Widening

Negotiations with four applicant states—Britain, Ireland, Denmark, and Norway—opened in June 1970, and were successfully completed by January 1972. Referendums were then held on membership in Ireland, Denmark and Norway. The first two produced clear majorities in favour of entry, but in September 1972 the Norwegian people, not for the last time, rejected membership. In Britain, the Conservative Government of Edward Heath refused to hold a referendum, arguing that it was not a British constitutional instrument; but parliamentary ratification was successfully completed. So on 1 January 1973 the six became nine.

While enlargement achieved the objective of widening the membership of the EC, it was to cause problems as well. The new member states entered at a time when the economic growth of the 1960s had already started to slow and was about to receive a further setback when OPEC quadrupled the price of oil in December 1973 (above, p. 138). Not having experienced the positive benefits of membership, neither the governments nor the peoples of these new member states had the same degree of psychological commitment to the idea of European integration as had those of the original six members. In addition, in Britain in particular there was considerable scepticism about the merits of the EC. Edward Heath was personally strongly committed to membership, but he never managed entirely to convince his own Conservative Party; and Heath was soon displaced as Prime Minister when he lost the general election early in 1974, and Harold Wilson once again formed a Labour government.

While in opposition, the Labour Party had been riven with dissension, and membership of the EC had been a central issue. Several of Wilson's cabinet ministers from 1964–70 were committed to British membership. Wilson himself was also convinced of the necessity of membership. But a majority in the party was still opposed, and the pressure from this majority meant that Wilson could not give unqualified approval to entry when Heath negotiated it. On the other hand his own certainty that membership was necessary, and the importance of the pro-membership minority within the leadership of the party, made it impossible for him to oppose entry. The result was an ingenious compromise of opposition to entry on the terms negotiated by the Conservative government. Labour went into the 1974 election committed to a full renegotiation of the terms of entry with a threat (or promise) of withdrawal if 'satisfactory' terms could not be agreed.

The renegotiation involved serious disruption to other business in the EC, at a time when there were several important issues on the agenda. It also involved a great deal of posturing and nationalist rhetoric from the British government. What it did not involve was any fundamental change in the terms of entry. Nevertheless, the renegotiated terms were put to the British people in a referendum in June 1975, with a recommendation from the government that they be accepted, which they were.

The two-to-one vote in the referendum in favour of Community membership was a passing moment of public favour. Soon the opinion polls were again showing majorities against membership. Britain had joined at a bad time, and the continuing economic difficulties of the country could conveniently be blamed on the EC. Although the Labour opponents of membership had to accept, for the time being, the verdict of the referendum, they lost no opportunity to attack the EC, and Wilson was prepared to accept this if it diverted attention away from his failure to solve the economic difficulties of Britain. He himself continued to take a strongly nationalistic line in EC negotiations, as did his Foreign Secretary, James Callaghan, who succeeded him as Prime Minister in March 1976.

By succeeding in widening its membership, the EC placed another barrier in the way of further integration. Yet it is a mistake to blame Britain alone for blocking further integration. Certainly Britain became an awkward partner; but as Buller (1995: 36) argued: 'everybody consciously attempts to be obstructive every now and again in European negotiations. It is all part and parcel of politics in this kind of environment.' The degree of awkwardness of all member states increased during this period of economic problems.

Deepening

Attempts at deepening co-operation between member states met with limited success. The two main objectives agreed at The Hague were 'economic and monetary union by 1980' and the creation of a common foreign policy.

Economic and Monetary Union (EMU)

This was the logical next step in the building of the EC. Economic union meant that the member states would, at most, cease to follow independent economic policies, and at least would follow co-ordinated policies. This would remove distortions to free competition and would help to make a reality of the common market. Monetary union meant, at most, the adoption of a single Community currency, at least the maintenance of fixed exchange rates between the currencies of the member states.

In 1969 there were the first major realignments of member states' currencies since the EC had started, and the prospect of monetary instability threatened to hinder trade within the common market by introducing an element of uncertainty into import and export deals. In this context, monetary union was seen as a means of making the common market effective.

Following the Hague summit, a Committee was set up under the chairmanship of Pierre Werner, the Prime Minister of Luxemburg, to produce concrete proposals on EMU. It reported within a few months, and in February 1971 the Council of Ministers adopted a programme for the achievement of EMU in stages between 1971 and 1980. The institutional centrepiece of the scheme was the 'snake-in-the-tunnel', an arrangement for approximating the exchange rates of member currencies one to another while holding their value jointly in relation to the US dollar. It was to be accompanied by more determined efforts to bring national economic policies into line, with Finance Ministers meeting at least three times per year to try to co-ordinate policies. Thus there would be progress on both monetary and economic union, the two running in parallel.

The 'snake' did not last long in its original form. It was destroyed by the international monetary crisis that followed the ending of the convertibility of the dollar in August 1971. Only after the Smithsonian agreements of late 1971 had restored some semblance of order to the world monetary system was it possible to attempt once again a joint Community currency arrangement, this time with the participation of the four states that had just completed the negotiation of their entry to the EC. That was in April 1972: but it took under two months for this second snake to break apart. In June the British government had to remove sterling from the system and float it on the international monetary markets. Italy was forced to leave in February 1973. France followed in January 1974, rejoined in July 1975, but was forced to leave again in the spring of 1976. In every case the currency had come under so much speculative pressure that it had proved impossible to maintain its value against the other currencies in the system.

By 1977 the snake had become a very different creature from that which had been envisaged. Of the nine members of the EC, only West Germany, the Benelux states, and Denmark were still members (Ireland had left with Britain, the Irish punt being tied to the pound sterling at that time). In addition, two non-member states, Norway and Sweden, had joined. Yet during 1977 even this snake was under strain, and Sweden was forced to withdraw the krona.

European Political Co-operation (EPC)

This was the more successful attempt at deepening, ironically since it was only included in the Hague objectives as a concession to France. President Pompidou was dependent for his majority in the French National Assembly on the votes of the Gaullist party of which he was himself a member. De Gaulle had opposed giving budgetary powers to the EP, and Pompidou agreed to this at The Hague. De Gaulle had also opposed British entry to the EC. He had made it clear when a second British application was tabled in May 1967 that there was no point in entering into negotiations, because he would veto British membership. Pompidou had made it equally clear that he was prepared to enter into negotiations, and perhaps even to accept British membership if satisfactory terms could be agreed. Both of these departures from Gaullist orthodoxy were controversial in his own party, and he needed concessions at The Hague in order to be able to sell the package to this domestic constituency.

One of de Gaulle's pet projects had been to set up a system of intergovernmental political co-operation between the member states of the EC. This was the basis of the Fouchet Plan, which had been under discussion at the same time as the first British application, and had finally collapsed as a result of the French veto on British entry (Ch. 9, p. 132–3). It was therefore unsurprising that Pompidou should look for a commitment to revive this project as part of the price for his co-operation on completion and widening. It was agreed at The Hague to set up a committee under the chairmanship of Viscount Etienne Davignon, a senior official in the Belgian Foreign Ministry, to devise machinery for co-operation between the member states on foreign policy issues. This committee reported in October 1970, and the system that it recommended became the basis for some successful diplomatic initiatives. Indeed, European Political Co-operation came to be seen as one of the few bright spots in the bleak years of the 1970s.

One of the successes was the formulation of a common position on the Middle East, which allowed the EC to pursue its clear interest in improving trade with the Arab OPEC states in the 1970s, through the Euro–Arab dialogue. In 1980 this common policy culminated in the Venice Declaration, which went further than the United States was prepared to go in recognizing the right of the Palestinians to a homeland. The nine member states were also extremely successful in formulating a common position at the Conference on Security and Co-operation in Europe (CSCE) in Helsinki in 1975, and at the follow-up conferences in Belgrade in 1977, and Madrid in 1982–3. Again the common position adopted by the EC ran somewhat contrary to the position of the United States, which regarded the Helsinki process with some suspicion as running the risk of legitimating Communist rule in eastern Europe. Third, the Community states achieved a high degree of unity in the United Nations, voting together on a majority of resolutions in the General Assembly, and developing a reputation for being the most cohesive group there at a time when group-diplomacy was becoming much more common.

Admittedly there were also failures for the policy of European political co-operation. On balance, though, there were more substantive successes than there were failures. However, all of this remained officially intergovernmental, rather than being rolled up into the more supranational procedures of the EC, so there was a question mark over whether it could be considered to be an advance for the process of European integration. On the other hand, the actual working of the system was less strictly intergovernmental than the formal procedures, a point that is explored further in Chapter 30 (see pp. 526–31).

The European Council

Mid-way through this period, there were again coinciding changes of government in both France and Germany, which strengthened the Franco-German relationship. Georges Pompidou died in office in 1974, and was succeeded by Valéry Giscard d'Estaing, who was not a Gaullist, although he was dependent on the Gaullist party for a majority in the National Assembly. In Germany, Brandt resigned following the discovery that an East German spy had been part of his personal staff, and was succeeded by his former Finance Minister, Helmut Schmidt.

These changes brought to office two strong national leaders who had an excellent *rapport*, and who dominated the EC for the next six years. They were not, though, particularly committed to reviving the process of supranational integration. Their approach was pragmatic rather than ideological, and they were prepared to use any instruments that presented themselves to deal with the problems that their countries faced.

In 1974 Giscard called a summit meeting to discuss his proposal that the EC should institutionalize summit meetings. The smaller member states were suspicious of this proposal, which sounded very Gaullist, but Giscard got strong backing from Schmidt, and it was agreed to hold meetings of the heads of state and government three times every year under the title the 'European Council'. At the same time, as a concession to the fears of those governments who saw in this a weakening of the supranational element of the EC, agreement was reached to hold direct elections to the EP in 1978. The British government was reconciled to this by concessions on the renegotiation of its terms of entry that was taking place at the same time.

Direct elections were not actually held until 1979 because the British government was unable to pass the necessary domestic legislation in time to hold the election in 1978. In the long run the decision to hold direct elections was far from insignificant. In the short to medium term, though, the creation of the European Council was much the more significant outcome of Paris, 1974.

The European Council was from the outset an intergovernmental body. It had no basis in the Treaties until the Single European Act came into force in July 1987. It became the overarching institution of the EU in the Treaty on European Union. Yet to this day it is not directly answerable to the EP, nor subject to judicial review by the ECJ (Ch. 20, pp. 278–81). In the 1970s it was symbolic of a profoundly inter-governmental era in the history of the EU.

CONCLUSION

In this period, when US hegemony began to falter, the EC had to deal with an increasingly turbulent international environment. The theme of the impact of the wider system on developments within the EC is clearly illustrated here, particularly trends in international political economy. The retreat into covert national protectionism, to preserve jobs for nationals, was a direct consequence of the shadow that recession cast over the process of European integration. The sceptical attitudes of the British and Danish people to the advantages of European integration were not produced by the recession, but the failure of membership of the EC to produce tangible economic benefits reinforced their prejudices.

The other part of the explanation for developments in this period is provided by the continuing importance of domestic politics. In the original six member states, the compromise on the principle of an ever closer union of the peoples of Europe reflected both the shallowness of that commitment among the political élites, and the fact that to retain office they needed to win votes among their own electorate. One of the consistent paradoxes of European integration has been an increasing divorce between politics and policy in the EC. Politics has remained firmly national, while policy has become increasingly Europeanized. This tension existed even in the early stages of the process, and the adverse economic conditions of the 1970s exposed it graphically.

Domestic politics can also be seen at work in the attitude of the British Labour government to the renegotiation of Britain's terms of entry to the EC. The objectives of the renegotiation could have been achieved, perhaps could have more easily been achieved, through the normal process of intergovernmental negotiations within the context of the EC. That the demands were made into a high-profile renegotiation was primarily due to the need of the Prime Minister, Harold Wilson, to satisfy the critics of EC membership within his own party, and to convince the British people that he had won a series of 'victories' on their behalf in the negotiations. The disruption that this approach caused to the functioning of the EC was a high price to pay, but the tension between domestic politics and European integration is again very apparent, as in this case is the primacy of domestic politics.

The impact of international economic factors and domestic politics was to apply the brakes to supranationalism. The main innovations of the period were the creation of the European Council, which to a large extent was an attempt to reclaim leadership of the EC for national heads of government, and the beginning of EPC, an intergovernmental process of co-ordinating foreign policy. The main integrative initiative, the 'snake in the tunnel' system designed to move the EC towards monetary union, collapsed in the face of the global turbulence in currency markets. There was little in the period onto which the neofunctionalists could cling as evidence of their theory being vindicated.

KEY POINTS

The Hague Summit

☐ Changes of leadership in France and Germany in 1969 appeared to free the way for further European integration. The result was The Hague summit, which declared the objectives of completion, deepening and widening.

☐ *Completion* was achieved through allowing the EC to have its own resources for the first time. The EP was also given some budgetary powers.

☐ *Widening* was achieved through the entry of Britain, Denmark and Ireland into the EC in 1973.

☐ *Deepening* of co-operation on foreign policy through European Political Co-operation had some success; less so co-operation on monetary union.

The European Council

- ☐ In 1974, Giscard d'Estaing called for the institutionalization of summit meetings of EC Heads of State and Government. He received support for this from Helmut Schmidt.
- ☐ It was agreed that these meetings be institutionalized under the auspices of the European Council and would be held three times each year.
- ☐ The creation of the European Council symbolized a profoundly intergovernmental period in the history of European integration.

FURTHER READING

This whole period is dealt with extensively by D.W. Urwin, *The Community of Europe: A History of European Integration since 1945* (London and New York: Longman, 2nd edn, 1995), 146–79. K. Middlemass, *Orchestrating Europe: The Informal Politics of European Union, 1973–1995* (London: Fontana, 1995), 73–110, calls the years between 1973 and 1983 'The Stagnant Decade'. A. Moravcsik, *The Choice for Europe: Social Purpose and State Power from Messina to Maastricht* (London: UCL Press, 1998), 238–313, focuses on monetary co-operation and the European Monetary System. British entry is ably dealt with in C. Lord, *British Entry to the European Community under the Heath Government of 1970–4* (Aldershot: Dartmouth, 1993).

@ online resource centre   **Visit the Online Resource Centre that accompanies this book for links to more information on European integration after the Luxemburg Compromise.**

CHAPTER 11

The European Community into the 1980s

CHAPTER OVERVIEW

The early 1970s marked a low point in European integration, but signs emerged in the late 1970s of the European Community (EC) turning a corner. A revived Commission, led by Roy Jenkins, secured agreement to be involved in international economic summits; the European Monetary System (EMS) was set up; and membership applications from Greece, Portugal, and Spain reflected positively on the external reputation of the EC. However, new problems also surfaced in this period, most notably the British government's claim for a rebate on its contributions to the EC budget. By the mid-1980s though, important domestic political changes and the resolution of the British rebate claim had provided a platform the relaunch of European integration.

" European integration was considered dead in the water in the 1970s and barely ten years later the European Community was being hailed as the new superpower for the twenty first century.
(Mutimer 1994: 42) "

Institutional Developments

The authority of the European Commission was strengthened by the presidency of Roy Jenkins between 1977 and 1981. Jenkins was an established political figure with considerable experience in government. He had held all the major posts in the British cabinet other than Prime Minister. As such, his appointment raised great expectations amongst those who regretted the decline in the authority of the Commission. Perhaps not all of those expectations were fulfilled. However, Jenkins did enhance the position of the president, and therefore of the Commission, by securing agreement from the Heads of State and Government that he should be present at meetings of the international economic summits, which had previously been restricted to the leaders of the major industrial nations. This development was strongly resisted by Giscard d'Estaing, but was strongly supported by the smaller member states, who felt excluded from an important economic decision-making forum, and who therefore wished to see the President of the Commission present to act as a spokesperson for the EC as a whole (Jenkins 1989: 20–2).

Jenkins also undertook a fundamental reform of the internal structure of the Commission, attempting, against considerable opposition from vested interests, to remove some of the causes of the bureaucratization that had been identified as one of the reasons for its decline in influence (Jenkins 1989: 310, 376). Although he was not completely successful, he did have some impact, and the strong leadership he demonstrated in tackling this problem was probably responsible for earning him the nickname that was a gallicization of his name, but also suggestive of an autocratic manner: 'Roi Jean Quinze'.

The other significant institutional development in this period was the introduction of direct elections to the European Parliament (EP) in 1979. Until this point, the demands of the EP for greater powers had always been countered by the argument that it lacked democratic legitimacy because it was only an indirectly-elected body. After it became directly elected, the EP was in a much stronger position to extract new powers from the member states. The decision to move to direct elections was made at the Rome European Council in December 1975. The politics behind the decision are analysed in Chapter 21 below (pp. 299–300). Further controversy had followed when the first elections were delayed for a year because of the failure of the British Parliament to pass the necessary enabling legislation in time for the May/June 1998 date agreed at Rome. However, the elections in June 1979 were relatively low-key affairs within the member states, with national parties taking a prominent role in the selection of candidates and campaign organization.

The European Monetary System

In the policy field there was one very significant development in the late 1970s. The decision taken at the Brussels European Council in December 1978 to create the European Monetary System (EMS) did not exactly constitute a revival of EMU, but it did provide a basis for a future step in that direction.

As explained in the previous chapter, the snake had by 1977 become a system that embraced only five member states of the EC, together with two non-members. During 1977 even this truncated snake was under pressure from international speculation, and Sweden was forced to withdraw. In this far from promising context, Jenkins launched an initiative that met with a certain amount of initial scepticism about its feasibility even from colleagues within the Commission. In a lecture at the European University Institute in Florence, in October 1977, he called for a new attempt to start the EMU experiment (Jenkins 1977).

The following year Helmut Schmidt and Giscard d'Estaing came up with a joint proposal for what became the EMS. In July 1978, the European Council meeting in Bremen agreed to pursue the idea, and in December 1978, meeting in Brussels, agreed to create what looked remarkably like another snake. It would be more flexible than its predecessor, allowing wider margins of fluctuation for individual currencies, and it would be accompanied by the creation of a new European currency unit (ecu). The ecu would take its value from a basket of the national currencies of the member states, and it would be used in transactions within the EMS. A stock of ecus would be created by each member state depositing 20 per cent of its gold and 20 per cent of its foreign currency reserves with a European Monetary Fund (EMF). If a government was having difficulty in holding the value of its currency in relation to the other currencies in the system, it could apply to the EMF for short-term loans, and later if necessary for medium-term loans, up to a predetermined limit, from the central reserve. The loans would be denominated in ecus. It was hoped that ecus would gradually become the normal means of settlement of international debts between EMS members, thus forming the basis of a common Community currency.

In addition to France and West Germany, the Benelux states and Denmark supported the EMS. After initial hesitation, Italy and Ireland agreed to become full participants. But Britain declined to put sterling into the joint float against the dollar, although it was included in the basket from which the value of the ecu was calculated. Despite the scepticism that had greeted Jenkins's initiative, the EMS did get off the ground, and this time the snake did hold together, so that the scheme must be judged a relative success in the context of the overall history of attempts to move towards EMU (see also Ch. 27, pp. 430–4).

The Mediterranean Enlargements

In 1974 two significant events took place in the Mediterranean. Turkey invaded Cyprus, and a revolution in Portugal overthrew the right-wing Caetano government. Each led to an application for membership of the EC. Subsequently, political developments in Spain led to a Spanish application.

Greece had concluded an Association Agreement with the EC in 1964. This had envisaged eventual membership, but in 1967 Greece entered a period of military dictatorship that precluded an application. The inability of the Greek military to prevent the Turkish occupation of Cyprus precipitated the collapse of the dictatorship, and in June 1975 the new democratic Greek government sought membership of the EC as a means of consolidating democracy. In January 1976 the Commission issued a very cautious Opinion on the ability of Greece to adapt to membership, but political and strategic considerations led the Council of Ministers to accept the application and order the opening of negotiations. Democracy had to be shored up; but also Greece had to be prevented from swinging to the far left and reorienting itself towards the Communist bloc. The negotiation of terms of entry for Greece was not easy, and it took up a great deal of the time of the Commission between July 1976 and May 1979, when the Accession Treaty was signed (membership began in January 1981). Nevertheless, the launching of the negotiations gave a new role to the Commission and put it back at the centre of the EC.

An application from Portugal followed the Greek application in March 1977. Again there were political and strategic reasons for accepting it. The Portuguese revolution threatened to run out of the control of the pro-capitalist forces, and to fall into the hands of extreme left-wing groups that would have emphasized relations with the Third World. The Socialist International, with the German SPD taking a lead, provided support to the Portuguese Socialist Party (PSP), and so when the PSP was elected to government in 1976 there was not much doubt that it would apply for EC membership, nor that the application would be accepted.

Similar political and strategic considerations applied in July 1977 to the acceptance of an application from Spain following the death of the dictator Franco and the restoration of democracy there. In the Spanish case, membership of the EC was held out as a bonus if it decided also to join the NATO alliance. Given Spain's strategic position in the Mediterranean, this was a vital interest of the western alliance.

Whereas the first of these applications stimulated a revival of the role of the Commission, handling three sets of difficult negotiations became a problem, and the Portuguese and Spanish Accession Treaties were not signed until 1985 (membership began in January 1986).

The British Budget Rebate

Another issue that caused problems for the EC in the 1980s was the British budgetary rebate. Although budget contributions had been central to the renegotiation, already by 1976, while transitional arrangements still limited the extent of its contributions, Britain was the third biggest net contributor to the EC budget, behind Germany and Belgium. In 1977, still under transitional arrangements, the British net contribution was the second highest to that of Germany. By mid-1978 it was becoming apparent that once the transitional period of membership ended in 1980, Britain would become the largest net contributor to the budget.

This situation arose because:

(1) Britain imported more goods, especially foodstuffs, from outside the EC than did other member states, and therefore paid more in import levies.

(2) Low direct taxes meant that British consumers spent more in proportion to the relative wealth of the country, and Britain therefore contributed more to the budget in VAT receipts.

(3) Payments out of the budget were dominated by the CAP, and Britain had a small and efficient farming sector that meant that it received less than states with larger agricultural economies.

The developing position was unacceptable to the Labour government. The Foreign Secretary, David Owen, told the House of Commons that the situation whereby 'the United Kingdom has the third lowest per capita gross domestic product in the Community' yet was already the second highest net contributor to the budget, 'cannot be good for the Community any more than it is for the United Kingdom', and promised that the government would 'be working to achieve a better balance, especially in relation to agricultural expenditure, to curb the excessive United Kingdom contribution' (*Hansard*, 14 November 1978, col. 214).

In fact the Labour government never had the opportunity to work for a better balance because it lost office in the June 1979 election to the Conservatives under Margaret Thatcher. The new government soon took up the same theme concerning the budget. Shortly after coming into office, Sir Geoffrey Howe, the Chancellor of the Exchequer, announced that the size of the problem was far greater than the Conservatives had realized while in opposition, and something would have to be done about it urgently.

Margaret Thatcher and the Battle for a Rebate

Margaret Thatcher raised the issue at her first European Council in Strasburg in June 1979, soon after her election victory. Her presentation there was moderate and reasonable, and the complaint was offset by an announcement on the first day of the meeting that Britain would deposit its share of gold and foreign currency reserves with the European Monetary Co-operation Fund that had been set up to administer the EMS.

The move was widely interpreted as a sign that sterling would soon join the exchange rate mechanism of the EMS. Discussion of the budgetary issue at Strasburg was brief and limited to agreeing a procedure for analysing the problem. The Commission was asked to prepare a report by September; this would be discussed by Finance Ministers, then revised in time for the next European Council in Dublin in late November.

At that November 1979 Dublin European Council Thatcher adopted an entirely different tone. She insisted that the Commission proposal of a rebate of £350 million was unacceptable, and that she would not accept less than £1 billion. The French said that they would not agree to more than £350 million, which the British would have to accept as full and final settlement of their claim. This provoked an argument that lasted ten hours, in the course of which Thatcher upset her partners by her uncompromising demands for what she insensitively described as Britain's 'own money back'.

This was the tone that Thatcher persistently adopted in negotiations for the next four-and-a-half years. During that time several temporary abatements of the British contributions were agreed, but a permanent settlement eluded all efforts to bridge the gap between what the British Prime Minister demanded and what the other member states were prepared to pay. British tactics became increasingly obstructionist on other issues, and relations with the other states became increasingly strained. Relations reached their nadir in May 1982. Britain was blocking agreement on agricultural price increases for 1982–3, linking agreement to a permanent settlement of the budgetary dispute. Finally, the Belgian presidency called a majority vote on the agricultural prices. Britain protested that this breached the Luxemburg Compromise, but the vote went ahead and was passed. Several of the other states, though, appeared shocked at their own behaviour. It seemed apparent that a settlement of the British dispute was necessary before progress could be made in other areas.

Leadership Changes

The confluence of challenges facing the EC at the beginning of the 1980s coincided with the appointment of Gaston Thorn to the Commission presidency in 1981. Member States generally welcomed Thorn's appointment. Although he took over at a difficult time, there was a feeling that he was uniquely well qualified for the job, as few people had a wider experience of the EC. Early in his presidency there were two significant changes among the national leaderships with which Thorn would have to work.

In May 1981 François Mitterrand defeated Giscard d'Estaing in the French presidential election. This result was consolidated a month later by a victory for Mitterrand's Socialist party in elections to the National Assembly. The change broke apart the Franco-German axis because Helmut Schmidt had less in common with the Socialist president than he had with the conservative Giscard. In particular, the Socialist government came into office committed to tackling unemployment rather than emphasizing low inflation as its predecessor government had done. However, a U-turn in economic policy in 1983 brought France more into line with the neo-liberal and deregulationist tendencies already evident in West Germany and Britain.

The second change in political leadership came in West Germany itself. Although the SPD/FDP won the 1980 Federal election, dissension within the coalition was increasing in the face of the economic problems the country was facing. Within the SPD, the left-wing and the trade unionist membership were demanding some measures of reflation to relieve unemployment, which in 1981 stood at 1 1/4 million. But at the same time, the FDP was returning to its basic principles of economic liberalism, represented most strikingly by the Economics Minister, Otto von Lamsdorff. The clash between the two parties over economic affairs led to the eventual breakdown of the coalition. The FDP changed partners and allowed the CDU/CSU into office, with Helmut Kohl, the CDU leader, as chancellor.

Kohl emphasized continuity in his foreign policy, but it was expected that he would develop a warmer relationship with Thatcher than Schmidt had. This was partly because the milder personality of Kohl was less likely to clash with the forthright manner of the British Prime Minister, and partly because of a mutual interest in attacking socialism.

Moves to Revive the EC

By the start of the 1980s there was an acceptance within both national governments and the Commission that the response to challenges facing the EC required, in part at least, institutional reform to facilitate easier and more effective decision-making.

The first response came in September 1981 from the foreign ministers of Germany and Italy, and was known as the Genscher–Colombo Plan. This plan called for a new European charter that would supersede the Treaties of Paris and Rome as the basic constitutional document of the Communities, and would bring European political co-operation, together with the EC, under the joint direction of the European Council. This would only be a formalization of the existing situation, although Genscher and Colombo also wished to improve the decision-making ability of the Council of Ministers by increasing the use of majority voting, to expand the functions of the European Parliament, and to intensify foreign policy co-operation in security matters.

The plan received a cool response in the Council, as had an earlier proposal led by Altiero Spinelli—now a senior figure in the European Parliament—that sought to diminish the institutional position of the Council in favour of the Parliament and Commission. Yet while these two sets of proposals made no immediate impact on integration, they contributed to the European Council beginning a new round of negotiations on the question of political union and possible revision of the treaties.

On the economic front, attempts by Thorn and his Vice-President and Commissioner for the Internal Market, Karl-Heinz Narjes, to highlight the problems faced by industrialists in trading across national borders within the EC met with little response from national governments. Governments were determined to reserve jobs for their own nationals (read 'voters') by tolerating, or even themselves erecting, non-tariff barriers to trade, and by giving public contracts exclusively to national companies. Yet Thorn, Narjes, and particularly Vice-President Etienne Davignon, the Commissioner for Industrial Policy, laid the groundwork for the agreement that was concluded under the following Delors presidency to free the internal market of all these obstacles by the end of 1992.

Thorn and Narjes maintained a constant propaganda campaign against barriers to a genuine internal market. This campaign had an effect in raising awareness of the issue, especially when it was taken up by a group of Members of the European Parliament (MEPs) who called themselves the Kangaroo Group because they wanted to facilitate trade that would 'hop over' national boundaries. The work of Davignon was less public, but possibly more influential in persuading governments to accept change. He called into existence a network of leading industrialists involved in the European electrical and electronics industries to discuss their common problems in the face of US and Japanese competition. Out of these discussions came the Esprit programme of collaborative research in advanced technologies; but more significantly there also arose the European Round Table of Industrialists, which was to become an influential pressure group pushing governments into taking measures to liberalize the internal market of the EC.

Fontainebleau

The European Council meeting at Fontainebleau in June 1984 marked a turning point in European integration. First of all, the summit resolved the British budgetary question, in the context of an agreement at Fontainebleau to cut back on CAP expenditure and to increase the Community's own resources through an increase in VAT contributions by member states. The agreement settled five years of dispute and opened the door for reform of the CAP.

The meeting also agreed to set up an *ad hoc* committee on institutional affairs, which came to be known by the name of its Chair, James Dooge of Ireland. The report of this committee became the basis for the institutional changes that were later to be made, alongside the fundamental policy commitment to completion of the internal market.

CONCLUSION

The first signs of the revival of the EC were ambiguous. The initiative to launch the EMS did not mark a new commitment to further European integration. Whatever Jenkins's motives for proposing a revival of monetary union, the EMS fell well short of being that. It was actually a response by West Germany to the threat posed to German exports by the US policy of benign neglect of the external value of the dollar. The themes that are relevant here are the impact of the international economic system on developments in the EC, and the defence of national interest by the larger member states. Later the EMS was to form the basis on which a new attempt at monetary union could be built, but this illustrates another consistent theme of the story: that steps taken in pursuit of national interest can often have unintended consequences that favour further European integration.

The continued decline of US hegemony drew the EC into playing a larger international role, and this was the main motive behind the Mediterranean enlargements of the EC in this period. The development of the EC was still being played out against the background of the Cold War, and it was a fear that political instability might open the way for Communist influence that inspired the leading states of the EC to push for the membership of Greece, Portugal, and Spain despite the obvious economic weaknesses of these states. Again, the unintended consequences of these decisions were arguably to advance European integration, because the new member states became a powerful lobby for the extension of the structural funds of the EC, which eventually accounted for one-third of the EC budget, second only to the CAP.

The influence of domestic politics came through again in the British dispute over the budget rebate. Margaret Thatcher used the technique that Harold Wilson had adopted very successfully in the renegotiation of British terms of entry. She adopted a confrontational and nationalistic tone, which played well to a domestic audience, but caused disruption to the smooth operation of the EC.

The introduction of direct elections to the EP enhanced the legitimacy of the EU decision-making process and provided a boost both to federalist aspirations and supranational interpretations of integration. At the same time there were the first stirrings of a more active role for the Commission in this period. The agreement to allow the President of the Commission to attend meetings of the economic summits reflected the concerns of smaller member states that the era of summitry might become the era of large states dominating smaller states. Again, a step that was negotiated from a viewpoint of defending national interest had positive implications for the strength of supranationalism.

On the other hand, the internal reforms by Jenkins indicated the problem of bureaucratization of the Commission, a problem that Jenkins did not manage to solve. Nevertheless, the increasing activism of the Thorn Commission, which is often unfairly treated as ineffective, showed the extent to which the presidency of Jenkins had marked a turning point in the self-confidence of the Commission, and paved the way for Delors.

KEY POINTS

Institutional Developments

☐ As Commission President, Roy Jenkins managed to secure a place at international economic summits for the Commission for the first time.

The European Monetary System

☐ Following a call from Jenkins to renew attempts at monetary union, the European Council passed a proposal by Schmidt and Giscard for a European Monetary System (EMS) in 1978.

☐ The new EMS would be more flexible than its predecessor, but Britain declined to put sterling in a joint float against the US dollar.

The Mediterranean Enlargements

☐ Following a difficult period of negotiations, the accession of Greece to the Community was agreed in 1979. Portugal and Spain, who applied later, were eventually accepted into the EC in 1985.

The British Budget Rebate

☐ Britain was set to be the largest net contributor to the Community budget by 1980. The tactics of the Thatcher government over the issue jeopardized progress in other areas until a satisfactory solution was found.

Leadership Changes

☐ The appointment of Gaston Thorn to the Commission presidency in 1981 coincided with important leadership changes in France and Germany.

Moves to Revive the EC

☐ The challenges facing the EC in the early 1980s demanded a response. The Genscher–Colombo plan proposed institutional reforms that received a cool response from the Council. However, Commission plans for freeing the internal market began to win over national governments.

☐ The resolution of the British budgetary question at Fontainebleau allowed for progress on both the internal market and institutional reform.

FURTHER READING

For an insider account of the early part of this period see R. Jenkins, *European Diary, 1977–1981* (London: Collins, 1989). The British budget rebate issue is explained more fully in S. George, *An Awkward Partner: Britain in the European Community*, 3rd edn (Oxford: Oxford University Press, 1998), 137–65. D.W. Urwin, *The Community of Europe: A History of European Integration since 1945* (London and New York: Longman, 2nd edn, 1995), 195–228, puts particular emphasis on the problems of enlargement and the initiatives for political integration such as the Genscher–Colombo plan.

online resource centre   **Visit the Online Resource Centre that accompanies this book for links to more information on the European Community in the 1980s.**

CHAPTER 12

The Single European Act

CHAPTER OVERVIEW

If the platform for the revival of European integration was laid in the early 1980s, the mid-1980s marked a turning point. The Commission under Jacques Delors, which assumed office in 1985, championed the scheme for a new integrative push starting with an ambitious project to free the internal market of the European Community (EC) of non-tariff barriers. This push led to the Single European Act (SEA), which marked a key moment in the history of European integration. It was the collective response of EC states to the global economic challenges of the late twentieth century and marked a new phase in European integration. By the end of the decade the EC had cast off the image of 'Eurosclerosis' and was demonstrating a dynamism that had hardly seemed possible five years earlier. This chapter examines the initiative taken by Delors, and the SEA itself. It looks at the provisions of the SEA, particularly the institutional reforms that it introduced, and then briefly at the debate over the role of the Commission in getting it accepted and problems of implementing what had been agreed.

> [T]he SEA ... had potential for revolution, suggesting a shift in the existing balance of power away from the member states towards the Community institutions.
>
> (Urwin 1995: 231)

When a new Commission assumed office in 1985 under the presidency of Jacques Delors (Insight 12.1) it offered a visible symbol of a new start under dynamic leadership. Delors proposed that the EC should set itself the target of removing a whole series of barriers to free trade and free movement of capital and labour that had grown up during the 1970s. This project would be pursued with a target date for completion of the end of 1992, and became known as the '1992 programme'. This economic project was linked to a programme of institutional reform that would have far-reaching implications for the way in which the EC made decisions, although those implications were not all immediately apparent.

From the outset the single market project was linked to certain institutional reforms, particularly the introduction of qualified majority voting (QMV) into the proceedings of the Council of Ministers, thus overcoming the blockage to progress imposed by the veto system. It was also intended to revive the momentum of integration, because Delors believed that the freeing of the internal market would lead to spillover into other policy sectors. In particular he believed that it would not be feasible to have the single market without strengthening the degree of social protection available to workers at the EC level; and that the single market would set up a momentum towards monetary union.

Despite British reluctance to see these further developments, the Thatcher government wanted to see the single market programme itself put into place. Subsequently the

---

INSIGHT 12.1

Jacques Delors

Jacques Delors was born in Paris in 1925. His father was a middle-ranking employee of the Bank of France, and the son went to work for the Bank straight from school. The young Delors was active in Catholic social movements, and became a devotee of the doctrine of 'personalism', a form of Christian socialism associated with the philosopher Emmanual Mounier. Delors was also an active trade unionist. In the 1960s he moved from the Bank to a senior position in the French Planning Commission, which had been created by Jean Monnet. Although he was an adviser to the Gaullist Prime Minister Jacques Chaban-Delmas at the end of the 1960s and in the early 1970s, he subsequently joined the reformed Socialist party of François Mitterrand, and was elected to the European Parliament in 1979 as a Socialist. When Mitterrand became President of France in 1981, Delors became Finance Minister in the Socialist government. He was instrumental in moving the government away from policies of economic expansion that were not working and were undermining the value of the currency. He played a crucial role in the negotiation of the 1983 realignment of currencies within the exchange rate mechanism of the European Monetary System, and won the respect of the German government in the process. In 1985, with strong support from Chancellor Kohl of Germany as well as from Mitterrand, he became President of the European Commission, a post that he retained for ten years.

British Prime Minister tried to block the further developments, but in the meantime the success of Delors's initiative revived the self-confidence of the Commission, which had already begun to recover under Jenkins and Thorn. It also led to a revival of theoretical interpretations of the EC that emphasized the role of the Commission and other supranational actors, thus rekindling the supranational—intergovernmental debate about the nature of the EC, which had lain dormant during the 'doldrums years' of the 1970s and early 1980s (see also Ch. 26, pp. 410–15).

1985: A Watershed Year

Delors had been Finance Minister in the 1981–3 French Socialist governments, which had tried to tackle the problem of unemployment in France by reflating the economy. The result had been a serious balance of payments crisis as the reflation did little to restore full employment, but did suck in imports. There had been two views on how to respond to this. One had been to withdraw from the European Monetary System, and to impose import controls, in contravention of France's EC obligations. The other, of which Delors had been the strongest advocate, had been to revert to national policies of balancing the budget by cutting public expenditure, and to develop a European solution to the problem of unemployment. That view had prevailed, and Delors's advocacy of it made him acceptable to both Germany and Britain as a nominee for the Commission presidency. It had been tacitly accepted that the presidency of the Commission would be given to a German candidate if the Federal Government wished to take it up; but Kohl chose to throw his weight behind Delors.

The Brussels European Council of February 1985 instructed the Commission to draw up a timetable for the completion of the single market. Within a few months of taking office, the British Commissioner for Trade and Industry, Lord Cockfield, produced a White Paper listing the barriers that needed to be removed for there to be a genuine single market inside the EC. This listed some 300 separate measures, later reduced to 279, covering the harmonization of technical standards, opening up public procurement to intra-EC competition, freeing capital movements, removing barriers to free trade in services, harmonizing rates of indirect taxation and excise duties, and removing physical frontier controls between member states. The list was accompanied by a timetable for completion, with a final target date of the end of 1992.

At the Milan European Council in June 1985, Heads of Government agreed the objectives of the White Paper and the timetable for its completion by the end of 1992. A massive publicity campaign would be organized to promote the project. It was also agreed, against the protests of the British Prime Minister, to set up an Intergovernmental Conference (IGC) to consider what changes were necessary to the original treaties in order to achieve the single market, and to consider other changes to the institutional structure that had been recommended by an *ad hoc* committee under James Dooge which had been set up at the Fontainebleau European Council a year earlier (Ch. 11, p. 154). This IGC drew up what became the SEA, which was agreed by the heads of government at the Luxemburg European Council in December 1985, and eventually ratified by national parliaments to come into effect in July 1987. Thus was born the 1992 programme, which did more than any initiative since the Treaties of Rome to revitalize the process of European integration.

The Single European Act

Although modest in the changes that it introduced in comparison with the hopes of federalists in the European Parliament and within some member states (particularly Italy), the SEA rejuvenated the process of European integration. The intention of the SEA appeared relatively modest, seeking to complete the objective of a common market set out in the Treaty of Rome. By the early 1980s, the need for member states to compete in world markets, especially against the United States and Japan, was an overriding concern. A single European market would increase the specialization of production at company level and allow greater economies of scale, leading to more competitive firms. The issue of monetary union as an accompaniment to the single market was not addressed at this stage of developments.

While ostensibly an economic project, the SEA had implications for a range of policy areas such as the environment and social protection (see Ch. 24, pp. 364–8). More broadly, in its proposals for institutional change, the SEA:

had potential for revolution, suggesting a shift in the existing balance of power away from the member states towards the Community institutions. The radical political implications of the economic target of a common market—the single internal market—were there for all to read in the document . . . while the issues of political and economic integration are closely interlinked, the parallel debates tended to muddy the waters of each.

(Urwin 1995: 231)

In retrospect at least, the political implications of the SEA are clear (Insight 12.2). At the time, though, the SEA was largely seen as a mechanism for implementing the commitment made at Milan to achieve the single market. This goal was not contested by member states. Moreover, the Commission was concerned with emphasizing the practical rather than the political implications of aspects of the reform. Only in the final section of the White Paper did the Commission refer to the wider implications of the internal market project, acknowledging that 'Just as the Customs Union had to precede Economic Integration, so Economic Integration has to precede European Unity' (European Commission 1985: 55). Despite the political implications of the single market being deliberately understated by the Commission, the proposed institutional reforms proved the most controversial aspect of the project.

Institutional Reforms

While ostensibly a project to complete the single market, the institutional reforms of the SEA were to be of lasting significance for European integration, in particular the introduction of QMV in the Council of Ministers. QMV was designed to speed-up

INSIGHT 12.2

The Political Provisions of the SEA

- It introduced qualified majority voting (QMV) for single-market measures.
- It increased the legislative powers of the European Parliament in areas where QMV applied.
- It incorporated European political co-operation (EPC) into a treaty text for the first time.
- It incorporated in the Preamble a reiteration of the objective of an economic and monetary union.
- It incorporated in the Preamble a commitment by the member states to 'transform relations as a whole among their States into a European Union'.

decision making by reducing substantially the number of areas in which individual states could reject progress by use of their veto. QMV would apply to measures related to the freeing of the internal market, although certain measures, including the harmonization of indirect taxes and the removal of physical controls at borders, were excluded at British insistence. Without the extension of QMV, the internal market project was likely to be delayed and possibly lost through intergovernmental disputes.

The codification of the commitment to QMV as a formal amendment of the founding treaties, and as part of a potentially wider reform of the institutional procedures for making decisions, was resisted strongly by Prime Minister Thatcher. The whole issue of institutional reform was one of several where the British government differed from most of its continental European partners. Mrs Thatcher insisted at Milan that no institutional reform, and so no IGC, was necessary. However, it seems that she was persuaded by her Foreign Secretary, Sir Geoffrey Howe, and her adviser on European affairs, David Williamson, that unless a legally binding commitment were made to an element of majority voting in the Council of Ministers the measures necessary to implement the Cockfield White Paper would never be agreed.

The freeing of the internal market was supported by all the member states, and it coincided with the belief of the British Prime Minister in universal free trade. On the other hand, it was also an excellent issue for the new Commission to make into the centrepiece of its programme. As Helen Wallace (1986: 590) explained:

The internal market is important not only for its own sake, but because it is the first core Community issue for over a decade ... which has caught the imagination of British policy-makers and which is echoed by their counterparts elsewhere ... The pursuit of a thoroughly liberalized domestic European market has several great advantages: it fits Community philosophy, it suits the doctrinal preferences of the current British Conservative government, and it would draw in its train a mass of interconnections with other fields of action.

Whereas doctrinal preferences may be sufficient explanation for British support of the internal market project, the support of other member states perhaps needs a little further explanation.

One important factor was the support given to the freeing of the market by European business leaders, some of whom formed the European Round Table of Industrialists in 1983 to press for the removal of the barriers to trade that had developed. This pressure occurred in the context of a generalized concern among governments about the sluggish recovery of the European economies from the post-1979 recession in comparison with the vigorous growth of the US and Japanese economies. In particular, the turning of the tide of direct foreign investment, so that by the mid-1980s there was a net flow of investment funds from western Europe to the United States, augured badly both for the employment situation in Europe in the future, and for the ability of European industry to keep abreast of the technological developments that were revolutionizing production processes.

It was in response to the worry that Europe would become permanently technologically dependent on the United States and Japan that President Mitterrand proposed his EUREKA initiative for promoting pan-European research and development in the advanced technology industries. This concern also lay behind the promotion by the new Commission of framework programmes for research and development in such fields as information technology, bio-technology, and telecommunications (Sharp and Shearman 1987). But when European industrialists were asked what would be most likely to encourage them to invest in Europe they replied that the most important factor for them would be the creation of a genuine continental market such as they experienced in the United States.

It was therefore in an attempt to revive investment and economic growth that governments other than Britain embraced the free-market programme. The pressure to break out of the short-termism that had prevented the EC from making progress in the 1970s and early 1980s came partly from interest groups, but also from the economic situation that faced governments. The EC, as only one part of the global capitalist economy, was seeing investment flow away from it to other parts of the global economy, and was already being left behind in rates of economic growth and in technological advance by rival core-areas within the system. It was a calculation of the common national interests of the member states that led them to agree a new contract, in the form of a White Paper and the Single European Act.

The Role of the Delors Commission

The emphasis that Delors put on the single market was part of a carefully considered strategy. During the autumn of 1984 he considered a variety of candidates for the role of the 'Big Idea' that would relaunch European integration (Grant 1994: 66). Initially attracted to completion of EMU, following the relative success of the EMS, Delors ultimately decided that the idea of completing the internal market was the best starting point. This project was firmly within the boundaries of integration established by the Treaty of Rome. Even more important, perhaps, with policies of market liberalization adopted by key member states, the single market project stood the best chance of winning the support of even the most Euro-sceptic governments, Britain's in particular. Moreover, successful completion of the 1992 project had implications for a wide range of Community policies. Most notably, the project would inevitably prompt reconsideration of the advantages of monetary union as a complement to the single market and would also lead to demands for strengthening EC social and regional policies from the member states most likely to be adversely affected by the internal market.

Few dispute that the Delors Commission played a pivotal role in developing and pushing forward the single market programme as a means to the end of ever closer union. The emergence of the programme and eventually the drive towards full monetary union and the adoption of a social charter, all bore the hallmarks of a plan devised in Paris in the light of the failures of the 1981–4 French economic experiment. Delors and the British Commissioner Cockfield worked together closely on developing and promoting the project. Cockfield faced accusations from the British Prime Minister that he had 'gone native' in his support for wide-ranging European integration, and it was no great surprise when Thatcher chose not to renominate him to the Commission in 1988.

Under Delors the Commission regained the high profile it had under Hallstein, and, irrespective of whether the Hallstein Commission had been the genuine motor of integration, the Delors Commission certainly appeared to play that role by the 1980s. But it was only able to play that role because of the support Delors received from Mitterrand, and because of the diplomatic skill of Mitterrand himself in ensuring that other member states, Germany above all, were carried along with the plan.

Implementing the SEA

While national governments were initially slow to implement the measures detailed in the SEA, businesses began to take advantage of the emerging opportunities offered by the 1992 project. Company mergers accelerated to take advantage of EC-wide economies of scale. The business publication *The Economist* (1988) noted that in 1987 there were 300 major mergers compared with only sixty-eight in the previous year. In comparison, by November 1987 the Council of Ministers had adopted only sixty-four of the measures set out in the White Paper (Dinan 1994: 150).

The core problem of implementation related to accompanying measures to the SEA, in particular, the demands of southern member states for adequate compensatory mechanisms to balance the adverse effects of market liberalization. While a number of member states were reluctant to commit greater resources to Community regional aid, ultimately these demands had to be satisfied to protect the 1992 programme. Subsequently, at the Brussels European Council of February 1988, Heads of Government agreed to a doubling in the allocations to the structural funds to promote greater cohesion as a complement to the internal market.

CONCLUSION

This was the period in which the EC was revitalized, and with it the theory of neofunctionalism. The debates surrounding the origins of the single market programme are considered further in Chapter 26 below (see pp. 408–15). Interpretations of the relevant importance of different factors certainly vary, but there is a considerable body of analysis that attributes a central role to the European Commission under Jacques Delors, and to the European Round Table of Industrialists. Two of the actors whom neofunctionalists had predicted would be influential appeared to be influential in this landmark decision: the Commission and transnational business interests. Neofunctionalism also received support from another development: the speed with which businesses responded to the announcement of the 1992 programme to conclude mergers and announce new investment plans vindicated the argument that changed circumstances would lead to changed attitudes and behaviour.

However, the interpretations that emphasized the role of supranational actors did not go along with neofunctionalism in seeing spillover as the dynamic force that produced the 1992 programme. There is general agreement that global economic developments were the catalyst for the acceptance of the single market. The remarkable economic recovery of the United States and Japan from the second oil crisis contrasted starkly with the sluggishness of the west European economies. Not only was there a marked difference in performance: the success of the United States and Japan was based on the adoption of new technologies into their production processes that threatened to leave western Europe with an obsolete industrial base unless investment could be revived.

In exploiting the problems that the changed global economic environment posed for national governments, Delors acted as a '**policy entrepreneur**'. However, he did not mobilize the Commission to support this role by carrying through the reforms that had eluded Jenkins. It remained a bureaucratized and fragmented body. Rather than reform its procedures, Delors chose to short-circuit them, using an informal network centred on his personal *cabinet* as the agents for pushing through the necessary initiatives. This was to store up problems for the future that would lead directly to a substantial crisis in the late 1990s.

KEY POINTS

1985: A Watershed Year

☐ In February 1985, the European Council instructed the Delors Commission to draw up a timetable for the completion of the single market. In June 1985, the Council agreed to the Commission's proposals and the 1992 timetable for completion.

☐ An IGC on institutional reform drew up what became the Single European Act.

The Single European Act

☐ The SEA rejuvenated the process of European integration, but the broad political significance of the institutional reforms of the SEA only became clear later.

☐ The British government was instinctively averse to QMV but accepted it as necessary to achieve the completion of the single market by 1992.

☐ On the whole, governments were persuaded of the need of the SEA by the desire to compete with Japan and the US.

☐ For Delors the single market programme was the 'Big Idea' that would relaunch European integration, but the support of key member governments was essential to its ultimate success.

☐ Companies were quick to take advantage of the opportunities provided by the single market project, but implementation of SEA measures varied across member states.

C. Grant, *Delors: Inside the House that Jacques Built* (London: Nicolas Brealey Publishing, 1994) and G. Ross, *Jacques Delors and European Integration* (Cambridge: Polity Press, 1995) both give accounts of what went on within the Delors Commission. For the analysis of the Single European Act, begin with D.R. Cameron, 'The 1992 Initiative: Causes and Consequences', in A. Sbragia (ed.), *Euro-Politics: Institutions and Policymaking in the 'New' European Community* (Washington, DC: Brookings Institution, 1992), 23–74; continue with W. Sandholtz and J. Zysman, '1992: Recasting the European Bargain', *World Politics*, vol. 45, 95–128; and then read A. Moravcsik, *The Choice for Europe: Social Purpose and State power from Messina to Maastricht* (London: UCL Press, 1998), 314–78, or his chapter 'Negotiating the Single European Act', in R.O. Keohane and S. Hoffmann (eds.), *The New European Community: Decision-Making and Institutional Change* (Boulder, San Francisco, and Oxford: Westview Press), 41–84.

online resource centre

Visit the Online Resource Centre that accompanies this book for links to more information on the Single European Act.

CHAPTER 13

Maastricht: The Treaty on European Union

CHAPTER OVERVIEW

The success of the 1992 project revived European integration, although the difficult issue of monetary union had yet to be addressed. Following the collapse of Communism in eastern Europe and the reunification of Germany, the future of European integration was once again brought into focus. The result was the Treaty on European Union (TEU), signed in Maastricht in December 1991, which brought agreement on moves towards a single currency and further institutional reforms. This chapter examines the moves towards monetary union, the impact of the collapse of Communism on the European Community (EC), the terms of the TEU, and the aftermath of its signing, when public opinion began to turn away from support for European integration.

> More than the SEA, the Maastricht treaty helps to clarify the rules of the game and the international *compétences* of the emergent Euro-polity.
>
> **(Schmitter 1996: 1)**

The 1992 project was a tremendous success. It led to a revival of investment in Europe, which had been stagnating. Companies anticipated the arrival of the single market by engaging in cross-border mergers and joint production arrangements. The EC experienced a wave of business euphoria, which ensured that the work of public officials in actually agreeing the necessary measures did not waver. By the target date of the end of 1992, 260 out of the consolidated list of 279 measures that had been identified in the White Paper had been agreed in the Council of Ministers, a staggering 95 per cent success rate (Pelkmans 1994: 103).

However, the freeing of the market was not the end of the project so far as Delors was concerned. He saw it as a first step that implied further extensions of integration. In particular he argued for a social dimension to the project, and for its completion by agreement on monetary union. On both of these issues he had the support of a majority of the governments of the other member states, but was implacably opposed by the British Prime Minister, Margaret Thatcher.

The British government rejected the proposed Social Charter, which Mrs Thatcher described as 'Marxist' (Urwin 1995: 231). The proposal for worker representatives on company boards was a particular problem for the Thatcher government. Despite subsequent revisions to the proposed Social Charter, the UK government refused to sign, leaving the remaining eleven governments to sign a protocol on social policy outside of the treaty (Insight 13.1).

INSIGHT 13.1

Objectives of the Social Protocol Annexed to the Treaty on European Union

- promotion of employment;
- improvement of living and working conditions;
- adequate social protection;
- social dialogue;
- the development of human resources to ensure a high and sustainable level of employment;
- the integration of persons excluded from the labour market.

Towards Maastricht

Monetary policy had been largely absent from the SEA (Ch. 12), but the logic of the internal market suggested at least some harmonization of taxation policies. Following the SEA there had been growing support for a single currency controlled by a European central bank, but the British government rejected this concept. Despite British opposition, the heads of government agreed in Hanover in June 1988 to set up a committee of central bankers and technical experts, under the chairmanship of Delors, to prepare a report on the steps that needed to be taken to strengthen monetary co-operation. The subsequent 'Delors Report' proposed a three-stage progress to monetary union leading to a single currency by 1999. The report was presented to the June 1989 meeting of the European Council in Madrid, which on a majority vote of eleven to one—Thatcher voting against—agreed to convene an IGC to prepare proposals for changes to the treaties to allow movement to a monetary union.

The dramatic collapse of Communism in the Soviet Union and other central and eastern European countries in the course of 1989 and 1990 added to the complexity of the situation. This forced a serious reconsideration of the political aspects of the EC. The immediate impact was the destabilization of the geographical area immediately to the east of the EC and, more positively for the EC, the opening up of potential new markets and new sites for investment for west European capital. In addition, the collapse of Communism raised the prospect of German reunification.

This 'acceleration of history' as Delors called it had an impact on the EC and on Delors's plans for its development. In particular, the prospect of a reunified Germany caused alarm in the neighbouring states, particularly over a possible resurgence of German nationalism. A more immediate concern was that the new Germany would turn its attention more to the east and become less concerned with its obligations to western Europe.

Chancellor Kohl of Germany shared these concerns. Kohl had not hitherto been noted for providing strong or dynamic leadership, but he seized the opportunity to go down in the history books as the person who reunified his country. At the same time, however, he did not want to be remembered as the Frankenstein who created a new monster in the centre of Europe. Such concerns led directly to the convening of a second IGC on political union to run alongside the one that had already been called on monetary union. Although Delors supported the move, it was not part of his plan. The IGC on political union, together with that on monetary union, meant that the Maastricht Treaty became a very high profile issue: 'a treaty too far' as Lady Thatcher later described it.

The two IGCs met throughout 1991, and their proposals were incorporated into the TEU which was signed in Maastricht in December of that year, and which created the European Union (EU). Britain, under the new premiership of John Major, agreed to the TEU only when a chapter on social policy had been removed from the main text, and only when it was agreed that Britain could opt out of the final stage of monetary union if its Parliament so decided.

The Treaty on European Union

Intergovernmental negotiations leading up the Maastricht Summit of December 1991 were tough and much of what was agreed reflected the lowest-common-denominator bargaining position of governments. The Treaty on European Union was signed in February 1992 and entered into force in November 1993. Despite the lowest-common-denominator position of governments, the Treaty marked a further big step on the road to European integration, with important implications for both internal and external activities (Insight 13.2).

The name of the 'European Economic Community' was changed to the 'European Community' and there were important new areas of co-operation in the fields of Common Foreign and Security Policy (CFSP) (Insight 13.3) and Justice and Home Affairs (JHA) (Insight 13.4). Along with the existing Community system (EC, ECSC and Euratom), CFSP and JHA became part of a three-pillar structure known as the European Union (see Ch. 18, Fig. 18.1, p. 232). While the first pillar remained an area of pooled sovereignty in which the community method of decision making would continue to predominate, the second and third pillars were explicitly areas of intergovernmental

INSIGHT 13.2

Extract from Treaty on European Union: Common Provisions

Article B

The Union shall set itself the following objectives:

- to promote economic and social progress which is balanced and sustainable, in particular through the creation of an area without internal frontiers, through the strengthening of economic and social cohesion and through the establishment of economic and monetary union, ultimately including a single currency in accordance with the provisions of this Treaty;

- to assert its identity on the international scene, in particular through the implementation of a common foreign and security policy including the eventual framing of a common defence policy, which might in time lead to a common defence;

- to strengthen the protection of the rights and interests of the nationals of its Member States through the introduction of a citizenship of the Union;

- to develop close cooperation on justice and home affairs;

- to maintain in full the acquis communautaire and build on it with a view to considering, through the procedure referred to in Article N(2), to what extent the policies and forms of cooperation introduced by this Treaty may need to be revised with the aim of ensuring the effectiveness of the mechanisms and the institutions of the Community.

The objectives of the Union shall be achieved as provided in this Treaty and in accordance with the conditions and the timetable set out therein while respecting the principle of subsidiarity as defined in Article 3b of the Treaty establishing the European Community.

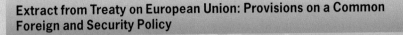

INSIGHT 13.3

Extract from Treaty on European Union: Provisions on a Common Foreign and Security Policy

Article J.1

(1) The Union and its Member States shall define and implement a common foreign and security policy, governed by the provisions of this Title and covering all areas of foreign and security policy.

(2) The objectives of the common foreign and security policy shall be:
- to safeguard the common values, fundamental interests and independence of the Union;
- to strengthen the security of the Union and its Member States in all ways;
- to preserve peace and strengthen international security, in accordance with the principles of the United Nations Charter as well as the principles of the Helsinki Final Act and the objectives of the Paris Charter;
- to promote international cooperation;
- to develop and consolidate democracy and the rule of law, and respect for human rights and fundamental freedoms.

(3) The Union shall pursue these objectives:
- by establishing systematic cooperation between Member States in the conduct of policy, in accordance with Article J.2;
- by gradually implementing, in accordance with Article J.3, joint action in the areas in which the Member States have important interests in common.

(4) The Member States shall support the Union's external and security policy actively and unreservedly in a spirit of loyalty and mutual solidarity. They shall refrain from any action which is contrary to the interests of the Union or likely to impair its effectiveness as a cohesive force in international relations. The Council shall ensure that these principles are complied with.

co-operation depending largely on unanimous decisions taken by the member governments (See Ch. 18, pp. 231–2).

Monetary union was the biggest single policy initiative in the TEU (see below, and Ch. 27, pp. 235–41), but in addition, the Treaty contained a number of other important provisions. In institutional terms, it strengthened the power of the EP through the extension of the co-decision procedure, which gave Parliament greater legislative power in a range of policy areas (Ch. 18, pp. 240–5); and it created a Committee of the Regions and Local Authorities, in recognition of the growing role of sub-national government in EC affairs, and in line with the principle of subsidiarity (see Ch. 18, pp. 237–8). The principle of subsidiarity was itself established as a general rule of the Community by the Treaty, having only applied to the field of environmental policy in the SEA.

The Treaty also introduced the concept of European citizenship, and gave the European citizen the right to circulate and reside freely in the Community; to vote and stand as a candidate for European and municipal elections in the State in which he or she

Extract from Treaty on European Union: Provisions on Co-operation in the Fields of Justice and Home Affairs

Article K.1

For the purposes of achieving the objectives of the Union, in particular the free movement of persons, and without prejudice to the powers of the European Community, Member States shall regard the following areas as matters of common interest:

- asylum policy;
- rules governing the crossing by persons of the external borders of the Member States and the exercise of controls thereon;
- immigration policy and policy regarding nationals of third countries:
  — conditions of entry and movement by nationals of third countries on the territory of Member States;—conditions of residence by nationals of third countries on the territory of Member States, including family reunion and access to employment;
  — combating unauthorized immigration, residence and work by nationals of third countries on the territory of Member States;
  — combating drug addiction in so far as this is not covered by (7) to (9);
  — combating fraud on an international scale in so far as this is not covered by (7) to (9);
  — judicial cooperation in civil matters;
  — judicial cooperation in criminal matters;
  — customs cooperation;
  — police cooperation for the purposes of preventing and combating terrorism, unlawful drug-trafficking and other serious forms of international crime, including if necessary certain aspects of customs cooperation, in connection with the organization of a Union-wide system for exchanging information within a European Police Office (Europol).

resides; to receive protection while in a non-EU country from diplomatic or consular authorities of a member state other than that of his or her state of origin; and to petition the EP or submit a complaint to the Ombudsman (European Union 2005).

In sum, these measures provided a strong political dimension to the economic imperatives that had dominated the integration process to date. More generally, EC competencies were established or extended in a number of areas including education and training, environment, health, and industry. Built on compromise, the TEU included something positive for the EC institutions and for each of the member states involved.

After Maastricht

Although agreed by the heads of governments, the decision to move to a single currency raised concerns within member states. Notably, this decision caused a collapse of support for the EU in Germany itself, where the Deutschmark was held in high regard as the factor that had facilitated post-war prosperity. Problems were made worse when the German currency union took effect, following the decision to convert East German Ostmarks at an artificially high rate into Deutschmarks. This led to inflationary tendencies in the unified Germany, which were suppressed by the Bundesbank (the German central bank) raising interest rates. This in turn solidified resistance within Germany to European monetary union, and therefore to Maastricht. It also pushed the buoyant European economies into recession, which made it more difficult to sell Maastricht to European citizens, who were already rather alarmed by the pace of change that was being proposed.

It was against this background that the Danish referendum in June 1992 rejected the Treaty by 50.7 per cent to 49.3 per cent. In Denmark farmers and fishermen had usually been strong supporters of the EC. Danish opposition to membership had been concentrated in Copenhagen and the other urban areas. In 1992, concern about the reforms of the CAP (see Ch. 25, pp. 392–4) and the Common Fisheries Policy reduced the 'yes' vote in rural areas, and may have been sufficient to make the difference between a narrow 'yes' and a narrow 'no'. It was only when concessions were made on monetary union—giving Denmark similar opt-out rights to those of Britain—and on some other issues of concern, that it was narrowly accepted in a second referendum in May 1993.

Perhaps even more significantly, the treaty was only accepted by the French public by the narrowest of margins (50.3 to 49.7 per cent) in September 1992. Guyomarch, Machin, and Ritchie (1998: 97–8) identified six factors that shaped this outcome: high unemployment and the argument of the No campaign that under the TEU the government would no longer be able to take effective action to create jobs; concern that further integration would lead to a weakening of the level of social security; hostility to the MacSharry reforms of the CAP (see Ch. 25, pp. 392–4); concern at the effects on previously protected sectors of the economy of the opening of the domestic market; concern at what was seen as interference by Brussels with aspects of the traditional French way of life, including the right to produce and eat unpasteurized cheese, and to shoot migrating birds; and splits in all the main parties on their attitude to the TEU, which deprived the electorate of clear leadership. The same authors pointed to the fact that the controversy generated by the referendum led to an increase in interest in the EU. This meant that in the 1994 elections to the EP the turnout in France increased against the EU-wide trend, from 50.4 per cent in 1989 to 55 per cent (Guyomarch, Machin, and Ritchie 1998: 101).

In Germany there was no referendum, but the strength of public concern about monetary union was such that the Bundestag demanded the right to vote on the issue again before any automatic abandonment of the Deutschmark in favour of a common European currency. This move, in effect, unilaterally claimed for Germany the opt-out that Britain and Denmark had negotiated. There was clear evidence of serious public discontent with the Treaty in other member states, not least in Britain.

The Commission after Maastricht

The Commission became caught in this wave of popular discontent about the pace of integration. Delors was personally associated with the proposals on monetary union, which were what caused the greatest concern in Britain and Germany. He had also adopted a very high profile in the run-up to the ratification débâcles. In particular, his ill-timed statement shortly before the Danish referendum, to the effect that small states might have to surrender their right to hold the presidency of the Council of Ministers in a future enlarged EC, was seen as a contributory factor in the negative vote in Denmark.

Delors's comments about small states were actually made in the context of an entirely different debate about enlargement of the EC. The success of the 1992 programme had led to concern among the members of the European Free Trade Association (EFTA) that they were not sharing in the investment boom that 1992 precipitated. Led by Sweden, these states began to broach the question of membership of the EC. Delors was against this because he believed that further enlargement would dilute the degree of unity that could be achieved, and he proposed instead a way in which the EFTA states could become part of the single market without becoming full members of the EC. Membership of the European Economic Area (EEA) would involve the EFTA states adopting all the relevant commercial legislation of the EC, without having any say in its formulation. It was never likely to be a satisfactory agreement for the governments of those states, who would thereby be surrendering sovereignty over large areas of their economies; more significantly, it did not convince the businesses that were already diverting their investments from EFTA to inside the EC. All the EFTA states decided to press ahead with membership applications, but Switzerland withdrew its application after the Swiss people rejected the EEA in a referendum in December 1992; and the Norwegians again rejected membership in a referendum in November 1994.

Sweden, Finland, and Austria became members of the EU on 1 January 1995 (Ch. 31, pp. 543–8). The EU that they joined was not the self-confident one that they had applied to join. As well as disagreement about the future direction, and signs of public disaffection with the whole exercise, the EMS had effectively collapsed during the ratification problems. Britain had withdrawn and floated sterling, and other states had only been able to remain inside because the bands of permitted fluctuation had been widened from 2.25 per cent either side of parity to 15 per cent.

Delors had started his long period as President of the Commission with a considerable triumph in the single-market programme. He ended it with that achievement somewhat overshadowed by the hostile reaction of public opinion in much of Europe to the Maastricht Treaty. Yet whether it was reasonable to blame the Commission for this débâcle is very doubtful. Delors had been upset at the extent to which the Commission had been ignored during the IGCs that prepared the TEU, and had opposed several of the provisions of the Treaty. However, he had adopted such a high profile during his period as President, and had been so closely associated personally with the most unpopular provision of the Treaty, for monetary union, that it was easy for the governments of the member states to pass the blame onto him personally and the institution of which he had been president for ten years.

Delors approached the single-market programme as the first step in a wider programme of integration. There is no doubt that he was familiar with the central concepts of neofunctionalist theory himself, as evidenced in his inaugural address to the sixth annual conference of the Centre for European Policy Studies (CEPS) in 1989 (CEPS 1990: 9–18). Delors expected and intended that the economic liberalization programme would be followed by both monetary union and an extension and deepening of social policy. Here the theme of the tension between contrasting types of capitalism re-enters the story, because the British Prime Minister, Margaret Thatcher, objected strongly to the idea that either of these things was entailed by the 1992 programme. While her objection to monetary union can be interpreted as a reflection of her commitment to an intergovernmental view of the EC, her objection to the social dimension of the single-market programme was clearly a reflection of her adherence to a different concept of how capitalism should be organized in the late twentieth century. That particular debate was to continue after the political demise of Thatcher.

While personal convictions cannot be written out of the explanation for Margaret Thatcher's opposition to both monetary union and an EC social policy, the question of the personal position of her successor, John Major, is less important. Major had little choice but to negotiate opt-outs for Britain on both issues at Maastricht, because of the domestic political constraints that he faced, which were in turn the legacy of the Thatcher years. The primacy of domestic politics, a consistent theme of these chapters, re-emerges here, as does the theme of the conflict between different ways of organizing capitalism.

The collapse of the exchange rate mechanism of EMS gives strong support to the argument that the evolution of the EC can only be understood against the background of an understanding of global economic forces. The globalization of monetary markets, and the increase in the quantity of liquid capital traded across the international exchanges, made it impossible for the system to be maintained in the form that had functioned for years to stabilize European exchange rates, and gave added force to the argument that only a single currency would provide the stability that was necessary to ensure the smooth and complete functioning of the single market, even though the British government chose to interpret the episode as evidence that the infrastructure was not yet in place for a single currency.

Neofunctionalism received some additional support from the applications for membership by the EFTA states. The idea of spillover was extended to cover the idea of geographical spillover, and this appeared to cover the case of the EFTAns. Once the single market was a reality, the attitude and behaviour of businesses changed—and not just of businesses based inside the EC, but also of businesses based in the rest of western Europe. The result was an inflow of investment to the single-market zone, and an imperative for those states that remained outside to join. When the half-way-house of the EEA failed to convince businesses that it would constitute full membership of the single market, the EFTA states were forced to reconsider their position on full membership. Again the relative impotence of the governments of individual states in the face of the forces of contemporary capitalism was illustrated.

It was in this period that the Cold War finally came to an end, although the impact of the uncertainty that this change in the background conditions of the EC produced was only fully felt in the next period, after Maastricht. The collapse of Communism may have given additional momentum to a process that was already under way, in the same way that Algeria, Hungary, and Suez gave additional momentum to the Messina negotiations in the late 1950s; but the 'acceleration of history' did not dramatically change the agenda of the IGCs that were already scheduled.

The Treaty on European Union focused on strengthening the legitimacy and effectiveness of the institutions and brought new areas of cooperation that marked a key stage in the process of European integration. The creation of the second and third pillars in particular marked a significant step forward, but these were explicitly intergovernmental. Yet the very formalization of co-operation in these areas may suggest a neofunctionalist logic at work, for example in the pressures to develop more systematic ways of dealing with effects of greater flows of people across borders caused by the single market programme.

Finally, the developments after Maastricht illustrate a theme that had been largely neglected by governments and analysts until then: the importance of legitimacy for the process of European integration. In a majority of member states, the EC had an independent legitimacy of its own because it represented European integration, which was perceived as a 'good thing'. The aftermath of Maastricht raised questions about whether this was still the case. At the same time, governments did not hesitate to undermine further the legitimacy of the EC/EU by blaming it for unpopular measures that they felt needed to be taken, but for which they were reluctant to accept the responsibility themselves, for fear of weakening their electoral position.

KEY POINTS

Towards Maastricht

- In June 1989, the European Council agreed to Delors's three-stage plan for monetary union by 1999, despite British opposition
- The collapse of Communism in Central and Eastern Europe and the prospect of a reunified Germany focused minds on the political aspects of European integration.
- In 1991, IGCs were held on both monetary union and political union. The proposals of these IGCs were incorporated into the Treaty on European Union, agreed at Maastricht in December 1991.

The Treaty on European Union

- The Treaty on European Union marked a major step on the road to European integration. It committed most of the member states to adopting a single currency, extended EC competencies in a range of areas, strengthened the powers of the European Parliament, created a Committee of the Regions, and introduced the concept of European citizenship.
- The Treaty created a three-pillar structure known as the European Union, consisting of the EC pillar and the intergovernmental pillars of the CFSP and JHA.

After Maastricht

- The decision to move to a single currency caused concern within member states, not least Germany, which had a strong attachment to the Deutschmark
- The TEU was rejected by the Danish following a referendum in 1992 and was only accepted in 1993 following major concessions. A referendum in France (1992) was only narrowly in favour.

□ By the time Austria, Finland, and Sweden became members of in 1995, the EU was not the confident one they had applied to join.

□ The Commission became caught up in the wave of unpopularity affecting the EU. Delors's high profile presidency ensured that he was the focal point of much criticism.

FURTHER READING

The negotiation of the Treaty is analysed by J. Baun, 'The Maastricht Treaty as High Politics: Germany, France and European Integration', *Political Science Quarterly*, 110 (1996): 605–24. A. Moravcsik, *The Choice for Europe: Social Purpose and State Power from Messina to Maastricht* (London: UCL Press, 1998), 379–471.

The aftermath of the signing of the Treaty is analysed in: B. Criddle, 'The French Referendum on the Maastricht Treaty, September 1992', *Parliamentary Affairs*, 46 (1993): 228–38; D. Baker, A. Gamble, and S. Ludlam, '1846–1906–1996? Conservative Splits and European Integration', *Political Quarterly*, 64 (1993): 420–34, and 'The Parliamentary Siege of Maastricht 1993: Conservative Divisions and British Ratification of the Treaty of European Union', *Parliamentary Affairs*, 47 (1994): 37–60; H. Rattinger, 'Public Attitudes towards European Integration in Germany and Maastricht: Inventory and Typology', *Journal of Common Market Studies*, 32 (1994): 525–40.

online resource centre

Visit the Online Resource Centre that accompanies this book for links to more information on Maastricht and the Treaty on European Union.

CHAPTER 14

The Road to Amsterdam: A Flexible Europe?

CHAPTER OVERVIEW

By the mid-1990s, the prospect of 'flexible integration' was clearly on the agenda. A majority of member states signalled their support for a single currency by 1999, but others were reluctant. As an alternative to making no progress until everyone was prepared to proceed, the idea of flexible integration—of allowing those states that wished to go ahead to do so—began to be discussed. The proposed enlargement to include states of central and eastern Europe was the other major issue of the period. Enlargement would bring with it a much greater variety of member states, which raised the prospect of even more issues on which there would be no unanimous agreement, thus providing another argument for allowing greater flexibility. Before looking at the debate over flexible integration, this chapter first examines the debates over monetary union, particularly over what form it would take, and reviews key changes in domestic politics. It then turns to the Treaty of Amsterdam, which contained procedures for flexible integration and attempted to prepare the ground for further enlargement.

> " ... flexibility, according to its proponents, promised a new principle and a new tool for responding to differences in the enthusiasms and capabilities of the member states of the EU to take on new tasks of policy integration. In the period following Maastricht, it had become evident that subsidiarity was both a contested concept and a muddled guide for practice. "
>
> (Wallace 2000: 175)

As the EU expanded to fifteen states on 1 January 1995 (see Ch. 13), Jacques Santer became president of the European Commission for a five-year term. He inherited an agenda that included further enlargement, an inter-governmental conference (IGC) to review the Treaty on European Union (TEU), and monetary union. He also inherited the legacy of the concerns and suspicions that had arisen over the TEU, and the role of the Commission in promoting integration. This led him to adopt as an unofficial mission statement a formula that had already been advocated by the British Foreign Secretary, Douglas Hurd: do less but do it better. However, not everyone in the EU wanted to do less. Despite the unfavourable move in public opinion, voices in both France and Germany were raised in favour of an arrangement that would allow those member states that wished to do so to forge ahead with closer integration, and not be held back by those states that were more hesitant. The field of monetary union was central to this issue.

Monetary Union

The agreement on monetary union that had been reached at Maastricht represented a compromise between the positions of states with very different perspectives on the issue. Those compromises had to be sorted out in order for the programme for a single currency to go ahead. During 1995, the decisions on the detail of the monetary union began to be settled, generally in favour of German views. These included agreement that the location of the European Central Bank (ECB) would be in Frankfurt, and that the new currency would be called the Euro, not the ecu as the French wished, because that name was not liked by the German public. More significantly, during 1996 it was agreed that the convergence criteria set out in the TEU (Ch. 27, pp. 435–6) would have to be met precisely, with no fudging of the issue, and that there would continue to be a stability pact after the single currency came into existence. French hopes for more political control over the monetary policy of the ECB were also dashed (Ch. 27, p. 438).

Continuing economic recession in Europe hindered the efforts of those member states that wished to participate in the single currency to meet the convergence criteria. During 1995, it was decided to abandon the earlier of the two possible starting dates for the single currency, i.e. 1997, because it was obvious that not enough states, if any, would fully meet the convergence criteria by then. There was also doubt about how many would achieve the targets by 1999, the second of the two possible starting dates. In France and Belgium the efforts of the governments to reduce the level of their budget deficits to the target of 3 per cent led to strikes and disruption. The imposition of lower public spending on economies that already had high levels of unemployment was a sure recipe for political problems.

However, in the course of 1996 and 1997 a surprising number of states did manage either to achieve or to approach the targets. This caused concern in Germany, because the idea that Italy in particular could possibly observe the conditions of the stability pact in perpetuity was not considered credible. There was a fear that the German public might reject a Euro of which Italy was a part. As the trend in the Italian economy moved in the direction of the targets, so the insistence of the Germans that the targets be treated as absolutes grew. On the budget deficit, which was treated as the most important criterion, the German Finance Minister, Theo Waigel, and the President of the Bundesbank, Hans Tietmeyer, insisted that 3 per cent meant exactly 3 per cent or less, not even 3.1 per cent. This was clearly an attempt to set the target at a level that Italy would not be able to reach. The irony was that Germany missed the deficit target of 3 per cent in 1996, and looked like missing it again in 1997. A single currency without German participation was inconceivable, yet the continuing problems posed for the German economy by the absorption of East Germany threatened to disqualify it from membership on its own criteria.

All of this caused some glee within the British Conservative government, which found the whole project of monetary union extremely difficult. For domestic political reasons the government could not join the single currency, even if it met the convergence criteria; but if the project went ahead without it there was a risk that British economic interests would be damaged, and that British political influence within the EU would be permanently diminished. So it was with a certain air of wishing rather than predicting that Prime Minister John Major had said in an article in 1993 that 'economic and monetary union is not realisable in present circumstances' (*The Economist*, 25 September 1993). While there might have been some justification for this view in 1993, by the end of 1997 it was apparent that the single currency would start on schedule in 1999, and although it was not clear which member states would be members, it began to look as though all those that wished to join, except Greece, would be in a position to do so.

Domestic Politics

There were significant domestic political developments during this period that affected the position of key member states on the EU. In Germany the government of Chancellor Kohl continued uninterrupted, but the authority of the Chancellor was called into question by a number of difficulties on policy and a number of electoral setbacks. In Britain the Conservative government of John Major experienced a series of defeats in parliamentary by-elections, which reduced its majority. This, combined with the increasingly militant anti-EU position of a significant number of its own MPs, left the government with little room for manoeuvre, and its discourse on the EU became increasingly negative. Just prior to the Amsterdam European Council in June 1997, at which the Treaty of Amsterdam was agreed, the Conservative government lost office in a general election and was replaced by a Labour government under Tony Blair.

In France there were two changes of government. In May 1995 the Gaullist Jacques Chirac was elected President in succession to the Socialist François Mitterrand. There was already a conservative majority in the National Assembly, from which Chirac nominated Alain Juppé as his Prime Minister. However, when parliamentary elections were held in April 1997, the Socialist Party won the largest share of seats, and formed a coalition with the Communists.

Chirac's initial actions as president were viewed with some concern in Germany. His decision to permit the testing of nuclear weapons in the Pacific met with protests throughout the EU, including in Germany. Only the British government supported Chirac on this. Together with the common experience of working together in Bosnia, this incident led to a measure of agreement between France and Britain. Chirac at one stage suggested that France might learn something from the British approach to the EU. However, he gradually came back into line with the position of his predecessor.

Flexible Integration

During 1994 the German Christian Democrat (CDU/CSU) parliamentary group produced a paper, jointly authored by Karl Lamers and Wolfgang Schauble, which suggested that a hard core of member states that wished to go ahead with closer integration should do so. A similar approach, envisaging a 'Europe of concentric circles' with France and Germany at its centre, had been outlined by the French Prime Minister, Edouard Balladur in an interview published two days before the German paper.

These ideas were prompted primarily by the increasingly obstructionist stand taken by the British Prime Minister, John Major, on all suggestions for further integration. Shackled by a small parliamentary majority and with a significant number of his own backbench MPs hostile to further integration of Britain with the rest of the EU, Major had become an increasingly unco-operative partner. Faced with the apparent determination of the French and German governments to push ahead with monetary union, and with other measures that would be unacceptable to the parliamentary Conservative Party, Major himself had begun to contemplate the possibility of extending the arrangements that had been agreed at Maastricht for Britain to opt out of both monetary union and an integrated social policy.

In September 1994 Major gave the William and Mary Lecture at the University of Leiden. He used it as an opportunity to expound the idea of flexible integration. On the basis that trying to force all the member states into the same mould would crack that mould, he called for an agreement that if some states wanted to integrate more closely, or more rapidly than others, they should be allowed to do so. On the other hand, it was important that no state should be excluded from participation in closer integration in any policy sector if it was willing and able to participate. This principle led Major to reject the idea of a 'hard core' Europe, although he did advocate a hard core of basic policies from which no state could opt out. These were international trade obligations, the single market, and environmental protection. Looking ahead, Major argued that bringing prosperity and stability to the states of central and eastern Europe was a historic task that required the enlargement of the EU. That enlargement would produce such a variety of member states in size, shape, economic and industrial profile, philosophy, history, and culture that it would require the introduction of the flexibility that he was advocating.

In January 1995, the former French President Valéry Giscard d'Estaing published two articles in the daily *Le Figaro* in which he went further and argued for a new Treaty with an explicitly federal aim. Since British membership, the existing EU had lost sight of that ultimate objective. Giscard believed that it would be impossible to get back on course for a federal Europe so long as the British government was able to block every step. The new treaty would be separate from the EU Treaties, and would exclude Britain and other countries that were reluctant to embrace the federal vocation of European integration. In common with the previous contributors to this debate, Giscard also mentioned the impending further enlargement of the EU to the east. This he considered inevitable; but in common with John Major, he believed that it would be impossible to proceed down a federal road with so many and so diverse a range of members. So as well as British obstructionism, the proposed enlargement figured prominently in this debate about the need for flexibility.

Enlargement

All member states paid lip-service to the principle of enlargement of the EU to the east, but some states were keener than others. For Germany the enlargement was an absolute priority; it was also strongly supported by Britain and the Scandinavian countries. However, France, Italy, and Spain had reservations. When the shift was made from the general issue of supporting enlargement to the discussion of the detailed steps that were needed to make a reality of the aspiration, even the strongest supporters were not necessarily prepared to accept the full implications.

Germany's commitment to enlargement was based largely on security considerations. Following reunification, Germany was once again a central European state, having borders with Poland and the Czech Republic. Instability in the region would be right on Germany's doorstep, and admitting its nearest neighbours to the EU was seen as a way of guaranteeing their stability. There were also economic considerations. Before the First World War, German companies and banks had been the leading foreign investors in central Europe, and soon after the collapse of Communism, German investment began to flow into the area. Guaranteeing the security of those investments was another reason for the German government's support of membership for the central European states.

British motives for welcoming enlargement were less immediately obvious, but reflected a combination of security, economic, and political considerations. In terms of security, British governments since the war had continued to support the principle of global stabilization even where British investments were not immediately involved. This was a habit of statecraft that dated back to the period before the First World War when Britain was the hegemonic power in the world and shouldered responsibility for policing the international capitalist system. That responsibility had largely passed to the United States in the period since the Second World War, but British governments had consistently supported such efforts at global stabilization. In the situation after the end of the

Cold War, the US administrations of both Bush and Clinton made it clear that they expected the EU states to play a leading role in stabilizing central and eastern Europe, and membership of the EU was specifically pressed by the Clinton administration as a means of achieving this.

In economic terms, British support for further enlargement reflected the hope that British business would be able to profit from access to a larger market. Politically, however, this enlargement would also imply a looser EU less likely to move in a federal direction. Thus in both economic and political terms, eastern enlargement suited the Conservative government of John Major.

Concerns of Member States about Enlargement

While the governments of France and the Mediterranean member states could see the arguments for enlargement to the east, and even accepted them, they were apprehensive about the effect that such an enlargement would have on the EU. First, they were concerned that an eastern enlargement would shift the balance of power in the EU decisively to the north, especially coming immediately after the accession of Austria, Finland, and Sweden. Second, and related to the first point, they were concerned that the problems of the Mediterranean, which affected them more than instability in the east, would be relegated to a secondary issue. Instability in North Africa, particularly civil war in Algeria, were already having an impact on them in the form of refugees, and threats to their companies' investments in the region. Third, they feared that EU funds that came to them through the CAP and the structural funds would be diverted to support for the central and east European economies.

The concern that attention would be diverted from the problems of the Mediterranean was recognized by the German government when it held the presidency of the EU in the second half of 1994. Agreement was reached at the Essen meeting of the European Council in December 1994 to launch an initiative on North Africa and the Middle East. This assumed more tangible form during 1995 under the successive French and Spanish presidencies, culminating in a major conference in Barcelona from 23 to 29 November 1995 involving the EU member states, the Maghreb states (Algeria, Morocco, and Tunisia), Israel, Jordan, Lebanon, Syria, Turkey, Cyprus, and Malta. The central and eastern European states were also represented. The conference agreed on a stability pact for the Middle East on the model of the Conference on Security and Co-operation in Europe (CSCE) and the EU agreed to contribute $6bn. in aid and $6bn. in **European Investment Bank** (EIB) loans to the economic development of the region.

The problem of accepting the implications of a commitment to enlargement to the east were apparent in November 1995 when the Commission proposed that agricultural imports from six central and east European states (Bulgaria, the Czech Republic, Hungary, Poland, Romania, and Slovakia) be increased by 10 per cent a year. Britain, Denmark, The Netherlands, and Sweden supported the proposal. France and the Mediterranean member states opposed it, indicating that they would only be prepared to accept an increase of 5 per cent a year. Germany, which was ostensibly the strongest supporter of enlargement, joined the Mediterranean states in opposing the Commission's proposal. This indicated the strength of the farming lobby in Germany, and the fragmented nature of decision making in the country, which allowed the Agriculture Ministry to adopt a line so clearly incompatible with the official policy as enunciated by the Chancellor's office.

The same contradiction in policy emerged after July 1997 when the Commission published its *Agenda 2000* report on the future direction of the EU in the likely context of enlargement. The German Farm Minister, Ignaz Kiechle, publicly stated that the proposed reforms of the CAP were unnecessary. He received no reprimand for this from Chancellor Kohl. In addition to the reform of key policies, the eastern enlargement had implications for the decision-making procedures of the EU. This came to be one of the key issues in the IGC that led up to the Treaty of Amsterdam. (On enlargement, see also Ch. 31.)

The 1996 IGC

Originally the 1996 IGC was intended to review the working of the TEU (Ch. 13, pp. 169–171). Provision for such a review was written into the agreements that were reached at Maastricht in December 1991. However, nobody expected the ratification of the TEU to take as long as it did, with the result that the review started after only two and a half years of experience of the new arrangements. The difficulties in ratifying the TEU (Ch. 13, pp. 171–172) also meant that there was little appetite for further fundamental change. Increasingly the IGC came to be seen as primarily about preparing the ground for the eastern enlargement. There were several institutional issues that needed to be addressed if the EU were to enlarge to over twenty members: the size of the Commission and the EP; the rotation of the presidency of the Council; the extent of qualified majority voting (QMV); and the weighting of votes under QMV.

The Commission already had twenty members in 1995, and that was already too many for the number of portfolios available, as Jacques Santer found out when he tried to allocate responsibilities without upsetting either national sensibilities or the *amour propre* of his colleagues in the College of Commissioners. Enlargement threatened to produce an unwieldy organization. The British government offered to relinquish its second Commissioner if the other large states would agree to do so, but this was not an easy concession for the others. For Italy and Spain in particular, having two Commissioners was a matter of national pride, singling out their countries as larger member states on a par with Germany, France, and Britain. Even if there had been unanimous agreement to dispense with the second Commissioners, the problem of too many Commissioners would have remained.

The EP would also become unwieldy if the same rough formula that had been used up to the 1995 enlargement were applied to further member states. Clearly there had to be some limit put on the numbers; but that had implications for the existing distribution of seats.

With twelve member states, and with the presidency of the Council changing every six months, there were six years between presidencies for any one state (see Ch. 20, pp. 287–90). This meant that all the expertise that had been acquired for one presidency was lost by the time the next one came round. There was also concern that the next enlargement would involve mostly small states, as had the 1995 enlargement. Small states often had problems with servicing the presidency. The problems had been eased since the Troika system had come into operation, whereby the present, previous, and immediate future presidents co-operated (see Ch. 20, p. 289). However, the impending enlargement heralded a situation in which there might not be a large state in the Troika for much of the time.

On QMV, the German and French governments wanted to see an extension to cover areas under the Justice and Home Affairs (JHA) pillar of the TEU, but the British Conservative government was adamantly opposed to any extension of QMV. The British government was also, along with Spain, one of the strongest advocates of a re-weighting of the votes under QMV. Because the number of votes allocated to a state was not directly proportional to its population, the increase in the number of small member states had produced a situation in which measures could be passed under QMV with the support of the representatives of a decreasing proportion of the total population of the EU. In the original EC of six states, votes representing 70 per cent of the population were needed to pass a measure; by 1995 this had been reduced to 58.3 per cent; and on the basis of reasonable assumptions about the identity of the members, and therefore about the numbers of votes to which they would be entitled on the existing formula, with twenty-six member states the proportion required could be as low as 50.3 per cent. The French government supported the idea of a re-weighting of votes, but the German Chancellor was hesitant because of the concern expressed by the smaller member states that this would be yet another step towards downgrading their role.

Beyond these specific institutional issues, each member state went to the IGC with particular issues that it wished to push. Sweden, Denmark, and the Netherlands were concerned to increase the accountability and transparency of Council business, and proposed that a freedom of information clause be written into the Treaty. Sweden was also a leading mover in pressing for a chapter on employment policy to be added to the Treaty. In March 1996 the Swedish government called a meeting in Oslo to build support for this proposal: France, Germany, Britain, and Italy were not invited. Britain wanted reform to the working of the European Court of Justice (ECJ), having suffered several adverse judgments at its hands. Britain and France both pressed for an enhanced role for national parliaments in the policy-making process. France and Germany pressed the flexibility issue hard; they also co-operated in putting forward proposals to move towards incorporating the Western European Union (WEU) into the EU, something that was strongly opposed by the neutral member states (Austria, Ireland, and Sweden) and by Britain.

The IGC was preceded by a 'Reflection Group', which met in the second half of 1995 under the Spanish presidency. This consisted of representatives of the Foreign Ministers and two members of the EP. It had a remit to seek the views of other institutions on progress towards European union, and possible amendments to the TEU, and to prepare a report on the issues that should form the agenda of the IGC. When he reported on the work of the Group in December 1995, the Spanish Foreign Minister Carlos Westendorp said that there was agreement that the IGC should not aim at fundamental reform, but be about necessary changes; in particular it should be seen as one part of the process of eastern enlargement. Werner Hoyer, the German representative on the Reflection Group, indicated publicly that the work of the Group had soon deteriorated into an exchange of national positions, and warned that there was a risk of the IGC turning into a confrontation between integrationists and intergovernmentalists.

The IGC and the British Beef Dispute

The IGC itself opened officially in Turin on 29 March 1996. The special European Council that was called to inaugurate it was dominated, though, by the ban on exports of British beef that had been imposed in the aftermath of the announcement that bovine spongiform encephalopathy (BSE) in cattle, with which British herds were particularly infected, could be the cause of Creutzfeldt–Jakob disease (CJD) in humans. As British efforts to get the ban lifted made little progress over the coming weeks, John Major threatened to block progress in the IGC, and to refuse to sign any Treaty that emerged from it until the ban was lifted. His government did in fact veto just about every item of EU business over which it could exercise a veto until an agreement was reached on a phased lifting of the ban.

This incident marked the final breach between the British Conservative government and the rest of the EU. Patience was already exhausted before Major threatened to block agreement on a new Treaty unless two changes were made to the existing one. First, he demanded agreement to allow the reversal of a decision of the ECJ that a directive on a 48-hour maximum working week must apply to Britain, despite the British government's opt-out from the social protocol, because it was a health-and-safety issue and so covered by the SEA. Secondly, he demanded that changes were made to the common fisheries policy, to prevent fishing boats from other member states buying quotas from British fishermen.

There were some indications that the IGC was deliberately prolonged into 1997 in the hope that the British general election would produce a change of government, which it did. The Labour government under Tony Blair indicated immediately that while its priorities would remain those of its predecessor, it would not block a Treaty over any issue other than that Britain must be allowed to retain its border controls. The way was thus cleared for agreement on the text of a new Treaty at the European Council in Amsterdam in June 1997.

The Treaty of Amsterdam

Agreement was reached at Amsterdam on a rather modest Treaty. In particular, no agreement could be reached on the institutional reforms that were believed to be essential to pave the way for enlargement. Also, there was little extension of QMV because Chancellor Kohl retreated from his earlier advocacy of the principle, and actually blocked its extension to cover industrial policy, social policy, and certain aspects of the free movement of labour.

As a result of what may have been an oversight, the failure to extend QMV to these three areas did not lead to withdrawal of the linked proposal to increase the powers of the EP in the areas, so when the EP was given the right to amend or reject proposed legislation in two-dozen areas that were brought under co-decision for the first time, the three areas that were not to be subject to QMV were still included.

Dutch plans to extend majority voting into eleven policy areas, ranging from cultural activities to industrial policy, ran into German resistance. Kohl insisted that these extensions would undermine the position of the German Länder. The only two extensions of QMV that were agreed were for research programmes and compensatory aid for imports of raw materials. In addition, new areas were agreed in which QMV would apply from the start, namely: countering fraud; encouraging customs co-operation; collating statistics; and laying down rules for the free movement of personal data.

On the number of Commissioners, a compromise was reached that if more than two and fewer than six new members joined, the Commission would continue to have one representative from each member state, although Spain insisted that it would only surrender its second Commissioner in return for changes in the weighting of votes in the Council, which could not be agreed.

Rules on allowing flexible integration were agreed. In the first pillar, if a group of member states wished to proceed with closer integration in a sector, but others did not wish to proceed, those who did wish to go ahead could do so provided that the Council of Ministers agreed to such a proposal by QMV, although if any member state insisted that the development would jeopardize its vital national interests it could veto the move. In the second pillar—the Common Foreign and Security Policy (CFSP)—the system would be 'constructive abstention'. This would allow a group of member states to undertake a joint action in the name of the EU, if those member states that did not feel they could take part were prepared not to vote against but to abstain, on the understanding that they would not then be required to contribute to the action (see Ch. 30, p. 523). In the third pillar, complete freedom of movement was pledged for all individuals within the EU, but the UK and Ireland were allowed to retain border controls. Decisions on immigration, visas, and asylum were to be subject to unanimity for at least five years, and then reviewed with a view to introducing more flexible arrangements, but with any member state being allowed to apply a veto on changing the procedure.

On CFSP, it was agreed that the Council Secretary-General would represent the EU to the outside world. QMV would be used on implementing foreign policy measures, but any state that believed its vital national interests were at stake could exercise a veto. The WEU might be incorporated into the EU in the future, but NATO was reaffirmed as central to Europe's defence. The Amsterdam Treaty also amended the TEU to distinguish between, on the one hand, deciding the principles and general guidelines of the CFSP, and common strategies in pursuit of these; and, on the other, the adoption of joint actions, common positions, and implementing decisions (Ch. 30).

Finally, it was agreed that a zone of freedom, security, and justice for EU citizens would come into force within five years of ratification. Member states that violated fundamental freedoms then faced loss of voting rights in the Council of Ministers.

CONCLUSION

The post-Maastricht period prepared the ground for flexible integration as the EU entered a period of tremendous uncertainty in both its global context and its internal functioning. Enlargement to eastern Europe was the biggest item on the post-Maastricht agenda, and threatened or promised to transform the EU itself beyond all recognition, clearly indicating the importance of external developments for the future of European integration. A definite tension developed between the will of all member states to consolidate democracy and capitalism in eastern and central Europe and the willingness of any member state to accept economic sacrifices to allow that enlargement to happen. Willing the end did not appear to mean necessarily willing the means. Domestic politics assumed priority too often when it came to trying to agree the details of reforms to the common policies and to the central institutions that everyone agreed were necessary to facilitate the enlargement.

As with the EC and the Mediterranean enlargements in the 1970s, eastern enlargement in the forthcoming twenty-first century was part of the enhanced security role for the EU in the world after the decline of US hegemony. So was the need to make progress on the CFSP, which had been incorporated into the TEU. Here immediate national economic interests were less directly involved, so there was the prospect of progress; but national cultural differences emerged, as did differing national security interests. The CFSP forum also provided Britain with an opportunity to be more centrally involved with the EU, alongside France as the two states with the most efficient professional armies. Germany remained hampered by a suspicion throughout central Europe of Germans in uniforms, and a reluctance among the German people themselves to see German forces committed to military operations in other countries.

The concern within Germany was partly about a re-emergence of German militarism, but it was also about the impact on the legitimacy of the EU if German lives should be lost in pursuit of objectives set through the CFSP. The attitudes of the publics of France and Britain were different, being accustomed to their national forces forming part of UN peacekeeping operations. The legitimacy of the EU in Germany was severely shaken by the decision to adopt the single currency, and by what appeared to be the centralization of functions that had previously been the responsibility of the Länder. It was this last concern that caused Helmut Kohl to backtrack at Amsterdam from his previous insistence that there should be more QMV.

Concern to prevent further slippage of powers from the national or sub-national level to the supranational level was apparent throughout the EU by the time of Amsterdam, indicating the increasing emphasis on intergovernmentalism. There were the first indications that a new form of co-operation was emerging, one that cast the Commission in a different role as an impartial arbiter and referee of agreements for co-ordinated national action rather than as enforcer of legally binding commitments, a development that would also have implications for the role of the ECJ.

KEY POINTS

Monetary Union

☐ In 1995, details of monetary union began to emerge. The ECB would be located in Frankfurt and the single currency would be called the 'Euro'.

- [ ] Although recession hindered attempts by some states to meet the convergence criteria, the single currency stayed on course for a 1999 launch.

Domestic Politics

- [ ] Significant domestic political developments during this period affected the position of key member states on the EU and shaped the prospects for flexible integration.

Flexible Integration

- [ ] In 1994 the idea of flexible integration became widespread. This was the notion that some member states should integrate further and faster than others.

Enlargement

- [ ] While member states were generally supportive of further enlargement to include countries of central and eastern Europe, there were a number of concerns over the impact this would have on key policies, such as agriculture, and also on decision-making procedures.

The 1996 IGC

- [ ] The 1996 IGC focused on the institutional changes necessary to prepare for further enlargement. This IGC was also marked by conflict over the British 'beef' crisis, which resulted in the Major government blocking agreement on a range of issues.

The Treaty of Amsterdam

- [ ] Resulting from the 1996 IGC, this Treaty was relatively modest in scope. In particular, it did not contain the decision-making reforms deemed necessary for enlargement.

FURTHER READING

Useful guides to the Treaty of Amsterdam are European Commission, *The Amsterdam Treaty: A Comprehensive Guide* (1999) and A. Duff, *The Treaty of Amsterdam: Text and Commentary* (London: Federal Trust/Sweet and Maxwell, 1997). On the politics that led up to the Treaty, see G. Edwards and A. Pijpers, *The Politics of European Treaty Reform: The 1996 Intergovernmental Conference and Beyond* (London, and Washington, DC: Pinter, 1997).

A reaction to Amsterdam from an intergovernmentalist perspective is given in A. Moravcsik and K. Nicolaïdes, 'Explaining the Treaty of Amsterdam: Interests, Influences, Institutions', *Journal of Common Market Studies*, 37 (1999): 59–85. Other analyses are offered by E. Philippart and G. Edwards, 'The Provisions on Closer Co-operation in the Treaty of Amsterdam', *Journal of Common Market Studies*, 37 (1999): 87–108 and Y. Devuyst, 'The Community-Method after Amsterdam', *Journal of Common Market Studies*, 37 (1999): 109–20.

online resource centre   **Visit the Online Resource Centre that accompanies this book for links to more information on flexible integration and the Treaty of Amsterdam.**

CHAPTER 15

From Amsterdam to Nice: Preparing for Enlargement

CHAPTER OVERVIEW

Following the agreement of the Amsterdam Treaty, the agenda of the EU was initially dominated by the opening of enlargement negotiations. However, the post-Amsterdam period began with both a symbolic milestone and an embarrassing setback. The milestone was the start of monetary union, thirty years after it had first been declared an objective of the EC at the Hague summit in 1969. The embarrassment was a crisis that led to the resignation of the European Commission. The period also saw significant steps taken in the formulation of a European Security and Defence Policy, and the declaration of a new approach to increasing the economic competitiveness of the EU. The period concluded with the longest European Council in history, which led to the Treaty of Nice. In these negotiations, concerns with flexible integration were soon overtaken by more traditional battles over institutional reform.

> " The Treaty of Nice may have paved the way for enlargement, but to many it provided sub-optimal solutions to the institutional challenges posed by a significantly larger EU
> **(Phinnemore 2003: 58).**

Following the Amsterdam European Council, momentum quickly began to build towards enlargement. Soon after the European Council meeting, in July 1997, the Commission produced a report entitled *Agenda 2000*, which outlined the internal reforms that would be needed to prepare the EU for enlargement, and the Commission's formal Opinions on the preparedness of the applicant states. However, before the enlargement process took its next significant step at the Helsinki European Council in December 1999, the EU achieved a major milestone in the field of monetary union and experienced a major setback in credibility through a crisis in the Commission.

The Euro

In January 1999, the Euro came into operation for eleven member states—Austria, Belgium, Finland, France, Germany, Ireland, Italy, Luxemburg, The Netherlands, Portugal, and Spain. This meant that the Euro became the official currency of these states, although national notes and coins continued in circulation until 2002. Greece was initially excluded from the Eurozone by failing to meet the convergence criteria, but its application to join was approved by the European Council in Santa Maria de Feira (Portugal) in June 2000, and it became a full member in January 2001. Britain, Denmark, and Sweden chose not to join the single currency. Britain and Denmark had negotiated opt-outs, while Sweden excluded itself on the technicality that it had not been a member of the ERM for two years and as such was not eligible. There were concerns over Italy's use of a one-off 'Euro-tax' to ensure it met the budget-deficit criterion in the qualifying financial year; and both Belgium and Italy had debt ratios that appeared to go beyond the criteria (see Ch. 27, pp. 440–1). Despite all of this, the completion of monetary union, almost thirty years after the Hague Summit had made it an explicit objective, was a considerable achievement.

Although the single currency came into existence more smoothly than many economists predicted, it soon ran into difficulties. The external value of the Euro fell steadily against the US dollar, and the 'Eurozone' itself began to exhibit some of the problems of having a single interest rate for such a diverse economic area. National economies on the fringes of the zone, particularly those of Spain and Ireland, began to experience the symptoms of repressed inflation, with rapidly rising property prices and shortages of labour. At the same time, the core economies of Germany and France were experiencing sluggish growth.

It was in this context that, as soon as the new currency came into existence, Oskar Lafontaine and Dominique Strauss-Kahn, Finance Ministers of Germany and France respectively, pressed the ECB to lower interest rates to stimulate growth (see Ch. 27,

p. 439). The ECB and its President Wim Duisenberg vigorously resisted such interference, though, and the pressure was reduced after Lafontaine resigned in March 1999. Nevertheless, a majority of states within the Eurozone continued to experience lower rates of growth and higher unemployment than the economies of those EU member states—Britain, Denmark, and Sweden—that remained outside the single currency. Against such a background it was perhaps unsurprising that the Danish people rejected membership of the Euro in a referendum in September 2000. The Swedes would follow suit three years later and the British government delayed holding a referendum on joining (see Ch. 16).

The Commission in Crisis

If the Amsterdam Treaty (Ch. 14) represented little advance on key areas of institutional reform, the Commission crisis of 1999 put the transparency and accountability of EU institutions under severe scrutiny. The report of the Court of Auditors on the 1996 budget had led the EP's Budget Committee in March 1998 to refuse to recommend discharge of the budget by the whole EP (the process of discharging the budget is explained in Chapter 18, pp. 238–40). The Committee was particularly concerned about alleged mismanagement of the Humanitarian Aid budget, which at that time had been under the control of Commissioner Manuel Marin, who was by 1998 a Vice-President of the Commission.

In October 1998 President Santer, together with Emma Bonino, who was by then in charge of the European Community Humanitarian Aid Office (ECHO), appeared before the Budget Committee to admit that an investigation by the Commission's internal fraud unit had indeed revealed irregularities in the expenditure of funds allocated to ECHO. In fact, ECHO had apparently not audited any of its external contracts until 1995, and the Commission therefore had no guarantees of how money had been spent between 1993 and 1995. The internal fraud unit had discovered that at least two contracts, for personnel and equipment for operations in Bosnia and in Africa, had been completely fictitious, and that most of the money appeared to have been spent on extra administrative staff for the Brussels office. However, some 400,000 to 600,000 ecus of the money had proved untraceable.

Despite an offer from Santer to re-create the fraud office as a separate agency outside of the Commission, the EP in December 1998 refused discharge of the 1996 budget. It expressed concern about the ECHO affair, and also about what appeared to be impropriety in making appointments under the LEONARDO Youth Training Programme, which was the responsibility of the French Commissioner, Edith Cresson. In the meantime, the Court of Auditor's report on the 1997 budget had appeared, and indicated that some 5 per cent of total EC expenditure could not adequately be accounted for.

The EP laid down a motion of censure on the Commission, which did not achieve the two-thirds majority required to remove the Commission from office, but which did achieve the largest vote for a motion of censure since the EC began: 232, with 293 against and 27 abstentions. This result was despite the Socialist Group, the largest single party group in the EP, officially deciding to vote against the motion. In an attempt to head off the censure, Santer produced a plan of action, which he put to the EP on 11 January 1999. This involved:

- new codes of conduct for Commissioners, their *cabinets*, and all Commission staff;
- the setting up of an independent fraud unit outside of the Commission itself;
- an audit of all the Commission's activities and departments, leading to proposals for restructuring;
- a promise of proposals to modernize the administration of the Commission;
- a review of budgetary management and of appointments to senior positions;
- the negotiation of an agreement with the EP on how MEPs would be kept informed on financial expenditure, and how to ensure effective EP scrutiny of spending.

This compromise at first seemed to have averted a crisis, but in March 1999 a committee of five independent experts that had been set up to look into the internal management of the Commission issued a damaging report, which suggested widespread malfunctioning of the system. Santer and his whole College of Commissioners then resigned, just after midnight on 15/16 March. The European Parliament claimed this as a great victory for its persistence in scrutinizing the activities of the Commission.

The European Council's preferred candidate to succeed Santer was the former prime minister of Italy, Romano Prodi, whose candidature was approved by the European Parliament in May 1999 by a majority of 392 to 72. Prodi's appointment was delayed by a case in the Italian courts over what proved to be false accusations of corruption relating to the Italian privatization programme. He came to the job in September 1999 committed to cleaning up the Commission's image and made clear his intention to discipline errant Commissioners. Prodi stated that his own staff would be multinational, to avoid claims of national 'cronyism'.

Enlargement

In December 1999, the Helsinki European Council agreed to open accession negotiations with Bulgaria, Latvia, Lithuania, Malta, Romania, and Slovakia, and also recognized Turkey as an applicant country (see Ch. 31, p. 548). In January 2000, accession negotiations with these states opened in Brussels. The key issues outlined by the EU delegation were the importance of formal transposal and implementation of Community law; ensuring effective functioning of the single market and EU policies; and alignment with EU policies on relations with third countries and international organizations. Later that year, in October, the Commission provided the Council with its report on enlargement, which consisted of progress reports on the preparations of each country and outlined the requirements for Turkey to begin accession negotiations. The Gothenburg European

Council of June 2001 agreed the framework for the successful completion of the enlargement negotiations, and in December of the same year the Council signalled its intention to conclude negotiations with the candidate countries by the end of 2002 so that they could participate in the 2004 European Parliament elections.

In order to be ready to take as many as twelve new members, the EU had to deal with some difficult issues requiring reforms of both policies and institutions. Two policy issues were particularly crucial to the prospects for enlargement: agriculture and the structural funds. The institutional questions were those that were already apparent at the time of the EFTA enlargement: the weighting of votes under QMV, and the size of the blocking minority; the abandonment of the national veto in more policy sectors; and the size of the Commission.

Agriculture accounted for 25 per cent of the GDP of the applicant states, with production concentrated in the products that were already the most problematic for the EU: meat, dairy products, and cereals. Productivity within the applicant states varied considerably, but was generally lower than in the EU. Application of the CAP directly to the new entrants would be likely to encourage higher output. It would have an unsustainable impact on the cost of the CAP, and would generate increased surpluses in the products that were already most of a problem. At the same time, the higher cost of food to the consumer would have an inflationary effect in the new entrants, where expenditure on food accounted for a higher proportion of total household expenditure than it did in the west. The struggle to get the existing member states to accept the sort of far-reaching reform of the CAP that was necessary to pave the way for enlargement is told in Chapter 25.

The reform of the structural funds was similarly dogged by the refusal of existing beneficiaries from the policies to accept that they would have to give up much of their funding in order to allow enlargement to take place within existing budgetary ceilings. The Commission's proposals unveiled in March 1998 would result in no state losing more than one-third of its eligibility for funding in terms of the percentage of its population covered by Objective 2. Long and generous transitional arrangements were made for regions that would lose Objective 1 status. Even so, it proved difficult to get agreement, leading the Commissioner, Monika Wulf-Mathies, to warn a Council of Ministers meeting in Glasgow in June 1998 that governments had to stop pretending that enlargement would be possible without making sacrifices on structural funding (see also Ch. 18 on Regional and Structural Policies).

Difficulties in getting agreement on policy issues were paralleled by problems in getting agreement on the institutional reforms that would also be necessary to facilitate enlargement. The Amsterdam European Council of June 1997 (Ch. 14, pp. 185–6) ended one IGC that was supposed to resolve these issues, but without agreement on them. A new IGC was convened in February 2000, and met throughout the year, but it also had produced no agreement on the most controversial issues by the time of the Nice European Council in December.

Other Developments

There were significant policy developments in this period in the areas of economic and social policy (with the agreement on 'the Lisbon strategy'), the Common Foreign and Security Policy (CFSP), and Justice and Home Affairs.

The Lisbon Strategy

In March 2000, a special European Council held in Lisbon agreed to a new EU strategy on employment, economic reform, and social cohesion, with the goal of making the EU 'the most competitive and dynamic knowledge-based economy in the world' by 2010. Its adoption was justified with reference to the challenge of globalization:

The European Union is confronted with a quantum shift resulting from globalization and the challenges of a new knowledge-driven economy. These challenges are affecting every aspect of people's lives and require a radical transformation of the European economy.
(Presidential Conclusions, Lisbon Special European Council, 23–4 March, para. 1)

The outcome subsequently became known variously as the Lisbon Strategy, the Lisbon Process, or the Lisbon Agenda. Success of the strategy depended on strengthening investment in research and development, reducing bureaucracy to stimulate innovation and entrepreneurship, and improving the employment rate to 70 per cent overall, including a minimum of 60 per cent for women.

Two features of the strategy were particularly significant. First, economic competitiveness and social cohesion were placed side-by-side as objectives. Critics of the strategy from the left maintained that the economic competitiveness elements represented a victory for the advocates of an Anglo-Saxon model of capitalism, while critics from the right argued that the social cohesion elements represented a victory for the advocates of a 'social Europe'. It seems more likely that the new approach represented less the victory of one model of capitalism over the other than a political compromise between the positions of the left and right. Second, the Lisbon strategy was to be pursued through what the Presidency Conclusions to the summit described as the 'Open Method of Co-ordination' (OMC). The OMC is described in more detail in Chapter 24 (pp. 357–8). Its main features, as delineated at Lisbon, were common guidelines to be translated into national policies, combined with periodic monitoring, evaluation, and peer review organized as mutual learning processes and accompanied by indicators and benchmarks as means of comparing best practice. In essence, this was an extension of the approach already adopted 'in the procedures for coordinating national economic policies under the EMU established in the Maastricht Treaty, and in the employment chapter of the Amsterdam Treaty' (Borras and Jacobsson, 2004: 187–8). As such, it was a departure from the 'classic community method' of decision making, whereby the Commission makes proposals for legislation and the Council of Ministers (increasingly in conjunction with the EP) adopts the legislation, which then supersedes national legislation. Most significantly, it was a departure in the direction of a more intergovernmental process, where policy competences would not be transferred to the EU, but would be retained at the national level, the Commission would play a less leading role as the facilitator of intergovernmental co-ordination, and the EP and European Court of Justice would have no real role at all. To strengthen this impression of firm national control over the process, it was agreed that one European Council out of three each year—the spring meeting—would be devoted to reviewing progress.

Common Foreign and Security Policy (CFSP)

In the immediate aftermath of agreement at Amsterdam to extend the scope of CFSP, the EU was once again embarrassed in the course of 1998 by its inability to take decisive action in former Yugoslavia. Attacks by Serb forces on ethnic Albanians in the province of Kosovo had to be countered by NATO, which launched a bombing campaign against the Serbs. Although EU member states participated in this, the lead came from the United States, which flew 60 per cent of all sorties, 80 per cent of strike sorties, and provided the crucial intelligence, communications, and logistical capabilities (Cornish and Edwards 2001: 588).

Kosovo provided the stimulus to a further push on the CFSP front. In December 1998 the French President, Jacques Chirac, and the British Prime Minister, Tony Blair, held a bi-lateral summit at St. Malo in France, at the end of which they declared their joint support for a European Security and Defence Policy (ESDP); and a year later, the Helsinki European Council announced the creation of a European Rapid Reaction Force. These moves served the interests of both Chirac and Blair. For Chirac, they were a further step towards a long-standing French goal, which was in line with the Gaullist aspiration for an EU that was capable of acting independently of the United States. For Blair, ESDP marked a new leading project for the EU in which British participation would be central, in marked contrast to the marginalization of Britain in the previous leading sector of monetary union.

Although Blair had an interest in seeing security and defence take the centre of the EU stage, there was no wish on the part of the British government to weaken the NATO alliance. For this reason, the appointment in November 1999 of Javier Solana, the then NATO Secretary-General, as the first EU High Representative for Foreign Affairs was an important decision. Solana was acceptable to the United States, and in moving directly from the NATO post to the EU post, he was in a strong position to ensure compatibility between the actions of the two organizations.

So, by the end of the decade, CFSP/ESDP looked as though it was about to become a significant new direction of advance for the EU. That it was not just a Franco-British enthusiasm was indicated by the fact that all fifteen of the then member states agreed to participate in the Kosovo Force (KFOR), which moved in to preserve the peace and assist in the reconstruction of the province after the end of the bombing campaign. It was widely noted at the time, though, that in this traditionally most intergovernmental of policy sectors, the member states had ignored a strong suggestion from the Commission that the office of the High Representative should be located within the Commission, and had instead opted to make it a position within the Secretariat of the Council. This was in line with the same mood for intergovernmental approaches that was evident in the adoption of the OMC as the basis for the Lisbon strategy. Also, seasoned observers of the CFSP, and its predecessor European Political Co-operation (EPC), might have wondered what would happen to the new spirit of EU co-ordination should another crisis like the Gulf War erupt, in which the United States opted for military intervention and demanded that its NATO allies follow its lead. Would European unity hold, or would the old differences of opinion on how to respond to US unilateralism re-emerge? (see also Ch. 30, pp. 522–5)

Justice and Home Affairs (JHA)

Following agreement at Amsterdam that a zone of freedom, security, and justice for EU citizens would come into force within five years of ratification, the Tampere European Council (October 1999) agreed a programme of action to address the problems raised by the free movement of people across its internal borders. This involved some 60 steps to be taken by 2004 relating largely to issues of asylum and immigration, and combating crime. The Commission was charged with the task of monitoring the progress towards the completion of these steps (see also Ch. 24, pp. 372–4).

The Nice European Council

The Treaty of Amsterdam made institutional reform a precondition of enlargement and contained a protocol anticipating further discussions on reform. The Cologne European Council of 1999 referred to this protocol in agreeing to set up an IGC to discuss the outstanding institutional issues that had not been resolved at Amsterdam, particularly in relation to the weighting of votes in the Council, the size and composition of the Commission, and the possible extension of QMV. The Commission was charged with putting forward options for change.

The IGC opened in February 2000, under the Portuguese presidency, and continued into the French presidency in the second half of the year. At the Biarritz European Council in October 2000 a number of points of contention remained. There were different political positions on the weighting of votes within the Council, with Germany arguing that its voting weight should reflect its size and population. France, however, was keen to retain the same voting weight as Germany. On the Commission, the larger member states joined forces to argue for a smaller Commission based on a rotation system, while smaller member states were critical of a proposed reduction in the number of Commissioners. On QMV there were clear and distinct positions. For example, Britain in particular was keen to prevent QMV from spreading to areas of taxation, Germany was keen to protect unanimity over asylum and immigration policies, and France was keen to prevent QMV from being applied to certain external trade issues in the area of trade in services.

Nice turned out to be the longest European Council in the history of the EC/EU. For four days the heads of government haggled over the areas that would become subject to QMV, and over the weighting of votes. Membership of the Commission proved less difficult, although really tough decisions were deferred by allowing the size of the College of Commissioners to grow to twenty-seven before there would be a move to having less than one Commissioner per member state; but in return for giving up their second Commissioner the large member states fought even harder on the weighting of votes in the Council. In the end an agreement was reached that just about opened up the prospect of the EU being ready for enlargement.

The Outcome

The veto was removed from 29 of the 70 Treaty articles where it still applied; but in important areas national interests prevented movement. Britain would not agree to the removal of the veto on tax or social security harmonization. Although QMV for trade negotiations was extended to services, at French insistence exceptions were made for audio-visual services, education, and health. Maritime transport was exempted from QMV at the insistence of Denmark and Greece. Many aspects of immigration and asylum policy were not transferred to QMV at German and French insistence. Perhaps most significantly, though, Spain, with the support of Portugal and Greece, retained the right to veto changes to the cohesion funds until after the conclusion of the negotiations on the 2007–12 Financial Perspective. This cast further doubt on the possibility of keeping the cost of enlargement to the common budget within limits acceptable to the net contributors.

On the way in which those areas subject to QMV would be decided, that is on the weighting of votes under QMV, the large member states seemed to gain an advantage over the small. The re-weighting, which would apply from 1 January 2005, left the small and medium-sized states with a smaller percentage of the total vote relative to the larger states than under the previous system. There was also the insertion of a clause requiring any measure agreed by QMV to comprise the votes of governments representing at least 62 per cent of the population of the EU. The effect was to put Germany, France, and Britain, or any two of these three plus Italy, in a position where they could effectively block progress on any measure on which they agreed to co-operate. In compensation the small states were allowed a clause that a measure agreed under QMV would also have to have the support of a majority of the member states. The cumulative effect of these two concessions to different coalitions of 'bigs' and 'smalls' was to make the decision-making system much more complex, and also to make it more difficult than previously to achieve a qualified majority, which now required a 'triple majority'—a majority of weighted votes, a majority of member states, and a 62 per cent or higher majority of the population.

The Treaty of Nice was formally signed in the following February, following eleven months of negotiation. The Treaty redistributed votes in the Council in favour of the more populous member states and also introduced the complex 'triple majority' voting procedure that would be in place from 2005 and which looked certain to slow down decision making in an enlarged EU. It also extended the use of QMV into around thirty new areas, but retained the veto in areas such as social policy and taxation. The Treaty strengthened the powers of the President of the Commission and provided for one commissioner per member state from 2005, with the proviso that the maximum number in future should be 26, and from that point onwards a rotation system would ensure parity among states. In relation to the EP, the Treaty extended the co-decision procedure and also changed the allocation of seats between states and set a maximum of 732 MEPs.

Commentators were critical of the achievements of Nice. Phinnemore (2003: 58) described the outcome as 'sub-optimal' in relation to enlargement, while Dinan (2004: 288) suggested that 'rarely did an intergovernmental conference devote so much time to so few issues with so few consequential results'. It undoubtedly made decision making more complex by increasing the number of thresholds for agreement in the Council, and deferred decisions in other areas. Moreover, the negotiations raised tensions between big states and small states that would re-appear when the outstanding issues were tackled in the negotiations over the Draft Constitutional Treaty (Chs. 16 and 18).

The Charter of Fundamental Rights

In a parallel initiative, also confirmed at Nice in December 2000, the EU set out its commitment to citizens' rights in the Charter of Fundamental Rights of the European Union. This Charter was drawn up by a Convention established by the Cologne European Council in June 1999 and set out a range of civil, economic, political, and social rights of European citizens for the first time in a single text. The 56 articles of the Charter fell under six headings, namely: Dignity, Freedoms, Equality, Solidarity, Citizens' Rights and Justice. The Charter was agreed by the Biarritz Council in October 2000 before being approved by the Commission and EP. The formal signing of this Charter by the Presidents of the Council, the EP, and the Commission at Nice was a political declaration that was not legally binding on member states. Its significance would have to await future events and, not least, the deliberations and outcome of the Constitutional Convention (Ch. 16).

CONCLUSION

This period highlights a number of the themes that were set out in the opening chapters of the book. The most prominent is perhaps that of intergovernmentalism (Ch. 1), which had by this time become the dominant tone of the EU. Though governments sought enlargement, in the negotiations over both the policy reforms and the institutional reforms that were necessary to assimilate the new member states, the protection and projection of national interests were never far from the surface. Developments in CFSP/ESDP point to the influence of external circumstances on internal EU relations, but the decision to locate the High Representative for Foreign Affairs within the Council Secretariat rather than the Commission again indicates the intergovernmental nature of this area of policy. Intergovernmentalism may also be seen as a prominent explanation of the move away from the traditional community method of decision making with the introduction of the OMC; but this development highlights as well the growing relevance of theories emphasizing new forms of governance in the EU (Ch. 2).

The Commission crisis raised questions about the legitimacy of the EU and its institutions (Ch. 4). As an unelected body, the Commission draws much of its legitimacy through its contribution to efficient and effective decision making—the 'performance' dimension. In this case, the Commission's failings in one particular area cast a shadow over its legitimacy more generally and, in doing so, added to wider concerns over the legitimacy of the EU as a whole. On a more positive note, the decisive response of the EP did something to redeem perceptions of the EU and added weight to arguments for its role to grow further for the sake of greater accountability.

If, on one level, this was a period in which governments were assertive, on another level it is important to see an underlying theme linking a number of developments: this is the need for the EU to compete economically in an increasingly globalized market. Monetary Union and the Lisbon Strategy have a clear and explicit link to European competitiveness, and there is also a strong economic dimension to enlargement. It should perhaps be no surprise, then, that this period was marked by a resurgence of academic interest in the links between economics and politics in explaining European integration. From a critical political economy perspective (Ch. 3), beyond the observable exchanges between governments, supranational institutions, and other actors, the balance of social forces provides a structural power that determines the trajectory of European integration. In particular, writers from this perspective would argue that the nature and pace of European integration is shaped by and for the dominant capitalist class, and that the changes in this period should be understood primarily as a response to the changing needs of European capitalism in the context of globalization.

KEY POINTS

The Euro

- ☐ In 1999 the Euro became the official currency in eleven member states. Greece was included the following year, but Britain, Denmark and Sweden remained outside the Eurozone.
- ☐ After a successful launch, the new currency soon experienced some difficulties and Britain, Denmark, and Sweden stayed outside.

The Commission in Crisis

- ☐ In 1999, the Santer Commission resigned following investigations into claims of fraud and mismanagement.
- ☐ The new President, Romano Prodi, came to office with a commitment to 'clean up' the Commission's image.

Enlargement

- ☐ Accession negotiations with opened with several states in 2000.
- ☐ Enlargement required difficult policy revisions (particularly in relation to agriculture and structural funds) and significant institutional reforms.

Other Developments

- ☐ The Lisbon Strategy responded to the challenges of globalization by aiming to make the EU 'the most competitive and dynamic knowledge-based economy in the world' by 2010. The Strategy was to be pursued using the Open Method of Co-ordination, which was a departure from the 'classic community method'.

- The EU's inability to respond decisively to the Kosovo conflict provided a push towards further co-operation on CFSP.
- The Tampere European Council (October 1999) agreed a 60-step programme of action to address the problems raised by the free movement of people across its internal borders.

The Nice European Council

- Nice became the longest European Council in the history of the EC/EU as leaders negotiated over institutional changes in preparation for enlargement. There was particular tension between large and small states over voting weights under QMV, and more widespread disagreement about the extension of QMV to new areas of policy.
- Reform of voting weights led to a complex 'triple majority' system, which seemed to advantage the larger member states against the smaller.
- QMV was extended into around 30 new areas, but the veto remained in others.
- In a parallel initiative, also confirmed at Nice in December 2000, the EU set out its commitment to citizens' rights in the Charter of Fundamental Rights of the European Union.

FURTHER READING

A distinctive interpretation of the enlargement negotiations is provided by A. Moravscik and M.A. Vachudova, 'Bargaining Among Unequals: Enlargement and the Future of European Integration', *EUSA Review*, 15, 4 (2002): 1–3. Two articles on the Open Method of Co-ordination contain a great deal of information on the whole Lisbon Strategy: D. Hodson and I. Maher, 'The Open Method as a New Method of Governance: The Case of Soft Economic Policy Co-ordination' *Journal of Common Market Studies*, 39 (2001): 719–46; and S. Borras and K. Jacobsson, 'The Open Method of Co-ordination and New Governance Patterns in the EU', *Journal of European Public Policy*, 11 (2004): 185–208.

On the Treaty of Nice see M. Gray and A. Stubb, 'Keynote Article: The Treaty of Nice—Negotiating a Poisoned Chalice?' in G. Edwards and G. Wiessala (eds.) *The European Union: Annual Review of the EU 2000/2001* (Oxford: Blackwell, 2001), 5–24; and K. Feus (ed.), *The Treaty of Nice Explained* (London: Federal Trust for Education and Research, 2001).

online resource centre Visit the Online Resource Centre that accompanies this book for links to more information on the Treaty of Nice.

CHAPTER 16

After Nice: Enlargement Overshadowed

CHAPTER OVERVIEW

Enlargement was the major ongoing concern of the EU post-Nice, but events in the United States on 11 September 2001 overshadowed enlargement and put security and defence to the top of the agenda. A desire to facilitate progress on this front, together with an awareness that Nice had probably not gone far enough to simplify decision making in an enlarged EU, led to the creation of a Constitutional Convention at the end of 2001. This seemed to mark a concerted effort to ensure the effectiveness of the EU, but the subsequent invasion of Iraq by the United States and an *ad hoc* coalition, in which Britain was a prominent participant, led to sharp disagreements between EU member states. This chapter covers these issues through to the successful enlargement in May 2004. It also tells the story of the collapse of the stability and growth pact, which had seemed to be one of the cornerstones of monetary union, but which was effectively abandoned in the face of the unwillingness of France and Germany to accept the fiscal discipline that it imposed.

> less than a year after the Nice summit, the terrorist attacks of 11 September
> 2001 rocked the world ... international politics came to be dominated by
> their aftermath.
> **(Menon 2004: 225)**

The Al-Qaeda terrorist atrocities in the United States on 11 September 2001 shocked the world and had a profound effect on international politics. The political climate in which the EU operated changed immediately, with implications for a range of internal policies—most obviously those concerned with security and defence.

European Security and Defence Policy (ESDP)

Up to September 2001, steady progress was being made on security and defence policy. The smooth progress ran into choppy waters, though, following the terrorist attacks in the US (see also Ch. 24, pp. 373–4 on the implications for EU co-operation on internal security matters and Ch. 30, pp. 524–5 on external security and defence).

The initial response from the EU was to declare solidarity with the United States, and this support was maintained during the subsequent US campaign in Afghanistan to unseat the Taliban government, which had undoubtedly harboured and supported the Al-Qaeda terrorists. Nevertheless, the effect of the united EU response was somewhat spoiled by Britain, France, and Germany trying to act independently of the EU as a whole. In October 2001, Blair, Chirac, and Schröder met outside of the EU forum to discuss their responses to September 11, and intended to do so again in London in early November; but on the second occasion vigorous protests by other member states led to the invitation to participate being thrown open to other states and to the EU High Representative, Javier Solana (Ch. 30, p. 524).

The most serious problems for the EU resulted from the determination of the Bush Administration to make Iraq the next target after Afghanistan. There was no evidence that the secular Ba'ath regime of Saddam Hussein supported Islamic terrorism, or had any involvement in the September terrorist attacks. Similarly there was no more than circumstantial evidence, which subsequently proved to be totally inaccurate, that Iraq possessed weapons of mass destruction with which it could attack the United States or its allies. In the build-up to the eventual invasion of Iraq, the EU split over how to react to the US initiative. France and Germany led a group of states that opposed any military action; Britain, Spain, and Italy were the leading supporters of a group that backed the US action.

Europe Split

In January 2003, in response to French and German statements implying that the EU was opposed to the US attitude towards Iraq, eight European states signed a letter indicating their support for the United States. Five of the eight were existing members of the EU—Britain, Denmark, Italy, Portugal, and Spain. The other three were prospective members—the Czech Republic, Hungary, and Poland. On 22 January, Donald Rumsfeld, the US Secretary for Defense, told a press conference that France and Germany posed 'a problem', but that they did not speak for Europe. They were, he said, 'old' Europe. The new Europe, of states to the east that had recently become members of NATO, was supportive. Both the letter and Rumsfeld's undiplomatic comments infuriated the French. When ten former communist states, seven of them EU applicants, jointly expressed their support for the US position in February, President Chirac publicly rebuked them, saying that they had shown bad manners, and had 'missed a good opportunity to keep quiet'. He pointedly went on to remind the prospective members who had already negotiated entry that the decision to admit them to the EU on 1 May 2004 had yet to be ratified by national parliaments; and he indicated that Bulgaria and Romania, who were still in the early stages of negotiating membership, had been particularly foolish to associate themselves with the statement.

In March 2003, France publicly declared that it would veto any resolution in support of military action against Iraq that might be presented by the United States and Britain to the United Nations Security Council. This caused a serious division between the two member states that had been in the forefront of efforts to create the European Security and Defence Policy (ESDP). On 18 March, Blair made a strong attack in the House of Commons on the French position. Following the invasion of Iraq in March 2003, Franco-British relations were at a very low ebb, and the prospects for an ESDP looked poor. Yet by the end of the year there were signs of improvement, particularly following Blair's agreement in principle that the EU should have the joint planning capacity to conduct operations without the involvement of NATO, a concession that appeared to alarm the United States. So, the signs were that the British wanted to facilitate the relaunch of the ESDP.

One other interesting phenomenon came out of this episode. On 15 February 2003 there were mass public demonstrations across Europe against the prospect of an invasion. These protests took place both in countries whose governments opposed the invasion, and in many of the states whose governments supported the United States. The possible significance of this is pointed up in the Conclusion to this chapter.

Enlargement: Towards an EU of 25

As international events unfolded, the momentum of the enlargement process continued despite the difficulties in achieving the desired institutional and policy changes (Ch. 15, pp. 192–3). In October 2002, the Commission declared that the applicant states—Cyprus, the Czech Republic, Estonia, Hungary, Latvia, Lithuania, Malta, Poland, the Slovak Republic, and Slovenia—were in a position to conclude negotiations successfully by the end of that year and would be ready for membership in 2004. The European Parliament gave its assent to the accession of these states in April 2003.

Two applications from Central and East European countries remained outstanding in 2004: Bulgaria and Romania, neither of whom was deemed ready for membership.

Negotiations opened with Croatia in 2004, and an application was accepted from Macedonia. Other Yugoslav successor states were expected to apply, and several Soviet successor states expressed an interest in joining, but were ruled out by the EU (Ch. 31, pp. 533–4). However, the major outstanding issue at this stage remained the Turkish question.

Turkey had had an association agreement envisaging membership since 1963. It was excluded from the enlargement process in 1997, largely through opposition from Greece and Germany. However, it was offered the prospect of future negotiations in 1999 following a change of government in Germany in 1998 and a dramatic improvement in Greek-Turkish relations in 1999. Further, a decision by the EU in 1999 to allow states to negotiate entry at their own pace made it easier to open negotiations with Turkey, and more difficult not to do so. A change of government in Turkey in 2002 produced rapid progress to meeting the Copenhagen criteria. Moreover, the international climate meant that geo-strategic factors were increasingly in Turkey's favour, although opposition to its accession remained strong in some states in 2004, particularly in France (Ch. 31, pp. 554–5).

The Constitutional Treaty

Alongside progress on enlargement were further moves to overhaul the EU's decision-making system. But these moves were not only linked to enlargement. They were also explicitly related to two other factors: the need to connect the EU more closely with its citizens; and the wish to put in place machinery to allow the EU to speak with one voice on international issues.

Existing concerns over the low level of public support for the EU were raised further when the Irish people rejected the Nice Treaty by a vote of 53.87 per cent to 46.13 per cent in a referendum in June 2001, with a turnout of only 32.9 per cent. Although this decision was reversed in a second referendum in October 2001, and the Treaty of Nice entered into force in February 2003, the Irish episode reflected the serious challenges facing the EU on the road to further deepening and widening.

In December 2001, the heads of government, meeting in Laeken (Belgium), agreed to move beyond the modest institutional changes agreed in the Nice Treaty. The adoption of the *Declaration on the Future of the European Union* committed the EU to transforming its decision-making procedures to make them more democratic and transparent and to prepare the ground for a European Constitution. The vehicle for moving forward reform was a Constitutional Convention, which brought together representatives of national governments and parliaments from both the member and accession states with representatives of the EU institutions (Insight 16.1), and which was chaired by the former French President, Valéry Giscard d'Estaing. It would be a unique forum in both its role and composition, designed to secure legitimacy for the reforms by incorporating the views of a broad range of actors. In addition to the formal members of the Convention and observers, various business representatives, non-governmental organizations, academics, and other interested parties would be consulted on specific topics. The

INSIGHT 16.1

Composition of the Constitutional Convention

In addition to its Chairman (Valéry Giscard d'Estaing) and two Vice-Chairmen (Giuliano Amato and Jean-Luc Dehaene), the Convention was composed of:

- Fifteen representatives of the Heads of State or Government of the Member States (one from each Member State);
- Thirteen representatives of the Heads of State or Government of the candidate States (one per candidate State);
- Thirty representatives of the national parliaments of the Member States (two from each Member State);
- Twenty-six representatives of the national parliaments of the candidate States (two from each candidate State);
- Sixteen members of the European Parliament;
- Two representatives of the European Commission.

There were alternates for each full member.

Observers were invited to attend from the Economic and Social Committee (three representatives), the Committee of the Regions (six representatives), the social partners (three representatives), and the European Ombudsman.

The Laeken Declaration provided for the candidate States to take a full part in the proceedings without, however, being able to prevent any consensus emerging among the Member States.

Source: http://european-convention.eu.int/organisation.asp?lang=EN

Convention's Chair would report on progress at each European Council meeting and receive the views of the heads of government, and the Convention's final report would provide the starting point for discussions and decisions at an IGC scheduled for 2004.

The proposals of the Convention for a Constitution for Europe were submitted by Giscard d'Estaing to the Thessaloniki European Council in June 2003. There followed a formal IGC, at which some of the proposals were amended, but the Treaty establishing a Constitution for Europe was signed by the heads of government and the EU Foreign Ministers in October 2004. Once ratified within member states, it would replace the existing Treaties.

The Treaty agreed had a four-part structure (Insight 16.2) and had implications for the founding principles of the EU, the institutions, the decision-making process and its policies, which are discussed in Chapter 18 (pp. 250–5). The Treaty also specified for the first time the areas that would be the exclusive competence of the EU (Article 1-13), and those areas that would be shared between the EU and the member states (Article 1-14). Both of these were long-standing federalist demands, although the governments of the member states had become increasingly aware of the possible protection that a clear demarcation of spheres of competence would offer against the creeping extension of competencies that had sometimes occurred as a result of the Commission's policy entrepreneurship (Ch. 19, pp. 264–8).

INSIGHT 16.2

Structure of the Constitutional Treaty

The Treaty was divided into four main parts, each of equal rank.

Part I was devoted to the principles, objectives and institutional provisions governing the new European Union and was divided into nine Titles: the definition and objectives of the Union; fundamental rights and citizenship of the Union; Union competencies; the Union's institutions; the exercise of Union competence; the democratic life of the Union; the Union's finances; the Union and its neighbours; and Union membership.

Part II comprised the European Charter of Fundamental Rights. It contained seven Titles, preceded by a Preamble: dignity; freedoms; equality; solidarity; citizens' rights; justice; general provisions.

Part III comprised the provisions governing the policies and functioning of the Union. The internal and external policies of the Union were laid down, including provisions on the internal market, economic and monetary union, the area of freedom, security and justice, the common foreign and security policy (CFSP), and the functioning of the institutions. It contained seven Titles: provisions of general application; non-discrimination and citizenship; internal policies and action; association of the overseas countries and territories; the Union's external action; the functioning of the Union; and common provisions.

Part IV grouped together the general and final provisions of the Constitution, including entry into force, the procedure for revising the Constitution and the repeal of earlier Treaties.

A certain number of protocols were annexed to the Treaty establishing the Constitution, in particular the: Protocol on the role of national parliaments in the European Union; Protocol on the application of the principles of subsidiarity and proportionality; Protocol on the Euro Group; Protocol amending the Euratom Treaty; Protocol on the transitional provisions relating to the institutions and bodies of the Union.

Source: http://www.europa.eu.int/scadplus/constitution/introduction_en.htm

Much will undoubtedly be said and written on the politics and significance of the European Convention that will provide insights that were not available at the time of writing, in its immediate aftermath—not only in relation to its proposals, but also in relation to its process. On content, some viewed it as a little more than a 'Nice II' or a 'tidying-up' exercise that mainly brought together existing rules and agreements into a single, more comprehensible Treaty. Others, particularly **Eurosceptics**, viewed it as a major step away from the sovereignty of nation states and towards the creation of a European super-state.

In terms of process, the Convention was, for its advocates, a model created to go beyond what had been and what might be achieved through IGCs. For some, the Convention was a new model of EU decision making that promoted deliberation, broad participation, and consensus-based politics. For others, it was dominated by hard bargaining, corridor politics, and political horse-trading. There was evidence of both sets of characteristics. While the process was clearly élite led, the range of actors from civil society that were involved in the process was unusual, and the style of proceedings sought to promote deliberation and consensus. By contrast, there were inevitable tensions between federalists and intergovernmentalists, and, as in the run-up to the Nice Treaty, serious tensions emerged between large and small states.

Commentators also disagreed on how far the Convention really extended consultation beyond the limits of official government positions. Moravscik (2004: 15) suggested that the negotiations were dominated by the member states. This view was rejected by Lord Kerr (2004: 17), the Secretary General of the Convention, who pointed out that in the Presidium the member states' representatives were in a minority. Moreover, there was a sense in which Convention members listened to each other and worked in a spirit of solidarity. However, he also suggested that the final months of the Convention did begin to resemble an IGC.

As with the earlier treaties, the Constitutional Treaty had to be ratified by the member states before entering into force. Some states chose to ratify through parliament, others by referendum. The ratification process was expected to last for two years and the Constitution expected to come into force on 1 November 2006. At the time of writing (mid-2005), the ratification process for the Treaty had not been completed and this process is discussed in the next chapter (Ch. 17, pp. 217–21).

Monetary Union

If the symbolic importance of the Constitutional Treaty was uncertain during this period, there was no doubting the symbolic importance of the appearance of a European currency. In January 2002, Euro notes and coins came into circulation for the first time in the twelve participating states and became the sole currency in these states the next month, following a short change-over period. Britain, Denmark, and Sweden were the non-participants (Ch. 15, pp. 190–1). Following the Danish precedent in 2000, the Swedish people voted against membership of the Eurozone in September 2003. The British government concluded in June 2003 that the time was not right to make an application to join, and at the time of writing had yet to name a date for a referendum on whether to apply. For the citizens of the participating states, the circulation of Euros was an important symbol of European integration.

However, the new currency was soon at the centre of disputes between member states. The stability and growth pact, which effectively made the Maastricht criteria on debt and budget deficits permanent requirements for the participating states (Ch. 27, p. 439), was proving difficult for some states to adhere to. In particular, the requirement that states keep their budget deficits below 3 per cent of GDP brought difficulties initially for Portugal and Ireland, and subsequently for France and Germany. How these difficulties were handled again brought out tensions between small and large states. While Portugal and Ireland were reprimanded for exceeding the budget-deficit target, France and Germany resisted criticism, and were viewed by the smaller states as abusing the conditions of the pact.

Initial Commission threats of sanctions against France and Germany were followed up by a formal proposal in November 2003 to impose sanctions unless France and Germany took steps to reduce their budget deficit for 2004 below the 3 per cent limit.

However, it became clear that there was no majority among the member states for the Commission proposal and the sanctions were suspended, henceforth effectively making the stability pact requirements mere guidelines for national policy rather than mandatory rules for fiscal discipline (Ch. 27, pp. 449–50). Despite this, both France and Germany did make efforts to meet the conditions of the pact, which raised the question of how much the issue was one of fiscal discipline and how much it was an issue of who was in charge—national governments or the Commission. The ECB—now under the presidency of a Frenchman, Jean-Claude Trichet—was very critical of the Council and expressed support for the pact.

CONCLUSION

Enlargement dominated concerns at the beginning of this period, and with the exception of Turkey, the process continued smoothly through this period. However, enlargement and the EU's internal developments were soon overshadowed by the threats to global security evident in the terrorist attacks on the US. In the EU, these attacks highlighted long-standing differences in the foreign-policy outlooks of key member states. Most obviously, Britain's support for the US over Iraq highlighted Atlanticist tendencies that were at odds with France in particular. However, while there may have been immediate problems for EU co-operation on ESDP, for some commentators this episode highlighted the need for such co-operation in the longer term.

On 31 May 2003, the German philosopher Jürgen Habermas and the French philosopher Jacques Derrida published a joint plea for a common foreign policy for Europe. Their joint essay was published in German in the *Frankfurter Allgemeine Zeitung*, and in French in *Libération*. They argued that the demonstrations of 15 February showed the existence of a European public opinion that supported a European foreign policy independent of the United States; but that such an independent policy, which would throw the weight of Europe into the scales against US global hegemony, could only be devised and led by France and Germany, together with those EU states that supported their position. Perhaps it was to head off the possibility of such a policy in opposition to the Unites States that Blair was so eager to get ESDP with British involvement back on tracks after the end of the Iraq war.

The decision to create a Constitutional Convention to make proposals for a Constitutional Treaty was in part a response to ongoing concerns over the EU's legitimacy (see Ch. 4, pp. 65–74) and the Convention model itself was seen as a step in the direction of more open and inclusive decision making at the EU level. However, the operation of the Convention was subject to contrasting interpretations. Intergovernmentalists emphasized the dominance of national governments and the hard-bargaining approach to negotiations, while others emphasized the supranational dimension and a process characterized largely by problem-solving rationality, rather than bargaining. The draft Treaty that emerged was viewed differently in different member states. For example, the right in Britain saw the Treaty as a major step towards a federal Europe and the loss of national sovereignty. By contrast, many on the left in France saw the Treaty as dominated by the Anglo-Saxon model of capitalism and a threat to French models of social welfare (see also Ch. 17, p. 217).

The circulation of Euro notes and coins in the member states that were participating in the single currency was a step of both practical and symbolic significance. For the citizens of the participating states the Euro was physical evidence of a closer Europe. From a social constructivist perspective (Ch. 3), this physical manifestation of European integration would serve to enhance citizens' attachment to and identity with Europe (Ch. 27, pp. 450–1).

KEY POINTS

European Security and Defence Policy (ESDP)

☐ EU progress on ESDP co-operation was stalled by the September 11 attacks in the US, with splits emerging between key member states on how to respond, in particular to the subsequent US decision to take military action against Iraq.

Enlargement: Towards an EU of 25

☐ In April 2003 the European Parliament assented to the accession of 10 new member states in 2004. Turkey's application remained the major outstanding issue at this stage.

The Constitutional Treaty

☐ The Constitutional Convention prepared the ground for a European Constitution. It was unique in its composition and purpose.

☐ The Convention's proposals were presented in June 2003 and, following some amendments, the Treaty establishing a Constitution for Europe was signed by the EU heads of government and the their Foreign Ministers in October 2004.

Monetary Union

☐ In January 2002, Euro notes and coins came into circulation in the twelve participating states. However, the stability and growth pact underpinning the new currency became difficult for some states to adhere to and led to a number of disputes.

FURTHER READING

For the exchanges on the nature of the Convention's deliberations, see the separate contributions of Andrew Moravscik, and Lord Kerr, to 'Plenary Session: The 2003–2004 Grand Bargain', *Towards a European Constitution: A Conference Organised by the Federal Trust and the University Association of Contemporary European Studies* (Goodenough College, London, 1–2 July).

The essay by Habermas and Derrida is reproduced, together with a wide range of responses to their proposals, in Daniel Levy, Max Pensky, and John Torpey (eds.), *Old Europe, New Europe: Transatlantic Relations After the Iraq War* (London: Verso, 2005).

online
resource
centre

Visit the Online Resource Centre that accompanies this book for links to more information on the Constitutional Convention and Draft Constitutional Treaty.

The EU at a Crossroads

CHAPTER OVERVIEW

The period began with the 2004 enlargement, an ambitious expansion creating a Union of 25 states. However, it closed with perhaps the biggest crisis in its history, leaving the EU at a crossroads. The rejection of the Constitutional Treaty in France and the Netherlands created uncertainty about the legitimacy and future direction of the European project. But the problems ratifying the treaty were not the only significant problems in this period. This chapter looks at the first year of membership for the new member states, which raised issues that challenged the public enthusiasm for membership in some states, but also illustrated some of the advantages. It then turns to the EU elections and the difficult approval process for the new Commission. It reflects on the progress towards the objectives set out at Lisbon before considering the ratification crisis.

> The danger is obvious. Locked between a rock of an unratifiable treaty and a hard place of dysfunctional institutions, the EU can only become more discredited in a vicious circle of decline, ever more obvious impotence and growing illegitimacy ... Europeans have to think straight, to talk honestly and recognise their commonality.
> **(Will Hutton 2005)**

On 1 May 2004, the EU's biggest enlargement brought in ten new member states and over 100 million more citizens, taking the size of the Union to 25 states and increasing its population by 75 million to 450 million. The date for the enlargement had been set to allow the new member states to take part in elections to the European Parliament (EP) that were scheduled for June 2004. This in turn was the first stage in a new constitutional timetable, which had applied for the first time in 1995, whereby the election of the new EP was followed by the nomination of the new Commission.

The New Member States

Accession to the EU was never going to be a painless process for the applicant states. The negotiations took four years, even though the earlier negotiations on the Europe Agreements had already dealt with the removal of an array of trade restrictions. The *acquis communautaire* to which the applicants had to adjust their domestic legislation consisted of some 80,000 pages of EC law. Yet the difficult negotiations did not seem to have any significant effect on public support for entry in the applicant states, as reflected in the opinion polls. Support generally held steady, albeit at different levels in different states, and it actually increased in the run-up to the referendums in 2003 to accept the terms of entry. After that, though, it sank quite markedly as the euphoria cleared and the full implications of the terms began to sink in. Some issues rankled, particularly:

- the determination of almost all the existing member states to restrict the free movement of workers from the new entrants for up to seven years after entry;
- the refusal of the EU to allow the new members permanently to restrict the right of citizens of other member states to purchase property and agricultural land, which the applicants feared would lead to their homes and farms being bought up by rich Austrians and Germans;
- the parsimony of the existing members over payments from the agricultural and regional funds to the new members, which for example would result in farmers in the new member states receiving only 25 per cent of the subsidies that went to their much wealthier counterparts in the older member states.

This disillusionment seemed to be reflected in the low turnout for the EP elections in June 2004. Although the turnout was everywhere low (see below), in some of the new member states it was only around 20 per cent.

Yet within a year sentiment had turned around. The Eurobarometer poll in autumn 2004 showed increases in the percentage of respondents who considered membership a good thing in almost all of the new member states when compared with the previous poll six months earlier (Eurobarometer 2004a, 2004b). Wagstyl (2005) attributed this change of sentiment largely to two developments, the first economic, the second political.

At a time when the core economies of the Eurozone were still performing badly, economic growth in the new members reached 5 per cent in 2004, partly as a result of a 20 per cent increase in exports, mainly to the old EU. Agricultural exports grew particularly vigorously, with the Czech Republic and Poland benefiting considerably. Even though the subsidies to their farmers were capped at a low level in comparison with those paid to farmers in the older member states, the first payments, combined with the increased exports, led to an increase in farm incomes in the new members estimated by the European Commission at 50 per cent overall, at 108 per cent for the Czech Republic, and at 73 per cent for Poland.

The second development was the attitude of President Putin's Russia to the Presidential elections in Ukraine in November 2004. The Russians were widely suspected to have been involved in blatant attempts to rig the Ukrainian election to hand victory to Russia's favoured candidate, the Prime Minister, Viktor Yanukovich. When that result was announced, Putin immediately congratulated the 'winner'; but tens of thousands of Ukrainians turned out in the streets of the capital, Kiev, in bitter winter weather, and maintained their vigil until the authorities agreed to a re-run of the poll, which was won by the pro-western Viktor Yuschenko. The role played by Russia underlined concerns in central and eastern Europe about the growing authoritarianism and aggressive nationalism of the Putin administration. Also, the role played by mediators from two of the new EU member states—the President of Poland, Aleksander Kwasniewski, and the President of Latvia, Valdas Adamkus—underlined that membership of the EU conferred a weight and importance in international affairs that these small states could not hope to attain separately.

Elections to the European Parliament

There was some hope that the publicity that enlargement had generated would result in an increased turn-out for the elections to the EP in June 2004. In fact turn-out, which had fallen in every election since 1979, declined further to a record low of 45.7 per cent. As noted above, in the new member states it was much lower. It is questionable, though, whether any clear conclusion can be drawn from this. Pat Cox, the President of the EP, expressed the view that the low turn-outs in the new member states reflected the fact that the citizens felt they had already shown their support for the EU in the referendums on accession in 2003.

The New Member States

In the new member states, the campaigns tended to be dominated by national political debates, and the results reflected this rather than attitudes to the EU. So although

Eurosceptic parties did well in the Czech Republic and Poland, this was more because they were the opposition parties that voters naturally turned to in order to express discontent with the incumbent government than because they were Eurosceptic. In Slovakia, which had the lowest turn-out in the EU at just 17 per cent, no nationalists or extreme Eurosceptics were elected.

The 'Pre-2004' Member States

In the 'pre-2004' member states there was no consistent pattern. In Germany the election was fought almost entirely on domestic issues, with the attempts of the Federal government to introduce structural economic reforms at the forefront of the debate. The big story of the results was that Gerhard Schröder's Social Democratic Party (SPD) recorded its lowest ever vote in any election that spanned the whole of the Federal Republic; but the turn-out, at 43 per cent, was very low by German standards, perhaps indicting disillusionment with the EU. In France the debate had an unusually strong focus on European issues, and particularly the question of what sort of EU the French people wanted to see. The big winners with 28.9 per cent of the vote were the Socialists, who campaigned in favour of a social Europe and against what they presented as the collaboration of the ruling Gaullists with the swing towards a liberal 'Anglo-Saxon' vision of the EU (Ch. 16, p. 208). Turn-out was again disappointing, though, at only 42.7 per cent, the lowest ever recorded in a European election in France.

Denmark and Sweden showed contrasting trends. In Denmark the rejection of membership of the Euro in the referendum of 2000 suggested a hardening of Eurosceptic sentiment; but the EP election campaign was marked by an aggressive pro-EU stance from the opposition Social Democrats, who were the big winners with 32.6 per cent, and turn-out went up to 47.9 per cent, above the EU average. In Sweden, on the other hand, the turn-out was very low—at 37.9 per cent it was the lowest of the pre-2004 members and lower than five of the new members—and the most notable trend was an increase in support for Eurosceptic lists and candidates.

Britain, which was also a traditionally Eurosceptic state with low turn-outs in EP elections, saw an increase in turn-out for the first time since 1979, up from 24 per cent to 38.4 per cent, the highest level ever recorded in a European election in Britain. However, this result was undoubtedly influenced in part by the coincidence of local elections in many parts of the country, and by the experimental adoption of postal ballots in some areas. Most of the significance of the results was purely domestic, but the United Kingdom Independence Party (UKIP), a hard Eurosceptic party, secured a surprisingly high 16.2 per cent of the vote, which did not augur well for the prospects of a 'yes' vote in a future referendum on ratification of the EU's Constitutional Treaty.

From these diverse experiences—and the experiences of other member states were equally as diverse—it is difficult to make any generalizations. The only strong trend was for the elections to be used as a chance to register a protest against the incumbent government, although even this did not apply everywhere—in Spain, the Spanish Socialist Workers' Party (PSOE), which had won a general election three months earlier, emerged as the clear winner in the European election with 43.3 per cent of the vote. Nevertheless, the general trend to vote against incumbent national governments, combined with the presence in government in most of the larger states—which have more seats in the EP than the smaller states—resulted in a centre-right majority in the new EP. The party composition of the new parliament can be found in Table 21.3 (p. 306).

The New Commission

In line with the new constitutional timetable, the EP elections were followed by the nomination of the new Commission. In June 2004, the European Council nominated Portuguese Prime Minister José Manuel Durao Barroso as the next Commission President. Formerly a Maoist Revolutionary, the conservative Barroso was appointed after some dispute within the Council over Romano Prodi's successor. The French and German governments had sought to install the Belgian Prime Minister Guy Verhofstadt, while Britain had backed Barroso. In the end, Barroso's appointment was not only seen as a compromise between federalists and Atlanticists, but also reassured the concerns of smaller states. It was also in line with the expectation of the EP that the nominee would be drawn from the same political 'family' as the majority that had been returned in the elections. This, combined with Barroso's competent and convincing manner in his own confirmation hearing before the EP, resulted in a comfortable majority in favour of his nomination.

Trouble really began for Barroso with the confirmation hearings for the proposed members of his Commission. The President had no choice in the nominations of the individuals, which were made by the governments of the member states, but he was responsible for the allocation of portfolios. At first his decisions were welcomed, particularly because he refused to bow to pressure from large member states to give the most central portfolios to their nominees. France's Jacques Barrot, for example, was allocated the transport portfolio, hardly the most important responsibility. However, during the parliamentary confirmation hearings, doubts arose about the suitability of several of the individuals for the posts for which they had been proposed. They included Mariann Fischer Boel of Denmark, who was criticized for a lack of rigour in answering questions about agricultural policy; Neelie Kroes of The Netherlands, whose nomination for the competition portfolio was criticized because her past involvement on the Boards of several leading Dutch and international companies might lay her open to suspicion of conflicts of interest; Laszlo Kovacs of Hungary, who was nominated Commissioner for energy policy, and whose technical competence in the energy field was questioned; Ingrida Udre of Latvia, nominated for the taxation and customs union portfolio, who was criticized for her negative view of the EU and for her reluctance to answer questions about an investigation into allegations of impropriety in the funding of her political party in Latvia.

The Buttiglione Affair

The biggest furore, though, arose over the hearing of Rocco Buttiglione, the Italian nominee for the justice, freedom, and security portfolio. Buttiglione was a devout Roman

Catholic, and in response to questions from MEPs he expressed the conventional Catholic views that homosexuality was a sin, and that the purpose of marriage was to allow women to have children and be cared for by their husbands. Socialist, Green, and Liberal MEPs felt that these were inappropriate sentiments for a Commissioner whose duties would include the protection of human rights and civil liberties. They threatened to vote down the whole Commission unless something was done about Buttiglione's position.

Barroso tried to reach agreement with the party groups, first on removing the relevant parts of the justice, freedom, and security portfolio from the responsibility of Buttiglione, and exercising them himself. Even that did not satisfy the MEPs, though, and despite pressure from national governments on their own parties to vote to confirm the Commission, it looked as though the vote would be lost. On 27 October, just days away from the scheduled transfer of responsibilities to the new Commission on 1 November, Barroso told the EP that he would not be presenting his team for the vote, but would instead look again at all the portfolios. By this time the MEPs scented blood, and it seemed unlikely that they would accept anything less than the replacement of Buttiglione. This was seriously embarrassing for Barroso, because he had no right to demand that the Italian government get him off the hook. He was saved by Buttiglione's decision to resign and so walk away from the what he insisted was systematic persecution of him for his religious beliefs.

The Final Outcome

Eventually the EP approved the Barroso Commission in a vote of confidence on 18 November, but not before Barroso had persuaded the Latvian government also to replace Udre, and then moved Kovacs from energy to taxation. The new Latvian nominee, Andris Piebalgs, was given the energy portfolio, and the new Italian nominee, former Foreign Minister Franco Frattini, was allocated the justice, freedom, and security portfolio. Frattini performed well at his hastily arranged confirmation. Barroso did not make changes to the responsibilities of Boel or Kroes, but overall the whole incident was seen as a clear victory for the EP in its struggle to extend its influence over individual Commissioners. (A full list of the Commissioners and their portfolios is given in Ch. 19, Table 19.2, p. 263.)

Progress on the Lisbon Strategy

In March 2004, the European Council appointed the former Dutch Prime Minister, Wim Kok, to convene a committee of experts who would carry out a mid-term review of progress towards the commitment made in Lisbon in 2000 to make the EU by 2010, 'the most dynamic and competitive knowledge-based economy in the world' (Ch. 16, pp. 194–5). The Kok Report, *Facing the Challenge*, was presented to the European Commission on 3 November 2004, and to the European Council the following day.

The report confirmed what everyone knew already: that delivery on the process of reform had been 'disappointing'. There had been some progress. Employment rates in the fifteen older member states had increased from 62.5 per cent in 1999 to 64.3 per cent in 2003. There had been a particularly good improvement in the rate of female employment. The use of information technology and the internet had increased, and twelve member states had met their target for household internet penetration. Against that, though, net job-creation had stopped, probably making the target of 70 per cent participation by 2010 already beyond reach; only two states were meeting their targets on research and development; only five were above target for transposing single market directives into national law; and environmental targets were being missed by some way. The report also noted that the EU was already facing new challenges: increased economic competition from China, India, and a revitalized United States; the problems of an ageing population; enlargement, which had brought in ten new member states that were even further from achieving the Lisbon targets; low investment; low rates of utilization of labour, with hours worked being well below the levels in the United States; and the weak fiscal position of many member states.

Blame for the relative failure of the process was partly attributed to unfavourable conjunctural factors. The collapse of the bubble in technology stocks and shares in 2000 had discouraged investment in the industries that were central to the Lisbon agenda. Two years of low growth in the United States and Europe had followed the September 2001 terrorist attacks. Business confidence had been hit not just by terrorism, but also by trade disputes, environmental problems, and rising oil prices. However, the report also pointed to an overloaded agenda, poor co-ordination of the process, and conflicting priorities. The biggest culprits were identified as the member states, which had shown a collective lack of political will in pursuit of the objectives.

Although it was already too late to meet some of the targets that had been set for 2010, the report argued that the date should not be abandoned, as there was a need to instil a sense of urgency into the process, and the embarrassment of reaching 2010 with results that were so bad that Lisbon would become 'a synonym for missed objectives and failed promises' might impart some momentum.

Beyond that, the report pointed to the need to focus on core objectives and to allocate responsibilities more precisely. So long as the Lisbon agenda remained so broad, it ran the risk of being about everything, and therefore about nothing. The number of key indicators should be reduced from over 100 to just 14; and the emphasis should be placed clearly on growth and employment, because they were essential to underpin the social and environmental objectives. While the governments of the member states had to accept the main responsibility for the relative failure to date, the Commission ought to be made the unambiguous co-ordinator of the process. It needed to be prepared to name and shame those member states that were simply not doing enough. To be able to do this without fear it needed to monitor the process closely, and the report recommended that the next President of the Commission should make driving the Lisbon agenda forward the main mandate for his period in office. This is exactly what Barroso sought to do.

Ratifying the Constitutional Treaty

Initially, members of the Constitutional Convention (Ch. 16, p. 205) had proposed that the Treaty be voted on in simultaneous referendums Europe-wide on the same date as the EP elections in June 2004. This proposal was rejected as being too federalist, and the decision on how to ratify was left to individual member states. Subsequently, some states chose to hold public referendums, while others chose to ratify through parliamentary procedures (see Table 17.1).

The ratification process began successfully with parliamentary ratification in Hungary, Latvia, and Slovenia; and the Treaty overcame its first referendum hurdle with the endorsement of the Spanish people in February 2005. The vote was 77 per cent in favour. While this was a decisive vote in favour, the low turn-out was a cause for concern. Only 42 per cent of eligible voters took part, particularly low in a country that was generally supportive of European integration, and one chosen to be the first to stage a referendum in the expectation of an outcome that would build momentum elsewhere.

The worst fears of the Treaty's supporters were realized in May 2005 when the French referendum returned a 55 per cent vote against. This was followed shortly afterwards by a negative vote in the Netherlands of almost 62 per cent (Table 17.1). The French vote in particular was significant, not only as the first major 'no' vote over the constitution, but because it came from a country at the heart of Europe, and one, perhaps more than any other, associated with driving integration forward. The vote prompted arguably the biggest crisis in the EU's history.

A range of factors contributed to the French 'no' vote. These included domestic factors such as the unpopularity of the Chirac presidency and the state of the French economy. Related to this last point was a growing resentment in France about the influx of cheap labour following the eastern enlargement at a time of rising unemployment. This resentment linked to concerns over the potential implications for immigration in France of the putative Turkish accession to the EU.

There was also a distinct strain of debate in France that linked the Constitutional Treaty to Britain and British preferences. It was widely portrayed as an Anglo-Saxon Treaty and one that would undermine the French social model. Ironically, in Britain the Treaty was opposed by the Eurosceptic right by not being Anglo-Saxon enough and threatening to institutionalize EU involvement in new areas of social policy. Less contentious was the view that the French vote almost certainly let the Blair government off the hook, faced as it had been with holding a referendum that most commentators believed it could not win. Although there had been a clear prior agreement by the heads of government that *all* member states would attempt to ratify the Treaty before the position was re-assessed, the British government maintained that there was no point in it proceeding to a referendum after the French and Dutch 'no' votes, and unilaterally announced an indefinite postponement.

TABLE 17.1

Procedures Planned for the Ratification of the European Constitution

Member State	Procedure	Date scheduled	Previous European referendums
Austria	Parliamentary (*Nationalrat* and *Bundesrat*).	Approval by the *Nationalrat* 11 May 2005. Approval by *Bundesrat* 25 May 2005.	1994: accession
Belgium	Parliamentary (Chamber and Senate + Assemblies of Communities and Regions). Indicative referendum ruled out.	Approval by the Senate: 28 April 2005. Approval by the Chamber: 19 May 2005. Approval by the Brussels regional parliament: 17 June 2005. Approval by the German Community Parliament of Belgium: 20 June 2005. Approval by the Walloon regional Parliament: 29 June 2005. Approval by the French Community Parliament: 19 July 2005. Approval by the Flemish regional Parliament: no date.	NO
Cyprus	Parliamentary	Approval by the House on 30 June 2005.	NO
Czech Republic	Referendum probable but no final decision so far.	Referendum should be postponed to end of 2006-beginning of 2007.	2003: accession
Denmark	Referendum	Previously scheduled on 27 September 2005. Now postponed (no new date).	1972: accession 1986: Single European Act 1992: Maastricht Treaty (twice) 1998: Amsterdam Treaty 2000: euro
Estonia	Parliamentary Referendum unlikely.	Debate in Parliament confirmed for Autumn 2005. Public debate should however be held before the final vote.	2003: accession

Member State	Procedure	Date scheduled	Previous European referendums
Finland	Parliamentary	Debate of Parliament previously scheduled in autumn 2005 and ratification envisaged at the end of the year or the beginning of 2006.	Consultative referendum:
		Decision of report of ratification process and presentation of a report to the parliament foreseen in autumn 2005.	1994: accession
France	Referendum	Referendum 29 May 2005 negative (NO) (54.68%; turn-out: 69.34%)	1972: enlargement EEC 1992: Maastricht Treaty
Germany	Parliamentary (*Bundestag* and *Bundesrat*).	Approval by *Bundestag*: 12 May 2005. Adoption by *Bundesrat*: 27 May 2005.	NO
Greece	Parliamentary. But the Left parties submitted a joint proposal for a referendum.	Approval by Parliament: 19 April 2005.	NO
Hungary	Parliamentary	Approval by Parliament: 20 December 2004.	2003: accession
Ireland	Parliamentary + referendum	Referendum postponed. A White paper would be presented in September 2005.	1972: accession 1987: Single European Act 1992: Maastricht Treaty 1998: Amsterdam Treaty 2001 and 2002: Nice Treaty
Italy	Parliamentary (Chamber and Senate).	Approval by the Chamber on 25 January 2005 and by the Senate on April 6th.	Consultative referendum: 1989: possible draft Constitution

(*continued overleaf*)

Member State	Procedure	Date scheduled	Previous European referendums
Latvia	Parliamentary	Approval by the chamber on 2 June 2005.	2003: accession
Lithuania	Parliamentary	Approval by Parliament 11 November 2004.	2003: accession
Luxemburg	Parliamentary (two votes) + consultative referendum.	Approval by the Chamber (first reading) on 28 June. Positive Referendum on 10 July 2005: 56.52% in favour, 43.48% against. Final approval by the Chamber must take place at least 3 months after the first reading.	NO
Malta	Parliamentary	Approval by Parliament: 6 July 2005.	2003: accession
Netherlands	Parliamentary (First and second Chambers) + consultative referendum.	Referendum 1 June 2005 negative (61.7%; turn out: 63%).	NO
Poland	No decision so far.	The Parliament failed on 5 July 2005 to vote on the ratification procedure. The decision should be taken by the next parliament.	2003: accession
Portugal	Referendum	Referendum previously scheduled for October 2005 along with the local elections (preliminary revision of the national constitution adopted by Parliament on 22 June 2005). Government wishes to postpone the process (no date fixed).	NO
Slovakia	Parliamentary	Approval by Parliament: 11 May 2005.	2003: accession
Slovenia	Parliamentary	Approval by Parliament: 1 February 2005.	2003: accession

Member State	Procedure	Date scheduled	Previous European referendums
Spain	Parliamentary (Congress and Senate) + consultative referendum.	Referendum 20 February 2005: 76.7% in favour. Turn-out: 42.3%. Approval of the Congress on 28 April. Approval of the Senate on 18 May 2005.	NO
Sweden	Parliamentary. No referendum envisaged at this stage.	Presentation of the Ratification Bill previously scheduled in Summer for approval in December 2005 has been postponed.	Consultative referendums: 1994: accession 2003: Euro
United Kingdom	Parliamentary (House of Commons and House of Lords) + referendum.	Parliamentary ratification process suspended (suspension announced by UK government on 6 June 2005).	1975: Continued membership of the EC.

Updated: 21 July 2005
Source: http://europa.eu.int/constitution/ratification_en.htm, accessed 19.08.05
Note: Some of the information in this table is subject to change. In particular, certain Member States might decide to hold a referendum.

CONCLUSION

To suggest that the EU is 'at a crossroads', as does this chapter heading, is hardly controversial—it is rarely anywhere else. However, in this period the crisis caused by the problems ratifying the Constitutional Treaty was perhaps as great as any in the EU's history. One commentator suggested that, 'If mishandled, the crisis may even lead to closure, protection, recession and the disintegration of the euro—and the balkanisation of Europe into mutually suspicious and hostile camps ... the entire EU edifice, and all the benefits it has brought in terms of trade, stability and peace, is at risk' (Hutton 2005: 18).

In relation to the conceptual themes that were identified in the opening part of this book, the period highlighted above all the issue of the legitimacy of the EU. Turn-out for the EP elections in 2004 reached a record low. As suggested in Chapter 4, low turn-outs can be read in more than one way. A low turn-out may be seen as tacit support by the public for the process of European integration—the notion of the permissive consensus (Ch. 4, pp. 65–6). Alternatively, it may be viewed as apathy or disenchantment with the political system. In most cases, the recent decline in participation in EU elections has been seen as the latter. Put together with the evidence from the ratification process for the Constitutional Treaty, this would seem to be the more persuasive argument.

At the same time, it should be noted that while we are concerned with the legitimacy problems facing the EU here, the trends in relation to voting in EP elections are broadly consistent with those for national elections. So while there are arguments that suggest that it is unfair to make comparisons between democracy at EU level and that in established political systems (Ch. 4), on this occasion it does the EU no harm: liberal democracy as a whole faces a growing problem of legitimacy.

The problems around the approval of the Barroso Commission can also be read in more ways than one in relation to democracy and legitimacy. One the one hand, the proposed appointment of certain individuals to particular portfolios can be viewed as clumsy, insensitive, and wholly avoidable, thus casting further public doubt over the efficiency of the EU system. On the other hand, the firm response of the EP on this issue and the way in which it was ultimately resolved may be taken as evidence of the growing maturity and effectiveness of the EU system, and, more specifically, of the growing influence of the most democratic body within that system.

The fourth enlargement demanded a more effective decision-making system, that the EU had thus far largely failed to deliver. As such, the larger EU brought a focus on the conflicting interests of large and small states and between richer and poorer states that promised continuing challenges to legitimacy. The fourth enlargement was in many ways a remarkable achievement, but already some were beginning to show signs of regret at the nature and scale of this enlargement, as was expressed in the French debates over the Constitutional Treaty. However, further expansion of the EU still remained on the agenda (Ch. 31).

Finally, we turn specifically to the Constitutional Treaty itself. Were it to be agreed it would put the EU, symbolically at least, onto a new footing. It was in large part an attempt to bring the EU closer to its citizens, but it was seen to have the opposite effect. At the same time, it did galvanize a widespread public debate on the EU in those states where a referendum took place.

In the French debate in particular, a key issue was the type of Europe that was being developed, which echoed the 'models of capitalism' debate (Ch. 3, pp. 51–2). French critics of the Treaty portrayed it as 'Anglo-Saxon', shaped by the British to take the EU closer to American-style capitalism. This interpretation of British motivations is seen as a distortion of the Blair government by many British commentators, who point to the Scandinavian influence on the government's social policies, such as tax credits for the poorest families, a national minimum wage and increased investment in public services. Collectively, these have been seen to justify a new 'Anglo-social label' (Pearce and Paxton 2005). Yet, irrespective of whether the British position has been mis-represented, this debate looks set to remain central in the near future, especially as the Kok Report seemed to indicate the failure of the attempt at Lisbon to find a compromise between the arguments for economic re-structuring and those for a social Europe.

While the EU has reached a crossroads, and was widely held by commentators to be in a crisis at the time of writing, it is important to try to retain some perspective on recent events. In the immediate aftermath of a crisis, there is a tendency to over-emphasize the significance of recent events at the expense of the bigger picture. The bigger picture is that the EU has provided over half a century of institutional development and active political and economic engagement between European states that will not be easily dissipated. The question raised by the current crisis is not whether the EU will survive—it surely will. The question raised is 'what kind of EU will emerge from the crisis'?

KEY POINTS

The New Member States

☐ Soon after entry, public support for the EU fell in a number of new member states. This was reflected in particularly low turn-outs for the EP elections in these states.

☐ This opinion soon began to turn around as economic and political benefits were realized.

Elections to the European Parliament

☐ Turn-out at EP elections fell to a record low in 2004, and national issues remained prominent in the election campaigns in most member states.

The New Commission

☐ Barroso's appointment was a compromise between federalists and Atlanticists, and also appeased smaller member states.

☐ The proposed Commission hit problems over a number of nominees, but particularly Rocco Buttiglione, whose views were deemed inappropriate by the EP.

☐ The strength of reaction against Buttiglione ultimately forced his resignation. The incident was seen as a victory for the EP.

Progress on the Lisbon Strategy

☐ The Kok report described progress on the strategy as 'disappointing', although there had been some achievements.

☐ There were several explanations for the disappointing progress, but the failure of member states to drive the strategy forward was prominent among them.

☐ The 2010 targets were not abandoned, although some had already become unrealizable, and Commission President Barroso made the strategy a priority of his term in office.

Ratifying the Constitutional Treaty

☐ The ratification process began successfully with parliamentary ratification in Hungary, Latvia, and Slovenia, and a 'yes' vote in the Spanish referendum of February 2005.

☐ The worst fears of the Treaty's supporters were realized in May 2005 when the French referendum returned a 55 per cent vote against. The vote prompted arguably the biggest crisis in the EU's history.

FURTHER READING

For a journalist's report on the new members' experience of their first nine months or so of membership see Stefan Wagstyl, 'The Pull of the West: Why the Benefits Bestowed by Brussels have come early for the EU's Former Communist Countries', *Financial Times*, 21 February 2005.

A series of country studies on the 2004 European elections was published by the European Parties, Elections, and Referendums Network (EPERN) based at the University of Sussex. These were available on-line: see the web-link below. The report on the Lisbon Agenda is available as *Facing the Challenge: The Lisbon Strategy for Growth and Employment,* Report from the High Level Group chaired by Wim Kok (Luxemburg: Office for Official Publications of the European Communities, 2004). A commentary and analysis is available in E. Jones, 'European Economic Governance: Forging an Integrated Agenda', Chatham House International Economics Programme 2005.

On the Constitutional Treaty ratification process, and particularly the contexts in the countries holding referendums, see N. Hussain, with G. M. Hudson, and R. Whitman (2005) *Referendums on the EU Constitutional Treaty: The State of Play*, Chatham House European Programme, Briefing Paper EP BP 05/02 (London: Chatham House).

 **online resource centre**

Visit the Online Resource Centre that accompanies this book for links to more information on the European Constitution, including updates on the ratification process.

Theories derived both from international relations and from the analysis of domestic policy-making include positions that emphasize the importance of institutions. In the international relations literature on international regimes, there is an emphasis on institutions as, 'persistent and connected sets of rules (formal and informal) that prescribe behavioral roles, constrain states, and shape expectations'
(Keohane 1989: 3). In the 'new institutionalist' approaches to the study of domestic policy making there is a similar emphasis on the importance of institutions, broadly defined. In short, *institutions matter*, although not only institutions matter, nor is it only formal institutions that matter. However, to understand the politics of the EU it is necessary to know something about the nature of the formal institutions and the relationships between them.

There are six chapters in this part of the book. The opening chapter on the *Institutional Architecture* provides essential introductory information on the institutions, the treaties, and the legislative and budgetary processes. It contains little analysis, but presents the context within which the institutions operate, and provides background to understanding the debates that are presented in later chapters. Since the first edition, a new section has been added on the Constitutional Treaty that was signed in June 2004. As explained in the Introduction to the book, the fate of this Treaty and the Constitution that it would have introduced hung in the balance at the time of writing. The tenses of all the verbs had to be changed between the first and second drafts as the Constitution moved from being something that looked sure to come into effect during the lifetime of the book to being something that might never come into effect at all. Perhaps by the time the book appears the picture will have changed again. Our decision to include this section of the chapter anyway reflects our feeling that the changes to the institutional architecture that the proposed Constitution would have introduced deserve to be widely known, even if they subsequently prove to be largely of historical interest.

For most of the rest of this part of the book, the choice of which subjects to include was straightforward. There is a broad consensus that the EU has four 'main' institutions: the *Commission*; the *Council*; the *European Parliament*; and the *European Court of Justice*. Each receives separate treatment. The final chapter in this part deals with *Organized Interests*, whose interaction with the formal institutions is a central component of the EU's decision-making process.

The Institutional Architecture

CHAPTER OVERVIEW

Up to now this book has introduced the institutions of the EU only as actors in the history of European integration, and their powers have only been briefly outlined. To understand the debates that surround the institutions themselves, though, it is necessary to understand their powers and their roles in relationship to one another in more detail. The same material is needed to understand the debates around the various policies of the EU, which are the subject of Part 4 of the book.

This chapter examines the pattern of institutions and the formal rules that govern them. It also gives information on the composition of the less-important institutions, although for the main institutions—the Commission, the Council, the European Parliament (EP), and the European Court of Justice (ECJ)—that information is provided in the separate chapters devoted to them.

The chapter starts with a review of the Treaties that form the founding 'constitutional' documents of the EU. The main institutions involved in the processes of decision making are then introduced. Decision making covers both the budgetary and legislative procedures, which are quite complex. They are explained. The chapter then looks at the implementation of decisions once they have been made. Finally, the rather different processes that operate in the intergovernmental pillars of the EU are outlined.

the institutional design is not stable, but subject to periodic debate, argument and revision
(Helen Wallace, 2005: 50)

The Treaties

A Constitutional Treaty was agreed at the Brussels European Council of 18 June 2004, but at the time of writing it had yet to be ratified. Unless and until the new Constitutional Treaty is ratified, the EU does not have a formal constitution. Instead various treaties govern its operation. There were three 'founding treaties'—the Treaty of Paris and the two Treaties of Rome. They were supplemented in ways that affected the powers of the institutions by three further Treaties in the 1960s and early 1970s. One merged the Councils and the Commissions of the three Communities, while the other two were concerned with budgetary provisions. After the last of these, in 1975, there were no further major revisions of the Treaties for another decade, but then there were four new Treaties in the next fifteen years: the Single European Act (SEA), the Treaty on European Union (TEU), the Amsterdam Treaty, and the Nice Treaty (Table 18.1). By 1997 the various Treaties had largely been consolidated into two: the Treaty on European Union (TEU), and the Treaty establishing the European Community (TEC). The Constitutional Treaty was agreed at the Brussels European Council on 18 June 2004.

The staff of the EU institutions constantly refer to the Treaties. They are always careful to check the Treaty base of any action that they take. In the preamble of any legislative proposal that it makes, the Commission is formally obliged to state under which article

---

TABLE 18.1

The Treaties

- The Treaty of Paris (signed 1951; took effect 1952) created the European Coal and Steel Community (ECSC).
- The two Treaties of Rome (signed 1957; took effect 1958). The first of these created European Atomic Energy Community (Euratom); the second created the European Economic Community (EEC).
- The Treaty Establishing a Single Council and a Single Commission of the European Communities, also known as the Merger Treaty (signed 1965; took effect 1967).
- The Treaty Amending Certain Budgetary Provisions of the Treaties (1970).
- The Treaty Amending Certain Financial Provisions of the Treaty (1975).
- The Single European Act (1985).
- The Treaty on European Union—also known as the Maastricht Treaty (signed 1992; took effect November 1993).
- The Treaty of Amsterdam (signed 1997; took effect 1999).
- The Treaty of Nice (signed 2001; took effect 2003).

of the Treaties it is making the proposal. This incessant engagement with the text of the Treaties has led to the internal discourse of the institutions being peppered with references to articles of the Treaties, usually just citing them by number.

However, as the founding Treaties were amended and added to by the later Treaties, the numbering grew more and more complex, with letters having to be used in addition to numbers. Finally, at Amsterdam in June 1997, the heads of government agreed to re-number the articles. This reasonable decision had the unfortunate consequence that familiar phrases in the discourse of the EU became obsolete. For example, everyone working in or studying the institutions knew what the Article 113 Committee was (see below, p. 494), or what an Article 177 referral to the ECJ meant (see below, p. 322). After Amsterdam they had to adjust to calling them respectively the Article 133 Committee and an Article 234 referral. Many other similar adjustments had to be made; and further adjustments will have to be made when the Constitutional Treaty is ratified, introducing a whole new set of numbers.

Authors of textbooks on the EU have also had to cope with the changed numbering system. In this book, the new number of a Treaty Article is given, followed by the old one in brackets, except where the reference is purely historical, when the numbering current at the time is given first followed by the new numbering in brackets. In all cases the reference is to what is now called the 'Treaty establishing the European Community' (TEC), unless it is indicated that it is to the Treaty on European Union (TEU). The articles of the Constitutional Treaty have not been indicated in the text, but if it should become operational during the lifetime of this edition, the new numbers will be found on the book's web site, where links to the TEC and TEU can also be found.

The Decision-Making Institutions

The main decision-making institutions of the EU are those that were set up in the Treaty of Rome (EEC):

- the Commission
- the Council of Ministers
- the European Parliament (EP).

There are also two consultative committees:

- the Economic and Social Committee (ESC), which was in the original Treaty of Rome (EEC);
- the Committee of the Regions and Local Authorities (CoR), which was set up by the TEU.

The original TEU introduced a structure consisting of three 'pillars': the EC pillar, governed by the TEC; and two intergovernmental pillars, covering the Common Foreign and Security Policy (CFSP) and Justice and Home Affairs (JHA) (Figure 18.1). Subsequent amendments to the original TEU, made by the Treaties of Amsterdam and Nice,

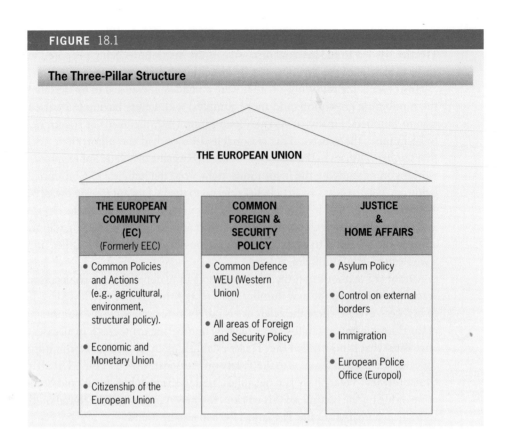

FIGURE 18.1

The Three-Pillar Structure

THE EUROPEAN UNION

THE EUROPEAN COMMUNITY (EC) (Formerly EEC)	COMMON FOREIGN & SECURITY POLICY	JUSTICE & HOME AFFAIRS
• Common Policies and Actions (e.g., agricultural, environment, structural policy).	• Common Defence WEU (Western Union)	• Asylum Policy
• Economic and Monetary Union	• All areas of Foreign and Security Policy	• Control on external borders
• Citizenship of the European Union		• Immigration
		• European Police Office (Europol)

eroded the distinctiveness of the JHA pillar, but CFSP remained distinctively intergovernmental.

In the EC pillar, the Treaties make the European Commission the sole proposer of legislation, and the Council of Ministers and the EP are the joint legislative decision makers. A similar division of functions exists for budgetary decision making. The ESC and the CoR also have a right to be consulted on legislative proposals. Implementation of legislation once it has been passed is partly a responsibility of the Commission, but mostly it is the responsibility of the member states. The Commission and the European Court of Justice act as watchdogs to ensure that the member states fulfil their obligations. The Court of Auditors performs a similar role for the budget. These powers and procedures do not apply in the two intergovernmental pillars, where the Commission has to share the right of initiative with the member states, and the EP has only a right to be consulted and informed about developments.

The Commission

In the formal decision-making system of the EC, the Commission has two important roles (Figure 18.2). It draws up the draft annual budget of the EC for discussion in the Council of Ministers and the EP, and it submits proposals to the Council of Ministers for EC legislation.

FIGURE 18.2

Decision-Making Institutions of the European Union

EUROPEAN COMMISSION

Initiates legislation
Drafts annual budget

COUNCIL OF MINISTERS

Makes decisions on
Commission proposals

EUROPEAN PARLIAMENT

Some co-decision powers
with Council
Approves budget

CoR & ESC

Consulted by Commission
and Council
Issue Opinions

The Commission is formally the sole institution with the right to propose legislation under the various EC Treaties, and it has vigorously defended this right. In the view of the Commission it is only its monopoly of the right of initiative that allows a coherent agenda to emerge for the EC as a whole. That monopoly was somewhat undermined by an amendment made to the TEC at Maastricht. Under Article 192, the EP 'may, acting by a majority of its Members, request the Commission to submit any appropriate proposal on matters on which it considers that a Community act is required for the purpose of implementing this Treaty'. Given that the democratic legitimacy of the EP is being increasingly emphasized, it would be difficult for the Commission to ignore such a request. Also, the sole right of initiative does not apply in the 'intergovernmental pillars' of the TEU (see below, pp. 248–50), where it shares the right of initiative with the member states. Even in the areas where it retains the right, to say that the Commission is the sole proposer of legislation should not be taken to imply that it works on legislative proposals in isolation. In practice it has always consulted widely with interest groups, and with committees of technical experts and representatives of national bureaucracies.

The Commission's legislative proposals can only be amended by the Council of Ministers if the Council acts unanimously, and the Commission may withdraw or amend its own proposals at any stage as long as the Council has not acted on them. However, where the EP has the right of co-decision with the Council, and where the Council and the EP cannot agree on the text presented by the Commission, they may agree an alternative in a Conciliation Committee that can be passed without unanimity on the Council (see below, pp. 243–5). The alternative does not have to be proposed by the Commission.

The Council of Ministers

The Council of Ministers consists of representatives of the member states. Most meetings under the Council heading are not of Ministers themselves, but of various committees of national government officials, known as 'working groups' (see Ch. 20, pp. 283–4). Nearly all business for the meetings of Ministers is filtered through these committees, and then through the Committee of Permanent Representatives (COREPER), which consists of the ambassadors from the member states to the EU (see Ch. 20, pp. 284–6). The Council makes decisions on proposals from the Commission on the basis either of unanimity or Qualified Majority Voting (QMV) depending on the issue. As was explained in Chapter 8, de Gaulle blocked the formal transition to QMV in 1965, but the SEA introduced it for legislative acts related to the single-market programme, and it was extended in the TEU to cover a range of other policies (Table 18.2). The weighting of votes that applied until 1 May 2004 is indicated in Table 18.3. These arrangements had to be adjusted to take account of the expansion of membership on 1 May 2004. A new system of QMV was agreed at the Nice European Council in December 2000, and incorporated into the Nice Treaty. The Nice voting arrangements are also indicated in Table 18.3.

Under the proposed Constitution the requirement for a qualified majority would have been changed completely, to require support for a measure from 55 per cent of the members of the Council, comprising at least 15 member states, and representing at least 65 per cent of the population of the EU. A blocking minority would have had to include at least four members, thereby limiting the ability of the biggest states to block measures. The figures were varied for votes on proposals that were not tabled by the Commission or the new EU Minister for Foreign Affairs. In that case, which could only arise within the CFSP pillar, the qualified majority would be 72 per cent of the member states representing at least 65 per cent of the population of the EU.

The European Parliament (EP)

In the original blueprint for the European Coal and Steel Community (ECSC), Jean Monnet did not include any parliamentary body; but in an attempt to make the new community more democratic a European Parliamentary Assembly was added to the Treaty of Paris (Diebold 1959: 62). This body was carried over into the Treaties of Rome.

The EP has consistently tried to insert itself more effectively into the decision-making process of the EC, especially since 1979 when it became a directly elected body. It has made some progress. In the original legislative process the Council of Ministers was obliged to consult the EP before disposing of legislative proposals made by the Commission, but it could ignore the EP's opinion if it wished. This remains the case in a few policy areas, but in most the EP now has further powers, culminating in a right to block legislation altogether, an ultimate power that makes it difficult for the Council to ignore

TABLE 18.2

Policy Areas Covered by Qualified Majority Voting

QMV applied in the following policy areas following the TEU:

- environment;
- development co-operation.
- the free movement of workers;

In the Treaty of Amsterdam, QMV was extended to:

- freedom of establishment;
- equal pay and treatment of men and women;
- mutual recognition of qualifications;
- the framework programmes for research and development;
- the internal market;
- public health;
- access to official documents;
- consumer protection;
- combating fraud;
- co-ordination of national provisions on the treatment of foreign nationals;
- customs co-operation.

QMV also applies to the implementation of the

- competition policy;
- the European Social Fund (ESF);
- the European Regional Development Fund (ERDF);
- transport policy;
- trans-European networks.

amendments proposed by the EP lest the legislation as a whole be lost. These powers are outlined under the heading 'Decision-Making Procedures' below.

The EP is formally a co-decision maker with the Council on the annual budget, and its approval is necessary for the budget to be given effect. The formal budgetary process is also outlined below in the section on Decision-Making Procedures. The other areas in which the EP has gained influence are in holding the Commission and the Council of Ministers to account, and these are examined in Chapter 21 (pp. 302–4).

The Economic and Social Committee (ESC)

The ESC consists of representatives of producers, farmers, workers, professionals, and of the general public. It is divided into three Groups representing employers, workers, and 'various interests', although Members are not obliged to join any of the Groups.

TABLE 18.3

Weighting of National Votes under Qualified Majority Voting

A. Up to 1 May 2004

Austria	4	France	10	Luxemburg	2
Belgium	5	Germany	10	Netherlands	5
Britain	10	Greece	5	Portugal	5
Denmark	3	Ireland	3	Spain	8
Finland	3	Italy	10	Sweden	4

A blocking minority consisted of 26 votes, but if there were 23 votes against a measure it was withdrawn for a period of reflection before being reintroduced.

B. As of 1 January 2005

Austria	10	Hungary	12	Slovenia	4
Belgium	12	Ireland	7	Spain	27
Bulgaria	10	Italy	29	Sweden	10
Cyprus	4	Lithuania	7	United Kingdom	29
Czech Republic	12	Luxemburg	4		
Denmark	7	Malta	3		
Estonia	4	Netherlands	13		
Finland	7	Poland	27		
France	29	Portugal	12		
Germany	29	Romania	14		
Greece	12	Slovakia	7		

TOTAL 345

The adoption of a proposal from the Commission required at least 258 votes in favour, cast by a majority of members.

Where the proposal was not from the Commission (as was possible, for example, under the intergovernmental pillars) at least 258 votes were required, cast by at least two-thirds of the members.

When a decision was to be adopted by the Council by a qualified majority, a member of the Council could request verification that the Member States constituting the qualified majority represented at least 62% of the total population of the Union. If that condition was not met, the decision could not be adopted.

The 'various interests' Group includes farmers, the professions, the self-employed, consumers, and environmental groups. Members are proposed by national governments and formally appointed by the Council of Ministers. They sit on the ESC in a personal capacity and formally may not be bound by any mandate or instructions from their organizations.

The main work of the ESC is carried out by its six Sections, which are the equivalent of the Committees in the EP. They are:

- Agriculture, Rural Development, and the Environment;
- Economic and Monetary Union and Economic and Social Cohesion;
- Employment, Social Affairs and Citizenship;
- External Relations;
- The Single Market, Production, and Consumption;
- Transport, Energy, Infrastructure, and the Information Society.

A secretariat-general is responsible for the Committee's administration.

The Commission, or the Council as appropriate, has to consult the ESC on a range of issues including agricultural matters, freedom of movement for workers, the right of establishment of companies, social policy, internal market issues, measures of economic and social cohesion, and environmental policy. In addition, the Commission may consult it on any matter that it thinks appropriate; and the ESC has the right to issue opinions on any matter on its own initiative, except for subjects that fall under the remit of the ECSC, which still has its own Consultative Committee.

In practice the ESC is not particularly influential. This is because it has chosen not to be selective in issuing opinions, which are of very variable quality. There is thus a lot of paper coming out of the secretariat of the ESC, much of it not very constructive, and as a result little of it is read with any great attention.

The Committee of the Regions and Local Authorities (CoR)

The CoR was created by the TEU, and was given the right to be consulted on proposals that affected regional and local interests, and the right to issue opinions on its own initiative. Its members are chosen by the member states and officially appointed by the Council of Ministers for a four-year, renewable term (Table 18.4). The members participate in the work of seven specialized commissions that are responsible for drafting the Committee's opinions.

The Bureau, which organizes the work of the Committee and its commissions, includes the chair, a first vice-chair, plus one vice-chair from each of the member states, whom the members of the assembly elect for two-year terms. They also include the chairs of the political groups. A secretariat-general is responsible for the Committee's administration.

At first sight the CoR appears to be another incarnation of the ESC, with which it originally shared a meeting chamber and support staff. However, there is an important difference: the CoR is strongly backed by political actors of considerable influence. It was put into the TEU at the insistence of the German Federal Government under pressure

TABLE 18.4

Membership of the Committee of the Regions and Local Authorities

Austria	12	Latvia	7
Belgium	12	Lithuania	9
Cyprus	6	Luxemburg	6
Czech Republic	12	Malta	5
Denmark	9	Netherlands	12
Estonia	7	Poland	21
Finland	9	Portugal	12
France	24	Slovakia	9
Germany	24	Slovenia	7
Greece	12	Spain	21
Hungary	12	Sweden	12
Ireland	9	United Kingdom	24
Italy	24	TOTAL:	317

Note: The number of members per member state were the same prior to the 2004 enlargement. There were only 222 members.

from the Länder, the states that make up the German federation. They appear to see it as an embryonic European equivalent of the Bundesrat, the upper house of the Federal German Parliament in which the Länder are represented. This interpretation of the future of the CoR is shared by regional authorities from some other member states, particularly Belgium and Spain. With the political weight and the resources of these significant regional actors behind it, there is a possibility that the Committee will turn into a much more influential institution than the ESC. The Commission therefore has every incentive to work closely with the Committee, particularly because the Commission itself has long favoured the emergence of a 'Europe of regions' that would break down the domination of all decision making by the central governments of the member states. So, as well as being another constraint on the freedom of action of the Commission, the CoR provides it with a potential ally against the governments.

Decision-Making Procedures

There are two types of decision-making procedure: that for adopting the annual budget of the EU—the budgetary procedure—and the various legislative procedures.

The Budgetary Procedure

The budgetary procedure is laid down in Article 272 (previously Article 203) of the Treaty, although it has been modified as a result of inter-institutional agreements

(Figure 18.3). The budget is divided into 'compulsory' and 'non-compulsory' items of expenditure. Compulsory expenditure consists mainly of agricultural expenditure, which remains the largest single item in the budget (Figure 18.4). The EP can only propose modifications to the compulsory items by an absolute majority of its members. However, it has the right to amend the draft budget for non-compulsory items with the effect that the EP has a final say on these items of expenditure within the constraints imposed by the multi-annual financial perspectives. The Constitutional Treaty proposed to abolish the artificial distinction between compulsory and non-compulsory items.

In 1988 the EP, the Council, and the Commission signed an Inter-institutional Agreement on Budgetary Discipline. This instituted multi-annual financial frameworks, and agreed ceilings for both compulsory and non-compulsory expenditure, which would have the effect of shifting the balance to the non-compulsory items. The balance between compulsory and non-compulsory expenditure in the budget, so long as it still holds, is obviously of considerable importance in determining the level of influence that the EP may exercise.

The first financial perspective covered the years 1988–92 and the second 1993–9. In March 1999, agreement was reached on a third financial perspective to cover the period 2000–6. Although they did increase the influence of the EP by shifting the balance of the budget away from compulsory expenditure, in practice the financial frameworks are predominantly negotiated between the Commission and the member states, and allow for only very limited change within budget headings. They thus provide little opportunity for the EP to increase or decrease expenditure in particular areas on a year-by-year basis.

The budget process begins with the Commission drawing up a Preliminary Draft Budget, which it has to do under the Treaty by 1 September of each year, but which it normally completes by June. The work is performed by the Budget Directorate-General (previously DG xix) in consultation with the other services of the Commission and under the supervision of the Budget Commissioner. In preparing this document, the Commission is constrained by the multi-annual budgetary framework agreements. The Budget Directorate-General holds a meeting with representatives of the Council and the EP to discuss the precise interpretation of the framework in the specific conditions of the current financial year. The Commission also takes the opportunity to establish the financial priorities of the other two institutions.

Once the Preliminary Draft Budget is prepared, and agreed by the Commissioners as a whole, it is sent to the Council of Ministers, which formally has until 5 October to adopt a Draft Budget. Often, however, the Draft Budget has been adopted by the end of the Council presidency for the first half of the year, which means by the end of June. Most of the detailed work at this stage is done by the Budget Committee of the Council—which consists of the financial attachés to the offices of the Permanent Representatives—operating under QMV. Before the adoption of the Draft Budget an informal meeting is held with the Budget Committee of the EP to try to resolve any issues that could delay the process later.

The Draft Budget is then sent to the EP for a first reading, which has to be completed within forty-five days. The Budgetary Committee of the EP takes the lead, co-ordinating with the other specialized committees. The EP can simply approve the budget at this stage, but it invariably proposes a lot of amendments to the Preliminary Draft Budget, most of which increase expenditure to the maximum permissible level. The maximum rate of increase is determined by the increase over the previous year of the gross national product of the EU, the increase in national budgets, and the rate of inflation. It can only be exceeded by agreement between the Council and the EP.

Once adopted by the full EP, the Draft Budget goes back to the Council. The Council then has fifteen days to consider its response to the amendments proposed by the EP. At this stage there is a meeting between the Council and the EP, with the full participation of the Commission, to try to reach agreement on priorities within the budget. Despite this 'conciliation' meeting, the Council usually rejects most of the amendments proposed by the EP.

The final stage is for the EP to complete a second reading within fifteen days of receipt of the Amended Draft Budget. The EP will restore whatever it has the power to restore of its original amendments. This is where the distinction between 'compulsory' and 'non-compulsory' expenditure is particularly important: the EP does not have the right to re-amend compulsory expenditure, only non-compulsory. To do this it has to muster the votes of a majority of all members, and three-fifths of those voting. It then has to adopt or reject the Budget as a whole. Rejection requires a majority of all members, and three-fifths of the votes cast. If the budget is rejected, as it was five times between 1979 and 1988, efforts to reach an agreement continue, but if no agreement can be reached by 1 January, when the new financial year begins, the EU has to operate on a system known as 'provisional twelfths'. This means that each month one-twelfth of the previous year's budget total is released to cover expenditure. This will obviously prove cumulatively more restrictive as the year progresses, and in particular it will mean that new programmes, which had no budget line the previous year, will not be able to begin operation. The introduction of the multi-annual financial perspectives has, though, considerably reduced the prospects of rejection.

There is one other part to the budgetary process. Every year the Commission is required to submit to the Council and the EP the accounts of the previous financial year. These are considered by both institutions in the light of the annual report from the Court of Auditors. The EP receives a recommendation from the Council, and in the light of this and its own deliberations, gives discharge to the Commission in respect to implementation of the budget. This means that the EP formally acknowledges that the Commission has implemented the budget properly and efficiently. It is not clear what happens if the EP does not feel that it can do so.

Legislative Procedures

So far as legislative proposals are concerned, there are many different procedures that operate under the EC pillar of the EU. The four main procedures with which students of the EU need to be familiar are:

- consultation (Figure 18.5);
- co-operation (Figure 18.6);
- co-decision (Figure 18.7);
- assent.

FIGURE 18.3

The Budgetary Procedure

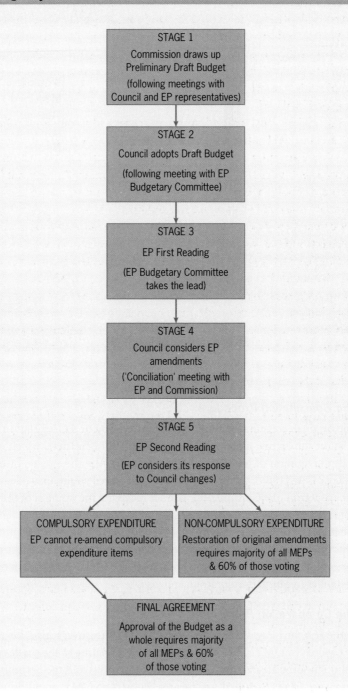

STAGE 1

Commission draws up
Preliminary Draft Budget

(following meetings with
Council and EP representatives)

STAGE 2

Council adopts Draft Budget

(following meeting with EP
Budgetary Committee)

STAGE 3

EP First Reading

(EP Budgetary Committee
takes the lead)

STAGE 4

Council considers EP
amendments

('Conciliation' meeting with
EP and Commission)

STAGE 5

EP Second Reading

(EP considers its response
to Council changes)

COMPULSORY EXPENDITURE

EP cannot re-amend compulsory
expenditure items

NON-COMPULSORY EXPENDITURE

Restoration of original amendments
requires majority of all MEPs
& 60% of those voting

FINAL AGREEMENT

Approval of the Budget as a
whole requires majority
of all MEPs & 60%
of those voting

INSTITUTIONS

FIGURE 18.4

Distribution of Expenditure from the Budget of the EU, 2005

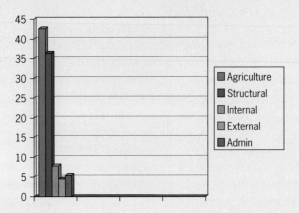

Agricultural expenditure = 42.6 per cent
Structural funds = 36.4 per cent
Internal policies = 7.8 per cent
External actions = 4.5 per cent
Administration = 5.4 per cent

These are the major items of expenditure. No other item accounts for more than 2 per cent of expenditure.

Source: Compiled from figures in European Commission, *General Budget of the European Union for the Financial Year 2005: The Figures* (Brussels and Luxemburg, January 2005).

The Consultation Procedure

The original 'consultation procedure' for deciding on EC legislation involved the Commission submitting a proposal to the Council of Ministers, which was then obliged to seek the opinion of the EP, and, where required by the Treaty, of the ESC. In the Isoglucose Case (1980), the ECJ ruled that the Council could not act legally in deciding on a proposal from the Commission without receiving the opinion of the EP. However, having received that opinion, the Council could if it so wished simply ignore it and agree to the proposal or reject it. Amendments could only be made by unanimity in the Council. This procedure still exists for certain categories of business, mainly agricultural policy issues and the policy sectors that were transferred under Amsterdam from the third to the first pillar (asylum, immigration, and visas).

The Co-operation Procedure

In the SEA the EP was given a right of second reading over legislation that was in future to be covered by QMV. This was most legislation relating to the single market programme, although some areas, such as veterinary regulations and the harmonization of taxation, were specifically excluded. In the areas subject to QMV, in addition to the right to be consulted, the EP was given a second chance to propose amendments. This procedure, often known as 'the co-operation procedure' is now almost only of historical interest, as in the Treaty of Amsterdam it was replaced by co-decision (see below) in nearly all areas to which it had applied. The exceptions were in the field of monetary union, which was not dealt with at Amsterdam. However, it is still worth explaining the co-operation procedure in full for two reasons. First, the procedure was of considerable historical importance, and students trying to understand institutional and policy developments between 1987 and 1997 will need to know how it worked. Second, the early stages of the co-operation procedure are the same as those of the later co-decision procedure, so an understanding of the earlier procedure will facilitate an understanding of the later.

Under the co-operation procedure, the Council adopted a 'common position' by QMV after the first round of consultation. This position was then communicated to the EP, together with a statement of the Council's reasons for adopting it, and a statement of the Commission's view on the position. The EP had three months in which to approve or reject the common position, or to propose amendments. If the EP approved the common position, or if it did not act at all within the three months allowed, the Council could adopt the common position as the final version of the proposal. To propose amendments, or to reject the common position, the EP had to be able to do so by an absolute majority of all its members. If the EP rejected the common position, the Council could only proceed to a second reading if it agreed to do so unanimously.

If the EP proposed amendments to the common position, the next stage was for the Commission to decide within one month whether to accept those amendments. If it did, the amended proposal went back to the Council of Ministers, which could only re-amend it if it acted unanimously. If the Commission did not accept the EP's proposed amendments, they were reported to the Council, which could decide to adopt them, but only by unanimity. This gave the Commission considerable discretion in the process. Under the co-operation procedure, the Council had the final say on the legislation adopted, unless the EP rejected the common position and the Council could not achieve unanimity, in which case the EP could block legislation.

The Co-Decision Procedure

Co-decision gave the EP stronger powers than co-operation. In its early stages it parallels the co-operation procedure; but if the EP rejects the common position, or the Council does not approve the EP's amendments, then a Conciliation Committee is set up. This consists of representatives of the members of the Council, and an equal number

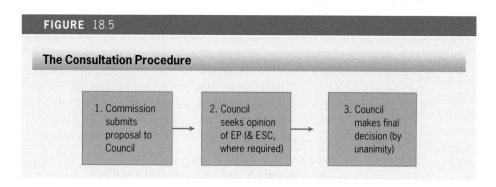

FIGURE 18.5

The Consultation Procedure

1. Commission submits proposal to Council → 2. Council seeks opinion of EP (& ESC, where required) → 3. Council makes final decision (by unanimity)

FIGURE 18.6

The Co-operation Procedure

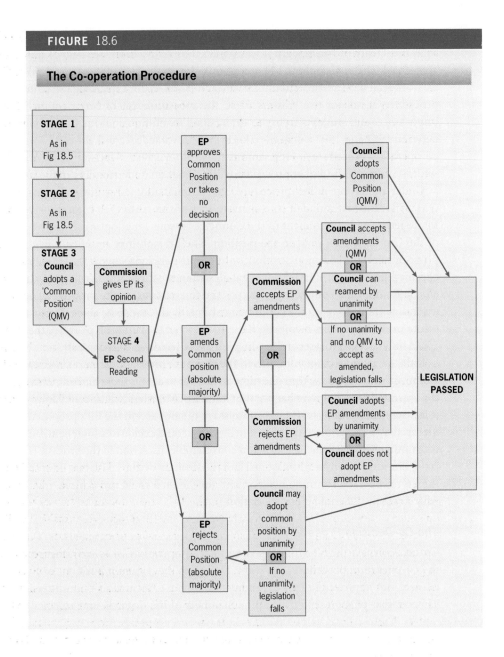

of representatives of the EP. With the help of the Commission, which acts in the role of a facilitator, the Conciliation Committee tries to negotiate a mutually acceptable compromise text, which can then be recommended to both institutions. The Committee has six weeks in which to do so, operating on the basis of QMV for the Council members and simple majority voting for the EP members.

If the Conciliation Committee agrees a joint text, the EP and the Council have six weeks in which to adopt it. The EP has to do so by an absolute majority, the Council

by a qualified majority. If either institution fails to adopt the text, the proposal is effectively dead. Under the rules adopted in the TEU, the next stage was very complex, but it
was simplified at Amsterdam. Under the original procedure, if the Conciliation Committee failed to agree a joint text, the Council could reaffirm its adoption of the original
text within six weeks. If it did not do so, the measure fell; if it did do so, the EP had a
further six weeks in which to reject the adopted text by an absolute majority. If the EP
did not reject the text, the measure was adopted; but if it did, the measure fell. Under
Amsterdam this extremely complex stage, which many felt advantaged the Council over
the EP, was simplified so that now, if the Conciliation Committee fails, the measure falls.
Amsterdam also simplified the co-decision procedure by allowing the Council to adopt
a measure where it and the EP are in agreement, or where the EP is unable to muster the
majority needed to pass amendments.

Other policy areas that became subject to QMV for the first time in the TEU, such as
environmental policy, were covered by the older co-operation procedure, but these were
changed to co-decision by the Treaty of Amsterdam. Under the TEU, two policy areas
that were subject to the co-decision procedure—cultural policy, and the multi-annual
technological research and development framework programmes—differed from the
other areas in that unanimity applied at the Council stages. At Amsterdam this was
changed for the framework programmes, which now come under QMV, but the anom-
aly was retained for cultural matters, and social security for migrant workers, the rights
of the self-employed, and citizens' rights were added to this category. It was also agreed at
Amsterdam that visa procedures and uniformity rules would be governed by co-decision
after five years.

Assent

The EP can also block legislation under the assent procedure. This was originally introduced for agreements with non-member states, but was extended in the TEU to cover
other areas. These included citizenship of the EU, amendments to the statute of the
European System of Central Banks, elections to the EP in accordance with a uniform
electoral procedure, and establishment and reform of the structural funds. Under Amsterdam, citizens' rights was transferred to co-decision (although with the Council acting by unanimity), while assent was extended to sanctions against a member state for
serious and persistent breach of fundamental rights. Assent is a simple extension of the
consultation procedure in which the assent of the EP is required for a measure to be adopted. There is no provision for the EP to amend proposals. However, the fact that its
assent is required does give it considerable influence at the stage when proposals are being prepared.

Implementation

The policy process does not end once agreement has been reached on a legislative proposal. The agreement still has to be implemented before the policy has any real existence.
In other words, implementation is an integral part of the policy process. For many types

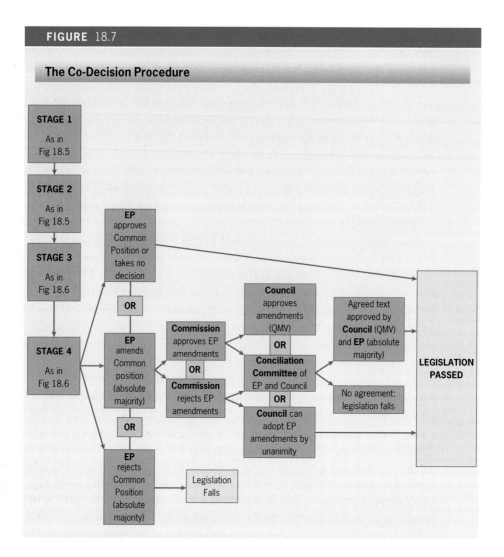

FIGURE 18.7

The Co-Decision Procedure

of legislation the primary implementers are the governments and administrations of the member states. The Commission has a central role in the case of other types of legislation, and is also charged by Article 211 (previously Article 155) of the Treaty to 'ensure that the provisions of this Treaty and the measures taken by the institutions pursuant thereto are applied'. In performing this latter task the Commission has recourse to judicial authority through the referral of cases to the ECJ. Finally, the implementation of all financial instruments is subject to scrutiny by the Court of Auditors.

National Authorities and Implementation

There are three main types of EC instruments that are legally binding: decisions, directives, and regulations. Decisions are addressed to particular individual legal actors such as companies or individual states. Directives are the most common form of general legislation agreed in the Council of Ministers; it is left to individual member states to decide how they are incorporated into national law. Regulations are directly applicable in all member states.

Where directives are concerned, there are two stages to implementation by national authorities. First, the directives have to be incorporated into national law through appropriate national legal instruments. Second, they have to be implemented on the ground; that is, they have to be applied by national administrative authorities. Regulations do not have to be incorporated into national law through national legal instruments, but it is still usually the responsibility of national administrative authorities to ensure that they are applied.

In the case of both aspects of implementation the record of member states in actually doing what they have agreed to do varies considerably. This means that the outcomes of EU decisions are not always the same as the intention. The Commission monitors the record of member states in implementing EU law in specific areas. For example, the varying record of member states in implementing single-market legislation is recorded in the successive reports on the implementation of the Internal Market Strategy (European Commission 2004*a*, 2005)

The Commission and Implementation

Formally, the Commission has overall responsibility for the implementation of EC decisions. There are several processes of implementation in the EU, in each of which the Commission has a role. First, there is the implementation of common policies that are centrally administered by the Commission itself. These are few, but some of the powers of the Commission under the ECSC and Euratom Treaties fall under this heading, as does competition policy, including the control of large-scale mergers. A slightly different area is the administration of international policies such as the provision of food-aid, where again the Commission is the sole responsible EU body, although it has to work in conjunction with other organizations. Second, there is the implementation of common policies which takes place partly at the European level and partly at the national level: the administration of the common agricultural policy (CAP) and the structural funds come under this heading. Third, there is the implementation of Council directives, where the Commission has a dual role as guardian of the Treaties: to ensure that directives are promptly and accurately incorporated into national law in the member states, and to ensure that they are actually implemented on the ground.

Under Article 226 (previously Article 169), if the Commission considers that a member state has failed to fulfil its obligations, it is required to deliver a reasoned opinion on the matter after giving the government of the member state concerned the opportunity to submit its own observations. If the state does not comply with the reasoned opinion, the matter may be brought before the ECJ. Another member state may also bring an alleged infringement of obligations to the attention of the Commission, which is required to act on the matter within three months, or the case automatically goes to the ECJ.

The European Court of Justice (ECJ)

Article 220 (formerly 164) of the Treaty charges the ECJ to ensure that the law of the EC is observed. It is the final arbiter on the interpretation of the Treaties and the application of EC law. As such it is a referee in disputes between institutions and member states.

Where the ECJ is asked to rule on whether a member state has fulfilled its obligations under EC law, its decision is final. Originally there was no penalty other than moral pressure if a member state still failed to fulfil its obligations after the ECJ had ruled against it. However, the TEU amended Article 171, EEC (now Article 228), to allow the Commission to return to the ECJ if it felt that a state was not complying with a ruling, and to request that a financial penalty be levied against the state.

The Court of Auditors

In 1975 the Treaty Amending Certain Financial Provisions of the EEC created a new institution, the European Court of Auditors. The Treaty confers upon the Court of Auditors the main task of auditing the accounts and the implementation of the budget of the European Union with the dual aim of improving financial management and the reporting to the citizens of Europe on the use made of public funds by the authorities responsible for their management.

It is based in Luxemburg, and consists of one member from each member state appointed for a renewable six-year period. Members must have belonged to national audit offices, or be especially qualified for the office, and their independence must be beyond doubt. The members of the Court themselves elect a President from among their number for a period of three years. It has 760 staff, of whom 250 are auditors.

This Court examines the accounts of all revenue and expenditure of the EC to determine whether the revenue has been received and the expenditure incurred in a lawful and regular manner. It provides the EP and the Council with a statement on the reliability of the accounts, and publishes an annual report. It also prepares special reports on aspects of the audit, either on its own initiative or at the request of another institution; and it delivers opinions on request from the other institutions concerning the financial implications of proposed legislation.

The Intergovernmental Pillars of the EU

The TEU introduced two new areas of co-operation to the Treaties (see Fig. 18.1, p. 232). CFSP was a renaming of what had first appeared in the SEA as 'European Co-operation in the Sphere of Foreign Policy' (Insight 18.1). JHA was entirely new as a Treaty commitment (Insight 18.2). In both cases actual co-operation had begun before incorporation in the Treaties. Because the member states were not ready to risk any surrender of control over such sensitive areas of national policy, these areas were not brought under the decision-making rules of the EC. Instead they were put into two separate 'intergovernmental' pillars where the Commission did not have the sole right of initiative.

INSIGHT 18.1

Common Foreign and Security Policy

Under Article 11 of the TEU, the CFSP has the following objectives:

- to safeguard the common values, fundamental interests, independence and integrity of the Union in conformity with the principles of the United Nations Charter,
- to strengthen the security of the Union in all ways,
- to preserve peace and strengthen international security, in accordance with the principles of the United Nations Charter, as well as the principles of the Helsinki Final Act and the objectives of the Paris Charter, including those on external borders,
- to promote international co-operation,
- to develop and consolidate democracy and the rule of law, and respect for human rights and fundamental freedoms.

Under Article 12 of the TEU, these objectives are to be pursued by:

- defining the principles of and general guidelines for the common foreign and security policy,
- deciding on common strategies,
- adopting joint actions,
- adopting common positions,
- strengthening systematic co-operation between Member States in the conduct of policy.

In these two pillars the Commission, the EP, and the ECJ did not have the same powers as under the EC pillar. In both pillars the Commission was to be 'fully associated' with actions taken, and it had the right to propose actions to the Council of Ministers, but it shared this right with the member states. The EP was to be consulted by the member state holding the presidency on the main aspects of both areas of co-operation, was to be regularly informed by the presidency and the Commission of developments, and was to be allowed to ask questions of the Council and make recommendations to it. It was also required to debate developments in each pillar annually.

These arrangements still apply to CFSP, but the Amsterdam Treaty modified the commitment under JHA. It split the previous bundle of JHA issues by transferring some of them to the TEC, where they were rolled in with issues of the free movement of persons that were already dealt with under the TEC. Together these issues formed a new Title IV (Articles 61-9) called 'Visas, Asylum, Immigration and other policies related to the Free Movement of Persons'. Although voting was to remain by unanimity, the transfer had the effect of bringing these areas within the jurisdiction of the ECJ. Amsterdam also formally changed the name of the previous JHA Title VI of the TEU (Articles 29–42) to 'Provisions on Police and Judicial Co-operation in Criminal Matters'. It should be noted, though, that the term 'JHA' is still commonly used to refer to all of these issues collectively.

INSIGHT 18.2

Justice and Home Affairs

Under the heading of JHA the TEU originally committed the member states to pursue co-operation in the following areas:

- asylum policy
- controls on people crossing the external frontiers of the Union
- immigration policy
- combating drug addiction
- combating fraud on an international scale
- judicial co-operation in civil matters
- judicial co-operation in criminal matters
- customs co-operation.

(Treaties Article 29, previously Article κ.1) Under the Treaty of Amsterdam, asylum and immigration policy were transferred to the EC pillar. The new Article 29 of the TEU therefore defines the objectives of 'Police and Judicial Co-operation in Criminal Matters' as:

- closer co-operation between police forces, customs authorities and other competent authorities in the Member States, both directly and through the European Police Office (Europol);
- closer co-operation between judicial and other competent authorities of the Member States including co-operation through the European Judicial Co-operation Unit ('Eurojust');
- approximation, where necessary, of rules on criminal matters in the Member States.

The Proposed Constitution of the EU

Several changes were made to the formal rules of the EU in the Constitution that was agreed on 18 June 2004. Some of these have been indicated in the relevant sections above. Together they affected:

- the rules covering QMV;
- the presidency of the Council;
- the size of the Commission and the rules for its installation;
- the rules for allowing a group of states to proceed further with co-operation than others wish to go ('enhanced co-operation');
- the powers of the EP;
- the role of national parliaments;
- the rules governing the Police and Judicial Co-operation pillar;
- the institutional shape of and the rules governing CFSP and ESDP;
- the rules governing the Euro Group.

In addition to these changes, which are considered in more detail below, the Constitution for the first time specified the areas that are in the exclusive competence of the EU (Article I-13), and the areas of shared competence (Article I-14).

The Rules Covering QMV

As was recorded in Chapter 15 (pp. 196–8), the changes to the rules covering QMV in the Council of Ministers proved extremely controversial. Failure by the heads of government to agree on the proposals of the Constitutional Convention on this point led to the failure of the European Council in December 2003 to adopt the Constitutional Treaty. The issue became one of division between the larger and the smaller member states. There was serious concern on the part of the majority of states that the EU was at risk of being dominated by the 'big 4' of Britain, France, Germany, and Italy.

The resistance of Poland and Spain to any change to the complex 'triple majority' system that had been agreed at Nice was undermined in March 2004 by a change of government in Spain, which left Poland isolated at the Brussels European Council in June 2004. Nevertheless, the agreements reached were marked by a continuing suspicion of the motives of the largest member states. Under the new 'double majority' system, support for a measure would have to include 55 per cent of the member states (i.e. 14 with 25 members), whose combined populations constituted 65 per cent of the total population of the EU. However, so that three big states acting together could not block measures that were strongly favoured by all the other members, there was also a requirement that a blocking minority consist of at least four states. A higher threshold applied for voting on proposals where the measure was not initiated by the Commission. This mainly applied to proposals under the CFSP pillar. Here, for a measure to be adopted it needed the support of 72 per cent of the member states (i.e. 18 while there are 25 members), whose combined populations constituted 65 per cent of the total population of the EU.

QMV was extended to a total of 44 new areas in the Constitution, although most of these are to do with implementation rather than the adoption of new legislation. Because of opposition from Britain, and some other member states, QMV was not extended to tax, to defence and foreign policy, or to budgetary contributions; and because of opposition from France, and some other member states, it was not extended to social, education, and health services, nor to policy on trade in cultural products. Article IV-444 permitted the European Council to adopt a decision allowing areas still governed by the unanimity rule to be decided instead by QMV, without the need for a full-blown treaty revision involving a new intergovernmental conference (IGC). To do this, the European Council had to agree unanimously, and it first had to consult the EP and get the consent of a majority of the Members (MEPs). Even then, the measure had to be agreed by all national parliaments, and could not be implemented if any one of them withheld that consent. This procedure was referred to by practitioners and commentators as the 'passarelle', although the term appeared nowhere in the Treaty.

In some of the new areas covered by QMV, a system that became known as the 'emergency brake' applied, although again the term did not appear in the Treaty. If a member state felt that its important national interests were threatened by a proposed measure, it could invoke this procedure, requiring the measure to be referred to the European Council, where it would be resolved by unanimity.

This applied to:

- proposals on the provision of social security benefits to nationals of one member state working in another (Article III-136), if a member state felt that the proposal would affect 'fundamental aspects' of its social security system;

- two areas of Police and Judicial Co-operation, concerning judicial co-operation itself, and the definition of serious crimes—such as terrorism, drugs trafficking, and money laundering—if a member state felt that the proposal would affect fundamental aspects of its criminal justice system.

The Presidency of the Council

Under the TEU and the TEC, one member state holds the presidency of both the European Council and the Council of Ministers for a six-month period, with the position rotating between the member states on a fixed rota (Ch. 20, pp. 287–90). Under the Constitutional Treaty, the European Council would elect an individual to act as its President for a period of two-and-a-half years. This would be a permanent full-time post: the President would not hold national office as well as the presidency. He or she would, in conjunction with the President of the Commission and on the basis of the work of the General Affairs Council: prepare the work of the European Council; chair the meetings of the European Council and 'drive forward its work'; and report to the EP after the meetings. In addition, the President would 'ensure the external representation of the Union on issues concerning its common foreign and security policy, without prejudice to the powers of the Union Minister for Foreign Affairs'. At the time of writing it was not at all clear how these distributions of duties would work themselves out in practice, and most commentators believed that the role was fraught with problems.

The Council of Ministers would also have a new system for its presidency. Instead of each member state in turn holding the presidency for six months at a time, a team of three member states together would hold the presidency for eighteen months at a time. The teams of three would then change over every eighteen months.

The Commission

Under the new rules, the College of Commissioners would consist of a number of individuals equal to two-thirds of the number of member states. This figure seems to have been arrived at arbitrarily. A system to be adopted by the European Council would ensure that there was a strict rotation of nationalities within the Commission, and that every Commission would reflect the geographical spread of the EU, and would be balanced between large, medium-sized, and small member states.

Whereas under the previous treaties, the governments of the member states nominated the President of the Commission 'by common accord', and the EP was required to approve the nomination, under the new procedure the nomination would be by majority vote in the European Council, and would have to take account of the results of the EP elections that would just have been held. Formally, the nominee would be appointed by the EP, not by the European Council. These changes, although subtle, represented a further extension of the powers of the EP, and particularly gave increased importance to the direct elections, as their outcome should have influenced the political family from which the President was drawn.

Enhanced Co-operation

Under Article I-44, the possibilities for enhanced co-operation were extended to any area that did not lie within the exclusive competences of the EU as defined in Article I-13. If the Council was satisfied that there was no prospect of being able to proceed within a reasonable period of time with closer co-operation across the EU as a whole, then a group of states could go ahead to develop closer co-operation between themselves, provided that at least one-third of the member states took part. This group of states could use the institutions of the EU for the purposes of their enhanced co-operation. Article I-44 specified the voting rules that would apply to such a group when it operated under QMV. A qualified majority was defined in the same way as for the Council as a whole: i.e. 55 per cent of the participating member states, representing at least 65 per cent of the total population of the participating states. A blocking minority was defined as a number of states representing at least 35 per cent of the population of all the participating states, plus one more participating state.

The European Parliament

One of the objectives of the Constitutional Convention was to consider ways of enhancing the democratic legitimacy of the EU. In pursuit of this objective, the Constitution extended the powers of the EP. Co-decision, a procedure that most observers believe gives the EP the maximum influence over legislation, was extended to cover almost all EC and Police and Judicial Co-operation matters, although the EP continued to have only a consultative role in CFSP matters. The budgetary powers of the EP were also extended by the abolition of the distinction between compulsory and non-compulsory items in the budget. As noted above, the EP was given a slightly stronger role in the appointment of the President of the Commission. Enhanced co-operation between a group of member states could only proceed with the agreement of the EP.

The Role of National Parliaments

A second approach to address the problem of democratic legitimacy was the greater involvement of national parliaments in the decision-making processes of the EU. Under a *Protocol on the Role of National Parliaments in the European Union*, the Commission was required to forward to national parliaments all green papers, white papers, and communications, its annual legislative programme, and draft legislative acts. No draft legislation could be considered in the Council of Ministers until six weeks after delivery to the national parliaments, and none could be passed for a further ten days after appearing on the agenda of the Council for the first time. This gave national parliaments time to consider the draft legislation. Under the *Protocol on Subsidiarity and Proportionality*, if a national parliament did not believe that the proposed legislation was in keeping with the principle of subsidiarity, they had a right to submit a reasoned opinion to that effect. The Commission was expected to take account of any such reasoned opinion, but if one-third of all national parliaments lodged such opinions, then the draft had to be reviewed and re-submitted.

In addition, the national parliaments had to be informed by the European Council if it proposed to use the procedure sometimes known as the *passarelle*, to change the system of voting from unanimity to QMV in any of the policy areas where unanimity still applied. The national parliaments had six months in which to lodge an objection. It only took one national parliament to object for the move to be blocked.

The Police and Judicial Co-operation Pillar

This is the area where the Constitution made the biggest changes. In effect the Police and Judicial Co-operation pillar (which prior to Amsterdam was the JHA pillar) ceased to be an intergovernmental pillar. Whereas in the TEU the Commission was only to be 'fully associated' with procedures under the Police and Judicial Co-operation pillar, in the Constitution it was given a full right of initiative, and member states could only make a proposal for a regulation if a quarter of them backed the initiative. Many measures would still be subject to unanimity, and the EP had only the right of consultation. QMV would apply in areas of the harmonization of laws, and here the EP had the same rights as under the co-decision procedure. However, there was an 'emergency brake' clause. Under Article III-271(3), if a member state believed that a measure that was passed under QMV would adversely affect fundamental aspects of its national judicial system, it could ask that the measure be referred to the European Council, where it would be decided on by unanimity. Against this, if such a measure was not agreed, the member states that supported it could go ahead under a procedure similar to enhanced co-operation, except that the unanimous agreement of the Council was not necessary for them to proceed in this way.

The ECJ, which was explicitly excluded from any role in this pillar originally, was in the Constitution confirmed in the right that it had already obtained to rule on whether a member state is acting in compliance with its obligations under Police and Judicial Co-operation agreements; and for the first time, the Commission had a right to refer a case of alleged non-compliance to the Court. However, the ECJ was still explicitly not allowed any competence to rule on the actions of police or judicial authorities.

CFSP and ESDP

Whereas the JHA pillar has been steadily eroded as an intergovernmental procedure through the Treaties of Amsterdam and Nice, a process that would have culminated in the effective disappearance of the separate pillar in the Constitution, CFSP has remained as intergovernmental as it was at its inception in the TEU. Under the terms of the Constitution, voting on CFSP matters would remain predominantly by unanimity. There were two exceptions. First, continuing the existing position, implementation measures could be agreed by QMV if the Council agreed unanimously to allow it. Second, if the new Union Minister for Foreign Affairs was requested by the European Council to bring forward proposals, these proposals could be voted on by QMV, but again only if the Council first agreed unanimously to do so. In neither case could QMV be used for measures having military or defence implications. There remained a provision for a member state to abstain in a vote, and make a formal declaration that it could not implement the decision if it was accepted. In that case the measure would be adopted if no other state vetoed it, and the abstaining state would be permitted not to implement the measure, provided always that it must also not take any action in conflict with the decision. However, if one-third of all the member states made such a declaration, the measure would not be adopted.

The main change in the CFSP/ESDP was the introduction of the new position of EU Minister for Foreign Affairs. This post combined the previous competences and duties of the Commissioner for External Relations and the High Representative for Foreign Affairs, with the incumbent straddling the Commission and the Council Secretariat—a potentially uncomfortable position. The appointment would be made by the European Council, acting by QMV, and with the agreement of the President of the Commission, and the appointee would automatically be a Vice-President of the Commission, but would also chair the Foreign Affairs Council, and would take part in the proceedings of the European Council.

The tasks of the Minister were to contribute to the development of the CFSP and the ESDP; to ensure that the policies were implemented; to ensure that all the external policies of the Commission were consistent with the CFSP/ESDP; to report on CFSP/ESDP to the EP; to engage in political dialogue with other states on behalf of the EU; and to represent the position of the EU in forums such as international organizations and international conferences. A new European External Action Service would be set up to assist the Minister, consisting of officials from the Commission, from the Council Secretariat, and from the diplomatic services of member states.

The Euro Group

There was a special Protocol to the Constitution devoted to the arrangements of meetings between Ministers of Finance of member states whose currency is the Euro. This was the first time that the Euro Group has been explicitly mentioned in a Treaty. The Protocol was very short: just two Articles. It specified that the meetings would consist of ministers only of those states that had adopted the Euro, that the Commission would take part in the meetings, and that the European Central Bank 'shall be invited to take part in such meetings'. It also made provision for the members of the Group to elect a Chair who would hold office for a period of two-and-a-half years.

CONCLUSION

The decision-making procedures of the EC are extremely complex. In particular, several different legislative procedures exist depending on the policy sector concerned. In many cases the procedure to be followed is by no means immediately apparent, and here the Commission can exercise some discretion in deciding under which articles of the Treaties it will bring forward its proposals. Sometimes this has been challenged. For example, in 1990 the Commission brought forward proposals on maternity rights under what was then the new Article 118A of the EEC Treaty (now Article 138), which the SEA had introduced. This meant that the measure was subject to QMV in the Council, rather than unanimity. The British government objected to the Treaty base, and threatened to refer the matter to the ECJ, before eventually accepting a compromise solution.

Whatever Treaty base is chosen, the main actors remain the same; only the relative balance of influence is shifted. The Commission, the Council of Ministers, and the EP are the dominant institutional actors. Behind the scenes of the formal constitutional arrangements, interest groups always exercise a considerable influence on both the content of proposals and the outcome of the decision-making process. At the implementation stage, the Commission and the ECJ are particularly important among the EU institutions, but national governments are often the key to how policies are implemented.

The formal relationships outlined in this chapter are only one part, although an important part, of the analysis of the role of the EU institutions. The informal relationships between the institutions themselves, and between the institutions and the member states, are the part not covered here. In the chapters that follow, these informal relationships become central to the discussion, and attention focuses on the academic debates that have been generated about these relationships and their implications.

A key issue of debate concerning the Commission has been the extent to which it is an actor with independent influence over the process of European integration. One view is that it is merely an agent of the member states, and acts only in accordance with their wishes; the alternative view is that it has a good deal of autonomy, and can push the member states in directions that they do not wish to go. This debate is central to the intergovernmental–supranational dichotomy outlined in Chapter 1, and is one of the debates considered in the next chapter. The other relates to the role of the Commission in the implementation of policy, where it is widely perceived to be less efficient than it is in making policy proposals.

The main issue of academic debate about the Council of Ministers centres on how far it is really an intergovernmental organization through which the member states successfully control the EU. Some analysts have argued that the complex nature of the structure of committees that make up the Council, and the frequency with which the same individuals meet in these committees, has weakened the control by central government actors over the processes and outcomes. From a social constructivist point of view (Ch. 3), officials experience a shared socialization process and the Council committees develop identities of their own, which mean they do not always follow the will of the core executives of their states. This debate is reviewed in Chapter 20.

For the EP the key academic debates have concerned the extent of its power and influence in the legislative process. Sociological institutionalists would argue that the member states have increased the powers of the EP not because it helps the governments of the states to achieve their narrowly-defined objectives, but because the EP has successfully argued that there is a democratic deficit that must be filled in order to give the decisions of the EU popular legitimacy (Ch. 4, p. 68). Rational choice institutionalists have contested the common observation that the EP has steadily increased its influence over legislative outcomes, sparking a considerable debate, which is reviewed in Chapter 21.

The ECJ is sometimes believed to have overstepped its proper judicial function as an interpreter of the treaties and an impartial referee in disputes between states. It is accused of having become a political actor, pushing forward European integration in a partisan manner. The evidence for this view is reviewed in Chapter 22.

Finally, although not part of the formal structure of institutions, organized interests play a considerable role in the decision making of the EU behind the scenes, as has been suggested from time to time in this chapter and emphasized by governance and network approaches set out in Chapter 2. The influence of organized interests is assessed in Chapter 23.

KEY POINTS

The Treaties

- ☐ The EC was founded by the Treaty of Paris and the two Treaties of Rome, which were amended and supplemented by later treaties.
- ☐ In 1997 the various treaties were codified into two: the Treaty on the European Community (TEC) and the Treaty on European Union (TEU).
- ☐ Together these treaties form the 'constitution' of the EU unless and until the Constitutional Treaty is ratified.

Decision-Making Institutions

- ☐ The Commission has the sole right to initiate legislation, although this has been somewhat undermined by new procedural rules.
- ☐ The Council of Ministers has to agree to proposals for them to become law. Originally it had to agree unanimously, but there has been a steady move towards the adoption of QMV.
- ☐ Since it became directly elected in 1979, the powers of the EP have grown, particularly in relation to the legislative process, until today it is effectively the co-legislator with the Council of Ministers in most policy areas.
- ☐ The EP is also effectively the co-decision maker with the Council on the annual budget.
- ☐ The ESC consists of representatives of producer and consumer groups, and has to be consulted before certain categories of legislation can be adopted, but its opinions are not often influential.
- ☐ The CoR consists of representatives of regional and local authorities, and is potentially an influential actor in the decision-making process, although that influence has not yet been manifested.

Decision-Making Procedures

- ☐ There are two main types of decision-making procedure in the EC: budgetary and legislative.
- ☐ The EU budget passes through a complex process, which involves the Commission, the Council, and the EP. The EP has gradually extended its role.

☐ Of the four main legislative procedures under the EC pillar, co-decision is now the most common, although consultation and co-operation remain for some matters, and the assent procedure covers mainly agreements on external affairs for which the approval of the EP is required.

Implementation

☐ Implementation is an integral part of the policy-making process.

☐ Three main types of EC instruments are legally binding: decisions, directives, and regulations.

☐ While the Commission has formal responsibility for implementation, in practice national authorities play an important role.

☐ The ECJ has the power to interpret EC law, and its decisions are final.

☐ The Court of Auditors checks the legality and regularity of EC expenditure.

The Intergovernmental Pillars of the EU

☐ The two intergovernmental pillars of the European Union cover Common Foreign and Security Policy (CFSP) and Justice and Home Affairs (JHA)

☐ Under these pillars, the Commission, the EP, and the ECJ have less authority than under the EC pillar.

The Proposed Constitution of the EU

☐ Agreed in June 2004, the Constitutional Treaty awaited ratification at the time of writing.

☐ The proposed Constitution listed for the first time the areas of exclusive competence of the EU, and the areas of shared competence.

☐ It made changes to the rules governing QMV; the presidency of the Council; the size of the Commission and the rules for its installation; the rules for allowing a group of states to proceed further with co-operation than others wish to go ('enhanced co-operation'); the powers of the EP; the role of national parliaments; the rules governing the Police and Judicial Co-operation Title of the JHA pillar; the institutional shape of and the rules governing CFSP and ESDP; and the rules governing the Euro Group.

FURTHER READING

The standard work on the institutional structure of the EU is N. Nugent, *The Government and Politics of the European Union* (Basingstoke: Palgrave Macmillan, 5th edn, 2002). Commentaries on the later treaties are provided by C.H. Church and D. Phinnemore, *European Union and European Community: A Handbook and Commentary on the 1992 Maastricht Treaties* (London: Prentice Hall, 2nd edn, 1995); A. Duff, *The Treaty of Amsterdam: Text and Commentary* (London: Federal Trust/Sweet and Maxwell, 1997), J. Monar and W. Wolfgang (eds.), *The Treaty of Amsterdam* (London: Pinter, 1999), K. Feus (ed.), *The Treaty of Nice Explained* (London: Kogan Page, 2002). On the budget the standard work now is B. Laffan, *The Finances of the European Union* (Basingstoke and London: Macmillan, 1997). Reading on other institutions is given at the end of each of the chapters devoted specifically to them.

 **online resource centre**

Visit the Online Resource Centre that accompanies this book for links to more information on the institutional architecture, including the text of the treaties and the proposed EU Constitution.

CHAPTER 19

The European Commission

CHAPTER OVERVIEW

When the European Community (EC) was established, the European Commission was expected to be the motor of European integration. Because of this, it attracted considerable academic attention, becoming a focal point for the theoretical disputes between intergovernmentalists and supranationalists (Ch. 1). This chapter explains the structure of the Commission before detailing its role in policy making, and reviewing the debate on the extent to which the Commission is an autonomous political actor or simply an agent of the member states. It then turns to the increasing challenges faced by the Commission in securing effective implementation of EU policies and its response to concerns over its financial management of EU programmes.

> To many observers, the Commission is a unique institution. It is not much more than an international secretariat, but not quite a government, though it has many governmental characteristics.
>
> **(Egeberg 2003: 131)**

Composition and Appointment

In an echo of debates between intergovernmentalists and supranationalists, the Commission has been pilloried by **Eurosceptics** as a bureaucratic monster that is out of control, and is usurping the rights of the member states. In fact it is a very small organization in comparison not just with national civil services, but even individual departments of state in national civil services.

The European Commission consists of a College of Commissioners and a permanent civil service of some 24,000 staff, of which only around 18,000 are administrators, the rest being employed either in scientific research or as translators and interpreters. This is the 'Brussels bureaucracy' that is frequently attacked or ridiculed by opponents of the EC. The term 'the Commission' is used to refer both to the Services of the Commission and to the College of Commissioners. However, these should be clearly distinguished, not least because, as Cram (2001: 776) pointed out, 'the members of each may have very different perspectives and, most importantly, very different interests or preferences'.

The Services are divided into twenty-six Directorates General (DGs), plus a number of special services. They are listed in Table 19.1. The DGs are the equivalent of national civil service departments of state. They used to be known by their number only (e.g. DGIV for the Competition Directorate-General, DGVI for the Agriculture Directorate General), but when he became President of the Commission in 1999, Romano Prodi abolished the numbering, and also tried to bring the structure of the DGs more into line with the designation of portfolios within the College. Students of the European Union (EU) will still find references to the DGs by number in historical case studies, but the DGs will always be identified as well so there is no need to list the old numbering, which anyway changed over time.

The Services are the bureaucracy of the EU. Political direction is given by the College of Commissioners. The members of the College—the Commissioners—are nominated by national governments, and appointed by the Council of Ministers. Originally they were appointed for a four-year renewable term, but this was extended to five years in the Treaty on European Union (TEU) (Ch. 13), and the term of office of the College was brought into line with the five-yearly elections to the EP. This allows the new EP to interview the European Council's nominee for President of the Commission, and the nominees for the various Commission portfolios.

Each state has one Commissioner, and the larger member states (France, Germany, Italy, Britain, and Spain) had two each until after the 2004 enlargement. There were therefore:

- Nine Commissioners when the EC had six member states;

TABLE 19.1

The Services and Directorates General of the Commission

Agriculture and Rural Development	European Anti-Fraud Office	Joint Research Centre
Budget	Eurostat	Justice, Freedom and Security
Competition	External relations	Legal Service
Development	Fisheries and Maritime Affairs	Personnel and Administration
Economic and Financial Affairs	Group of Policy Advisers	Press and Communication
Education and Culture	Health and Consumer Protection	Publications Office
Employment, Social Affairs and Equal Opportunities	Humanitarian Aid Office—ECHO	Regional Policy
Energy	Informatics	Research
Enlargement	Information Society	Secretariat General
Enterprise and Industry	Infrastructure and Logistics	Taxation and Customs Union
Environment	Internal Audit Service	Trade
Europe Aid—Co-operation Office	Internal Market and Services	Translation
	Interpretation	Transport and Energy

- Thirteen after the accession of Britain, Denmark, and Ireland in 1973;
- Fourteen following Greece's accession in 1981;
- Seventeen following the accession of Spain and Portugal in 1986;
- Twenty following the 1995 enlargement to take in Austria, Finland, and Sweden.

In the Treaty of Nice (Ch. 15, pp. 197–8) it was agreed that starting with the Commission that took office on 1 January 2005, the number of Commissioners would be limited to one per member state. The Constitutional Treaty (Ch. 16, pp. 204–7) made provision for the number to be reduced further, so as to correspond to two-thirds of the number of member states, selected on a basis of equal rotation between the member states.

The current Commissioners (at the time of writing), and the portfolios are listed in Table 19.2. Commissioners are sworn to abandon all national allegiances during their tenure of office, and they are bound by the principle of collegiality—all actions are the responsibility of the Commission as a whole.

One Commissioner acts as President for the five-year term. This person is chosen by agreement between the governments of the member states ahead of the rest of the Commission, and is consulted about the other nominations. The Treaty of Amsterdam strengthened this right to be consulted, saying that the other Commissioners would be appointed by common accord of the member states with the President. The President allocates the portfolios to the other Commissioners.

The term of the President is also renewable: Jacques Delors held office for two full terms of four years each, plus an interim two-year period to bring the period of office of the Commission into line with that of the EP following the change to the rules made

TABLE 19.2

Commissioners and their Portfolios (as of January 2005)

Jose Manuel Barroso	President
Margot Wallstom	Vice President; Institutional Relations and Communications Strategy
Gunter Verheugen	Vice-President; Enterprise and Industry
Jacques Barrot	Vice-President; Transport
Siim Kallas	Vice-President; Administrative Affairs, Audit, and Anti-Fraud
Franco Frattini	Vice-President; Justice, Freedom and Security
Viviane Reading	Information Society and Media
Stavros Dimas	Environment
Joaquin Almunia	Economic and Monetary Affairs
Danuta Hubner	Regional Policy
Joe Borg	Fisheries and Maritime Affairs
Dalia Grybauskaite	Financial Programming and Budget
Janez Potonic	Science and Research
Jan Figel	Education, Training, Culture and Multilingualism
Markos Kyprianou	Health and Consumer Protection
Olli Rehn	Enlargement
Louis Michel	Development and Humanitarian Aid
Laszlo Kovacs	Taxation and Customs Union
Neelie Kroes	Competition
Mariann Fischer Boel	Agriculture and Rural Development
Benita Ferrero-Waldner	External Relations and European Neighbourhood Policy
Charlie McCreevy	Internal Market and Services
Vladimir Spidla	Employment, Social Affairs and Equal Opportunities
Peter Mandelson	Trade
Andris Piebalgs	Energy

in the TEU. There are no formal rules on the nationality of the president, but there are unwritten understandings that the presidency rotates between member states. A list of Presidents of the Commission is given in Table 19.3. There are also two vice-presidents, but their position is nowhere near as influential as that of the president has become.

Each Commissioner has a team of five or six personal assistants, known by the French word *cabinet* (pronounced 'cab-ee-nay'). The President's *cabinet* is larger, approximately double the size of the others. The members of the *cabinet* act as the eyes and ears of the Commissioner within the organization, and perform a valuable co-ordination function—particularly valuable because the structure of the Commission tends to produce fragmentation of policy making between the Directorates General. It is widely accepted that the dynamism of Jacques Delors' presidencies would not have been possible without the sheer energy and effectiveness of the President's *cabinet* under the leadership of Pascal Lamy, who later went on to become a Commissioner himself.

Each member of the *cabinet* will have responsibility for monitoring one or more areas of policy, and there are weekly meetings of these specialists chaired by the relevant member of the President's *cabinet*, to discuss issues that are current and to monitor the progress of draft legislation. The heads of the units—*chefs de cabinet*—also meet weekly,

TABLE 19.3
Presidents of the European Commission
Walter Hallstein (West Germany) 1958–1967
Jean Rey (Belgium) 1967–1970
Franco Maria Malfatti (Italy) 1970–1972
Sicco Mansholt (Netherlands) 1972
Francois-Xavier Ortoli (France) 1973–1976
Roy Jenkins (UK) 1977–1980
Gaston Thorn (Luxemburg) 1981–1984
Jacques Delors (France) 1985–1995
Jacques Santer (Luxemburg) 1994–1999
Romano Prodi (Italy) 1999–2004
Jose Manuel Barroso (Portugal) 2004–

two days prior to the weekly meetings of the College of Commissioners. All draft legislation that has been prepared within the Directorates General has to go to the College for final approval, in keeping with the principle of collegiality. Before it gets there it is considered by the *chefs*, and if difficulties that can be resolved are spotted at that stage, the draft will be referred back for amendment or further consideration. Where differences are highly politicized, the matter will be allowed to go through to the College for discussion.

The Commission in the Policy-Making Process

There is considerable academic debate around the role of the European Commission in the policy-making process. There is no doubt about its formal role. It has the sole right to initiate proposals for legislation. Without a proposal from the Commission, neither the Council of Ministers nor the EP can act. However, the debate centres on whether the Commission can actually determine the direction in which the EU moves. A question has also recently arisen about the possible erosion of the autonomy of the Commission as a result of changes made to the powers of the EP. Successive amendments to the Treaties have increased the powers of the EP in an attempt to close the democratic deficit of the EU (Ch. 21, p. 298). These increases in power have been at the expense of the Commission, leading some observers to argue that it faces extinction as an independent political entity (De Gucht 2003: 165).

The Commission and the Member States

The story of the decline and revival in the fortunes of the Commission has been told in Chapters 10 to 17 (pp. 137–224). Theorizations of the role of the Commission moved from the neofunctionalist view of it as the 'motor of integration' to the intergovernmental view of it as no more than the servant of the member states. This balance of opinion swung back after the launch of the single market programme in the mid-1980s. After this development, it rapidly became a widely-accepted view that:

The renewed drive for market unification can be explained only if theory takes into account the policy leadership of the Commission.

(Sandholtz and Zysman 1989: 96)

This view did not go unchallenged, though (Ch. 26, pp. 410–12). The disagreements over the role of the Commission in the single-market programme represented fundamental disagreements about the nature of the Commission in more general terms. Is it simply an agent of the member states, acting at their behest and under their control; or is it an autonomous actor in its own right, capable of playing a leadership role in the EU?

If the argument that the EU is an intergovernmental organization is to hold, then those who defend the position have to confront the assertion that the Commission is the prime mover of the process of European integration. This assertion was made from the early days of the EEC by Lindberg (1963) and other neofunctionalists (Ch. 1). The counter-argument is that the Commission is simply an international secretariat like many others that help the member states of international organizations to achieve their collective aims. It is simply an agent of the member states, acting on their behalf and in accordance with their will. This view has been strongly argued by intergovernmentalists, notably Andrew Moravcsik (Ch. 1).

The Commission as an Agent of the Member States

The intergovernmentalist view of the Commission is that it is only an agent of the member states. On this view, the Commission is like the secretariat of any other international organization. Its function is to make it easier for governments to find agreement on the details of co-operation with each other. Where there is agreement on the broad agenda for co-operation, it is convenient for member states to delegate some control over the detailed agenda to the Commission. They see it as a reliable source of independent proposals because it has technical information, and is a neutral arbiter between conflicting national interests. Delegating the making of proposals to the Commission in this way reduces the costs of co-operation by reducing the risk that 'decisions will be delayed by an inconclusive struggle among competing proposals, or that the final decision will be grossly unfair' (Moravcsik 1993: 512). Where there are alternative proposals that might win majority support, the choice is often decided by which proposal is backed by the Commission.

Although this delegation of the right to make detailed proposals gives the Commission a certain formal power to set the agenda, in the intergovernmentalist view the Commission does not determine the direction in which the EU moves. It is only helping the member states to agree on the details of what they have decided that they want to do anyway. Nor is the Commission always effective. It is not the only potential source of proposals, nor of package deals to facilitate compromise between different national positions. Other actors are able to perform these functions, and often do so.

The Commission may use the margin of discretion that the member states allow it to try to manoeuvre the member states towards objectives that they had not anticipated. It is difficult for the states to keep a check on exactly what the Commission is doing because it is in possession of more information than they are. That is, after all, the point of delegating to it. Nevertheless, there are ways in which the member states can keep a check on the Commission (Pollack 1997). First, they have set up a whole complex of committees of national experts to monitor the actions of the Commission: Management Committees, which operate mainly in the agricultural policy sector, can refer a Commission decision to the Council of Ministers for review by qualified majority voting (QMV); Regulatory Committees, which operate in a range of policy sectors, have to support the Commission by QMV, or the proposed measure is referred to the Council of Ministers for review. Second, Article 230 (previously Article 173) of the Treaty allows challenges through the European Court of Justice (ECJ) to the actions of the Commission should any individual member state, or any directly-affected individual or company, believe that it has overstepped its mandate. Other EU institutions, such as the EP and the Court of Auditors, also monitor the activities of the Commission, providing member states with the information that they need to keep a check on it.

The Commission as an Autonomous Actor

The alternative to the view that the Commission is no more than an agent of the member states is that it can and does act autonomously to provide policy leadership to the EU. Defenders of this view point to key resources that allow it to do so: its sole right of initiative in the legislative process of the EC; its ability to locate allies among influential interest groups; and its powers under the competition clauses of the Treaties to act against monopolies. (For a more comprehensive list, see Nugent 1995: 605–13).

The Commission does not have to wait passively for the member states to ask it to bring forward proposals. It can identify a problem that has already started to concern governments, and propose a European solution, as it did with the single-market programme. It can use its sole right of initiative to package issues in the form least likely to engender opposition in the Council of Ministers. Where there is opposition from member states to the full-blown development of a policy, the Commission may propose instead a limited small-scale programme; where there is resistance to a directive or regulation, the Commission may propose a less threatening recommendation or opinion. In each case, the limited step establishes a precedent for action in the policy sector and can be followed up later with further steps if and when the environment in the Council of Ministers is more conducive (Cram 1997: 162–3).

The Commission can also act to put the Europeanization of a policy sector onto the agenda of governments. By involving domestic interests at the EU level, through instruments such as advisory committees, the Commission seeks to win converts to the idea that an issue can best be handled at the European level. These allies may help to soften up the governments of the member states to allow the development of a European competence in that policy sector (Cram 1997: 164–5).

Similarly, the Commission can utilize, and if necessary create, transnational networks of producers who will be its allies in the private sector and bring pressure to bear on governments to transfer competence in a sector to the EU level. It did this in the case of technology policy (Sharp and Shearman 1987; Sharp 1989; Peterson 1991), and in the cases both of telecommunications (Dang-Nguyen *et al.* 1993; Fuchs 1994) and energy (Matlary 1993). In each of these latter sectors it encouraged industrial users to press governments to move away from national monopolies to create a European market under European regulation.

Once governments have become aware of a problem, and faced up to the possibility of a European solution, the Commission can use technical experts to increase the pressure on governments, as it did with the Cecchini report of economists for the single market (see Ch. 26, p. 411), or for monetary union, the Delors Committee which consisted mainly of central bankers (see Ch. 27, p. 442).

Nevertheless, any move to develop a European competence in a policy sector will produce counter-pressures from groups that benefit from the status quo. The Commission can break down this opposition by threatening the use of its existing powers under the competition clauses of the Treaties if actors in the sector will not co-operate to find a negotiated way forward. Again it did this to achieve the opening up of national monopolies in telecommunications and energy supply. In each case DGIV (the Directorate-General for Competition) threatened to use its powers under what was then Article 90 (now Article 86) of the Treaty. This Article specifically said that national public monopolies were subject to the rules prohibiting the prevention of competition within the common market. The vested interests against change were therefore faced with the alternative of either reaching an agreement with the relevant Directorate-General of the Commission to allow phased and regulated competition, or having DGIV make a full-frontal attack on its protected position. In both the cases cited, the alternative of having some say in *how* the transition from national monopoly to European market was carried out proved more attractive than the uncertainty of the alternative of legal proceedings, and the resistance to the Commission's proposals was seriously weakened as a result (Ch. 26, Insights 26.2 and 26.3, pp. 419 and 421).

The Commission and the European Parliament

While most attention has been paid to the relationship between the Commission and the member states, sympathetic practitioners have recently expressed concern about the erosion of the autonomy of the Commission resulting from the extension of the powers of the EP (De Gucht, 2003). Several academic observers have identified an erosion of the Commission's powers and independence within the decision-making process (Tsebelis and Garrett 2000, 2001; Majone 2002; Burns 2004). Four main ways in which this has happened are identified.

(1) Although the Commission and the EP have traditionally been allies in attempting to wrest powers away from the member states, the Commission has always vigorously resisted suggestions that the EP be given an equal right of legislative initiative. The Commission argued that sharing the right to determine the legislative agenda would weaken its ability to give coherence and strategy to European legislation. Formally, the Commission has maintained its monopoly of initiative. Yet, since Maastricht, the EP has the right to request that the Commission 'submit any appropriate proposal on matters on which it considers that a Community act is required for the purpose of implementing this Treaty' (TEC Article 192). Majone (2002: 376) considered that this 'comes close to a true right of legislative initiative'.

(2) The introduction of co-decision (Ch. 18, pp. 243–5) made it more difficult for the Commission to play the role of motor of integration because its proposals had to satisfy a larger number of actors. Whereas under co-operation it was only necessary for the Commission to draft proposals that would meet with approval from a qualified majority in the Council of Ministers, under co-decision it needs to satisfy also a majority in the EP. The more actors that have to be brought into

agreement, the more the proposals are likely to become compromises rather than reflecting the autonomous preferences of the Commission.

(3) Co-decision also left open the possibility of the Council and the EP agreeing an entirely different legislative text from that put forward by the Commission. If the Council and the EP cannot reach agreement on an amended version of the original Commission proposal, a conciliation committee is convened, where the representatives of the two legislative institutions seek to reach agreement directly with one another. This may mean agreement on an entirely different text. The compromise text then has to be agreed in the Council by a qualified majority, and by the EP by a simple majority. Thus, the formal requirement for the Council to amend the Commission's proposal only by unanimity is circumvented. Again, the Commission's autonomy is eroded.

(4) The changes made to co-decision in the Treaty of Amsterdam further eroded the Commission's influence. Because the Council and the EP can reach agreement at first reading under the revised procedure, there is an incentive for them to open direct informal contacts at a much earlier stage than under the original co-decision procedure. This deprives the Commission of the pivotal role in the negotiations around the legislation. However, claims that it rendered the Commission irrelevant were rebutted by Burns (2004: 6), who pointed out that the Commission can still affect the chances of the EP's amendments being accepted by the Council, because if the Commission adopts the amendments, the Council can accept them by QMV, but can only reject them by unanimity; whereas if the Commission rejects the proposed amendments, the Council can only reinstate them by unanimity, whereas it can accept the unamended version by QMV.

Burns (2004) found evidence that the Commission's influence had declined under co-decision, but argued that its weakness should not be overstated. She provided a case study in which the Commission was actually excluded from conciliation (Insight 19.1), thus at first sight supporting the more far-reaching claims about the weakening of its autonomy. However, she concluded that the outcome was a result of the Commission playing its hand badly: it was more a result of agency than an illustration of a clear-cut structural loss of influence. In this context, she stressed the importance of informal relationships in the actual working of the co-decision procedure: 'by being flexible and seeking to improve its informal relationship with the Parliament, [the Commission] has been able to strengthen its legislative position' (Burns 2004: 14). The role of informal relationships is something of which rational choice models do not take much account.

The Commission and Implementation

The EC has a management deficit at least as significant for its future effectiveness as its more widely recognised democratic deficit.

(Metcalfe 1992: 118)

INSIGHT 19.1

The Novel Foods Regulation

The Novel Foods regulation concerned the rules that would apply to the sale of new categories of foodstuffs in the EU, primarily genetically modified (GM) foods. The Commission was under pressure to produce legislation because until the rules had been defined, the import of GM foods was banned, and this had led to a serious trade dispute with the United States, which was the main exporter of GM foods. A key issue was what labelling requirements there would be, if any. Opponents of GM food insisted that if they were to be allowed onto the EU market, they should be clearly labelled as genetically modified. This position was strongly represented in the EP. On the other hand, the supporters of GM foods took the same view as the United States, which was that to label GM foods would appear to indicate that there was something wrong with them. It would stigmatize them in the eyes of the consumers. The Commissioner in charge of the legislation, Martin Bangemann, strongly held the latter view.

The original draft legislation contained no requirement for GM foods to be labelled as such, but the EP's amendments on first reading added in such a requirement. The Commission refused to accept the amendment, which meant that the Council of Ministers could only reinstate it by unanimity. This made a big difference to the fate of the amendment on second reading. There were sufficient member states that were sympathetic to the labelling requirement for the amendment to have been accepted by QMV had the Commission adopted it, but the viewpoint was not unanimous. As a result, the amendment disappeared from the draft legislation that went from the Council to the EP for second reading, although a much weaker labelling requirement was included. Predictably, the EP re-amended to impose more stringent labelling requirements, although these were less stringent than on first reading. The signs of a willingness to compromise were emerging, but the Commission refused to accept the EP's second-reading amendments. The issue therefore went to conciliation.

In the meetings of the Conciliation Committee there were signs that a compromise might be reached between the positions of the Council and the EP, but the EP delegation felt that the position taken by the Commission was unhelpful, and asked that the conciliation proceed without the presence of the Commission. The Council delegation agreed, with the result that the Commission was excluded from future meetings. A compromise was then agreed, and the legislation was passed by both the Council and the EP.

At first sight this incident illustrated perfectly how conciliation had rendered the Commission impotent. It seemed that if it were to participate in future conciliations, it would have to abandon all attempts to pursue its own agenda, and would have to play the role of impartial mediator between the Council and the EP. However, this is not the way in which the main actors perceived the issue. Neither the Council nor the EP wanted to exclude the Commission. When the procedures for conciliation were codified, the task was given to the Commission, which naturally inserted a role for itself in conciliation. This was accepted by both the Council and the EP. Whatever the formal rules allowed, the main actors preferred to operate the system as a trialogue rather than as a dialogue.

(*Source:* Burns, 2004)

In 1991 the Secretary General of the Commission, David Williamson, in a lecture to the Royal Institute of Public Administration in London, admitted to the failings of the Commission when it came to implementing the growing body of EC legislation. He argued that the Commission had to enhance its capacity to manage the post-1992 EC without becoming a central monolith.

This analysis echoed that of Metcalfe (1992) and other academic observers, who had noted that the Commission was better adapted to proposing policies and legislation than to implementing them once they were agreed. It has long been argued that the two functions of initiation and implementation require different types of organizational structure, which Coombes (1970) identified as *organic* and *mechanistic* organizations. He described the Commission as an organic organization, well equipped to generate proposals, but lacking sufficient of the qualities of a classical mechanistic bureaucracy to implement them effectively. Others have seen this bias against implementation as embodied in the culture of the Commission.

There has always been a bias within the Commission in favour of policy formulation as opposed to policy execution.
(**Ludlow 1991: 107**)

After Williamson's lecture in 1991, the implementation problems of the Commission increased as a result of several factors.

(1) The success of the 1992 programme and other policy initiatives taken under Delors' presidency left the Commission with a much larger body of legislation to implement.

(2) The extension of EU competences into new policy sectors, such as social and environmental policy, raised different problems of implementation from those that the Commission had previously encountered (Peters 1997: 191).

(3) The question of consistent implementation of single-market rules became an issue because of the wide disparities between member states that were shown up by Commission monitoring reports. The states with the better records felt that they were being placed at a competitive disadvantage in comparison with states that were less meticulous about applying the rules.

(4) The crisis over the ratification of the TEU, and the subsequent renewed emphasis on the principle of subsidiarity, further complicated the relationship between the Commission and the member states (Laffan 1997*b*: 425).

The Commission as Implementer

There are very few policy sectors where the Commission has direct implementation powers. The most notable is competition policy, which has been called 'the first supranational policy' (McGowan and Wilks 1995). Others are fisheries and some of the programmes involved in the external relations of the EU, such as the Humanitarian Aid Programme, and the programmes for assisting the transition to capitalism and liberal democracy in the former communist states of central and eastern Europe. For most internal policies, the Commission sits at the apex of a multi-level system of implementation that extends down to the central authorities of the member states, then below them to sub-national authorities and agencies. Whereas for both policy making and direct implementation, the Commission acts as the agent of the member states, for the bulk of implementation, national and sub-national actors are the agents of the Commission.

The problem for the Commission is ensuring that these agents do not pursue their own agendas.

This problem is compounded by two circumstances. First, the Commission does not have the resources to ensure effective performance, lacking both adequate staffing levels and independent information (Metcalfe 1992: 126). Second, the number of agents that it has to monitor has been increased by the fragmentation of public administration that has taken place in many member states under the banner of the 'New Public Management' (Peters 1997: 198). Under these circumstances, Metcalfe (1992) argued that it was necessary for the Commission to learn to function as the manager of European networks, rather than seek to manage European integration alone. In this role, it would seek to prompt the development of organizational capacities and inter-organizational co-ordination. Although he did not use the phrase, Metcalfe here was also talking about how the Commission could adapt to the process of governance—governing in a situation where there is a variety of actors with shared or contested responsibility for policy implementation rather than one identifiable unitary authority as had traditionally been the case (Ch. 2).

Ten years after Metcalfe, Majone (2002) came to essentially the same conclusion. He argued that the transfer of new competences to the EU had not involved increasing the exclusive competences of the EU, but had involved the extension of the number of areas where the EU and the member states shared competence, or where competences were dispersed to new institutional actors such as the European Central Bank (ECB) or the High Representative for the Common Foreign and Security Policy (Majone 2002: 376). The reluctance of member states to transfer further exclusive competences to EU institutions reflected their concern about the loss of control that earlier transfers had involved. However, it also reflected a realization that the implementation role of the Commission could not be increased further without an increase in its size and resources that the member states were unwilling to sanction (Majone 2002: 382). In the view of Majone (2002: 382–3), this situation obliged the Commission to share responsibility with national administrative authorities, even though it was difficult to do so because of differing national regulatory philosophies and differing levels of national administrative competence.

At the same time the Commission faced the prospect of becoming increasingly subject to political interference with its performance of its implementation function because of the measures taken in the TEU and the Treaty of Amsterdam to deal with the democratic deficit (see above, pp. 267–8). These had shifted the balance between the Commission and the EP. Moves by the EP to have the political composition of the Commission reflect the political balance of the EP itself would, if successful, increase this tendency to politicization. Such politicization would reduce the policy credibility of the Commission in comparison with earlier periods, or in comparison with independent agents such as the ECB.

Majone (2002: 387) argued that there was a case for a 'fourth branch of government' on the model of US federal regulatory agencies. In fact, some further independent agencies were created in connection with the transfer of new competences, but they were not given regulatory powers, being mainly charged to collect and collate information. A list of these agencies is given in Table 19.4. This reluctance to transfer regulatory powers to the new agencies reinforced Majone's argument that federal agencies such as

TABLE 19.4

Independent Agencies

CdT—Translation Centre for the Bodies of the European Union
Cedefop—European Centre for the Development of Vocational Training
CPVO—Community Plant Variety Office
EAR—European Agency for Reconstruction
EASA—European Aviation Safety Agency
EEA—European Environment Agency
EFSA—European Food Safety Agency
EMCDDA—European Monitoring Centre for Drugs and Drug Addiction
EMEA—European Agency for the Evaluation of Medicinal Products
EMSA—European Maritime Safety Agency
ENISA—European Network and Information Security Agency
ETF—European Training Foundation
EUMC—European Monitoring Centre on Racism and Xenophobia
EU-OSHA—European Agency for Safety and Health at Work
EUROFOUND—European Foundation for the Improvement of Living and Working Conditions
OHIM—Office for Harmonization in the Internal Market (Trademarks and Designs)

those that operated in the United States would not be acceptable in the context of the EU. Instead, he argued that the fourth branch should take the form of 'transnational regulatory networks, including both national and European regulators and enjoying a large measure of autonomy in rule-making and enforcement' (Majone 2002: 387). The model would be the European System of Central Banks (ESCB), which involves the central banks of the member states of the Eurozone, together with the ECB, which acts as the co-ordinator of the network. The Commission would play the role of co-ordinator of these new regulatory networks, which is very close to the role advocated for it by Metcalfe (1992).

Financial Management

Alongside the Commission's burgeoning implementation problems, concern has also grown about effective financial management of EC programmes. As Laffan (1997*b*: 427) noted, for many years the annual reports of the Court of Auditors highlighted weaknesses in the Commission's financial management. However, concern only began to grow as the EC budget grew, and the number of member states that were net contributors to EC funds also grew. The 1995 enlargement added three more net contributors (Laffan 1997*b*: 427). Both increased payments and an increase in the number of net-contributor states led to greater concern that EC money should be spent effectively. This concern was reflected in changes made in the TEU. The TEU raised the status of the Court of Auditors to that of a full EC institution, and raised the status of budgetary discipline and sound financial management to central EC principles (Laffan 1997*b*: 429).

In the context of increasing concern from member states, the Santer Commission made improvements in financial management central to its programme. Santer appointed the Finn, Erkki Liikanen, as Budget Commissioner, and enhanced his status by requiring all proposals that had expenditure implications to be sent to Liikanen for approval before being circulated to the College of Commissioners. Santer also appointed Anita Gradin from Sweden to be in charge of an anti-fraud unit within the Commission. However, despite the efforts of the Santer Commission to put this aspect of implementation on a sound footing, in 1999 the Commission was almost voted out of office on a motion of censure from the EP because of alleged lax financial control, and eventually resigned over the issue (Ch. 15, pp. 191–2).

Despite the events leading up to the 1999 crisis, it is still uncertain exactly how much fraud there is within the EU (Peterson 1997). There is no doubt that the issue of fraud has been blown up to inflated proportions by media attention. However, it is equally certain that the public perception of fraud and financial mismanagement contributes to undermining the legitimacy of the EU among citizens and changing this perception remains an outstanding challenge for the Commission.

CONCLUSION

The debate over the role of the Commission remains central to explanations about the nature and pace of European integration. It is clearly central to one of the themes of this book: the debate about the nature of the EU itself. If the Commission can be shown to be an autonomous actor, the argument that the EU is an intergovernmental organization is severely weakened. Up to now the debate is inconclusive.

The Commission has been fiercely criticized in its role as manager of EC policies and finances. While policy implementation is never straightforward within member states, it becomes even more difficult to achieve policy objectives in a union of fifteen member states, where the Commission is dependent on national governments and national administrations for effective compliance. Added to this, the proliferation of actors involved in the policy process nationally and the increased role of agencies generally, has made the Commission's task even more difficult. Such developments have been central to the increased interest in the application of the concepts of governance and policy networks to the EU (Ch. 2).

The impact of these challenges has fed into the debate about one of the other themes of the book: the issue of the legitimacy of the EU (Ch. 4). While there is a lot of discussion about the democratic deficit, Beetham and Lord (1998) pointed to a wider legitimation deficit, of which the democratic deficit was only one aspect. Another aspect that they identified as feeding the legitimacy deficit was performance: 'the ability [of the EU] to deliver effective policy in the areas it undertakes, to meet some basic criteria of effective decision making, and to demonstrate a capacity for correction and renewal in the event of "failure"' (Beetham and Lord 1998: 23–4). The relevance of this to the above discussion of the Commission's 'management deficit' should be obvious. The loss of freedom that the Commission has experienced as a result of well-intentioned moves to make it more answerable to the EP may even reduce its efficiency further.

KEY POINTS

Composition and Appointment

- ☐ The Commission consists of a College of Commissioners and the Services.
- ☐ The Services are the bureaucracy—the permanent civil service—of the EU.
- ☐ The Commissioners are appointed by the Council, subject to approval by the EP.
- ☐ There is one Commissioner per member state. They are sworn to abandon national allegiances.
- ☐ The President is a particularly influential figure, and is consulted on the nomination of other Commissioners.

The Commission in the Policy-Making Process

- ☐ Formally the Commission has the sole right to propose EC legislation.
- ☐ There is debate about how much autonomy it actually has.
- ☐ The intergovernmentalist view is that the Commission is merely the agent of the member states; the supranationalist view is that the Commission can and does achieve a degree of autonomy from the member states, to pursue its own agenda.
- ☐ Treaty changes designed to deal with the democratic deficit have reduced the autonomy of the Commission by increasing the control over it by the EP.

The Commission and Implementation

- ☐ The Commission has always been more active as a proposer than as an implementer of legislation. Recent developments have emphasized its failings in this respect.
- ☐ In most areas the Commission has to work alongside the national administrations of the member states, leading to suggestions that it should evolve as a manager of European networks of implementation agents.
- ☐ Increasing politicization of the Commission because of its subjection to closer control by the EP threatens its perceived independence, and also points to the need for the emergence of transnational regulatory networks.

Financial Management

- ☐ Concern about fraud and financial mismanagement have led to reforms within the Commission, but they have not solved the problems.

FURTHER READING

N. Nugent, *The European Commission* (Basingstoke: Palgrave Macmillan, 2000) is the most comprehensive introduction to the institution. An alternative is M. Cini, *The European Commission: Leadership, Organisation and Culture in the EU Administration* (Manchester: Manchester University Press,

1996). G. Edwards and D. Spence (eds.), *The European Commission* (Harlow: Longman, 1994) is a useful collection of articles, as in more analytical mode is N. Nugent (ed.), *At the Heart of the Union: Studies of the European Commission* (Basingstoke and London: Macmillan, 1997). B. Laffan, *The Finances of the European Union* (Basingstoke and London: Macmillan, 1997) has an excellent discussion of the implementation deficit of the Commission.

online resource centre   Visit the Online Resource Centre that accompanies this book for links to more information on the European Commission, including the European Commission's own web site.

CHAPTER 20

The Council

CHAPTER OVERVIEW

The term 'the Council' is used here to cover a complex of institutions (Insight 20.1). It includes both the European Council, which is the correct name for the periodic summit meetings of heads of state and government, and the Council of Ministers, which itself is a multi-part institution that does not have a constant membership, but involves different ministers depending on the policy under consideration. Even that, though is not the full extent of the complexity of the Council. The work of the meetings of ministers is prepared by a myriad of committees consisting of national and European officials and experts that is brought together by the Committee of Permanent Representatives (COREPER). Below, each of the manifestations of the Council is examined in turn: the European Council, the Council of Ministers, COREPER, and the technical committees. The coordination of this complex institutional conglomerate falls to the Presidency and the Council Secretariat, which are considered separately.

> **The Council of the European Union is the institutional heart of decision making in the EU.**
>
> **(Lewis 2003b: 149)**

The Council of Ministers itself meets in several guises, with different ministers present depending on the subject under discussion. Those that meet more frequently may start to develop a collegiality that will erode the pure intergovernmental nature of their discussions. The European Council, the meetings of heads of government, was originally set up in part to reassert national government control over the EC, and it remains the most unambiguously intergovernmental of the manifestations of the Council.

However, a large majority of decisions are made before they reach the ministers, at the level of the Permanent Representatives or technical committees. There is some evidence that these groups do develop a collective identity that undermines the simple description of them as intergovernmental bargaining forums.

The question of the relationship between the intergovernmental and supranational features of the Council is a theme that runs through this chapter. The theme is closely related to the debate covered in Chapter 19 (pp. 264–7) about whether the Commission is an autonomous actor in the policy-making process. The discussion here is not about

---

INSIGHT 20.1

The Structure of the Council

The European Council

Summit meetings of the Heads of Government (and the French Head of State), held at least twice per year, with provision for additional meetings.

The Council of Ministers

Consists of a representative of each member state 'at ministerial level', authorized to commit the government of the member state. It meets in more than twenty different forms depending on the subject matter under consideration.

The Committee of Permanent Representatives (COREPER)

The Permanent Representatives are the ambassadors of the member states to the EU. Their deputies meet as COREPER I and the Representatives themselves as COREPER II. They filter business for the meetings of ministers.

The Presidency

A representative of the member state currently holding the presidency chairs all meetings of the Council. The presidency rotates on a six-monthly basis.

The Secretariat

The state holding the presidency is assisted by a Council Secretariat of around 2,000 staff, about a tenth of whom are senior administrators.

the relationship between the Council and other institutions: it is about the relationships within the Council; about whether the constituent parts of the Council act as agents of the core executives of national central governments. By 'the core executive' we mean the Prime Ministers, Foreign Ministers, and other members of what in Britain is called 'the cabinet', and in other member states is known as 'the council of ministers' (which is where the EU institution gets its name from).

The European Council

Meetings of the heads of governments of the member states of the EU are officially called meetings of the European Council. The origins of the European Council were in the summit meetings that started with the 'relaunching of Europe' at The Hague in 1969 (see Ch. 10, p. 144). Agreement was reached in Paris in 1974 to institutionalize the summit meetings and to call them meetings of the European Council. The first formal meeting of the European Council was in Dublin in 1975.

Originally meetings were scheduled to take place three times per year, but in the Single European Act (SEA) that was reduced to twice per year, or once per presidency. However, such is the prestige of hosting a meeting of the European Council, and such are the opportunities for attracting a lot of business into hotels, bars, and restaurants in major cities, that presidencies often managed to find an excuse to have more than one European Council in their country during their six months in charge. Under the terms of the Constitutional Treaty (Ch. 18, pp. 250–5), the European Council would have met quarterly.

Reasons for Inventing the European Council

There are a number of reasons why the European Council was set up in the first place. In an era of events such as currency fluctuations, crises in energy supplies, and **stagflation**, summitry was a prominent feature of the international system in the 1970s as governments sought to maintain economic control (see Ch. 20, pp. 278–9). It was at this time of recurrent global crises that the international economic summits, now known as the G7/G8, began (Insight 20.2). Just like these wider forums, the European Council was a response by states to the demands of complex interdependence.

However, the European Council was also an attempt by governments to reassert national control over the development of the EC. After de Gaulle's resignation in 1969 there was a wish by the national governments to start the development of the EC moving again, but in the direction that they, not the Commission, decided; hence the Hague summit. The 1965 crisis led to a crisis of confidence inside the Commission, which partly explains the lack of movement in the 1965–9 period. If the Commission was not going to drive the EC forward, another motor would be needed. The agreement to formalize summits in the form of the European Council was an indication that the governments were determined to keep control.

The G7/G8

Like the European Council itself, the origins of the present G8 meetings lie with an initiative by French President Giscard d'Estaing. He convened an economic summit at Rambouillet in November 1975, at which he and Chancellor Schmidt of West Germany proposed that such economic summit meetings should become regular events. Originally there were five members of the group: France, Germany, Britain, the United States, and Japan. In 1976–7 the group's membership was extended to seven with the addition of Italy and Canada. At the same time it was agreed that the President of the European Commission could attend summit meetings to represent the views of the other member states of the EC. The group came to be known as the G7.

Initially the summits were concerned purely with economic issues, but in the 1980s political and strategic-defence issues began to appear on the agenda. At the same time meetings of Finance Ministers started to take place separately from the summits. Following the end of the Cold War, Russia started to participate in the meetings, originally as an observer, but eventually as a full member of what is now the G8.

A further explanation for the establishment of the European Council was that as the EC increased the number of policy sectors in which it had competence, the risk emerged of policy segmentation through there being no single body that could take an overview of events. As explained above, the Council of Ministers meets with a different membership depending on the policy under discussion. The General Affairs Council (GAC), consisting of Foreign Ministers, is supposed to act as the co-ordinator, but the heads of government have more authority to play that role.

Finally, the European Council was also an attempt to present a united front to the outside world. It has always been in effect what it has been constitutionally since the Treaty on European Union (TEU), i.e. the highest body of both the European Community (EC) and European Political Co-operation (EPC)/Common Foreign and Security Policy (CFSP). It was therefore an attempt to co-ordinate overall policy towards the rest of the world. This is another function that the heads of government have usurped from the Foreign Ministers meeting in the GAC and in the EPC/CFSP Council of Foreign Ministers.

Functions and Dysfunctions

The European Council has four important functions:

- As a court of appeal for the resolution of problems that cannot be resolved lower down the system. If agreement cannot be reached in the Council of Ministers, the issue is pushed further up the hierarchy to be resolved at the next meeting of the European Council.

- As a 'Board of Directors' giving general guidance to the EU on its future direction. Although the details have to be filled out by interaction between the Commission and the Council of Ministers, if the European Council gives a lead, the presumption is that the Commission will make proposals and the Council will try to reach agreement on a policy.

- As a means of attracting publicity to the EU. Much of the work of the EC in particular is technical and unexciting—except to the specialists—hence it is rarely reported. European summits are probably the only occasion when most members of the public hear about the EU other than when there is crisis. The European Council feeds the desire of the media to have pictures of pomp and ceremony, and to focus on individuals. Perhaps Kirchner (1992: 113) slightly overstated the case when he said, 'European Councils are a media stunt', but there is an element of truth in the accusation.

- As a forum for personal contact between heads of government. The meetings have become more formal, but the original intention was that they would be informal get-togethers by heads of government to help them to understand each other's problems, and just to get to know each other. European Councils do still fulfil this function to a certain extent, and it is the reason given for meals being scheduled to last for long periods, because during meals the heads of government are free of officials and able to relate to each other as individuals.

In carrying out these functions, the European Council faces some serious problems. These can be considered the *dysfunctions* of the European Council. They can be summarized as problems of overload, over-optimism, over-cautiousness, and over-expectation.

- Overload: During the late 1970s and into the 1980s there was a tendency for more and more problems to be referred up from the Council of Ministers to the European Council, so that it often found itself considering quite detailed and technical issues. Because it only met three times a year, and later only twice a year on a routine basis, there was a danger of it becoming overwhelmed with mundane business at the expense of its more strategic functions. However, since the introduction of qualified majority voting (QMV) into the work of the Council of Ministers in the SEA and TEU, the tendency for matters not to be resolved at lower levels has receded.

- Over-optimism: Sometimes the atmosphere of mutual co-operation that can be generated, together with the expectation that something will come out of every European Council, can lead to commitments being made that subsequently prove difficult to honour. When they go home after the meeting, heads of government may not be able to get the agreement of their own political parties or their cabinets/councils of ministers to carry through the commitment. At a press conference on 20 March 1996, the then President of the European Commission, Jacques Santer, complained about the phenomenon of over-optimism, which had resulted in heads of government not putting up the money to fund the projects that they had launched at various European Council meetings. He gave a list of things that European Councils had said should be supported, but for which the money had not been forthcoming: Trans European Networks (i.e. infrastructure projects in transport and power supply); the Northern Ireland peace initiative;

financial aid to Armenia and Georgia; extra Commission posts for the 1995 entrants. Some of these commitments went back to 1994, but adequate funds had never been made available.

- Over-cautiousness: The publicity can make it more difficult for heads of government to make concessions that might be made in a less exposed bargaining context.

- Over-expectation: If the meetings do not produce dramatic results, this can cause disillusionment amongst the European public because the media has built up expectations.

Intergovernmentalism and Informality in the European Council

Although the European Council 'is the body universally recognized as the ultimate intergovernmental protectorate in the EU', it is also 'one which has paradoxically increased the supranational character of the EU over its three decades of operation' (Lewis 2003: 1006). It has increased the supranational character of the EU because it provides the political framework for supranational legislation and other agreements. Although the heads of government cannot themselves formally agree legislation, if they say that something should happen, it will be acted upon by the Commission and the Council of Ministers. Thus, the European Council gives legitimacy to supranational actions that might otherwise be contested at the level of the Council of Ministers.

An important aspect of the work of the European Council is that it proceeds entirely informally. For over a decade it was not even mentioned in the Treaties, until it received legal recognition in the SEA in 1986. Even now, it operates with no formal rules of procedure (Lewis 2003: 1006). This means that it is subject to no formal constraints on what it may or may not discuss. Because the main actors are heads of government, it is able to discuss whatever it wishes, and so can and does trespass onto areas that are not formally within the competence of the EU. In this way, the boundaries between areas of national sovereignty and areas of EU competence are made less impermeable by being crossed, even if initially only in discussion.

The fourth of the functions of the European Council identified above—as a forum for informal contact between heads of government—increases the degree of collegiality of the institution. If leading members of the European Council remain in post for several years, they can become socialized into more co-operative working with the other heads of government. This effect is never likely to work as strongly for the heads of government as it does for some manifestations of the Council of Ministers, and for some of the committees of the Council (see below), because the frequency of interaction is lower and the level of politicization of the heads of government is higher; but in reading the analyses that follow of the Council and its committees as supranational phenomena, it should be borne in mind that some of the same effects may operate even at the highest level of the European Council.

The Council of Ministers

The Council of Ministers is not an institution with a constant membership. It meets in a variety of manifestations depending on the subject under discussion. Formally there is no hierarchy between different Councils, but there is a recognized unofficial hierarchy. The GAC, consisting of Foreign Ministers, normally meets monthly, and has a co-ordination function between the various technical councils. It is therefore perceived to be the highest level at which the Council of Ministers meets. It also has some direct responsibility for external relations, but the same participants meet under different rules of procedure as the Council of Foreign Ministers in the CFSP pillar of the EU.

The Council of Economic and Finance Ministers (ECOFIN) also normally meets every month. These meetings have a high position in the unofficial hierarchy because of the importance and centrality of the subject matter with which they deal. This position was enhanced in the late 1990s because the issue of monetary union dominated the agenda of the EU. The start of the single currency (the Euro) on 1 January 1999 complicated the institutional position because now the Finance Ministers from those member states that are also members of the Eurozone meet prior to the full meetings of ECOFIN to discuss single-currency matters. The existence of this 'Eurogroup' would have been formally recognized had the Constitutional Treaty been ratified. Meetings of ECOFIN are prepared by a specialist group, which was known as the Monetary Committee prior to the arrival of the single currency, but is now called the Economic and Financial Committee (EFC).

The Council of Agriculture Ministers also has a privileged status because of the importance of agriculture to the EU, although this position is threatened by attempts to reduce the extent to which agricultural expenditure dominates the budget. Like the other senior councils, the Agriculture Council meets monthly during most of the year, and sometimes more frequently when negotiations are taking place on the annual fixing of agricultural prices in the first half of each year. Its business is prepared, not by COREPER, but by a Special Committee on Agriculture (SCA), indicating the unique position that agriculture occupied in the early years of the EC, as the only common policy.

Other Councils can be divided into those that cover subjects for which there is a recognized EC competence, and those such as education where the member states are attempting to co-ordinate their policies (Kirchner 1992: 74). The frequency of meetings varies considerably, though most of the sectoral councils meet between twice and four or five times a year (Hayes-Renshaw and Wallace 1997: 30).

Fritz Scharpf (1989) contrasted 'problem solving' and 'bargaining' as modes of negotiation within the EC. His distinction at least partly corresponds to the differences between theorists about how to understand the operation of the Council. For intergovernmentalists the Council is simply 'a forum for hard bargaining' (Lewis 1998: 479; 2000: 261). For those who adopt a more supranational perspective, combined with a social constructivist theoretical position, bargaining takes place between actors whose positions are influenced, at least partially, by their social interaction with their ministerial colleagues from other member states; 'communicative rationality' is at least as important as 'instrumental rationality', which means that the discussion is about how to find a solution to common problems rather than just about playing a negotiating game to win; and there is an instinct to proceed consensually (Lewis 1998: 480–81).

The hypotheses that these theories generate are fairly clear. If the supranational theorists are correct, one would expect to find more collegiality, and a discourse more oriented to joint problem solving, in Councils that meet more frequently than in those that meet less frequently, and also in the more technical Councils rather than in the more political Councils (although deciding what is technical and what is political is notoriously difficult).

The extent to which ministers meeting in the different Councils engage in hard-headed intergovernmental bargaining, or adopt a more supranational approach, is difficult to research because of the secrecy that surrounds such meetings. Minutes are not publicly available. Anecdotal evidence suggests that some manifestations of the Council are more collegial than others. For example, it was said that after John Major became British Prime Minister in late 1990, he became increasingly disillusioned with the political nature of interactions between the heads of government, having previously only experienced meetings of ECOFIN, which were much more oriented towards common problem solving than to political points scoring.

One particularly interesting research finding in this respect is that very few issues are actually decided by the ministers themselves. Hayes-Renshaw and Wallace (1997: 78) estimated that approximately 85 per cent of all decisions are effectively made either at the level of COREPER, or at the level of the technical committees that operate below COREPER. The issues are either decided before they go to the Council, which just rubber-stamps them (the 'A-points' on the agenda), or they are decided in outline by the Council of Ministers but then referred back to the committees for the details to be negotiated.

Van Schendelen (1996: 542), who managed to obtain the Minutes of all meetings of the Agriculture Council for 1992 and 1993, calculated that only 13 per cent of decisions were finally made in the Council, while 65 per cent were left to be made by auxiliary bodies (the remainder were still under consideration when he wrote). The interest of this lies in the expectation that negotiations in COREPER and the technical committees are more likely to be oriented to problem solving than to bargaining. This is because the national representatives meet more frequently than ministers, and they are both less political and more concerned with the minutiae of technical issues than are ministers.

COREPER and the Technical Committees

It is at the level of the Council committees, up to and including COREPER, that the argument is most convincing that the Council is not an intergovernmental organization at all, but a supranational institution.

Although it formally only prepares the agenda and meetings of the Council, COREPER has a great deal of discretion about what it classifies as A-points or B-points on the agenda. A-points are simply accepted by the ministers without discussion. It is also the case that issues move up and down the hierarchy of committees. So although

COREPER and the working groups formally prepare the meetings of the ministers, in one sense the ministers can be said to prepare the meetings of the committees. This is the case where an issue has been discussed at ministerial level, and broad consensus has been reached, but the issue is then referred back down the hierarchy for the detail to be filled in.

COREPER

The Permanent Representatives are the Ambassadors from the member states to the EU. They perform some formal functions in Brussels, but their main task is to co-ordinate the work of the various committees that meet under the banner of the Council of Ministers, and to sift through the reports of these committees before they go to the Council of Ministers. This they do in the context of COREPER.

COREPER meets at least weekly at ambassador level as COREPER II, and at deputy level as COREPER I. Both prepare the agendas of meetings of the Councils of Ministers, except that of the Agriculture Council, for which the SCA performs the same task. COREPER II is responsible for the agendas for meetings of the GAC (consisting of Foreign Ministers), the Development Council, the Economic and Finance Ministers Council (ECOFIN), and the Budget Council. It also prepares the agendas for meetings of the European Council. The Antici Group of officials, named after the Italian official who was the chair of the first such group, assists it in this task. COREPER I is responsible for the agendas of all other Councils except Agriculture.

COREPER divides the agendas of Council meetings into points A and points B. The A points are normally agreed at the Council meeting without discussion, although any member state can request at the start of a meeting that an item be moved from the A to the B list, but this is usually only done as a gesture by a member state that has lost the argument at committee level yet wishes to enter a further reservation (Van Schendelen 1996: 40). It is also the case that issues move up and down the hierarchy of committees. So although COREPER and the working groups formally prepare the meetings of the ministers, in one sense the ministers can be said to prepare the meetings of the committees. This is the case where an issue has been discussed at ministerial level, and broad consensus has been reached, but the issue is then referred back down the hierarchy for the detail to be filled in.

All studies of COREPER indicate that its members consider themselves to have a dual role. According to Hayes-Renshaw *et al.* (1989: 136), while the Permanent Representatives 'are the trustworthy executors of the instructions from their respective capitals', they also have strong ties of solidarity with their colleagues in COREPER. These ties are developed as a result of intensive social interaction in Brussels. Committee members eat, drink, and breathe EU issues seven days a week. Every six months they and their spouses go on trips to tourist locations in different member states, which helps to cement the bonds between them (Barber 1995: I). Lewis (1998: 487) argued that this constant interaction between the same individuals built up a considerable legacy of what he called 'social capital', meaning that the individuals concerned trust one another, and understand and have sympathy for each other's points of view.

The ties are also the result of all the Permanent Representatives being in the same position vis-à-vis their national governments. All of them will have sympathy with one of their number who is bound by a tight mandate on a particular issue, because they are sometimes placed in that position themselves. In such a situation they will try to help each other out, perhaps by persuading their own government to make concessions if they feel that the issue is not so important for them. The attitude of the Permanent Representatives to a negotiation is ambivalent: they all want their government's position to prevail; but they also want to reach agreement even at the cost of not achieving all of their own government's objectives in the negotiation (Hayes-Renshaw *et al.* 1989: 136).

One explanation of this approach is based on rational choice and games theory. It is also compatible with an intergovernmental-bargaining image of the committee. On this view, when Permanent Representatives make concessions, or urge their governments to make concessions, it is not just because they feel a sense of social solidarity with their counterparts from other member states. It is also indicative of the strong sense that they have of being involved in a continuous process of bargaining with the same partners. In the language of games theory, they are involved in *iterated* games (i.e. the same game is repeated several times with the same participants). This changes the calculation of what is rational as compared with isolated games. In a one-off game it is rational to take any step to damage your opponent's position and to further your own, even so far as cheating on the rules if you can get away with it. In iterated games the use of such tactics is likely to backfire during a subsequent round. If you have reneged on a deal in one round of negotiations, it will be difficult to get anyone to conclude a deal with you in subsequent rounds.

This logic of iterated games in EU bargaining is more apparent to Permanent Representatives than it sometimes is to ministers, who have many other concerns and are less intensively socialized into the Community method of bargaining. It means that Permanent Representatives are often involved in trying to educate their governments about the nature of the EU bargaining-process. This can lead to them being seen as the representatives of the EU in the national capitals: one German Permanent Representative punned that he was known in Bonn not as the *ständiger Vertreter* (Permanent Representative) but as the *ständiger Verräter* (permanent traitor) (Barber 1995: I; Lewis 1998: 483). Although this sort of suspicion may occasionally exist in national capitals, it would be a foolish government that did not listen seriously to the advice of the Permanent Representative when deciding on its national negotiating position. This could be taken as evidence that the intergovernmentalist view, that national preferences are formulated independently of influence from the EU level, is false.

Another explanation of the approach of COREPER, which also challenges the intergovernmentalist view, is based on social constructivism. Lewis (2000) identified five main features of the operation of COREPER that resulted from the circumstances and socialization processes identified above. He labelled these: diffuse reciprocity, thick trust, mutual responsiveness, a consensus-reflex, and a culture of compromise.

- Diffuse reciprocity means that the Permanent Representatives will support one of their number on an issue that is important to that individual's member state but less important to their own, and in return will expect to receive such support when they themselves have a problem. This is not the same as the sort of formal agreement that is allowed for in rational choice bargains, where deals are done that A will support B on issue C in return for the support of B on issue D. The reciprocity is diffuse, not specific. It relates to the collectivity of COREPER across the whole range of issues.

- Thick trust—as opposed to 'thin trust'—means that the Permanent Representatives feel they can be honest and open with one another without anything that they say being reported back to other governments. In restricted sessions they feel that they speak freely, knowing that what they say will not come out.

- Mutual responsiveness means that the Permanent Representatives, because they work together so closely, come to understand one another's perspectives and problems, and will try not to approach an issue in a way that they know will cause problems for other members of COREPER.

- The consensus-reflex is deeply embedded in the culture of COREPER. Although there is provision for QMV where the Treaty specifies, it is hardly ever used, and is always the last resort. COREPER will continue to seek a consensus long after it is apparent that a qualified majority could be mustered if a vote were called.

Other Preparatory Committees

Lewis (2000) went on to ask whether these same criteria applied to other senior committees that prepare business for meetings of the Council of Ministers. He looked at five: the Special Committee on Agriculture (SCA), which takes over the role of COREPER with respect to meetings of the Ministers of Agriculture; the Article 113/133 Committee, which monitors the activity of the Commission in international trade negotiations and prepares reports for the Council of Trade Ministers (see Ch. 29, pp. 294–5); the Budget Committee, which has the very specific role of preparing for meetings of the Council to discuss the annual budgetary proposals; the EFC, which prepares for meetings of ECO-FIN; the Political Committee, which prepares for Ministerial meetings under the Common Foreign and Security Policy (CFSP); and the K-4 Committee, which performs a similar function for meetings of ministers under the 'third pillar' of Justice and Home Affairs/Police and Judicial Co-operation (see Ch. 24, pp. 372–4). The conclusion of this investigation (Lewis 2000: 282) was that of these senior committees, only the EFC came close to exhibiting the five features to anything like the same extent as COREPER. This weakens somewhat the thrust of the supranationalist argument, but not the validity of the social constructivist approach, because the empirical findings underlined the need to investigate the 'sociality and normative environment in which interests are defined and defended' (Lewis 2003: 262). Sometimes this environment will be more supportive of an intergovernmental-bargaining approach to business; in other forums it will be more supportive of a co-operative, and therefore more supranational approach.

The Technical Groups

Moving down the hierarchy from COREPER, the technical groups that prepare recommendations for the Permanent Representatives involve intensive interaction between national and Commission officials. The processes of socialization that Lewis and others argued apply to COREPER also apply here. Although the people who sit on these committees are national representatives, research by Beyers and Dierickx (1998: 307–8) showed that members of working groups soon started to judge other members on the basis of the level of expertise that they showed in the committee rather than on nationality. Ludlow (1991: 103) went further to argue that 'Commission officials act as thirteenth members of the Council machinery', implying that the distinction between national and Commission representatives was almost meaningless in the work of these groups.

The thrust of all these arguments is that the members of the technical groups develop a sense of collegiality and engagement in a joint enterprise that makes it more sensible to see them as individuals participating in a team effort than as representatives of individual states. Here we are operating very much at the 'problem-solving' end of Scharpf's spectrum of types of negotiation. Agreements are reached on the basis of convincing arguments, not political weight or bargaining skill.

The relationship between the ministers on the one hand and COREPER and the technical groups on the other can be seen as similar to the relationship between the member states and the Commission as outlined in Chapter 19 (pp. 264–7). In an argument similar to that used to define the degree of autonomy available to the Commission, Van Schendelen (1996: 543) said that members of these 'auxiliary bodies' had a discretionary freedom within broadly defined parameters because of:

- the technical nature of the dossiers, which the ministers struggle to understand;
- the fact that the ministers are too busy to monitor their agents' performance in detail;
- the fact that instructions from national governments are often loosely drawn, arrive late, or are weak;
- the discretion that the agents are allowed in response to the argument that they need to be given room for manoeuvre in negotiations;
- the agents' ability themselves to influence the national negotiating position, and to educate the national ministry on what is feasible.

The Council Presidency

Every six months a different member state assumes the presidency of the Council. During its period of office, that member state has responsibility for organizing and chairing meetings of the European Council, and the Council of Ministers and its various committees. In the course of its six months in charge, the presidency can expect to arrange and chair some ninety separate meetings of ministers, and many more times that of committees. In addition, there will be at least one European Council meeting during the

The Council Secretariat

The Secretariat is a relatively small body of 2,300 people, a tenth of whom are at the senior A-grade. It is based in Brussels in the Justus Lipsius building. It is internally divided into the private office of the Secretary-General, a Legal Service, and ten Directorates-General.

The Secretariat is another potential mediator in disputes between member states, a role that it came to play more prominently after Niels Ersbøll of Denmark became Secretary-General in 1980. Ersbøll gave the Council Secretariat a new role through the active support he gave to successive presidencies during the 1985 inter-governmental conference (IGC) (Dinan 1994: 236). He was actively involved in the discussions about institutional reform in 1990–1, and in the drafting of documents for the IGC on political union (Dinan 1994: 18–81). Ersbøll was also widely credited with having brokered a deal at the Edinburgh European Council on the concessions that needed to be made to the Danish government to allow them to win a second referendum on the TEU.

As Wessels (1991: 140) put it, the Secretary-General 'intentionally maintains a low profile but is known to be highly influential in attaining consensus'. From the viewpoint of intergovernmentalist theorists, this further undermines the claim of the supranational theorists that the Commission is essential to the process of reaching agreement in the EU. However, the Secretariat-General itself is also a supranational body, so its role hardly disproves the contention that supranational actors are influential in the EU.

six months. In this considerable task, the civil service of the state holding the presidency is assisted by the Council Secretariat (Insight 20.3). However, much of the burden of administering the presidency inevitably falls on national officials.

Kirchner (1992: 72–3) argued that the increase in the role of the presidency in the 1970s was a result of several developments. First, the 1970s saw national positions diverging because of the differential impact on the member states of the international economic crises. Reaching agreement between the member states thus became more difficult at the very time that the Commission was at its least effective. In this context the Council presidency's role as mediator became more salient. Second, the development of EPC in the 1970s emphasized the intergovernmental method, sidelined the Commission, and again increased the salience of the presidency. Third, the increased role of the European Council also enhanced the presidency, because it prepared the agenda, drafted compromises between heads of government, and drafted the final communiqué.

The current system has been subject to two main criticisms: that six months is too brief a period for the tenure of the presidency; and that the scale of demands on the country holding the presidency has grown to outstrip the capacity of all but the largest member states to cope.

Brevity of Tenure

Six months is not long to hold the presidency, 'scarcely longer than the learning curve' (de Bassompierre 1988: 153), and the frequency of changes disrupts continuity. With fifteen members, the presidency came around only once every 7 1/2 years, and following enlargement it will come around on the present system only once every twelve years. This is too long a gap for collective expertise to be retained because staff have moved on, so the learning has to begin anew with every turn at the presidency.

In an attempt to get round this problem, a system known as the Troika was introduced in 1983, whereby the current presidency works in close liaison with the immediate past and next presidency states. The Troika system also provides a partial solution to the problem that the frequent changes in the presidency can confuse the EU's partners in other parts of the world.

Domestic political instability can seriously disrupt a six-month presidency. For example, of the seven presidencies between January 1993 and June 1996, only that of Belgium (January to June 1994) was not disrupted by either elections or political crisis. Perhaps the worst crisis was during the Danish presidency (January to June 1993), when the government resigned weeks before it was due to take over, and everything had to be put on hold while new ministers came into office and mastered their briefs. But other presidencies in this period were severely disrupted by domestic politics. Germany (July to December 1994) had a federal election and France (January to June 1995) had a presidential election during the presidency. Spain (July to December 1995) faced a crisis over the domestic budget, and was in a pre-election phase with a government seriously weakened by scandals. Italy was without an elected government for most of its presidency (January to June 1996), and held elections during the presidency.

Scale of Demands

Some of the smaller member states have difficulties in coping with the sheer range of topics on which they might be expected to produce papers during a presidency. There is a lot of room for concern about whether the political and administrative infrastructure of the new members who joined in 2004, as well as those who are expected to join in the next few years, will be up to the task. It is also the case that enlargement means there are more small and medium-sized states than large states, and the turn of a large state will not come around very often. Sometimes it takes the resources of a large state to break the backlog that has built up.

Reforms Proposed in the Constitutional Treaty

Under the terms of the Constitutional Treaty, changes were made to the presidency to try to respond to the problems identified above. The European Council would have elected its own president for a term of two-and-a-half years, renewable once. It would have been the job of this individual to chair meetings of the European Council, to 'drive forward its work', and to represent the EU externally on matters relating to the CFSP. The presidency of the Council of Ministers would have continued to be held by member states on a rotating basis, but the Troika system would have been extended so that a team of three member states would have held the presidency jointly for eighteen months. This arrangement would not have applied to the Council of Foreign Ministers, which would have been chaired by the new European Foreign Minister, nor to the Eurogroup of member states that are part of the single currency, which would have elected its chair for a period of two-and-a-half years.

CONCLUSION

At first sight it seems obvious that the Council is an intergovernmental organization. However, this is a simplification of a complex situation. First, it is clear that the Council as a collective entity is a supranational institution, because it can and does agree to legislation that is then binding on all the member states. Second, it is not clear that the Council, in all its manifestations, operates simply as an intergovernmental bargaining forum. Wessels (1991: 136) insisted that 'the Council is not an "interstate body"... but a body at the supranational level'. Hayes-Renshaw and Wallace (1997: 278) were less sure of that, but were clear that it was 'not a wholly "intergovernmental" institution'. As they put it,

For the analyst the Council and its processes embody the recurrent tension in the construction of the EC between the supranationalists and the intergovernmentalists.
(Hayes-Renshaw and Wallace 1997: 2)

To try to analyse the role of the Council as a whole would be a mistake. It is important to disaggregate the Council's component institutions in order to understand at exactly which point in the machinery issues are dealt with. Only with this knowledge can an informed judgment be made concerning the key actors involved and their motivations. Even then, the task is complicated by the secrecy that surrounds Council activity in virtually all of its manifestations. The usual justification for this is that the Council meetings are intergovernmental negotiations, and if they were subject to public scrutiny it would become more difficult to reach agreements. There is an echo here of one of the arguments about the problems faced by the European Council: that the publicity given to meetings encourages excessive caution. Ironically, it is very difficult to establish whether the premiss of this argument is correct because of the secrecy that is justified by reference to that premiss. Under the Constitutional Treaty, the Council of Ministers 'shall meet in public when it deliberates and votes on a draft legislative act' (Article I-24.6). However, the same Article goes on to explain that 'each Council meeting shall be divided into two parts, dealing respectively with deliberations on Union legislative acts and non-legislative activities', thus leaving open plenty of scope for the secrecy of the negotiating process to continue.

The most informed research suggests that a high proportion of Council decisions are taken relatively low down in the decisional hierarchy. It is here, within COREPER and the technical committees, that observers find the greatest evidence of supranationalism in Council activities. At the ministerial level, decisions tend to be more politicized and national positions less open to negotiation. However, to complicate matters further, anecdotal evidence suggests that even at the ministerial level, some Councils are more collegial than others. Lewis (2000) also concluded that there is considerable variation in the degree of collegiality exhibited by the senior preparatory committees. The conclusion must be, therefore, that the argument between intergovernmental and supranational theorists cannot be settled finally so far as the Council is concerned, but that there are some grounds for not assuming too readily that because the Council is the institution where the governments of member states are most directly represented, it is necessarily an intergovernmental body.

The other theoretical debate around the Council concerns whether to approach it using the techniques of rational choice institutionalism and games theories, or whether to understand it as a case study in social constructivism. To some extent this division corresponds with the division between intergovernmental and supranational theories of the nature of the Council. Intergovernmentalists tend to favour rational choice approaches to understanding the workings of the Council because they see it as a forum for hard bargaining around national interests, and it is in understanding the operation of such forums that rational choice and games theory have made some of their biggest contributions. Supranationalists tend to rest their arguments on evidence that the representatives of the member states on the various committees and Councils become socialized into a different construction of what they are trying to achieve from a simple defence of national interests, and into informally institutionalized procedures that emphasize consensus and co-operation rather than instrumental bargaining. However, it is possible to accept a social constructivist **epistemology** and still come to the conclusion on the basis of empirical evidence that the socialization process does not operate very effectively in some of the committees and some of the manifestations of the Council.

While the debate between academics continues, the Council faces major practical problems in the context of enlargement. Some of these concern the viability of the presidency. Others concern related issues such as the weighting of votes under QMV. However, these practical concerns are not as far removed from the academic debate as might appear at first sight. Whether the Council can continue to operate with over twenty members may depend on how far it is only a forum for intergovernmental bargaining, or how far it is a genuinely collegial, problem-solving body. In the first case, the prospects for it functioning effectively after enlargement are not good; in the second, after a period of socialization of new members, they are much better.

KEY POINTS

The European Council

- ☐ The European Council was established in the 1970s to provided a collective response to the challenges of economic interdependence; to allow national governments collectively to control the direction of the EC; to avoid policy segmentation; and to present a united front to the outside world.

- ☐ The functions of the European Council include: to resolve disputes that cannot be resolved lower down the decisional hierarchy; to provide general direction to the EU; to attract publicity; and to provide a forum for heads of government to get to know each other.

- ☐ The European Council faces problems of overload, over-optimism, over-cautiousness, and over-expectation.

- ☐ Although it is recognized as an intergovernmental institution, its informal methods of operation and its political authority have resulted in it increasing the supranational character of the EU.

The Council of Ministers

- ☐ The Council of Ministers meets in a variety of manifestations depending on the subject under consideration.

☐ Although there is no formal hierarchy of Council meetings, informally the General Affairs Council and those sectoral Councils concerning foreign affairs, finance, and agriculture have the highest status.

☐ The frequency with which ministers meet in sectoral Councils can lead to the emergence of a sense of collective enterprise, marked by communicative rationality rather than instrumental rationality.

☐ Because of the secrecy in which the Council of Ministers meets, it is difficult to research the degree to which individual Councils engage in problem solving rather than bargaining around national interests.

COREPER and the Technical Committees

☐ Research has indicated that a large proportion of 'Council' decisions are actually taken lower down the decisional hierarchy, within COREPER and the various technical committees. Arguments that the Council is a supranational entity are strongest at this level.

☐ The Permanent Representatives of national governments interact regularly and develop trust and solidarity, which makes agreement between them easier than between politicians who are less regularly engaged and who have broader concerns.

☐ The operation of COREPER can be explained either from a rational choice bargaining perspective, as the behaviour appropriate to actors involved in iterated games; or from a social constructivist perspective as the building of a new sense of identity among the Permanent Representatives.

☐ Other senior preparatory committees have not achieved the same degree of trust and solidarity as COREPER, with the exception of the Economic and Financial Committee.

☐ National representatives on technical groups also undergo a process of socialization that produces a problem-solving approach where decisions are taken more on the strength of evidence than political considerations.

The Council Presidency

☐ The role of the presidency of the Council increased during the 1970s because of the ineffectiveness of the Commission at a time when economic divergences increased the need for a mediator between member states. Other factors were the start of EPC and of the European Council.

☐ The Council presidency rotates between member states every six months. This system has been criticized on the grounds of brevity of tenure and for the scale of the demands it places on smaller member states.

☐ Under the Constitutional Treaty the European Council would have had its own President, selected by the member states; the Council presidency would have been jointly held by three states at a time for eighteen months.

An extremely comprehensive treatment of the functioning of the Council, which remains a standard work on the subject, is F. Hayes-Renshaw and H. Wallace, *The Council of Ministers* (Basingstoke and London: Macmillan, 1997); but M. Westlake, *The Council of the European Union* (London: John Harper Publishing, 3rd edn, 2004) is more up-to-date, and informed by something of an insider's perspective (Westlake works for the Commission).

An early assessment of the strengths and weaknesses of the institutionalized summit meetings, which remains relevant, is in S. Bulmer and W. Wessels, *The European Council: Decision-Making in European Politics* (Basingstoke and London: Macmillan, 1987). A later assessment from one of the same authors is provided in W. Wessels, 'The EC Council: The Community's Decision-Making center', in R.O. Keohane and S. Hoffmann (eds.), *The New European Community: Decisionmaking and Institutional Change* (Boulder, San Francisco, and London: Westview Press, 1991), 133–54.

Some of the most interesting work on the Council has been done by Jeff Lewis. In addition to the articles cited above, for which references may be found in the Bibliography, the theme of rationalism versus social constructivism is explored in J. Lewis, 'Institutional environments and everyday EU decision making—Rationalist or constructivist?' *Comparative Political Studies*, 36 (2003): 97–124.

online resource centre   **Visit the Online Resource Centre that accompanies this book for links to more information on the Council.**

CHAPTER 21

The European Parliament

CHAPTER OVERVIEW

The European Parliament (EP) is the one directly elected institution of the EU. The Members of the EP (MEPs) are elected once every five years, and since the first direct elections in 1979 the EP has campaigned for more power and influence. Although it is still not satisfied with the situation, there has been a considerable increase in its powers. This struggle for increased powers is discussed in more detail below, after the basic structure and functions of the EP have been summarized. The chapter then turns to look at debates and research on the EP, which have been more extensive than on any of the other institutions. One theme of the academic debate is the extent to which the EP has become an effective independent actor in the affairs of the EU, and how far it will continue to move in that direction in the future. This clearly parallels the discussion in the previous two chapters, on the Commission and the Council.

> "...of all the Union institutions, it is the EP whose developmental trajectory is the most impressive"
>
> **(Warleigh 2003: 78)**

Composition and Functions

The EP consists of 732 MEPs, divided between the member states on a basis that is approximately proportionate to size of population, although the small countries are somewhat over-represented. The distribution of the 732 seats following the 2004 enlargement is shown in Table 21.1.

The EP meets in plenary session for three or four days every month, except August, in Strasburg; and additional plenaries are held in Brussels; but most of its work is channelled through twenty standing committees (Table 21.2). In addition, it can establish temporary committees and committees of enquiry. Committee meetings are normally held in Brussels, although they do meet in Strasburg as well during plenary sessions.

The EP has a President, a Bureau, a Conference of Presidents, and a Secretariat. The President is elected by the MEPs from among their number for a $2\frac{1}{2}$-year renewable term. The President represents the EP on official occasions, and in relations with other institutions; presides over debates during plenary sessions; and chairs meetings of the Bureau and the Conference of Presidents. The Bureau consists of the President, the fourteen vice-presidents, and five 'quaestors' who deal with administrative and financial matters relating to MEPs. The members are elected by the MEPs for a term of $2\frac{1}{2}$ years. The Conference of Presidents consists of the President and the Chairs of the Political Groups. It draws up the agenda for plenary sessions, fixes the timetable for the work of

TABLE 21.1

Distribution of Seats in the European Parliament

Austria	17	Greece	22	Poland	50
Belgium	22	Hungary	20	Portugal	22
Cyprus	6	Ireland	12	Slovakia	13
Czech Republic	20	Italy	72	Slovenia	7
Denmark	13	Latvia	8	Spain	50
Estonia	6	Lithuania	12	Sweden	18
Finland	13	Luxemburg	6	United Kingdom	72
France	72	Malta	5		
Germany	99	Netherlands	25		

In addition 33 seats have been reserved for Romania and 17 for Bulgaria pending their anticipated admission to membership.

TABLE 21.2

Committees of the European Parliament (as from July 2004)

- Foreign Affairs Committee
  - — Security and Defence Sub-Committee
  - — Human Rights Sub-Committee
- Budgets Committee
- Budgetary Control Committee
- Civil Liberties, Justice and Home Affairs Committee
- Economic and Monetary Affairs Committee
- Legal Affairs Committee
- Internal Market and Consumer Protection Committee
- International Trade Committee
- Industry, Research and Energy Committee
- Employment and Social Affairs Committee
- Environment, Public Health and Food Safety Committee
- Agriculture Committee
- Fisheries Committee
- Regional Development Committee
- Transport and Tourism Committee
- Culture and Education Committee
- Development Committee
- Constitutional Affairs Committee
- Women's Rights and Gender Equality Committee
- Petitions Committee

parliamentary bodies and establishes the terms of reference and size of parliamentary committees and delegations. The Secretariat consists of approximately 3,500 administrative and clerical staff, headed by the Secretary-General. Around one-third of the staff are in the language service, concerned with translation and interpretation. In addition to the secretariat, the political groups have their own administrative support.

The powers of the EP are summarized in Insight 21.1. It has legislative, budgetary, and supervisory functions. In the legislative field, it has emerged as a co-legislator with the Council of Ministers in most areas of EC legislation. The various legislative procedures, and the powers of the EP in each of them, are discussed in Chapter 18, pp. 240–6. The EP and the Council of Ministers are the joint budgetary authorities on the EC. The budgetary procedure, and the role of the EP in it, is described in Chapter 18, pp. 238–40.

The supervisory functions of the EP refer to both the Commission and the Council. Under the Treaty of European Union (TEU), the EP was given the right to be consulted by the governments of the member states when they were agreeing on a new president

INSIGHT 21.1

The Powers of the European Parliament

Political

- Approves appointment of Commission President
- Approves appointment of Commission after public hearings
- Questions the Council and Commission
- Can censure and dismiss whole Commission

Legislative

- Delivers opinions on Commission proposals
- Shares final decision on most proposals with Council (co-decision procedure)
- Assent required for enlargement of European Union and agreements with third countries

Budgetary

- Can modify certain proposed expenditures
- Annual approval required for annual budget
- Budgetary Control Committee Checks expenditure (together with Court of Auditors)

of the Commission. The Treaty of Amsterdam extended this power so that the nomination had to be formally approved by the EP. A new Commission is subject to a vote of approval by the EP, and the EP has the power to dismiss the whole of the Commission on a vote of censure; but in neither case can it target individual Commissioners. A motion of censure requires a positive vote from an absolute majority of MEPs and two-thirds of the votes cast. The EP also has the right to ask the Commission written and oral questions. Following the resignation of the Santer Commission, agreement was reached with the incoming President of the Commission, Romano Prodi, that if the EP expressed a lack of confidence in an individual Commissioner, the President of the Commission would consider whether to demand the resignation of that individual (see below, p. 303).

In respect to the Council of Ministers, the powers of the EP are more limited. It can table written and oral questions about the activities of the Council of Ministers; and the Foreign Minister of the state holding the presidency of the Council reports to the EP at the beginning and end of the presidency. For the European Council, there is no mechanism of parliamentary accountability, although the presidency does give the EP a report on European Council meetings. The Council Presidency consults the EP on the main aspects of the Common Foreign and Security Policy and ensures that Parliament's views are taken into consideration. The EP is regularly informed by the Council presidency and by the Commission of developments in the Union's foreign and security policy.

The Struggle for Power

In the original Treaties, the forerunner of the present EP was neither directly elected nor endowed with significant powers. Members of the European Parliamentary Assembly (EPA) were members of national parliaments who were seconded to the EPA. They were full-time national MPs and part-time European MPs. The EPA had the right to be consulted by the Council of Ministers before legislation was agreed, but its opinion could be, and frequently was ignored; and it could dismiss the Commission as a whole on a vote of censure, but only if it could achieve the difficult degree of unity needed to reach the double majority requirement (two-thirds of those voting, constituting an absolute majority of members). From the outset, though, the EPA set about trying to extract the right to be directly elected, and to have stronger powers.

The main steps in the transformation of the weak EPA into the much stronger EP were listed by Corbett, Jacobs, and Shackleton (2003: 354) as:

the budget treaties of 1970 and 1975; the introduction of direct elections by universal suffrage in 1979; the 1980 Isoglucose *ruling of the European Court of Justice, giving Parliament a de facto delaying power; the Single European Act in 1987, introducing the co-operation procedure and the assent procedure; the Treaty of Maastricht in 1993, bringing in the co-decision procedure, and giving Parliament the right to allow (or not) the Commission as a whole to take office through a vote of confidence; and the Treaty of Amsterdam, which greatly extended the scope of co-decision, modified it to Parliament's advantage, and gave Parliament the right to confirm or reject a designated President of the Commission.*

In achieving these gains, the EP has used a number of tactical devices. First, most of its members have acted as an interest group pressing for increased powers for the EP within their national parties. Here the most significant step forward was the introduction of direct elections. Direct elections, 'created a new class of elected representatives in Europe . . . whose career depended on making something of the European dimension (Corbett, Jacobs, and Shackleton 2003: 356). Second, the argument that the powers of the EP needed to be increased in order to close the 'democratic deficit' has been consistently used by the EP. The academic debate about the democratic and legitimacy deficits is reviewed in Chapter 4, pp. 65–74. Third, it has made the most extensive use possible of its existing powers, and tried to stretch the definition of those powers, 'on the supposition that anything not explicitly forbidden the EP by the EC treaties is permitted' (Lodge 1990: 11). In this the EP found an ally in the European Court of Justice (ECJ). A number of judgments of the ECJ, on cases brought to it by the EP, have given a more far-reaching interpretation of the constitutional powers of the EP than the member states had foreseen, starting with the 1980 *Isoglucose* judgment that was mentioned by Corbett, Jacobs, and Shackleton. These judgments are examined in Chapter 22, pp. 319–25. Alongside this 'minimalist' approach, the EP has also pursued a 'maximalist' approach, 'based on the overt goal of advancing European Union through not merely treaty amendment but the supplanting of the old treaties by a new one, a constitution for the European Union'

(Lodge 1990: 12). In this the EP has been remarkably successful, although the question of why it has been so successful has never been fully answered.

In what follows, the powers of EP and how they were gained are discussed in more or less the order that they were granted. The grant of additional budgetary powers came before direct elections, but so fundamental were direct elections to the use that could be made of those powers that direct elections are discussed first, then the budgetary powers. Then the increased legislative and scrutiny powers are considered. The discussion of the rulings of the ECJ comes in the next chapter (pp. 319–25).

Direct Elections

Agreement to replace the EPA with a directly-elected body was reached at the Rome meeting of the European Council in December 1975. The date agreed for the first direct elections then was May/June 1978; but the first elections were not held until 1979, because of delay in passing the necessary enabling legislation in Britain. Why was this decision taken; and what were its consequences?

The reason why the heads of government agreed to direct elections is concealed by the aura of secrecy that surrounds all the work of the European Council. However, Germany, Italy, and the Benelux countries had long favoured a directly elected EP. The governments of these states appear to have been convinced by the argument that transferring competences to the EC would lead to a democratic deficit unless there were a directly-elected parliament at that level that could take over the role of scrutiny that would be lost to national parliaments. The crucial shift was on the part of France. Valéry Giscard d'Estaing was the first President of the Fifth Republic not to belong to the Gaullist party. Although his own Independent Republicans did not support direct elections to the EP prior to Giscard becoming President, the small parties in the centre of the French political spectrum did, and Giscard needed their support to move away from dependence on the Gaullists for his parliamentary majority in France. So the agreement to direct elections to the EP may have been the result of domestic political calculations.

Britain, newly joined in 1973, was more reluctant to accept direct elections because it implied a degree of federalism in the constitution of the EC that was greater than British politicians from either of the main political parties wanted to see. Why the Labour government agreed is difficult to understand, but there may have been a deal behind the scenes on French support for the renegotiated terms of entry.

The British Labour government found it difficult to get acceptance of direct elections in the British Parliament. At this time Labour was not a pro-European party; but the government, which did not have a majority in the House of Commons, was dependent on the support of the Liberal Party, which was pro-European. The Liberals were also strong supporters of proportional representation (PR) as a system of election, which most Labour MPs strongly opposed. In response to Liberal demands, the government introduced a European elections bill that incorporated PR, but had to retreat to a system based on single-member constituencies in the face of the combined opposition of the Conservatives and a majority of its own backbenchers. This delayed the legislation, but it delayed implementation even further because the constituency system required extensive work to draw boundaries. As a result of domestic British politics, the first elections were put back a year, until June 1979.

The EP's 'sense of its own dignity and tactical responsiveness increased with direct elections' (Middlemas 1995: 91). The first directly-elected Parliament therefore had the temerity to challenge the Council of Ministers over the annual budget. It was also emboldened to demand more powers of decision making and control over the Commission, now that the member states could not rebuke it with being merely an indirectly elected institution of doubtful legitimacy.

Budgetary Powers

The first grant of additional powers to the EP came in the Treaty of Luxemburg in 1970, when it was given the right to amend 'non-compulsory' items of expenditure in the budget. This agreement was the outcome of an intergovernmental negotiation about the settlement of the long-running budgetary dispute that had led to the 1965 crisis (Ch. 9, pp. 133–4). France continued to be reluctant to grant any budgetary powers to the parliamentary assembly, which was still the indirectly-elected EPA at that time, but President Pompidou was anxious to get the system of 'own resources' agreed prior to the opening of entry negotiations with Britain. For France, the goal was to set up a budgetary system to fund the Common Agricultural Policy (CAP) in a way that would leave France a large net beneficiary from the system. As Britain would inevitably lose out from such a system, agreement could not be left until after British entry because the British government would block any such settlement. However, the other five member states insisted that the loss of parliamentary control over national budgetary contributions must be redressed by an increase in the control of the EPA. As with all such intergovernmental negotiations, the outcome was a compromise.

A distinction introduced by the French between expenditure items that followed directly from Community legal acts (compulsory expenditure) and expenditure that did not, such as administrative expenses (non-compulsory expenditure), was accepted, albeit grudgingly by some delegations (the Dutch delegation most notably) as it gave the EP a final say over only about 4–5 per cent of the entire Community expenditure (that is, non-compulsory expenditure).
(Rittberger 2003: 217)

Subsequently, in the 1975 Budget Treaty, the EP was granted the formal right to reject the budget as a whole. Working with these limited powers, the EP pushed its budgetary role to the maximum, especially after the first direct elections in 1979, so that, '[i]n the early 1980s the annual budgetary cycle was punctuated with unending disputes between the institutions on what were relatively small amounts of money' (Laffan 1997a: 77).

In December 1979, the first directly elected EP blocked the passing of the budget for 1980 in a test of strength against the Council. For several months the EC had to survive on the system of 'provisional twelfths', whereby it is allowed to spend each month an amount equivalent to one-twelfth of the previous year's budget. Eventually the MEPs came under tremendous pressure from their national parties to lift their veto, which they did without winning any further concessions on the substance of the budget from the Council; but a marker had been put down that the Council should not treat the directly elected EP with disdain. An informal agreement was reached on resolving such disputes should they arise in the future, although this did not prevent another crisis the following year, when the EP passed a budget that exceeded the maximum rate of increase. The EP was taken to the Court of Justice by the Council, but an out-of-court agreement was reached in June 1982. Again the EP gave way on the substance of the dispute, but in return got agreement on a joint declaration on the definitions of compulsory and non-compulsory expenditure, and on the respective roles of the two institutions in the budgetary process (Laffan 1997a: 82).

After further acrimonious exchanges in each of the next two years, in 1985 another serious crisis erupted. The EP was becoming increasingly agitated at the failure of the member states to provide adequate funds for new common policies that had been agreed. The main reason for this failure was an inability to bring under control expenditure on the CAP, over which the EP did not have the power of amendment. At first reading on the 1986 budget, the EP inserted amendments to reduce agricultural expenditure, which it had no right to do. The Council removed the amendments, but the EP restored them, and declared the budget passed. The case went to the Court again, where the budget was declared illegal, but the ECJ also banged heads together, telling the Council and the EP that they were joint budgetary authorities, that neither could act unilaterally, and that they had to find means of reaching agreement (Laffan 1997a: 82; Corbett, Jacobs, and Shackleton 2003: 360–2).

It was clear that the disputes and delays in agreeing the annual budgets could not go on indefinitely. Out of this awareness arose the 1988 Inter-institutional Agreement on Budgetary Discipline (Ch. 18, p. 239), which agreed ceilings for both compulsory and non-compulsory expenditure that would have the effect of shifting the balance to non-compulsory items. After this, the budget ceased to be at the forefront of the EP's struggle for power.

Influence in the Legislative Process

The EP from the outset argued the case for it to be an effective co-legislator with the Council of Ministers. This was gradually introduced, first through the co-operation procedure, and then through the co-decision procedure (Ch. 18, pp. 242–6). The crucial breakthrough was the introduction of the co-operation procedure in the Single European Act (SEA). This was insisted upon by the governments of those states—especially Germany and Italy—that were most convinced by the federalist arguments and the arguments about widening the democratic deficit (Rittberger 2003: 220). Consensus gradually emerged between the governments that for the single market to be created, they would have to accept qualified majority voting (QMV), otherwise every individual measure would be vetoed by the government of the state that stood to be most adversely affected. This implied, though, that national parliaments would no longer be able to reject a proposed measure by instructing their government's representative to veto it in the Council. The democratic deficit argument implied that the loss of control by the national parliaments should be made up by an increase in the role of the EP.

Once the principle of a larger role for the EP in the legislative process had been established, the extension of that role followed as experience of operating the new system made it clear that co-operation was a clumsy procedure, and that the EP would use its powers to improve legislation, not just to be obstructive. Whether the movement from the co-operation procedure to co-decision actually did increase the effective influence of the EP in the legislative process was, though, the subject of considerable academic debate. This is reviewed at length in the next main section of the chapter, on Debates and Research. As far as practitioners are concerned, though, they have no doubt that co-decision has increased the influence of the EP.

The EP and the Commission

There are two main aspects of the ability of the EP to exercise control over the Commission. The first is in its powers over the appointment of the College of Commissioners. The second is in its power to dismiss Commissioners if it disapproves of their conduct.

The power of the EP in the appointment of a new Commission was originally zero. This is an area, however, where the maximalist strategy produced results: Treaty amendments gave the EP limited powers that were then exploited fully under the minimalist strategy. At Maastricht the heads of government agreed to consult the EP on the choice of the President of the Commission and to give it the right to consent (or not consent) to the appointment of the College of Commissioners as a whole. They also agreed to bring the term of office of the Commissioners into line with that of the EP, so that the newly-elected Parliament would be asked as one of its first acts to approve the proposed new Commission. In the Amsterdam Treaty there was a further extension of these powers, when the EP was given a formal right of approval of their nominee for President. These changes were made with an eye on the need to address the democratic deficit. It was hoped that the new powers would persuade voters that the EP was an institution that had the characteristics of a real parliament, and thereby contribute to increased interest in the European parliamentary elections (Smith 1999: 68).

Having gained the right to approve the appointments of the President, and separately of the other Commissioners as a whole, the EP reverted to its minimalist strategy of making the most extensive use possible of its powers. It adapted its internal rules of procedure so that the approval or rejection of the Commission President required only a simple majority, and if the nomination was rejected, the member states would be asked to make a new nomination. It also adopted a rule of procedure that the approval of the Commission as a whole would follow parliamentary hearings in which each of the Commissioners would be subjected to cross-examination *in public* by the members of the relevant Specialist Committee of the EP (Judge and Earnshaw 2002: 355). These procedural adaptations increased the leverage of the modest extra powers granted in the Maastricht Treaty in ways that will be explored below.

The other aspect of parliamentary control over the Commission is in its power to dismiss Commissioners. Here the Treaty gives the EP what at first sight is a powerful weapon. If a motion of censure on the Commission is passed by a two-thirds majority of the votes cast, representing a majority of MEPs, then the Commission must resign as a body (TEC, Article 201). However, this right is less powerful than it seems for at least two reasons. First, the majority required is very difficult to attain. Of nine such motions tabled prior to 1998, none came close to achieving the double majority required. Second, the most likely reason for a censure is because of the behaviour of an individual Commissioner or Commissioners, yet there is no possibility of targeting the censure against individual Commissioners, only against the College as a whole.

Despite these problems, at the end of the 1990s the EP managed to use the blunt instrument given it by the Treaty to effect a shift in its influence. In 1998 its Budgetary Affairs Committee postponed a decision on whether to discharge the 1996 budget (see Ch. 18, p. 240), because it was unhappy with the response of the Commission to certain charges of lax financial administration. Although the Committee subsequently decided by one vote to recommend the grant of discharge, the EP meeting in plenary rejected the recommendation. Jacques Santer, the President of the Commission, then made the issue one of confidence by challenging the EP either to give discharge to the budget or to lay down a motion of censure on the whole Commission. This the EP did, although when it was voted on in January 1999 it failed to get even a majority, let alone the two-thirds majority that was required. However, the vote of 232 for and 293 against was the biggest vote ever for a motion of censure, and prompted the Commission to agree to set up a committee of independent experts to report to the EP on fraud, mismanagement, and nepotism in the Commission. When the report appeared in March 1999 it was so damning of the level of mismanagement by some Commissioners, that the whole Commission resigned. Although the EP had not managed to summon the substantial majority needed to censure the Commission formally, it had managed to raise the public awareness of the issues identified by the Court of Auditors to the point where the position of the Commission became untenable. By adept use of its limited powers, the EP achieved a considerable victory (see Ch. 15, pp. 191–2).

At this point, the powers of the EP to approve the new Commission President and College of Commissioners took centre-stage. The new nominee for President was Romano Prodi. He anticipated that the EP would want to seek some assurance that in future it would not need to attack the whole Commission if, as had been the case with the Santer Commission, the problem lay with certain individuals. In fact, the Santer Commission probably could have survived had one individual Commissioner agreed to resign, but her refusal to do so left the Commission with no option but to resign as a whole. Prodi therefore told the EP at his own confirmation hearing that he would require every individual Commissioner to promise to resign if asked by the President to do so. Although this did not give the EP the right to dismiss individual Commissioners, it did mark a further advance towards that goal. The EP then underlined the importance that it set on this development by requiring each of the proposed new Commissioners to make a public declaration at their confirmation hearing that they would resign if asked by the President to do so. In July 2000 a new *Framework Agreement on Relations between the European Parliament and the Commission* was adopted by the EP. In it, the commitment of Prodi to hold Commissioners individually responsible was strengthened by a commitment that if the EP expressed a lack of confidence in an individual Commissioner, the President would consider whether to ask that individual to resign.

Five years later, the EP again flexed its muscles during the confirmation hearings for the incoming Barroso Commission, when the EP expressed an unwillingness to confirm the new Commission in office if the Italian nominee Rocco Buttiglione was a member of the team, and expressed doubts about the competence of other nominees (Ch. 17, pp. 214–15). After something of a stand-off, Barroso agreed to re-think the position. Buttiglione's nomination was withdrawn and the Italian government put forward another Italian nominee, and two other changes were made to national nominations. This outcome was achieved because of the impressive degree of independence demonstrated by MEPs in the Socialist and Liberal groups, in the face of intense pressure from national governments to allow the contested nominations. This leads, then, into the discussion of the extent to which individual MEPs and the party groups are liable to appear as autonomous actors.

Debates and Research

Whereas academic debates on other institutions have tended to focus on one issue, both debate and research on the EP have been more far-reaching and diverse. In a very useful summary, Hix, Raunio, and Scully (2003: 193–6) classified contemporary research on the EP into four areas:

- work on the general development and functioning of the EP;
- research on political behaviour and EP elections;
- research on the internal politics and organization of the EP;
- examinations of inter-institutional bargaining between the EP, the Council, and the Commission.

The first of these has been dealt with already in this chapter. In this section of the chapter, each of the other three categories of research will be briefly reviewed to indicate the main academic concerns.

Political Behaviour and EP Elections

The strongest argument for the direct election of the EP was that it would increase the legitimacy of the institution and thereby of the EU as a whole. Yet turn-out in European elections has been consistently low. Overall turn-out declined from 63 per cent in 1979 to 49 per cent in 1999 and to 45 per cent in 2004. It varied between member states, but Mattila (2003) showed that the bulk of the variation in turn-out could be explained by the same variables as affected national elections. The more significant fact is not the variation, but that in every state the turn-out is much lower than for national elections.

Successive European Elections Studies have examined this phenomenon (Reif and Schmitt 1980; van der Eijk and Franklin 1996; Schmitt and Thomasen 1999). The thrust of the argument of these studies is that European elections are treated by the electorate as 'second order national elections', which means that they are seen as being on a par with local-government elections. This reflects the fact that the European elections do not affect which party or coalition governs the EU. The outcome affects neither the composition of the Commission nor that of the Council of Ministers, the two most powerful institutions in the system. So, the campaigns are fought predominantly on domestic issues rather than European issues. Although the main party groups issue European manifestos, these are framework documents from which the national parties draw when they prepare their national manifestos. Most of the actual campaigning centres on the record of the national government rather than on the differences between the parties on European issues. This held true in 2004 as much as in earlier elections.

One consequence of this is that the results tend to reflect the protest nature of voting in second-order elections. The party that is in office nationally will tend to do badly if it is in the middle of its term because voters use the European election as a means of indicating their dissatisfaction. Of course, the national electoral cycles of member states map onto the schedule of European elections in different ways; and there may well be parties of different political complexions in office in the different member states. However, there is a tendency for European electorates to move to the right or left in a manner that may not be co-ordinated, but does produce clusters of conservative or socialist governments at any one time. So, during most of the 1980s and 1990s there was a majority of conservative governments in Europe, and the socialist parties formed the largest group in the EP because protest votes in European elections were directed against the national conservative governments. Following a swing to the left in the large majority of member states in the late 1990s, it was predictable that the conservative parties would overtake the socialists in the EP elections of 1999 and again in 2004.

This effect of having different ideological majorities in member states from the majority in the EP was perhaps less significant in a situation where the main concern of the EP was to press for further European integration. There has been a tendency for individuals who stood for election to the EP to be pro-European whether they were from the right or left of the political spectrum. In the aftermath of the completion of the single market, though, the issues that face the EU are classic left-right issues of how much public control there should be over business, how much legal protection should be given to workers, etc. Research indicates that '[w]hen taking legislative decisions, the EP parties tend to split along left-right lines' (Judge and Earnshaw 2002: 362). For this reason, the disjuncture between the ideological orientation of the national and European majorities could become a serious barrier to effective governance.

Internal Politics and Organization of the EP

Hix, Raunio, and Scully (2003: 194–5) divide research under this heading into three categories. One of these, research on the work of the committees of the EP, is almost a blank category. The only significant research that they identify is a study by Bowler and Farrell (1995) on the determinants of committee membership. Much more attention has been focused on the party groups. Their third category is 'other aspects of political behaviour inside the EP', which raises the issue of the independence of MEPs as demonstrated by their behaviour in the EP.

The Party Groups

Just as the EP cannot expect to extend its power and influence unless MEPs show themselves to be competent, so it cannot do so by definition if it lacks independence and autonomy. The main constraint on MEPs acting autonomously is the influence of national political parties. Unless the party groups in the EP can establish their autonomy from national parties, the EP will be constrained.

MEPs do not sit in the EP in national delegations, but in transnational party groups. A party group may be established by twelve MEPs if they are drawn from three or more member states; by eighteen MEPs if they are drawn from two member states; or by twenty-three MEPs if they are drawn from only one member state.

Each party group has its own administrative and support staff, paid for out of the central budget of the EP. Groups are co-ordinated by a Bureau, consisting of a Chair, a Vice-Chair, and a Treasurer as a minimum. The members of the Bureau are elected by the members of the group as a whole. The groups play an important role in setting the agenda of the EP, choosing the *rapporteurs* for committees, and allocating speaking time in plenary sessions. A full list of the groups, and their level of representation in the 2004–9 Parliament is given in Table 21.3.

TABLE 21.3

Membership Numbers of Political Groups in the European Parliament (as at January 2005)

Group	MEPs
The European People's Party and European Democrats	268
The Party of European Socialists	200
Alliance of Liberals and Democrats for Europe	88
Greens/European Free Alliance	42
European United Left/Nordic Green Left	41
Union for a Europe of Nations	27
Independence and Democracy Group	37
Non-affiliated	29
Total	**732**

There are definite advantages to being a member of one of the party groups. The groups receive funding from the EP to cover their administrative costs. Memberships of committees, and their chairs and rapporteurs, are allocated to groups in proportion to their size. (For a list of EP committees see Table 21.2, p. 296.) It is not surprising, therefore, that national parties and individual MEPs who cannot find an ideological group to join will seek to band together to form a disparate group of their own. This was the nature of the Rainbow Group in the 1984–9 Parliament. It consisted of members of environmentalist parties, regionalist parties, and anti-EC Danish MEPs; the only thing that they had in common was a wish to draw down the funding and other advantages that would be denied them if they did not join a group.

However, even the groups that may appear to be more homogeneous can contain within them a wide variety of divergent ideological positions. The Liberal and Democrat Group contains economic liberals, who believe in free-market economics and are conservative on social issues, and social liberals, who are nearer to social democrats on social issues and on the need to regulate the market than they are to some of their colleagues in their own Group. Even bigger divergence existed over many years between the French and Italian Communists in what used to be the Group of the Democratic Left: the Italian Communists were pro-European integration, whereas the French Party was hostile.

Even within the ideologically more cohesive groups, which include the two largest groups of the Party of European Socialists (PES) and the conservative European People's

Party (EPP), differences can emerge around national perspectives on issues. In early 1999, when the EP voted on a censure motion against the Santer Commission, the Socialist Group officially said it would vote against the motion. However, almost all its German members voted for the censure. This reflected the fact that criticism of the Commission had become a popular cause in the press in Germany, to a greater extent than in other member states.

Not only can genuine differences of national perspective lead to divergence in voting behaviour: the MEPs in the party groups are subject to pressure from their national parties. In many, although not all member states, the PR electoral systems that operate make it easier for national party leaders to put pressure on their MEPs, because European elections are held on the basis of closed party lists—that is, the voter is presented with a list of the candidates for that party in the order of preference decided by the party, and is unable to change the order. The chances for an individual of being elected on any particular level of vote for the party depend on where he or she is placed on the list. As the lists are drawn up by the national party organizations, the MEPs face the prospect of being dropped down the list, and of their seats being jeopardized, if they offend the national party leadership too much.

This raises directly the issue of the independence of MEPs. The system is still dominated by national parties, and this has a number of adverse consequences for MEPs, not least in denying them greater electoral legitimacy. The observation is made above that voters treat European elections as second-order national elections. The main reason that this situation persists is the domination of the process by national political parties and national debates.

The central aim of domestic political parties in any electoral contest is gaining control of national government offices. European elections are thus fought on the performances of the parties holding national government offices. . . . As long as national parties decide who are the candidates in the elections and control the attention of the media during campaigns, there is little the EP groups or the party federations can do to break their hold over the process.

(Hix and Lord 1997: 211)

Despite these pressures on the party groups, research (Hix 2000; Faas 2003) indicates that the internal cohesion of party groups has generally increased over time. Analysis of voting within the EP demonstrated that:

In terms of party cohesion, the studies have revealed a surprisingly high degree of party group cohesion. An exception is those party groups that exist for mere technical reasons, like the Technical Group of Independent Members in the 1999 European Parliament. Large, as well as leftist, party groups were usually found to be more cohesive than smaller or rightist ones.

(Faas 2003: 850)

In addition, groups containing larger numbers of different national parties were less likely to be cohesive than those with fewer different nationalities, and some national groups—such as the British—were more likely to defect on group votes than others.

Kreppel (2002, 2003) correlated the increasing group cohesion with the increased power of the EP. As the powers of the EP were increased under successive revisions of the Treaties, so the party groups tended to become more cohesive in order to be more effective. They also became less ideological, because of the need to form alliances across groups; and following Maastricht, the two biggest groups (the PES and EPP) co-operated in pushing through changes to the rules of procedure that allowed them to dominate (Kreppel 2003: 900). At the same time, with more power there also came more pressure from national parties, and particularly from national governments, to defect from the position of the transnational group if it conflicted with the national position. This is how Hix (2000: 3) explained a statistical dip in the level of group cohesion in the first session of the 1999 parliament. However, Faas (2003: 860) argued that, 'national parties will only precipitate a breakdown of party group cohesion by putting pressure on their MEPs on specific questions that are of special importance to them, but not on a general basis'. As a result, it can be expected that group cohesion will remain high, an expectation that was borne out by the research reported in Faas (2003).

A test of the strength of group cohesion in the face of pressure from national governments occurred with the confirmation crisis of 2004 (Ch. 17, pp. 214–15). Despite pressure from several national governments on the MEPs from their own parties to break ranks and vote for the confirmation of the Commission as a whole, the groups generally held firm, forcing the withdrawal of the most controversial nominee, and obliging President-elect Barroso to reshuffle his College. This incident underlined one of the arguments of Kreppel (2002), that MEPs were always likely to unite around the drive to secure more influence for the EP within EU decision making. That the MEPs held firm on this occasion, though, contrasts with the eventual capitulation in the confrontation over the budget in 1979–80, perhaps again indicating that the EP as a whole has attained more autonomy along with its increased authority.

The Independence of MEPs

As suggested above, one of the factors that will affect the ability of the EP to extend its power and influence further is the independence of MEPs from national influence. In the early years of the EP, few MEPs had any real incentive to assert their independence from their national parties. They were predominantly either older or younger than most national MPs. Most of the older politicians had exhausted their career options in their home state and were serving out their years to retirement in the well-paid but relatively undemanding role of MEP. The young politicians were mostly keen to pursue a national political career, but found that it was easier to get started with a European seat than with a national seat.

There is a problem about the lack of an obvious career route at the European level. National MPs can aspire to enter government, or at least to become an official spokesperson for their party if it is in opposition. At the European level the executive is not drawn from the EP, which means that there is little obvious progression. However, as Hix and Lord (1997: 117) pointed out, if the Commissioners from the then new member states were excluded, eleven out of seventeen members of the Santer Commission had been MEPs. Another point about career progression, is that in the United States the executive is not chosen from members of the legislature, but that has not prevented the emergence of professional members of Congress who aspire to occupy senior committee chairs. As the powers and influence of the EP grow, so a similar career route might come to be followed by MEPs.

Over the years this seems to have been happening. Research by Martin Westlake (1994) indicated that there was increasing professionalization and careerism among MEPs. Although this still had far to go, the European Parliament might be becoming 'more, rather than less, attractive' to ambitious politicians (Westlake 1994: 268). These findings were supported in a later study by Scarrow (1997), who saw the proportion of European career politicians steadily increasing, and similarly predicted that MEPs would become increasingly independent of national parties.

The EP and Inter-Institutional Bargaining

This is an area that has attracted a lot of academic attention, which has centred on the extent to which the effective influence of the EP over the legislative process has really increased. Although the general view of the progression from consultation through co-operation to co-decision was that 'the consecutive institutional reforms are moving the EU towards a genuinely bicameral system' (Crombez 2000: 366)—i.e. that each stage represented an increase in both the power and influence of the EP—some analysts argued that the EP had less effective influence on legislation under the co-decision procedure than it had under co-operation (Garrett and Tsebelis 1996; Tsebelis and Garrett 1996). Their argument was as follows.

Under the *consultation* procedure the Council had the strongest say on the final form of legislation, because although the Commission drafted the proposal, the Council had to accept it unanimously. The Commission therefore had to formulate each proposal in such a way that even the member state least favourably disposed towards integration would be able to accept it, which meant that the Commission had little room to exercise its own discretion. After the SEA introduced QMV in the Council, the Commission became more influential in those few areas that still came under consultation. This was because the Commission only had to draft a proposal that would be preferred to the *status quo* by a qualified majority of members of the Council. Here, the EP was restricted to a consultative role, and its opinion could be ignored whether the voting rule was unanimity or QMV.

Under the *co-operation* procedure the Commission and the EP shared the power to determine the final form of the legislation. This was because of the combination of QMV in the Council, and the introduction of a second reading with a conditional power of veto for the EP. At the second reading, if the EP was unhappy with the version of the draft legislation that had been adopted by the Council as its 'common position' (which in effect meant if the EP's proposed amendments had largely been ignored), the EP could reject the common position by an absolute majority of its members. This constituted a veto, but the Council could override it if it acted by unanimity. A key element in the balance of influence here was the attitude of the Commission to the EP's proposed amendments at second reading. If the Commission accepted the amendments, the Council had to act by unanimity to overturn them; but the Council could accept the amended proposal by QMV. This meant that if the EP and the Commission could agree on a proposal that was acceptable to a coalition in the Council that constituted a qualified majority, they together had the decisive influence on the form of the legislation.

Under the *co-decision* procedure, according to Tsebelis and Garrett, the formal power to determine the final wording of the legislation passed to the Council of Ministers. This was in complete contrast to the general view that co-decision was a significant increase in the power of the EP. The procedure gave the EP:

* three readings of legislation
* the right to negotiate directly with the Council via a conciliation committee on any amendments for which there was an absolute majority in the EP but with which the Council did not agree
* an absolute right of veto.

The reasoning of Tsebelis and Garrett was as follows:

(1) The position of the Commission was fatally weakened because after the second reading the Council and the EP could convene a conciliation committee and negotiate a text bi-laterally which could overrule the Commission text.

(2) On the assumption that the EP would normally prefer to see some legislation rather than no legislation, it was engaged in an uneven negotiation with the Council. If agreement could not be reached in the conciliation committee, the Council could either allow the proposal to drop by simply not acting on it, or could adopt the original common position. In the latter case the EP could reject the common position by an absolute majority, but the effect was to revert to the status quo.

These conclusions were strongly contested by several writers (Crombez 1996, 1997, 2000; Moser 1996, 1997; Scully 1997*a*, 1997*b*). They accepted the general framework of the model put forward by Tsebelis and Garrett, but pointed to certain flaws in the argument. In particular, the role of the Commission was underestimated. It still had the sole right of initiative for legislative proposals, and drafted the initial text. If it worked in conjunction with the EP at this stage, and if the two institutions acted strategically to agree proposals that could command a qualified majority in the Council, then they had the same joint influence as under the co-operation procedure. Also, Tsebelis and Garrett were incorrect to argue that after the EP's second reading the Commission was marginalized. The Commission did consider the proposed amendments, and if it rejected them it effectively forced a conciliation committee to be convened. At this stage the Commission could still play an effective role as a negotiator, and try to find a position that was still based on its original text but which would avert conciliation, where both sides stood to lose everything that they hoped to gain from the legislation.

Another criticism was that Tsebelis and Garrett seriously underestimated the importance of the EP's power of veto under both the co-operation and conciliation procedures. If the issue was a matter of detail, then the willingness of the EP to threaten to veto a proposal might produce concessions from the Council, which would be reluctant to lose a measure on which it was agreed in principle because of a detail.

In practice much of Tsebelis and Garrett's analysis was based on ignoring the informal aspects of the inter-institutional bargaining process. This failing is perhaps related to the rational choice framework of analysis that they adopted, which does not place much emphasis on empirical research. Scholars whose approach involved intensive research 'in the field' were clear that, 'the informal dimensions of inter-institutional relations are of major significance in understanding policy-making in the EC' (Judge, Earnshaw, and Cowan 1994: 45).

The importance of the informal aspect is related to the EP's vigorous pursuit of the minimalist strategy of making the greatest possible use of its formal powers. This first emerged with reference to the consultation procedure in the aftermath of the Isoglucose judgment (Ch. 22, pp. 319–20). As a result of the judgment, the EP was able to force the Commission to interact more intensively with it to try to ensure that it would not delay legislation. Under the *renvoi* procedure the EP refused to deliver a formal opinion until it had received some indication from the Commission of how it proposed to react to the amendments that the EP was suggesting. The level of informal interaction in particular increased, and in 1990 the Commission offered a code of conduct that committed it to keeping the EP informed. This was accepted, and was extended in 1995 in the light of changes in the TEU.

On the same theme, Earnshaw and Judge (1997: 560) made the following assessment of the effect of the co-operation procedure:

the co-operation procedure served to 'hyphenate' the relationship between Parliament and the other two institutions and so to transform the Council–Commission dialogue into an asymmetrical Council–Commission–Parliament trialogue. However, in strict constitutional terms, Parliament still remained the 'outsider' in this relationship. Nonetheless, the true importance of the formal procedure was that it facilitated the exertion of greater informal parliamentary influence over EU legislation. Thus, in interview, MEPs and officials alike pointed to the importance of informal negotiations between Parliament and the Commission in determining the eventual legislative impact of the EP.

On the co-decision procedure, the same researchers (Earnshaw and Judge 1995: 645) agreed with Tsebelis and Garrett that the role of the Commission had been weakened. It was placed in 'a considerably more ambiguous, and weaker, position than in the co-operation or consultation procedures'. However, they disagreed that the procedure had left the EP with less influence than previously:

Under co-decision Parliament is certainly a more equal partner in the legislative process, and now has a rightful place alongside the Council in several important policy areas—despite the weighting of the procedure towards the Council.

(Earnshaw and Judge 1995: 647)

As with the other developments treated above, though, the biggest impact of the change was on the informal contacts: 'informal inter-institutional linkages have expanded as a result of co-decision' (Earnshaw and Judge 1995: 647–8). In practice, the formal changes to the rules made under Maastricht led to the emergence of informal institutional changes.

Initially, the Council attempted to minimize the impact of the changes on the way in which legislation was dealt with. However, the determination of the EP to make the maximum use of its new powers soon convinced the Council that it could not carry on as before. The EP showed itself willing to take even relatively uncontroversial legislation to conciliation unless its positions were taken seriously. As a backlog of legislation began to mount, the Council agreed to institute informal 'trialogues' or 'trilogues' with the Commission and EP in an attempt to ease the passage of important measures.

The determination of the EP was demonstrated further when the Council attempted to use the clause that allowed it to re-introduce its final common position should conciliation fail. In 1994 the Conciliation Committee on the 'Open Network Provision Directive on Voice Telephony' failed to reach a compromise that was acceptable to both Council and EP. In response the Council re-instated its common position, defying the EP to muster the absolute majority needed to throw it out. The EP had already adopted an internal rule that it would reject any attempt by the Council to invoke this power, whatever the merits of the case, and the measure was indeed thrown out.

Subsequently, the experience of trying to make the system introduced at Maastricht operate effectively led to further changes to the formal rules at Amsterdam. These changes allowed the Council and EP to conclude the process at first reading if they could reach agreement, and changed the rules of conciliation so that there was no longer the possibility of legislation that had been rejected by the EP being passed if the Conciliation Committee failed to reach agreement. The decision to allow agreement after the first reading reflected the concern of the Council Secretariat that, with the transfer of even more areas to co-decision, the system needed to be streamlined. However, the new rule implied a further extension of informal discussion, effectively involving the EP in the formulation of legislative proposals at the same early stage as the Commission consulted with the Council.

The change of rule on what happened after an unsuccessful conciliation simply reflected acceptance that the EP would never accept the re-instatement of a Council common position, as it had demonstrated in 1994. According to Shackleton and Raunio (2003: 173), in an assessment that is given authority by the fact that Shackleton was the Head of the Conciliations Secretariat of the EP at the time:

Co-decision is now seen as an interlinked, continuous procedure where it is essential and normal that there be intensive contacts throughout the procedure from before first reading onwards. Such contacts offer the opportunity of coming to agreements without having recourse to the time-consuming procedure of conciliation.

The other change—to the rules governing the final stage of the process—led Tsebelis and Garrett (2000) to conclude that equality had been reached at last because the Council could no longer carry its common position if conciliation failed. However, an empirical study by Kasack (2004) indicated that the revised procedure did not lead to an increase in the rate of adoption of the EP's amendments, and that the big step forward for the EP had indeed been the introduction of the original co-decision procedure under Maastricht. The role of the Commission had been diminished as a result of the changes made at Amsterdam, but not that of the EP. As Kasack (2004: 256) summarized in a sub-heading: 'The Parliament keeps its influence while the Commission loses power.'

CONCLUSION

The themes of the book that are brought out in this chapter are particularly those concerned with the supranational or intergovernmental nature of the EU, and with the democratic and legitimacy deficits of the EU. The debate between rational choice and social constructivist approaches to the analysis of the EU also emerges when the process by which the EP has extended its influence is analysed.

The issue of the nature of the EU as an organization is clearly affected by the view that is taken of the effective influence of the EP. If it is accepted that the successive changes in its formal role have made it a co-legislator with the Council of Ministers, then the view that the EU is no more than an intergovernmental organization cannot be sustained. There is no other such organization where the member states have to share decision making with a directly-elected institution. This is true whether or not the formal role translates into effective influence. It can be dismissed as no more than an appearance of supranationalism, though, if there is no real power attached to the role.

On legitimacy, the main reason why the powers of the EP have been extended has been in response to the argument that this would help to close the democratic deficit, and therefore the legitimacy deficit of the EU. The evidence does not indicate that much has been achieved in that direction. There are clear limits to the legitimacy of the EP's democratic mandate, which may only be eased with the development of a stronger sense of European identity among EU citizens. For now, the best prospect of reducing the democratic deficit appears to lie in closer working relations between the EP and national parliaments.

In other respects, though, the EP may be helping to close the legitimacy deficit. Its strong line towards the management failings of the Commission, culminating in what was effectively the forced resignation of the Santer Commission, may be helping to convince European publics that the efficiency issue is being addressed. Also the role of the EP as an alternative point of access to the policy-making process for interests that feel excluded elsewhere by the domination of business interests could help to build a sense of European identity among such groups in the longer term.

The debate between rational choice and social constructivist approaches to the analysis of the EU is apparent in the explanations that each side offers for the way in which the EP has extended its powers and influence. The social constructivist position is apparent in the argument of Pollack (2003), which is examined in Chapter 2 (p. 25), that the governments of the member states have largely extended the formal powers of the EP in response to arguments about the need to address the 'democratic deficit' rather than in an attempt to reduce transaction costs. However, the process whereby formal rule-changes led to informal changes that were subsequently formalized, was analysed by Farrell and Héritier (2003) using a game-theoretical approach. Although the insight that informal procedures are central to the operation of inter-institutional relationships is usually associated with historical institutionalists and constructivists, the adoption of the idea of *iterated games*, instead of treating each round of bargaining as a 'one-off-shot', allows the rational choice models to be adapted to take account of the informal developments. So, there is no definitive judgment that can be made between the explanatory power of the two approaches.

KEY POINTS

Composition and Functions

☐ The EP has 732 seats, which are distributed between the member states approximately in proportion to population.

☐ It meets monthly in plenary in Strasburg, but most of its work is done in Committee in Brussels.

☐ Organizationally it has a President, a Bureau, a Conference of Presidents, and a Secretariat.

The Struggle for Power

☐ The forerunner of the EP was not directly elected and had limited powers.

☐ The EP has steadily increased its powers by putting pressure on national parties and governments, arguing that it needed increased powers to close the democratic deficit. It has also made the maximum use of its existing powers and campaigned for a Constitution for Europe.

☐ The first direct elections to the EP took place in June 1979. Direct election emboldened MEPs to challenge the member states over the budget and to demand more powers.

☐ In 1970 the power of the EP over the budget was increased, when it was given the power to amend 'non-compulsory expenditure', which excluded the CAP. In 1975 it was given the power to reject the budget as a whole. By provoking budgetary crises in 1980, 1984–5, and 1986, the EP forced a move to multi-annual budgetary programmes negotiated between itself and the Council.

☐ The EP can force the Commission as a whole to resign by a motion of censure, but it has to achieve a demanding majority to do so, and it cannot dismiss individual Commissioners.

☐ Originally, the EP had no say in the appointment of the Commission. Under successive Treaty amendments it gained the right to withhold consent for the new Commission to take office, and to approve the nominee for President.

Debates and Research

☐ The electorate in all member states treats European elections as 'second-order' national elections. They are fought primarily on domestic issues, and turn-out is lower than for national elections.

☐ MEPs sit in transnational party groups, which can contain within them a wide variety of ideological positions, but research indicates that the degree of group cohesion has increased as the powers of the EP have increased.

☐ The lack of a European-level career structure acts as an obstacle to MEPs acting independently of their national parties, but research has indicated that being an MEP is increasingly attractive to ambitious politicians.

☐ The role of the EP in the legislative process has moved from the weak position in the consultation procedure, through successively stronger positions under co-operation and co-decision.

☐ Tsebelis and Garrett argued that, contrary to popular belief, co-decision actually weakened the influence of the EP over EC legislation. Critics of this argument suggested that it underestimated the importance of the informal powers of the EP in the inter-institutional bargaining process.

FURTHER READING

For general guides to the EP see F. Jacobs, R. Corbett, and M. Shackleton, *The European Parliament* (London: Catermill, 4th edn, 2000), and M. Westlake, *The European Parliament: A Modern Guide* (London: Pinter, 1994). More grounded in political science are J. Smith, *Europe's Elected Parliament* (Sheffield: Sheffield University Press/University Association for Contemporary European Studies, 1999), and D. Judge and D. Earnshaw, *The European Parliament* (London: Palgrave Macmillan, 2003).

A less technical supplement to the European Election Studies, which are referenced in the text, is a series of edited books on several of the European elections by Juliet Lodge. The series since the 1989 election are: J. Lodge (ed.), *The 1989 Election of the European Parliament* (Basingstoke and London: Macmillan, 1990); *Euro-Elections 1994* (London: Continuum, 1995); *The 1999 Elections to the European Parliament* (Basingstoke and London: Macmillan, 2001); *The 2004 Elections to the European Parliament* (Basingstoke and New York: Palgrave, 2005).

On the political parties, the most impressive survey is S. Hix and C. Lord, *Political Parties in the European Union* (Basingstoke and London: Macmillan, 1997). Tapio Raunio, *The European Perspective: Transnational Party Groups in the 1989–1994 European Parliament* (London: Ashgate, 1997) is more narrowly focused. Amie Kreppel, *The European Parliament and Supranational Party System: A Study in Institutional Development* (Cambridge: Cambridge University Press, 2002) makes an important contribution to our understanding of the relationship between the power of the EP and the behaviour of its party groups.

online resource centre   **Visit the Online Resource Centre that accompanies this book for links to more information on the European Parliament, including the EP's own web site.**

CHAPTER 22

The European Court of Justice

CHAPTER OVERVIEW

The European Court of Justice (ECJ) makes binding decisions on disputes over Treaty provisions or secondary legislation. It therefore plays an essential role in the developing EU. This chapter looks first at the structure and functions of the ECJ, and than at some of its main rulings and their significance. It considers rulings on the powers of the institutions, then judgments on issues of EC law made in response to questions referred to the ECJ by national courts. The chapter then turns to look at, first the political reactions to the judgments of the Court, and then the debate over whether the member states have lost control of the process of European integration because of the radical jurisprudence of the ECJ.

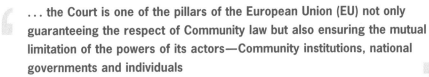

> ... the Court is one of the pillars of the European Union (EU) not only guaranteeing the respect of Community law but also ensuring the mutual limitation of the powers of its actors—Community institutions, national governments and individuals
>
> **(Costa, 2003: 741)**

There is consensus on the need for the ECJ to exist as an authoritative interpreter of both the Treaties and the secondary legislation (directives, regulations) put in place by member states; but in carrying out this task, it has been criticized for stepping beyond its legal role into the realm of politics. Specifically, it has been accused of generally ruling in favour of integrationist solutions to disputes. This has provoked hostility from member states who see their national sovereignty being undermined by Court rulings. In the period after the Maastricht ratification crisis, the ECJ was subjected to increased criticism from member states for its radical jurisprudence. The British and German governments were at the forefront of this criticism. Yet while the 1990s may have seen some questions raised about the Court's influence, its centrality to the process of European integration remains intact.

Structure and Functions

The Court of Justice meets in Luxemburg. It comprises twenty-five judges and eight advocates general, who are appointed by common accord of the governments of the member states and hold office for a renewable term of six years. They are chosen from persons whose independence is beyond doubt and who are of recognized competence. Half of the judges and half of the advocates-general are replaced every three years. The judges select one of their number to be President of the Court for a renewable term of three years. The President directs the work of the Court and presides at hearings and deliberations. The advocates general assist the Court in its task. They deliver legal opinions on the cases brought before the Court.

In 1989 a Court of First Instance was created to help the ECJ with the sheer volume of business that it had to get through. It also comprises of twenty-five judges, with one from each member state. There are no advocates-general in the Court of First Instance. As with the ECJ, its members are chosen from among persons whose independence is beyond doubt, and who possess the ability required for judicial appointment; they are appointed by common accord of the governments of the member states, for a renewable six-year term, with the membership being partially renewed every three years.

It is the responsibility of the ECJ to ensure that the law is observed in the interpretation and application of the Treaties establishing the European Communities and of the provisions laid down by the competent Community institutions. To enable it to carry out that task, the Court has wide jurisdiction to hear various types of action and to give preliminary rulings.

The types of action the Court may hear are: proceedings for failure to fulfil an obligation; proceedings for annulment of EC legislation; proceedings for failure of an EU institution to act; actions for damages; and appeals against judgments of the Court of First Instance. Each of these categories is now explained in a little more detail.

(1) Proceedings for failure to fulfil an obligation (Treaty establishing the European Community (TEC) Articles 226, 227, and 228).

A member state may be taken to the Court by the Commission or by another member state for failing to act to meet its obligations under the Treaties or EC secondary legislation. If the Court finds against the state so charged, it must comply without delay. If it fails to do so, the Commission may go back to the Court and ask for a fine to be imposed on the state.

(2) Proceedings for annulment (TEC Articles 230 and 231).

A member state, the Council, the Commission and, in certain circumstances, the EP, may apply to the ECJ for the annulment of all or part of an item of EC legislation, and individuals may seek the annulment of a legal measure that is of direct and individual concern to them. The annulment may be sought and granted on grounds of lack of competence, infringement of an essential procedural requirement, infringement of the Treaty, or mis-use of powers.

(3) Proceedings for failure to act (TEC Articles 232 and 233).

The Court may review the legality of a failure to act by a Community institution, and penalize silence or inaction.

(4) Actions for damages (TEC Article 235).

In an action for damages, the Court rules on the liability of the Community for damage caused by its institutions or servants in the performance of their duties.

(5) Appeals (TEC Article 225).

The Court may hear appeals, on points of law only, against judgments given by the Court of First Instance in cases within its jurisdiction.

The Court of First Instance has jurisdiction to rule at first instance on: all actions for annulment, for failure to act and for damages brought by natural or legal persons against the Community; actions brought against the Commission under the ECSC Treaty by undertakings or associations of undertakings; disputes between the Community and its officials and servants. The TEC also allows all other categories of cases to be transferred upon decision taken by the Council, to the Court of First Instance. The explicit exception is preliminary rulings.

Preliminary rulings are judgments by the Court on the interpretation of the Treaties or secondary legislation arising under the Treaties. Under TEC Article 234 (formerly Article 177), national courts that are hearing cases involving EC law may request a ruling from the ECJ on the interpretation of the law, and where the issue is raised before a national court against whose judgment there is no appeal in domestic law, that court must seek a preliminary ruling from the ECJ. The ECJ cannot deliver a preliminary ruling unless it is asked to do so by a national court. Preliminary rulings are discussed at length below (pp. 322–5).

Although judges are usually thought of as conservative, that cannot be said of the ECJ judges. It has been argued that the ECJ has done more than any other institution to advance European integration (Freestone 1983: 43). Its approach has been heavily criticized by some commentators as stepping beyond the bounds of legal interpretation to become political (Ramussen 1986; Smith 1990). Perhaps this lack of conservatism is because many of the members of the ECJ are not judges by profession. Many of the appointees have been academics rather than professional lawyers. Whatever the reasons, the ECJ has followed a radical jurisprudence that has involved it in consistently reaching decisions that have advanced the process of European integration. It has done this both in judgments on the proper powers of the institutions arising from actions brought under the Articles listed above, and in Article 234 (formerly 177) referrals from national courts seeking clarification of points of EC law.

ECJ Rulings on the Powers of the Institutions

The biggest beneficiary of the ECJ's distinctive approach to institutional relations has been the EP. In a series of judgments the ECJ has interpreted the powers of the EP in an expansive manner. The key cases, which are considered here, were:

- Roquette v. Council (1980) (the 'Isoglucose' case) Case 138/79.
- Parti Écologiste, 'Les Verts' v. Parliament (1986). Case 294/83.
- European Parliament v. Council (1988) (the Comitology case). Case 302/87.
- European Parliament v. Council (1990) (the Chernobyl case). Case c-70/88.

The Isoglucose Case (1980)

In March 1979 the Commission submitted to the EP a draft regulation on fixing quotas for the production of isoglucose—a food sweetener produced from cereals—to take effect from the beginning of July. The draft regulation went to the EP's Committee on Agriculture, which reported to the May plenary session of the EP. However, the plenary rejected the report of the Committee containing an opinion on the regulation. This effectively meant that the quotas could not be introduced at the beginning of July (1979 was an election year for the EP, so there was no June plenary). In the meantime, the Council had considered the draft regulation and agreed to adopt it. Faced with a possible delay of four months or more, the Commission acted on the approval of the Council and published the directive in the Official Journal.

Subsequently, an individual who was directly affected by the directive brought a case to the ECJ under Article 173 (now Article 230), claiming that the Council and Commission had acted beyond their powers by adopting the directive without having received the opinion of the EP. The Court could have decided that the EP had been consulted, and the fact that it had been unable to deliver an opinion in time for the regulation to take effect at the date planned was its own fault. In other words, it could have decided that 'consultation' meant submitting the proposal a reasonable time before a decision was needed. Instead it upheld the complaint, choosing to interpret 'consult' to mean that the formal opinion of the EP had to be delivered before the Council could act.

In its judgment, the Court insisted that the EP had a duty to give an opinion within a reasonable length of time, without defining what would be considered reasonable. Thus, the judgment did not give the EP an effective power to veto legislation under the consultation procedure, but it did give it a significant power to delay legislation by holding back on formally delivering its opinion.

Les Verts v. European Parliament (1986)

In 1984 the French Green Party (*Les Verts*) stood candidates for election to the EP for the first time. In doing so it discovered that those of its opponents that had been represented in the previous Parliament had been voted funds by the EP to defray their election expenses. Subsequently the Greens brought a case to the ECJ under Article 173 claiming that the EP had acted beyond its powers in effectively supporting the election of existing parties at the expense of new parties.

The immediate issue here was whether any such case could be brought to the Court. Article 173 explicitly said: 'The Court of Justice shall review the legality of acts of the Council and the Commission.' There was no mention of the ECJ reviewing the legality of acts of the EP. The Court nevertheless accepted the case on the grounds that, although the Treaty did not explicitly make the actions of the EP subject to judicial review, this omission was not in keeping with the spirit of the Treaty.

The Court argued, without any real evidence to support the assertion, that the EP must have been omitted from Article 173 because when the Treaty was signed the EP had no real powers. Subsequently it had acquired powers that would normally be subject to judicial review. These included the powers that were contested in this case, and as these *should* be subject to judicial review, the Court would review them.

In this judgment the ECJ increased its own powers by a unilateral reinterpretation, some would even say rewriting, of the Treaty. Although apparently acting in a way that would restrict the powers of the EP, the judgment also took the first step towards giving the EP a legal personality that it had not been granted by the member states when they signed the Treaty. Once it had been decided that the EP could be a defendant in an Article 173 hearing, it seemed logical that it should also be accorded the right to be a plaintiff; that is, that it be allowed to bring cases to the Court under the same Article. The Court was given the opportunity to take this step in the next case reviewed below.

Parliament v. Council (The Comitology Case) (1990)

This case was brought by the EP under Article 175 (now 232), which said:

Should the Council or the Commission, in infringement of this Treaty, fail to act, the Member States, and the other institutions of the Community may bring an action before the Court of Justice to have the infringement established.

The EP argued successfully that it was allowed to bring a case under this Article because it was one of the 'other institutions of the Community'. But it also argued that it should be allowed to bring a case under Article 173 if the issue was one of another institution acting beyond its powers, rather than of not acting at all. The EP argued that it was illogical for it to be allowed to bring a case under 175, but not under 173. It also quoted the Court's judgment in *Les Verts* that the EP could be a defendant under Article 173, and argued that if it could be a defendant it was illogical that it should not be allowed to be a plaintiff.

Surprisingly, the Court rejected the EP's arguments. It said that there was no logical link between the circumstances outlined; that the EP could normally rely on the Commission to take up a case under Article 173 on its behalf; and that the member states had recently had the opportunity to grant this right explicitly to the EP in the Single European Act and had declined to do so, despite a submission from the Commission to the intergovernmental conference (IGC) explicitly recommending this revision. However, within a short period of time the Court appeared to have a change of heart on the issue.

European Parliament v. Council (The Chernobyl Case) (1990)

In this case, the EP applied to the Court for a review of the procedure adopted for agreeing a regulation on public health. This regulation set limits for the permissible radioactive contamination of food that could be sold for public consumption following the Chernobyl disaster (Insight 22.1). The Commission proposed the regulation under Article 31 of the Euratom Treaty, which dealt with basic standards for the protection of the health of the general public arising from radiation. Proposed legislation under this Article was subject to the consultation procedure. The EP maintained that the matter was a single-market issue, and therefore should have been introduced under Article 100A of the EEC Treaty, as revised by the SEA (now TEC Article 95). This would have brought it under the co-operation procedure, and given the EP a second reading. The EP wished to challenge the treaty base under which the regulation was adopted, but first had to establish that its case was admissible because it was invoking Article 173.

Although the Court's decision in the *Comitology* case was surprising, its decision in this case, coming so soon after, was even more surprising. Here, the Court decided that the EP could bring the case after all, despite what it had said in its *Comitology* judgment. Its reasoning was that the job of the Court was to preserve the institutional balance. In the *Comitology* judgment the Court had asserted that the Commission could normally be relied upon to protect the prerogatives of the EP where Parliament required an Article

---

INSIGHT 22.1

Chernobyl

On 26 April 1986 a major accident occurred at the Chernobyl nuclear power station in Ukraine. Radioactive pollution extended over a vast geographical area. Contamination was detected in the food chain as far west as Ireland. The EC introduced standardized rules on the permissible levels of radioactive contamination, and provided financial support for the farmers worst affected.

173 case to be brought. However, in this instance the dispute over the treaty base pitted the Commission against the EP. Therefore in this, and similarly limited circumstances, the EP had to be granted the right to be a plaintiff in an Article 173 case. The other argument that had appeared in the *Comitology* judgment, that the member states had only recently declined to grant this power explicitly to the EP, now disappeared from view. A sceptic commenting on the *Chernobyl* judgment, soon after it appeared, said:

The fundamental flaw in this decision is of course the Court's failure to give effect to the wholly unambiguous provision of Article 173 . . . the judgment rests on the unsatisfactory concept of 'institutional balance', which is not to be found, still less defined, in the Treaties. Moreover, the Court's own failure to define the notion adequately means that, should it decide in future cases that the prerogatives of the Commission or the Parliament in other areas are not sufficiently safeguarded, the requirement of 'institutional balance' may be used to justify providing a remedy.

(Smith 1990: 20)

ECJ Rulings on the Nature of EC Law

If the jurisprudence of the ECJ has pushed back the limits of the Treaty in judgments based on Article 173/230 cases, it has been even more radical in its judgments on Article 177 (now Article 234) referrals from national courts. In a number of controversial judgments the Court laid out principles of EC law that took it beyond the limits that the member states would like to put on it. The following cases were particularly important:

- Van Gend en Loos (1963). Case 26/62.
- Costa v. ENEL (1964). Case 6/64.
- Van Duyn v. Home Office (1974). Case 41/74.
- R. v. Secretary of State for Transport, ex parte Factortame (1991). Case C-221/89.
- Francovich v. Italy (1991). Cases C-6 and 9/90.

Van Gend en Loos (1963)

In this early case, the Court first asserted the principle that EC law conferred rights on individuals as well as on member states. This was the principle of 'direct effect', which has no explicit authority in the Treaties, and is a dramatic departure from international law. Under international law, treaties are held to impose obligations on the states that sign and ratify them, but neither to confer rights nor impose obligations directly on individual citizens.

A Dutch company claimed that its rights under the EC Treaty had been breached by the Dutch government, which had levied a higher rate of duty on formaldehyde—a chemical used as a disinfectant and preservative, and in the manufacture of synthetic resins—after the date on which it was agreed in the EEC Treaty that there would be no increase in internal EEC tariffs. The Dutch government maintained that the company had no power to claim a right deriving from an international treaty. The Court disagreed. It maintained that a new legal order had come into existence with the signing of the Treaty, in which citizens could claim rights against their governments. The ruling of the Court contained the following famous phrase:

the Community constitutes a new legal order of international law for the benefit of which the states have limited their sovereign rights, albeit within limited fields, and the subjects of which comprise not only member states but also their nationals. Community law therefore not only imposes obligations on individuals but is also intended to confer upon them rights that become part of their legal heritage.

(Quoted in Kuper 1998: 5)

The full significance of this doctrine only became apparent years later.

Costa v. ENEL (1964)

In this case, the year after *Van Gend en Loos*, the Court first asserted the supremacy of EC law over national law. Again there was no explicit authority for this in the Treaty. An Italian court referred the case to the ECJ, but the point of law at issue was also pertinent to the United Kingdom, because the Italian constitution, while it is a written constitution, was originally modelled on British practice and principles. This is mentioned to clarify that the principle was established well before Britain became a member of the EC, and should have been known to the British government when it made its second and third applications.

Under both Italian and British law, Parliament is sovereign (strictly speaking in Britain it is the Queen in Parliament). This means that statute law (that is, a written law that has been passed by Parliament) takes precedence over all other forms of law. Where statutes come into conflict, the principle that prevails is '*lex posterior priori derogat*': the later law over-rides the earlier. This is necessary if the democratic principle that no Parliament can bind its successor is to be observed.

In the Italian case, the issue was whether an Act of the Italian Parliament, passed later in time than the Act that embodied an EC directive into Italian law, took precedence over the earlier EC law. The Court said it did not, because if there was to be a single body of EC law throughout the Community, it could not be subject to interpretation in each member state in the light of the individual laws of that state. This was a perfectly logical position, but it did directly conflict with both Italian and British constitutional principles.

Van Duyn v. Home Office (1974)

A Dutch national who had been debarred from entering Britain because she was a member of the Church of Scientology, which the British Home Office considered to be a socially undesirable organization, brought a case in the English courts challenging the ruling. This case was brought on the grounds that Article 48 of the EEC Treaty (now TEC Article 39) committed the member states to allow free movement of workers, and that the British government had accepted Directive 64/221 which implemented this Treaty provision as part of the *acquis communautaire* when it joined the EC. The Court was asked to decide whether rights could be acquired directly in this way from a directive that had not yet been incorporated into national law.

The extension of the principle of direct effect to directives seemed unlikely because Article 189 (now Article 249) made a very clear distinction between a regulation, which 'shall be binding in its entirety and directly applicable in all Member States', and a directive, which 'shall be binding, as to the result to be achieved, upon each Member State. . . but shall leave to the national authorities the choice of form and methods'.

Despite this apparently clear distinction between an instrument that was directly applicable and one that was not, the Court still decided that the directive did have direct effect. Although the relevant directive had not yet been explicitly incorporated into English law, the Court maintained that the defendant could still quote it as grounds for her opposition to the British government's position.

Factortame (1990)

This was a highly publicized case in which Spanish fishermen had been purchasing British fishing vessels, and with them the quotas that the boats had been allocated to catch fish under the Common Fisheries Policy of the EC. In effect the Spanish fishermen had been catching fish on the British quota and landing it in Spain. The British government had responded by passing the 1988 Merchant Shipping Act, which required 75 per cent of the shareholders and directors of a company to be British in order for the company to be able to register as British. The Spanish fishermen claimed that this was a breach of their rights as EC citizens to be given equal treatment with other EC citizens.

The Court first granted an injunction to the Spanish fishermen, which the government agreed that the Law Lords could instruct British courts to recognize. This was the first time that British courts had been allowed to set aside an Act of Parliament. The ECJ subsequently agreed with the Spanish fishermen that the Merchant Shipping Act was in breach of EC law on the equal treatment of citizens, thus overturning the British Act of Parliament. Each of these steps caused a furore in the British Parliament, both because of what was seen as the manifest unfairness of allowing Spanish fishermen to take fish on the British quota, but also because of the constitutional implications. Here was a stark example of the ECJ overruling an Act of Parliament. Although no new principles were enunciated by the Court, the full impact of its radical jurisprudence only really came home to many British parliamentarians with this case.

Francovich v. Italy (1991)

Before this case arose, the Italian government had already been taken to the ECJ by the Commission and charged with not incorporating into Italian law a directive that gave redundant workers the right to compensation, and made such compensation the first claim against the assets of a bankrupt employer. It had still not been incorporated when workers for a bankrupt Italian company took a case to court in Italy because they had received no compensation for redundancy. On an Article 177 referral, the advocate-general argued that the Italian government should be liable for damages because it had already been found in breach of its obligations. The full Court went further. It said that the fact that the Italian government had been taken to the Court previously was irrelevant. Any government that did not properly implement EC law was liable to damages claims by its own citizens.

Subsequently the Court used the same principle, that a government that did not properly implement EC law was liable to damages claims, to decide that the Spanish fishermen in the *Factortame* case were eligible for compensation from the British government for loss of earnings during the period when they were prevented from catching fish on the British quota. It also decided, in another case (*Brasserie du Pêcheur*), that a French brewery could claim damages from the German government for the period when the German government enforced its beer purity laws, which the Court had subsequently ruled to be an illegal barrier to trade. So in these two cases, the liability of a government that had not properly applied a directive to be sued for damages was extended beyond its own citizens to cover other citizens of the EU.

Political Reactions to the Radical Jurisprudence of the ECJ

After a long period during which the pro-integration stance of the ECJ was tolerated by the governments of the member states, there was something of a backlash against the process of European integration generally, and against the ECJ more particularly, in the 1990s. The difficulties that were encountered in several member states in getting ratification of the TEU reinforced a tendency that had already been apparent in the inclusion in that Treaty of clauses on **subsidiarity** (Insight 22.2). The desire to limit the transfer of competences from member states to the EU institutions was not confined to Britain, although John Major's government pressed the case for subsidiarity to be written into the Treaty. The French government actually pressed for the whole *acquis communautaire* to be reviewed in the light of subsidiarity. The importance of this step should not be underestimated.

The formal introduction by the Maastricht Treaty (TEU) of subsidiarity as a general principle into EC . . . law both symbolized and contributed to a gradual change in the political and legal culture of the European Community. If much of the Community's legal activity before the 1990s reflected a self-conscious teleology of integration, the teleology of subsidiarity suggests a rather different future.

(De Búrca 1998: 218)

As well as the general change of mood away from pro-integration sentiments, the implications of the Court's judgments in the *Francovich*, *Factortame*, and *Brasserie du Pêcheur* cases led the British and German governments to sponsor a proposal to the 1996 IGC that the right to damages should only apply where there was 'grave and manifest disregard of their obligations' by governments; that is, not where governments believed

> ### INSIGHT 22.2
>
> **Subsidiarity Articles of the TEC and TEU**
>
> **Article 5 (formerly Article 3b) of the TEC**
>
> In areas which do not fall within its exclusive competence, the Community shall take action, in accordance with the principle of subsidiarity, only if and insofar as the objectives of the proposed action cannot be sufficiently achieved by the Member States and can therefore, by reason of the scale or effects of the proposed action, be better achieved by the Community.
>
> **Article 1 (formerly Article A) of the TEU**
>
> This Treaty marks a new stage in the process of creating an ever closer union among the peoples of Europe, in which decisions are taken as closely as possible to the citizen.

in good faith that they were abiding by EC law and applying the relevant directives. The Court, not surprisingly, did not want to get into having to make these decisions, which are far from clear-cut.

It should be noted at this point, though, that even the attitude of the British Conservative government to the Court was not uniformly hostile. The 1996 White Paper (HMSO, 1996) said:

> *The Government is committed to a strong, independent Court without which it would be impossible to ensure even application of Community law, and to prevent the abuse of power by the Community institutions. . . . The ECJ safeguards all Member States by ensuring that partners meet their Community obligations.*

Is the ECJ out of the Control of the Member States?

The evidence that the ECJ has been instrumental in considerably advancing the cause of European integration is convincing. However, the question then arises of how the Court is able to get away with its radical jurisprudence. In the 1990s an academic debate emerged on this question that paralleled the intergovernmental versus neofunctionalist debate of the 1960s (Ch. 1). The intergovernmental case is considered first, and then the 'legal neofunctionalist' argument.

The Intergovernmental Case

Geoffrey Garrett and his collaborators (Garrett 1992, 1995; Garrett and Weingast 1993; Garrett, Keleman, and Schultz 1998) put the intergovernmental case. Essentially their argument was as summarized by another contributor to the debate (Carrubba 2003: 78), that 'the ECJ helped to facilitate integration, but only to the degree that member state governments desired it'. Although governments did sometimes contest cases brought to the ECJ, they often accepted and applied the judgment after it was handed down. This reflected the fact that governments were under pressure from domestic interests that would be adversely affected by a particular interpretation of EC law, and so argued against it. However, member states all accepted that they would be better off in the long term if the rules of the single market were implemented by everyone, and for that to happen required an independent and impartial referee to adjudicate on disputed interpretations of the rules, which is the role of the ECJ. To refuse to accept an adverse ruling would weaken the legitimacy of the impartial referee, and that was a cost that member states would be loath to pay.

In some cases, Garrett (1995) argued, the strength of a domestic interest that was adversely affected by a ruling of the ECJ would be sufficiently great that the government of a member state would attempt to placate it by unilaterally but covertly not implementing the ruling. In that way it could avoid weakening the legitimacy of the independent arbitrator, while possibly avoiding the political costs of not doing so. Whether this course was followed would depend on the relative gains to the member state from the existence of an efficiently functioning internal market when set against the political cost of upsetting a powerful interest group. The states that stood to gain the most from the single market—generally the more northern member states—would be most reluctant to risk damaging the legitimacy of the ECJ even by covert non-compliance. Those that stood to gain less—mainly the southern member states—might be more inclined to engage in unilateral non-compliance to try to evade the political costs of displeasing a powerful domestic vested interest. Even then, the government would try to conceal evasion, and would plead implementation problems if caught.

On its part, the ECJ was very aware that its legitimacy was dependent on the behaviour of the member states. If governments were openly to flout its decisions, its legitimacy would be seriously damaged, and pressure might build for its powers to be weakened by revision of the treaties. As a result, the ECJ avoided making decisions that would place powerful governments in a difficult position. It was able to do this because although Article 30 of the Treaty [TEC Article 28] prohibited restrictions on internal trade, Article 34 [TEC Article 30] allowed exceptions that could be 'justified on grounds of public morality, public policy or public security; the protection of health and life of humans, animals or plants; the protection of national treasures possessing artistic, historic or archaeological value; or the protection of industrial and commercial property'. This gave the ECJ plenty of scope to find a reason for allowing an exception if it would be politically uncomfortable not to do so (Garrett 1995: 178).

The Neofunctionalist Case

Burley and Mattli (1993) and Mattli and Slaughter (1995) argued that the ECJ had been the prime mover in European integration, and that the governments of the member states had passively accepted this lead. The ECJ had used European law as a 'mask' to cover its integrationist agenda, wrapping its promotion of integration in the discourse of legal logic and necessity. It had also used the law as a 'shield' to protect itself from political attack. If the governments of the member states did not like the activism of the ECJ, they had the means available to counter it, either by non-compliance with the rulings or by amendment of the treaties. Yet the first had not been done to any significant degree, and the second had not been done at all. Burley and Mattli (1993) used the example of the famous *Cassis de Dijon* case to illustrate their argument, and were subsequently challenged specifically on their interpretation of this case by Garrett (1995).

The 'mask and shield' part of the argument was frequently quoted in later contributions to the debate (Garrett 1995: 171–2; Garrett, Keleman, and Schultz 1998: 149–50). However, it was never a particularly strong element in the neofunctionalist argument. As Carrubba (2003: 78) pointed out:

First, to assume that law 'masks' the political ramifications of a decision is to suggest that governments are incapable of evaluating what outcome would serve their purposes best. Since governments make observations on ECJ cases on a regular basis, it seems demonstrably implausible that the governments do not have well-formed preferences over outcomes. Further, to say that the legal venue 'shields' decisions from political interference, owing to the domestic norms of the rule of law, is to assume that governments will obey court rulings because governments have been observed doing so in the past. There are a number of reasons why governments may obey court rulings in one situation and not in another.

The threat of Treaty revisions could also 'be dismissed fairly easily' (Carrubba 2003: 76) because it required the unanimous consent of all member states' governments, which was unlikely to be achievable given the commitment of some states to the enforcement of the single market, and of others to the enhancement of integration. Even to change secondary legislation, which could not be used to weaken the general power of the ECJ but could be used to mitigate the effect of an individual adverse judgment, required a qualified majority difficult to achieve given that the adverse effect on an interest group in one member state would be an opportunity for advantage for interest groups in others.

The second part of the legal neofunctionalist argument was stronger. It started with the observation that for the legal doctrines of the ECJ to be effective they had to be accepted by national courts. This seemed to have happened. By making Article 177/234 references, national courts had been the main accomplices of the ECJ in its 'constitutionalization' of the Treaties. Why had this collaboration taken place? Burley and Mattli (1993) suggested that a legal version of neofunctionalism was at work. Spillover was implicit in the concept of EC law itself, but it was cultivated by the ECJ to give the most integrationist interpretation possible to the existing laws. Other actors—national courts, private individuals—fed the process simply by pursuing their own self-interest in a rational manner within the changed context: e.g. individuals did so by bringing cases against their own governments under European law when they felt that their rights had been breached.

Alter (1996, 1998) went further, arguing that the Article 177 procedure actually empowered lower national courts. They were used to having their judgments overturned on appeal by higher national courts, but by making Article 177 references they could directly influence the evolution of national legal principles. Higher courts might be able to overturn the substance of their judgments, but they were unable to challenge the points of European law on which they were based.

The ECJ has also been careful always to get the national courts on its side by proceeding in what another advocate of this theory, Mancini (1991: 185), described as a 'courteously didactic' manner. The judges:

developed a style that may be drab and repetitive but explains as well as declares the law, and they showed unlimited patience vis-à-vis the national judges, reformulating questions couched in imprecise terms or extracting from the documents concerning the main proceedings the elements of Community law that needed to be interpreted with regard to the subject matter of the dispute.

(Mancini 1991: 185)

In this way the European judges won the confidence of their national colleagues. Those who presided over even the lowest courts knew that they would receive sympathetic treatment if they made an Article 177 referral, and were therefore more inclined to do so.

This co-opting of national courts raised the stakes for national governments that might be inclined to defy the jurisprudence of the ECJ, for it would also be defying the jurisprudence of its own domestic courts. The indirect political costs of undermining the legitimacy of the rule of law in the domestic arena were considerably higher than the costs of undermining the ECJ. Research reported by Carrubba (2003: 95) indicated that European publics would be inclined to support their own government if it were in dispute with the ECJ, but not if it were in dispute with national courts.

A criticism of this analysis is that the alliance forged between the ECJ and lower national courts is not the whole of the story. The reception of the jurisprudence of the ECJ by national supreme courts has been less enthusiastic. Problems have arisen with the reception of the judgments of the ECJ by the Italian, French, British, and German supreme courts (Kuper 1998: 19–27). In no case has a national supreme court attempted to negate a decision of the ECJ. Were one to do so it would cause a constitutional crisis. In several cases, though, the national supreme court has disagreed with the reasoning of the ECJ, while finding alternative lines of legal reasoning to arrive at the same substantive decision. In particular, the doctrine of the supremacy of EC law over national law has not been universally accepted by member states. However, this is compatible with the argument that lower courts were prepared to collaborate with the ECJ on preliminary rulings because that increased their influence within their national legal hierarchies. The corollary of that argument is that higher courts would see their influence weakened, and so would be expected to resist the jurisprudence of the ECJ.

CONCLUSION

This review of the role of the ECJ particularly raises two of the themes that run through the book. The first is the theme that has been most prominent in the chapters on the institutions: the intergovernmental–supranational debate about the nature of the EU. A second theme is that of legitimacy.

If the role of the ECJ is approached in the same way as was the discussion about role of the Commission in Chapter 19 (see pp. 264–7), that is, whether it is an agent of the member states or an autonomous actor in its own right, there is little doubt that the judgments of the Court have gone beyond what the governments of the member states were expecting. The radical jurisprudence of the Court may represent the logical consequences of the actions of the member states, but it is not a logic that was thought through by their governments, nor is it always welcome to them. In this sense the ECJ has proved itself to be an autonomous actor in the process of European integration.

As intergovernmentalists would point out, the member states can rescind those powers that they have given to the Court; but this is not easy, because without an independent and authoritative interpreter of the law, all the rules put in place by the Treaties and by EC secondary legislation would be subject to different interpretation by different parties. There has to be an authoritative source of interpretation, and it has to be unquestionably independent. Some parties to any dispute will not like some of the decisions of the independent arbitrator, but they will abide by them rather than see the collapse of the system from which they benefit generally. The 'ratchet effect' also makes it difficult to recall powers once delegated. Treaty changes require unanimity, and if even one member state is happy with the thrust of the ECJ's decisions, it will not be possible to reduce its powers because its one supporter has a veto on any attempt to do so.

There is no doubt that the ECJ has the formal right to reach the decisions that it does. Whether those decisions are accepted as legitimate is another matter. Most decisions of the Court have not impinged on the consciousness of national politicians or members of the public. They have received legitimacy through being accepted by national courts, especially those lower down the legal hierarchy. When ECJ judgments have come to the attention of national politicians, there has sometimes been a strong negative reaction, suggesting that the legitimacy of the Court's doctrines does not extend beyond the national courts and professional judges. The strength of reaction in Britain to the *Factortame* judgment is indicative of this. As Carrubba (2003: 96–7) noted: 'public perceptions of institutional legitimacy are critical to the EU legal system being able to act as an effective democratic check', but 'the ECJ remains woefully short on public legitimacy today'.

The highest courts in the member states have been less comfortable than have lower courts with the judgments of the ECJ, which have often raised difficult constitutional issues. Essentially the ECJ has been in the business of forging a new constitution for the EU from the raw material of the Treaties. It has had plenty of scope to impose its own interpretation of what that constitution should look like, because treaties are not carefully crafted legal documents: they are the outcome of diplomatic negotiations and compromises. These far-from-watertight documents leave judges plenty of space to fill in the gaps. In doing so, the ECJ has enunciated principles that conflict with some fundamental national constitutional principles. The legal conflict shows the impossibility of taking several different national constitutions and reconciling them with one overarching European constitution. The political reaction raises again the issue of identity, which appears in the discussion of the legitimacy of the EP in Chapter 4 (pp. 68–9). National politicians and publics find it difficult to accept that decisions made by their democratically elected national institutions can be overruled by an organization that has far less legitimacy in their eyes.

Structure and Functions

☐ The Court consists of fifteen judges and nine advocates-general.

☐ It is charged to ensure that the law of the EC is observed.

☐ It has wide-ranging powers to hear various types of action and to give preliminary rulings.

ECJ Rulings on the Powers of the Institutions

☐ The EP has been the major beneficiary of the Court's radical jurisprudence.

☐ Although on occasions, the Court has found against an extension of the EP's legal position, it has also reversed this in subsequent judgments.

☐ In particular, the Court has used the principle of 'institutional balance' to extend Parliament's prerogatives.

ECJ Rulings on the Nature of EC law

☐ The ECJ has been most radical in cases referred by national courts under Article 177 (now 234).

☐ In early rulings, the Court stated the principles of 'direct effect'—that EC law confers rights on individuals—and the supremacy of EC over national law. Subsequent rulings confirmed these principles.

☐ A series of later cases also produced rulings that surprised the governments of the member states, because they imposed on them obligations to which they did not think that they had agreed.

Political Reactions to the Radical Jurisprudence of the ECJ

☐ The ECJ has been criticized for stepping beyond its legal role and behaving politically in favouring judgments that advance European integration.

☐ Partly because of a general anti-integrationist mood in the 1990s, the ECJ was subjected to increased criticism by member states for its perceived political activism.

☐ At the same time, even the British Conservative government declared itself to be committed to a strong, independent Court.

Is the ECJ out of the Control of the Member States?

☐ Intergovernmental and neofunctionalist explanations have been offered of why member states have accepted the radical jurisprudence of the ECJ.

☐ The intergovernmental argument was that member states tolerated the rulings of the ECJ because it was important to them to have an independent arbitrator who could enforce the single-market contract between them, and they did not want to undermine the legitimacy of the arbitrator by defying its rulings.

☐ The neofunctionalist case was that the ECJ had used the legal system as a 'mask' and a 'shield' to advance integration further than the member states wished; and that it had recruited national courts to assist it in this process.

☐ Explanations of why national courts have accepted the radical jurisprudence of the ECJ point to shrewd tactics on the part of the Court.

☐ Despite the advances of the ECJ, the principle of the supremacy of EC law over national law has yet to be fully accepted by national supreme courts.

FURTHER READING

An excellent, non-technical introduction to the role of the ECJ is provided by R. Kuper, *The Politics of the European Court of Justice* (London: Kogan Page, 1998). Readers of this book who turn to that one, as they should, will recognize the debt that the present authors owe to it. Another clear non-technical introduction to the ECJ is R. Dehousse, *The European Court of Justice: The Politics of Judicial Integration* (Basingstoke and London: Macmillan, 1998).

More technical accounts of the impact of EC law, including the controversial rulings of the Court are T.C. Hartley, *The Foundations of European Community Law* (Oxford: Clarendon Press, 5th edn, 2003), and, J. Steiner, L. Woods, and C. Twigg-Fleisner, *Textbook on EC Law* (Oxford: Oxford University Press, 8th edn, 2003).

A view of the relationship between the ECJ and both national courts and national governments that is in line with what has here been described as the 'legal neofunctionalism' perspective is presented in K.J. Alter, *Establishing the Supremacy of European Law: The Making of an International Rule of Law in Europe* (Oxford: Oxford University Press, 2001).

online resource centre Visit the Online Resource Centre that accompanies this book for links to more information on the European Court of Justice, including the ECJ's own web site.

CHAPTER 23

Organized Interests

CHAPTER OVERVIEW

The term 'interest group' is used to describe a range of organizations, outside of the formal institutions, that seek to influence decision making. They provide a link between state actors and the rest of society. Within the political systems of member states, interest-group activity is long established and it has increased considerably in the EU arena since the launch of the single market programme in the mid-1980s. This chapter looks first at the general growth of interest-group activity at the European level, before analysing the types of groups that try to influence EU policy making and the forms of representation open to interests. The resources that interest groups bring to the task are considered, and how these resources gain the groups access to institutional actors. The chapter then looks at the strategies and tactics that groups use to try to influence the different institutions, and at attempts to regulate their activity.

> easy access to the European institutions and the dependence of those institutions on interest groups have allowed certain interests to have a substantial say in the European policy process
>
> (Eising 2003: 205)

The Growth of Interest-Group Activity at the EU Level

Interest-group activity aimed at EU decision makers has grown spectacularly, particularly from the launch of the single-market programme in the mid-1980s. By the end of the 1990s, Mazey and Richardson (1999: 105) could speak of 'a dense European lobbying system. . . which now exhibits many of the features of interest group intermediation systems long familiar in Western Europe'. Finding precise statistics on this growth is more difficult, but Commission figures suggested that in the mid-1990s there were around 3,000 interest groups active in Brussels, with around 10,000 individuals involved in the lobbying industry (Greenwood 1997: 3), and later estimates placed the number of individuals involved at between 10,000 and 30,000 (Greenwood 2003: 9).

For many organized interests, the development of direct representation at the EU level is in addition to their continuing attempts to influence national governments as part of their overall strategy to shape EU policy. However, the Brussels end of the strategy is increasingly important. Factors that contribute to this include:

- the growing policy competence of the EU;
- changes in the formal rules of decision making;
- the receptiveness of EU officials to interest group representations;
- the 'snowballing' effect of groups following the lead of others, so as not to risk being disadvantaged.

In line with the maxim that 'where power goes, interest groups follow', the increasing competence of EU institutions is an important reason for the rapid growth in interest-group activity at the European level. Whereas in the early years, the coal and steel industries and agriculture were the most affected by the setting up of the European Communities (EC), there are now very few policy sectors that do not have an EU dimension (see Ch. 24).

Increased competences have been accompanied by changes in the rules of decision making (Ch. 18, pp. 238–45). The switch within the Council of Ministers to qualified majority voting (QMV) for most policy sectors makes it less sensible to lobby only at the national level, because a single state no longer has a veto over legislative proposals. There has also been a perceived shift of power within the policy-making process away from the Council of Ministers to other institutions, particularly the European Parliament (EP), to access which it is essential to have a base in Brussels.

The EU provides relatively easy access for those seeking to influence decision making, which provides 'part of the explanation for the intensity of participation in the process by so wide a range of political and economic actors' (Wallace and Young 1997: 250). There are several advantages for policy makers of good relations with interest groups:

Put simply, it is very difficult to make effective public policy without the specialized expertise *which interest groups possess. Moreover, their cooperation in the* implementation *of public policy is a prime condition for implementation success. Finally, from the bureaucratic perspective, the mobilization of a constituency of* support *is vital to the long-term survival of bureaucracies.*

(Mazey and Richardson 1999: 106)

The importance of organized interests to policy makers, particularly in the complex emerging system of the EU, means that many groups find themselves greeted by an open door when they seek discussions in Brussels.

Although no one can be sure of the benefits of lobbying activities in Brussels, the fear of missing out has become a motivating factor for EU-level activity. Once some groups start to shift their activity to Brussels, a momentum builds up that carries other groups along with it. Mazey and Richardson (1999: 107) suggested that: 'rather like bees around a honey pot, interest groups are attached to regulatory institutions in swarms. Once one set of groups begins to exploit incentives and opportunity structures at the European level, others are bound to follow; they cannot afford to be left out, whatever the cost'. Brussels has acquired the reputation of being 'an insider's town' (Greenwood 1997: 55; 2003: 2), in which those who do not have an established presence operate at a disadvantage.

Types of Interest Group

Interest groups that operate in Brussels can be classified under seven headings (Mazey and Richardson 1999: 108):

(1) *European associations* (e.g. Association of Petrochemicals Producers of Europe, Greenpeace International–European Unit);

(2) *National associations* (e.g. Confederation of British Industry, Federation of Swedish Industry);

(3) *Individual firms* (e.g. Imperial Chemical Industries, Ford Motor Company);

(4) *Lobbying consultancy firms* (e.g. European Public Policy Advisers);

(5) *Public bodies* (e.g. regional governments and local authorities);

(6) *Ad hoc coalitions for single issues* (e.g. European Campaign on Biotechnology Patents; Software Action Group for Europe);

(7) *Organizations of experts and epistemic communities* (e.g. European Heart Network; Federation of Veterinarians of Europe).

Each of these seven types of organization has grown in the past two decades.

Different types of organizations can represent any given set of interests at the same time. Business interests provide a good example. Business representation in Brussels takes the form of individual companies, collective national organizations (such as the Confederation of British Industry), and collective European organizations. The last category includes the Union of Industrial and Employers' Confederations (UNICE), which brings together national business associations, and the European Round Table of Industrialists (ERT), which is made up of Chief Executives of major firms. The ERT was particularly active in moves to launch the single-market programme in the mid-1980s (see Ch. 26, p. 411). In addition, firms individually or collectively might employ lobbying consultancy firms to advance their case.

Business interests were represented in Brussels from a very early stage in the existence of the EC. Hix (1999: 192) noted that individual firms were initially the most numerous type of interest represented there. Nevertheless, following the logic that activity by one set of interests stimulates competing interests into similar activity, there is now a wide range of groups that act as countervailing forces to business lobbying in Brussels. Trade unions, consumer groups, and environmentalists are examples of countervailing forces to business interests, although these groups were late to the game and only really became prominent in the 1990s. The other type of group that has exploded in numbers in Brussels is the lobbying consultancy firm.

Forms of Interest Representation

Several forms of interest representation coexist in the EU:

- the full institutionalization of representation through the Economic and Social Committee (ESC);
- the semi-institutionalized 'social dialogue';
- a **pluralist** system based on competitive lobbying;
- informally institutionalized policy networks;
- legal representation.

The ESC has its origins in the '**corporatist**' institutions that were set up between the wars in Germany (the Economic Council) and France (the *Conseil Economique et Social*) to bring together labour, management, the self-employed, and the government. Similar institutions were created or recreated in five of the six member states after the war, Germany being the exception.

The ESC did not prove to be a particularly effective institution (Ch. 18, pp. 237–8), and when new forms of institutionalized relations between government, business, and trade unions were tried in several member states of the EC during the 1970s, attempts to replicate them at the EC level did not involve the ESC. Instead, the ministers of social affairs and economic and financial affairs organized a series of Tripartite Conferences bringing together European business and trade union organizations in an arrangement that is often referred to as **neo-corporatism**. The Tripartite Conferences met six times in 1978 to discuss issues such as employment, inflation, wage restraint, fiscal policy, vocational training, and measures to increase productivity. The business groups were reluctant participants, though, and by the end of 1978 the European Trade Union Confederation (ETUC) had withdrawn from the process because of lack of progress.

The idea was revived by Jacques Delors when he became President of the Commission. In 1984 he proposed the creation of a 'social space', a term that had first been used in 1981 by the French Socialist government of which Delors was a member. Subsequently Delors linked this phrase to the 1992 project to free the internal market. In 1985 an approach was made to both ETUC and UNICE to open a 'social dialogue'. Delors suggested that if the idea were accepted, the Commission would refrain from introducing further items of social legislation, and would instead let them emerge out of the dialogue. Initially two working parties were set up, on employment policies and on new technology and work. They met at the chateau of Val Duchesse outside Brussels, and the dialogue therefore became known as the 'Val Duchesse process'.

From the outset there were difficulties about the status of the discussions. UNICE insisted that they should lead to the publication of 'joint opinions', not 'agreements', and that the opinions should not lead to legislation. ETUC wanted the process to result in legislation. Despite these difficulties, the social dialogue was incorporated into the social protocol of the Treaty on European Union (TEU). It was agreed that where the social partners could negotiate agreement on any aspect of social legislation, that agreement would automatically be accepted by the Commission and formulated as a proposal to the Council of Ministers, with the expectation that it would become part of the social legislation of the EC—although it would not apply to Britain, which at that time had an opt-out from the social protocol. The first piece of legislation to be agreed in this way, in 1995, concerned paid parental leave. However, there was little subsequent progress, because UNICE was reluctant to make the system work. The fact that the British government signed the social protocol at Amsterdam, thereby allowing it to be incorporated into the Treaty as the social chapter, obviously owed something to the change from a Conservative to a Labour government in 1997, but it is also indicative of how little the system was seen as a threat even by the state that had always been least keen on it.

The continuous lack of enthusiasm of UNICE and its member organizations for EU-level neo-corporatism reflects the fact that business interests are in a stronger position to get their views heard under the alternative, pluralist system of interest representation. Schmitter and Streeck (1991) argued that the shift of policy-making competences from the national to the EU level would be accompanied by a shift in the pattern of interest mediation from the neo-corporatism that prevailed in most European states to a pattern much more akin to the pluralism of the United States. European business interests welcomed the opportunity to circumvent the influence of labour by supporting a shift of policy competence to the EU. Moves under Delors to reconstitute neo-corporatist arrangements at the European level were successfully resisted, and a pluralist system emerged instead. If this argument is correct, it is less surprising that EU policy resembles the business-friendly policies of the Anglo-American model of capitalism rather than some average of the different national policies of the member states. It is precisely to achieve this outcome that business, and perhaps the governments of member states also, collaborated in the shift of policy competences to the EU.

In theory, this pluralist system could be just a temporary stage in the evolution of interest representation. Once the EU system settles down, it could move to an informal institutionalization based on policy networks. This seems to have happened with agricultural policy making, the policy sector with the longest-established EU competence. However, against this view Grossman (2004: 648) argued that:

> *even after learning and institutionalization European policy-making remains unstable and unpredictable for interest groups, mainly because of the characteristics of the policy process . . . While it is often assumed that the Commission and EU policy making are still in an 'infant' stage, it is more likely that these are long-term structural characteristics related to the overall institutional architecture of the EU polity.*

This is not a disagreement that can be easily resolved. It can only be subjected to detailed empirical investigation in individual sectors. It is likely that the degree of informal institutionalization will vary from one sector to another, depending on the specific circumstances of policy making in each sector. Yet, even if the pluralist stage is a passing phase, the dominance of large firms in that stage would put them in an advantageous position to become core members of any emerging policy networks.

Finally, although it constitutes a very different activity from lobbying, for certain categories of interest groups, targeting the European Court of Justice (ECJ) has been a particularly fruitful activity. Mazey and Richardson (1999: 115) noted that: 'Women's and environmental groups (and also trade unions) have been adept in securing favourable ECJ decisions which have been just as, if not more, effective than bringing about change in EU policy via other means.' Here, 'whistle-blowing' activity of groups in highlighting non-compliance with EU decisions by member states has been prominent.

Resources

The extent to which groups command resources of varying types is crucial to understanding their relative influence. The control of key resources is an important factor in deciding whether a group will secure 'insider status' with policy makers or remain outside the core process.

Greenwood (1997: 18–20) identified eight types of resources as important to interest groups (Insight 23.1). When it comes to such resources, size matters. Larger organizations generally are better resourced than smaller ones. At the level of individual firms, big-business interests possess far more of the resources that are needed to operate effectively than do small-business interests. For example, large firms will often have their own research and development units, which means that they are better equipped to provide institutional actors with up-to-date expert knowledge than are smaller firms. Also, the complexity and multi-level nature of EU decision making puts a premium on being able to deploy sufficient personnel to cover all possible access points.

The diffuse character of the Brussels process within and between institutions means that to be a participant often requires covering several access points in order to find the most useful one. Small groups, and small firms, thus find it much harder to engage than the better resourced organizations or firms.

(**Wallace and Young 1997: 244**)

INSIGHT 23.1

Resources Available to Interest Groups

- Information and expertise
- Economic muscle
- Status
- Power in implementation
- The organization of the interest into a non-competitive format
- Coherent organization with representative outlets able to make decisions with ease and alacrity
- The ability to help the overloaded Commission with carrying out policies
- The ability of a group to influence its members

Only large individual firms or other particularly well-resourced interest groups are able to pursue their own information gathering and lobbying without joining forces with other actors. To become more effective, smaller organizations have to pool resources. Kohler-Koch (1997: 58) provided the example of business: 'Large firms find it easy to become privileged interlocutors of the political-administrative system, thanks to their economic importance, while small and medium-sized firms rely more heavily on their collective force.' However, while there are resource advantages in separate interests coming together, such combinations of interests increase the risk that they will encounter problems of collective action: the interests aggregated within a combined group may find it difficult to agree among themselves about priorities and tactics.

This disparity in material resources does not necessarily mean that large individual firms have the best access to the policy-making process, though. Bouwen (2002, 2004*a*, 2004*b*) argued that the degree of access that an interest group can achieve to any of the EU's institutions depends on its ability to offer each institution the type of information that it most needs to perform efficiently its functions within the decision-making system. He identified three types of information that are important in differing degrees to the various EU institutions:

- expert knowledge;
- knowledge of the needs and concerns of actors in the relevant sector across Europe;
- knowledge of the specific concerns of national actors in the relevant sector.

Expert knowledge is essential for the institution to understand the technical working of the market into which the legislation is an intervention. It results in legislation that is better adapted to its purpose, and is therefore likely to work better. Information about the needs and concerns of actors in the relevant sector, both across Europe as a whole and in specific national contexts, enhances the legitimacy of the decision-making process, because a wide range of affected actors will feel that they have been listened to, and this ought to contribute to their compliance with the legislation and therefore to the chances of successful implementation.

Different types of interest groups possess these different types of information in varying degrees. Interests that pursue their own lobbying—which will most often be large firms, because they have the resources to do so—are very good at providing expert information. European and national associations are less efficient at providing expert information, but they are very good at providing information on the concerns of actors across Europe in the case of European organizations, and on the concerns of national actors in the case of national associations. On the basis of this theoretical analysis, Bouwen (2002) drew up a number of hypotheses about the degree of access that different types of groups would have to the different institutions of the EU. These are reviewed in the next section.

Organized Interests and the Institutional Actors

The Commission

For a number of reasons, the Commission is an important target for interest groups:

- it has a central role in setting the agenda;
- all proposals have to pass through it;
- it is there that the detail of proposals is decided;
- it is receptive to approaches from interest groups.

The Commission's agenda-setting role is of particular importance to interest groups. If they want to get particular issues placed on the agenda of the EU, the Commission is a good place to start lobbying. Alternatively, if they want to prevent measures from coming onto or rising up the agenda, influence in the Commission is vital. All policy proposals 'have to pass through the Commission gateway and are subject to detailed *processing* at that institutional site' (Mazey and Richardson 1999: 112). This means that the Commission is an important channel to monitor. It also means that it is the primary place for influencing the detail of proposals, which is often what concerns interest groups.

The Commission is widely recognized as being receptive to interest-group representations. This is not least because the Commission's limited human resources make it more dependent than other institutions on the information and expertise that interest groups can offer. Bouwen (2002: 379) argued that, in terms of the three types of knowledge that he had identified, the Commission needed expert knowledge most, to allow it to construct viable legislation that successfully addressed the problem and was most likely to be implemented successfully. Second, it required information on the concerns of actors across Europe in order to boost both its own legitimacy and that of the specific piece of legislation. It needed information on the concerns of specific groups of national actors only in so far as it proved necessary for it to broker a deal within the Council of Ministers between differing national preferences.

Mapping the Commission's demand for each type of information against the supply from different types of actors, Bouwen (2002: 382) hypothesized that large individual firms, which could provide good-quality expert knowledge efficiently, would have the best access to the Commission, followed by European associations, which could provide reliable information on the concerns of the sector across Europe. While national associations would enjoy the lowest level of access during the crucial drafting stage of legislation, at the later stages of the passage of the legislation through the Council of Ministers they might well find that their particular expertise on the concerns of national actors was sought by the Commission. However, subsequent research indicated that European associations actually had the best access to the Commission, despite the fact that they were 'often considered to be internally divided, poorly resourced and unable to respond quickly to Commission requests for information' (Bouwen 2004a: 355). Large firms were close behind in second place, while national associations were far behind.

This finding was not predicted in Bouwen's original model of access to the Commission, but it was consistent with the observation of Greenwood (1997: 4) that the Commission preferred interaction with Euro-groups where possible:

Places on its advisory committees are handed out to Euro groups first. Drafts of directives and other policy initiatives are often given to European business sector associations to comment on. Although single-firm representations to the Commission are heard, the firm concerned is usually told that the Commission would wish to explore the issue further by talking to the interest group concerned in order to ensure that it gets a more representative opinion.

Kohler-Koch (1997: 53) noted further that the Commission 'has actively promoted the organization of the less represented social interests in order to achieve more balanced participation'. It has also sought alliances with influential groups to strengthen its position vis-à-vis the Council in the EU system. Authoritative and representative interest groups can provide the unelected Commission with legitimacy in its arguments with the Council. The Commission has produced a guide for its own staff which lists interest groups by policy sector, 'as part of a "procedural ambition" to maximize Commission consultation with European civil society', and, 'where the Commission identifies that a European-level group is missing, it attempts to create and sustain one' (Hix 1999: 206).

The Council

The authority of the Council makes it an important target for interest groups. Yet in reality there is little opportunity for them to lobby either the European Council or the Council of Ministers directly. These institutions meet behind closed doors and, generally, groups do not have direct access. Because its members are supported by national administrations and permanent officials in Brussels, the Council has less need for the information resources of interest groups than does the Commission, and is thus less receptive to approaches. The consequence is that most lobbying of the Council is indirect rather than direct.

To influence the Council indirectly, groups seek contact with individual national governments. Initially, of course, they will try to influence their own national government;

but as understanding of the EU policy process has grown, interest groups' lobbying techniques have become more sophisticated, and interest groups in one member state will now seek to influence governments in other member states. Which governments matter will vary with the issue. For obvious reasons, the government holding the Council presidency will be a particular target.

Although lobbying national governments is only an indirect way of influencing EU affairs, it is a process that is familiar to most interest groups. It is, as Greenwood (2003: 39) argued, an arena 'where established policy networks and dependency relationships operate which can equally well be used for the purposes of EU representation as for the governance of domestic affairs'. Moreover, for those groups that do not have the necessary resources to lobby EU institutions, the national route may remain the only real option. However, the value of lobbying individual governments has declined with the extension of QMV in the Council. Even where a group has successfully persuaded a government of its case, under QMV it is far from certain that the government will be able to assist. As such, 'it is one thing to argue that the majority of groups still rely on the national opportunity structures, but quite another to conclude that this is an efficacious form of behaviour. It is no accident that large firms appear to show a growing preference for Euro-level lobbying' (Mazey and Richardson 1999: 119).

Bouwen (2002: 381) noted that at the ministerial level, the Council is the most intergovernmental of the institutions; but at the level of the officials involved in the preparation of the ministerial meetings there is also a considerable degree of supranationalism. In terms of his model, the governments of member states primarily need information on the needs and concerns of their own state's actors in the policy sector, so that they can formulate their national preferences on any legislation. However, at the level of officials there is considerable concern for the impact of legislation on the European market as a whole, as well as the narrower focus on national interests, so the expert committees might well be open to representations from European associations. Expert knowledge is less needed from outside sources, as there is plenty available from national officials who staff the committees that consider the proposed legislation.

On this basis, Bouwen (2002: 382) expected national associations, together with large national firms that constituted 'national champions', to have the best access to the Council of Ministers via the national route. European associations were expected to have some access via the European route, with large individual firms (except 'national champions' who gained access through the national route) having the least access. These hypotheses were largely supported by the subsequent research (Bouwen 2004a). The best access was for national associations, closely followed by large firms that were national champions. Other large firms and European associations had very much less access.

The European Parliament

Despite the fact that the EP traditionally had less influence over decision making than either the Council or the Commission, it has always attracted considerable attention from interest groups. This is largely because of its long-standing advisory role, which has been viewed as an indirect route to influencing the other institutions. Moreover,

Members of the European Parliament (MEPs) are relatively accessible. In particular, those with a constituency interest in an issue will be the focus of attention.

More generally, the EP is seen as a 'natural ally' for groups lobbying on behalf of consumers, human rights, and the environment. This is 'not because MEPs necessarily favour their demands, but because their interests match. MEPs are eager to take up those issues which attract a broad public interest and are grateful for any external support which mobilizes public attention, because this will increase their political weight in the decision-making process' (Kohler-Koch 1997: 55–6). In addition to representations to individual MEPs, they can also be targeted collectively through the numerous inter-groups that bring together MEPs with similar interests in a relatively formal arena. As the logic of interest-group activity suggests, activity around EP plenary sessions and committee meetings has increased with the enhancement of Parliament's powers under first the Single European Act (SEA), and subsequently the TEU and Amsterdam (Ch. 18, pp. 238–45).

Like the Commission, the EP lacks the national administrative support that is available to the members of the Council, but it does have a considerable amount of in-house expertise. Bouwen (2002) argued that while the EP does rely on interest groups for expert knowledge to some extent, it initially has a much greater need for information on the concerns of the relevant actors in the sector across Europe, to alert it to impending legislation that might not meet the needs and interests of the European market as a whole. If it seeks to amend legislation in detail, it will need expert knowledge. On the other hand, individual MEPs need information on the concerns of their own national actors in the relevant sector to alert them to legislation that might be damaging to their own constituents.

On this basis, Bouwen (2002: 382) expected European associations to have the best access to the EP as an institution, because they could provide the initial, and crucial information on the likely impact of impending legislation on the sector at the European level. National associations were expected to have a lower level of access, but might well be able to gain access via the national route, through the offices of MEPs. Large firms were expected to have the lowest level of access. These hypotheses were again supported by subsequent research: European associations had the best access to the EP, closely followed by national associations, with individual large firms a long way behind (Bouwen 2004b: 492).

Strategies and Tactics

The strategies and tactics of interest groups will vary depending on the targeted decision maker and/or the issue concerned. There is no magic formula for success in lobbying. There are, however, tried and tested practices that suggest some approaches are better than others. Greenwood (1997: 8) offered some advice for lobbying Brussels (Insight 23.2, p. 344). Much of this advice amounts to good common sense. Policy makers are often under great pressure, and even those who respond to interest-group approaches need to feel this is a good investment of their time. Those interests that are

INSIGHT 23.2

How to Lobby in Brussels

- Have a clear strategy.

- Develop long-term, even permanent, relations with authorities. Establish a track record as a provider of useful, accurate, well-researched information.

- Find out who is drafting an item and make your representations early.

- Prepare well for meetings. Beware of using hired hands to present cases where their knowledge of your issue will inevitably be limited.

- Present with brevity and clarity.

- Be aware of all sides of the argument. Keep it low-key; do not over-lobby. Appreciate the limits of what can be achieved.

- Keep all viable channels of communication open.

- Know the system, and get to know the points of entry to the decision-making process.

- Remain vigilant.

Source: Greenwood 1997: 8

professional in their approach, that keep to the point and do not waste time, and that have realistic expectations of the policy process, are likely to develop the best relationships with decision makers.

This advice also indicates clearly the importance of timing in the lobbying process. For many groups, making representations early is vital, particularly in relation to policy formation. As Greenwood noted (1997: 8), 'If you have not been able to influence the Commission draft proposal you have probably lost the case.' Related to this is the need to maintain ongoing relationships with Brussels policy makers to ensure that there is a good flow of information so that issues can be identified quickly. Ongoing relations are also important in responding to issues, in that '[i]f you need to start forming a relationship when there is a problem it is probably too late' (Greenwood 1997: 8).

Moreover, the impact of lobbying is affected by the extent to which the views of an interest group 'chime with the emerging prevailing wisdoms of policy and with the quest of European policy makers (including those from national governments) for a form of legitimation for their proposed actions' (Wallace and Young 1997: 245–6). Even interests that are effective in every way advocated by Greenwood may well find that their efforts are without success if they advocate views that are out of line with the views of key decision makers.

As any card player knows, skill in playing the hand that you have been dealt can allow you to win even when your opponents have better cards. There are limits, though, to how far effective strategy and tactics can equalize the disparity of resources. As argued above, attempts by other interests to combine resources may reduce the effectiveness with which they can be deployed, because of tensions within the coalition about priorities. Also, big business has the financial resource to buy the expertise that it needs to take the maximum advantage of its already strong hand. Perhaps it is in order to gain some insight into how to play their hand more effectively that smaller players turn to Brussels-based consultancy firms, despite their apparently poor record in gaining access to the institutional actors.

There is one other strategic approach open to interests that fail to achieve insider status. They can in effect turn over the gaming table by politicizing the issue. Pluralist lobbying usually is most effective when it takes place out of the view of the public, and well away from the political debate. Similarly, policy communities are cosy relationships between organized interests and officials. Politicians are sometimes included in these relationships, but are usually peripheral to them. The policy community can get on with the business of making public policy without interference so long as the issues do not attract the notice of the politicians or the public. In either case, if the profile of the issue is raised above the political threshold, then the nature of the process changes. The strategy of excluded groups with interests in the field is therefore to seek access by politicizing issues. As issues become politicized, they disrupt the exclusive relationships between public agencies and insider interests (Greenwood 1997: 23). The adoption of such disruptive techniques may be more common in the EU context than is sometimes supposed. Research by Jan Beyers (2004) rejected the idea that the technocratic nature of decision-making processes in the EU meant that interest groups would avoid public activism. Beyers (2004: 211) found that, although the institutional supply of access favoured specific interests, the EU contained important institutional opportunities for other ('diffuse') interests that aimed to expand the scope of political conflict or signal policy concerns by using 'public political strategies'.

Regulating Lobbying

It is a sign of the development of EU lobbying that the issue of regulating the activities of interest groups emerged as an important issue in the 1990s. The first moves were taken by the EP, in response particularly to concerns expressed by the Socialist Group. A report produced by the Belgian MEP, Marc Galle in October 1992 ran into problems over the definition of what constituted a lobbyist. However, the Galle Report raised an important issue that the Commission soon sought to address. In 1993, Commission attempts to persuade interests to introduce a self-regulatory code failed, despite warnings that the absence of a voluntary code would probably prompt regulatory instruments drawn up by other institutional actors, who might be less sympathetic. The code that was ultimately produced by lobbying firms in 1994 provided minimum standards in line with the Commission's wishes (Greenwood 1997: 86). This, however, did not satisfy the EP, which returned to the issue following the elections of 1994. The result was a report produced by Glynn Ford MEP, a British member of the Socialist Group.

Ford rejected the self-regulatory approach to lobbying. He was also able to get around the problem of defining lobbying activities by developing an approach based on incentives. The proposal was to issue passes to those who sought to access the EP on a regular basis because they wished to provide information to MEPs. These passes would ensure easy regular access, rather than requiring individuals to apply for a one-day pass on each occasion. In exchange for passes, the recipients would agree to register their interests and activities with the EP.

The attractive simplicity of the Ford Report got lost when its fate became linked to the more complex and more controversial Nordmann Report on members' interests. In effect, 'what started life as a debate about the regulation of lobbying in the Parliament ended as a highly politicised contest between party groupings over the declaration of members' assets and receipts of gifts' (Greenwood 1997: 97). The effect was to delay acceptance of Ford's proposals, along with those of Nordmann, until they were eventually passed together by the EP in July 1996. This decision required that passes would be issued to interested parties in exchange for their agreement to the establishment of a code of conduct and the creation of a register of interests. While action on the regulation of lobbyists was generally welcomed, there was concern that this format might formalize the role of insider groups at the expense of those interests in less frequent contact with EU actors. In other words, these proposals, even if fully implemented, would not achieve the level playing-field sought by many.

Despite these reservations, the acceptance of the Ford and Nordmann schemes did at least mark a starting point in regulating lobbying activity, which could be built upon in future. It is clear that key institutional actors in the EU have a vested interest in ensuring the effective participation of organized interests. The Commission in particular has developed a consultative approach that encourages broad participation, which is part of its wider strategy for mobilizing support for European integration. In this context, the Commission is likely to be an important force in the future of interest-group intermediation. Mazey and Richardson (1999: 125) suggested that: 'the Commission seems intent on a process of *institutionalization* as a means of creating stability and predictability in the policy process. . . it means a growing number of permanent consultative structures.' The outcome of this is likely to be 'the emergence of more and better organized groups, and the further proliferation of EU opportunity structures accompanied by institutionalization, which will further bind interest organizations into the European project' (Mazey and Richardson 1999: 126).

CONCLUSION

This chapter raises issues connected with two of the themes of the book. The first is the theme of supranational versus intergovernmental interpretations of the nature of the EU. The second is the theme of national models of capitalism, and the model that will emerge at the EU level.

Interest-group activity may provide a litmus test for the degree to which the supranational institutions of the EU exercise independent influence over the policy process. If interest groups transfer their lobbying activities away from national governments to Brussels, this might be taken as an indication that the EU is a supranational organization. However, such a conclusion has to be modified in the light of arguments and evidence presented in this chapter. First, the increased level of interest-group activity in Brussels has not replaced activity at the national level, but has generally supplemented it. Second, although groups must have some reason to expend financial resources on establishing a presence in Brussels, this does not mean that the reasons are well founded. They may simply be afraid of missing out on something. There is a point at which the sight of other groups swarming to Brussels will lead groups to follow, on the assumption that there must be something going on, even if there is not.

Once located in Brussels, groups will not all be equally effective in influencing the institutions. Most studies suggest that business interests are more influential than other interests, such as organized labour, consumers, or environmental groups. Within the category of business interests, large firms are more influential than small firms. Whether this relative influence matters, of course, depends on the answer to the question of how much independent influence the supranational institutions have over policy outcomes. If they do have some influence, and if it is true that big-business interests have the most influence over the supranational institutions, then this could provide one explanation for the observation that the policies that emanate from Brussels tend to be in line with an Anglo-American model of capitalism.

On the other hand, the domination of the process by big-business interests may not be as clear as several writers suggest. Beyers (2004) showed that interests that feel themselves excluded can make their voice heard by politicizing the process, while the research undertaken by Bowen (2002, 2004a, 2004b) indicated that business interests do not have the privileged access to the institutions that is often asserted. It should also be noted, though, that formal access is not the same as effective influence: from a critical political economy perspective (Ch. 3) it could be argued that big business can exercise a structural power over decisions by influencing what Wallace and Young (1997: 245–6) called the 'prevailing wisdoms of policy'.

KEY POINTS

The Growth of Interest-Group Activity at the EU Level

☐ Interest-group activity in Brussels has increased greatly since the mid-1980s.

☐ Factors in this growth are: the growing policy competence of the EU; the perception of a shifting balance of institutional power in Brussels, most notably in favour of the EP; the receptiveness of EU officials to interest-group representations; and the 'snowballing' effect of groups following the lead of others so as not to risk being disadvantaged.

Types of Interest Group

☐ There are several different types of interest organization active in Brussels.

☐ Business interests were the first to locate in Brussels, and still account for the largest number of groups.

☐ Interest groups representing workers, consumers and the environment have become increasingly active.

Forms of Interest Representation

☐ Five forms of interest representation co-exist in the EU: 'corporatist', 'neo-corporatist', pluralist, policy networks, and legal representation.

☐ Of these three, pluralism is the dominant form.

Resources

☐ The most effective interest groups in a pluralist system are generally those that control key resources such as information and expertise, economic muscle and status.

☐ Small organizations can pool resources, but they may then find problems in agreeing on priorities and tactics.

☐ Different types of interest groups can provide different types of information to the institutions.

☐ The three types of information sought by the institutions are expert knowledge, information on the needs and concerns of actors in the relevant sector across Europe, and information on the needs and concerns of national actors in the sector.

Organized Interests and the Institutional Actors

☐ For some EU actors, interest groups are an important source of information and legitimation and as such are enthusiastically consulted.

☐ The Commission is in need of the expert knowledge that big-business interests can provide most effectively, but it has also sought to cultivate links with European-level associations and to promote less represented social interests.

☐ The Council is less reliant on organized interests than other institutions and as such is less open to approaches. Much lobbying of the Council is indirect, through individual national governments.

☐ The EP is a key target for organized interests, particularly following the growth of its powers since the mid-1990s. MEPs are thought to be particularly sympathetic to representations on issues of broad public interest.

Strategies and Tactics

☐ Effective strategies and tactics can increase the influence even of interest groups with limited resources at their disposal.

☐ It is possible to identify good practice in lobbying. Developing good ongoing relationships with policy makers, and the timing of interventions are important.

☐ To be influential groups need to be in tune with the prevailing thinking of policy makers.

☐ Groups that find it difficult to gain access to the institutions often seek to politicize issues.

Regulating Lobbying

☐ Attempts to regulate lobbying have been made in recent years, indicating its increased importance in the system.

FURTHER READING

For a thorough and comprehensive review of organized interests in the EU, see J. Greenwood, *Interest Representation in the European Union* (Basingstoke: Palgrave Macmillan, 2003). In addition to considering interest group strategies, resources, and channels of influence, this book includes separate chapters on some of the major interests, including business, labour, and territorial interests.

The edited collection by J. Greenwood and M. Aspinwall (eds.), *Collective Action in the European Union: Interests and the New Politics of Associability* (London and New York: Routledge, 1998) looks at the motivation for and problems of collective action in the EU, drawing on a number of case studies including business, the professions and consumer groups. The edited collection by H. Wallace and A.R. Young (eds.), *Participation and Policy-Making in the European Union* (Oxford: Clarendon Press, 1997) focuses on participation in the fields of market regulation and policies for industry, while S. Mazey and J. Richardson (eds.), *Lobbying in the European Union* (Oxford: Oxford University Press, 1993) brings together contributions on the European lobbying process in general and in specific sectors.

online resource centre

Visit the Online Resource Centre that accompanies this book for links to more information on organized interests.

PARTFOUR
Policies

So many policy sectors now have an EU dimension that it is difficult to provide comprehensive coverage, especially in a general textbook where the policies are just one part of the overall book. We had to make a choice between coverage in breadth or in depth. We settled for depth. While Chapter 24 outlines the main patterns of policy making, and gives an overview of those policies that do not subsequently have separate chapters to themselves, each of the remaining chapters provides a detailed account and analysis of an area of policy that has been central to the development of the EU and to academic theorizing.

Agriculture and *Regional and Structural Policies* between them account for over three-quarters of EU spending. Early theories of European integration were built around the agricultural policy, assuming that this first common policy would form the model for future policies. When it did not, explaining why not advanced theory further. Regional and structural policies have taken an increasing share of the budget of the EU, now around one-third of all spending, and have been at the forefront of experiments with innovative programmes and modes of governance.

Creating a common market was a central objective of the process of European integration from the signing of the Treaty of Rome (EEC) in 1957, while the project to complete the *Single Market* in the mid-1980s revived the faltering process of European integration. Attempts to understand the success of the single-market programme, and the spillover from it to other common policies, generated a parallel revival of theory.

The most significant spillover was from the single market to the creation of a single currency. *Economic and Monetary Union* had been an objective since 1969, but had progressed little, so there was some scepticism at attempts to use the momentum from the single-market programme to move to a single currency. This time, though, the effort succeeded, although not all member states participated. The success generated heated academic debates about the explanation. At the same time, those problems that the sceptics had believed would prevent the formation of the single currency put the system under pressure from the outset, providing the sceptics with ammunition to continue their academic critique.

External relations have two aspects: economic and political. Each has developed at a different pace, and has generated its own academic debates, so there is a chapter on each. *Enlargement* is also a part of external relations—the promise of accession is an important incentive allowing the EU to bring about changes in the politics and governance of neighbouring states; but it is also a process in which they are transformed into internal relations, and so has profound implications for the operation and nature of the EU as a whole.

CHAPTER 24

Policies and Policy Making in the European Union

CHAPTER OVERVIEW

Starting in 1958 with policy on internal tariffs, agriculture, and overseas development, the EC/EU has gradually acquired a competence in more and more areas of policy. A complex system of policy making has emerged to deal with these responsibilities. This chapter reviews the main patterns of policy making, and looks at those policies that have not been given separate chapters to themselves in the rest of this section of the book.

> both member states and supranational institutions 'matter' in EU policy-making, but their respective roles and influence remains highly variable across different modes of EU policy-making
>
> (Pollack 2005: 46)

In July 1988, in a speech to the European Parliament (EP), Jacques Delors predicted that, 'In ten years, 80 per cent of economic legislation—and perhaps tax and social legislation—will be directed from the Community' (European Parliament 1988: 140). The prediction infuriated the British Prime Minister of the day, Margaret Thatcher, yet after sixteen years the range of EU activity had increased to such an extent that in 2004 the Europa web site listed an EU competency in some thirty-one policy areas. This list is reproduced in Table 24.1.

These policy areas vary both in their significance and in the degree to which the EU exercises competence, which means that they have received very different levels of attention in academic studies. Nine of the most significant policy areas, both from a practical and from an academic viewpoint, are considered in separate chapters in this section of the book. The remainder are considered in more cursory form in this chapter. They in turn are divided into policy areas that could have justified separate chapters had space been unlimited, and those that are relatively minor or derivative.

Before turning to the policies, though, the chapter looks at how the European policy agenda is formed, and at the main patterns of policy making that have emerged to handle that agenda. Much of this material recaps what has already been said in the section on the institutions, so it will be briefly covered here with cross-references to the relevant sections of Part III where appropriate.

TABLE 24.1

Policy Competencies of the European Union

Agriculture	Employment and Social Affairs	Humanitarian Aid
Audiovisual	Energy	Human Rights
Budget	Enlargement	Information Society
Competition	Enterprise	Internal Market
Consumers	Environment	Justice and Home Affairs
Culture	External Relations	Public Health
Customs	External Trade	Regional Policy
Development	Fisheries	Research and Innovation
Economic and Monetary Affairs	Food Safety	Taxation
Education, Training, and Youth	Foreign and Security Policy	Transport
	Fraud	

The European Policy Agenda

What is meant by 'the policy agenda'? The domestic policy agenda for governments is comprised of issues that pose problems demanding solutions. Some of these issues arise from domestic political pressures, either from interest groups or from public opinion, or both. Others arise from the international environment, such as security concerns or the effects of the globalization of production on economic interests. These two sources of inputs can interact. International events can raise an issue up the domestic political agenda, which is what happened with environmental policy in the 1970s. Disasters such as oil tankers polluting seas and shores, and accidents at nuclear power stations elsewhere in the world increased public awareness in Europe of the potential environmental consequences of industrialization in the 1970s, and made it easier for domestic environmental pressure groups to recruit and to draw attention to long-term environmental damage, such as the effects of acid rain on the Scandinavian and German forests.

How do such issues find their way onto the EU agenda, rather than remaining domestic issues? Sometimes it is because there is an obvious functional logic to trying to solve the problem collectively. Even the British government, often hostile to the adoption of European solutions, recognized in the 1980s that the economic problems of Europe could only be effectively tackled by joint action to create a genuine single European market (Ch. 26). Sometimes it is because the problem itself arises from *spillover* from other EU policies (see Ch. 1, pp. 10–12), and therefore demands a European solution. The single European market led to a spate of cross-border mergers, some of which threatened to create monopolistic enterprises that would prevent the achievement of greater competition, which was the purpose of the single-market initiative. This put pressure on national governments to agree to regulation of mergers at European level (see below, pp. 362–4). Sometimes the pressure on governments from domestic interest groups is specifically for the transfer of regulation to the European level, as it was for the deregulation of national telecommunications (Ch. 26, Insight 26.2, pp. 419–20). Sometimes some governments are receptive to European approaches to problems because it allows them to escape political unpopularity for the measures that are necessary. There was a strong element of this in the commitment of most EU member states to the creation of a single currency (Ch. 27).

Within this complex picture there are plenty of opportunities for an actor with a commitment to increased European integration to exploit the various pressures on governments. The usual suspect here is the European Commission, an institutional actor that owes its existence and importance to the process of European integration and therefore has every incentive to try to maximize the extent to which governments are prepared to transfer policies to the European level (Ch. 19, pp. 266–7). However, much of this shift of activity is voluntary on the behalf of national governments, in search of collective solutions to problems that are increasingly difficult to resolve to the satisfaction of organized interests and public opinion domestically.

The EU Policy Process

Once an issue is accepted as a legitimate item on the policy agenda of the EU, a complex political and bureaucratic process is set in motion, which involves a plethora of actors. This used almost always to be based around the formal institutional procedures that are described in Chapter 18 (pp. 240–5), and it often still is, although other options have been used more frequently in recent years (see below, pp. 357–8).

Although the details of the involvement of different institutional actors varies according to the procedure that is relevant to a particular policy area, all the formal procedures begin with the Commission formulating a proposal for legislation. In doing this, the Commission normally consults widely. It will usually discuss the range of options with the most obviously relevant interest groups at an early stage. There is no point in coming up with proposals that stand no chance of being accepted by governments because there will be strong lobbying against them by interest groups at national level. The Commission will also consult widely with technical experts in the field, either on an *ad hoc* basis or through its own complex of committees of experts. Just as there is no point in formulating proposals that interest groups will work hard to block, there is no benefit in pushing through legislation that will prove to be impossible to implement, and by consulting experts that can be avoided. Finally, the Commission will sound out national government officials to discover the parameters within which it might prove possible to get an agreement in the Council of Ministers.

Of course, the Commission will receive conflicting opinions and advice when formulating its proposals, and will have to make judgments of its own between these viewpoints. There is sometimes an element here of the Commission being forced to go for the lowest common denominator in order to ensure that it can get some legislation through. This is most often likely to be the case where the policy area is a new one for the EU, when the premium for the Commission is to make a start on building an *acquis communautaire* that can form the basis for further advance at a later date. Often, though, the Commission will take risks in order to push a certain position. This can backfire, but in many cases the Commission has already ensured that it has allies, either among powerful interest groups or within the bureaucracies of national governments, who will back its proposals against opposition from elsewhere.

In preparing its proposals, the Commission will also often consult MEPs who have a particular interest in a policy area, especially those who are members of the relevant specialist committee of the EP. This is most important for those policy areas that are covered by the co-decision procedure (Ch. 18, pp. 243–6) because the EP can block measures that it does not like. Life has become more difficult for the Commission since the introduction of the co-operation (Ch. 18, pp. 242–3) and the co-decision procedures, because the role of the EP in the formal legislative process has been enhanced considerably by these developments. The EP is sometimes theorized as being an inevitable ally of the Commission, because it too is considered to be an institution with a vested interest in further European integration (Garrett and Tsebelis 1996; Tsebelis and Garrett 1996). However, the relationship between the EP and the Commission is much more complicated than that. MEPs have to respond to democratic pressure from their constituents, they face party-political pressures, and they are subject to lobbying from a wide variety of interest groups. Also, the EP has a vested interest in standing up to the Commission to prove its independence and importance. Whereas under the consultation procedure the crucial consideration for the Commission was to ensure that it could get its legislation through the Council of Ministers, there is now a trilateral negotiation to be conducted.

Not only has life become more difficult for the Commission because of the greater role of the EP in the formal procedures, but also in recent years other procedures have appeared for governments to pursue European solutions to their policy problems without delegating as much responsibility to the Commission. In the Treaty on European Union (TEU) (signed 1992, took effect 1993) two new 'pillars' were created alongside the EC pillar (Ch. 18, pp. 231–2). These covered Justice and Home Affairs (JHA; see below, pp. 372–4), and the Common Foreign and Security Policy (Ch. 30). In neither of these pillars did the formal rules of the EC apply. They were explicitly 'intergovernmental' pillars, and although the Commission had a role to play, it did not have the sole right of initiative, as it did in the EC pillar. Subsequently, less formal and more intergovernmental procedures were introduced into the EC pillar, in the form of what is known as the 'Open Method of Co-ordination' (OMC) (Ch. 15, pp. 194–5).

Under the OMC, the member states have a much stronger control over the policy process, from the formulation of objectives through to the implementation of the policy. The process begins with the agreement by the European Council of the objectives to be achieved in the policy sector, and a timescale for achieving them. The Commission and the Council of Ministers then work jointly to produce a series of performance indicators and 'benchmarks' indicating best practice in the field; and to translate the European-level targets into national and regional targets. Member states draw up their own action plans to achieve these targets. The action plans are reviewed by the Council, with input from the Commission, and recommendations may be made for adjustments to the plans, although these are suggestions and are not binding. Progress towards the achievements of the targets is monitored on a regular basis, usually through reports from the Commission to the Council of Ministers, which engages in a system of peer review. There are no sanctions involved in the process, other than the disapproval of the other member states for the failure of states to adjust to criticism, and the fact that this disapproval is made public and could therefore feed into the domestic political process.

The open method thus allows both co-ordinated and individual responses, as appropriate with the possibility of convergence, but with an emphasis on policy learning.
(Hodson and Maher 2001: 740)

How, and how well, the method would work was still to be seen at the time of writing. Wincott (2003: 534) suggested that,

The OMC might be seen as a form of 'cheap talk', perhaps not even able to deliver effective 'co-ordination' across a range of policies and over a medium- or long-term period.

On the other hand, it could turn out to be a transitional phase to the transfer of new policy competencies to the EU-level under the classical method. After all, the Commission had in the past used various forms of 'soft' co-operation as a starting point to build support for the later formal transfer of competencies. However, Borras and Jacobsson (2004: 189–90) pointed to seven distinct differences between the new OMC and previous exercises in co-ordination of policies:

- there is no involvement of the European Court of Justice (ECJ), which in the past has been prepared to interpret commitments entered into under soft co-ordination mechanisms as though they were in some degree binding, so helping to convert 'soft' law into 'hard' law;
- there is a much higher level of political input, especially in monitoring implementation;
- it is a much more systematic process;
- it links different areas of policy;
- it links national and EU-level action in novel ways;
- it aims to mobilize a wide range of actors, in the private sector as well as the public sector, and to foster networking;
- instead of sanctions, it aims to promote learning and self-improvement.

As a result of all these distinctive features, it may well be that the OMC is a new permanent method of governance, in which case its effects will need further study. If it does persist, it certainly changes the dynamics of policy making by reconfiguring the policy-making arena. The lack of any role for the ECJ has been noted above. In addition, it should be noted that there is no role for the EP, nor indeed for the Committee of Permanent Representatives (COREPER; Ch. 20, pp. 284–6). The lack of any input from the EP raises questions about the democratic legitimacy of the process, although the involvement of a wide range of actors, the transparency of the process, and the retention of control over policy instruments in the hands of national governments, which are directly answerable to national parliaments, all seem to point in the opposite direction.

Whatever the uncertainties about the OMC, there is no doubt that it has rapidly spread across a variety of policy sectors. In 2004 it was being applied to the co-ordination of the policies listed in Table 24.2.

TABLE 24.2

Policies where OMC was used in 2004

- economic (Ch. 27);
- education;
- employment (below, pp. 364–7);
- enlargement (Ch. 31);
- enterprise;
- entrepreneurship;
- information society;
- pension reform;
- research.

Minor Policy Areas

To classify any areas of EU competence as 'minor' is likely to be controversial. Certainly they are not minor for the actors directly affected; and some of the areas so classified here actually have quite a high profile with the general public. However, the extension of EU competence to these policy areas did not have major implications for the development of European integration, and consequently they did not attract a great deal of academic attention or analysis.

These minor policy areas can be roughly divided into four groups: those that have some independent functional justification of their own; those that arise largely as a result of functional spillover from the single-market programme; those that are really about building a sense of European identity among the citizens; and those that arise from the commitment made at the Lisbon European Council in 2000 to make the EU into 'the most competitive knowledge-based economy in the world' by 2010. However, several of these policy areas show aspects of more than one of these types.

Those policies that arise from independent functional logics include: fisheries, fraud, and some aspects of both public health and food safety. Those that arise largely as a result of spillover from the single European market include: consumers, customs, taxation, and some aspects of both food safety and the information society. Those that arise from efforts to build a sense of European identity include culture and education. Those that arise directly from the Lisbon commitment include enterprise and many aspects of policy on the information society.

The Common Fisheries Policy (CFP)

The CFP arose from the need to regulate the exploitation of the EU's fish stocks. It originally also had the objective of encouraging the modernization of the less efficient national fishing fleets; but as depletion of fish stocks reached critical levels, the policy was reformulated in a comprehensive review in 2003, after which grants were available only to improve the safety and comfort of boats, not to provide them with the most modern equipment for taking as many fish out of the sea as possible.

Although the allocation of strict quotas to national fleets is invariably unpopular with the fishing industry, and every new allocation produces new predictions of the demise of fishing in one region or another, there is a clear functional logic to regulating fishing in EU waters. The alternative is either a new 'tragedy of the commons', where every national fleet insists on taking as much as it can from the common pool until fish stocks collapse to unsustainable levels, or the emergence of national protectionism for coastal waters. The latter option is not feasible because of the overlap of coastal waters; and even if the boundaries could be sorted out, fish would be unlikely to recognize them, so that one state's efforts to conserve stocks could be easily undermined by a neighbouring state's persistence in over-fishing.

Fraud

Fraud against the EU started almost as soon as the first common policies emerged. The first positive common policy, agriculture, was the victim of some very elaborate schemes to obtain payments outside of the rules. Some farmers mis-stated the amount of land that they had under cultivation, and claimed subsidies for non-existent herds.

Middlemen returned fraudulent figures for the quantities of produce that they held in storage. Export subsidies were claimed for grain that had never left the EU.

When the structural funds were expanded following the Mediterranean enlargement in the 1980s (see Ch. 28, p. 464, and Ch. 31, pp. 542–3), many figures for the costs of projects were artificially inflated, and some money simply disappeared. The existence of different rates of indirect taxes on goods such as cigarettes and alcohol within a frontier-free EU has led to big increases in the smuggling of such goods from countries with low tax rates for sale in countries with higher rates.

So, once the EU existed, fraud against it existed; and this clearly needed to be invest-igated centrally given that the perpetrators of the fraud often operated in several differ-ent states. Today there is a European Anti-Fraud Office (OLAF) that operates within the Commission, but with a special status to ensure its independence.

Public Health and Food Safety

Public health policy has several aspects, one of which is the control of communicable dis-eases. In a world where people travel extensively, diseases quickly cross national bound-aries. This is especially true in an area without frontiers, such as the EU. Although the outbreak of Severe Acute Respiratory Syndrome (SARS) in 2003 did not affect Europe as badly as it did other parts of the world, it did show up the inadequacy of the EU's existing system of exchange of information between national public health authorities. As a dir-ect result it was agreed to set up a European Centre for Disease Prevention and Control, based in Sweden, which would take the leading role in co-ordinating efforts to combat the spread of disease and responding to threats of bio-terrorism.

This aspect of public health policy is a function that is more efficiently performed at a European level than at the national level, and is therefore directly justified by func-tional logic, as are harmonized regulations on the use, storage, and distribution of blood products, and on ensuring access to health care for citizens of one member state while they are resident in another member state. Much the same arguments about the appro-priate functional scale of policy making apply to food safety, especially where trade in food products crosses national boundaries, as it does in the single European market.

The creation of a single European market (Ch. 26) gave the biggest boost to European integration since the creation of the EEC, not only because of what it meant for pro-ducers and consumers directly, but also because of the spillover effects. These included strengthening the independent functional logic of regulating food safety at a European level, which already existed but was enhanced by the need to ensure that consumers were not wary of buying food from other member states because they were worried about whether it was safe to eat. Similarly, the need to remove the real or imagined concerns of consumers about the safety of manufactured products, and about their ability to claim their rights in the event of the failure of a product bought from another member state, created a spillover to the need for an EU-wide policy on consumer protection and con-sumer rights.

Customs

By creating a single European market, the EU paved the way for a geographical area without internal border controls. With the exception of the United Kingdom, which insisted on maintaining its border controls with the rest of the EU (and, by default, the Republic of Ireland, which has long-standing special travel arrangements with the UK, and therefore cannot unilaterally abandon border checks on arrivals from within the EU without forfeiting those privileges), anyone entering the EU, and any goods entering, can thereafter travel freely within the area. This has meant that customs and immigration officials now operate mainly on the external borders of the EU to control the arrival of people and goods from outside of the EU. Under these circumstances, it is considered appropriate that the EU has a role in the co-ordination of the work of national customs services, and the harmonization of the training of customs officials. (Immigration is covered under Justice and Home Affairs below, pp. 372–4).

The Information Society

For producers, the need to ensure a level playing-field of opportunity led to moves to open up cross-national competition in telecommunications (Ch. 26, Insight 26.2, pp. 419–20), which was the beginning of an EU policy on the information society. Once national regulation of telecommunications had been swept away, it became necessary to re-regulate the industry at the European level. Mostly, though, this policy arose in pursuit of the commitment made by the Heads of Governments at Lisbon in 2000, to transform the EU into 'the most competitive knowledge-based economy in the world by 2010'. This led directly to the 'eEurope' programme, which set ambitious targets such as ensuring that all businesses, schools, and universities of EU members had broadband access to the Internet by 2005, with further targets for enabling new members to catch up. Facilitating broadband access for remote and rural areas also became a major priority of the Regional and Social Funds.

Building a European Identity

A few of the minor policy areas date back to an earlier commitment to try to build a stronger sense of European identity among the members of the EC/EU. Although the cultural dimension to European integration was only formally recognized in the TEU in 1992, attempts to build a stronger European cultural profile date back at least to 1985 when the practice began of naming one or more cities annually as the 'European capital of culture'. The funding of the capital of culture and of other initiatives to develop artistic and literary creation, to develop heritage sites, and to stimulate inter-cultural dialogue come under a budget head known as 'Culture 2000'.

The Directorate-General for Education, Training and Youth oversees the administration of two main programmes that also fall under this heading of building identity: Leonardo da Vinci and Socrates. Leonardo supports international vocational training exchanges. Socrates is an umbrella programme, the oldest element of which is the Erasmus scheme to support exchanges of university students and staff. Other elements under the Socrates umbrella are: Gruntvig, which supports adult learners and their teachers in developing teaching materials and building trans-European networks; Comenius, for schools; Lingua to support language learning; and Minerva to support the educational application of new technologies. While formal EU competence over education policies generally has been strictly limited by national governments, the Commission has been an active participant in pan-European initiatives on higher education that fall under the heading of the 'Bologna process' (see Bache 2006; Corbett, forthcoming).

Major Policy Areas

As well as these minor policy areas, there are several major policy areas for which it is not possible to include full chapters in this book. These are policies that have considerable practical significance in their own right, and that have attracted a certain amount of academic attention as well. They are: competition, employment and social policy, energy, environment, research, transport, and JHA. Like the minor policy areas, most of these can be justified either through independent functional arguments, as spillover from the single European market, or as part of efforts to build a sense of European identity. The academic analyses also allow us to say more about the political logic behind these policies.

Competition

Competition policy has been called 'first common policy' of the EC/EU (McGowan and Wilks 1995). Yet, although some elements of competition policy did exist prior to the adoption of the single-market programme, it was considerably enhanced as a direct spillover from the single market. As McGowan and Cini (1999: 177) pointed out, competition policy is a necessary adjunct to the single European market because if large firms reacted to the opening of national markets by adopting anti-competitive practices, such as collusion through cartels, or mergers to create effective European monopolies, the aim of the single market—to increase efficiency and benefit consumers by enhancing competition—would be frustrated. To counter such anti-competitive practices, EU competition policy has four main aspects: antitrust and cartels, merger control, state aids, and liberalization.

Antitrust activity is aimed at preventing cartels. The Commission investigates reports of collusion between producers, for example to fix prices, and penalizes through fines those companies found guilty of acting in restraint of competition. This is necessary to prevent large producers from colluding to stop new producers from breaking into the market, or to maintain profits at artificially high levels by not passing on cost-savings to consumers.

Merger control is a centralized system for approving mergers that have Europe-wide implications. Unlike the Treaty of Paris, the Treaty of Rome contained no provisions for merger control. Various attempts by the Commission to persuade the member states to redress this omission failed, until the single-market programme led to a big increase in the number of cross-border mergers (McGowan and Cini 1999: 178–9). Concern about the possible emergence of monopolistic market conditions put the issue firmly on the agenda. It was pushed to the top of the agenda by the ruling of the ECJ in the Philip Morris case (1987) that the power to prevent market domination through mergers could be inferred from other Articles of the Treaty. This introduced a major element of uncertainty into the calculations of industry about how extensive the inferred powers of the Commission might be, and this uncertainty led in turn to demands from big companies for the member states to adopt clear and explicit legislation defining those limits. The Council of Ministers responded by indicating to the Commission in November 1987 that, despite having rejected four previous proposals, it would now welcome a draft merger regulation. The proposal led to protracted debates and negotiations, but the regulation was eventually adopted in December 1989 and became effective in September 1990 (McGowan and Cini 1999: 180). Under the regulation adopted, a proposed merger must be cleared by the Commission if the merged company would have a turnover within the EU in excess of 250m Euros, and a world-wide turnover of more than 5bn Euros, unless more than 2/3 of the turnover would be within one country, in which case the merger is subject to national scrutiny.

The Commission has considerable autonomy in merger control. Proposed mergers are considered by a merger task force within the Directorate General for Competition (previously DGIV). Merger control is very political because it raises issues such as whether large European companies should be allowed to emerge to act as 'European champions' in global competition with companies from the United States and Japan. This is the position particularly of French governments, and contrasts with the position of the British, Dutch, and other governments that the most important issue is the preservation of competition in the European market. Under the guidance of a series of Commissioners who have shown a strong commitment to the free-market interpretation (Leon Brittan, Karel van Miert, Mario Monti), the Directorate-General has moved in that direction, but all rulings have to be approved by the full College of Commissioners, and here the outcome is not always certain as political considerations can intervene.

Politics is even more in the forefront of policy on state aids, which involves the Commission investigating instances where the government of a member state grants any of its own companies subsidies, loans, tax breaks, loan guarantees, or preferential purchase deals on goods and services, to ensure that this is not giving those companies an unfair competitive advantage. As Smith (1998: 58) pointed out, the difference between merger control and state aids is that in the latter the Commission is confronting governments directly. Autonomous powers were granted to the Commission at an early stage in the history of the EEC, because there was a widespread wish among governments to remove distortions to competition in the common market, and it was obvious that an impartial arbitrator was needed. The powers granted, though, proved to give the Commission more autonomy than envisaged.

Were Member States given the choice today, they would probably not delegate the same powers to the Commission as they did 40 years ago.

(Smith 1998: 76)

However, rolling back those powers would require a revision of the Treaty, and could jeopardize the success of the single market.

Liberalization prevents natural monopolies, such as domestic postal service providers, which are not subject to competition, from cross-subsidizing their commercially competitive activities, such as, in the case cited, postal deliveries to businesses. This is another area where the Commission is likely to come into conflict with national governments, because of the domestic political implications of restrictions on the activities of national providers, which might as a result find it difficult to maintain profitability and have to receive bigger subsidies for the service that they provide to the public.

Employment and Social Policy

There has always been a social dimension to the EC/EU. The Treaty of Rome, generally a *laissez-faire* document, contained mention of the need to achieve social cohesion, to improve health and safety at work, to facilitate the free movement of labour, to promote equality between men and women in the workplace, to harmonize social security provision, and to promote a social dialogue between management and workers. However, the change of name for this policy sector to 'employment and social policy' is indicative of a shift in the priorities, which in turn may be indicative of how far the Anglo-Saxon model of capitalism and changing economic circumstances have shifted thinking within the EU as a whole.

Originally, EC social policy was predominantly about the protection of workers. Although a large part of the European Social Fund (ESF) has always been used to retrain workers, the emphasis of the social policy articles of the Treaty of Rome was much more on creating a level playing-field of competition by imposing on all producers the same levels of protection for employees as applied in the most regulated markets. An example of this is gender equality, which was given its own Article of the Treaty of Rome (originally Article 119, now Article 141) because France had extensive domestic legislation on equal pay between men and women before the EEC was set up, and wanted to ensure that the competitiveness of French companies was not damaged by this in comparison with other member states. After the common market had been established, some of the first pieces of social legislation to be passed concerned the equal rights of women and men in work-related matters. The Equal Pay Directive of 1975 imposed a legal requirement of equal pay for equal work; the Equal Treatment Directive of 1976 made discrimination illegal in access to employment and training and in respect to rights concerning dismissal; and the Social Security Directive of 1978 required equal treatment in access to state benefits. All of these were rights that were already embodied in French domestic legislation, and the other member states were now obliged to accept them under pressure from trade unions and women's groups. Other than in legislation on gender equality, social policy had made little progress by the mid-1980s. Jacques Delors tried to revive it by arguing that the single market needed a social dimension if it were to be acceptable to those who would initially lose out. Yet the member states were prepared to make only health and safety in the workplace subject to qualified majority voting (QMV) in the Single European Act (SEA). Although the opposition of the British Conservative government to social policy was the usual explanation for this lack of progress, it was very convenient for other governments to hide behind the British veto.

Delors's argument pointed most obviously to the need for some element of redistributive social expenditure controlled at the EU level, to redress the large divergences in prosperity that existed between different social groups. The only significant element of such redistributive expenditure that did exist already—other than for specific groups of workers, such as for farmers through the CAP—was the European Regional Development Fund (see Ch. 28). Expenditure on redressing regional disparities did increase considerably as a result of the SEA, and again as a result of the TEU.

However, no large-scale social programme emerged as a complement to the SEA. Not only were there financial limits to what the richer member states would pay as compensation for the single-market programme, governments generally remain sensitive to the transfer of policy competencies in this domain. In addition, the variety of national types of welfare provision among the member states has made even harmonization of policy impossibly complicated (Majone 1993: 160–1).

In one area, though, Delors did lay the foundations for what at one stage began to look like a promising approach to extending the social dimension. Soon after becoming President of the Commission he instituted a 'social dialogue' with representatives of employers and employees at the European level. In 1985, Delors approached both the Union of Industries in the European Community (UNICE) and the European Trade Union Confederation (ETUC) to propose an ongoing negotiation on social legislation. He suggested that if the idea were accepted, the Commission would refrain from introducing further items of social legislation, and would instead let them emerge out of the dialogue. Initially two working parties were set up, on employment policies and on new technology at work. The meetings took place at the chateau of Val Duchesse outside Brussels, and were therefore known as 'the Val Duchesse process'.

A fundamental difference of opinion soon emerged between UNICE and ETUC. The employers wanted the discussions to lead to publications but not legislation: the unions wanted them to result in legislation. The first of the two working parties produced an anodyne report, based on the lowest common denominator of what the two sides could agree, while the second one failed to arrive at an agreed report of any sort.

Following this false start, the Commission made an attempt to revive the process in January 1989. At a meeting in Brussels it was agreed to set up a steering group to sustain the momentum of the process, and to extend the dialogue to all areas covered in the 'Social Charter' that had just been agreed by the heads of government. Although it had no great achievements to its name, the social dialogue—involving UNICE, ETUC, and also the European Centre of Public Enterprises (CEEP)—was incorporated into the Social Protocol of the TEU, and became part of the Social Chapter of the Treaty after the British Labour government signed up to the Protocol at Amsterdam in 1997.

Under the terms of this 'social agreement', the Commission is obliged to consult the 'social partners' on proposed legislation under the Social Chapter twice, first on the principle and then on the content of the draft legislation. At either stage, the social partners may inform the Commission that they wish to initiate discussions to reach a collective agreement. This effectively stops the formal procedure for at least nine months. If a collective agreement is reached in that time, the partners can ask the Commission to present it to the Council of Ministers for formal approval, which is normally expected to be given, so that their agreement then becomes law.

This institutionalization of the social dialogue appeared for a time to offer what Wendon (1998: 343) called 'alternative venues' for the Commission to pursue integrative measures. Strøby Jensen (2000: 86), using neofunctionalist concepts, talked about 'institutional-legalistic' spillover, a similar idea whereby once the institutional basis for the social dialogue was established, it provided a forum for Commission activism. In practice, though, the legislative achievements of the social agreement were very limited. The first item that was taken under the new procedure, on European Works Councils, could not be agreed, although legislation was subsequently adopted under the normal procedures in September 1994 (Falkner 2000: 707–8). This was at a time when the British government was still not a signatory to the Social Protocol, and was therefore not involved in the discussions in the Council of Ministers. That deprived UNICE of its generally most reliable ally. The message that if it failed to reach agreement with ETUC, it might find unwelcome legislation being pushed through anyway, encouraged UNICE to be somewhat more co-operative. Subsequently directives were adopted through the new procedure on parental leave (December 1995, adopted by Council in June 1996), and two on 'atypical work' in 1999—one on the rights of part-time workers and one on the rights of workers on fixed-term contracts (Falkner 2000: 709–11). By 1999, though, this method had already been overtaken by a change of emphasis away from protecting the rights of workers towards providing opportunities for work for the unemployed, and by the introduction of the OMC into employment and social policy.

Persistent unemployment throughout the EU led to the introduction in the Amsterdam Treaty of a new title on Employment, which called for a 'co-ordinated strategy for employment'. A special 'jobs summit' was held in Luxemburg in November 1997 at which a strategy was agreed that became the model for what the later (2000) Lisbon European Council was to entitle the OMC. The Luxemburg process involves agreement on a common set of European targets, with member states drawing up National Action Plans for Employment (NAPs). The NAPs are then submitted to the Commission and Council for scrutiny and recommendations may be made. The Commission then produces an annual report on the performance of member states and of the EU as a whole in achieving its objectives, and targets may be adjusted accordingly (Adnett 2001: 353–9). Although no member state is obliged to adopt a particular approach to achieving its objectives, the emphasis on emulating best practice has led to an emphasis on freeing labour markets of restrictions and providing training for the unemployed, an emphasis more in line with the Anglo-Saxon model of capitalism than with the various continental models that have traditionally put more emphasis on protecting the rights of those in work. On the other hand, Adnett (2001: 360) reported that there was little evidence of a convergence of national policies, and that indeed in some areas there was evidence of increasing diversity.

Since the Lisbon European Council (2000), the OMC has also been applied to social policy as more traditionally understood in the EU. At Lisbon member states committed themselves to draw up national action plans to combat poverty and social exclusion, to devise indicators for assessing progress, and to develop mechanisms for ensuring the achievement of objectives in these fields (Hodson and Maher 2001: 726, Table 1). This commitment underlines the argument of Borras and Jacobsson (2004: 190) that the Lisbon strategy addresses *both* competitiveness and social cohesion. As they go on to emphasize, though, the outcome of adopting the OMC is likely to be a change in the nature of the social dimension, which 'had arrived at a stalemate' because 'more EU rights would have invariably undermined the socio-economic agreements and social contracts upon which each national welfare arrangement has been historically built . . . There was simply no political support for the further transfer of legal competencies to the EU in these areas' (Borras and Jacobsson 2004: 190).

In the area of employment and social policy, the OMC has allowed progress where the traditional method of European legislation was severely hindered by the lack of any consensus over priorities, and where the prospect of more such legislation risked further damaging the legitimacy of the EU. The result has been to change the nature of the policy sector, both the content of policy outputs and the process. While the changed policy process was still in flux at the time of writing, it seems clear that the power of the EP and the ECJ must be weakened by their effective and formal exclusion from the OMC. On the other hand, 'it is not obvious that the OMC has weakened the Commission' (Borras and Jacobsson 2004: 198), but it has changed the nature of the game for the Commission, and seems to have sidelined the institutional forum centred on the social dialogue that was identified by Wendon (1998) and Strøby Jensen (2000).

Environment

Environmental policy has an independent functional logic to it. Environmental pollution is no respecter of national boundaries. Also, the equalization of environmental conditions is important to facilitating the free movement of labour within the single market. Skilled workers in particular will be reluctant to relocate to countries where their health and that of their families could be adversely affected by less pure water or air than is available in the countries with the highest standards. It is also a policy area that demonstrates well the organic process by which European integration can develop.

There was no mention of environmental protection in the treaties until the SEA of 1986. Yet by that time there was already a considerable body of environmental legislation in operation. As noted above (p. 355), that development was the result of growing concern over environmental issues in the original member states, combined with the obvious functional logic of tackling the problems at a level above that of the individual state. Given a green light by the member states, the Commission was not slow to propose environmental legislation, and in 1973 the first EC 'Environmental Action Programme' was agreed. This was followed by further programmes in 1977 and 1982, with the programmes becoming successively less vague. Environmental directives and decisions increased steadily from ten in 1975, to thirteen in 1980, twenty in 1984, and twenty-four in 1985 (Majone 1993: 164). All of this was before environmental policy was incorporated into the treaties via the SEA.

The legislation agreed by the Council of Ministers has consistently gone further than the lowest common denominator of domestic legislation. This is partly a reflection of the strength of feeling on the issue among the leading environmental states, particularly Germany, which was the main advocate of strong environmental legislation in the early days. Member states with lower levels of concern were not prepared to defy Germany on an issue that was so important to German governments because they did not want to damage their prospects of getting support from Germany on other issues. Another factor may also have been helpful in allowing far-reaching legislation through the Council of Ministers: for many years the Environment Ministers were allowed to get on with forging a body of EC law without much interference from higher levels of their governments. The issues were technical, and not easily understood by the offices of Prime Ministers or the Economics Ministries, or indeed often by the political appointees to the position of Minister of the Environment. The Environment Ministries tended to be staffed by officials who wanted to see their own countries introduce more stringent environmental legislation, and so the representatives of the 'laggard' states were very willing to go along with the 'leader' states in concluding far-reaching agreements. It took a long time before the cost of some of the legislation, for example on the purity of drinking water, became apparent. When it did, the Finance Ministries in particular were not very pleased, but by that time the legislation was already binding.

Perhaps the governments of the 'laggard' states also thought that they would never need to apply the legislation very rigorously. They were wrong, though. Environmental pressure groups have brought pressure on the Commission to report to the ECJ infringements of environmental legislation by their own governments (Fairbrass and Jordan 2001: 499). Also, as Cichowski (1998) illustrated, when faced with referrals from national courts under former Article 177 (now Article 234) of cases where varying national interpretations of environmental-protection directives conflict with free-market rules, the ECJ has consistently obliged the member states with the weaker legislation to upgrade their levels of environmental protection, rather than allow the reversion of protection to the lowest level.

Because the southern member states had the lowest levels of domestic environmental protection, the impression was formed that they would be the most unwilling to implement the much higher EU levels, many of which had been agreed before Greece, Portugal, and Spain joined. However, Börzel (1999) argued that there was no 'southern problem', and that there was considerable variation in successful implementation both across member states generally, and even across different environmental sectors within one member state. Problems arose when there was a lack of 'policy fit', that is, where the European policy did not adopt a similar approach to that which had been adopted previously in that country. This was consistent with the research of Knill and Lenschow (1998), which had shown how implementation of environmental directives was influenced by national traditions in Germany and Britain. It is an issue that is of considerable interest in the context of Europeanization (Ch. 4, pp. 58–65; see Börzel 2002; Jordan 2005).

Energy

Energy is another area where policy objectives have changed as a result of changing circumstances. Over a long period of time the main objective of energy policy was the liberalization of national markets, which were dominated by monopolistic national suppliers. This resulted in high energy costs, which damaged the global competitiveness of European manufacturers. The situation came to the fore in the aftermath of the single-market programme, with the Commission acting as a **policy entrepreneur** to cultivate spillover.

Matlary (1997) analysed the approach that the Commission used to push forward a common energy policy. The energy sectors were dominated by national monopolists, which were most commonly publicly-owned. An open market in energy was originally part of the White Paper on the single market, but the opposition of national monopoly suppliers led to it being excluded. However, the Commission returned to the issue in 1989, making proposals for a phased dismantling of national monopolies over the electricity grids and gas supply networks. It was unlikely that the national monopolists themselves would support liberalization moves, but the Commission was able to mobilize the support of large industrial users of energy, working through the existing institutionalized networks of UNICE and the European Round Table of Industrialists.

The linking of energy policy to the single-market programme was explicit. In April 1991 Sir Leon Brittan, the Commissioner for Competition Policy, said that there were two sectors that were vital to the internal market, telecommunications and energy. At the same time as the proposals for a phased dismantling of national monopolies were being negotiated, DG IV (Competition) was stepping up its attacks on monopolistic practices using its powers under Article 90 of the EEC Treaty. Although the threat never became as explicit, the vested interests resisting integration were faced with a choice between a hard-line free-market approach from DG IV or a negotiated softer approach from another DG, in this case from DG XVII (Energy).

Negotiations in the Council of Ministers were protracted. The French government in particular was reluctant to end the monopoly of *Electricité de France* (EdF) over the distribution of electricity in France. It claimed that its primary concern was to protect the access of rural French domestic consumers to electricity at the same price as was available everywhere else in France. This was the 'public service' argument. However, it was also bowing to intense lobbying from the trade unions, which feared that liberalization would mean job losses. Eventually, in June 1996, agreement was reached on a phased liberalization of electricity supply over six years, but it would only apply to large industrial users. The whole process of negotiation then had to be repeated to secure an agreement on liberalization of the market in gas supply, with the French government fighting as hard to protect the position of *Gaz de France* as it had to protect EdF. Eventually another compromise deal was reached in December 1997.

Once the principle had been established that national energy markets would be opened up to competition from other member states, the potential existed to shift other aspects of energy policy to the EU level. In 2004 the Commission identified problems concerning the high level of dependence of the EU on fossil fuels and on imported sources of energy. Fossil fuels are finite, and burning them contributes to global warming. The supply of imported energy is liable to disruption from international crises, which can also increase prices quite dramatically. From these problems arises the need to develop co-ordinated programmes to save energy, to use it more efficiently, and to develop alternative sources. In 2004 the EU had ambitious targets to double the amount of energy generated from renewable sources—wind, bio-mass, hydro, and solar—by 2010. The main hope for diversifying supply, though, was hydrogen. The 'European Hydrogen and Fuel Cell Technology Platform' was drafting a blueprint for a transition from coal, oil, and natural gas to hydrogen-based sources of energy. Spillover from energy policy into transport and into research policy was also recognized by the Commission. Thus the transfer of energy supply from a national to a European market brought in its train the prospect of a whole set of new competencies for the EU.

Transport

A common transport policy was one of the Titles of the original Treaty. There is an obvious functional necessity for efficient cross-border transport, to make a reality of the ideal of a common market, and a functional logic to organizing it at the European level. Arising from this, the European Commission has responsibility for the planning and part-financing of Trans-European Networks (TENs) for different modes of transport. Despite several statements of support for the TENs, though, the member states have never been prepared to provide adequate funding, so that the programme is always lagging behind the aspirations.

Spillover from the single-market programme allowed the Commission to push through measures to open national transport markets to competition. The liberalization of air transport contributed to a reduction in fares and a consequent increase in passengers; and the liberalization of rail transport, which began with the implementation of a first package of measures in March 2003, held out the prospect of opening 70 to 80 per cent of rail freight traffic over main lines to competition. In the road-haulage industry, internationally competitive firms had long argued against the principle of cabotage with respect to loads, a principle that had reserved to national transport firms the right to transport national goods. This had meant that lorries carrying goods from their own state to another member state had to return home empty, which was obviously uneconomical. It was possible to get agreement on the abolition of this principle once the single market was in operation.

As with energy, other problems were exacerbated with the opening of the markets, and these provided a continuing agenda for action by the Commission. Problems with road congestion, pollution, and the continuing fragmentation of some transport infrastructure were highlighted in a 2001 White Paper on Transport, which also set ambitious targets:

- to reduce road deaths;
- to improve the speed of freight trains by eliminating the causes of delay;
- to reduce flight delays by developing an integrated air-traffic control system;
- to regulate the allocation of airline landing slots;
- to promote investment in inland waterways;
- to improve maritime safety standards;
- to improve port services;
- to introduce integrated ticketing and baggage handling for mixed-mode journeys.

Through a combination of these measures it was hoped to move the EU away from its heavy dependence on road transport, to eliminate some of the consequent congestion, and to reduce the consequent pollution.

Research

Although a European technological community had been part of the original vision of Jean Monnet, technological research was not included in the Treaty of Rome. The main reason was that the idea of developing 'national industrial champions' held strong sway in the 1950s, as it continued to through until the 1980s. Despite several periods of concern about the technological lead of the United States over Europe—for example, the furore sparked by Jean-Jacques Servan-Schreiber's book *The American Challenge* (Servan-Schreiber, 1968)—attempts by the Commission to persuade member states to institute collaborative research programmes had little effect until the 1980s, when a major breakthrough occurred with the approval by the Council of Ministers in 1982 of the European Strategic Programme in Information Technology (ESPRIT).

The reasons for this breakthrough were similar to those that brought about the even bigger breakthrough of the single-market programme (Ch. 26, p. 410). The weak recovery of Europe from the 1979 oil-price shock, in comparison with the vigorous recovery of the United States and Japan, led to much of talk of 'Eurosclerosis'. The policy of supporting national champions was clearly not working. In particular, the crucial electronics sectors in Europe were 'showing a poor performance in both capital and consumer goods' (Sharp 1991: 63). At the same time national research budgets were under pressure because national budgets were being pushed into deficit by high unemployment, and the cost of research was increasing. It was increasingly apparent that the United States and Japan had a range and scale of research and technological-development programmes that no individual European state could afford to match (Peterson 1992: 231).

Those were the structural factors that made the 1982 breakthrough feasible. Agency was provided by Etienne Davignon, the EC's Commissioner for Industry from 1977 to 1985. Davignon responded to the concern about Europe's technological performance in electronics by convening the 'Big 12 Round Table' of leading European electrical and electronics firms. This organization provided the model for the later, more extensive, European Round Table of Industrialists. The consensus among the Big 12 was that EC-level support for research and development was essential if the European electronics industry were not to slip even further behind its competitors. This consensus was then pressed on national governments by the powerful large corporations (Sharp and Shearman 1987: 49). What made their lobbying even more effective was that Davignon had used his own network of contacts to ensure that the Round Table met not only at a technical level, but also at the level of Chief Executives:

Until then the Commission had tended to work with research directors or their equivalents and initiatives had come unstuck because they had been unable to carry them higher up the hierarchy.
(Sharp 1991: 64)

Here, then, was a prime example of the Commission, in the form of Davignon, playing the role of a policy entrepreneur: identifying a problem, suggesting a solution at the European level, and creating then mobilizing a transnational network of producers to act as its allies in the private sector and to bring pressure to bear on governments to adopt the European solution.

Once the principle of centrally-funded research was established in the field of electronics and information technology, other industries soon began to demand that they get similar support. In 2004 the EU's Sixth Framework Programme accounted for €4 billion a year and funded 6 per cent of all civil research in the EU. Around three quarters of this budget was devoted to seven priorities:

- genomics and biotechnology for health;
- information society technologies;
- nanotechnologies, intelligent materials and new production processes;
- aeronautics and space;
- food safety and health risks;
- sustainable development;
- economic and social sciences.

Justice and Home Affairs (JHA)

This is another policy sector that originally had no Treaty basis. It did not enter the treaties until the TEU, where it appeared as a separate intergovernmental pillar. In the Treaty of Amsterdam, provisions on visas, asylum, and immigration, which had originally been part of the JHA pillar, were transferred to the TEC—although only visa procedures were to come under QMV—and the remaining Title VI of the TEU was renamed 'Provisions on Police and Judicial Co-operation in Criminal Matters'.

Although there was no treaty base until the TEU, co-operation began in the 1970s, although it 'took place in [a] range of poorly co-ordinated intergovernmental groups which lacked adequate institutional structures, legal instruments and objectives' (Monar 2001: 748). In the 1990s, though, co-operation in this area really took off. A large amount of new legislation was adopted, and at the Tampere European Council in October 1999 the Heads of Government agreed to make the creation within the EU of a 'European area of freedom, security and justice' a central Treaty objective.

Monar (2001) explained these developments as the result of a series of increasingly urgent 'driving forces' encountering a fertile ground for rapid development because of the 'laboratory' nature of the earlier efforts at co-operation through the Council of Europe, 'Trevi', and the work of the Schengen group (see below). Despite the somewhat disparaging description quoted above of the earlier forums for co-operation, they were the 'laboratories' where experiments in co-operation took place that prepared the ground for the rapid advances in the 1990s.

Council of Europe texts on extradition, mutual legal assistance in criminal matters, the international validity of criminal judgments, and the transfer of sentenced persons were so central to JHA co-operation between EU member states that they were added to the *acquis* that applicant states were required to adopt before they could become new members. Perhaps more importantly, though, through co-operation in the Council of Europe the traditionally parochial outlook of Interior Ministries began to be broken

down. National officials gained experience of working co-operatively with their counterparts in other European states, and everyone's awareness of national sensitivities and
peculiarities, and of the problems involved in co-operation, was raised.

'Trevi' was a loose form of co-operation within European Political Co-operation
(EPC). It lasted from 1975 until it was overtaken by the institutionalization of JHA co-
operation in 1993. It started as a response to increasing terrorist activity in Europe, but
was later extended to the fight against drugs trafficking and organized crime. As with co-
operation through the Council of Europe, it provided the experience of working together
that paved the way for more structured co-operation under JHA.

Some of the benefits of Trevi were passed on to the third 'laboratory', the 'Schengen
group' of those member states that signed the Schengen agreement to eliminate internal
border controls. The group was set up to study the implications of this move, which
proved to be more far-reaching than envisaged. It did valuable work that paved the way
for JHA agreements on asylum policy, visa policy, extradition, and police co-operation.
It also created a 'culture of co-operation' (Monar 2001: 752) and laid the basis for the
transnational networks of police and judicial authorities that are essential to the successful implementation of JHA measures.

The experience gained in these forums meant that when the external and internal
pressures for closer co-operation under JHA built up, the member states did not have to
start from a blank sheet. The driving factors that built the pressure were already present
before the 1990s, but were dramatically increased by the collapse of communism. International crime increased rapidly following the end of the USSR, with Russian criminal gangs muscling their way into activities such as drugs dealing with a ruthlessness
that shocked even hardened police operatives. The civil wars in former Yugoslavia led to
massive increases in asylum applications, especially with the Kosovo conflict at the end
of the 1990s. Although only connected to the collapse of communism indirectly, terrorist
incidents accelerated in the chaotic world that followed the end of the cold war, culminating in the atrocities in New York in September 2001, which produced another rapid
escalation in JHA legislation within the EU (see below). Alongside these developments,
the unconnected phenomenon of the spread of the internet provided opportunities for
new types of criminal activity, such as child pornography, that could only be tackled by
cross-border co-operation.

Spillover from the single-market programme also opened up new criminal
opportunities. Free movement of goods facilitated smuggling, especially of goods
such as cigarettes that attracted very different levels of tax in different parts of the EU.
Free movement of people allowed criminals to commit crimes in one member state and
retreat to another to evade detection and capture. Free movement of capital facilitated
financial crime, including the 'laundering' of money obtained from activities such as
drugs dealing and smuggling. Also, individuals and businesses who took advantage of
the single market to buy or sell in other member states found it difficult and prohibit-
ively expensive to gain access to the system of justice if things went wrong, which is what
sparked the Tampere commitment to the European area of justice.

Despite these driving forces, progress was slow prior to 11 September 2001 because the decision-making system in the Police and Judicial Co-operation pillar was
intergovernmental, and agreement on any measure had to be unanimous. The terrorist

attacks in the United States 'put enormous pressure on justice and home affairs' cumbersome decision-making system to produce substantial legislative action in a very short time' (Monar 2002: 121). Several measures were agreed, including a common definition of terrorism, and a 'European arrest warrant'—making provision for automatic extradition from one member state to another—that had been blocked for some time previously. Even under such extreme pressure, though, the agreements were delayed until the middle of 2002 by objections to particular clauses by individual member states. This concentrated the minds of the member states on the need to improve the efficiency of decision making in the JHA field when they came to agree the new Constitutional Treaty.

Under the terms of the Constitutional Treaty (Articles III-257 to III-277) the intergovernmental character of the Police and Judicial Co-operation pillar would largely disappear, with the introduction of QMV for voting in the Council, and a role similar to that under co-decision for the EP. A scrutiny role is given to both the EP and national parliaments, thus ensuring that some of the extreme secrecy that has surrounded the implementation of JHA agreements is removed. The role of the Commission is also strengthened, both by strengthening its right of initiative and by giving it the right to take a member state to the ECJ for failing to implement JHA agreements, something that previously only another member state could do. To allay the concerns of some member states that the changed rules might threaten fundamental aspects of its judicial system, an 'emergency brake' procedure is available that would block the adoption of any such measure. However, there is also provision for any number of member states in excess of one-third of the total to agree to go ahead among themselves with any measure that is blocked by application of the emergency brake.

CONCLUSION

One of the first conclusions that leaps out from this brief review of the policy process and of various policy sectors is that there is no one consistent pattern of policy making. As suggested by governance and networks approaches, different elements are important in different sectors and, as such, there is a need to disaggregate analysis of the policy process to understand these different patterns. At the same time, however, some patterns emerge that highlight the value of other conceptual contributions.

The extent to which policies have either originated, or more often have accelerated because of spillover from the single European market is clear. This emphasises the central importance of the single-market programme, but also the continuing theoretical relevance of neofunctionalism. The validity of neofunctionalism is also clear in the role played by the Commission in exploiting the spillover pressures to engineer transfers of competencies to the EU, often through forming alliances with interest groups. It fits well, too, with the way in which the deregulation of national markets in energy and transport led to the involvement of the EU in finding solutions to other problems in these sectors.

Intergovernmentalism obtains less support from the review given above. There are some elements of intergovernmentalism in the way that social policy was blocked for so long, often apparently by the British government alone, although this may be a bit of a mis-representation given that other governments did not have to declare their opposition if the British were going to veto measures anyway. The danger of European social policy interfering with the operation of very different national welfare systems was a barrier to progress that applied to all member states. The contrast between the lack of progress on social policy, which had a treaty base, and the progress on environmental policy, which did not, is indicative of the importance of a policy having support and sponsorship from influential states, Germany in the case of the environment.

Another support for intergovernmentalism comes from the introduction of the OMC into an increasing number of policy areas. This allows the governments to keep a tighter control over developments. Implicitly it is an acknowledgement that there was validity in the arguments of neo-functionalists and of supranationalist theorists more generally that once the initial step was taken in a process of integration, it would become difficult for the member states to keep control of how far they went. On the other hand, the reassertion of control is evidence of the resilience of national sovereignty. This development also adds weight to governance approaches that emphasise the increasing importance of informal modes of co-ordination rather than formal legislative initiatives. Interest-based explanations have predominated over ideas-based explanations in the sectors reviewed here, but this may just reflect the choice of sectors, which is based on significance and prominence, and therefore is random from the point of view of rational versus social constructivist approaches. Constructivist ideas do get support from the way in which co-operation was developed under JHA through the 'laboratories' of the Council of Europe, Trevi, and Schengen. This also lends support to historical institutionalist approaches, as does the observation of Smith (1998: 58) on competition policy relating to state aids, that member states are locked into commitments that were made forty years earlier because of the difficulty of changing them without causing damage to other policies, and the concept of 'institutional-legalistic' spillover developed to explain social policy by Strøby Jensen (2000: 86).

It is important to note, though, that the policies reviewed here are selected on the theoretically arbitrary basis that they are not the most central to the EU. Before drawing too many theoretical conclusions, it is necessary to look in depth at the nine policies that have been selected for especial attention in the chapters that follow.

KEY POINTS

☐ The policy competencies of the EC/EU have expanded considerably, although not all policies are of equal significance or have received equal academic attention.

The European Policy Agenda

☐ Policy agendas are composed of problems that governments face as a result of domestic political pressure and/or international developments.

☐ Issues on domestic policy agendas are pushed up to the EU level because of functional logic, because they arise from spillover from other EU policies, because domestic interest groups seek action at the EU level, or so a government can escape domestic unpopularity for a necessary reform.

☐ The Commission is often able to exploit these circumstances to promote a European solution.

The EU Policy Process

☐ Much policy is still processed through the formal rules of the EC.

☐ These begin with the Commission drawing up proposals for legislation, at which stage it will consult widely with interest groups, technical experts, and national government officials.

☐ Since the introduction of the co-operation and co-decision procedures, the Commission will also consult MEPs.

☐ The TEU introduced two intergovernmental 'pillars' of the EU—CFSP and JHA—where EC rules did not apply.

☐ In recent years the OMC has been introduced into the EC pillar, giving the member states stronger control and excluding the EP and ECJ.

Minor Policy Areas

☐ Of the more minor policy areas, fisheries, fraud, and some aspects of both public health and food safety arise mainly from the functional logic of handling problems at the EU level.

☐ Policies on consumers, customs, taxation, and some aspects of both food safety and the information society arise predominantly from spillover from the single European market.

☐ Policies on culture and education look back to an earlier commitment to strengthen a sense of European identity.

☐ Policies on enterprise and many aspects of policy on the information society arise directly from the Lisbon commitment to make the EU the world's most competitive knowledge-based economy.

Major Policy Areas

☐ Competition policy developed largely through spillover from the common market and single market. It is an area in which the Commission has considerable autonomy, but in exercising its powers it is often brought into conflict with national governments.

☐ Social policy was included in the original Treaty, but made little progress before the 1980s, and was boosted in the 1990s by a new emphasis on combating unemployment and the introduction of OMC into both employment and social policy.

☐ Environmental policy developed from the 1970s, despite having no treaty base. National environmental pressure groups seized on EU legislation to take their own governments to court if they did not comply, and the ECJ adopted an expansive interpretation of the obligations.

☐ Spillover from the single market allowed the Commission to mobilize a coalition of industrial users of energy in favour of liberalization of national energy markets. Once an EU-wide energy market had been established in principle, it became logical to handle other problems, such as security of supply and environmental effects, at the EU level.

☐ A similar process operated for transport: spillover from the single market allowed the Commission to push through liberalization of national markets, and then other issues needed to be handled at the European level.

☐ Research policy started with the ESPRIT programme in the electronics and information technology sectors. The Commission exploited European concerns about US and

Japanese advances in these sectors to pressurize governments to adopt an EC-wide programme of support for research.

☐ JHA saw rapid advances in the 1990s as a result of increasing problems with organized crime and terrorism. It was possible to make such rapid progress because the foundations had been laid by co-operation in the Council of Europe, Trevi, and Schengen.

FURTHER READING

The standard text on policy making in the EU is H. Wallace and W. Wallace (eds.), *Policy-Making in the European Union* (Oxford: Oxford University Press, 3rd edn, 1996). Students should especially read the introductory chapters by H. Wallace, but also the individual chapters on specific policies are the best possible starting point for following up on the other policies included in this chapter—competition, energy, environmental, research, social, and transport policy, and justice and home affairs.

Because of its influence on later analysis of policy making, it is important to read J. Peterson, 'Decision-making in the European Union: Towards a Framework for Analysis'. *Journal of European Public Policy*, 2 (1995): 69–93.

On the Open Method of Co-ordination, there are two articles that, read consecutively, will give a good overall picture of the method and of its strengths and weaknesses. They are, D. Hodson and I. Maher, 'The Open Method as a New Mode of Governance: The Case of Soft Economic Policy Co-ordination', *Journal of Common Market Studies*, 39 (2001): 719–46; and S. Borras and K. Jacobsson, 'The Open Method of Co-ordination and New Governance Patterns in the EU', *Journal of European Public Policy*, 11 (2004): 185–208.

 **online resource centre**

Visit the Online Resource Centre that accompanies this book for links to more information on European Union policy-making processes.

CHAPTER 25

Agriculture

CHAPTER OVERVIEW

The common agricultural policy (CAP) has been at the centre of controversy throughout its history. Developed to ensure security of food supplies in the Community, the CAP has proved highly expensive, with overproduction by farmers keen to maximize subsidies. Despite widespread criticism, the CAP has proved notoriously difficult to reform. Farmers' groups have fiercely resisted change and their importance in the domestic politics of key member states has ensured that reform has been slow and piecemeal. Only in the context of external pressures in the 1990s was significant change secured. Yet the CAP still claims a major proportion of the EU budget and pressure for further reforms continues.

> **simply by its persistence the CAP constitutes a continuing source of tension on all levels of governance, internationally, supranationally, nationally, and regionally**
>
> **(Rieger 2005: 188)**

The common agricultural policy (CAP) was the first redistributive policy of the EC, and for many years the only one. The success of agriculture sustained the hopes of the advocates of integration during the 1960s, when it was seen as the start of a process that would lead to other common policies; but the other common policies did not appear. As a result, agriculture dominated payments from the common budget. This became one of the bases for the protracted dispute over British net contributions to the budget in the 1970s and early 1980s.

The main features of the CAP, as it operated before reform in the 1980s, are summarized in Insight 25.1. Every year the national Ministers of Agriculture decided the level of prices for agricultural products that were covered by the CAP. These prices were ensured by the intervention of the Commission in the market to buy up enough of each product to maintain the agreed price. If prices subsequently rose above the agreed level, the produce that the Commission had purchased and placed into storage would be released onto the market to bring the price back down; but in practice this did not occur.

Prices tended to be set at the level that would ensure the least efficient farmers in the EC an adequate income. However, this was also a level that encouraged the more efficient, large-scale farmers to maximize their output, because the price was more than adequate to guarantee them a return on their investment. Thus surpluses in most products

---

INSIGHT 25.1

The Price-Support System of the CAP

The system of price support for different commodities uses slightly different terminology, but the basic principles are the same.

The Target Price is the wholesale price that Ministers of Agriculture agree on every year, commodity by commodity. This is the price that the EU is aiming to see prevail in the market. It is supported by import levies, export subsidies, and intervention buying.

The Market Price is the price level that prevails within the EU without intervention by the authorities. If the market price falls too far below the target price, the authorities will intervene to buy up produce so as to raise the price; if it rises too far above the target, the authorities will intervene to release stored produce onto the market to depress the price.

The Intervention Price is the level at which the EU will start to buy up produce on the open market in order to prevent the market price from falling below the target price. It is set at a level a little below the target price. All produce that is offered for sale at this price will be purchased.

The Threshold Price is the price of imports from outside of the EU below which levies will be charged. It is set below the target price by an amount that takes account of transport and handling costs.

became permanent. The Commission's interventions in the market were all in one direction: to keep up prices by intervention buying. The amounts of produce in storage constantly grew and became an embarrassment, prompting press reports of 'food mountains' and 'wine lakes'. The cost of storage in itself became a significant burden on the Community budget, so attempts were made to reduce stocks by subsidizing exports. This, though, incurred the anger of the United States, which saw the subsidies as a threat to its own agricultural exports.

These problems stemmed from the failure of agricultural policy itself to develop. What was commonly known as the CAP was in effect only one part of a common agricultural policy: it was a policy on agricultural price support. Sicco Mansholt, the Commissioner in charge of agriculture during Hallstein's presidency, saw a clear line of spillover from price support to the restructuring of European agriculture to create fewer, larger, more efficient farms. This would have allowed guaranteed prices to be reduced. At the request of the Council of Ministers, Mansholt introduced proposals for such a restructuring in the late 1960s. However, in the end there was no agreement on a Community approach that would have placed responsibility in the hands of the Commission, nor was there progress on restructuring by national governments. Despite repeated attempts, no effective reform was achieved until the 1990s.

This chapter, then, addresses the following questions:

- What was peculiar about agriculture that it was possible to agree a common policy in this sector?
- Why was the price-support system chosen as the basis of the CAP?
- Why did restructuring of the farming sector not follow agreement on price support?
- Why did reform of the CAP prove so difficult?
- Why did reform eventually succeed in the 1990s?
- How have these reforms changed the CAP?

The Peculiarities of Agriculture

The most obvious difference between agriculture and other sectors where integration could occur is the extent of the commitment to a common policy actually written into the Treaty of Rome. Agriculture was one of only four common policies that had its own Title in the Treaty. (The others were the free movement of goods; the free movement of persons, services, and capital; and transport.)

The privileged position afforded to the sector reflects other peculiarities of agriculture, particularly the importance that French governments of the Fourth Republic attached to it. For them, agriculture was both politically and economically important. Politically, there was constant electoral pressure on all the parties of the centre-right from small farmers who were inefficient producers but were determined to retain their independence. This, in effect, meant that the farmers had to be subsidized by the state through the national price-support system. Economically, France also had an efficient agricultural sector, and produced a considerable food surplus.

Part of the price that the French insisted on for their participation in the common market in industrial goods was the subsidization of the cost of maintaining their small farmers, and the guarantee of a protected market for French agricultural exports. France was assisted in placing agriculture at the head of the list of possible common policies by the agreement of all the other participants that agriculture was different from other economic sectors. All the member states, including West Germany, had national support policies for agriculture, and it was generally accepted that the social and environmental implications of allowing a completely free market in agricultural products would be unacceptable.

Had the EC simply abolished restrictions on free trade in foodstuffs, the effect would have been to produce a competition between member states to see which government would be prepared to give the highest level of support to its farmers. So free trade was not viable. Yet it was also recognized that the equalization of food prices was an important factor in ensuring fair competition in industrial products, because of the effect of food prices on wages. Higher food prices meant that workers demanded higher wages, thus raising industrial production costs. The argument was that to have a level playing field of competition between different national industrial producers, cost differences arising from the effect of food prices needed to be limited. The same reasoning could be applied to other elements in industrial production costs, such as tax levels or energy costs. The difference in the case of food was that West Germany, which had low tax rates because of low social security benefits and low energy costs because of efficient production plant, had high food costs because of the political influence of its farmers. Thus the equalization of costs was more acceptable to West Germany where food was concerned than where other costs were concerned. This created something near to unanimity within the Community of six.

The existence of high food prices in West Germany was indicative of the problems that the CDU/CSU governments had in reconciling their commitment to economic modernization with their conservative political image. The same difficulty faced the Gaullist governments of the Fifth Republic in France. On the one hand, their commitment to modernization meant that they wished to keep down labour costs and to see the movement of workers from agriculture to industrial employment. This was essential if industrial expansion was to be maintained during the long post-war boom. On the other hand, these parties depended on votes from the agricultural population to keep them ahead of the parties of the left in electoral terms. As such, they were under pressure to maintain farm incomes, although the cost would be a burden on industry, and they were reluctant to see too rapid a reduction in the rural population lest their electoral position be undermined. Hence there was the basis for a Franco–German agreement on agriculture: the French would get their subsidy to maintain a significant rural population and the Germans would get the equalization of food prices throughout the common market.

West Germany was less happy on the issue of agricultural protection against the rest of the world. West German industry felt that its exports to countries such as Argentina would be adversely affected if West Germany stopped importing foodstuffs from them in order to give preference to EC produce. There was also the influence on the West German government of the United States, which was very unhappy about the idea of any restriction on trade in agriculture.

However, another peculiarity of agriculture in the policies of the EC was relevant here: it was the only issue on which the French government was on the same side as the Dutch government. As a major agricultural producer itself, The Netherlands also wished to gain guaranteed access to the West German market. This unity of ambition meant that France and The Netherlands were in alliance against West Germany, whereas on almost every other question that arose during de Gaulle's presidency, the Dutch government opposed what it saw as France's attempt to dominate the smaller states. This was an important factor in overcoming West German resistance, because The Netherlands was normally closely allied to the German position. In addition, Adenauer did not wish West Germany to appear to be throwing its weight around where small states were concerned: there was a reputation to be lived down.

The Price-Support System

The detail of the agricultural policy was not included in the Treaty of Rome. In negotiations that took place in Stresa, Italy in July 1958 it was agreed that the CAP would be based on a system of common prices (see above, Insight 25.1, p. 379). It was this system that eventually became the cause of the high cost of the CAP, and of the high price of food. As such, the system came in for sustained criticism, especially in Britain, where the high cost of food under the CAP was an important issue in the debate on entry.

For many British consumers it was impossible to understand why the original six Community member states ever set up such a patently irrational system of farm support, and why they were so reluctant to see it changed. For most people in Britain it was obvious that the old British system of deficiency payments to farmers, to compensate them for loss of income due to low prices, was much more sensible. It meant lower food prices for the consumer, and it allowed the government to bring pressure on individual farmers to improve their efficiency.

The first point that British critics of the CAP price-support system overlooked was that French peasant farmers rejected any suggestion of a system that would allow the government to put pressure on them to do anything other than they wished. In fact, any system involving a direct and obvious subsidy from the government would have upset the peasant spirit of independence. There were, then, good political reasons for choosing a price-support system and these were strengthened by administrative considerations. It is much more difficult to operate a system of direct deficiency payments where there are large numbers of small farmers concerned.

It was not so much the price-support system in itself that was irrational, but the level at which prices were set in a context of mixed farming sizes. The original price level that was set for cereals, in 1964, was not particularly high. This was because the French cereal producers were mostly large scale and efficient, so there was no reason for the French government to hold out for a price that would raise the cost of living and put pressure on industrial wages. But the reaction in West Germany to a cereals-price level that was below the prevailing national price was instructive as a guide to why later price agreements were consistently high.

The West German farmers were uniformly small-scale, high-cost producers. They opposed the whole idea of the CAP, fearing that it would reduce their incomes, and they vehemently opposed the low level of cereal prices as a vindication of their worst fears. But on this occasion a combination of industrial pressure in favour of lower food prices and the personal commitment of Adenauer to the process of integration overruled them. In fact, in the early 1960s de Gaulle exerted considerable influence over Adenauer and made German agreement to the cereal-price settlement a test of their friendship. The corollary of Adenauer's support on cereal prices was de Gaulle's continued support for Adenauer's hard line towards Eastern Europe. The consequence of Adenauer's adherence to this deal was a further undermining of his position within the CDU, and the political enmity of the FDP, which was determined to pose as the protector of the farmers. Adenauer's removal from the Chancellorship in October 1963 was thus made more certain, and it in turn put Ludwig Erhard in the hot seat. His defence of the agreement helped to strain his relations with the FDP. At the same time the neo-Nazi National Democratic Party (NPD) was formed, and was to enjoy some success among disillusioned rural CDU supporters.

Under the pressure of these political developments, the West German government held out for a higher level of prices for the beef and dairy sectors. These they obtained because in those sectors the French, who had small producers of their own, were more interested in a generous support level than in reducing food costs. But at this stage in the story it was the West Germans who were most concerned about setting higher price levels because of the need of the CDU/CSU to retain the farm vote in the face of the threat from the NPD and the challenge from the FDP. The influence of the FDP continued to be exerted on the side of high price settlements after the arrival of the SPD/FDP coalition in office in 1969.

Although the French are often blamed for high support prices, successive German governments have often been supporters of high prices for domestic political reasons. This is not to argue that the French had no responsibility for the high prices. In the early years of the CAP they were perhaps less responsible than were the Germans, partly because in the 1960s the rapid growth of the French economy meant that policies fostering a movement off the land were favoured rather than those aimed at maintaining a rural population. But after 1973 the slow growth of the economy shifted this emphasis in French policy quite markedly. There was more need to maintain a rural population for social reasons, because there were not enough jobs available for the existing non-agricultural work force. High support prices therefore became more important to the French government.

The change in economic circumstances is a factor often overlooked by critics of the price-support system. At the time that it was set up it was predictable that political pressures would tend to push price levels upwards, but that situation was not expected to persist. It was a period of rapid change in agriculture, with a fast rate of depletion of the rural population. In the 1960s, the problem seemed to be how quickly the last remaining areas of agricultural inefficiency could be eliminated in order to free more labour for industry, which was beginning to suffer from labour shortages in all parts of the EC. It seemed that the elimination of the smallest farms would soon reduce the pressure for high support prices, which would allow the system to function without placing too great a burden on the Community budget.

In the meantime Commissioner Mansholt saw the burden that high prices would place on the budget as an incentive for the member states to press forward to the next stage of the agricultural policy, the restructuring of European agriculture. This had been an agreed priority of the Stresa Conference of July 1958. It was reasonable to assume that it would be handled as a Community policy rather than through national policies, because in that way governments could maintain a certain distance from measures that might be electorally dangerous. By the late 1960s the cost of the price-support system was already causing concern, and the Council asked the Commission to examine the problem in October 1967.

Restructuring Agriculture: The Mansholt Plan

The Council's request that the Commission examine the price support system came in the year that West German GDP actually fell by 2 per cent. The issue was pressed by the CDU/SPD coalition at a time when budget problems and the problems of industry were understandably dominant concerns. It came also at a time when the French government was itself thinking along the same lines. In 1968 the Vedel Plan for the reform of French agriculture appeared, which showed that labour supply for industrial expansion was taking precedence over the maintenance of a rural population in the thinking of the government. Rising inflation increased for all member states the incentive for a reduction in farm prices. The signs for agricultural restructuring were favourable.

In December 1968 the Commission produced a memorandum entitled 'Agriculture 1980', which came to be known as 'the Mansholt Plan' (European Commission 1969). It proposed a restructuring of agriculture, based upon encouraging small farmers to leave the land and giving financial support to the amalgamation of holdings. The 'carrot' of incentives would include grants, pensions to farmers over fifty-five, and assistance to younger farmers in finding new jobs. The other side of the scheme was the 'stick': a proposal that price levels be cut so that inefficient farmers would be forced off the land. This last proposal was considered by the Community's farming pressure group, COPA, to be a 'psychological blunder' (Rosenthal 1975: 88). It certainly guaranteed the hostility of the French and West German farmers.

In France the larger farmers took the lead in organizing opposition to the plan, arguing that it would mean the death of the family farm. Their concern with the family farm may have been sentimental, but it is also clear that they did not like the prospect of the removal of their high profits once the small farmer disappeared. 'Save the family farm' was a better campaign slogan than 'Save our excess profits'.

Yet despite the outcry, the reaction of the French government was not too hostile to the plan. As was explained above, the Vedel Plan for French agriculture appeared in the same year as the Mansholt Plan. The Gaullists gained a large majority in the 1968 elections to the National Assembly, which were held in the aftermath of the strikes and riots of May, and were in a strong position to go ahead with their rationalization proposals. So the French government's reaction to the Mansholt Plan was moderate, but emphasized the need for the implementation of the plan to be in the hands of national governments and not of the Commission. This was in line with de Gaulle's general approach to Community policies. Had the position of the government been less secure, the French might not have insisted on national control: they might have preferred to hide from political unpopularity behind the Commission. Circumstances, though, made it more important for de Gaulle that the nationalist principles of Gaullism be observed.

The main opposition to the Mansholt Plan came from West Germany. This was for a combination of reasons. First, the reaction of the German farmers was very much the same as that of the French farmers, but their influence was enhanced because there was a Federal election due in 1969. Neither of the parties in the Grand Coalition wished to argue too strongly for Community proposals that upset the farmers: the CDU/CSU feared that their position might be damaged by a loss of votes to the NPD; the SPD was hoping to conclude a coalition agreement with the FDP. Second, the government parties collectively were worried about the potential cost of the proposals. They foresaw a considerable short-term burden on the Federal budget, since West Germany would be bound to provide the largest share of the funding. The government therefore announced that it was unhappy with the Plan and would prefer to see the problem of surpluses tackled by a system of quotas on the amounts that would be bought into intervention.

When Mansholt produced his revised plan ('mini-Mansholt') in 1969 (European Commission, 1970) he rejected the West German suggestion, arguing that it would be a cumbersome bureaucratic system which would have to be permanent, whereas his restructuring scheme was a long-term solution to the problem. But the political doubts slowed down progress on the plan, and it was overtaken during 1969 by changes of government in France and West Germany, and by the Hague summit at the EC level. The exchange-rate crises of 1969 (see Insight 10.1, Ch. 10, p. 138) put economic and monetary union higher on the agenda than agricultural reform, and once enlargement was accepted in principle it constituted another reason for delay on the CAP. This was because the applicant states, particularly Ireland and Denmark, would find it difficult to negotiate terms of entry if there was uncertainty about agriculture, which was of central importance to them.

The one applicant likely to favour the Mansholt Plan was Britain, and Mansholt attempted to gain advantage from this by visiting the country in late June 1969. He met agricultural interest groups, gave a press conference, and recorded a BBC interview. His message was that unless his proposals were implemented, the Community market for some products, particularly butter, would simply collapse. He also warned the British people that without reform of the CAP they would find themselves paying high food prices and making high contributions to the Community budget to finance the intervention buying. He was right, of course, but his message did not prompt the British government to make reform of the CAP a condition of entry. Edward Heath, the British Prime Minister, was too eager to conclude negotiations to want to introduce new difficulties. All that Mansholt succeeded in doing was infuriating the French government, which saw his intervention as an attempt to interfere with the decision-making process within the Council of Ministers.

When the Council of Agricultural Ministers eventually met to discuss the plan, in March 1971, it was accompanied to Brussels by 80,000 demonstrating farmers. The farmers hung Mansholt in effigy, burned cars, tore up street signs, broke windows, killed one policeman, and injured 140 more of the 3,000 deployed to restrain them (Rosenthal 1975: 92). Their anger had been increased by low price rises in 1970, which had resulted in a drop in their incomes, yet had not solved the problem of the surpluses. But the presence of the farmers in the streets probably did not have a great influence on the outcome of the meeting. The French were angry with Mansholt for his attempt to ally Britain to his cause, and were determined to get the issue settled before Britain became a member, in case the Mansholt intervention had worked. They were also determined to get it settled in a way that would leave responsibility for the implementation of restructuring in the hands of national governments. The West German government was equally determined to keep the cost of the restructuring exercise as low as possible, and, under the SPD/FDP coalition, was not prepared to commit the country to measures that would anger its farmers too much.

The modified version of the plan that the Council of Ministers finally accepted did not significantly increase the amount to be spent on restructuring over what was already available through the Guidance section of the CAP. It also left the member states full discretion for the implementation of the restructuring. Although Mansholt welcomed the agreement as 'the beginning of a vast process of reform' (*The Times*, 26 March 1971), he was putting a brave face on what was obviously a personal defeat. He retired the following year.

The vast programme of reform never even got started. In 1972–3 a combination of bad weather, poor harvests, and an increase in world demand led to big price rises on international markets, so that world prices actually exceeded EC prices. This removed the immediate pressure for reform. Then in 1973 the OPEC oil-price rises sparked off the world recession that led to high unemployment, and meant that all governments had an incentive not to force labour off the land. A combination of national political and economic considerations and international economic developments therefore led to the complete failure of the attempt to extend the CAP beyond the level of guaranteed prices.

Agriculture in the 1970s

The economic recession of the 1970s led to resistance to the introduction of restructuring measures from those governments that had considerable agricultural populations. There was also a tendency for price settlements to remain high because of the political influence of farmers, which was everywhere considerable. Even the British government, despite loud protestations about the cost of the CAP, connived in allowing high price settlements through the Council of Agricultural Ministers. At the same time, the high prices acted as a burden on the Community budget, and put a particular burden on the national budgets of West Germany and Britain, the two largest net contributors to the Community budget.

West Germany here, as in other areas, faced a dilemma. On the one hand its belief in balanced budgets and sound finance meant that the West German government wished to reduce its budgetary commitments to the minimum. This was especially so at a time when the recession meant that the Federal government was receiving less in tax revenue, and was having to disburse more in social security payments. On the other hand, the electoral salience of the farm vote remained high, especially for the FDP. When Helmut Schmidt took over as Chancellor in 1974 it looked for a time as though he was determined to resolve the dilemma in favour of budgetary restraint. In September 1974 he vetoed the farm-price settlement that had been accepted by Josef Ertl, the FDP Minister of Agriculture. It was a move that shocked the rest of the EC, though not nearly so much as it shocked Ertl and the FDP. The consequent strain on coalition relationships led to the veto being revoked, and though Schmidt continued to speak out in favour of reform of the CAP, West Germany did not seek to take the lead in forcing the issue.

Britain eventually provided that lead. The British problem with the CAP was that as a net importer of food, and an efficient producer with a small farming sector, it ended up contributing more to the EC budget than it should have on the basis of its relative prosperity within the Community. The domination of the budget by the CAP distorted the pattern of disbursements, giving Britain the greatest incentive to press for change. Yet the 1974–9 Labour governments made no real effort to bring about change. John Silkin, the Secretary of State for Agriculture for much of this period, adopted a tough image in his dealings with the EC, presumably for domestic political purposes. But he repeatedly acquiesced in high price settlements, claiming victory if he could offset the effect on British prices by obtaining special subsidies on butter or by manipulating the artificial 'green' rate of exchange that was used for calculating agricultural prices in national currencies (see below, Insight 25.2, p. 388). The government as a whole seemed to prefer to engage in bruising public fights for annual rebates on Britain's budgetary contributions rather than going for fundamental reform.

The difficulty for the Labour government may have been that it could see little prospect of gaining agreement to the modification of the CAP from the other members of the EC. France was opposed to any fundamental changes: and the fact that it was Britain, a late-comer to the club and an uncooperative member on almost every other issue, that was leading the challenge, led to a closing of ranks by the original members. This was where an unambiguous West German commitment to reform would have been useful, but it was not forthcoming.

Of the other new members, neither Ireland nor Denmark wished to see the CAP dismantled because they too were big beneficiaries. The only other alternative solution to the problem was a considerable expansion of the budget to accommodate other common policy funds from which Britain would benefit, so that British payments would increase but so would British receipts, leaving it a net beneficiary. But this line of approach was ruled out for the Labour government because of the hostility of so much of the Labour Party to any increase in integration, which was seen as a further loss of sovereignty.

The Conservative government that succeeded Labour in 1979 followed a very similar line. For it, the blockage to a permanent settlement that would involve a larger Community budget was formed more by economic doctrine than by nationalism. Prime Minister Margaret Thatcher's approach was opposed to increased governmental

388

Green Currencies and Monetary Compensatory Amounts

A Green Currency was an artificial rate of exchange between a national currency and the European unit of account (EUA) used to calculate agricultural prices, which were set in EUA but had to be applied in national currencies. They originated at the end of the 1960s, and disappeared in January 1999 with the start of the single currency.

When, in August 1969, the French franc was devalued, the French government declared that it would like to phase in the effect of the devaluation on agricultural prices so as to alleviate the inflationary effects. Had the full devaluation been applied to agricultural prices they would have increased sharply because the Community support-price levels were calculated in EUA. This was a fictional currency based on the average value of the member states' national currencies, so the devaluation would have meant that the same price expressed in EUA would have translated into a higher price expressed in francs. To accommodate the French government, the Council of Ministers agreed that for a limited period the agricultural prices would be calculated as though the franc had not been devalued. The CAP would operate on the basis of a fictional 'green' franc for the purpose of calculating national agricultural price levels. The intention was that the green franc would be devalued in stages until it eventually came into line with the real franc's international value.

Almost immediately a problem arose. The green-currency arrangement meant that it became more profitable for French agricultural produce to be sold in Community markets outside France than in France itself. This was because the EUA price could be obtained in another national currency, which could then be converted into francs at the normal rate of exchange, so yielding more francs than if the produce had been sold in France at the artificially low translation of the EUA price. As speculators began to buy up agricultural produce throughout France, the Community moved more swiftly than usual to correct the price imbalance by inventing Monetary Compensatory Amounts (MCAs).

An MCA is either a levy or a refund that is paid to an exporter or importer at the border between two states. In the French case, a levy or tax was charged on all agricultural produce leaving France to bring its price up to the difference between the rates of exchange of the green franc and the real franc. All importers were paid a subsidy of the same amount to compensate them for the lower price that they would receive in France.

There is little doubt that the French government did see these measures as purely temporary and exceptional. As a net exporter of food to the rest of the EC, France had no interest in seeing such obstacles to free trade become a permanent feature. But in October the green-rate system was extended to the Deutschmark. The upwards revaluation of the Deutschmark should have led to a drop in farm incomes in West Germany. The effect of a revaluation was to lower food prices in the revaluing state, for precisely the opposite reasons to those that increased prices in devaluing states: the rate of exchange against the EUA was changed, so that the same price translated into Deutschmarks came out at a lower price on the West German market. Lower prices would mean lower farm incomes. This was politically unacceptable to the FDP, which had just re-entered government in coalition with the SPD. So, for far less worthy reasons than the French, the West German government requested that the currency revaluation should not be reflected in agricultural prices, and a green mark was created.

expenditure either at the national or the Community level, and she adhered to that position even where its relaxation would have benefited the British Treasury.

The failure to reform the CAP led to ever-larger surpluses being kept in storage, and the cost of storage itself added to the budgetary burden. In an attempt to address at least this part of the cost, a decision was made in the course of the 1970s to encourage the export of the surpluses instead of storing them. As world market prices for all products covered by the CAP were consistently lower than the guaranteed internal prices, it was necessary for the EC to pay farmers the difference between the price they received for the exports and the guaranteed price. Such export subsidies technically constitute what is known as the 'dumping' of products on world markets. It had the adverse effect of lowering world prices by adding to supply; but it also encouraged other agricultural producers to subsidize their own farmers so that they could compete with the EC farmers. This move from storage to export of surpluses was eventually to produce irresistible external pressure for reform of the CAP, although these pressures did not hit home until the 1980s. In the meantime, the main pressures that the CAP generated were internal.

The tensions set up by a single common policy standing alone provided vindication of the neofunctionalist idea of functional spillover pressures (Chapter 1, pp. 10–11). But there was no spillover into other policy areas, only an uneasy and unstable condition of immobility. Political spillover pressure was not succeeding, though the interest groups in the agricultural sector were acting as effective gatekeepers, barring the way to a retreat from the level of integration already achieved. Governments were trying to avoid the implications of their position, but the strains were threatening to break something, possibly even the EC itself. In only one direction had the governments been able successfully to fudge the issue of spillover, and that was in the direction of monetary union, one of the ways in which it had been expected by the Commission that spillover from agriculture would occur.

The Commission believed that the CAP would act as an incentive for the EC to move rapidly towards economic and monetary union, as stable exchange rates between national currencies were essential to the system of common agricultural prices. In fact, when exchange-rate instability hit the EC in 1969 it was not allowed to destroy the CAP, but the defence was not to move to monetary union either. Instead a complex arrangement of green currencies and monetary compensatory amounts (MCAs) was introduced (Insight 25.2).

In the international monetary chaos that followed the ending of the convertibility of the dollar in 1971, frequent changes in the relative values of Community currencies were prevented from destroying the CAP only by allowing six green currencies to grow. In this way, the linkage between the CAP and monetary policy, which the Barre Report on economic and monetary union had made the centrepiece of its argument in 1969, was avoided. However, this was only at the expense of destroying one of the main justifications for the CAP, the argument that food prices should be the same in all member states so as to equalize the pressure on wage rates.

Agriculture in the 1980s

In the course of the early 1980s the pressures built up for reform of the CAP. The main sources of pressure were its escalating cost, increasing concern about its environmental effects, spillover from the single-market programme, and external pressures. Together these did produce some reforms in 1984 and 1988. In 1984 a system of quotas for dairy products was agreed. In 1988 agreement was reached on a complex package that put a legal limit on agricultural price support for 1988 and fixed future increases above that level at an annual maximum of 74 per cent of the increase in Community GDP. If this limit were breached there would be automatic price cuts for the relevant products in subsequent years until the ceilings ceased to be breached. Also money was made available to encourage farmers to set aside arable land and to let it lie fallow (Butler 1993: 116–17).

The Cost of the CAP

Between 1974 and 1979 the cost of the CAP rose by 23 per cent, twice the rate of increase of incomes. It then stabilized between 1980 and 1982 because the exceptionally high value of the dollar in 1981–2 brought higher world food prices and reduced the cost of export subsidies and the need for intervention buying. In 1983, as the value of the dollar declined, the cost of the CAP soared by 30 per cent. Even with the true cost of the CAP obscured by the high dollar, the EC reached the ceiling of expenditure that could be covered from its own resources. Agreement to lift the limit had to be unanimous, and the British government would not agree to any increase without firm measures to curb the cost of the CAP. This led to the 1984 agreement on dairy quotas, and on a system of budgetary discipline whereby a maximum limit would be set to the size of the budget each year before the annual round of negotiations on agricultural prices. Ministers of Agriculture would therefore be negotiating within fixed parameters. Any budgetary overshoot would be clawed back in the following years.

In the event, this system did not work because there was no automatic mechanism for making the necessary adjustments to costs in the years following an overrun. Between 1985 and 1987 the cost of the CAP increased by 18 per cent per annum. Dairy products remained largely under control thanks to the system of quotas set in 1984; but cereals were the new cause of difficulty, due to increased yields that resulted from technological advances and a consequent decline in world prices that increased export subsidies.

Although the EC did not appear to face the immediate exhaustion of its financial resources as it had in 1984, there was an estimated budgetary shortfall of 4 to 5 million European currency units (ecus) in 1987. This was covered by creative accountancy that simply pushed the problem forward in time. By this time, also, Spain and Portugal had joined the EC, bringing new demands on the budget that could only be met by either diverting money away from existing beneficiaries or expanding the size of the budget. This situation was compounded by the insistence of the Spanish, Portuguese, and Greek governments that they would not be able to participate in the freeing of the internal market of the EC by the end of 1992 unless the structural funds were substantially increased. At the London meeting of the European Council in December 1986 agreement was reached in principle on the doubling of the structural funds by 1993 (see Ch. 28, p. 465), thus requiring an increase in the resources of the EC.

Environmental Pressures

Environmental pressures were less pressing than financial pressures, but in the 1980s there was growing concern about the environment in general, and about the effect of the CAP in particular. The main beneficiaries of the CAP were large farmers who responded to the high prices by maximizing output. To do this they pumped more and more fertilizer into the land, and hormones into animals, to improve yields. The rise of environmentalism provided a counter-weight to the general sympathy of European public opinion for farmers, and made it politically easier for governments to respond to the financial pressures with reform measures.

Spillover from the Single-Market Programme

The 1992 programme to free the internal market did not directly involve agriculture, but the fact that the CAP had not achieved one of its original objectives, that of equalizing food prices, did act as a barrier to a genuine level playing-field of competition. Also, the existence of 'green' exchange rates and MCAs did offer a barrier to the removal of internal frontiers, which was one of the ultimate objectives of the single market for most member states (Warley 1992: 121).

External Pressures

External pressures proved the most formidable incentive for change in the CAP. The United States made the phasing out of agricultural subsidies a central part of its negotiating position for the Uruguay Round of GATT talks, which began in 1986. It was joined by the Cairns Group of fourteen agricultural-producing states, including Australia, Canada, New Zealand, and several Latin American states. All felt that they suffered from the dumping of the EC's agricultural exports onto world markets, which drove down prices and prevented them selling some of their own production.

These pressures led to the reforms described at the start of this section. But those reforms were ineffective in restraining the growing cost of the CAP. They were both too modest in their aims, and lacked effective enforcement mechanisms. This reflected two aspects of the reforms. First, that they were drawn up by an EC agricultural policy community that consisted of the Agriculture Directorate-General (DGVI) of the Commission, the European Agriculture Commissioner, and the representatives of farmers in COPA. These groups had developed close working relationships, and were unlikely to produce proposals that would seriously damage the interests of farmers, or reduce the importance of agriculture as an EC policy sector. Second, the proposals had to be agreed by the Council of Agriculture Ministers, most of whom were strongly influenced by national farmers' representatives.

These circumstances operated most strongly for the 1984 reforms. By the time of the 1988 reforms, according to Moyer and Josling (1990: 86–7), the coalition against change had been weakened by the formation within the Commission of an inner circle. This inner circle consisted of the president, Jacques Delors, the Agriculture Commissioner between 1985 and 1989, Frans Andriessen, and the Budget Commissioner, Hening Christophersen. Delors's reason for supporting reform was the damage that failure to achieve it might do to the single-market programme. 'Delors had made the single European market something of a personal crusade and could not easily see this goal frustrated by agricultural stalemate.' (Moyer and Josling 1990: 86) Under pressure from the Commission, which was prepared to take the Council of Ministers to the European Court of Justice if it did not agree a budget for 1988, a system of price stabilizers for agricultural produce was accepted in February 1988. That did not resolve the problems, though, and further reform was planned within the Commission during 1990.

Agriculture in the 1990s and Beyond

In the 1990s the external pressures for reform of the CAP finally forced effective action to be taken. Initially this was in the context of the Uruguay Round of GATT negotiations. Subsequently the pressure for reform was maintained by the need to prepare for the eastward enlargement of the EU.

The MacSharry Reforms

In May 1992 the EC member states reached an agreement to cut guaranteed prices for cereals by 29 per cent over three years, together with smaller but still significant reductions for other surplus products. The price reductions were accompanied by a rural development dimension that encouraged set-aside, early retirement, reforestation, and the adoption of more organic forms of farming (Ross, 1995: 200).

These reforms were the result of the same combination of internal and external pressures that had produced the 1988 reforms, but the real change had come from an intensification of the external pressures (Insight 25.3). Delors and the new commissioner for agriculture, Ray MacSharry, saw particularly the linkage between reform of the CAP and the GATT negotiations as a useful way of pressing the necessity for reform on the member states. 'The threat of trade war inherent in the GATT negotiations could lessen internal opposition to CAP reform while the gestation of CAP reform might give the United States pause before pushing too hard on trade' (Ross 1995: 141). However, as Grant (1997: 77) explains, there was also frequent denial of the linkage because any suggestion that the reforms were being forced on the EU from the outside would have stiffened the resistance of the Ministers of Agriculture.

Commissioner MacSharry introduced his reform proposals in July 1991, and they were agreed with some modifications, and side-payments to sweeten the pill, in a very rapid ten months, by May 1992. Although known as the 'MacSharry reforms', they nevertheless bore the imprint also of President Delors and his *cabinet*. The package

INSIGHT 25.3

External Pressures for CAP Reform in the 1990s

- Budget pressures again became significant as the USA allowed the value of the dollar to decline and reintroduced agricultural export subsidies of its own. This forced down world prices, and so increased the cost of export subsidies.

- The reunification of Germany brought into immediate membership of the EC considerable grain-producing areas, as well as extra dairy and beef livestock, adding to the problems of overproduction.

- The need to stabilize democracy and capitalism in the states of Central and Eastern Europe demanded that the West buy exports from them to allow them to obtain the hard currency necessary to buy from the West to re-equip their industries. These countries had few products in which they had any comparative advantage. Agricultural products were among the few. If the CAP had not prevented it, several of the states could have exported their agricultural goods to the EC.

- By 1992 the Uruguay Round of the GATT had reached a critical stage. In previous rounds of the GATT, agriculture had been raised as an issue, but had always been eventually left on one side because the participants did not want the overall package to collapse. This time the fate of farmers was so serious that both the USA and the Cairns Group appeared to be prepared to collapse the deal unless it were included. Eventually in 1992, with the original deadlines for agreement already well past, the Cairns Group agreed to allow the United States to negotiate directly with the EC on agriculture.

involved a sharp decrease in the prices for cereals and beef, to bring them more into line with world prices, linked to a move from supporting farmers through subsidies on production to direct support for rural incomes. More land was to be taken out of production altogether, with the farmers being compensated by direct payments; an early retirement scheme was introduced to encourage older farmers to cease production; and more environmentally friendly farming was encouraged, with the implication that this would lower yields.

Sceptics claimed that the reforms would not solve the problem, and in the short term would even increase the cost of the CAP. However, at the end of November 1993 MacSharry's successor, René Steichen, claimed that cereal production for 1993 was 16 million tons lower than it would have been without the reforms (*The Week in Europe*, 2 December 1993). More significantly, the reforms accepted for the first time that support for farmers could be separated from production. Surprisingly, in his farewell speech to the European Parliament in January 1995, Delors said that getting this agreement on reform of the CAP was in his own view his greatest achievement.

The Uruguay Round: The Blair House Agreements

Acceptance of his reform package allowed MacSharry to turn his attention to negotiating with the United States in the context of the GATT talks. Agreement was reached in December 1992, but the implications caused widespread protests from French farmers, and the Socialist government, faced with elections before the end of the year, chose not to reinforce its unpopularity by implementing the agreement. However, the conservative government of Edouard Balladur, which was elected in March 1993, had little choice but to accept the agreement because of the implications for the French economy if the GATT round were not successful. France was the world's fourth largest exporter after the United States, Germany, and Japan; and it was the second largest exporter of services, with ten per cent of total world trade (*Independent*, 7 November 1993).

Even this proved not enough to satisfy the United States within the GATT negotiations, though. In November 1992 Delors reached the limit of his willingness to compromise. MacSharry had almost reached a deal in direct talks with the United States at the Blair House hotel in Chicago, when he received a telephone call from Delors telling him that the concessions he was proposing to make were not acceptable. They went beyond the limits of the CAP reform that had been agreed, and would not be acceptable to the member states. If MacSharry persisted with the deal, Delors would oppose it in the College of Commissioners.

MacSharry flew back to Brussels and took up the challenge from Delors by resigning as one of the Commission's negotiators for the GATT. Delors was outvoted in the College of Commissioners, MacSharry resumed his mandate and reached an agreement with the United States. Delors suffered a severe blow to his prestige, which contributed to undermining his future effectiveness.

Agenda 2000

The external pressure on the EU to continue the process of reform of the CAP became greater as the former communist states of East-Central Europe, outside of what had been the Soviet Union, began to press ever more strongly for full membership of the EU. After some initial reluctance, most member states came round to the realization that this would be necessary. Germany in particular became a strong advocate of eastern enlargement. However, reports prepared by the Commission indicated that the existing CAP could not simply be applied to the applicant states without dramatic consequences for the budget of the EU.

Extension of the Common Agricultural Policy in its present form to the acceding countries would create difficulties. Given existing price gaps between candidate countries and generally substantially higher CAP prices, and despite prospects for some narrowing of these gaps by the dates of accession, even gradual introduction of CAP prices would tend to stimulate surplus production, in particular in the livestock sector, thus adding to projected surpluses. World Trade Organization (WTO) constraints on subsidized exports would prevent the enlarged Union to sell its surpluses on third markets.

(quoted in Avery and Cameron 1998: 153)

However, the difficulties of negotiating the political obstacles to further reform of the CAP were clearly demonstrated in November 1995. At this stage, Germany joined France and the Mediterranean states in rejecting a proposal from the Commission that the permitted exports of agricultural produce from six Central European states (the Czech

Republic, Poland, Hungary, Slovakia, Bulgaria, and Romania) be increased by ten per cent per annum. Five per cent annual increase was all that these states were prepared to accept (*Financial Times*, 17 November 1995). Despite paying lip-service to the need to allow the eastern states into the EU, they were not prepared to risk the wrath of their own farmers to facilitate this.

Pressure also increased on the world-trade front. At the conclusion of the Uruguay Round of GATT it had been agreed to open a further round of trade talks at the end of 1999. It was clear that the compromises reached at Blair House were provisional, and that agriculture would be a central element of the new round. In June 1996 the British National Farmers' Union (NFU) produced a paper explaining why the EU would come under great pressure in these trade talks to reform the CAP further. At the end of the Uruguay Round, agreement had been reached to allow both the EU and the USA to continue to subsidize cereal and livestock farmers. These measures had, in the terminology of the agreement, been placed in a 'blue box'. This meant that the subsidies did distort production, but could be continued without legal challenge until 2003 provided that they were not increased. Another 'green box' was created, consisting of support for farmers that did not distort production. These included measures such as those that had already been introduced into the CAP by the MacSharry reforms: measures to take land out of production, or to encourage environmental protection. Since the agreement, the USA had unilaterally moved almost all of its support measures out of the blue box into the green box, leaving the EU alone in the blue box. Although the blue-box measures could be sustained until 2003, the EU would now be under tremendous pressure to reciprocate the unilateral US gesture (NFU 1996).

It was in this context that Frans Fischler, Agriculture Commissioner in the Santer Commission, produced a package of proposals for further reform in November 1995. These continued the pattern of the 1992 reforms, decoupling support for farmers from production and linking it to social and environmental objectives (European Commission, 1995). They were subsequently incorporated into the Commission document *Agenda 2000: For a Stronger and Wider Europe* (European Commission 1999*b*). This document 'consisted essentially of the Commission's recommendations for the Union's financial framework for the period 2000–6; the future development of the Union's policies, and in particular its two most important spending policies—the cohesion and structural funds, and the Common Agricultural Policy; and the strategy for enlargement of the Union.' (Avery and Cameron 1998: 101). On CAP it proposed large reductions in support prices and giving compensation to farmers in the form of direct payments, with a ceiling on the level of aid that any one individual could receive. Although explicitly linked to the eastern enlargement in *Agenda 2000*, these reforms were in line with shifting support from the GATT 'blue box' to the 'green box'.

When negotiations began on the CAP proposals of *Agenda 2000* in February 1999, the French government predictably pressed for more limited reform. This position was supported by 30,000 farmers—mainly from France, Germany, and Belgium—protesting on the streets of Brussels, the biggest demonstration since those against the Mansholt reforms in 1971. After a temporary suspension of the negotiations, the Agriculture Ministers agreed on 11 March to cut cereal prices by 20 per cent, as proposed by the Commission, but to do so in two stages—a half in 2000–1 and the other half in 2001–2. They agreed to lower milk prices by 15 per cent in line with the Commission's proposals, but only over three years starting in 2003, and dairy production quotas were actually raised slightly. They also agreed that beef prices should be cut by 20 per cent, but this was only two-thirds of the cut proposed by the Commission.

Fischler hailed the agreement as the most far-reaching reform of the CAP for forty years; but the states that had most strongly supported reform—Britain, Italy, Sweden, and Denmark—expressed their disappointment. They did not like the delays in implementing the cuts that had been forced through by France and Germany (which held the Presidency of the Council). They were to be even more disappointed following the Berlin European Council that was intended to approve the reform.

In Berlin, President Chirac of France simply refused to accept what the French Minister of Agriculture had negotiated. This reflected the fact that Chirac was a conservative President who was forced to work with a Socialist government. He was blatantly playing domestic politics. However, so important was it to the German government to get an agreement during its presidency, and not to break publicly with France, that Chancellor Schröder eventually agreed to support a significant further dilution of the reform package. The dairy reforms were further delayed, and the cuts in cereal prices were scaled back from the compromise level reached by the Ministers of Agriculture. The other member states went along in return for side-payments: Spain and Greece got agreement to continuation of the Cohesion Fund (see Chapter 28, pp. 470–2); Britain got agreement to the continuation of the British budgetary rebate with only minor concessions.

The Agenda 2000 outcome was thus deeply compromised and must be judged a missed opportunity to reform the CAP.
(**Lowe** *et al.* 2002: 4)

But Commissioner Fischler did not give up. Helped by difficulties in the new Doha round of trade negotiations, which became bogged down at an early stage by disputes over agricultural subsidies, he put forward a revised proposal for the full decoupling of agricultural subsidies from production by the end of 2004. The amounts of money that each member state would receive would be the same as under the system that had been agreed at Berlin, but the money would be paid in a lump sum to the governments, which could then distribute between their farmers as they saw fit, so long as it was not paid in the form of a production subsidy. So, governments that did not wish to enter into a confrontation with their larger farmers, who received the bulk of the subsidies under the existing system, could simply pay the money out according to historic distributions; whereas those that were keen to bring about a domestic restructuring of agricultural holdings could divide the money up differently. In either case, the payment would be linked to requirements for farmers to comply with EU-wide standards on environmental protection, food safety, and animal welfare.

After almost a year of debate, the Council of Agriculture Ministers reached a compromise on 26 June 2003. The essence of the Commission's proposals was adopted, although the shift to direct payments was deferred until 2005, and individual member states could apply for exceptions until 2007 to continue to subsidize production where there was a risk of farmers withdrawing from production altogether.

The Effect of Reform

Although it had been a long and sometimes frustrating series of negotiations, the cumulative effect on the CAP of the reform process that started in 1992 was to bring about a considerable shift in the pattern of support for farmers away from price support to direct support. By 2002–3 direct payments, or 'compensatory payments', accounted for 65 per cent of CAP support, and the June 2003 agreement meant that by 2007 all support should be in this form. This, when combined with 'set aside' requirements, did have the effect of reducing the production surpluses that had plagued the system since it was set up, but it did nothing to redress the problem that the bulk of receipts from the CAP went to a small number of large farmers. In 2003 the OECD estimated that 70 per cent of CAP support still went to the richest 25 per cent of farms.

Large farmers had always benefited more than small farmers from the CAP because they were able to achieve larger yields. Thus, when payments were related to output, the larger and more efficient farmers pocketed the largest share. Direct payments were introduced under MacSharry to compensate farmers for the reduction in guaranteed prices towards world market prices. In order to minimize opposition to the changes, the direct payments were based on the size of farms. Farmers received payments linked to the number of hectares that they farmed. This reduced the incentive to maximize yields, which was the primary aim of the exercise. Production was further curtailed by making it a requirement of receiving the direct payments that 15 per cent of arable land be set aside and not used to produce crops. Similarly, meat producers were required to reduce the density of livestock per hectare in order to qualify for the direct payments. Agenda 2000 extended the same principle further. It did nothing, though, to redirect subsidies from rich farmers to poor farmers. This political hot potato was effectively dropped into the laps of national governments by the June 2003 agreement to move to a 'single farm payment' that governments could distribute between different categories of farms as they chose.

The decoupling of subsidies from production gained the EU some credit in the Doha round of trade negotiations, especially as the United States under the Bush Administration had moved in the opposite direction. The 2002 US Farm Trade Bill considerably increased subsidies to farmers, including direct production support. The situation that had prevailed between the US and the EU when the Uruguay Round was concluded appeared to have been reversed, with the EU more virtuous than the United States on agricultural subsidies.

As well as helping the EU to meet the requirements of the Uruguay Round of GATT, the shift to direct payments at first appeared to provide a solution to the problem of how to accommodate the very large farming sectors in the states of Central Europe that were negotiating for membership of the EU. Because the direct payments were 'compensatory payments' for income lost as a result of the reduction in the level of price support, the Commission argued before the opening of the accession negotiations that these payments should not be available to farmers in the new member states because they had never received the benefit of the previous high prices, and therefore could not expect to be compensated (Commission 1995). However, such was the strength of feeling in the applicant states on this issue, it was agreed that the direct payments would be paid eventually, but the Commission refused to shift from its opening proposal to pay only 25 per cent of aids to the new member states initially, with the rest being phased in over ten years.

CONCLUSION

Elements of neofunctionalism can be seen in history of the CAP. Setting up a system of support for agriculture that was based on fixing the prices of commodities, in a context of mixed farming sizes, inevitably caused problems. The price level that was needed to keep inefficient small farmers in business was so high that it encouraged more efficient farmers to increase output to the maximum level. When combined with technological advances, this led to the food surpluses that became one of the biggest headaches of the EC. This outcome was not an unanticipated consequence of the CAP, though. It was foreseen by the Commission, and Sicco Mansholt tried to use it as a lever to get member states to take the next step, of rationalizing farm sizes. So this was an example of cultivated spillover. However, it did not work because the governments of the member states retreated from radical reform in the face of domestic political pressures, thus providing some support for the intergovernmental critique of neofunctionalism.

Neofunctionalism predicted also that the creation of a single common policy would set up spillover pressures for the adoption of other common policies. This did appear to be working in the 1970s, when frequent changes in the exchange rates of the currencies of the member states threatened to render the CAP unworkable. Again, though, the governments of the member states avoided the apparent implication that they would either have to fix their exchange rates or abandon the CAP, by improvising a solution based on 'green currencies', regulated by levies and rebates when produce crossed national boundaries. The spillover pressures certainly existed, but the governments proved able to resist them until they felt that they wanted to take the next step. Again this seemed to vindicate Hoffmann's intergovernmental analysis (Ch. 1, pp. 12–13).

The same argument applied to the pressure on the budget. Having only one policy with major expenditure implications led to a distortion of budgetary payments. Britain in particular suffered from this imbalance, ending up at the end of its transitional period of membership as the second biggest net contributor to the budget despite being one of the less prosperous economies. This problem could have been solved by adding other common policies from which Britain would benefit, but in the face of opposition to increasing levels of public expenditure from the Thatcher government, the preferred solution was to give Britain a rebate on its contributions.

Ultimately, though, these *ad hoc* solutions were unstable. Neofunctionalism might be thought to have been vindicated when agreement between governments on the single-market programme, and the consequent removal of customs checks between states, forced the abandonment of the 'green currency' system. On the other hand, this was only made necessary by the intergovernmental decision to proceed with the removal of customs checks, and it was only made feasible by the adoption of the single currency, which again was the result of an independent decision by governments. The British budgetary rebate still existed at the time of writing, but its future was constantly in question. That it might persist illustrates another theoretical theme.

Historical institutionalism argues that decisions made at one point in time can influence the future path of decisions, particularly if they are embodied in formal institutional rules. It can be argued that the British budgetary rebate was fought against long and hard by both the Commission and the other member states partly because it embodied a principle that was alien to the spirit of European integration. If it was accepted that states should receive payments from the budget that reflected their payments into it, the principle of *juste retour* as it was known, then the basic ideal of a community of the peoples of Europe was replaced by an intergovernmental idea of an alliance of states. This argument is also consistent with a social constructivist analysis that emphasizes the role of ideas in politics. Once the arrangement had been agreed, though, rational choice considerations come to the fore. The institutional rules for agreeing the budgetary arrangements of the EC/EU require unanimity. By securing a rebate, Margaret Thatcher changed the *status quo* in such a way that subsequent British governments could retain the financial benefit by simply blocking any budgetary agreement that removed the rebate.

Such behaviour is entirely consistent with liberal intergovernmentalism, which stresses the economic motivation for the positions taken up by national governments. It is more difficult, though, to interpret earlier episodes in the evolution of the CAP purely in terms of economic advantage. Certainly successive French governments were set on concluding the CAP before allowing British entry because it would benefit France economically and disadvantage Britain. On the other hand, the reluctance of French governments in the 1990s to agree to radical reform of the CAP, even when failure to reform threatened the conclusion of a GATT agreement that would tremendously benefit the much more economically significant French industrial and service sectors, indicates that politics has to be taken into account.

Similarly, the unwillingness of the Thatcher government to resolve the British budgetary problems consequent on the CAP by negotiating further common policies that would benefit Britain, can only be explained by economic interest if ideology is also taken into account. Moravcsik's essentially rational choice approach would therefore appear to need to be supplemented by a social constructivist focus on ideas.

Turning to the theories of governance, the CAP appears at first sight to be a prime example of a sector where supranational governance applies. Support for agriculture had been transferred from the national to the EC/EU level. Policy communities of national farmers' organizations and bureaucrats in national ministries of agriculture were apparently replaced by a European policy community of EU farmers' organizations and Commission officials in the Directorate General for Agriculture. However, decisions both on fixing annual price levels and on the regulation and reform of the system remained firmly with national Ministers of Agriculture meeting in the Council of Ministers. The extent to which these Ministers became identified with the interests of their sector rather than with the interests of their governments is a question for empirical research, but examples of Ministers having to be overruled by the Heads of Government suggest that this particular Council may have developed a supranational tinge. More significantly, perhaps, the national bureaucrats in Agriculture Ministries remained involved, if for no other reason than that the actual implementation and administration of the policy remained at national level. The CAP may always, then, have been more accurately analysed as a system of multi-level governance rather than an example of supranational governance, and the reform process that was concluded in June 2003 enhanced the multi-level nature of the sector by restoring considerable discretion over the expenditure of CAP receipts to the national level.

Perhaps the strongest theoretical message from this study of the CAP, though, is that while the policy may have resisted reform for so long because of institutional and political factors, it ultimately had to change because of external pressures. Analysis of European integration cannot proceed very far without bursting through the bounds of the EU and incorporating into the analysis the wider processes of global economic and political change.

POLICIES

KEY POINTS

Peculiarities of Agriculture

☐ Agriculture was politically and economically important to France. The French government made it a condition of agreeing to the common market in industrial goods that agriculture be included in the Treaty.

☐ There was general agreement between the governments of the Six that agriculture was special and could not be subject to market rules.

☐ It was necessary to equalize food prices between the member states to ensure a level playing field of competition in the common market because food prices were an important determinant of industrial wage costs.

☐ France and The Netherlands were allies on this issue, forming a powerful lobby in favour of an agricultural policy.

The Price-Support System

☐ The price-support system was introduced for both political and administrative reasons, with the concerns of French peasant farmers paramount.

☐ Political resistance to the CAP in Germany was exacerbated when Adenauer, as part of a political deal with de Gaulle, forced acceptance of lower prices for cereals than had previously been guaranteed to German farmers. Because of the reaction to the cereals price level, the German government held out for high guaranteed prices for beef and dairy products.

☐ After the collapse of the post-war economic boom there ceased to be any advantage in forcing farmers off the land because they would only be adding to the level of unemployment. The CAP then became a system of welfare support for farmers.

Restructuring Agriculture: The Mansholt Plan

☐ The Mansholt Plan proposed a restructuring of agriculture, based upon encouraging small farmers to leave the land and giving financial support to the amalgamation of holdings. This provoked hostility from farmers' groups.

☐ The French government objected to allowing the restructuring to be in the hands of the European Commission.

☐ The main opposition came from West Germany. The elections in 1969 enhanced the already considerable political influence of German farmers on the government.

☐ The Mansholt plan faced further difficulties as the 1969 exchange-rate crisis put economic and monetary union higher up the agenda than agricultural reform. Reform was further delayed by the need to negotiate enlargement.

☐ The modified version of the plan that the Council of Ministers finally accepted did not significantly increase the amount to be spent on restructuring. It also left the member states full discretion for the implementation of the restructuring.

Agriculture in the 1970s

☐ In the 1970s, economic recession and the political influence of farmers blocked reform, despite the high cost of the CAP distorting the overall Community budget.

☐ The move from holding intervention stocks in storage to paying export subsidies caused tensions in trade relations with the United States.

☐ Spillover pressures from agriculture to monetary union were circumvented by inventing the system of 'green currencies' and monetary compensatory amounts.

Agriculture in the 1980s

☐ Some progress on CAP reform came in the 1980s. This was driven by:
— escalating costs;

— growing environmental concerns;

— the single-market programme;

— other agricultural producing countries, particularly the United States.

☐ Reform was resisted by farmers and, when it did come, was rendered ineffective by the policy community of the Commission DGVI and COPA, and the reluctance of Ministers of Agriculture to upset farmers.

☐ Towards the end of the 1980s the forces for reform began to be manipulated by key figures in the Commission who feared that an unreformed CAP would damage the single-market programme.

Agriculture in the 1990s and Beyond

☐ External pressures were crucial in forcing CAP reform in the 1990s: the collapse of communism increased pressure to allow the East European states to export their agricultural produce to the EU; and, agricultural reform became linked to the success of the Uruguay Round of GATT talks.

☐ In the face of these pressures the MacSharry reforms were agreed in 1992, establishing the principle of separating support for farmers from production subsidies.

☐ The agreements on agriculture made at the end of the Uruguay Round left unfinished business for a further round of trade talks at the end of the 1990s when the EU would face strong pressure to reform the CAP further.

☐ Applications for membership of the EU from the states of Central and Eastern Europe meant that the CAP had to be revised to accommodate their agricultural sectors once they became members, otherwise the EU budget would be bankrupted.

☐ The Agenda 2000 reforms of the CAP continued the process begun by the MacSharry reforms, but were so watered down on French insistence in particular that they were still an unsatisfactory basis for the future.

☐ Under an agreement reached in June 2003, CAP payments were decoupled from the level of production, reducing surpluses.

FURTHER READING

W. Grant, *The Common Agricultural Policy* (Basingstoke and London: Macmillan, 1997) is a general introduction to the CAP, which also has an interesting dedication. The same academic has established a web site that is an invaluable reference tool for up-to-the-minute comment on developments in the CAP, which can be accessed via our Companion Web Site (see below). R. Ackrill, *The Common Agricultural Policy* (Sheffield: Sheffield Academic Press/UACES 2000) is written from the perspective of an economist, and concentrates on the mechanisms of market intervention, and the interaction between the CAP and the budget of the EU. An interestingly different perspective, linking the CAP to the post-war European welfare state, is presented in E. Rieger, 'The Common Agricultural Policy', in H. Wallace and W. Wallace (eds.), *Policy-Making in the European Union* (Oxford: Oxford University Press, 3rd edn, 1996), 97–123.

On the difficulties and emerging prospects of reform of the CAP, in chronological order see: H.W. Moyer and T.E. Josling, *Agricultural Policy Reform: Policy and Process in the EC and the USA* (Ames: Iowa University Press, 1990); A. Swinbank, 'CAP Reform in 1992', *Journal of Common Market Studies*, 31 (1993): 359–72; W. Grant, 'The Limits of Common Agricultural Policy Reform and the Option of Renationalization', *Journal of European Public Policy*, 2 (1995): 1–18; W.D. Coleman, 'From Protected Development to Market Liberalism: Paradigm Change in Agriculture', *Journal of European Public Policy*, 5 (1998): 632–51; P. Lowe, H. Buller, and N. Ward, 'Setting the next agenda? British and French Approaches to the Second Pillar of the Common Agricultural Policy', *Journal of Rural Studies*, 18 (2002): 1–17.

online resource centre

Visit the Online Resource Centre that accompanies this book for links to more information on the development of the common agricultural policy.

CHAPTER 26

The Single Market

CHAPTER OVERVIEW

Although the EU is much more than just a **common market**, the economic ideal of a common or single European market lies at its core. The aspiration to create a common market was fundamental in the decision in the mid-1950s to set up the EEC. Thirty years later, the decision to institute a drive to achieve a single internal market by the end of 1992 was fundamental to the revival of European integration. It is hardly surprising, therefore, that analyses of the causes and consequences of these decisions have also been fundamental to theoretical debates about European integration.

This chapter looks at the original decision to create a common market, the patchy record of progress from the 1960s through to the 1980s, then at the moves to complete the internal market, what became known as the single-market programme, in the 1980s. It also reviews the development of internal-market policy, and the record of implementation beyond 1992.

> **The single market programme marked a turning point in European integration.**
> (Young 2005: 93)

Article 9 of the Treaty of Rome (EEC) states, 'The Community shall be based upon a customs union'; also, a substantial section of the Treaty (Title III, Articles 39–69, previously 48–73) is devoted to the free movement of persons, services, and capital. Together these objectives constitute the construction of a single European market. Progress in achieving the objectives has varied in line with fluctuations in the world economic cycle. After rapid initial progress in the 1960s there was a period of stagnation and even retreat from the unified market in the 1970s and early 1980s, before the adoption in 1985 of a new programme to free the internal market by the end of 1992 sparked off a second period of rapid progress. The single-market programme gave a tremendous boost to European integration, bringing many other measures in its wake. Yet even today the internal market is still incomplete in certain important respects, and other measures have only been agreed on the basis of unsatisfactory lowest-common-denominator bargains.

The Common Market: The Original Decision

The decision to create a common market reflects two of the main motivations for setting up the EEC: to avoid any return to the national protectionism that had been economically disastrous for Europe between the wars, and to promote economic expansion by creating a large internal market for European producers that would rival the large US market. The history of the decision is recounted in Chapter 7.

There is little evidence of supranational actors playing a key role in this original decision. Whereas the scheme for Euratom emerged from the lobbying activities of Jean Monnet's Action Committee for the United States of Europe, the proposal for the EEC, although it was adopted by the Action Committee, originated with the Dutch government supported by the Belgian government, and was a revival of a scheme that they had long favoured and had implemented on a more limited scale between themselves in the form of the Benelux economic union. The initiative was taken by the political and administrative élites in small states, in pursuit of what they perceived as their national interest in being part of a larger economic grouping.

Neofunctionalism (Ch. 1, pp. 8–12) does not provide an adequate framework for understanding the original commitment in the Treaty of Rome to the common market; but it was, after all, a theory about what would happen once the first steps had been taken in the integrative process. In one sense the first steps were taken with the Treaty of Paris, but in another sense the ECSC was something of a false start, based upon a view of integration as a process that would proceed sector by sector. It was only with the EEC Treaty that the framework was laid for a form of integration based on a general common market.

Initial reaction from producer groups in the member states of the ECSC to the proposal for a general common market were much more mixed than neofunctionalist theory might have predicted. According to neofunctionalism, the success of the ECSC ought to have led other groups of producers to put pressure on their governments to extend the common market to their products so that they too could benefit. Yet there is no evidence that any national group of producers lobbied for the extension of the ECSC.

Although the experience of the coal and steel industries with the ECSC had been generally beneficial, it was also clear, especially in the case of coal, that as well as winners from a common market there would be losers. The reactions of different national interest groups reflected the extent to which they expected to be winners or losers from a general common market. German industrialists were mostly supportive of the idea; they were in buoyant mood because of their experience of remarkably high rates of economic growth in the early 1950s, and they saw the common market as an opportunity to sustain that expansion (Haas 1968: 172). French industry, on the other hand, had not by the mid-1950s shaken off the generally negative, safety-first culture that had dominated between the wars, and the CNPF campaigned against French participation in the EEC (Haas 1968: 191–3). They were, however, overruled by the French state élites.

So the experience of the creation of the EEC does not lend support to the neofunctionalist concept of political spillover. Nor does it support the view that important steps in the process of European integration have been taken as a result of the lobbying of national governments by economic interests. Rather it illustrates the inadequacies of a simple pluralist view of the nature of politics and the way in which public policy is made in capitalist democracies. The state is not just a cipher, a black box into which demands are fed, and which processes those demands to produce outputs that reflect the balance of the forces making those demands. It is an independent actor, consisting of politicians and administrators who may sometimes take a short-term view of policy (especially perhaps the elected politicians, who wish to be re-elected), but who also have to take a view of what will be in the longer-term interests of the country. Of course, in this respect, economic interests are often prominent. If they do not take that longer-term view, governments find that they run into more and more intractable problems. Short termism has its limits, and they are soon reached.

Thus it was clear that the creation of a customs union would result in an uneven distribution of benefits and losses between the member states; and although the precise distribution of those benefits and losses could not be predicted in advance, there were reasonable grounds for believing that West German industry might gain more than French industry would. That is why French negotiators were anxious to ensure that other commitments were made in the Treaty of Rome, to develop policies in areas where their country could be expected to benefit more than West Germany, particularly agriculture. But the reason why the plunge was taken to create the EEC was that all six states expected their economies to be better off as a result of creating the internal market, even if some benefited more than others.

Towards Completion of the Internal Market

After the original decision had been taken to create a common market, there was rapid progress in that direction; but the progress faltered in the mid-1960s, and there was no further advance in the 1970s. It was not until the 1980s that the programme was revived, in a form that was updated to take account of the changed global circumstances in the meantime.

Progress in the 1960s

Although the original decision to create a common market did not lend support to the neofunctionalist idea of political spillover, the surprisingly rapid progress that was made in the 1960s towards achieving the common market did seem to do so. In particular, a decision taken by the Council of Ministers in 1960 to accelerate the original timetable for removing internal tariffs and quotas, and erecting a common external tariff, was celebrated by Leon Lindberg (1963: 167–205) as a graphic illustration of political spillover at work.

The EEC Treaty specified (Article 14) a precise timetable for the progressive reduction of internal tariffs. On the original schedule it would have taken at least eight years to get rid of all internal tariffs. This rather leisurely timetable reflected the concerns of some industrial groups about the problems of adjustment involved in ending national protection. However, once the treaty was signed and it became obvious that the common market would become a reality, those same industrial interests responded to the changed situation facing them. Even before the treaty came into operation on 1 January 1958, companies had begun to conclude cross-border agreements on co-operation, or to acquire franchised retail outlets for their products in other member states. Just as the neofunctionalists had predicted, changing circumstances led to changed behaviour.

Corporate behaviour adjusted so rapidly to the prospect of the common market that companies became impatient to see the benefits of the deals concluded and of the new investments made. This led to pressure on national governments to accelerate the timetable. Remarkably, the strongest pressure came from French industrial interests, which had opposed the original scheme for a common market.

On 12 May 1960, the Council of Ministers agreed to a proposal from the Commission to accelerate progress on the removal of internal barriers to trade and the erection of a common external tariff, and on the creation of the CAP. Interest groups had only pressed for the first of these to be accelerated. Progress was slow on agriculture; the negotiations had been dogged by disagreements over the level of support that ought to be given to farmers for different commodities. But the issues were clearly linked: progress on the CAP to accompany progress on the industrial common market had been part of the original deal embodied in the EEC treaty.

In keeping the linkage between the two issues in the forefront of all their proposals to the Council of Ministers, the Commission played a manipulative role that coincided with the view of neofunctionalism about the importance of central leadership. As described by Lindberg (1963: 167–205), the progress of the EEC between 1958 and 1965 involved the Commission utilizing a favourable situation to promote integration. Governments found themselves trapped between the growing demand from national interest groups that they carry through as rapidly as possible their commitment to create a common market, and the insistence of the Commission that this could only happen if the same governments were prepared to overrule the conflicting pressures on them from other groups and reach agreement on the setting of common minimum prices for agricultural products. It should be noted, though, that this interpretation has been contested by Andrew Moravcsik (1999: 159–237; see Ch. 9, p. 135)

The Dark Ages: The 1970s

In July 1965 President de Gaulle withdrew France from all participation in the work of the Council of Ministers, plunging the EC into crisis (Ch. 9, p. 133). This 1965 crisis was to blame for taking much of the momentum out of the EC. However, de Gaulle did not stop the completion of the customs union, which was complete by July 1968. He did cause a delay, though, in the implementation of the rest of the treaty. The wait turned out to be much longer than just for the retirement of de Gaulle. By the time that Pompidou became President of France, and adopted a more accommodative attitude to the EC, world economic circumstances had begun to shift away from the high growth of the 1950s and 1960s. By the time that the negotiation of the entry of Britain, Ireland, and Denmark had been completed, clearing the way for a further deepening of the level of economic integration, the capitalist world was teetering on the brink of recession, and was soon to be pushed over the edge by OPEC (Ch. 11, p. 138).

Throughout the 'stagflation' years of the 1970s further progress on the creation of a genuinely free internal market became almost impossible (Hodges and Wallace 1981; Hu 1981). Given the economic problems that they were experiencing, and the political problems that resulted, governments became particularly prone to short termism, and sensitive to the protectionist impulses of domestic interest groups and public opinion. This was not a favourable environment for strengthening the internal market. Indeed, throughout the 1970s there was a marked retreat from the common market by the member states. Unable to raise tariffs or quotas against imports from other members of the EC, governments became adept at finding different ways of reserving domestic markets for domestic producers. Non-tariff barriers (NTBs) proliferated.

These NTBs took a wide variety of different forms. Some, such as state aids to industry, were against the competition clauses of the EEC Treaty, and the Commission frequently took member states to the European Court of Justice (ECJ). However, the compliance of guilty states with the rulings of the ECJ was often tardy, and only effected once an alternative system for supplying the aid had been devised. The long process of investigation by the Commission, issuing of warnings, reporting to the ECJ, and waiting for the case to make its way to the top of the Court's increasingly long agenda then had to begin all over again.

Other non-tariff barriers were more subtle. Particularly prevalent were national specifications on the safety of products, some of which were so restrictive that only nationally produced goods could meet them without modification to their basic design.

Differing regulations could prevent a single manufacturer from producing on the same production line for the whole EC market; in effect the market was fragmented into a series of national markets again. Governments also used border customs formalities to make importing difficult, and only placed public contracts with national companies (Pelkmans and Winters 1988: 16–53).

Project 1992: Freeing the Internal Market

In the mid-1980s the situation in the EC began to change rapidly, again in response to the changing international economic environment. In June 1984, at the Fontainebleau meeting of the European Council, two major steps were taken in breaking out of the *immobilisme* that had been afflicting the EC. First, agreement was reached on the long-running dispute over British contributions to the Community's budget; second, a committee was set up to look into the need for reform of the institutional structure and decision-making system of the EC.

At the beginning of 1985 a new Commission took office under the presidency of Jacques Delors, and in June 1985 Lord Cockfield, the British Commissioner for Trade and Industry, produced a White Paper on the freeing of the internal market from NTBs to trade in goods, services, people, and capital (European Commission 1985). This listed some 300 separate measures, later reduced to 279, covering the harmonization of technical standards, opening up public procurement to intra-EC competition, freeing capital movements, removing barriers to free trade in services, harmonizing rates of indirect taxation and excise duties, and removing physical frontier controls between member states (Insight 26.1). The list was accompanied by a timetable for completion.

At the Milan European Council in June 1985 the Heads of Government accepted the objectives of the White Paper and the timetable for its completion by the end of 1992. It was also agreed, against the protests of the British Prime Minister, Margaret Thatcher, to set up an IGC to consider what reforms of the decision-making process should accompany the initiative to free the market. The outcome of this IGC was the Single European Act, which was agreed by the Heads of Government at the Luxemburg European Council in December 1985, and eventually came into force, after ratification by national parliaments, in July 1987. It introduced qualified majority voting (QMV) into the Council of Ministers, but only for measures related to the freeing of the internal market, and even here certain areas—including the harmonization of indirect taxes and the removal of physical controls at borders—were excluded at British insistence.

Explaining the 1992 Programme

The decision to adopt the 1992 programme provoked a fierce academic debate about the explanation. All voices in this debate agreed that structural factors favoured the single market. The differences concerned the role of supranational versus national actors.

The Commission's White Paper on Freeing the Internal Market

The White Paper provided no simple definition of what 'freeing the internal market' constituted, but it dealt with four 'freedoms':

- free movement of goods
- free movement of services
- free movement of labour
- free movement of capital.

The aim of the White Paper was to remove physical barriers, fiscal barriers, and technical barriers to these four freedoms of movement.

The removal of physical barriers was dealt with by a series of proposed directives to end elaborate border checks on goods crossing from one EC member state to another, which were costly in themselves and caused long delays.

The removal of fiscal barriers was dealt with in a series of proposals to harmonize rates of VAT and excise duties.

'Technical barriers' was a portmanteau term covering a range of different things, including national standards for products, barriers to the free movement of capital, the free movement of labour, and public procurement rules.

National standards were dealt with by the adoption of the so-called 'new approach'. This was based on the principle enunciated by the ECJ in its judgment in the *Cassis de Dijon* case (case 120/78, 1979). Ruling that the German government had acted illegally in preventing the sale of a French liqueur in Germany because its alcohol content was lower than specified in German law, the ECJ stated that any product that could legally be offered for sale in one member state should also be allowed to be offered for sale in every other member state. The only exceptions permitted to the principle were those imposed on health and safety grounds. In order to overcome this potential barrier, the Commission proposed that minimum health and safety standards for all products should be laid down by two European standards authorities, each of which is known by the initial letters of its name in French: CEN (the European Committee for Standardization), CENELEC (the European Committee for Standardization of Electrical Products). If products met these minimum standards, they would be awarded a 'CE' mark, and could not legally be prevented from being put on sale in any member state.

Barriers to the free movement of capital had already started to disappear within the EC, and the White Paper simply proposed to complete this process through three directives covering cross-border securities transactions, commercial loans, and access to stock exchanges in other countries.

Barriers to the free movement of labour were to be tackled by directives covering the extension of rights of residence that already existed for workers, to citizens who were not active members of the labour force (students, retired people, the unemployed), and guaranteeing non-discrimination in access to social and welfare benefits. The Commission also undertook to prepare guidance and draft directives on the mutual recognition of professional and educational qualifications.

Public procurement referred to the purchasing policies of public authorities, which in most member states discriminated in favour of national suppliers and contractors. The aim was to open the largest contracts to competitive bidding by firms from across the EC.

Structural Factors

The structural context was the sluggish recovery of the European economies from the post-1979 recession in comparison with the vigorous growth of the US and Japanese economies. In particular, the tide of direct foreign investment turned, so that by the mid-1980s there was a net flow of investment funds from Western Europe to the United States. This augured badly both for the employment situation in Europe in the future, and for the ability of European industry to keep abreast of the technological developments that were revolutionizing production processes.

It was in response to the worry that Europe would become permanently technologically dependent on the United States and Japan that President Mitterrand proposed his EUREKA initiative for promoting pan-European research and development in the advanced technology industries. It also lay behind the promotion by the new Commission of framework programmes for research and development in such fields as information technology, bio-technology, and telecommunications (Sharp and Shearman 1987). But European industrialists indicated that what would be most likely to encourage them to invest in Europe would be the creation of a genuine continental market such as they experienced in the United States.

It was therefore in an attempt to revive investment and economic growth that governments embraced the single-market programme. The pressure to break out of the short termism that had prevented the EC from making progress in the 1970s and early 1980s came from the economic challenges facing key European governments. The EC, as only one part of an increasingly globalized economy, was seeing investment flow away from it to other parts of the world, and was being left behind by its rivals in both economic growth and technological advances. It was thus a strategic calculation of the common economic interests of key member states in this changing structural context that led the EU to agree a new contract, in the form of the White Paper and the Single European Act.

The Role of Supranational Actors

Among scholars and commentators . . . a conventional wisdom has emerged about the origins of the SEA . . . The decisive impulse stemmed from far-sighted Commission officials like Etienne Davignon, Jacques Delors, and Arthur Cockfield . . . backed by a coalition of visionary multinational businessmen who, strongly supportive of market liberalization, convinced or circumvented reluctant national leaders.

(**Moravcsik 1998: 316–17**)

Although in the above quotation he is setting up a position in order to knock it down, Andrew Moravcsik is not entirely erecting a straw man. According to Sandholtz and Zysman (1989: 96): 'The renewed drive for market unification can be explained only if theory takes into account the policy leadership of the Commission'. In their explanation, the Commission manipulated a conjunction of international events and domestic circumstances to push forward the process of European integration in much the way that neofunctionalists had expected it would back in the 1960s. It was seen as providing the essential leadership to exploit the prevailing international and domestic circumstances. In one of the earliest assessments of the single-market programme, Stanley Hoffmann (1989), who had been the main advocate of intergovernmentalism in the 1960s, emphasized the importance of Jacques Delors.

Before assuming office in January 1985, Delors spent much of the autumn of 1984 casting around for a 'big idea' that would provide a focus and an impetus for the incoming Commission (Grant 1994: 70). Institutional reform, monetary union, and defence co-operation were all considered, but eventually the completion of the single market was chosen. There were two main reasons for this decision. First, extensive consultations indicated that each of the other possibilities would be strongly resisted by the governments of some member states, but the opening up of the European market would command general support. Indeed, there was already a momentum underway to dismantle the barriers that were fracturing the market and hindering economic development. Second, Delors believed that market integration would inevitably bring other important issues onto the agenda. For example, it would only be possible to pass all the laws necessary to complete the single market if there was a reform of the decision-making process; and movement towards a more integrated market would raise the question of monetary integration. So, Delors was instrumental in giving the single-market objective a high priority. He promoted it in the early months of his presidency through speeches, interviews, and in his dealings with national governments. He encouraged the members of the European Round Table of Industrialists (ERT) to bring pressure to bear on governments to support the single-market programme, so utilizing a **transnational network** to push forward the issue. He commissioned the Cecchini Report (Cecchini *et al*1988) of leading European economists to put the weight of technical experts behind the project. The issue was already on the agenda, but Delors singled it out and pushed it to the top of that agenda. He acted as a **policy entrepreneur**, recognizing an opportunity to promote a policy that went with the grain of existing thinking, that would increase the level of integration between the member states, and that would put other integrative measures onto the agenda in its wake.

Sandholtz and Zysman (1989) also emphasized the role of supranational business interests in pushing the single market, mentioning particularly the role of the ERT. This too became almost accepted wisdom, with Cowles (1995) making the strongest statement of the importance of the role of the ERT.

Against this 'accepted wisdom', though, Moravcsik (1991) contested all explanations that stressed the role of supranational forces. He considered two broad explanations for developments that furthered European integration: supranational institutionalism and intergovernmental institutionalism. His first category, supranational institutionalism, covered explanatory factors such as pressure from the EC institutions (primarily the European Parliament (EP) and the ECJ), lobbying by transnational business interests, and political entrepreneurship by the Commission; it was therefore a model consistent with neofunctionalist theory. Moravcsik tested it against the empirical evidence relating to the Single European Act (SEA) and found it wanting. He argued that the EP was largely ignored in the negotiation of the SEA; the transnational business groups came late to the single market, when the process was already well under way as a result of a consensus between governments on the need for reform; the Commission's White Paper on the single market was 'a response to a mandate from the member states' rather than an independent initiative from a policy entrepreneur (Moravcsik 1991: 45–8).

His second category, intergovernmental institutionalism, stressed bargains between states, marked by lowest-common-denominator bargaining and the protection of sovereignty. It was an example of what Keohane (1984) had described as the 'modified structural realist' explanation of the formation and maintenance of international regimes, but it took more account of domestic politics. Indeed, in his application of the model to the SEA, Moravcsik put a good deal of emphasis on domestic politics, and he ended his article with a plea for more work on this aspect of EC bargaining.

Against Moravcsik's interpretation, Budden (2002: 82) argued that, 'the outcome of the IGC ... cannot be explained *solely* by reference to the policy preferences of the national governments, let alone those of the biggest three. The Council Presidency (with the Secretariat), the European Commission and the transnational EPP [European People's Party] also influenced the IGC outcome.' Nevertheless, Budden also accepted the importance of the role of national actors, although he considered that Moravcsik overstated the extent to which they behaved as single unified actors in the IGC.

National Actors and the Single-Market Programme

Britain

The adherence of the British government to the single-market programme is not difficult to explain. The Thatcher government had a strong ideological commitment to liberalization. It had carried through a programme of domestic economic liberalization within Britain, and had been advocating international liberalization in a variety of fora for some time. Indeed, it was because of the predictable support that the Thatcher government was prepared to give to the programme that it was chosen as the centrepiece of Delors's strategy to relaunch the EC. As Helen Wallace (1986: 590) explained:

The internal market is important not only for its own sake, but because it is the first core Community issue for over a decade ... which has caught the imagination of British policy-makers and which is echoed by their counterparts elsewhere. ... The pursuit of a thoroughly liberalized domestic European market has several great advantages: it fits Community philosophy, it suits the doctrinal preferences of the current British Conservative government, and it would draw in its train a mass of interconnections with other fields of action.

It was with the 'mass of interconnections in other fields of action' that the British government was to have most difficulty (see below). Initially, though, its problems were with just one aspect: the link that was made between the single market and institutional reform.

The codification of the commitment to QMV as a formal amendment of the founding treaties, and as part of a potentially wider reform of the institutional procedures for making decisions, was resisted strongly by Margaret Thatcher. The whole issue of institutional reform was one of several where the British government differed from most of its Continental European partners. Thatcher insisted at Milan that no institutional reform, and so no IGC, was necessary. However, it seems that she was persuaded by her Foreign Secretary, Sir Geoffrey Howe, and her adviser on European affairs, David Williamson, that unless a legally binding commitment was made to an element of QMV in the Council of Ministers, the measures necessary to implement the Cockfield White Paper would never be agreed.

That such persuasion of the Prime Minister was necessary indicates that the British government was perhaps not as united as intergovernmentalist theorizing would assume. Budden (2002: 79) argued that divisions throughout the IGC between Thatcher and her two most senior ministers, Howe and Chancellor of the Exchequer Nigel Lawson, weakened the ability of the Prime Minister to prevent discussion in the IGC from ranging beyond the single market, and particularly to block all discussion of the EC's monetary capability. Her failure to take complete control of the British position allowed the Commission to keep monetary issues on the agenda, and although Budden does not explicitly say so, may well have contributed to the symbolic commitment to the ideal of monetary union in the preamble to the SEA, which became the peg on which the Commission subsequently hung proposals for the single currency.

Germany

Any West German government would have been expected to support the single-market programme. West Germany was an export-oriented economy, and over half of its exports went to the rest of the EC. Although business support for market liberalization varied according to sector, the German federation of industrialists (*Bundesverband der Deutschen Industrie*—BDI) came out in favour of the proposals in the White Paper (Moravcsik 1998: 328). In addition, public support in Germany for European integration in general was high. Unlike the situation in Britain, it was a vote-winning platform.

The government that was in office had particular reasons to support the proposals. A coalition government made up of the Christian Democratic Union (CDU), the Christian Social Union (CSU), and the Free Democrat Party (FDP) took office in 1982 and was returned in the 1983 Federal election. All three of the coalition partners were pro-EC, and the FDP was particularly associated with such policies through its leader, Hans Dietrich Genscher, who was the Foreign Minister in the coalition government. Helmut Kohl, the Chancellor, was himself personally committed to European integration, but it was also important for internal unity within the coalition for him to embrace a relaunching of the EC.

Another element in the equation was that the new government wanted to reform the German economy to make it more competitive. This meant introducing domestic liberalization measures that would be sure to run into opposition from economic vested interests, and particularly from the trade unions. Signing up to the single-market programme allowed the government to pursue unpopular policies that it believed necessary under the cover of pursuing European integration, which was popular (Moravcsik 1998:

330). Here was a prime example of a phenomenon that was referred to earlier (Ch. 13, p. 175): the tendency of governments to hand responsibility to the EC for unpopular measures that they felt needed to be taken, but for which they were reluctant to accept the responsibility themselves, for fear of weakening their electoral position. Unfortunately, the long-term effect of doing this can be to undermine the support for European integration.

France

The position of the French government was pivotal in ensuring the acceptance of the 1992 proposal. The turning point was the decision of President Mitterrand to keep the French franc in the EC's exchange rate mechanism (ERM) in 1983. Faced with high unemployment in the aftermath of the second oil-price shock of 1979, the Socialist government that was elected in 1981 had embarked on an expansionary economic policy, which had sucked in imports from the other EC economies, plunged the **balance of trade** into deficit, and put severe downward pressure on the French franc, threatening its position within the ERM. The left wing of the Socialist Party wanted the government to continue on the same course, and if necessary leave the ERM. Instead, Mitterrand backed his Finance Minister, Jacques Delors, and negotiated a realignment of the relative value ('parity') of the franc within the ERM. Delors even persuaded the Germans to shoulder some of the cost of this adjustment by revaluing the Deutschmark upwards. In return, though, the Germans insisted on a change of economic policy by the French government. This began with a freeze on wages and prices in June 1982, which had to be extended when the problem continued and a further readjustment of ERM parities was needed. By the beginning of 1984 the Socialist experiment in France had ended.

Mitterrand's reversal of policy required justification to his electorate, which had voted for the socialist policies of the first three years. Mitterrand chose to justify the new direction by declaring a European mission for himself and for the Socialist Party. This was a strategically clever move. It had a base of support within the French socialist movement: the influential socialist trade union federation, the *Confederation Française Democratique du Travail* (CFDT), had always been closely associated with support for European integration, and its leadership supported both domestic and external policies of liberalization (Moravcsik 1998: 337). The abandonment of the socialist experiment implied that the French economy must be opened up to international competition, which meant that it was necessary to pursue modernization of the less competitive sectors. As in Germany, this was bound to stir up opposition. It was therefore convenient for the socialists to be able to hide behind Brussels to force through the reforms. At the same time, the drive to remove NTBs throughout the EC was likely to benefit the more dynamic sections of the French economy, which were heavily export oriented, and were concerned about the adverse effect of NTBs elsewhere, particularly in Germany.

Moravcsik (1991) analysed the French position in the negotiations over the single-market programme as a straightforward defence of the preferences determined by domestic economic considerations. As with Britain, Budden (2002: 79) argued that France could not be treated as a unitary actor to that extent. He identified a clear division within the French government over whether the IGC could be used as a vehicle to make progress towards President Mitterrand's preferred goal of monetary union. Having committed France to a 'European vocation', Mitterrand wanted to block any future pressure for a reversal of that policy. Monetary union would be an irrevocable step that would tie France into the EC. So, Mitterrand would have preferred to have moved straight to a single currency, but he was convinced by Delors that that would be a step too far, and that the single-market programme needed to be agreed first. France's Europe Minister, Roland Dumas, nevertheless favoured keeping monetary union on the agenda; but the Finance Ministry was opposed; while Elizabeth Guigou, the President's adviser on European affairs, feared that pushing monetary union would jeopardize the IGC, and so she sided with the Finance Ministry. These divisions gave the Commission room to manoeuvre around this issue, and Budden (2002: 79) was quite clear that this 'had a direct impact on the IGC's outcome'.

Beyond 1992

The deadline of the end of 1992 was the target date for the Council of Ministers to agree all the 279 measures in the White Paper. To facilitate meeting the deadline, the Commission drew up a timetable for proposals to be made and to be agreed. As a result of this, over 95 per cent of the measures mentioned in the White Paper had been agreed by the end of 1992 (Calingaert 1999: 157). This remarkable record of success, however, needs to be set against three further considerations:

- Council agreements have to be implemented. Thus, agreement in the Council did not in itself mean that the single market was working. Before that stage would be reached there were two further requirements: transposition and enforcement.

- The 5 per cent of the measures that had not been agreed included some of the most intractable and controversial in the White Paper.

- The White Paper did not cover some areas where businesses wanted to see liberalization, because they were considered too controversial.

Transposition

Once a directive has been agreed by the Council of Ministers, it has to be transposed into the national laws of the member states. This process was slower in some states than in others, which meant that there were transposition problems ongoing over a decade after the 1992 agreement. The Commission kept a running tally of the record of member states on transposition, and published the results annually as a league table. Concern about the low level of transposition overall, and particularly in certain member states, led to agreement in 2003 on an Internal Market Strategy that set the target for every state of keeping its 'implementation deficit' below 1.5 per cent. This meant that at any one time no state should have failed to transpose more than 1.5 per cent of all single-market directives that had been agreed at EU level. Some member states responded vigorously to the target. For example, Ireland more than halved its implementation deficit between May 2003 and January 2004 to get below 1.5 per cent. Other member states, however, responded less to the target. Although there was variation in the performance of member states, a small group of persistent offenders emerged, consisting of France, Germany, Luxemburg, Greece, and Italy. At the other end of the spectrum, Denmark, Spain, Finland, and Britain (in approximate order of merit) consistently kept within the target (European Commission 2004a).

Enforcement

Even when the member states have transposed internal market legislation, it still has to be enforced, and the record of national governments on this is very variable. The Commission has had to deal with a constant flow of complaints from member states about infringements of the rules by other member states, although the records of different states vary considerably. In January 2004, France and Italy together accounted for 28 per cent of single-market infringement cases, more than Denmark, Finland, Sweden, Luxemburg, Portugal, Ireland, and the Netherlands combined. Two areas where the record on enforcement is particularly bad are those products for which there are no harmonized EU standards, and **public procurement**.

Where there is no uniform EU standard for a product, internal-market regulations require national authorities to accept the standards of other member states. However companies have often found their products being subjected to a battery of national test and certification requirements, especially in France and Germany. The British Department of Trade and Industry even set up its own Single Market Compliance Unit in the mid-1990s, to pursue cases where British manufacturers felt they had been discriminated against in this way, and if necessary to report the offending state authorities to the Commission. Largely in response to the same problem, a network of national officials was established in 1997 in the hope that disputes might be resolved by negotiation rather than litigation. The network, called SOLVIT, did not prove very effective, but it was reformed following a Commission Communication on Effective Problem Solving (European Commission 2001; 2002). This approach was in line with the general drift away from centralized supranational control towards decentralized international co-operation to solve problems. It is also in line with the recommendation of Metcalfe (1992) and others for the Commission to handle implementation by putting itself at the centre of networks of national implementers (Ch. 19, pp. 270–2).

Similar problems of non-recognition in the absence of harmonized standards arose in the services field, where there was a marked reluctance to recognize the qualifications of individual workers, thus putting limits on the free movement of labour, and there were also barriers placed in the way of service companies operating across frontiers. In February 2004, Erkki Liikanen, the Commissioner for Enterprise and the Information Society, launched an initiative to set voluntary pan-European standards on training and quality assurance. The new standards would not be mandatory, but would be legally recognized across the EU. Firms taking up the standards would be able to ask for certification that they were in compliance. The hope was that the best firms and individuals would adopt the voluntary standards and, in doing so, raise the quality threshold. This would then make it more difficult for national authorities to find spurious grounds for excluding firms and individuals from other member states from their market. The system would cover firms and individuals offering a wide range of services, from funeral directors to language translators (*European Voice* 26 February–3 March 2004).

On public procurement, eight directives were agreed by the end of 1993 that obliged all public authorities to advertise for tenders for public contracts worth over 5 million ecus in the *Official Journal* of the EC. Despite these directives, very few contracts were ever actually awarded to non-national firms, and there were a number of celebrated cases of governments blatantly flouting the rules. In 2004 the Commission was still complaining that many public administrations continued to award contracts without effective competition, and urged member states to tackle the problem, noting that a recent study had shown that public procurement costs could be as much as 34 per cent higher where EU rules were not applied (European Commission 2004*a*). Again, in the post-Maastricht political climate, the Commission was approaching the problem by exhortation rather than with threats of legal action. New legislation to improve the efficiency of public procurement procedures had meanwhile not been passed by the target date of the end of 2003.

Problem Areas

Some issues that were included in the White Paper have proved particularly difficult for member states to agree on, and this is why only 95 per cent of the programme had been agreed by the end of 1992. Two that stand out are tax harmonization and company law. Arguably, agreement on both is necessary if there is to be a genuine single market in which companies can operate without regard to national boundaries. Without harmonization of taxes and a common company statute, companies that operate in several different states face a complex of regulations and paperwork.

Pressures for tax harmonization have grown through spillover. The removal of restrictions on the purchase of goods across borders, such as alcohol, has led to cross-border shopping by consumers taking advantage of lower levels of excise duty and value-added tax (VAT) in other states. This has particularly hit countries such as Denmark, which has high duties but is close to Germany, which has low duties, resulting in Danes travelling to Germany to buy alcohol more cheaply.

Ironically, cross-border shopping has also hit Britain. In 1988 the British government argued that rates of excise duty and VAT should be allowed to adjust through market mechanisms. To compete for customers, states with higher rates of excise duty and VAT would have to lower their rates to match those of their neighbours. The British government believed that this would benefit consumers by reducing taxes across the EU. At the same time, it clearly believed that Britain would suffer little from cross-border shopping (George 1998: 196–7). Yet by mid-1995 the British Brewers' and Licensed Retailers' Association was arguing that unless the level of excise duty on beer was reduced, many pubs and off-licences would be driven out of business by the influx of cheap beer bought by British day trippers to France. Predictably, though, the states with low excise duties refused to consider raising their levels.

A second spillover from the single market to tax harmonization came from the freeing of capital movements. This led to competition between states to attract savings from other countries by reducing taxes on the interest paid on them. Germany has suffered most from lower levels of taxes on savings elsewhere, particularly those in Luxemburg. In all cases, the reduction of taxes on savings has led to the lost revenue for governments being replaced by them introducing higher taxes on less mobile factors such as labour. The Commission frequently identified this as one of the reasons why the single market had not produced the numbers of extra jobs predicted in the Cecchini report. Yet it proved difficult for the Commission to make progress on the issue. Britain in particular opposed agreement on a harmonized level of withholding tax on savings, reflecting the determination of the British government to resist the principle of tax harmonization. After a long campaign by the British government, the idea of a common withholding tax was abandoned in favour of a commitment by member states to exchange information on interest payments to investors, thus allowing the state in which the investor resided to levy tax on the interest. However, three member states—Austria, Belgium, and Luxemburg—insisted that they could not reveal such information unless the same principle applied to non-EU tax havens, specifically Switzerland, Andorra, Liechtenstein, Monaco, and San Marino. This reflected the importance of confidentiality to cross-border investors. The EU opened negotiations with these non-members, and in the meantime Austria, Belgium, and Luxemburg were given permission to levy a withholding tax on the savings of non-nationals instead (Council Directive 2003/48/EC).

Agreement on a European company statute was blocked for over a decade by the insistence of the German government that it must contain a requirement for workers' representatives to sit on supervisory boards and to be consulted on all management decisions that affected the workforce, as was the practice within Germany. The German trade unions feared that if this was not made a requirement at EU level, German firms would operate under the European rules, reducing the influence of workers. Other member states were opposed to this German system being introduced at the EU level, resulting in stalemate. Again the solution was a rather awkward compromise. In October 2001, the Council of Ministers formally adopted a Regulation (Council Regulation (EC) 2157/2001) that allowed companies to register themselves as European companies (*Societas Europaea,* or SE). This would enable them to operate in more than one member state with a single set of accounting and reporting rules. There would be no central registration of SEs: they would register in a member state. At the same time a related directive on the involvement of employees was adopted (Council Directive 2001/86/EC) which specified that employer and employee representatives should formally discuss the arrangements for employee consultation prior to the registration of the SE. If agreement could be reached, these arrangements would apply to the new company. If agreement could not be reached, then rules laid out in the directive would come into effect. The rules specify that if a certain percentage of employees of the new company (varying depending on the type and size of SE) were previously covered by national rules on employee participation, then these must continue to apply to the new company. Individual member states could refuse to embody such rules into their national company laws, in which case the SE concerned could not be registered in that member state. The complexity of these rules indicated the difficulty of finding a middle way between entrenched national positions. The agreement itself was something of a false achievement, because for companies in states with existing laws that did not provide for employee consultation, the incentive to register as an SE was weakened. This is perhaps why none had been registered by the end of 2003.

Areas Omitted from the White Paper

Cockfield's White Paper made no mention of extending the single market to telecommunications. Although it did mention energy, this was subsequently dropped. Yet these were identified by businesses in the EU as two of the areas that most raised their costs of production in comparison with the United States. They were omitted from the White Paper because they were both sectors that had traditionally been in public ownership in the member states, and they both had a public-service aspect to them. However, the Corfu European Council in June 1994 recognized that the extension of the internal market to the two sectors was a priority action to raise European competitiveness. The Commission then tried, and to a certain extent succeeded, in liberalizing these market sectors (Insights 26.2 and 26.3).

INSIGHT 26.2

The Liberalization of Telecommunications

Telecommunications in Europe is traditionally dominated by national monopoly suppliers—the Post, Telephone and Telegraph (PTT) public utilities. Attempts by the Commission to involve itself in the sector prior to 1982 proved fruitless. It was a sector dominated by national policy communities, which collaborated with each other at the international level to preserve the *status quo*.

An opportunity was opened for the Commission by the implications of deregulation of the telecommunications market in the United States in the early 1980s. This led to pressure from the government of the United States for the EC to open its markets for telecommunications equipment. AT&T, which had been forced to open up its domestic operations, was anxious to recoup lost revenue by moving into Europe, and IBM was looking to diversify into what promised to be an increasingly profitable market (Dang-Nguyen *et al.* 1993: 103).

The Commission (DGXIII) responded by commissioning a number of reports on how Europe was losing out to the United States following US deregulation. It used these to build a momentum in the same way that Delors and Cockfield used the Cecchini Report on the 'Costs of Non-Europe' (Cecchini *et al.* 1988) to build-up momentum for the internal market. It also mobilized producer groups that had an interest in seeing an increase in the efficiency and a decrease in the cost of telecommunication services: UNICE, and the Information Technology User Group (INTUG).

Another element in the strategy was that the Commission tried to ride its project on the back of the single-market programme. Its discourse on telecommunications drew heavily on the 1992 programme. Its approach assumed that a single market required a common infrastructure, of which telecommunications would be a part. Thus the creation of a European policy for telecommunications gathered momentum by association with the 1992 programme (Fuchs 1994: 181).

Having established the legitimacy of a European policy for the sector, the Commission produced in 1987 a *Green Paper on the Development of the Common Market for Telecommunications,*

Services and Equipment. This discussion document became the basis for the development of a policy in the sector much as the White Paper on the internal market had been the basis for the 1992 programme. It advocated deregulation and increased competition, proposals that were consistent with developments in those member states that had begun to respond to the problem at national level.

The Green Paper advocated the separation of regulation of the sector from operation of the system, a reform that had already been introduced in Britain, France, and Germany; and the introduction of Open Network Provision (ONP), so that rival operators could compete using a common infrastructure. A concession to the PTTs was that they would remain in control of the provision of network services.

In 1988, the year after the publication of the Green Paper, the Directorate General for Competition (DG IV) issued an administrative directive on the liberalization of the terminal-equipment market. The Commission argued that it had the right to act without specific approval by the Council of Ministers because it was acting in pursuance of Article 90 paragraph 3 of the Treaty of Rome (EEC), under which the Commission is charged to ensure that special rights conferred on national companies by their governments do not prevent the completion of the common market. Although the Council of Ministers had approved the Green Paper—which listed liberalization of the market amongst its objectives—France, Belgium, Germany, and Italy took the Commission to the ECJ, alleging that it had exceeded its powers by not seeking the approval of the Council for the directive. In March 1991 the Court found in favour of the Commission.

Dang-Nguyen, Schneider, and Werle (1993: 108) interpreted this incident as evidence of a conflict between the interventionist philosophy of DG XIII and the free-market philosophy of DG IV, and stated that: 'The Directive was issued by DG IV without consulting DG XIII'. However, given the internal procedures of the Commission on consultation of all DGs with an interest in a sector, it is difficult to see how this could have been the case. An alternative explanation is that the directive was another element in the strategy of the Commission as policy entrepreneur. In effect DG IV was playing the 'hard cop' to DG XIII's 'soft cop'. Faced with the prospect of an enforced opening of telecommunications monopolies by DG IV's exploitation of Article 90 of the Treaty, the PTTs were more likely to co-operate with a negotiated process under the auspices of the Task Force.

The Services Directive

Telecommunications and energy supply are specific examples of service industries, which as a whole proved to be much more difficult to liberalize than did trade in goods. By 2005 only 20 per cent of sales of services in the EU were traded across frontiers. This slow progress led the Lisbon European Council in March 2000 to request that the Commission produce an action plan to remove barriers. Liberalizing services was therefore part of the 'Lisbon agenda' (Ch. 17, pp. 215–16; Ch. 24, pp. 366–7). Following widespread consultations, in July 2002 the Commission published a *Report on the State of the Internal Market for Services*. This was followed in January 2004 by a proposed Services Directive.

The Services Directive ran into vocal political opposition because it proposed to apply to services the 'country-of-origin principle' that had applied to trade in goods since the *Cassis de Dijon* judgment of the ECJ in 1979 (Insight 26.1, p. 409). Under the *Cassis*

The Liberalization of Energy Supply

According to Matlary (1997), a similar approach to that used in the case of telecommunications was used to push forward a common energy policy. Like telecommunications, the energy sectors were dominated by national monopolists, which most commonly were publicly owned. An open market in energy was originally part of the White Paper on the single market, but the opposition of national monopoly suppliers led to it being excluded. However, the Commission returned to the issue in 1989, making proposals for a phased dismantling of national monopolies over the electricity grids and gas supply networks. The linking of energy policy to the single-market programme was explicit. In April 1991 Sir Leon Brittan, the Commissioner for Competition Policy, said that there were two sectors that were vital to the internal market, telecommunications and energy.

It was unlikely that the national monopolists themselves would support liberalization moves, but the Commission was able to mobilize the support of large industrial users of energy, working through the existing institutionalized networks of UNICE and the ERT.

At the same time as the proposals for a phased dismantling of national monopolies were being negotiated, DG IV was stepping up its attacks on monopolistic practices using its powers under Article 90 of the EEC Treaty. As in the case of telecommunications, although the threat never became as explicit, the vested interests resisting integration were faced with a choice between a hard-line free-market approach from DG IV or a negotiated softer approach from another Directorate General, in this case from the Directorate General for Energy (DG XVII).

Negotiations in the Council of Ministers were protracted. The French government in particular was reluctant to end the monopoly of Electricité de France (EdF) over the distribution of electricity in France. It claimed that its primary concern was to protect the access of rural French domestic consumers to electricity at the same price as was available everywhere else in France. This was known as 'the public service argument'. However, it was also bowing to intense pressure from the *Confederation Générale du Travail* (CGT) trade union, which feared that liberalization would mean job losses.

Eventually, in June 1996, agreement was reached on a phased liberalization of electricity supply over six years, but it would only apply to large industrial users. The whole process of negotiation then had to be repeated to secure an agreement on liberalization of the market in gas supply, with the French government fighting as hard to protect the position of Gaz de France as it had to protect EdF. Eventually another compromise deal was reached in December 1997.

judgment, if a good could be sold legally in one member state, it could be sold legally in any member state. This meant that where there were no EU-level standards for a product, it had only to meet the national standards of the state in which it was produced, and could then be legally exported to any other member state. Although it had caused some protest at the time, this principle had come to be accepted for trade in goods. The application of the same principle to trade in services, though, was not readily accepted.

For services, the country-of-origin principle meant that if the company that provided a service met the legal requirements of the member state in which it was based, it could offer the service in other member states. This implied, for example, that a British building firm could build a house in Germany using British workers whose terms and conditions of employment complied with British law, even if they did not comply with German law. From the outset this alarmed both employers and trade unions in those member states that had the highest wages and conditions of service. The concern really became focused, though, in the aftermath of the 2004 enlargement. Whereas there might be a small difference in employment standards between Britain and Germany, the differences between the established member states and the new entrants were considerable. Fierce opposition was mounted to the directive in the run-up to the 2004 European election, especially in Germany, France, and Sweden. In France, the directive was given the name 'the Frankenstein directive', a rather poor pun on the name of the Commissioner who introduced it, Frits Bolkestein, suggesting that the directive was a monstrous creation that would destroy jobs and social consensus.

When the new Commission took office in late 2004, the Services Directive became the responsibility of the Irish Commissioner, Charlie McCreevy. He quickly indicated that he would listen to the criticisms that had been voiced, and consider amending the directive. Some such action was considered prudent because the directive had become one of the issues around which discontent had crystallized in the French debate on the EU Constitution. President Chirac had called a referendum on whether to ratify the Constitution for 29 May 2005, but as polling day approached opinion polls were showing a majority in favour of a 'no' vote, which would have plunged the EU into crisis. Those member states whose governments favoured the Services Directive agreed to re-examine its provisions in an attempt to assist Chirac win his referendum. This did not mean that there were no underlying tensions. The new member states in particular were extremely keen to see the directive adopted in something like its existing form, as they expected to benefit considerably from it.

CONCLUSION

The story of the various moves to create a single internal market in the EC illustrates several of the themes that run through this book. In particular it has been a key intellectual battleground for the supranational-intergovernmental debate. This has also involved debate about the role of interests and ideas. The influence of the external environment, on the other hand, has been accepted by all sides in the debate.

The supranational–intergovernmental debate on this issue remains as contentious as ever. The original decision to create a common market was taken by national governments against a background of enthusiasm for federalist ideas, but in response to urgent practical problems, particularly the need to sustain the post-1950 economic expansion. There were no significant supranational actors to cloud the analysis of the original decision; but disagreement continues over the role that the Commission played in promoting market integration subsequently. Even less is there consensus on the relative role of the Commission in the 1985 decision to adopt the single-market programme.

As for the role of organized interests, there is agreement that larger businesses have supported the single market, while smaller businesses have been more hesitant about its impact on them. This did not apply across the board to the original decision on the common market: business interests were divided on essentially national lines; but it did apply to the 1985 decision. However, there is disagreement about whether the channel used for exerting influence was through national governments, or through supranational institutions, with the ERT being identified by some analysts as a key ally of the European Commission. Once the first steps had been taken, the pressure from the larger industrial interests helped to prevent any backsliding from governments, and helped to sustain, even to accelerate the momentum; just as in the 1960s industrial pressures led to the acceleration of progress to the original common market. Once industrial interests began to gear themselves up to the existence of a genuine internal market they were anxious that it should come about, otherwise their efforts and investments would prove in vain. As one of their number put it, 'it is the entrepreneurs and corporations who are keeping the pressure on politicians to transcend considerations of local and national interest' (Agnelli 1989: 62). The support of large users of telecommunications and energy was important to counteract the pressure of vested interests within the states against extension of the single market to these sectors.

Knowledge and ideas played a role in promoting market integration. The manipulation by the Commission of the Cecchini report, which the Commission itself had requested, illustrated the importance of knowledge. The group of economists involved in the production of this report comprised an epistemic community (Ch. 2, pp. 32–3), in the sense that they did not have an obvious material interest in the outcome, as did sectors of business, but they did have a commitment to the ideas that underpinned the programme. In terms of ideas, it was clearly important that the philosophy of market integration chimed with the neo-liberal outlook of the British government, which had a track record of being generally opposed to further integrationist measures. More generally, once the single market was accepted, the ideas that informed the project became part of the common outlook of the Commission and the member states, making much easier the extension of the competitive principles to sectors such a telecommunications and energy supply.

The role played by the global economic environment in fostering both the original common market decision and the 1985 decision is clear. The background of the Cold War and the threat of communism in the 1950s was combined both with pressure from the United States, and with the hope on the part of European, especially French, leaders that they could make Europe as strong an economic actor as the United States. The background of the relative failure of the EC to recover from the recession of the end of the 1970s, and the sight of both the United States and Japan establishing what might prove to be a permanent lead in an increasingly globalized economy, were crucial in prompting the 1985 decision.

The form taken by the single-market programme gave an extra twist to globalization. It led to the dismantling of a whole array of protectionist devices that individual states had used to try to shelter their populations from the full impact of global competition. It did not replace these with EC-level protection against the encroachment of US and other non-European companies into the European market. At the same time, the failure to provide the accompanying social measures that Delors had envisaged helped to structure EC capitalism on a pattern that looked more like the Anglo-Saxon or American model than it did the various continental European models.

By making it more difficult for national governments to protect jobs, and by failing to deliver effective compensatory social policies, the single market contributed to undermining the legitimacy of the EC. This in turn made it often more difficult to implement the European legislation at national level, and also to secure agreement on some of the important measures that had not been dealt with by the end of 1992, including trade in services. Although the single European market was far more of a reality by the end of 2004 than it had been immediately prior to the launch of the 1992 programme, the post-Maastricht political climate, to which the early single-market measures themselves had contributed, left the structure still incomplete.

KEY POINTS

The Common Market: The Original Decision

- ☐ The original decision to create a common market was based on avoiding national protectionism and providing a large market to rival that of the USA.

- ☐ This decision was not promoted by supranational actors, but primarily by the Dutch and Belgian governments.

- ☐ Support for the common market from national interest groups was ambiguous and varied by country and by sector. The acceptance of the common market reflected the commitment of key national political élites.

Towards Completion of the Internal Market

- ☐ Industrial interests responded to the creation of the common market by adjusting their commercial behaviour. They became advocates of faster completion of the common market, and pressured governments to accelerate progress.

- ☐ The Commission responded by linking acceleration on the common market with acceleration of the CAP in a classic package deal to 'upgrade the common interest'.

- ☐ The 1965 crisis slowed momentum on completing the common market.

- ☐ A focus on enlargement in the early 1970s and developing economic problems for member states throughout the decade held back further market integration

- ☐ Changing economic circumstances in the early 1980s prompted new attempts to revive the EC

- ☐ In 1985 a new Commission under the presidency of Jacques Delors published a White Paper on freeing the internal market. This was approved the European Council, which agreed 1992 as the target date for completion of the necessary measures.

Explaining the 1992 Programme

- ☐ All commentators agree on the importance of the global economic context to the decision to take the 1992 initiative.

- ☐ There is a commonly accepted view that the initiative was driven by a combination of supranational actors: the Commission and supranational business interests organized in the ERT.

- ☐ The Commission (and specifically President Delors):
  — raised the issue to the top of the agenda;
  — mobilized experts to produce reports arguing the advantages of the single market;
  — mobilized business interests (the ERT) to press the case on governments.

- ☐ The alternative view, put by Andrew Moravcsik, is that the initiative came from national governments, and reflected the coincidence of the policy and political priorities of the governments in Britain, Germany, and France.

National Actors and the Single-Market Programme

☐ The British government embraced the single-market programme enthusiastically because of its ideological commitment to free markets, but it had difficulty with some of the associated policies, including the introduction of QMV into the Council of Ministers.

☐ The German coalition government was intent on modernizing the German economy, and the single-market programme allowed it to do this, while linking unpopular restructuring measures to the project for European integration, which had popular support.

☐ The French socialist government had just turned away from the policies on which it was elected, and hoped to use the single market as an alternative popular platform. Like the German government, it was looking to modernize the national economy behind the cover of a commitment to European integration.

Beyond 1992

☐ The Council had agreed 95 per cent of the White Paper's measures by the end of 1992, but transposition of Council agreements into national law has been much slower and effective enforcement of legislation varies both by member state and by sector.

☐ No progress has been made on tax harmonization, but an awkward compromise was eventually reached on a European company statute, although this was so unsatisfactory that no European companies were set up under it.

☐ The Commission successfully extended the single market to telecommunications and energy.

The Services Directive

☐ Trade in services proved more difficult to liberalize than trade in goods.

☐ Liberalizing services became part of the 'Lisbon agenda' in 2000.

☐ A proposal from the Commission for a Services Directive ran into strong political opposition in some of the older member states, and had to be revised.

☐ This caused a split with the new entrants, which had hoped to benefit from the directive.

FURTHER READING

The great debate between theorists about the single market began with Wayne Sandholtz and John Zysman, '1992: Recasting the European Bargain', *World Politics*, 42 (1989): 95–128; and continued with Andrew Moravcsik, 'Negotiating the Single European Act', *International Organization*, 45 (1991): 19–56. Philip Budden responded to Moravcsik's arguments from a pluralist perspective in his article, 'Observations on the Single European Act and the "Relaunch of Europe": A Less "Intergovernmental" Reading of the 1985 Intergovernmental Conference', *Journal of European Public Policy*, 9 (2002): 76–97. Another contribution worth reading is that by Maria Green Cowles, 'Setting the

Agenda for a New Europe: The ERT and EC 1992', *Journal of Common Market Studies*, 33 (1995): 501–26.

online resource centre Visit the Online Resource Centre that accompanies this book for links to more information on the single market.

CHAPTER 27

Economic and Monetary Union

CHAPTER OVERVIEW

Economic and monetary union (EMU) first became an official objective of the EC in 1969, but it was not achieved until thirty years later. This chapter examines the various attempts at EMU between 1969 and 1999, and analyses the reasons for the relative successes and failures, up to and including the launch of the single currency, the Euro. It then looks at the interpretations and explanations that have been given by various academic commentators for the success of the latest attempt. The chapter goes on to examine the record of the Euro since it was set up.

> The euro and the ECB, while certainly dramatic developments, have not been overnight successes; rather EMU has deep roots in the history of European integration
>
> **(McNamara 2005: 143)**

Economic and monetary union (EMU) first came to the fore as a primary objective of the EC in 1969. Each element in the term—economic union and monetary union—has a minimum definition and a maximum definition. The minimum definition of economic union is that states cease to follow completely independent economic policies and instead follow closely co-ordinated policies. The maximum definition of economic union is that economic policies are made centrally for all the economies of the member states. The minimum definition of monetary union is that states maintain fixed exchange rates between their national currencies. The maximum definition of monetary union is the adoption of a single currency.

Over the years, the economic aspect of EMU has been emphasized less, and the monetary aspect more. This is partly because co-ordination of economic policy has occurred quietly and away from intense public scrutiny, while monetary union has been more politically sensitive in some member states and has had a history of false dawns.

The First Attempts

In February 1969 the Commission produced the Barre Report, arguing the case for EMU, and in December of the same year the Hague summit meeting of the EC heads of government made a commitment to the achievement of EMU 'by 1980'. What followed then is recounted in Chapter 10 (p. 142). Analysing the reasons for these first attempts to move to EMU, and the reasons for their relative success and failure, provides a basis for understanding the later efforts that resulted in the Euro.

The discussion of EMU that preceded the Barre Report centred on spillover from the customs union and the Common Agricultural Policy (CAP); but already by the time the Report was published the motivation for EMU was changing. By 1969, international considerations were already coming to the fore. In the background to the Hague summit were the first symptoms of the disintegration of the international monetary system that had been agreed at **Bretton Woods** in 1944. These symptoms included a devaluation of the French franc and a revaluation (upwards) of the West German Deutschmark, changes in exchange rates that disrupted both the system of common agricultural prices and trade relations between the EC states. They gave added weight to the argument in the Barre Report that the common market and the CAP would be threatened by fluctuating exchange rates.

To make the commitment to EMU was one thing, but to agree how to do it was another. International considerations prompted the commitment, but different national economic strategies caused problems in implementation. The French government wanted a system for the mutual support of fixed exchange rates. It argued that this in itself would produce economic convergence (Dyson 1994: 79–80). The West

German government rejected that approach because it believed that it would involve using up West Germany's considerable foreign currency reserves to support the currencies of states that were following what the Germans saw as irresponsibly lax and inflationary economic policies. For West Germany, common economic policies had to come first; and they wanted their preference for monetary stability, rather than the growth-orientated policies of France, to be the basis of the common policies. At the time, the French position was described as 'monetarist', because it advocated monetary union ahead of economic union, while the German position was described as 'economist' because it advocated economic union ahead of monetary union (Tsoukalis 1977a; Dyson 1994: 79–80).

This fundamental disagreement produced the compromise proposals of the Werner Committee in November 1970 (Ch. 10, p. 142). Werner proposed that the co-ordination of economic policy and the narrowing of exchange-rate fluctuations should proceed in parallel. This arrangement for approximating the exchange rates of member currencies one to another became known as the 'snake-in-the-tunnel'. In its first stage the snake was to contain no institutionalized mechanism for mutual support of currencies. Each state had to maintain its own currency within the parameters of the system. Even in the second stage, the aid from one member to another would be in the form of loans, not grants, the bulk of which would be short term and repayable within three months. Where longer-term credits were granted they would be accompanied by conditions on the economic policies to be adopted by the recipient.

Even such a limited arrangement was entered into reluctantly by West Germany. However, concern about the way in which the United States handled the world monetary crisis of 1971 (Ch. 10, p. 138) increased the German wish to establish some degree of autonomy from United States domination of the world monetary system. So, although the original 'snake' collapsed following the ending of the convertibility of the dollar in August 1971, it was reconstituted in April 1972, only to run into the same problems as its predecessor because of the reluctance of West Germany to support weaker currencies. In 1972 the German Federal Bank (Bundesbank) refused to intervene in the foreign exchanges to support the pound, with the consequence that speculation forced sterling out of the snake.

In an attempt to prevent a repetition of this incident, in April 1973 the Council of Economic and Finance Ministers (ECOFIN) agreed to move at the start of 1974 to the second stage of the original Werner plan. This involved setting up a European Monetary Co-operation Fund (EMCF), which would co-ordinate mutual support measures and the payment and repayment of loans in an acceptable currency. The West German government agreed to this only reluctantly: it was very unhappy with the lack of progress on the co-ordination of economic policies.

In fact co-ordination of economic policy was always going to prove difficult simply because the French, and other member states, could not accept that they should follow the German policy priority of restraining inflation. For the governments of these states it was more important to achieve high rates of economic growth so as to keep unemployment low, and they were prepared to risk higher inflation in order to do so. This difference of viewpoint was exacerbated by the international economic developments of the early 1970s.

Slower economic growth affected different national economies very differently, as did the oil-price rises of December 1973 (Ch. 10, p. 138). By 1974 economic divergence was glaringly apparent in the EC, indicating that there were definite structural weaknesses in the economies of the peripheral states, including Britain. France sat delicately balanced on the edge between centre and periphery. These strains caused the complete collapse of the original EMU experiment after 1973. They were made worse by a US policy of allowing the dollar to depreciate on the foreign exchanges, at a time when all the currencies in the snake were being pulled upwards by the strength of the Deutschmark. Hence the departure of Italy in February 1973, finding itself unable to compete with US products even on its domestic market, but unable to boost its exports to its biggest customer, West Germany, because it could not devalue the lira against the Deutschmark. The French struggled against the same competitive disadvantage for longer, in the interests of encouraging West German independence from the United States, but finally capitulated after the oil-price rises, in order to ease the resulting deficit in their balance of trade. With the departure of the franc, the snake ceased to be even a possible route to EMU.

The EMS: Origins

Despite the failure of the snake to move the EC towards EMU, it still served a purpose in 1977. It held together, within tight margins of fluctuation, seven currencies covering an area of high economic interdependence based on strong mutual trading links. In effect the snake constituted a Deutschmark zone within which West Germany conducted 25 per cent of its export trade. The proportion was even higher for the other participants. Given the failure to hold all the EC currencies together, this was a reasonable alternative, and few people thought that West Germany would be interested in any attempt to revitalize the original conception of the snake. Roy Jenkins's initiative in October 1977 to revive EMU (Ch. 11, p. 149) was therefore greeted with some scepticism (Tsoukalis 1977b).

Jenkins's initiative was taken up by the West German Chancellor Helmut Schmidt, largely because of the effect on the Deutschmark of the US policy of 'benign neglect' of the dollar. Since the start of the 1970s the dollar had been going down in value, and there had been a corresponding upward pressure on the Deutschmark. The Deutschmark and the Yen were the safest currencies to hold. There was no chance of a devaluation, or depreciation of the Deutschmark, and every prospect of an upward movement that would represent a profit. The extent of the movement of funds into the Deutschmark ensured that it would appreciate in value. This was what made it so difficult for the other EC currencies to remain in the original snake.

The influx of funds into the Deutschmark increased long-term inflationary pressures, and the appreciation of the currency adversely affected the price competitiveness of West German exports. After France and Italy left the snake their currencies depreciated, making their goods more competitive than West German goods. Even the exclusion of a million migrant workers could not prevent the growth of unemployment in West Germany, and consequent political strains, including a widening rift on economic policy between the Social Democratic Party (SPD) and the trade unions.

Even worse, despite the best efforts of the Bundesbank to prevent it, there were signs that the Deutschmark was about to become an international reserve currency. International trade and investment deals were being concluded in Deutschmarks, and Deutschmarks were increasingly being accepted as payment by non-German commercial banks and financiers, who then loaned them on to non-German clients, so creating a 'Euromark' market to rival the Eurodollar market as an uncontrolled source of credit. This was the last thing that the West Germans wanted. They had seen the effect on Britain and the United States of having to conduct economic affairs through the medium of a national currency that was also an international reserve currency. It was with this prospect in mind that Schmidt proposed the creation of a European Currency Unit, or 'ecu', which could provide an alternative reserve currency to the dollar without having the same damaging effect on West German economic freedom.

At the same time as these considerations were encouraging the West German leadership to reconsider an EC monetary arrangement, one of the main factors that had been a barrier to German enthusiasm about the original snake was now removed. Gradually the governments of the other member states were coming round to accepting the West German economic priority of controlling inflation.

Mainly this reassessment of policy was because of the acceleration of inflation following the 1973 oil-price rises. It was obvious that the economies that were having the least success in controlling inflation were also those with the highest rates of unemployment, and the poorest record on growth. The trade-off between inflation and growth did not appear to be working, and accelerating inflation threatened economic collapse. In these circumstances the economic doctrine known as 'monetarism' came increasingly to be accepted in western Europe. Confusingly, monetarism in this sense meant something completely different to the French approach to EMU, which had earlier been described as 'monetarist' because it advocated monetary union ahead of economic union. This economic doctrine of monetarism returned to the orthodox economists' view that governments could only control inflation by balancing their budgets. They must either cut spending or raise taxes. The difficulty was in implementing the policy. The refusal of both organized and non-union workers to accept willingly a decline in their living standards meant that anti-inflationary policies were politically dangerous. It is in this light that the acceptance of the EMS idea by the French President, Giscard d'Estaing, can be understood.

The victory of the anti-inflation priority in French economic policy was marked by the appointment of Raymond Barre as Prime Minister in succession to Chirac in 1976. But Giscard and Barre had difficulty in convincing the centre parties of the necessity of such policies, and the participation of the centre parties in the government coalition was essential to maintain a majority in parliament. The EMS was an ideal opportunity for Giscard to remove internal dispute within his coalition government on the issue of domestic economic policy. Acceptance of the EMS could be presented as a pro-EC and integrationist move. As such it was pleasing to the centre parties, which had always strongly supported European integration. But it could also be used as an argument for following deflationary policies, since only by reducing France's rate of inflation to the West

German level could the franc be kept in alignment with the Deutschmark. The EMS therefore served the French President as a useful external constraint on domestic economic policy, allowing him to plead that he could do no other than he was doing, and avoiding the admission that he would have chosen to do it anyway.

In December 1978 the Bremen European Council created the EMS. The central element was the exchange rate mechanism (ERM) for holding fluctuations in exchange rates within narrow bands. Britain joined the EMS, but did not enter the ERM.

The EMS in the 1980s

Despite predictions of its early demise, the new monetary system, which began operations in March 1979, did survive. The main reason for its survival in the early stages was the surprising weakness of the Deutschmark. Partly this was due to the end of the weakness of the dollar. The new strength of the US currency meant that there was no speculative pressure on the West German currency to revalue. Partly also it was a reflection of the very real problems for the West German balance of payments caused by the second oil-shock of 1979 (Ch. 26, p. 410). For a time the balance of payments was in deficit, and there was even speculation at one stage that the Deutschmark might have to be devalued within the EMS. Under these circumstances it was relatively easy for the other member states to remain within the system.

The ease with which the other currencies were able to live with the Deutschmark had a negative aspect: the EMS did not have the anticipated disciplinary effects on national economic policies. Member states were not obliged to adopt stringent measures against inflation in order to keep up with West Germany. The result was greater economic divergence, and inflation rates in particular moved wider apart. Under these circumstances the West German government was not prepared to accept the automatic movement to the second stage of the scheme, the setting up of the EMCF, and in December 1980 this was postponed indefinitely.

The postponement of the second stage was partly a reflection of the domestic political difficulties of the scheme's two main architects. Although Helmut Schmidt had won the October 1980 Federal election, his health was not good, and growing dissension within the government coalition weakened his position. The financial élite in the Economics Ministry and at the Bundesbank, who had always opposed the EMS, were therefore able to become the dominant voice in the West German camp (Ludlow 1982: 136–8). In France, Giscard faced a difficult presidential election campaign in which he would have to defend himself against Gaullist charges that he was intent on compromising France's monetary sovereignty, so he could hardly fight too openly on behalf of the EMCF.

The result of the French presidential election was the victory of François Mitterrand, soon followed by parliamentary elections that produced a Socialist government (Ch. 11, p. 152). The new government faced a rapid flow of funds out of the franc, putting it under tremendous pressure to devalue. This combined in the autumn of 1981 with a revival in the strength of the Deutschmark. The West German balance of payments began to move back into surplus, while the dollar weakened temporarily. Funds flowed back into the Deutschmark from the dollar, and funds leaving the French franc were also converted into Deutschmarks. The combination of downward pressure on one and upward pressure on another of the main currencies within the EMS inevitably produced a major realignment. In October 1981 the Deutschmark and the Dutch guilder were revalued upward, while the French franc and the Italian lira were devalued. Within five months the Belgians and the Danes were also obliged to devalue.

Stability did not last long. The French franc remained under pressure, as the Socialist government increased its budgetary deficit in an attempt to reduce unemployment. The effect was to produce another realignment of EMS currencies in June 1982. This time, though, there was a significant new development. The French franc was devalued, but the Deutschmark was also revalued, although it had not experienced great upward pressure. The revaluation was to improve France's relative trade position without France having to devalue by as much as it really needed to in order to take account of the weakness of the franc. The advantage for France was that every percentage point that it devalued increased the cost of imported oil proportionately. The cost to West Germany was a reduction in the price competitiveness of its exports. But the German gesture came with conditions. It was accompanied by commitments from the French Finance Minister, Jacques Delors, to reverse the expansionary economic policies of the government, to attempt to cut the budgetary deficit, and to introduce a prices freeze. The Italians, who also devalued, made the same commitments.

The EMS now seemed to be working as originally intended by Schmidt. The importance of the West German economy as a market for other EC states' exports allowed the West Germans to offer them help in maintaining the value of their currencies, while extracting the price of economic policies that followed the West German priority of restraining inflation. The EMS looked like creating a zone of monetary stability.

Nevertheless, the change of course by the French did not take the pressure off the franc, and in March 1983 there had to be yet another realignment. This time there were recriminations. The new West German government of Helmut Kohl was not happy at the idea of revaluing the Deutschmark yet again in order to help the French, particularly since the new course for the French economy had already been marked out, so that there were few concessions that could be extracted in return. But the French threatened to withdraw from the system if the West Germans did not agree to bear the bulk of the burden of readjustment. Chancellor Kohl was hesitant about causing the collapse of his predecessor's achievement: it might rebound against him in the forthcoming Federal elections. So the West German government agreed to a $5\frac{1}{2}$ per cent revaluation of the Deutschmark, against only a $2\frac{1}{2}$ per cent devaluation of the franc. The West German press reaction was uniformly hostile, but the hostility was directed at France, not at Kohl.

This wrangle did spoil somewhat the image of the EMS as a symbol of unity; but just as serious was the continued non-participation of Britain. When the Conservatives took over from Labour in 1979 there were hopes that Britain would enter the ERM. But the new government at first maintained that it was against its economic principles to intervene in any way to control the value of the pound. According to this view, the market should decide the value of currencies, and the correct exchange policy was to float the national currency. This dogmatic phase of British external monetary policy lasted only until mid-1981, after which the Bank of England did begin to intervene to prevent large fluctuations in the value of sterling; but Britain still refused to enter the ERM. This was seen within the EC as one example among many of the lack of pro-European spirit in Britain.

The Single-Market Programme and Monetary Union

Moves to strengthen and extend the EMS were part of the programme of the Delors Commission from the outset. However, the issue really came into the forefront of debate in the aftermath of the decision to free the internal market by the end of 1992, and it became the most serious issue of dissension between the British government and the rest of the EC.

Delors, in presenting the programme of his new Commission to the European Parliament (EP) in January 1985, said that he wanted to develop the EMS by bringing sterling into membership and making the ecu a reserve currency (*Debates of the European Parliament*, 12 March 1985, 2–324/3–6). At the end of that year the Luxemburg European Council agreed on the terms of the Single European Act (SEA), including a commitment to monetary union despite the objections of the British.

Further progress had to wait until the June 1988 Hanover European Council, but in the meantime there was growing support for the idea of a single currency controlled by a European central bank, a concept that British Prime Minster Margaret Thatcher totally rejected. The Hanover European Council agreed to set up a committee of central bankers and technical experts, under the chairmanship of the President of the Commission, to prepare a report on the steps that needed to be taken to strengthen monetary co-operation. The report of this committee (Insight 27.1) was accepted by the June 1989 European Council meeting in Madrid.

Thatcher made it clear that she was unhappy about both the route and the destination mapped out by Delors. However, at Madrid she did lay down concrete conditions for putting sterling into the exchange-rate mechanism, going beyond her previous

---

INSIGHT 27.1

The Delors Report

The 'Delors Report' proposed a three-stage progress to monetary union.

(1) The EC currencies that remained outside the exchange-rate mechanism of the EMS (those of Britain, Greece, Portugal, and Spain) would join, and the wider band of fluctuation would disappear.

(2) Economic policy would be closely co-ordinated, the band of fluctuation of currencies within the EMS would be narrowed, and the governors of central banks would meet as a committee to prepare the ground for the institution of a European Monetary Co-operation Fund (EMCF).

(3) National currencies would be irrevocably locked together, and the ecu would become a real currency in its own right, administered by the EMCF.

formulation that Britain would join 'when the time was ripe'. The conditions were that the British rate of inflation must be on a falling trend towards convergence with the rates in other member states, that there must have been tangible progress towards the achievement of the internal market, and that other member states must have dismantled their controls on the movement of capital. The momentum was sustained when the December 1989 European Council in Strasburg agreed to set up an inter-governmental conference (IGC) to consider the institutional changes that would be necessary in order to move towards monetary union. The British Prime Minister voted against the IGC on monetary union, but she made it clear that Britain would continue to play a full role in the EC despite its differences with the other members.

Events in eastern Europe gave a new urgency to the timetable for unity within the EC in the latter part of 1989. François Mitterrand told the EP in December that the EC needed to accelerate its integrative moves in response to developments in the East (*Debates of the European Parliament*, 25 October 1989, 3–382/150). These comments were the prelude to a Franco-German proposal for an IGC on political union to run alongside that on monetary union, but the acceleration argument applied also to monetary union. Although the British government rejected the logic of treating the collapse of communist regimes in eastern Europe as a reason for changing the internal plans of the EC, most other member states seemed prepared to accept the argument. This put additional pressure on the British Prime Minister not to allow Britain to be left behind; pressure that was eventually central to her political downfall in 1990 (George 1998: 229–30).

Monetary Union in the 1990s

Before the two IGCs began to meet in 1991, West Germany was reunified with East Germany in October 1990, and Margaret Thatcher was replaced as British Prime Minister by John Major in November 1990. Germany entered the negotiations as clearly the largest state as well as the largest economy in the EC, while Britain entered the negotiations adopting a new and more co-operative tone of voice (George 1998: 238–40). Despite the more co-operative British approach, the IGC on monetary union took as its negotiating text the report of the Delors Committee, which recommended that movement to monetary union should be to a timetable, rather than adopting the British idea for an evolutionary approach.

Early in the negotiations there was a consensus that a monetary union would only be sustainable if it were underpinned by a considerable degree of economic convergence. The Treaty on European Union (TEU) provided five convergence criteria that would have to be met by any state before it could take part in the monetary union. Prospective members would have to have:

- a budget deficit of not more than 3 per cent of GDP;
- a public debt of not more than 60 per cent of GDP;
- a level of inflation no more than 1.5 percentage points above the average level achieved by the three states with the lowest levels of inflation;

- interest rates that were no more than 2 per cent above the average level of the three states with the lowest levels;
- a record of respecting the normal fluctuation margins of the exchange rate mechanism for two years.

These criteria reflected the policy priorities of the German government in that they were all concerned with monetary stability.

Although the criteria were stringent, the Treaty did appear to leave room for some relaxation if states were moving in the right direction on all the relevant indicators. At the same time, it was written into the Treaty that any state that did qualify would join the monetary union when it was set up, which would be in 1997 if possible, and not later than 1999. Only Britain was initially allowed to opt out of signing up for the monetary union in advance.

For John Major it would have been extremely difficult to persuade his party, and the British Parliament, to ratify the Maastricht Treaty if it had tied Britain into a commitment to joining the monetary union. The influence of his predecessor on the thinking of the Conservative Party was too strong. The governments of the other member states understood this, and were prepared to let him off the hook by granting Britain the right to decide whether it would participate when the union was about to come into effect. The British government would have preferred the right to decide later to be a general right, thus avoiding the appearance that Britain was isolated yet again. However, the other member states were not prepared to accept this because of fears that the German parliament, the Bundestag, might decide against taking Germany into the monetary union. That would have defeated the object of the exercise. Following the rejection of Maastricht in the Danish referendum in June 1992, Denmark was granted a similar opt-out clause in a protocol to the Treaty.

On 16 September 1992 Britain was forced out of the exchange rate mechanism by intensive speculation against the pound (Insight 27.2). The incident damaged Anglo-German relations because the Chancellor of the Exchequer, Norman Lamont, accused the Bundesbank of making little effort to support the British currency, whereas full support was given to the French franc when it came under pressure. The next day the Italian lira also had to leave the mechanism. Then in August 1993 the system came under so much pressure that the 'narrow bands' had to be widened to 15 per cent either side of parity to allow it to survive.

One interpretation of these developments was that the member states were not ready for a single currency if they could not hold their exchange rates. Another interpretation was that the episode showed how important it was to move to a single currency so that speculators could not push the economies of the members apart. Certainly the problems deflected neither the French President nor the German Chancellor from their commitment to monetary union.

It was not entirely clear, though, how much support the President and Chancellor had in their own countries. In France high unemployment made the policy of tying the franc closely to the Deutschmark increasingly unpopular, and the country was paralysed by strikes in the later months of 1995, as the government tried to introduce policies that would allow it to meet the convergence criteria. In Germany, public opinion

'Black Wednesday': Britain's Exit from the ERM

(1) The Background

In October 1990 the British government finally took the pound sterling into the ERM. The Prime Minister, Margaret Thatcher, had resisted taking the step despite pressure from her senior cabinet colleagues. When she did agree to go in it was at a parity of 2.95 Deutschmarks. This was a parity of her choosing, and reflected her wish that the pound should be seen as a strong currency. Many observers in both Britain and the rest of Europe thought it too high. The rate at which sterling entered should have been a matter for negotiation with the other members, but they were presented with a take-it-or-leave-it offer, which caused some resentment, particularly on the part of the German central bank, the Bundesbank, which would be expected to defend the parity in case of a crisis.

(2) The Run-up

In mid-1992 German interest rates were high following the monetary unification between the Deutschmark and the Ostmark at a politically-determined one-for-one rate of exchange. ERM membership meant that the interest rates of other members of the system had to be set in line with German rates, even if this was not an appropriate rate for their economies.

In mid-1992 the British economy was in recession. The British government had been urging the Bundesbank for some time to lower rates, and had been supported by the other governments, including the French.

On 1 July 1992 Britain assumed the presidency of the EC. The Chancellor of the Exchequer, Norman Lamont, convened a meeting of ECOFIN in Bath over the weekend of 5 September to discuss the forthcoming annual meeting of the IMF. Lamont used the occasion to attack the policy of the Bundesbank, and angered its president, Helmut Schlesinger, who was present at the meeting, by repeatedly demanding that the Bundesbank lower interest rates.

(3) The Crisis

Over the next week both the pound and the Italian lira came under intense speculative pressure to devalue from their internal parities within the ERM.

On the following weekend, 12 September, the lira was devalued. The British government refused to apply to devalue the pound.

On 15 and 16 September the pound came under irresistible pressure to devalue. The Bank of England spent over $30 billion of its foreign currency reserves defending the value of the currency, an unprecedented amount. The Bundesbank refused to intervene in the markets to assist by buying sterling. Eventually the British government had to admit defeat, withdraw sterling from the ERM altogether and let it 'float' (i.e. allow it to find its own level against other currencies through free-market transactions).

Source: Dyson and Featherstone 1999: 682–6.

polls showed growing opposition to abandoning the Deutschmark, despite a conspiracy amongst the political élite to insist that the monetary union was the only course for the country. In November 1995 a poll published in *Die Woche* indicated that 61 per cent of the German people were opposed to the single currency (*Financial Times*, 11–12 November 1995).

Because of public scepticism about the single currency, the German government was in a strong position in the bargaining about the detail of the arrangements. It could always argue that unless the German public was confident in the arrangements made, there would be no German participation, and therefore no single currency. In this way, Germany won all the main arguments. First it was agreed that the European Central Bank (ECB) (Insight 27.3) would be located in Frankfurt; then, that the name of the new currency would not be the 'ecu', which the French preferred because it was the name of an old French coin, but the 'Euro', because the German people did not have confidence in the existing ecu.

France put up a stronger fight on three other issues:

(1) the level of political control that would be exerted over the ECB;

(2) the rules that would govern budgetary policy after the start of the single currency;

(3) the identity of the first President of the ECB.

On the level of political control, the Kohl government insisted that the ECB should be as independent as it was possible to make it. This was the only way that the German people would have confidence that the single currency would be run on a sound basis. The French conservative government prior to June 1997 never accepted this. It wanted the ECB to be answerable to national governments.

This fundamental philosophical clash also underlay the differences between the two governments on the terms of the budgetary rules that would apply after the start of the single currency. The German government wanted the Maastricht convergence criterion for budget deficits—that budget deficits should not exceed 3 per cent of GDP—to

---

INSIGHT 27.3

The European Central Bank

The TEU set up a European Central Bank (ECB) charged with conducting the monetary policy of the Eurozone. Its governing council consists of an Executive Board plus the governors of the national central banks. The Executive Board consists of a President, a Vice-President plus four other members. They are appointed by common accord of the member states for a non-renewable term of eight years, and must be 'of recognized standing and professional experience in monetary and banking matters' (Treaty A. 109a).

In May 1998 there was an unseemly dispute at the special European Council meeting in Brussels which had been called to launch the single currency, when the French President, Jacques Chirac, refused to accept the nomination of the Dutchman Wim Duisenberg as the first President of the ECB. Duisenberg had been the President of the forerunner of the ECB, the European Monetary Institute, and was the first choice of the clear majority of member states, including Germany. Eventually, in order to satisfy the intransigent French President, Duisenberg apparently agreed to step down half-way through his term of office to allow the Governor of the Banque de France, Jean-Claude Trichet, to take his place (*Financial Times*, 4 May 1998). However, Duisenberg subsequently told the EP that he had not made such a precise commitment on when he would retire, and that he would decide when was the time for him to go (*Financial Times*, 8 May 1998).

become permanent. It also wanted a system to penalize states that overshot this target, and proposed a fine that would be automatic. The French government argued that the fine should be discretionary, and that the Finance Ministers should decide the issue in the light of prevailing economic circumstances.

At the Dublin European Council in December 1996, it was agreed that states that ran a deficit in excess of 3 per cent of GDP would be fined, but the fine would be automatically waived if the GDP had fallen by more than 2 per cent in the previous year. If GDP had fallen by less than 2 per cent, but by more than 0.75 per cent, the Finance Ministers would have discretion to decide whether a fine should be imposed. This compromise allowed everyone to claim that they had won, but the fundamental principle was that of the German government.

When a Socialist government was elected in France in June 1997, it made clear that it was unhappy with the stability pact that had been agreed at Dublin. Although the Finance Minster, Dominique Strauss-Kahn, said that he did not want to renegotiate the pact, he also said that he was not sure that it could be accepted in its existing form. Once again a compromise had to be found to keep both Germany and France on board. At the Amsterdam European Council in June 1997, it was agreed that the stability pact would be supplemented by a growth and employment pact, and this was written into the Treaty as a new Title 6a. However, the terms of the employment pact did not involve any commitments to new EU expenditure, nor were they particularly interventionist in nature. The member states committed themselves: to review their tax and benefits systems to see whether there were any measures that were disincentives to job creation that could be removed; to pursue measures to make their labour markets more flexible; and to institute programmes of education and training to improve the employability of the workforce.

Over the five months following Amsterdam, national plans of action were drawn up. These were debated at a special 'jobs summit' in Luxemburg in November 1997, and adjustments were made to co-ordinate the measures. Nevertheless, the outcome at Amsterdam on monetary union has to be seen primarily as a success for the German government. The French government accepted the stability pact in return for much less than the employment chapter that it had originally wanted to be written into the Treaty; and the principles of the pact were based on the ideas of the modernizing social democrat parties, particularly those of the British Labour government, rather than the socialist principles of intervention that the Jospin government claimed to represent.

The French position received a temporary boost following the election victory of the SPD/Green coalition in the October 1998 German federal election. The new German Finance Minister, Oskar Lafontaine, declared himself to be in favour of the same sort of interventionist principles as his French counterparts. He formed a strong bond with his French opposite number, Dominique Strauss-Kahn, and together they put pressure on the national central banks to lower interest rates to boost employment. After 1 January 1999, when the third stage of EMU became operative, they put the same pressure on the ECB. However, the independent bank resisted the pressure, and in March 1999 Lafontaine resigned following heated exchanges with the German Chancellor, Gerhard Schröder. Thereafter, German policy reverted to something similar to its priorities under the Christian Democrat/Free Democrat coalition governments, and France was once again isolated in its demands for a political input to the setting of monetary policy.

Having lost the major arguments on EMU to Germany, the French government made an issue of the identity of the first president of the ECB. In 1996 Alexandre Lamfalussy of Belgium, the first head of the European Monetary Institute (EMI), the predecessor institution to the ECB, retired. This was unexpected. Most governments had assumed that he would retire when the EMI came to the end of its term, leaving them to choose a new president for the ECB. Lamfalussy was replaced by the president of the Dutch central bank, Wim Duisenberg. This was resented in France, and elsewhere, as a move by the central bankers to influence the decision on the first ECB president; but the German government favoured Duisenberg for the post anyway. Given that it would clearly be unacceptable to the rest of the EMU members to have a German head the bank, Duisenberg was the German government's preferred choice.

In November 1997, the French President Jacques Chirac and the Prime Minister Lionel Jospin jointly proposed the president of the French central bank, Jean-Claude Trichet, as a candidate to be the first president of the ECB. This was a surprise initiative, coming so late in the process and more than a year after Duisenberg had succeeded Lamfalussy at the EMI. There followed several months of open lobbying by the Dutch and French governments for their respective nominees, with increasing talk of a compromise whereby Duisenberg would be nominated as the first president, but would agree to step down half-way through the eight-year term in favour of Trichet. Although Duisenberg publicly rejected this solution at the end of January 1998, in May 1998 agreement on just such a deal was announced following the special Brussels European Council that was called during the British presidency of the EU to launch the single currency.

The deal was widely criticized in both Germany and France. It was also condemned by the EP, which approved the nomination of Duisenberg, but also voted an amendment that called on him to avoid a situation in which there would be 'early or simultaneous succession of both the president and vice-president'. The first vice-president, a Frenchman, was appointed for four years. The clear implication was that the EP would cause trouble if asked to approve the nomination of Trichet to replace Duisenberg after four years. Duisenberg himself subsequently indicated that he had no intention of being forced to retire after four years: he would decide for himself when it was appropriate for him to retire.

The launch of the single currency was only slightly marred by this political controversy, and the financial markets reacted calmly to the shenanigans. The Euro formally came into existence on 1 January 1999 with eleven members. Only Greece in the end was excluded by the convergence criteria. Britain, Denmark, and Sweden met the criteria but excluded themselves. Britain and Denmark were allowed to do this under the terms of their 'opt-outs'. Sweden was able to claim on a technicality that it had not fulfilled the conditions because it had not been a member of the ERM for two years prior to the launch of the Euro.

The inclusion of Italy caused some misgivings because the budget-deficit criterion had been met partly by what seemed to be a purely temporary expedient: the Italian government levied a one-off 'Euro tax' to offset the deficit in the year for which the criteria were applied. The inflation criterion did not prove to be a problem because of a slowing in European economic activity. The criterion relating to the debt-to-GDP ratio was effectively ignored on the grounds that it only required the ratio to be moving in the right direction. As Belgium and Italy both had ratios that were double the 60 per cent target, and that were not showing clear evidence of coming down, this seemed to be a fudge. Even more serious doubts were raised about the statistics on the basis of which Greece joined in mid-2001; indeed, eventually a new Greek government admitted that its predecessor had massaged the figures to gain entry, but nobody suggested that Greece should therefore be expelled from the system.

Despite all the dubious accounting, the remarkable fact is that monetary union happened. Almost thirty years after the Hague summit declared EMU to be a priority objective, half of the union was achieved by a majority of the member states. The existence of a single currency made at least the minimum definition of economic union inevitable. Close co-ordination of economic policy was required by the stability pact, and by the necessity of living together in the same currency area. The question is why those states that signed up to the Euro chose to abandon their monetary sovereignty in this way, and especially why the key states of France and Germany chose to do so.

Explanations of EMU

Academics have vigorously debated both why the decision was finally made to adopt a single currency, and why the particular form that the monetary union took was agreed. Among supranationalist explanations that have been debated have been spillover, the role the Commission, and the role of central bankers as an epistemic community. Among intergovernmental explanations have been some that have stressed geo-political factors and some that have stressed domestic economic factors. International factors form the background to both supranational and intergovernmental explanations.

Spillover

It could be argued, as it was argued by the Commission, that pressure for monetary union came as spillover from the decision to free the internal market. Making a reality of the single market implied eliminating the fluctuations in exchange rates that were a source of interference with trade across national boundaries. However, Sandholtz (1993: 20–22) rejected the argument that there was a clear functional spillover from the single market to a single currency. The reasoning behind it was contentious:

Among economists, there is no consensus on the desirability of monetary integration, much less on its functional necessity.

(Sandholtz 1993: 21)

However, he argued that there was clearly what others have called 'cultivated spillover'. This occurs when the Commission 'cultivates' pressure on the governments of member states to adopt further measures of integration (Ch. 1, p. 12).

The Role of the Commission

The Commission used 1992 as an argument to press for a single currency, and it met with a receptive audience among the public, business, and political élites because the success of the single-market programme had provided a favourable environment. Tsoukalis (1996: 293) reinforced this argument. He suggested a strategic approach by the Commission that resembled that identified in Chapter 26 (p. 411) as the approach of the **policy entrepreneur.**

In terms of decision making, the negotiation on EMU during the Maastricht IGC bore considerable resemblance to earlier European initiatives and especially the one that had led previously to the adoption of the single-market programme. The gradual build-up of momentum, the steady expansion of the political base of support through coalition building, and the isolation of opponents were combined with an effective marketing campaign orchestrated by the Commission and addressed primarily towards opinion leaders and the business community. Central bankers were closely involved early on, notably through their participation in the Delors Committee, which produced the report on EMU. Later, they played an active role in the drafting of the relevant articles of the Treaty. Arguments about functional spillover were also successfully mixed with high politics and the appeal to 'Eurosentiment'—a recipe that had proved quite successful in the past.

Central Bankers as an Epistemic Community

Verdun (1999: 317) identified the central bankers as an 'epistemic community' in this process (see Ch. 2, pp. 32–3). They all agreed that the aim of monetary policy was to achieve price stability. They all agreed that to achieve this, monetary policies had to be freed from political influence. They all supported a supranational regulatory agent in the form of the European System of Central Banks (ESCB). She also argued (Verdun 1999: 320) that the Delors Committee itself fulfilled the four main requirements laid down by Haas (1992) for an epistemic community:

(1) a shared set of normative beliefs: that monetary union would benefit the EC;

(2) a shared set of causal beliefs: on the causes of inflation, on the importance of stable exchange rates, that the dominance of European monetary policy by the Bundesbank was unsatisfactory; that it was undesirable to have economic policy centrally directed;

(3) shared notions of validity;

(4) a common policy enterprise.

Verdun appeared to accept the intergovernmentalist view of the dynamics of monetary union, arguing that the member states invoked the assistance of this epistemic community in order to legitimate policy decisions that they wished to take. An alternative interpretation is to see Delors's use of the epistemic communities as entirely in line with the way in which he had used the epistemic community of economists in the form of the Cecchini Report to push forward the single-market programme (Ch. 26, p. 411).

Kaelberer (2003) agreed that the central bankers exhibited the characteristics of an epistemic community, but he warned against overstating either the extent to which they functioned as such a community during the that the EMU process, or the extent of their influence.

The internal functioning of the Delors Committee and the central banking community did not fully correspond to the ideal of an epistemic community. While consensus was certainly widespread, it was not complete. Moreover, the functioning of the group of central bankers was quite hierarchical. This hierarchy was not the result of epistemic criteria but rather structural positions.

(Kaelberer 2003: 371)

There was a lack of consensus between the central bankers on how to approach monetary union, with the old division between the French monetarist and the German economist positions re-emerging (see above, p. 429). The French central bank argued for rapid movement to a single currency, which would automatically bring about convergence in economic performance, while the Bundesbank insisted that monetary union must be preceded by economic convergence, with the onus on the governments of the states that wished to participate to meet the convergence criteria. Each position was backed by solid academic arguments, but the lack of consensus weakens the argument that the central bankers functioned as an epistemic community (Kaelberer 2003: 371–2).

The dispute was not resolved by consensus, either, as it should have been had the central bankers been operating fully as an epistemic community. According to Kaelberer (2003: 372), the President of the Bundesbank, Karl-Otto Pöhl, was not held in particularly high regard for his technical competence among the group of European central bankers. Rather than being resolved on the balance of technical arguments, or 'epistemic' criteria, the disagreement was resolved in favour of German policy priorities because of the political strength within the Delors Committee of the Bundesbank. Contrary to the definition of an epistemic community, there was a clear hierarchy within the Committee because of the strong bargaining position held by the Germans.

Kaelberer (2003: 375) also made the point that the influence of the central bankers on the transition to a single currency was limited by the fact that the Delors Committee was charged only to study how to achieve monetary union, not whether there should be a monetary union. The central bankers, who had not been supportive of the idea of a single currency, were 'trapped' into the process by governments that had already made the fundamental decision for political reasons. In this respect, Kaelberer (2003) agreed with Verdun (1999) in adopting an intergovernmentalist view of the dynamics of European monetary integration.

Intergovernmentalist Explanations

Acceptance of the explanation that both Kaelberer and Verdun appeared to offer would involve stressing the wish of national governments to transfer decision making on monetary policy to central institutions. This would allow them to disclaim responsibility for some of the unpopular economic measures that might be necessary to maintain competitiveness in the single market. Votes are closely correlated to the sense of economic well-being of the population of a state, and this has been a powerful factor encouraging parties in office to bow to protectionist demands that they may know not to be in the long-term national interest. If governments were increasingly losing their room to influence the short-term performance of the national economy, it would clearly be in their interest to make this as obvious as possible to the electorate. The EU could then be blamed for adverse economic fortunes.

Linked to this argument are concerns about the credibility of anti-inflationary commitments. Sandholtz (1993: 34–6) argued that the commitment of some governments to combating inflation was in doubt because of their previous record on this issue, and because of the political obstacles in the way of carrying through the necessary policies. In this context, a government might welcome having its hands tied by commitments to the EC/EU:

monetary union would provide price stability for governments that would be unable, for domestic political reasons, to achieve it on their own.

(Sandholtz 1993: 35)

This hypothesis might explain why German preferences prevailed on the issues of the independence of the ECB and the constitutional commitment that the ECB should aim for price stability above other goals. Whatever other governments' public protestations that they found the German preferences too restrictive, in private they welcomed the opportunity to be tied into policies that they believed to be right, but did not believe that they could persuade their electorates to support. In states where the general value of the EU was never in doubt, this technique could be used without undermining the legitimacy of EU membership itself. In other states the outcome of the monetary union negotiations contributed to undermining the legitimacy of the EU.

Another explanation for EMU starts from the experience that member states had of the EMS. Sandholtz (1993: 27–30) noted that the EMS was working well, but that there was growing discontent in France and elsewhere with the way that decisions on interest rate were made by the Bundesbank in the light of conditions only in West Germany, and these were then transmitted throughout the EMS member states because of the need to keep all currencies aligned in a context of open capital markets. This was the main motivation for the French government, in a paper circulated in January 1988, proposing to move beyond the EMS to a single currency. Sandholtz (1993: 30) argued, though, that this explanation ignored the possibility that a greater say for the other members of the EMS could be achieved by reforms to the system. The goal of a greater voice for France and for other countries in EC monetary policy could have been achieved by other means and did not require movement toward EMU.

This objection was met in part by the argument of Cameron (1997), who identified three asymmetries in the EMS that were unwelcome to France and other participants. First, there was the asymmetry of influence in making decisions on interest rates, which has already been noted above. Second, there was an asymmetry in adjustment costs, which fell particularly heavily on the weak-currency states. If the exchange rate of a weak-currency country threatened to fall below the range of its parity, it was expected to take the necessary action to support its currency. Failure to maintain the parity could lead to a devaluation, which would again place adjustment costs on the weak-currency state by feeding inflationary tendencies. Third, there was an asymmetry in the impact on the prosperity of strong-currency and weak-currency states. If realignments could be avoided (and they became less frequent the longer the system lasted) states that had higher levels of inflation would find that their exports were becoming relatively less competitive. States with lower rates of inflation would find their exports becoming steadily more competitive. This is how West Germany came to run large surpluses with all its main EC trading partners. To these, Loedel (1998) added a fourth asymmetry: in international monetary influence. It was with West Germany that the USA conducted such dialogue as it held with Europe on international monetary matters. Other members of the EMS had no say in such monetary diplomacy.

On this argument, then, the experience of the EMS led member states other than West Germany to want to transfer control of monetary policy from the national to the European level. As things stood under the EMS, the German central bank had effective control over the monetary policy of other member states. While reform of the exchange rate mechanism might have tackled this problem, there were other disadvantages to the system that made movement to full monetary union preferable.

It is clear, though, that the asymmetries in the EMS do not explain why West Germany supported the single currency. After all, it was a system that favoured German interests. Here Sandholtz (1993: 31–4) invoked West German foreign policy aims. The West German Foreign Minister, Hans Dietrich Genscher, who initially welcomed the French proposal, had a long record of wanting to balance West German policy to the east with strengthening its links within the EC. In the context of the accelerating collapse of communism in eastern and central Europe, this aim came to be shared by Chancellor Kohl. The issue also became linked to German reunification. In late 1989 Kohl produced a ten-point plan for German unification. Shortly afterwards, the EC states agreed to convene the IGC on EMU in 1990. Sandholtz suggested that this decision was precipitated by the concern of France and other neighbours of Germany that the reunified German state would lose interest in the EC, and might even become nationalist again. This danger became a theme of speeches given by Helmut Kohl in defence of the single currency. He repeatedly associated the single currency with European integration, and European integration with the avoidance of war in Europe. The single currency was an essential step on the way to political union, which in turn was essential to peace and stability.

In contrast, Moravcsik (1998: 381) was dismissive of the explanation based on German reunification because, he maintained, the timing was wrong. Firm commitments by France and West Germany to move decisively forward with EMU—and opposition by Britain to that goal—predated the fall of the Berlin Wall and remained unchanged after unification was completed in August 1990. On the other hand, Moravcsik did allow that in this decision the influence of the commitment of both Kohl and Genscher to European integration could not be dismissed:

Genscher and Kohl appear to have been strongly predisposed toward integration, even in advance of a clear economic justification for it.

(Moravcsik 1998: 403)

At the same time he argued that there was a German economic interest in monetary integration. The steady appreciation of the Deutschmark against other currencies was reducing the competitiveness of German exports, and merging it into a wider European currency offered the opportunity to dampen down this trend. Concerns about currency appreciation intensified in the 1990s in the face of the large costs of reunification and the collapse of the ERM in 1992 (Moravcsik 1998: 392).

Kaltenthaler (2002) attempted to cut through the dichotomy between explanations of German policy that stressed geo-political factors and those that stressed economic interests by distinguishing three distinct groups of actors who influenced German policy on monetary union whenever it was proposed. The first group was a 'foreign policy coalition', consisting of the Foreign Ministry and the Chancellor's office. The second group was a 'monetary stability coalition' of state actors with responsibility for financial and monetary policy, consisting primarily of the Finance Ministry and the Bundesbank. The third group consisted of societal actors, predominantly bankers and industrialists operating through organizations such as the Federation of German Banks (BDB), the Federation of German Industry (BDI), and the German Chambers of Commerce (DIHT). There was always a tension between these actors. The foreign policy coalition had the primary aim of 'embedding Germany in western institutions' (Kaltenthaler 2002: 70), and was particularly concerned to maintain the key diplomatic relationship with France. The monetary stability coalition, as the name implies, was concerned to ensure that domestic monetary stability was maintained. Which of these coalitions had the greater success in influencing policy was largely determined by their ability to attract the support of the third group, the societal actors (Kaltenthaler 2002: 72–3).

When the French government, dissatisfied with the asymmetrical operation of the EMS, first proposed moving to full monetary union in early 1988, the immediate reaction of the West German government was cool. This reaction reflected the combined opposition of the monetary stability coalition and the societal interests, which saw the French proposal as a device to gain control of German monetary policy and move it away from its emphasis on price stability. Chancellor Kohl and Foreign Minister Genscher both supported the proposal for geo-strategic reasons, to shore up the alliance with France. The balance of power shifted, though, with the fall of the Berlin Wall and the prospect of reunification. The banking and industrial interests saw tremendous prospects for expansion into East Germany, and therefore very much favoured reunification. France, though, held a veto over reunification, because it was one of the four powers that had occupied Germany after the war (together with Britain, the United States, and the Soviet Union), and the agreement of all four was needed for reunification to proceed.

Kaltenthaler (2002: 80) disagreed with Moravcsik (1998) that reunification was unimportant in explaining the commitment to monetary union, but whereas Sandholtz (1993) emphasized the strategic thinking behind the decision—that Kohl and Genscher wanted to reassure France and the other EU member states that it was still committed to the EU—Kaltenthaler emphasized the politics behind the decision. The foreign policy coalition won the support of the societal interests when it seemed as though monetary union was the price that would have to be paid to get France to agree to reunification. However, in the IGC the monetary stability coalition was able to dictate the terms of monetary union because on the principle of monetary stability it still had the backing of the societal interests.

Turning from Germany back to more general explanations of monetary union, Sandholtz (1993: 23–7) argued that key domestic interest groups came to support the single currency. The 1992 programme led to a big increase in cross-border mergers, which increased the constituency of firms that would benefit from the disappearance of currency-exchange costs. However, he acknowledged that the business support came after the single currency had become the leading project of the member states, so that it could not be used as the explanation for the commitment, although it could help to explain why the commitment was carried through against all obstacles. Public opinion was generally pro-EC in the aftermath of the successful agreement on the 1992 single-market programme, but it also could not be seen as a cause of the commitment to the single currency. Rather it was a permissive factor in most member states. Later, when it came to ratification of the Maastricht Treaty, less enthusiastic public opinion became an obstacle to carrying through the commitment.

International Pressures

Pressures for monetary union from the global system were present at several stages in the story. The debate about the impact of the collapse of communism has been reviewed above. In addition, from at least the early 1980s on, there was continuing and growing concern about the extent to which the United States was prepared to use the still-dominant position of the dollar in the international monetary system to benefit the US domestic economy. Large fluctuations in the value of the dollar threw off course the economic and budgetary plans of the EC, and gave it a strong incentive to develop a single European currency that could displace the dollar from its position of pre-eminence in the international system, which it continued to hold more by default than because of the strength of the currency.

EMU after 1999

Although the single currency came into existence more smoothly than many economists predicted, it soon ran into difficulties. The external value of the Euro fell steadily against the US dollar, and the 'Eurozone' itself began to exhibit some of the problems of having a single interest rate for such a diverse economic area. National economies on the fringes of the zone, particularly those of Spain and Ireland, began to experience the symptoms of repressed inflation, with rapidly rising property prices and shortages of labour. At the same time, the core economies of Germany and France were experiencing sluggish growth.

It was in this context that, as soon as the new currency came into existence, Oskar Lafontaine and Dominique Strauss-Kahn, Finance Ministers of Germany and France respectively, pressed the ECB to lower interest rates to stimulate growth (see above, p. 439). The ECB and its President Wim Duisenberg vigorously resisted such interference, though, and the pressure was reduced after Lafontaine resigned in March 1999. Nevertheless, a majority of states within the Eurozone continued to experience lower rates of growth and higher unemployment than the economies of those EU member states—Britain, Denmark, and Sweden—that remained outside the single currency. These problems became much worse following the terrorist attacks in the United States in September 2001, after which the global economy dipped. Against such a background it was perhaps unsurprising that the Danish people rejected membership of the Euro in a referendum in September 2000, the British government concluded in June 2003 that the time was not right to make an application to join, and the Swedish people followed the Danish example in September 2003.

While Britain and Sweden were in the process of deciding that they did not want to be part of the Eurozone, serious disputes broke out among the member states that were in the single currency over the application of the stability and growth pact. The pact effectively made the Maastricht convergence criteria permanent requirements for the participating states. In particular, they were expected to keep their budget deficits below 3 per cent of GDP. This proved very difficult to achieve in the context of low growth, teetering on the brink of recession. Although agreement was reached on making both Portugal and Ireland come into line when they breached the spending limits, by 2003 the states in the dock were the two giants of the Eurozone, France and Germany.

France was already in breach of the deficit limit, and in receipt of a warning from the Commission, which monitored compliance, when presidential and parliamentary elections were held in May/June 2002. During the two election campaigns, President Chirac made pledges that meant it would be impossible for the new government to remain within the 3 per cent deficit limit. When challenged about this after the elections, the new French Prime Minister, Jean-Pierre Raffarin, asserted that while the pact ought to be observed, 'France is not a run-of-the-mill country' (*Financial Times*, 8 January 2004). This implied that although Portugal and Ireland might be expected to abide by the rules, France was too important to be told what to do.

Such an attitude no doubt played well within France, where the EU was unpopular because of attempts by the Commission to get the government to abide by its commitments under the single-market programme on issues such as state aids and market access. It did not play so well, though, elsewhere within the EU, especially among smaller states that had grown concerned about the way in which the Franco-German alliance was steamrollering through decisions on matters such as agricultural reform.

The possibility of a Franco-German alliance on the stability pact opened up because the German government was also failing to keep its budget deficit within the 3 per cent limit. In February 2002 the Commission proposed issuing an 'early warning' to Germany over its rising deficit, but political manoeuvring led the Finance Ministers to reject the proposal. Although it exerted diplomatic pressure to avert the embarrassment of a formal warning in an election year, the German government did implement advice from the Commission on how to avoid exceeding the deficit limit, but it was still in breach of the limit in 2003 when it drew up its budget plans for 2004.

These budget proposals included a package of tax cuts that the German government believed were necessary to sweeten the structural economic reforms that the Commission had also been urging it to adopt for some time. The tax cuts, taken in the context both of the budget as a whole and of projections for rates of economic growth, implied that Germany would exceed the 3 per cent limit again in 2004. In this light, Pedro Solbes, the Commissioner for Monetary Affairs, warned in May 2003 that it might prove necessary to implement sanctions against Germany, a statement that, according to press reports, infuriated the German Finance Ministry (*Financial Times*, 26 November 2003).

Matters came to a head in the autumn of 2003, against the background of increasingly difficult negotiations in the Convention on the Future of Europe over the voting rules that would apply in an enlarged EU (Ch. 16, pp. 204–7). That debate was about whether the agreement reached at Nice in December 2000 should be replaced with a 'dual vote' system that would be more favourable to the three largest member states—Britain, France, and Germany. The Spanish government was a leading opponent of re-opening the Nice agreement, which had given Spain votes that were almost equal to those of the larger states. Against the background of this dispute, Spain became one of the stronger advocates of the strict application of the rules of the stability pact to both France and Germany. The other advocates of this position were Austria, the Netherlands, and Finland from within the Eurozone, and Denmark from outside.

On the night of 24–5 November the Eurozone Finance Ministers met over dinner ahead of a scheduled meeting of ECOFIN, to discuss a formal proposal from the Commission that sanctions be applied against both France and Germany unless they took steps to reduce their budget deficit for 2004 below the 3 per cent limit. Once it became obvious that there was no majority for the Commission's proposal, the Italian presidency proposed a suspension of the sanctions, and this was accepted by a majority vote. With this decision, the stability pact in effect ceased to exist as a mandatory set of rules for fiscal discipline and became no more than a set of guidelines on policy to national governments.

Yet neither Germany nor France ever challenged the principle of the pact, and in an attempt to minimize the damage that their action might cause, both agreed voluntarily to try to reduce spending for 2004: Germany by 0.6 per cent, which was only marginally less than the 0.8 per cent that Solbes had tried to insist on; France, less credibly, by 0.8 per cent. This seemed to make it clear that the principle at stake was not the need for fiscal discipline, but who was in charge: national governments or the European Commission. That principle was also the reason for the decision of the European Commission, in January 2004, to take the Council to the European Court of Justice (ECJ) under Article 230 (ex. 173) of the Treaty. The decision was taken by a majority vote in a badly divided College; but the view prevailed that it was the duty of the Commission in its role as guardian of the Treaty to test the legality of the act.

For its part, the ECB was extremely critical of the decision of the Council. Duisenberg had finally given way to Jean-Claude Trichet on 1 November 2003. Perhaps to emphasize the extent to which he was above all a central banker, despite his French nationality, Trichet made several statements in the course of 2003 in support of the pact, urging both Germany and France to take steps to comply with it. Following the November 2003 decision, he made it clear that the ECB regretted the step. The President of the Bundesbank, Ernst Welteke, reinforced this message in an article in the *Financial Times* (4 December 2003). Welteke used the same article to draw attention to proposals in the draft European Constitution that would weaken the ECB by making it into an EU institution, whereas the TEU had created it as an institution *sui generis*, and allowing the European Council to change the composition, decision-making rules, and functions of the ECB on a majority vote without having to get ratification either through national parliaments or by referenda.

So the epistemic community of central bankers held together in its support for the principles of fiscal stability to support monetary stability, and of independence of the ECB from political interference. Indeed, the governments of the member states continued to pay lip service to these underlying ideals of monetary union, but their actions were increasingly in contradiction to those principles. This does not seem to have been a case of different ideas prevailing, but of political interests taking priority over abstract economic principles. Nevertheless, if press reports of the position of the German Finance Ministry are correct, the incident did appear to mark a split within the 'monetary stability coalition' of the Finance Ministry and the Bundesbank identified by Kaltenthaler (2002: 72).

Political interest also drove forward the attacks on the Commission, which after all was only doing its job of monitoring the compliance of member states with the commitments into which they had voluntarily entered. Unfortunately for the Commission, the message that it had to deliver was extremely unwelcome to the French and German governments, and rather than publicly accept that they were at fault, they chose to 'shoot the messenger'. The referral to the ECJ of the November 2003 decision on the stability pact was a risky move for the Commission to take, but it is difficult to see what else it could have done under the circumstances. At the same time, Romano Prodi promised that the Commission would bring forward proposals for changes to the pact that would accommodate the criticism that it was too restrictive in a context of economic downturn. In July 2004 the ECJ ruled that the Council had acted illegally in suspending the pact's mechanism for sanctioning member states, but affirmed that responsibility for making the member states observe budgetary discipline lay with the Council, not the Commission (*Financial Times*, 14 July 2004).

The other main development in monetary union after 1999 was the introduction of Euro notes and coins on 1 January 2002. Between 1999 and 2002, the Euro officially existed as an international currency, but national currencies continued to be used for domestic purposes. The replacement of the national currencies with the Euro notes and coins was a significant development because it gave physical form to the new currency for ordinary citizens of the Eurozone, and made it a part of their daily lives. The creation of a single currency in physical form provided an important symbol of European integration and for some signalled an important step towards the development of a European identity.

Risse (2003: 501) made the claim that within a year of the introduction of the notes and coins there was evidence that their use had 'already begun to affect citizens' identification with the EU and Europe in general'. However, the evidence, taken from Eurobarometer polls, was not unambiguous enough to support the claim. Between November 2001 and January 2002 the percentage of respondents who agreed that by using Euros instead of national currencies they would feel more European rose from 51 per cent to 64 per cent; but it then fell back again in September 2002, after the respondents had experienced nine months of actually using the new notes and coins, to 58 per cent. The strongest evidence in support of Risse's claim was that when in the spring 2002 Eurobarometer, respondents were asked what the EU meant to them personally, the Euro came second, mentioned by 49 per cent of respondents, very close to the 50 per cent who said 'freedom of movement and travel', which was the first most common choice. Thus, although Risse (2003: 492) claimed that 'the data show that the Euro is beginning to leave its mark on the construction of European identity', he accepted that 'the effects of the Euro on collective identities remain ambivalent' (Risse 2003: 495). The ready availability of Eurobarometer data on-line makes it possible for readers to check whether more recent polls indicate a significant change in the development of European identity through the Euro.

CONCLUSION

Economic and monetary union raises many of the issues that are consistent themes of this book. The debate between supranational and intergovernmental interpretations of the nature of European integration rages as fiercely here as it does for the single-market programme, and the creation of another independent supranational institution, the ECB, feeds the argument between the same positions about the nature of the EU and its institutions. The form of monetary union that has been adopted gives another twist to the erosion of different national models of capitalism, and in doing so further helps to undermine the legitimacy of the EU, which the symbolic aspects of the move had already damaged.

In terms of the supranational—intergovernmental debate, while there is some evidence of spillover from the single-market programme, it is largely of what the neofunctionalists called 'cultivated spillover'. The Commission, and Jacques Delors in particular while he was president of the Commission, repeatedly asserted that the single market needed to be completed by a single currency, but there was no consensus on this among economists. Nor is there strong evidence that the project was driven forward by interest groups. It seems to have been an intergovernmental project, specifically a project taken forward by two national leaders, Mitterrand and Kohl.

The previous history of attempts to achieve EMU clearly indicated that the attempt at the end of the 1980s would have to face up to the difficult issue of the form that the monetary union would take. French and German views on the matter had long differed. France favoured institutional arrangements that would put the ECB directly under the guidance and ultimate control of the governments of the member states. West Germany favoured an independent central bank, not because the West German government wanted to increase the degree of supranationalism inherent in the EC's institutional architecture, but because the West German post-war tradition was that the value of the currency should not be subject to political interference, but should be determined by an independent bank. The Bundesbank had always been fiercely independent of the Federal government in West Germany, and the confidence of the West German people in the new currency would be vitally dependent on similar arrangements applying to the ECB. The German view prevailed, with the result that the degree of supranationalism of the EU may have been increased, even if that was not the intention.

German priority to preserving the value of the currency was a fundamental and indigenous aspect of the West German model of capitalism. However, an emphasis on keeping control of inflation through a rigorous monetary policy was also part of the Anglo-Saxon model. The British government, although operating with an opt-out from the single currency, supported the German position in the negotiations on the institutional form of monetary union, as did the epistemic community of central bankers who formed the core of the Delors Committee. Institutionalizing this anti-inflation priority undermined the ability of other member states to protect employment at the risk of higher inflation. This was a fundamental part of the models of capitalism that operated in France, Italy, and elsewhere in the EU. The removal of another policy instrument from the toolkit of national governments took the EU nearer to adopting the Anglo-Saxon model, and risked undermining the legitimacy of the EU when recession cost jobs and the government could not respond effectively. This led directly to the confrontation between France, Germany, and the Commission in 2003, the outcome of which weakened both the stability pact and the position of the Commission.

Even before the form of monetary union had been negotiated, the decision to abandon national currencies caused an undermining of the legitimacy of the EU. National currencies are a symbol of national identity. In Britain in particular the debate about entry to the single currency became a debate about national identity more than about the economic merits of the move. Similar considerations applied in Germany. The decision of the German government at Maastricht to agree to monetary union led to a rapid drop in the level of public support for the EU in Germany. The government did not suffer directly, because the main political parties took common cause in defence of the move; but the German people, who were not consulted in a referendum on the abandonment of the Deutschmark, made clear their distaste for being forced into a monetary union with countries that had very different traditions when it came to preserving the value of the currency. When low growth and high unemployment persisted and became worse after 1999, the German people inevitably blamed the Euro, even though the problems owed more to the combination of the aftermath of reunification and unfavourable global economic conditions (Barysch 2003).

The international context was not so clearly important in the decision to move to a monetary union as it had been in the case of the single market, but throughout the history of EMU there was a persistent tendency to see a single currency as means of establishing greater European independence of the United States. US hegemony meant that the dollar became the main international reserve currency, and commodities such as oil were traded in dollars. If the EU is to challenge the dominant position of the United States, escaping from the dominance of the dollar is an important part of any such project.

KEY POINTS

The First Attempts

☐ Moves to EMU took place in the context of the collapse of the Bretton Woods international monetary system.

☐ There was tension over EMU between Germany and France. Germany made anti-inflationary policies the priority; France made economic growth the priority even at the risk of higher inflation. This disagreement led to the compromise proposals of the Werner Committee for closer co-ordination of economic policy accompanied by tying together the exchange rates of member states within narrow margins of fluctuations (the 'snake in the tunnel').

☐ First established in 1971, the snake collapsed following the ending of dollar convertibility in August 1971; it was reconstituted in April 1972.

☐ The snake was ultimately broken by a combination of divergence in the economic performance of the members and the US policy of allowing the dollar to devalue.

The EMS: Origins

☐ In October 1977 the Commission President, Roy Jenkins, called for a new attempt at EMU.

☐ This initiative was supported by German Chancellor Helmut Schmidt, who feared the Deutschmark was about to become an international reserve currency, which would have a detrimental effect on West German economic freedom.

☐ In the period following the oil crisis, other member states began to follow Germany's lead in supporting a low-inflation policy. This removed a major barrier to greater currency co-operation. Also important, the deflationary effects of the EMS would provide President Giscard with a politically helpful external constraint to facilitate domestic policies of budget restraint in France.

The EMS in the 1980s

☐ The EMS survived initially because the Deutschmark was weak.

☐ In 1981, a change of government in France coinciding with an upturn in the fortunes of the Deutschmark led to currency realignments. Further alignments were necessary in 1982 and 1983.

☐ In return for taking some of the burden of the adjustment in rates, Germany forced policy changes onto the French government.

☐ Britain remained outside of the ERM.

The Single-Market Programme and Monetary Union

☐ Moves to strengthen the EMS after the single-market programme became a major point of contention between the British government and the Commission

☐ The rapid collapse of communist regimes in Eastern Europe persuaded most member states of the need for greater cohesion within the EC: Britain rejected this logic.

Monetary Union in the 1990s

☐ The 1991 IGC set a timetable for completion of monetary union, which would be not later than January 1999.

☐ The Maastricht Treaty (1991) set stringent criteria to ensure the convergence of member state economies prior to participation in monetary union

☐ Only Britain was initially allowed to opt-out of signing up for the monetary union in advance. Following the rejection of the Maastricht Treaty in the Danish referendum in June 1992, Denmark was granted a similar opt-out.

☐ In September 1992 Britain was forced out of the ERM by intensive speculation against the pound. The following day the Italian lira also had to leave the mechanism.

☐ In August 1993 the 'narrow bands' of the ERM had to be widened to 15 per cent either side of parity to allow it to survive.

☐ German public scepticism about monetary union placed the German government in a strong position to negotiate the detail of monetary union. One consequence was that the ECB was located in Frankfurt.

☐ Franco-German tensions over the conditions for sustaining monetary union after 1999 culminated in a dispute over who should head the new ECB. This controversy only slightly marred the launch of the Euro in January 1999. Only Britain, Denmark, and Sweden refused to take part, while Greece failed to meet the qualifying criteria.

Explanations of EMU

☐ Supranationalist explanations have included spillover, the role the Commission, and the role of central bankers as an epistemic community.

☐ Intergovernmental explanations have stressed geo-political factors and domestic economic factors.

☐ International factors form the background to both supranational and intergovernmental explanations.

EMU after 1999

☐ Soon after it started, the Euro ran into problems. Its value fell against the dollar, and the outlying economies experienced inflation at the same time as the core economies experienced recession.

☐ The economies that remained outside of the Eurozone experienced high levels of growth. Between September 2000 and September 2003 Britain, Denmark, and Sweden all decided not to apply for entry.

☐ When France and Germany breached the rules of the stability pact, they refused to come into line, and in November 2003 the mandatory system was effectively abandoned and replaced by a set of voluntary guidelines.

☐ Euro notes and coins were introduced at the start of 2002. Risse claimed that this reinforced a sense of European identity amongst citizens of the Eurozone, although the evidence was rather ambiguous.

FURTHER READING

The essential starting point for further reading is D.R. Cameron, 'Economic and Monetary Union: Underlying Imperatives and Third-Stage Dilemmas', *Journal of European Public Policy* 4 (1997): 455–85, which examines why the member states perceived EMU to be in their national interest, and considers some of the practical problems involved in operating a single currency. W. Sandholtz, 'Choosing Union: Monetary Politics and Maastricht', *International Organization* 47 (1993): 1–39, reviews the history of the decision on monetary union, and analyses it in the light of theoretical perspectives, including neofunctionalism and intergovernmentalism. Unsurprisingly, the intergovernmental viewpoint is best represented by A. Moravcsik, *The Choice for Europe: Social Purpose and State Power from Messina to Maastricht* (London: UCL Press, 1998), 379–471. An excellent, detailed history is provided by K. Dyson and K. Featherstone, *The Road to Maastricht: Negotiating Economic and Monetary Union* (Oxford: Oxford University Press, 1999); while the perspectives of a political scientist and an economist are combined in M. Levitt and C. Lord, *The Political Economy of Monetary Union* (Basingstoke and London: Macmillan, 2000).

online resource centre

Visit the Online Resource Centre that accompanies this book for links to more information on the Economic and Monetary Union, including the web site of the European Central Bank.

CHAPTER 28

Regional and Structural Policies

CHAPTER OVERVIEW

The EC had a problem of regional disparities in economic performance from its inception, but serious efforts to tackle them at EC level only began in the 1970s. From modest beginnings, EU regional and structural policy has grown to account for over a third of the EC budget. This chapter traces key developments and highlights shifts in the intergovernmental-supranational nature of policy control in the sector that first gave rise to the notion of multi-level governance.

> The increasing involvement of the European Union in the development of European regions is one of the clearest examples of transnational policy cooperation...
>
> **(Adshead 2002: 7)**

Disparities between Europe's regions have been long reported by both the Commission and independent experts. As early as 1958 it was noted that the regional GDP in Hamburg was five times greater than in Calabria (Halstead 1982: 55). Yet the Treaty of Rome made no specific commitment to the creation of a Community regional policy. It did though provide a more general objective of promoting throughout the Community 'a harmonious development of economic activities, a continuous and balanced expansion' (Article 2). The preamble to the Treaty also made reference to 'reducing the differences between the various regions and the backwardness of the less favoured regions' (Swift 1978: 10). At this stage, it was not clear whether these disparities would be addressed through member state or Community regional policies, or a combination of both.

For almost two decades, the responsibility for regional policy remained with the member states, but wide disparities between EC regions persisted. In 1970 the gap in GDP per head between the ten richest and the ten poorest regions in the EC was approximately 3 : 1. This represented a narrowing of the gap that had existed in the mid-1960s, when the ratio was nearer to 4 : 1; but this narrowing was based on a high level of labour migration from the poor to the rich regions (Eurostat 1980). Eventually, agreement was reached at the Paris summit in October 1972 to create a European Regional Development Fund (ERDF). This move reflected the increased salience of the issue following the first enlargement of the EC, and subsequent enlargements have also been significant in producing reform of the ERDF and other structural funds that were subsequently added to the budget (Insight 28.1).

This chapter looks first at the early moves to try to co-ordinate regional policies between the member states, before turning to the formation of the ERDF. The negotiations around the ERDF are considered in some detail as an illustration of how the process of intergovernmental bargaining has from the outset been critical to the development of regional and structural policy. The subsequent rounds of reform in 1988, 1993, and 1999 are also considered in some detail. The central question of the chapter is whether the experience of regional and structural policy lends more support to intergovernmental theories of the nature of the EU or to supranational theories.

Early Moves

The Commission showed recognition of regional problems in 1961 when it convened a conference in Brussels to consider what a European regional policy would constitute. This set in train a process of deliberations that led to the establishment in 1967 of a Commission Directorate General (DG xvi) for regional policy. This brought together those

POLICIES

INSIGHT 28.1

The European Structural Funds

Several terms that have quite specific meanings are often used interchangeably in this policy field. EU *regional* policy is concerned with correcting economic and social disparities between European regions that are caused by the creation of a single European market. The main financial instrument of EU regional policy is the European Regional Development Fund (ERDF). Other EU policies have regional dimensions, but are primarily aimed at assisting specific social groups. Of particular importance among other EC financial instruments in this respect are the European Social Fund (ESF) and the 'Guidance' section of the European Agricultural Guarantee and Guidance Fund (EAGGF).

Since 1988, the ERDF, ESF, and EAGGF collectively have been known as the *structural funds*, informed by *structural policy*. Thus structural policy has both regional and non-regional dimensions. In 1993, the Financial Instrument of Fisheries Guidance (FIFG) was added to the structural funds. To complicate the picture further, the term *cohesion policy* came into use after the Single European Act of 1986. This term describes a range of EU measures, including the structural funds, which are aimed at reducing economic and social disparities in Europe. The main non-structural-fund financial instrument is the Cohesion Fund.

parts of the Commission of the EEC and the High Authority of the ECSC with responsibility for existing regional measures. The merger provided additional impetus to the development of Community regional policy.

In 1969, the Commission made proposals to the Council for the co-ordination of member states' regional policies and of Community policies with a regional impact, and for the creation of a European Regional Development Fund (ERDF). The ERDF would be targeted through regional programmes and overseen by a standing committee on regional development made up of representatives from member states' governments and the Commission.

The Commission's proposals were not well received by the Council. Only Italy, which contained the poorest regions in the EC, was really keen to see progress in that direction. West Germany was already feeling concern at the financial implications of the CAP, and was not keen on making any further open-ended commitments of a similar nature. France had both political and economic reasons for opposing a common regional policy. Politically, President Pompidou had to avoid antagonizing his Gaullist supporters by appearing to cede further member state sovereignty to the EC; economically, France's exceptional growth rates in the 1960s, which were continuing with a 7.9 per cent increase in GNP in 1969 (OECD 1970: 1), meant that despite her own problem regions, she might well become a net contributor to any ERDF.

After 1969, a combination of factors elevated the status of regional policy: the issue of economic and monetary union (EMU); the proposed enlargement of the Community to include Britain and Ireland; and the issue of member state aids to industry. The Werner Report of 1970 gave impetus to the Treaty of Rome's objective of completing economic and monetary union (Ch. 27, p. 429). This Report planned to achieve economic and monetary union in the Community within ten years, requiring further institutional reform and closer political integration. The Report argued that continued regional disparities within the Community would work against this objective. From the subsequent agreement to work towards EMU, taken at the Hague Summit of 1969, came recognition from the Council that action was necessary to address the problem of regional imbalances.

The proposed enlargement of the Community to include Britain, Denmark, and Ireland would bring a new set of disadvantaged regions to deal with in two of these countries. While the problems of Ireland, largely related to agriculture, might have been dealt with by reforming the European Agricultural Guarantee and Guidance Fund (EAGGF), Britain had a number of regions suffering industrial decline. Moreover, Britain was also likely to be a net contributor to Community funds and was keen to explore potential forms of reimbursement.

The third factor providing the context for the introduction of EC regional policy was the Commission's plans for controlling member states' aid to industry. In June 1971, the Commission recommended to the Council that state aids should be clearly measurable (transparent) and that a distinction should be made between the 'central' or wealthy areas of the Community and the 'peripheral' regions. It proposed that the level of state aid to central areas should be no more than 20 per cent of total investment. In line with the commitment to fair competition in the Treaty of Rome, the Council endorsed this proposal in October 1971. The effect was to encourage a higher proportion of member states' aid to be targeted at poorer regions. This decision placed constraints on member states' regional policies and consequently intensified interest in developments at Community level.

The Creation of European Regional Policy

In the changing circumstances of the early 1970s, a new coalition in favour of European regional policy emerged, but the British position was crucial (Insight 28.2). As a result, the Commission's regional policy proposals were accepted unanimously by the European Parliament in March 1972 and the Council agreed to decide on the issue by October. At the Paris Summit of October 1972, the new member states were involved in discussing future priorities for the first time and it became clear that senior political leaders had accepted the case for a regional policy. The final communication of the summit outlined the agreement that a 'high priority' should be given to correcting the Community's structural and regional imbalances that might affect the realization of economic and monetary union. Further, the heads of government instructed the Commission to prepare a report on the Community's regional problems and suggest appropriate solutions. It was also agreed that member states would undertake to co-ordinate their regional policies and that a regional development fund would be established.

> **INSIGHT** 28.2
>
> ### British Entry to the EC as an Incentive to Create the ERDF
>
> Both West Germany and France wanted to see Britain settle in as a member of the EC. For West Germany the reasons were primarily economic: the decline of British self-sufficiency in capital goods offered an important potential export market which might be dominated by the United States if Britain remained outside the EC. For France the reasons were primarily political: President Pompidou had made British entry one of the bases of his *rapprochement* with the centre parties, and he had staked his personal prestige on the exercise; he was also on good personal terms with the British Prime Minister, Edward Heath. For his part, Heath knew that there was a lack of enthusiasm in Britain for Community membership, and that the domination of the Community budget by the CAP meant that Britain might become a net contributor after the end of the transitional period. To head off the possibility of financial loss from membership, and to produce tangible benefits as quickly as possible, Heath made the creation of a regional fund a high priority. It would be an institutionalized subsidy from the EC for British expenditure in the regions.

The Thomson Report

The problems posed for the EC by the existence of wide and growing divergences in economic performance were summarized in the Commission's first major report on the subject, published in May 1973. The 'Thomson Report', as it became known after the British EC Regional Policy Commissioner, argued that regional problems prevented balanced expansion of the Community. Moreover, the poverty of the weaker regions limited the size of the potential market for the products of the stronger regions, thus limiting the potential for continuous expansion of the economy as a whole.

Thomson also emphasized that the commitment to EMU was jeopardized by regional disparities. While regional weaknesses did not coincide exactly with member states' boundaries, there was a tendency for the weakest member states' economies to be comprised predominantly of regions that had the most serious problems, and for the stronger member states' economies to contain few problem regions. This placed pressure on the governments of countries with serious regional problems to follow national economic policies to alleviate them. In the context of a common market, manipulation of the exchange rate of the national currency was one of the few policy instruments still available to governments for this purpose: EMU implied the loss of that instrument. If they were expected to abandon this important means of assisting their economies, the governments of the weaker states would expect Community aid for those regions that subsequently found themselves in difficulty.

Finally, the Thomson Report pointed out the threat of ongoing regional disparities to the common market, and so to the basis of the Community itself. The Report put this point bluntly: 'No community could maintain itself nor have meaning for the peoples which belong to it so long as some have very different standards of living and have cause to doubt the common will of all to help each Member to better the conditions of its people' (European Commission 1973: 550). This warning took on a new immediacy in the context of the recession of the 1970s, as pressure began to grow for governments to take protectionist measures as a means of alleviating the unemployment problem.

The Oil Crisis

While the EC took a major step towards a regional fund at Paris in 1972, it was a difficult journey from this declaration to the establishment of the ERDF in 1975. The insistence of Britain, Ireland, and Italy that they could not take the first steps towards EMU if there were no regional fund was an important factor in securing West German acceptance. But the size of the proposed fund remained a serious point of contention between the potential recipients and the potential contributors.

Before this issue could be tackled, the 1973 oil crisis intervened to place discussion of energy at the top of the Community agenda. And on this issue the British reluctance to consider any Community interference with the distribution of North Sea oil drove a wedge between Britain and West Germany. The German government, keen to get an agreement on energy-sharing, attempted to link the issue to that of a regional fund. It was a time-honoured Community method of working, but the British government, not used to such methods, rejected the linkage, annoying the Germans even further. West Germany then decided to take a hard line on the ERDF, and refused to continue negotiations. As the OPEC price-rises had thrown the international economic systems into such disarray that 'EMU by 1980' was no longer feasible, the German government felt that it could afford to retract the commitment to set up the fund, as it now had little to lose.

Domestic Politics

Changes of government in 1974 in Britain, West Germany, and France also had their effect on the dispute. The election of a minority Labour government in Britain in February 1974 introduced a new dimension into negotiations. The new government was committed to renegotiating the British terms of entry into the Community and to holding a referendum on continued membership. With the British government's interest in the proposed regional fund marginalized, the prospects for agreement on regional policy became even more distant. The change of Chancellor in West Germany brought Helmut Schmidt into office, a man unlikely to compromise West German national interests and more concerned than his predecessor about the cost to the Federal German budget of membership of the EC. This made him less likely to agree to any further common funds to which his country would be a net contributor. The arrival in office in France of Giscard d'Estaing, and the rapport that rapidly developed between him and the new German Chancellor, meant that the two leaders were able to work together on the issue of Britain's renegotiation. This marked the beginning of the Franco-German alliance that was to dominate the EC for the next seven years; an alliance that was not inclined to look favourably on any revival of the ERDF proposal. Yet agreement *was* reached on the setting up of an ERDF at the summit in Paris in December 1974.

This unexpected development was a direct result of desperate action by the Irish and Italian governments, which still had a major interest in seeing such a fund come into existence. They threatened to boycott the summit unless they were promised progress on the creation of the fund. Such a move would have been unwelcome to Giscard. He had called the summit to establish his position as a leading European statesperson, and to launch his scheme for the institutionalization of summits in the form of the European Council. To save his summit, Giscard was prepared to accept the demand for an ERDF, and to persuade Schmidt to do so. In fact, the removal of the British from the coalition of states pressing for the ERDF made it easier for West Germany to agree to the Italian and Irish demands. Relations between Britain and West Germany were so cool at this time that Schmidt would have been reluctant to back down on his refusal to create a regional fund if it had been the British asking for it. Since it was not, the summit was able to reach agreement on the size and distribution of the ERDF. Concerns remained primarily about the Fund's distribution and the eligibility criteria. However, largely in response to Irish and Italian threats, member states agreed at the Paris Summit to establish a regional fund for a three-year period to begin on 1 January 1975. Initially the French government interpreted this as a trial period, but following the angry reaction of the Irish and Italian governments, all parties accepted that the Fund would be permanent but should be reviewed triennially.

The 1975 Agreement

While the agreement to create a regional fund was politically significant, the imbalance of influence between the member states pressing for the fund and those resisting it limited the initial allocations significantly. Commissioner Thomson had initially proposed a fund of 3 billion European Units of Account (EUA) (approximately £1,260 million), which was reduced to 2.4 billion EUA before the proposal even left the Commission. Already this was a 'political' figure, designed to gain Council approval, rather than a realistic figure in view of the size of the problem. The supplicant states had considered it inadequate. Eventually the Paris summit reached agreement on a fund of 1.3 billion EUA (approximately £540 million), only just over 50 per cent of what the poorer member states had originally considered an inadequate sum.

The Fund would provide up to 50 per cent of the cost of regional development projects in targeted regions. It was a requirement under the funding rules that the remainder had to be provided domestically. This 'match funding' requirement was designed to ensure that EC and member states' regional policy initiatives would be co-ordinated and complementary. In addition to this requirement, the Fund regulations called for close co-operation between Community and member states' authorities in implementing regional policy.

ERDF-funded projects were concerned either directly or indirectly with job creation. Applications for funding were to be submitted by member states to DG XVI of the Commission, which was authorized to select projects for approval by the Fund Management Committee (composed of representatives of the member states and chaired by the Commission). A Regional Policy Committee was also created, consisting of two representatives of each member state and one from the Commission, with the Commission also providing the secretariat. The chief tasks of this Committee were to co-ordinate domestic regional policies and to set the overall framework for regional policy in the Community. The Regional Policy Committee also considered funding applications for large-scale infrastructure projects (over 10 million EUA).

Member states' governments refused to accept the Commission's proposals for 'objective' Community criteria, insisting instead that the regional fund should be allocated according to national quotas. Moreover, each government demanded a quota, even though this meant regions in richer member states were eligible for assistance despite having a greater per capita GDP than some ineligible regions in poorer member states. This intergovernmental carve-up meant funding was dispersed rather than concentrated on areas of greatest need. In its first phase, the ERDF was to cover some 60 per cent of the geographical area of the Community and 40 per cent of the total population (Mawson, Martins, and Gibney 1985: 30). Three member states would be net beneficiaries of the fund—Britain, Ireland, and Italy—with the other six being net contributors. The quotas agreed are set out in Table 28.1.

TABLE 28.1

ERDF National Quotas (1975)

	Percentage (%)
Belgium	1.5
Denmark	1.3
France	15.0
Germany	6.4
Italy	40.0
Ireland	6.0
Luxemburg	0.1
Netherlands	1.7
United Kingdom	28.0
Total	100.0

Note: Ireland was also to receive a further 6 MUA taken proportionally from the other countries, with the exception of Italy.
Source: Preston 1984: 75.

Guiding Principles

The German government was an important ally for the Commission in seeking precise rules for the implementation of regional policy. This was particularly the case with the principle of *additionality*. The intergovernmental disputes following the outbreak of the Yom Kippur War led the German government to adopt a firmer approach to the ERDF, particularly in seeking to ensure rules that would prevent governments spending grants as they saw fit. Consequently, the wording on additionality in the original ERDF regulations stated that,

the Fund's assistance should not lead Member States to reduce their own regional development efforts but should complement these efforts (European Commission 1975).

Securing the additionality of regional funds would have been a major step towards a genuine supranational element in EC regional policy. However, effective implementation of this key principle could not be assumed.

The 1988 Reform of the Structural Funds

EC regional policy underwent reforms in 1979 and 1984, the history of which was 'largely one of a struggle to throw off the many restrictions imposed by the Council of Ministers in the original 1975 Fund Regulation' (Armstrong 1989: 172). The package introduced in 1975 was subject to much criticism. The ERDF was considered too small and too dispersed. It had also become clear that the principle of additionality was largely ignored by member states. In short, progress towards the development of a Community regional policy had 'been marred by national control over all the major aspects of the policy' (Keating and Jones 1985: 54).

Where the Commission did make progress before 1988, it did so through its agenda-setting powers. Thus, while member states' governments rejected and diluted many of the Commission's proposals for regional policy from the 1960s through to the early 1980s, some were adopted. The introduction of a non-quota section of funding and the development of programme contracts were both illustrations of this. Both allowed the Commission greater controls over the allocation of funding and were moves towards a genuinely supranational policy (Bache 1998: 53–66). Yet advances for the Commission depended on securing sufficient support within the Council, which often did not materialize. Additionality was an important example of this and the Commission's failure to make progress on such a key principle was an illustration of the member states' governments' resilience on matters of public expenditure.

The reform of the structural funds in 1988 provided another opportunity for the Commission to strengthen the redistributive impact of regional policy. While the reforms of 1979 and 1984 failed to convert ERDF from a system of reimbursement to an effective instrument of regional policy, they contained the seeds for future policy development as seen in the 1988 reform.

The 1988 Reform

Two important developments provided the political and economic context of the major reform of the structural funds that came into effect on 1 January 1989: the enlargement of the Community to include Portugal and Spain in 1985; and the push towards greater economic and social cohesion given expression in the Single European Act (SEA) of 1986.

The accession of Spain and Portugal meant a considerable widening of regional disparities in the EU, leading to a doubling of the population of regions with a per capita GDP of less than 50 per cent of the Community average (European Commission 1989: 9). This in itself required an increase in regional allocations. The accession of Spain and Portugal was also important in prompting the introduction of a new type of regional development programme in 1985, the Integrated Mediterranean Programmes (IMPs). These programmes involved the Commission in all aspects of programming and also, for the first time, involved subnational actors with detailed knowledge of local problems. This was the Commission-inspired concept of 'partnership'. Through the development of this principle in particular, the IMPs proved to be important forerunners for the reform package of 1988.

Moves to complete the internal market in the mid-1980s led to talk of a 'Golden Triangle' connecting the prosperous parts of the Community that would benefit most from the single market. This 'served to alert the poorer regions of the Community that the completion of the internal market could lead to a concentration of wealth in the EC's core economies' (McAleavey 1993: 92). In response to the concerns of the poorer regions, Article 130A of the SEA (now Article 158, TEC) set out the need to strengthen 'economic and social cohesion' within the EC, in particular through 'reducing disparities between the various regions and the backwardness of the least-favoured regions' (European Commission 1989: 11). The term *cohesion* subsequently came into use to describe a range of Community policies, including structural policy, aimed at reducing regional and social disparities. The concept was developed within the Commission as the counterpart of the moves to completing the internal market. Cohesion had a dual meaning:

It summarized a novel policy rationale to deal more effectively with the old problem of regional economic disparities, but it also held a political promise to involve subnational actors more openly in European decision-making . . . subnational mobilization was crucial to its success.

(Hooghe 1996b: 89)

Article 130D of the SEA (now Article 161 of the TEC) called for a reform of the three structural funds (ERDF, ESF, and EAGGF), through a framework regulation on their tasks, their effectiveness 'and on co-ordination of their activities between themselves and with the operations of the EIB and other financial instruments' (European Commission 1989: 11). The Brussels European Council of February 1988 agreed the draft regulations in principle and also agreed to a doubling of structural fund allocations by 1993. The final details were agreed in three main Regulations that came into effect on 1 January 1989.

Provisions of the 1988 Reform

The Council agreed that allocations to the three structural funds would double in real terms between 1987 and 1993, with allocations in the final year of this period up to ECU 14 billion; approximately 25 per cent of the EU budget. This contrasted sharply with the initial allocation of ECU 257.6 million in 1975, which had represented 4.8 per cent of total EC spending, and the 1987 allocation of ECU 3,311 million (9.1 per cent) (Marks 1992: 194). Approximately 9 per cent of the structural fund budget would be allocated

---

INSIGHT 28.3

Principles Guiding the Operation of the Structural Funds

concentration of the funds on the areas of greatest need as defined by the accompanying objectives (see Insight 28.4, p. 466).

programming: multi-annual programmes would be the norm for all funding, to ease the Commission's administrative burden and promote a more coherent approach.

partnership: partnerships would be established to oversee the administration of the funds and would require the formal involvement of local and regional actors for the first time.

additionality: the additionality requirement would be strengthened by a new regulation and by the greater involvement of the Commission and local and regional actors in the new partnership arrangements.

through CI programmes, for which the Commission had greatest influence over both design and implementation. CIs superseded the existing non-quota allocations.

The operation of the structural funds would be guided by four complementary principles (Insight 28.3), which were essentially those the Commission had advocated throughout the development of regional policy. Several 'Objectives' were defined on the basis of which eligibility for funds would be determined (Insight 28.4). Together with allocations from the non-regional Objectives 3, 4 and 5a the share of structural funding received by each member state is detailed in Table 28.3 (p. 471).

Despite the creation of new Objectives with detailed criteria for eligibility, the decisions on which regions (and thus member states) received assistance under both Objectives 1 and 2 were either taken or heavily influenced by member states' governments. Yet, as McAleavey (1995a: 159) put it: 'Even if an element of the "carve-up" approach did remain, the advances made by the European Commission on the other key principles were more radical.'

Programming

After more than a decade of trying, the Commission finally secured Council support for multi-annual programmes for all structural funding. This switch promised more coherence in formulating strategies for regional development and brought greater certainty to the spending process. Objective 1 regions received programme funding for five years and

---

INSIGHT 28.4

Priority Objectives of the 1988 Reform

Following the principle of concentration, structural-fund expenditure was focused on five objectives, three with an explicit regional dimension (Objectives 1, 2, and 5a). The bulk of spending was focused on the most disadvantaged regions eligible under Objective 1 (approximately 65 per cent of total structural-fund allocations).

Objective 1: promoting the development of 'less developed regions', i.e. those with per capita GDP of less than, or close to, 75 per cent of the Community average under 'special circumstances' (ERDF, ESF, and EAGGF—Guidance Section)

Objective 2: converting the regions seriously affected by industrial decline (ERDF, ESF)

Objective 3: combating long-term unemployment: assisting people aged over 25, unemployed for over a year (ESF)

Objective 4: assisting the occupational integration of young people, i.e. people below the age of 25 (ESF)

Objective 5: (a) accelerating the adjustment of agricultural structures (EAGGF—Guidance Section); (b) promoting the development of rural areas (EAGGF—Guidance Section, ESF, ERDF)

In addition to the 'mainstream' structural funds allocated according to the five objectives, approximately 9 per cent of the ERDF budget was retained for 'Community Initiatives' (CIs). These were programmes devised by the Commission to meet outstanding regional needs. As with the non-quota and Community programmes, such as RESIDER (steel areas) and RENAVAL (shipping and shipbuilding areas), CI programmes would primarily address the needs of particular categories of regions, such as those suffering from the decline of a dominant industry.

Objective 2 regions for a shorter period of three years to allow flexibility for structural funding to respond to problems caused by unforeseen industrial decline.

Programming would follow a three-stage process. First, after full consultation with the sub-national implementers, national governments were to submit regional development plans to the Commission. Each of these would detail regional problems, set out a strategy indicating priorities and provide an estimate of required funding. Second, the Commission would incorporate member states' views in Community Support Frameworks (CSFs) that would prioritize spending, outline the forms of assistance, and provide a financial plan. Third, detailed operational programmes would be agreed by the partners to provide the basis on which they would implement the objectives of the CSFs. These would identify appropriate measures, beneficiaries, and costings. Beyond this, each programme would be monitored and assessed to ascertain whether money had been spent appropriately (European Commission 1989).

Partnership

The principle of partnership formed part of the Commission's view of regional policy from the 1970s (McAleavey 1995*a*: 167). However, early Commission attempts to involve sub-national authorities in the making of regional policy had received a mixed response. In Britain, for example, the 1984 reform agreement on this had little impact on a government, 'reluctant to allow local authorities much say in the preparation of the non-quota programmes. . .' (Mawson, Martins, and Gibney 1985: 49). The partnership principle of the 1988 reform made the consultation of appropriate local and regional authorities a formal requirement for the first time. The framework regulation adopted by the Council in 1988 formally defined partnership as: close consultation between the Commission, the member states concerned and the competent authorities designated by the latter at national, regional, local or other level, with each party acting as a partner in pursuit of a common goal (Regulation (EEC) 2052/88).

In addition to addressing the broader goal of cohesion, the partnership principle was an attempt to make regional policy more effective by engaging in policy making those actors closest to the problems and priorities of targeted regions. Partnerships were to be active in the management, presentation, financing, monitoring, and assessment of structural fund operations, including: preparation of regional development plans for submission to the Commission; negotiation of the CSFs; implementation of the Operational Programmes; and monitoring and assessment of measures taken.

Additionality

The 1988 reform provided the Commission with a major opportunity to strengthen its position for securing additionality. The final wording on additionality agreed by the Council stated: In establishing and implementing the Community Support Frameworks the Commission and the member states shall ensure that the increase in the appropriations for the (structural) funds ... has a genuine additional impact in the regions concerned and results in at least an equivalent increase in the total volume of official or similar (Community and national) structural aid in the member states concerned, taking into account the macro-economic circumstances. . . (Article 9 of Regulation 253/88 EEC)

The Commission also believed that more widespread use of programming would enhance additionality. While the 1988 reform appeared to improve the Commission's prospects of ensuring effective implementation, the issue provided one of the major obstacles in the negotiations, with the British government being the key objector to the rewording of this part of the regulation (Bache 1999).

Environmental Protection

The 1988 ERDF framework regulation reflected increased awareness of the potential environmental threat posed by economic development operations. The regulation stated that: Measures financed by the Structural Funds receiving assistance from the EIB or from another existing financial instrument shall be in keeping with the provisions of the Treaties with the instruments adopted pursuant thereto and with Community policies, including those concerning ... environmental protection (Official Journal of the European Communities 1988, L185/9, Art. 7).

The CSF for Objective 1 regions also included a requirement that measures should satisfy Community legislation on the environment and that member states should supply appropriate information to allow the Commission to evaluate the environmental impact of measures funded (Scott 1995: 81).

The 1993 Reform of the Structural Funds

The general thrust of the 1993 reform was one of continuity rather than radical change, with the principles and structures of the 1988 reform remaining largely intact. Yet the political and economic context in which the 1993 reform took place was very different from that of 1988, and so, consequently, was the scope for advancing Commission preferences.

While enlargement again formed part of the context, negotiations to include Austria, Finland, and Sweden were relatively straightforward. The new members were relatively prosperous and posed no major sectoral problems for the EU to deal with. In terms of regional policy, this enlargement involved three concessions: part of Austria gained Objective 1 status; Objective 6 status was created for sparsely populated areas; and EC competition rules were adapted to accommodate the subsidy practices of the Nordic states (Wishlade 1996: 57). However, the crucial factor in shaping the context of the 1993 reform was the signing of the Treaty on European Union (TEU) at Maastricht in December 1991.

The TEU upgraded the importance of EC regional policy in the context of further moves towards closer economic and political union. Yet the period between the Maastricht European Council and the 1993 reform of the structural funds was marked by a change in the political and economic climate. In particular, 'growing unemployment and other economic difficulties within some northern member states heightened concerns about the costs and the cost-effectiveness of Community policies' (Wishlade 1996: 48). Subsequent problems involved in ratifying the Treaty prompted concern over the progress and timetable for economic and monetary union (Ch. 13, p. 172).

By the Edinburgh European Council of December 1992 'agreement on the future Community budget (providing funding for the commitments entered into at Maastricht) was the most critical item requiring decision' (Bachtler and Michie 1994: 790). The compromise that was reached included an increase in the structural funds' budget to ECU 27.4 billion by 1999, virtually doubling the amount previously allocated. The context of monetary union was crucial in securing this increase.

Following the budgetary envelope agreed at Edinburgh, the Commission's proposals for the 1993 reform were framed within the principles of concentration, partnership, programming, and additionality set out in the 1988 reform. The main proposals related to eligibility criteria, programming periods, and administrative arrangements. When agreement was reached by the European Council in July 1993, following the intervention of Commission president Delors, 'secrecy surrounded the final compromise figures . . . and uncertainty remained as to whether the promised allocations matched or exceeded the sums agreed at Edinburgh' (Bachtler and Michie 1994: 790).

Provisions of the 1993 Reform

The Commission's initial proposals for the 1993 reform were intended to address member states' concerns over the operation of the funds after 1988. Despite this, member states' governments 'proceeded to change the substance of the Commission's proposals in several nontrivial ways to respond to concerns about the distribution of funds, efficiency, and member state control of the funds' operation' (Pollack 1995: 381). Thus, while the major principles adopted in the 1988 reform—concentration of effort, partnership, programming, and additionality—were maintained, governments secured important modifications to some of these principles.

The principle of concentration continued attempts to focus aid on the areas of greatest need. To do this, some amendments were made to the existing priority objectives (see Insight 28.5). More controversial was the designation of eligible areas. Here again, a number of governments pressed for, and secured the inclusion of regions that did not meet the objective Community criteria.

More generally, governments again pressed their claims for a share of the total fund allocations. In particular, the Irish government claimed to have been promised a 13.5 per cent share of allocations at the Edinburgh European Council of December 1992 in return for concessions on allocations to the new Cohesion Fund (below). The Irish government threatened to veto the 1993 reform agreement if this promise was not honoured, which ultimately it was (Pollack 1995: 381–2).

In addition to conflicts over redistributive matters, the Council also amended the Commission's proposed administrative arrangements. Four issues were important (Pollack 1995: 382–3):

(1) Provisions for the monitoring and assessment of structural fund operations were strengthened, largely at the insistence of the British government.

(2) Member states were given a more important role in the designation of Objective 2 and 5b regions. Here the governments of France, Germany and Britain were most influential.

Priority Objectives of the 1993 Reform

Objectives 1 and 2 were not changed from 1988. Objectives 3 and 4 were merged to create a new Objective 3. This aimed at 'facilitating the integration . . . of those threatened with exclusion from the labour market' (European Commission 1993*b*: 11). The new Objective 4 was designed to give effect to new tasks laid down in the Maastricht Treaty to, 'facilitate workers' adaptation to industrial changes and to changes in production systems' (European Commission 1993*b*: 11). Objective 5a maintained its initial goal of accelerating the adjustment of agricultural structures as part of the CAP reform, but a new fund was added to assist the fisheries: the Financial Instrument of Fisheries Guidance (FIFG). Problems arising from the decline in fishing and fish-processing activities would also be addressed through Objectives 1, 2, and 5b. Objective 5b changed slightly from the 'development of rural areas' to the 'development and structural adjustment of rural areas' (European Commission 1993*b*: 11). Objective 6 status (above) was added to the list.

Objective 1: promoting the development of 'less developed regions' (ERDF, ESF, and EAGGF—Guidance Section)

Objective 2: converting the regions seriously affected by industrial decline (ERDF, ESF)

Objective 3: combating long-term unemployment and promoting entry into the labour market (ESF)

Objective 4: facilitating the adaptation of workers to industrial change (ESF)

Objective 5: (*a*) accelerating the adjustment of agricultural and fisheries structures (EAGGF—Guidance Section, FIFG); (*b*) promoting rural development and structural adjustment (EAGGF—Guidance Section, ESF, ERDF)

Objective 6: developing sparsely populated Nordic areas (ERDF, ESF, EAGGF—Guidance Section)

(3) The Council made amendments to the Commission's proposed wording on additionality, adding that it should take account of 'a number of specific economic circumstances, namely privatizations, an unusual level of public structural expenditure undertaken in the previous programming period and business cycles in the national economy'. This allowed member states to reduce spending on domestic structural measures without contravening the additionality requirement.

(4) The Council insisted on the creation of a management committee to facilitate greater national government control over CI programmes

The Cohesion Fund

During the negotiations over the Maastricht Treaty, the Spanish government argued for a new compensatory mechanism additional to the structural funds. Spain was worried it would be a net contributor to Community funds by 1993. While the Spanish government did not convince other governments to introduce a compensatory financial instrument, it did secure the support of the governments of other relatively poor member states—Portugal, Greece, and Ireland—in arguing for additional resources to compensate for ongoing regional disparities. Ultimately, faced with the threat of veto from the Spanish government, the Council agreed to establish a new Cohesion Fund (Morata and Munoz 1996: 215). This had allocations of approximately ECU 16 billion for the period 1993–9 (European Commission 1996a: 147).

The Cohesion Fund provided broadly equal amounts for environmental improvements and transport infrastructure projects. The Fund was targeted at member states with a GDP of less than 90 per cent of the Community average, not at specific regions. It would support up to 85 per cent of the costs of projects, a higher intervention rate than with any of the structural funds. As with the structural funds, the Cohesion Fund—and the interim instrument established before the Fund came into operation—was subject to indicative allocations: (Greece 16–20 per cent; Spain 52–58 per cent; Portugal 16–20 per cent; and Ireland 7–10 per cent) (Scott, 1995: 38) (Tables 28.2, and 28.3).

TABLE 28.2

Cohesion Fund Allocations 1994–1999 (estimated)

	%	ECU m.(1994 prices)
Spain	55	7950
Portugal	18	2601
Greece	18	2602
Ireland	9	1301
	100	14454

Source: Commission 1996a: 147

TABLE 28.3

Scale of Structural Intervention (including Cohesion Fund and Community Initiatives) 1994–1999 (allocations for 1989–1993 in brackets)

	% Share of EU aid	EU aid as % of national GDP
Austria	1.13 (0)	0.19 (0)
Belgium	1.25 (1.18)	0.18 (0.11)
Denmark	0.50 (0.59)	0.11 (0.08)
Germany	12.97 (11.46)	0.21 (0.13)
Greece	10.58 (12.51)	3.67 (2.65)
Spain	25.30 (20.57)	1.74 (0.75)
Finland	1.19 (0)	0.40 (0)
France	8.92 (9.46)	0.22 (0.14)
Ireland	4.42 (6.68)	2.82 (2.66)
Italy	12.92 (16.0)	0.42 (0.27)
Luxemburg	0.06 (0.10)	0.15 (0.17)
Netherlands	1.56 (1.11)	0.15 (0.07)
Portugal	10.53 (12.9)	3.98 (3.07)
Sweden	0.93 (0)	0.37 (0)
United Kingdom	7.75 (7.27)	0.25 (0.13)

Source: Calculated from figures in Commission 1996a: 144

Some key principles guiding the structural funds did not apply to the operation of the Cohesion Fund. As Scott (1995: 39) noted: 'In the first instance, nowhere in the interim instrument or in the European Council guidelines regarding the main elements of the forthcoming Cohesion Fund Regulation is there any reference to the concept of partnership.' Instead, decisions on the projects (*not* programmes) to be funded would be made by the Commission in agreement with the 'member state' concerned. In terms of additionality, the preamble to the interim regulation stipulated that member states should not 'decrease their investment efforts in the field of environmental protection and transport infrastructure', but the more tightly defined principle of additionality included in the structural-fund regulations did not apply.

While the relaxed requirements on additionality and partnership left the implementation of these principles to the discretion of member states, this had to be understood in the context of moves towards monetary union that required severe constraints on public expenditure. In this context, governments were left with considerable discretion over how Cohesion Fund allocations would be spent. In particular, insistence on additionality would have created serious tension with the objective of reducing public expenditure in the 'Cohesion Four' countries.

Implementing the Structural Funds 1988–1998

As noted above, the framework of implementation provided by the regulations for the period after 1988 was relatively consistent. This section focuses on the implementation of the principles of partnership, additionality, and environmental protection.

Partnership

Hooghe (1996*a*) co-ordinated a comprehensive study of the impact of the partnership arrangements across member states. This study considered the impact of the partnership arrangements on 'territorial restructuring' within eight member states. It sought to answer two related questions: 'Have diverse territorial relations converged under pressure of this uniform EU policy, hence moving towards a systematic involvement of subnational authorities in all member states? Or are uniform European regulations being bent and stretched so as to uphold existing differences in member states?' (Hooghe 1996*a*: 2). The study found that the implementation of the partnership principle varied considerably across member states. Actors at different levels—national, sub-national, and supranational—controlled different resources in different member states, influencing their ability to shape policy implementation within the framework set by EU-level agreements. The study of Britain (Bache, George, and Rhodes 1996) also illustrated variations in implementation across regions within a member state.

In centralized member states, where central government actively sought to play a gatekeeper role over the political impact of the new arrangements, such as in Britain, it met with considerable success. There was sufficient scope within the requirements for governments to dominate partnerships, where they had the will to do so. Here, sub-national actors were mobilized, but not necessarily empowered. In more decentralized member states, sub-national authorities—normally regional governments—were better placed to take advantage of the opportunities provided by the partnership requirement. In 1998, the Commission (1998*b*: 11) stated that: 'While significant progress has been made in involving regional authorities, in particular where regionalization is least developed, the involvement of local authorities most directly concerned . . . is still very patchy.'

Additionality

After 1988, the European Commission singled out Britain as the only member state to continue breaching the principle of additionality. The additionality problem in Britain culminated in a dispute over the Rechar programme for declining coal-mining areas. The way in which the British government tried to implement the expenditure of Rechar funds led directly to a confrontation with the Commission. The dispute began in December 1990 and lasted for over a year.

The details of the dispute are complex. The British government had long been suspected of not providing genuine additionality, but the Treasury had always maintained that it built into each year's regional expenditure plans an element to cover expected ERDF funds. Without the ERDF, spending in the regions would be less. However, this excuse did not hold for Rechar because the programme had not even existed when the British budgetary plans for the Rechar funding period (1990–3) were made. After a prolonged struggle between the government and the Commission, during which Commissioner Bruce Millan withheld the British share of the Rechar money, the government backed down and in February 1992 announced its intention to introduce new arrangements for implementing additionality.

This dispute, and the generally enhanced autonomy of the Commission in the regional policy sector, was central to the development by Gary Marks (1993) of the theory of multi-level governance (Ch. 2, pp. 33–6). However, the Commission's success on additionality in Britain proved to be short-lived. An assessment of additionality following the implementation of the government's new arrangements showed little evidence of extra spending in targeted regions as a result (Bache 1999).

Environmental Provisions

Despite provisions in the 1988 reform seeking to address the environmental problems caused by structural developments, in practice environmental concerns took a low priority. The Commission was inadequately resourced to monitor environmental impacts, with only six Commission officials dedicated to overseeing this aspect of operations across all member states. Moreover, member states were reluctant to supply full information on environmental implications and the Commission had no clear powers under the regulations to insist that governments comply with the request in the regulations (Scott 1995: 82). Non-governmental environmental organizations were equally powerless to ensure adequate implementation of environmental requirements. Scott (1995:

83) noted that these groups were 'entirely excluded from national or regional monitoring committees in theory as well as practice—committees which at any rate do not have an explicit environmental remit'.

The 1993 structural-fund regulations sought to strengthen the Commission's powers for regulating the behaviour of member states in ensuring respect for the environment, but these provisions fell short on a number of counts (Scott 1995: 94–7):

(1) The 1993 reform provisions were so vague as to leave member states with considerable discretion.

(2) There remained a need for environmental assessment to be strategic, rather than project-based.

(3) The amendments failed to take account of the limited effectiveness of the Environmental Impact Assessment Directive of 1985 in relation to structural-fund operations.

(4) The new regulations failed to open up the structural-fund planning-process to non-governmental organizations.

Assessing Implementation

The 1988 reform of the structural funds provided a classical illustration of how EU-level agreements could be frustrated at the policy-implementation stage. The principles of partnership and additionality were implemented very differently by member states in practice. Yet the partnership principle remained key to the Commission's pursuit of an effective regional policy. In its proposals for the 1999 reform, the Commission argued for a deepening of partnerships, so that partners would be more involved throughout the process of financing from the structural funds (below). Perhaps more significantly, the Commission noted the 'very patchy' involvement of local authorities, environmental authorities and other bodies (the social partners, local voluntary organizations, non-governmental bodies etc.) who were 'dealing with matters of major concern to the Community, such as employment, sustainable development and equal opportunities for men and women' (European Commission 1998b: 11).

In terms of theoretical developments, perhaps the main lesson from the implementation of the 1988 reform was that:

Analysts who want to predict developments in EU cohesion policy from the great bargains risk overlooking the ambivalence in the regulations; the active role of the European Commission, national administrations, and subnational actors in exploiting these ambiguities; and the effects of policy learning.

(Hooghe 1996b: 119)

In particular, where governments were determined to resist unwanted outcomes from developments at EU level, they could often operate as effective 'gatekeepers' at the policy-implementation stage.

The 1999 Reform of the Structural Funds

Negotiations over policy reforms for the post-2000 period took place in the context of a majority of member states joining the single currency and ongoing negotiations to enlarge the EU to include countries of central and eastern Europe. As one commentator put it:

The political climate in which the latest round of regional policy reforms is being negotiated is very different from that surrounding previous exercises over the past decade. After the successive expansion of regional and social funding in 1988 and 1993, the emphasis now is very much on budgetary consolidation.

(Watson 1998: 16)

Enlargement to include countries from central and eastern Europe, with an average GDP per capita typically at around one third of the existing EU average, required a change to the existing structural-fund criteria. Under the structural-fund regulations for 1994–9, the entire territories of the countries of eastern and central Europe would have qualified for Objective 1 and Cohesion Fund assistance. Extending the existing funds only to Poland, Hungary, the Czech Republic, and Slovakia would have increased the total cost of the funds to approximately ECU 48 billion. Somehow, the Commission's proposals for reform had to strike a balance between the demands of existing member states and the need to facilitate enlargement. The context did not favour Commission advances on the principles of regional policy. In addition to the challenges of proposed enlargement, EMU was crucial in framing a mood of uncertainty within member states, creating a political atmosphere against further integration.

Commission Proposals

In March 1998, the Commission presented its proposed regulations for governing the structural funds for the period 2000–6. The proposed reform was centred on three priorities: greater concentration, decentralized and simplified implementation, and a strengthening of efficiency and control set against a background of budgetary discipline (European Commission 1998a: 2).

The Commission proposed to maintain the four governing principles of the structural funds—partnership, concentration, additionality, and programming (Insight 28.6). However, the partnership principle would be reformed so that the responsibilities of each of the partners would be defined 'so as to implement better the principle of subsidiarity and permit improved application of Article 205, under which the Commission is responsible for implementation of the Community budget' (European Commission 1998b: 10). The Commission proposed introducing a fifth principle—efficiency—to reassure people that public money allocated to the structural funds was well used. While the four principles of 1988 remained intact, and a fifth principle of 'efficiency' would be added, the Commission's proposals were relatively modest and in some areas hinted at a further renationalization of the funds.

INSIGHT 28.6

Priority Objectives of the 1999 Reform

Objective 1: would continue to assist the least-developed regions, defined as those with a GDP per capita at 75 per cent or less of the EU average over the previous three years. Henceforth, this criterion would be strictly enforced. In addition, the new Objective 1 included the regions that previously qualified under Objective 6, which were the sparsely populated regions of Finland and Sweden.

Objective 2: The changes to designation here were more significant. The existing Objectives 2 and 5b were merged into the new Objective 2, which thus covered 'areas undergoing socioeconomic change in the industrial and service sectors, declining rural areas, urban areas in difficulty and depressed areas dependent on fisheries' (Wishlade 1999: 39). Also significant was that Objective 2 would be concentrated on no more than 18 per cent of the EU population, with the safety-net mechanism ensuring that no member state's Objective 2 population would be less than two-thirds of its coverage under the 1994–9 programme period.

Objective 3: would apply across the EU, except for Objective 1 regions, and would assist in modernizing systems of education, training, and employment.

The Commission signalled its intention to take a lesser role in the day-to-day management of the funds. This meant withdrawing its officials from involvement in partnership activities below programme monitoring committees, where involvement had been the practice. In defence of this withdrawal, Commission officials emphasized that they would still be involved in programme monitoring committees, and these would take on a more strategic role than previously. In addition, the Commission proposed retaining 10 per cent of the structural funds as a 'performance reserve' for it to allocate during the programme period to those regions spending funds most effectively. The proposed enlargement of the EU focused the Commission's efforts on concentrating the funds on a smaller proportion of the existing EU's population. While existing member states accepted the need for concentration in principle, agreeing which areas would be affected by greater concentration in 1999 would be fiercely contested. Moreover, the proposed regulations suggested that in addition to determining Objective 1 areas, the Council would also have more control over the designation of Objective 2 areas.

The convergence criteria for monetary union established at Maastricht had provided a loose interpretation of the additionality requirement after the 1993 reform. While the Commission's proposal for 'negotiated additionality', if accepted, appeared to be an improvement on this, its success would depend in large part on what the Commission would be able to negotiate with member states, most of whom were about to experience the first challenges of monetary union to their national budgetary policies. The Commission proposed taking a specific indicator of additionality for each objective to facilitate more effective monitoring.

Programming remained a relatively uncontroversial principle of structural funding in 1998. Its value had been widely accepted. One proposal for improvement was to reduce the three-stage programming process to two stages, except for very large allocations. Partnership remained at the core of Commission thinking and the principle would be strengthened if the proposals for 1999 were accepted. The Commission sought to build on the existing provisions by increasing the emphasis placed on involving the social partners, environmental agencies, and other non-governmental organizations that had a role in social and economic development. The need to reduce the number of CIs to simplify procedures and reduce duplicative structures was accepted by the Commission. While CIs were reduced to three in number, this meant more resources for each remaining CI.

Provisions of the 1999 Reform

The General Affairs Council formally adopted the new structural-fund regulations in June 1999, following political agreement at the Berlin European Council in March and approval by the European Parliament in May. The same meeting also adopted the regulations for the Cohesion Fund and the Instrument for Structural Policies for Pre-Accession (ISPA), which would be used to help the applicant states adjust their economies in preparation for membership.

Financial allocations to the structural funds were EUR195 billion over the period 2000–6, with a further EUR18 billion provided for the Cohesion Fund. In addition, EUR7.28 billion was set aside for pre-accession structural assistance to applicant states. Total funding under these measures remained at 0.46 of the EU's GNP over the period. Allocations by member state and by Objective are outlined in Table 28.4.

The guiding principles proposed by the Commission were accepted. On *concentration*, this meant that the number of structural-fund Objectives would be reduced from six to three (see Insight 28.6, p. 476). Also, as proposed by the Commission, the number of CIs would be substantially reduced from the existing thirteen. The Commission had proposed three Initiatives:

- Interreg (cross border, transnational and inter-regional co-operation)
- Leader (rural development)
- Equal (tackling discrimination in the labour market).

However, at the insistence of the European Parliament, a fourth programme was retained:

- Urban (to regenerate inner cities).

Although having no clear Treaty mandate for urban policy, the Commission had made imaginative use of this programme to develop innovative practices in an increasing number of cities (Tofarides 2003).

The *programming* process was retained, with the Commission adopting a more strategic role and delegating greater responsibility to domestic actors for the day-to-day implementation and monitoring of programmes. The reworded *partnership* principle required the involvement of organizations that reflected the 'need to promote equality between men and women and sustainable development through the integration of environmental protection and improvement requirements' (OJ L161, 26/6/99: 12). The principle of *additionality* was maintained, although its verification would depend on baseline figures of domestic spending that member states' governments would play a key role in

TABLE 28.4

Structural Funds: Breakdown by Member State for the Period 2000–2006 (in Million Euros at 1999 prices)

Member State	Obj. 1	Transitional support for former Obj. 1 areas	Obj. 2 for former Obj. 2 and 5(b) areas	Transitional Instrument (outside Obj. 1 areas)	Obj. 3	Fisheries	Total
Belgium	0	625	368	65	737	34	1829
Denmark	0	0	156	27	365	197	745
Germany	19229	729	2984	526	4581	107	28156
Greece	20961	0	0	0	0	0	0
Spain	37744	352	2553	98	2140	200	43087
France	3254	551	5437	613	4540	225	14620
Ireland[a]	1315	1773	0	0	0	0	3088
Italy	21935	187	2145	377	3744	96	28484
Luxemburg	0	0	34	6	38	0	78
Netherlands	0	123	676	119	1686	31	2635
Austria	261	0	587	102	528	4	1473
Portugal	16124	2905	0	0	0	0	19029
Finland	913	0	459	30	403	31	1836
Sweden[b]	722	0	354	52	720	60	1908
UK[a]	5805	1166	3989	706	4568	121	15635
EU15[c]	127543	8411	19733	2721	24050	1106	183564

Note: [a]Including Peace (2000–2004). [b]Including the special programme for Swedish coastal zones. [c]EU totals for all fifteen member states.
Source: Inforegio Newsletter No. 65, June 1999, pp. 3–4.

determining. Finally, in line with the principle of *efficiency*, a performance reserve was agreed by member states. However, this was limited to 4 per cent of each member state's share of funding, rather than the 10 per cent the Commission had proposed.

Developments in Implementation

Partnership

Research funded by the European Commission (Kelleher *et al.* 1999) confirmed the findings on partnership of the earlier Hooghe study. It highlighted continuing differences in the implementation of the principle across member states, emphasizing again the degree of internal decentralization or deconcentration. Central governments were again seen as key actors in shaping partnership arrangements and dominating and delimiting partnership functions. The role of social partners was often limited and Non-Governmental Organizations often absent from partnerships. However, there were also examples of governments increasingly seeing advantages in the partnership model, leading to extended participation and reduced conflict.

This pattern was reflected within Britain, where national control of partnerships had been particularly strong. The change of government from Conservative to Labour in 1997 partly explained the relaxed approach to partnership, but there were signs before 1997 that a learning process was taking place that led to a reassessment of the costs and benefits of the model. Over time, and accelerated by the change of government, this resulted in central government relaxing its firm grip on partnership composition and decision making (Bache 2004). In relation to Spain, there was evidence of a strong central presence in the implementation process and varying degrees of subnational empowerment according to internal patterns of devolution, with 'those regions on the fast track to devolution . . . generally more able to participate effectively in the policy-making process' (Bache and Jones 2000: 18). In her study of the Basque region, Bourne (2003) went further by suggesting not only that partnership had no significant empowering effect, but that the process of European integration as a whole undermined Basque political power. A study by Gualini (2003: 633) of implementation of the structural funds in Italy placed more emphasis on the constraints facing central government actors, both in relationships with the Commission and with subnational governments, which hindered its ability to play the gatekeeping role in the regional programming process.

Additionality

After the high-profile arguments on additionality in the early 1990s, the issue quickly faded from the political agenda. The 1999 reform did not in practice make the Commission's task of securing compliance, or proving non-compliance, any easier. Besides, by this stage in the history of EU regional policy, other issues were more urgent: in particular, resolving disputes over how the structural funds should operate and be distributed in the context of enlargement.

In Britain, again a particularly reluctant implementer, there were changes in the domestic approach. In this instance, the change of government was decisive. The election of Labour in 1997 brought a British government less hostile than its predecessor to both the EU and the principles of interventionist regional policies. The result was Labour increased public spending limits in the regions benefiting from additional structural funding from 2000, and provided some assistance with matching funds. Significantly, however, there was no significant change in the financial mechanisms through which structural funds were allocated: the Treasury kept control. This left open the possibility that the additional spending capacity given to assisted regions in this period could at some future date be taken away if central government preferences were to change (Bache and Bristow 2003).

Post-2000: Preparing for Enlargement

As discussed above, the 1999 reform signalled a general acceptance that the bulk of funding would have to be redirected towards the new member states of Central and Eastern Europe (CEE). The financial implications of simply extending eligibility to the new member states meant this was never a serious option. However, the Commission reaffirmed its commitment to the core principles of structural funding post-enlargement. This would present a number of challenges to states that had little or no experience with the EU's model of regional development and, in particular, the concept of multi-level and cross-sectoral partnerships. In the period before the transition from communism, regional imbalances in the CEE states were dealt with by the central direction of investment. In the period immediately following transition, limited central resources and a reduced role of the state in the economy reduced the scope for regional measures. Moreover, emphasis on market economics implied that regional imbalances would be corrected through that mechanism.

As these states began to look more seriously at the prospect of EU membership, regional policy measures began to develop alongside the institutional capacity necessary for effective regional policy making. Bailey and De Propris (2002a: 409) argued that over the period 1989–97, one explanation for the continuing lack of convergence across European regions was that some regions lacked the institutional capability to participate effectively in the policy-making and implementation process. Moreover, this failing would be replicated in the CEE states without sufficient capacity building. However, this trend was generally slow and uneven across the accession states.

To assist this process, a number of structural funding instruments were developed to provide financial aid over the period 2000–6. ISPA provided funding for transport and environmental projects, SAPARD (Special Accession Programme for Agricultural and Rural Development) provided assistance for agriculture and rural development, while the PHARE (Poland and Hungary: Aid for Economic Restructuring) programme aimed to strengthen economic and social cohesion and administrative and institutional capacity in the accession states. These three programmes would be worth 3 billion Euros a year in the pre-accession period, and PHARE alone would continue for the period 2004–06 at the rate of 1.6 billion Euros. In this period, Bulgaria and Romania would also be eligible for this funding. In addition, the new member states would be eligible to claim up to 21.8 billion Euros of structural funding in the period 2004 to 2006 (European Commission 2004b: xxii–xxiii).

Bailey and De Propris (2002b) considered the extent to which these instruments had brought about institutional change and, specifically, accelerated a shift to multi-level governance in the accession states. They noted that the Commission had been the 'dominant player' in the use of these funds, 'dictating the terms of institutional changes required, the size of territorial units (NUTS II), the institutional capabilities needed and so on to candidates countries' national governments which are eager to comply with the new rules of the game' (Bailey and De Propris 2002b: 319–20). As such, this raised the prospects for multi-level governance. However, their empirical study of five accession states suggested that national government 'gatekeepers' remained 'firmly in control' of domestic sub-national actors, who were able to participate in but not significantly influence the policy process. Here, it was important to distinguish between the development of institutional *capacity*—offices, staff and buildings—and institutional *capability*—the ability of institutions to carry out the functions assigned to them. The latter was slow to develop during the accession process, but would be crucial to the effective participation of these regions in the EU in the longer term (Bailey and De Propris 2002b: 320).

Proposals for Post-2006

Following enlargement, socio-economic disparities in the EU doubled and the average GDP of the EU decreased by 12.5 per cent. In this context, the Commission set out its proposals for the structural funds for the period 2006–17 in its Third Report on Economic and Social Cohesion (European Commission 2004*b*). It argued that the three existing objectives (1, 2, and 3) should be replaced by three new priorities:

- Convergence: supporting growth and job creation in the least developed member states and regions (Cohesion Fund; ERDF; ESF);
- Regional competitiveness and employment: anticipating and promoting change (ERDF; ESF);
- European territorial co-operation: promoting the harmonious and balanced development of the Union territory (ERDF).

The *Convergence* priority would cover those regions with a per capita GDP of less than 75 per cent of the Community average (previously covered by Objective 1) and would account for approximately 78 per cent of the structural-fund budget. The *Competitiveness* priority, effectively replacing Objectives 2 and 3, would have two strands: regional programmes to promote the attractiveness and competitiveness of industrial, urban and rural areas; and national programmes to promote full employment, quality and productivity at work and social inclusion. The *Co-operation* priority would build on experience of Interreg, to promote co-operation on issues at cross-border, transnational and interregional level. Interreg, along with the other CI programmes (Equal, Leader, and Urban) would no longer exist separately, but their strengths would be incorporated into the new mainstream programmes. For example, in relation to Urban, the Commission proposed that there be a sub-delegation of responsibilities to city authorities (European Commission 2004*b*: xxxii). Finally, the Commission proposed that the EAGGF and FIFG (Financial Instrument for Fisheries Guidance) be removed from the structural-fund programmes and be incorporated into mainstream policies for agriculture and fisheries.

In terms of the long-standing principles, it suggested that while the *programming* approach had increased planning capabilities, there had also been increasing concerns over the complexity of the programming process. *Partnership* was seen as a success that was increasingly inclusive and leading to more effective policies. *Concentration* was seen to have increased, but there was still concern that resources were being spread too thinly. Finally, the Commission suggested that additionality had been 'largely respected' in Objective 1 regions, but that 'verifying that this has also been the case as regards Objective 2 and 3 programmes, especially the latter, has proved more difficult' (European Commission 2004*b*: xxii). In response, the Commission proposed a simplification of the programming approach; offered member states greater responsibility for ensuring additionality; sought to strengthen the partnership requirement; argued for increased concentration of resources on the less prosperous member states; and placed a greater emphasis on performance.

As with previous reforms, the Commission proposals marked only the beginning of the serious bargaining process. An early shot was fired across the bows by the British Chancellor, Gordon Brown, who supported the need to focus on the poorest member states post-enlargement, but suggested that there should be an end to the financial transfers to the richest member states. This would reduce the gross contributions to the EU budget of the richer states, who would then use the savings for their own regional policy purposes: a partial renationalization of EU regional policy (Bache 2004). At the Commission-organized Third Cohesion Forum in Brussels in May 2004, which brought together a range of relevant stakeholders, differences of opinion began to emerge. Giordano (2004) suggested that there was a division between, on the one side, those in favour of the Commission's proposals, including the Commission President Romano Prodi, and member states such as Portugal and Greece; and, on the other side, the government ministers of net contributors to the budget, including Britain, France and Germany, who had concerns over the coverage and costs of the proposals.

CONCLUSION

Since 1975, the regional policy sector has been subject to significant fluctuations in the influence of key actors. While the Commission has long pushed for a genuinely redistributive policy, the Council has intervened at key moments in ways to protect member states' allocations and governments' control over the distribution of funds.

All the major decisions on the creation of regional policy were taken by the heads of government, in particular at the summits in Paris in 1972 and 1974 and in Copenhagen in 1973. The Commission's influence over initial allocations and policy guidelines was at first limited, although the Commission was important in keeping the issue of the regional policy alive in the difficult circumstances of the 1960s and early 1970s. Yet while the eventual establishment of the ERDF in 1975 owed a great deal to the Commission's persistence, intergovernmental politics ensured that it fell some way short of the redistributive policy instrument that the Commission sought.

While a number of member states sought to limit the increase in the fund allocations in the 1988 reform, the doubling of allocations owed much to the commitment of larger member states to the single-market programme. Although the funds continued to benefit regions in the more prosperous member states, the main impact of the doubling of the funds was to transfer resources from Belgium, Denmark, Germany, France, and the Netherlands to Greece, Spain, Ireland, Italy, and Portugal, with the impact on Britain largely neutral (Marks 1992: 194).

Pollack (1995) argued that agreement to major reform in 1988 could be explained by changes in the preferences of the various member states—in particular net contributors such as Britain, France, and Germany—and as a result of the accession of Greece, Spain, and Portugal. The preferences of the net contributors changed in three ways. First, with the Iberian enlargement, the proportion of structural funds received by the 'big three' member states decreased significantly. This meant that for these governments, 'the idea of greater Commission oversight seemed less like an intrusion into the internal affairs of one's own state, where EC spending was minimal, and more like a necessary oversight of the poor member states where the bulk of EC money was being spent' (Pollack 1995: 372). Second, the Iberian enlargement made France, like Britain and Germany, a net contributor to the EC budget, thus giving the 'big three' governments a common interest in the efficient use of the structural funds. Third, the spiralling costs of both the CAP and the structural funds made the level and efficiency of EC spending a 'political issue' of increasing concern to the governments of France, Germany, and Britain in the 1980s (Pollack 1995: 372).

In terms of the budgetary envelope agreed in 1988, an intergovernmentalist interpretation found favour amongst most commentators. The more prosperous member states strongly supported the completion of the single market and wanted this market extending to include Spain and Portugal. In this context, the doubling of the structural funds was accepted by the likely paymaster governments as a 'side-payment to Ireland and the Southern nations' in exchange for their political support on other issues (Moravscik 1991: 62). Marks (1992: 198) conceptualized the side-payment argument as an illustration of *forced spillover*, 'in which the prospect of a breakthrough in one arena created intense pressure for innovation in others'.

Consensus between scholars over other aspects of the 1988 reform is harder to find. For example, Hooghe (1996b: 100) argued that the Commission emerged 'as the pivotal actor in designing the regulations' through its 'monopoly of initiative on the institutional design'. A good example was the inclusion of the partnership principle in the regulations, which was the major innovation of the 1988 reform. In contrast, Pollack (1995) suggested that this shift was a response to national government pressure to secure 'value for money' in the funds' administration. While there is some truth in Pollack's argument, in the context of the single-market programme and enlargement, negotiations over the reform of the structural funds in 1988 allowed the Commission to advance its objective of an effective supranational regional policy. Yet securing changes in the regulations was one thing; effective implementation could not be taken for granted, as later evidence proved.

While the context of the 1988 reform gave the Commission considerable scope for advancing its policy preferences, the 1993 reform represented a reassertion of control by the member states' government in key areas. A good example was additionality. The tenacity with which the Commission had sought the implementation of additionality after 1988 was met by member states' governments effectively diluting the requirement in 1993. Indeed in the context of the convergence criteria for monetary union agreed at Maastricht, for the Commission to pursue genuine additionality at this time would have been difficult: while additionality required member states to demonstrate additional public expenditure, the Maastricht convergence criteria put a squeeze on domestic public spending.

Other changes in 1993 reflected the reassertion of government preferences. For example, while the partnership principle was confirmed, governments remained in control of the designation of 'appropriate partners'. Finally, the creation of the Management Committee to oversee CIs created a degree of national government involvement that would curtail Commission discretion. In the conflict over the implementation of additionality after 1988, the Commission had used its control over the content, coverage and timing of CIs to undermine the British government's arguments. The 1993 changes meant this would be less possible in future.

In summary, the 1993 reform provided a measure of how the relative influence of actors fluctuated over a short period of time. The context of regional-policy reform changed dramatically in the five years after the 1988 reform. This led to a shift in the balance of political resources away from the Commission to the Council at the EU level, which was reflected in the 1993 outcome.

As with previous reforms, the budgetary envelope for the 1999 reform of the structural funds was decided at Council level. In addition to limiting total allocations, member states' governments were also instrumental in securing safety-net mechanisms and transitional arrangements to protect their assisted regions from a sudden and dramatic reduction of funding. Moreover, the reduction of the proposed performance reserve from 10 to 4 per cent was accompanied by provisions for member states' involvement with the Commission in determining the allocation of this reserve to regions that were performing well.

While the partnership principle was maintained, and its requirements made more precise, the selection of partners remained with governments. The additionality principle was also retained, but the new regulations did not suggest that member states' compliance would be any easier for the Commission to ensure. The reduction in the number of and financial allocations to CIs would limit the Commission's scope for autonomy and innovation somewhat, although in its proposals the Commission had acknowledged the need for such a reduction. Institutional politics aside, CIs had been subject to much criticism from a broad range of actors who deemed some programmes to be unnecessarily bureaucratizing the structural-fund process further.

If the 1999 reform was not simply a renationalization of the structural funds, a number of changes from the Commission's initial proposals reflected the preferences of governments. Perhaps more significantly, in the context of proposed enlargement, the Commission's initial proposals were themselves relatively modest. Yet the Commission retained a key role in the process, for example over issues of eligibility, programming, allocating the performance reserve, and in the design and implementation of CIs. Moreover, the key principles guiding the operation of the funds essentially remained those developed by the Commission.

The implementation of key principles of the structural funds after 2000 displayed familiar characteristics: verification of additionality proved difficult and the partnership experience varied. However, in relation to the latter there was perhaps growing evidence of a learning process, such that 'policy formulation is increasingly characterised by consensus-seeking and communicative rationality rather than political-ideological divides' (Bache and Olsson 2001: 234).

In the run-up to enlargement, the Commission experienced familiar difficulties with seeking to empower regional actors as national governments in the accession states demonstrated their gate-keeping capabilities and evidence of multi-level governance remained limited.

Inevitably, enlargement provided the context for the Commission's proposals for the operation of the structural funds after 2006. The Commission's emphasis was on efficiency, with a streamlining of objectives, programmes and funds. However, even at this early stage of the reform process, national governments were raising concerns over the finances and focus of the proposals, with the British government calling for a partial renationalization of EU regional policy. In this policy domain at least, the intergovernmental-supranational theoretical debate remained highly relevant.

KEY POINTS

Early Moves

☐ The Treaty of Rome made no specific commitment to regional policy.

☐ Until the 1970s, regional policy remained a domestic matter for member states.

☐ In the early 1970s, three factors combined to make European regional policy more likely: the issue of economic and monetary union (EMU); the proposed enlargement of the Community to include Britain and Ireland; and the issue of member states' aids to industry.

The Creation of European Regional Policy

☐ The Paris Summit of 1972 agreed to set up the ERDF.

☐ Commissioner Thomson's (1973) report emphasized the importance of regional policy to the project of European integration as a whole.

- ☐ The 1973 oil crisis and political changes within member states threatened to jeopardize agreement on regional policy.
- ☐ A deal was eventually reached only when the Italian and Irish governments threatened to boycott the Paris Summit of 1974.
- ☐ Initial ERDF allocations were disappointing. Moreover, there were no guarantees that the funds would be spent by member states as the Commission intended.

The 1988 Reform of the Structural Funds

- ☐ After 1975, ERDF was criticized for being inadequate to meet the needs of disadvantaged regions.
- ☐ Member states' governments dominated the policy process and there was no major movement towards the creation of a supranational policy. However, developments before 1988 provided the seeds for policy change.
- ☐ Enlargement and the single market programme provided the context for a major reform of the structural funds in 1988.
- ☐ The 1988 reform doubled financial allocations, strengthened the additionality principle, and introduced the principle of partnership.

The 1993 Reform of the Structural Funds

- ☐ The 1993 reform of the structural funds maintained the guiding principles established in 1988, although aspects of the reform reflected a reassertion of member states' government control.
- ☐ In 1993, the Cohesion Fund was established as an additional compensatory instrument for the poorer member states.

Implementing the Structural Funds 1988–1998

- ☐ The implementation of the principles of additionality, partnership, and environmental protection left much to be desired from a Commission perspective.
- ☐ Evidence suggested that member state governments have considerable scope for frustrating EU-level agreements at the implementation stage.

The 1999 Reform of the Structural Funds

- ☐ Proposed enlargement and completion of monetary union provided the context for the 1999 reform. In this context, the Commission's proposals were relatively modest.
- ☐ The final agreement maintained allocations at 0.46 per cent of EU GNP and retained the principles of additionality, concentration, partnership, and programming while adding the principle of efficiency.

Developments in Implementation

- ☐ Implementation of the partnership principle continued to vary across and within states, but there was evidence of a learning process taking place that reduced conflict.
- ☐ Verifying compliance with additionality proved difficult, although in the short term at least the British response improved.

Post-2000: Preparing for Enlargement

- ☐ The applicant states of CEE had little or no experience with key aspects of EU regional policy. There were concerns that they lacked the institutional capacity to deliver the policy effectively.

□   A number of funding instruments were introduced to develop institutional capacity in the accession states. However, central governments were acting as 'gatekeepers' to limit the development of sub-national capability.

Proposals for Post-2006

□   The Commission's proposals for the operation of the structural funds from 2007–13 recognized the need for concentrating the bulk of funds on the new member states and focused operating reforms on efficiency

□   Net contributors to the budget were critical of the proposals in terms both of finance and focus, and the British government proposed a renationalization of some EU regional policy.

FURTHER READING

There has been no recent book-length analysis of EU regional and structural policies. As such, the most relevant books remain two volumes that were published in the mid- to late-1990s: I. Bache, *The Politics of European Union Regional Policy: Multi-Level Governance or Flexible Gatekeeping?* (Sheffield: Sheffield Academic Press/University Association for Contemporary European Studies, 1998) provides a conceptually informed overview of the key developments in the politics of EU regional policy from the 1950s to 1998, focusing on the struggle for policy control at EU level and during policy implementation; L. Hooghe (ed.), *Cohesion Policy and European Integration* (Oxford: Oxford University Press, 1996) is an edited collection that brings together detailed coverage of the political impact of the partnership principle in eight member states, assessing the degree of multi-level governance evident.

A more recent book is M. Tofarides (2003), *Urban Policy in the European Union: A Multi-Level Gatekeeper System* (Aldershot: Ashgate), but it is also more specialized, focusing on the urban component of structural policy. It examines not only the development of urban-policy instruments at the EU level, but also their implementation in Britain and France. As with the two books above, this one is also situated in the context of intergovernmental-supranational debates.

There are also a lot of shorter pieces on structural policy. From his analysis of the 1988 reform of the structural funds and subsequent disputes over implementation, G. Marks, 'Structural Policy and Multi-level Governance in the EC', in A. Cafruny and G. Rosenthal (eds.), *The State of the European Community*, vol. 2, *The Maastricht Debates and Beyond* (Boulder and Harlow: Lynne Rienner and Longman, 1993), 391–410, developed his arguments about multi-level governance. M. Pollack, 'Regional Actors in an Intergovernmental Play: The Making and Implementation of EC Structural Policy', in C. Rhodes and S. Mazey (eds.), *The State of the European Union*, vol. 3, *Building a European Polity?* (Boulder and Harlow: Lynne Rienner and Longman, 1995), 361–90, reflects on both the 1988 and 1993 reform and provides an essentially, though 'not mindlessly', intergovernmental response to the arguments of Marks. I. Bache, 'The Extended Gatekeeper: Central Government and the Implementation of EC Regional Policy in the UK', *Journal of European Public Policy*, 6 (1999): 28–45, argues that in these accounts, either inadequate or insufficient attention is given to the process of implementation in shaping regional policy outcomes.

The most recent contributions to this debate are studies on Italy by E. Gualini, 'Challenges to Multi-Level Governance: Contradictions and Conflicts in the Europeanization of Italian Regional Policy',

Journal of European Public Policy, 10 (2003): 616–36; on Britain, by I. Bache and G. Bristow, 'Devolution and the Core Executive: The Struggle for European Funds', *British Journal of Politics and International Relations*, 5 (2003): 405–427; and on five of the accession states, by D. Bailey and L. De Propris, 'EU Structural Funds, Regional Capabilities and Enlargement: Towards Multi-Level Governance?', *Journal of European Integration*, 24 (2002): 303–324.

For an overview of the Commission's most recent reform proposals, see European Commission, 'A New Partnership for Cohesion: Convergence, Competitiveness, Cooperation', *Third Report on Economic and Social Cohesion* (Luxemburg: European Communities 2004).

online resource centre

Visit the Online Resource Centre that accompanies this book for links to more information on European regional and structural policies, including the web site of the Commission's Directorate-General for Regional Policy.

Note to Reader: This chapter focuses on the financial aspects of regional policy. However, the EU's control of national state aids that differentiate between regions is also seen as part of EU regional policy (Thielemann 2002; Conzelmann 2005). For a discussion of EU policy on state aid, see Chapter 24.

CHAPTER 29

External Economic Relations

CHAPTER OVERVIEW

Up to now, this section of the book has dealt primarily with the internal policies of the EU. At this point the focus shifts to those policy areas that concern the relations of the EU with the rest of the world. External political relations are examined in the next chapter; in this chapter the external economic relations of the EU are under scrutiny.

The EU is the world's largest trading bloc. As such it is obliged to have an external economic policy. Economic relations with the rest of the world fall into a number of categories, although these different categories are gradually being overtaken by global trade agreements. This chapter reviews the different categories of external economic relations, with especial emphasis on relations with the United States, on the global economic agreements that are being negotiated in the context of the World Trade Organization (WTO), and on relations with the developing world.

> Free trade and preferential trade agreements are a major element in EU foreign policy and are at the forefront of EU policy towards developing countries and neighbouring countries in Europe.
>
> (Brenton and Manchin 2002: 1)

The external economic relations of the EU have developed in the context of a global economic system that has itself evolved and changed throughout the post-war era, and they are conducted in the light of a central economic relationship with the United States that has strong elements of both rivalry and co-operation. Within these twin contexts, the EU has a complex set of agreements that govern its economic relations with the rest of the world. The main categories are: multi-lateral free-trade agreements, bi-lateral free-trade agreements, agreements with other European states, the Euro-Med agreements with non-European states of the Mediterranean basin, and Development Co-operation Agreements.

The Post-War International Economic System

When the EEC came into existence, economic relations were governed by the agreements reached at negotiations in **Bretton Woods**, New Hampshire in 1944. These agreements set up several institutions designed to help an international economic system to emerge. At the heart of the structure was a monetary system nominally based on gold, but in practice based on the US dollar as the anchor currency. To assist the development of other states' economies, the International Bank for Reconstruction and Development (IBRD), or World Bank was created. To help states that got into temporary difficulties with their balance of payments, the International Monetary Fund (IMF) was set up. There was also intended to be an International Trade Organization (ITO), to facilitate the gradual introduction of global free-trade agreements, and to regulate the emerging system by arbitrating and ruling on trade disputes between states. However, the US Congress would not agree to the ITO, so instead a series of intergovernmental negotiations were initiated, known as the General Agreement on Tariffs and Trade (GATT).

Within the GATT framework, a key concept was that of 'most favoured nation' (MFN) treatment. This meant that states would not negotiate more favourable deals with some partners than they were prepared to offer to all the participants in GATT. Exceptions were allowed to the rule, though. The EEC received special dispensation from the MFN principle to allow it to dismantle tariffs on internal trade between the member states, because there was special provision in the rules to allow the creation of customs unions and free-trade areas that might speed up the process of dismantling barriers to free trade globally. The other area where the EEC concluded preferential trading deals was in relation to the former colonies of the member states. There were also special agreements with prospective future members of the EEC. These were not uncontroversial arrangements, though, and they became more liable to challenge when the GATT was superseded by a World Trade Organization (WTO) in 1995.

The GATT was a weak organization. It was never intended to stand alone, and only became the arbiter of international trade relations because the ITO failed to appear. Although it had a procedure for resolving disputes, it was easy for a state that was losing a case to block a ruling against it. The arrangements began to collapse in the late-1970s and 1980s with the growth of protectionism in the face of the global economic downturn. In response, GATT launched a marathon round of trade negotiations in 1986, known as the Uruguay Round. The negotiations were scheduled to be completed by 1990, but stretched out until 1994. The difficulty of reaching agreement, and the prospect of having to enforce a much more complex package of arrangements, led to the creation of the WTO, a much stronger body than GATT. In particular, under WTO rules on dispute settlement, a state cannot prevent a ruling being made against it.

Partly because of the increased complexity of the rules, and partly because of the advent of more effective machinery, recourse to dispute panels has increased considerably, averaging forty disputes a year since 1995 as compared to six under the old procedures (McQueen 1998: 436). This has affected the EU because of increased challenges to its practices, particularly from the United States.

Trade Relations with the United States

Relations with the United States are central to the external relations of the EU in both economics and politics. There is a high degree of commercial interdependence between the EU and the United States. In 2003 exports of EU goods to the United States were worth 266 million Euros, and accounted for 25.8 per cent of total EU exports; while EU imports of goods from the United States were worth 157.2 million Euros, 16.8 per cent of total EU imports. Each accounted for about one-fifth of the other's bi-lateral trade (*Source*: *Europa* web site). The public authorities on the two sides of the Atlantic would therefore seem to have a strong incentive to work together to maintain open trading relations. However, EU–US trade has been dogged by a series of intractable disputes. Yet at the same time as these disputes were causing tensions, steps were being taken to improve commercial relations.

Trade Disputes Between the EU and the United States

It is not difficult to find examples of tensions in the trade relations between the EU and the United States. Since the WTO began operation in January 1995, the United States and the EU have struggled to dominate the procedures and the agenda, or at least to ensure that the other does not dominate. Each side has brought complaints against the other.

The United States objected to the proliferation of free-trade agreements between the EU and other states in the 1990s. The EU justified them as stepping-stones to global free trade, but the United States saw them as bilateral measures that damaged US access to the third markets. The United States also treated enlargements of the EC/EU as being the same as an extension of free-trade agreements, and in 1995 it demanded compensation for the trade-diversion effects of the northern enlargement of the EU, as it had after every previous enlargement, and threatened to make a formal complaint to the WTO before agreement was reached in December.

In October 1996 the EU made a formal complaint to the WTO against the United States' policy of operating sanctions against companies that invested in Cuba. Under the 1996 Helms-Burton Act, the US reserved the right to impose financial penalties against non-US companies trading with Cuba, and even to deny access to the United States to individuals who were shareholders, directors, or executives of the companies concerned. The US Congress also passed legislation (the D'Amato Act) in May 1996 allowing similar action to be taken against companies dealing with Libya or Iran. As well as making a complaint to the WTO, the EU in 1996 gave itself the power to retaliate against US companies and individuals if the United States implemented the terms of Helms-Burton or D'Amato against EU companies or citizens. These disputes have been put on the back-burner by the US Administration, which is in effect declining to use the powers given it by the acts, but the issue of the United States passing legislation with extraterritorial applicability continues to be a cause of resentment in the EU.

Extraterritorial legislation was also involved in a fierce dispute that blew up in 1998 over the EU's banana regime. This was part of the Lomé agreements with former French and British colonies (see below). It gave preferential access to the EU market for bananas grown in those Caribbean and Pacific states that were parties to the agreement. The United States objected to the discrimination against bananas produced in Latin America, mainly by US-owned companies.

The WTO had already ruled against the EU's banana regime in September 1997, and had given it until January 1999 to produce a revised scheme that complied with WTO rules. The EU produced a revised scheme, but the United States insisted that it still did not comply with WTO rules, and in October 1998 threatened unilaterally to impose sanctions. The EU maintained that this would be a breach of WTO procedures, and that if the United States was not satisfied with the new banana regime it would have to start the complaints procedure all over again. The United States said that that was a recipe for endless delay. The EU then asked the WTO to rule on the legitimacy of Section 301 of US trade law under which the unilateral sanctions were threatened, which is where the issue of extraterritorial legislation arose.

Eventually, in April 1999, the WTO did authorize the imposition of sanctions by the United States, although at a much-reduced level from those originally proposed. The whole issue generated a surprising amount of bitterness and heat considering that it concerned a product that was grown in neither the EU nor the United States.

In 1999 the United States won a complaint to the WTO against a ban by the EU on the import of hormone-treated beef. The ban reflected the strong prejudice of EU consumers against meat that contained hormones, and was first imposed in 1987. The United States maintained that this action was against WTO rules because there was no scientific evidence that there was any risk to human health from eating such meat. The EU insisted that it wanted to complete its own scientific tests before agreeing to lift the ban. Early in 1999 the WTO ruled against the EU, and the United States said that it would impose retaliatory sanctions unless the ban was lifted, but the EU refused to lift the ban in the face of intense consumer opposition. It did offer to allow the import of hormone-treated beef if it was clearly labelled as such, but the United States rejected this compromise because it said that the labelling itself implied that there was something wrong with the beef.

The dispute over hormone-treated beef should really be seen as a just a sub-issue within the larger issue of the use of bio-technology in the production of foodstuffs. In 1999 the EU placed an effective moratorium on the granting of licences for genetically modified (GM) crops. This move was attacked by the United States as imposing a non-tariff barrier on agricultural trade. In 2001 the Commission proposed to introduce rules on the labelling of foodstuffs that contained GM crops, and a requirement that the origins of foodstuffs be traceable back to the crops from which they were produced. The United States considered these to be unreasonable requirements that would probably be impossible to implement, and would certainly be very costly, eliminating any advantage that US farmers gained from adopting the new technology, and requested a WTO panel on the issue.

Both the issue of hormone-treated beef and that of GM foodstuffs point to a fundamental problem with devising rules to govern the emerging global economy. Legislation in a democracy reflects the balance of opinions on the issue among the citizens. US farmers have adopted new technologies to increase yields, secure in the knowledge that most US consumers are indifferent to the production methods used, provided that the food is cheap and plentiful. Consumer attitudes in Europe are different. Although there has been some variation from country to country, generally European consumers are much more wary about departures from traditional production methods. This wariness has been increased by a series of health scares concerning food, such as the outbreak in 1996 of Bovine Spongiform Encephalopathy (BSE), or 'mad cow' disease as it was known, where the cause was feeding the animals non-traditional foodstuffs that scientists had not considered to be unsafe. Europeans are also generally much more concerned about the impact of bio-technology on the environment. When economic vested interests based in one country (US farmers) come into conflict with democratic sentiments in another, there is a real difficulty in resolving the stand-off without the governments of the two being drawn into a conflict that neither may relish.

The tensions in the trade relations between the EU and the United States are also indicative of the differences of interest between two large trading blocs, which are inevitable. Politics comes into it. The strength of the US reaction to the EU's defence of its banana regime was widely believed to reflect the influence in Congress of Carl Lindner, the Chairman of Chiquita Bananas, and a large contributor to the funds of both the major US political parties. On the EU side, the sensitivity of the relationship with their former colonies for the two large ex-imperial member states (France and Britain) clearly counted for a lot, especially when it is borne in mind that the German public was hostile to the banana regime because of their passionate attachment to the larger 'dollar bananas'.

Another factor that weighed heavily was the refusal of the EU to be pushed around in world trade matters by the United States. This is why extraterritorial legislation was such a sensitive issue for the Europeans. For the same reason, the EU was not prepared to allow the United States to pick fights with it in the WTO only on grounds of its own choosing. In the face of the US appeals against it on beef and bananas, in 1998 the EU launched its own WTO appeal against the Foreign Sales Corporation (FSC) provisions of US tax law.

The FSC came into effect in 1984, and allowed US corporations to claim exemption on between 15 and 30 per cent of their earnings from exports. The EU maintained that this amounted to an export subsidy in breach of WTO rules. The United States considered that the appeal was simply EU retaliation against its appeals on bananas and beef, pointing out that it taken the EU fourteen years to get round to protesting about the FSC, and that there was no evidence of pressure on the Commission from European businesses for the complaint to be made at this time (Ahearn 2002: 4). However, in October 1999 a WTO Disputes Panel found in favour of the EU, and the United States was told to come into compliance with its WTO obligations by October 2000. In November 2000 the FSC was repealed and replaced by the Extraterritorial Income (ERI) provisions. This allowed tax breaks up to the same amount to US corporations on all foreign earnings, including their earnings from foreign investments. By extending the provision beyond export earnings in this way, Congress hoped to redefine the tax provision. Predictably, the EU appealed and the WTO ruled against the ERI, and against the counter-appeal from the Bush Administration (Ahearn 2002: 5). In August 2002, the WTO dispute panel ruled that the EU could impose up to $4 billion of sanctions in retaliation.

The result of these moves and counter-moves was that the United States and the EU entered the 21st century each armed with the right to impose WTO-approved sanctions on the other. Tensions flared in March 2002 when President Bush announced 30 per cent tariffs on a wide range of steel products, triggering an immediate EU complaint to the WTO; eventually the tariffs were rescinded in late 2003. Then, during the early part of the second Administration of George W. Bush, further tensions arose over accusations and counter-accusations of illegal subsidies by both sides to their major producers of civil aircraft. The United States accused the EU of granting illegal aid to Airbus for the development of its new A380 'super-jumbo'; and the EU accused the United States of providing illegal subsidies to Boeing for the development of its new 7E7 'Dreamliner' aircraft. The whole situation held the potential to develop into a trade war, which would have benefited neither party. Although it is inevitable that trade disputes will continue, the mutual desire to avoid a trade war has led to several attempts to improve relations.

Attempts to Improve EU–US Commercial Relations

During 1995 a Transatlantic Business Dialogue (TABD) was instituted with the aim of developing EU–US co-operation on issues such as mutual recognition of standards. This represented an attempt to overcome the risk of non-tariff barriers being used as means of restricting trade (Ch. 26, pp. 407–8). In November 1996 the TABD produced a declaration on Mutual Recognition Agreements, advocating the recognition by public authorities on each side of the Atlantic of the testing procedures for health and safety that were in force on the other side. In June 1997 a pact on mutual recognition of testing and certification procedures was signed between the EU and the USA covering trade worth £29 billion ($47 billion) a year. It involved each side agreeing to accept the other's procedures as adequate to ensure safety, thereby reducing the barriers to imports and exports.

In December 1995 a New Transatlantic Agenda was signed in Madrid by US President Bill Clinton, EU Council President Felipe Gonzalez, and Commission President Jacques Santer. Under this heading the EU and the United States agreed a transatlantic action-plan to develop four areas of collaboration:

(1) promotion of peace, stability, democracy, and development;

(2) responding to global challenges such as environmental threats and drugs trafficking;

(3) contributing to the expansion of world trade;

(4) building 'Atlantic bridges' through collaboration in areas such as education.

The most obvious common interest of the EU and the United States, though, has been in constructing and extending multi-lateral trade agreements under the GATT and now the WTO.

Multi-Lateral and Bi-Lateral Free Trade Agreements

In the negotiation of multi-lateral trade agreements, the EU operates under the rules of its own common commercial policy as outlined in the EC Treaty, Title IX (ex. VII), Articles 131–4 (ex 110–15).

Article 133 of the Treaty (ex Article 113) gives the EC exclusive competence in commercial policy, including external trade negotiations. However, the trade negotiations are to be conducted by the Commission, 'in conjunction with a special committee appointed by the Council'. This committee, known as the Article 133 committee (previously the Article 113 committee), consists of senior civil servants of the member states who monitor the position taken by the Commission at every stage of trade negotiations to ensure that it is in line with a negotiating mandate laid down by the Council of Ministers. The senior committee meets monthly throughout the year, and there are weekly meetings of deputies. Once an agreement has been reached in the negotiations, it has to be ratified by the member states meeting in full Council, using QMV.

Not only is the Commission closely monitored in trade negotiations: except for trade in goods it formally does not have full competence. Trade in services and intellectual products are not included. Originally this was because they were not the subjects of trade negotiations when the Treaty of Rome was drawn up. In 1994 the European Court of Justice (ECJ) ruled that the Commission did not have sole competence in negotiations on such matters, but shared the competence with the member states. In September 1996 the Commission asked the Council of Ministers to extend its remit to these sectors, but met with a cool response. Young (2000: 101) suggested three considerations that made the member states, and especially the larger of them, reluctant to extend competence in these new trade issues to the EU:

- the new issues are more sensitive domestically than trade in services;

- some member states do not trust the Commission to represent their interests in these areas;

• if competence were ceded to the EU there would be no possibility of those states that wanted to go further in liberalizing these areas concluding agreements independently of the EU where common agreement was blocked by a coalition of unwilling states.

In the Treaty of Amsterdam the member states inserted a clause that allowed them to give the Commission full competence in these sectors for specific future negotiations, without further change to the Treaties, but only if they were unanimous in agreeing to do so.

Shared responsibility for trade negotiations produces a complex pattern of bargaining. Putnam described the making of foreign policy for a state as a 'two-level game'. Moravcsik (1991, 1993, 1998) incorporated this insight into his theorizations of the nature of the relationship between the EC/EU and its member states (Ch. 1, p. 14). At one level the government of each member state has to find a position that will satisfy the balance of pressures in its domestic political arena. It then has to play a game at the level of negotiations with the other member states to try to achieve an agreement that falls within the parameters of what is acceptable domestically. Already there is a complicated bargaining situation to analyse. However, the position in EC trade negotiations is even more complex. The nature of the relationship between the member states, the Commission, and the trade partners means that it is a three-level rather than a two-level game (Collinson 1999). The three levels are:

(1) The government of each of the member states has to find a negotiating position that reflects the domestic constraints.

(2) All the governments then have to negotiate around these positions in determining together the negotiating mandate for the Commission in the wider trade talks.

(3) The Commission then has to negotiate in the wider talks within the tight parameters of this mandate.

If it is necessary to go beyond these parameters to reach a deal, the Commission has to refer back to its constituency in the Council, and the members of that constituency (the governments of the member states) have to refer back to their domestic constituencies.

Matters are made even more difficult by the multi-issue nature of trade talks. It has already been suggested that when the Treaty of Rome was drawn up, certain issues that are central to contemporary world trade were not considered to be part of the trade agenda. Trade in the 1950s was predominantly in goods. Today there is growing trade in services and intellectual property. Foreign direct investment has also grown rapidly and become a matter of concern, with some governments wishing to regulate it and others wishing to embed international rules that ban national discrimination against foreign investment. In addition, agriculture, which was effectively excluded from the earliest rounds of GATT negotiations by a tacit agreement between the participants, has become a central issue.

Each of these sectors has its own policy networks (Collinson 1999), and some, especially agriculture and the cultural industries (part of intellectual property issues), are politically extremely sensitive. For example, the French government had great difficulty in accepting the November 1992 Blair House agreements between the European Commission and the USA on agricultural trade (Ch. 25, pp. 393–4), and almost collapsed the whole GATT package-deal because of the difficulty of selling the agreement to its domestic political constituency. France also objected to the inclusion of cultural industries in the GATT package because of fears that the dominance of US films and television programmes would undermine its distinctive national culture.

Indicative of the clash of interests in making EC trade policy was the 1997 dispute over the imposition of anti-dumping measures against imports of unbleached cotton cloth. The measures against China, Egypt, India, Indonesia, and Pakistan were demanded by Eurocoton, the association of European producers of cotton fabrics; but they were opposed by European producers of finished cotton goods who benefited from the cheaper semi-finished products imported from the non-EU countries. The member states were evenly divided, with Germany abstaining when the first vote was taken in March 1997. This reflected the balance of industrial interests between producers of raw cotton cloth and producers of finished cotton goods in the different member states. Eventually, in May 1997, the German government decided to oppose the anti-dumping measures, to the fury of the French. Underlying the specific issue, which was a straight division on the basis of national economic interest, there was also a more general issue about free trade versus managed trade.

This difference was nicely illustrated at a meeting in Otranto in Italy in April 1996, when during a discussion of the twenty-six bi-lateral free-trade agreements that the Commission had negotiated, the French representative said that the Commission appeared to want to have free trade with the whole world. This might well have been the ultimate aim of the British Commissioner for trade, Sir Leon Brittan. The extent of the philosophical difference is indicated by the fact that the French representative apparently considered it to be a bad thing.

The thrust of EC trade policy has been in the direction of free trade. Given the qualms of France and other southern member states, some of the explanation must lie in the role of the Commission, and particularly that of Commissioner Brittan. The divisions within the EU between member states, combined with the need for the Council to approve trade agreements by a qualified majority rather than unanimity, opened up an opportunity for active and committed Commission leadership to influence the direction of policy. Brittan provided such leadership, a task made easier by the 1995 enlargement, because all three of the new member states were favourable to free trade. He became a vigorous defender of the view that the single market gave the EU the opportunity to set the future trade agenda, rather than responding to the lead of the United States. This may also have helped his cause in building support within the Council of Ministers, because French governments have generally been favourably disposed toward any policy of European leadership in defiance of the United States.

In the Prodi Commission, the Trade portfolio was held by a Frenchman: Pascal Lamy, who had been Jacques Delors's *chef de cabinet* when Delors was President. Some concerns were expressed when the appointment was made that the French wanted to secure the post in order to slow or even reverse the progress towards free trade, but these concerns proved to be unfounded. Lamy continued to press the cause of free trade through both bi-lateral and multi-lateral means. Although he was vigorous in his defence of EU interests in the WTO, particularly against the United States, he had a good working relationship with his US counterpart in the Bush Administration, Robert Zoellick, and together they endeavoured to clear the blockages that had emerged in Seattle in 1999 to a new round of global trade negotiations.

One of the major obstacles remained the level of support for their own agricultural exports applied by both the EU and the United States. In May 2004, Lamy and Agriculture Commissioner Franz Fischler jointly signed a letter to all 148 members of the WTO offering to eliminate all export subsidies on agricultural goods provided that the United States matched the offer by eliminating all subsidies on its agricultural exports. This initiative was condemned by the French government, which claimed that the Commission was exceeding its negotiating mandate in making the offer (*Financial Times*, 11 May 2004). In making this move, Lamy showed that he was prepared to incur the displeasure of France in order to achieve his objectives as Trade Commissioner. Lamy's professional pursuit of the same objectives as his predecessors perhaps indicates the force of institutional factors in shaping behaviour.

An institutionalist approach to analysing the common commercial policy has been advocated by Young (2000). According to this analysis, the three-level game is structured by the institutionalization of the policy sector. The treaties are only one basis for this institutionalization. Two others are the jurisprudence of the ECJ and the accumulation of secondary legislation and policies (*acquis communautaire*). Despite the refusal of the ECJ to accept the Commission's argument that the common commercial policy should be deemed to extend to new trade issues, it did extend the scope of the policy considerably in a series of decisions in the 1970s. In particular, the ECJ ruled that where member states agreed to new internal policies, they implicitly gave up their right to negotiate external agreements that had implications for the viability of those internal policies; and that the Commission had competence to negotiate external agreements that were necessary in order to make a reality of internal policies that had been agreed and incorporated into EC law (Young 2000: 102–4). The accumulation of common internal policies therefore has implications for the extent of the competencies of the EC in external economic policies. Young (2000: 111–12) concluded that 'the EU is constantly evolving, and thus a focus only on treaty reforms misses much of the story of European integration'.

Agreements with Other European States

As the EU does not cover the whole of Europe, various economic arrangements have been made with other European states. Because many European states wish to become members of the EU, Association Agreements have been the most common type of arrangement, but an attempt was made in the early 1990s to find a more permanent arrangement short of full membership, a scheme known as the European Economic Area. Subsequently, 'Europe Agreements' were entered into with the applicant states from Central Europe.

Association Agreements are in effect pre-accession agreements with states that want to become full members of the EU. The agreements involve a variety of trade concessions by the EU, with partial reciprocation by the other parties. One of the earliest such agreements was with Turkey in 1973. In recognition of the disappointment of Turkey at not being treated as a candidate for membership of the EU in the enlargement round that ended in 2004, in 1996 the Association Agreement with it was extended into a special customs union.

The European Economic Area (EEA) began in January 1989 as a scheme devised by Jacques Delors to allow the member states of the European Free Trade Association (EFTA) to share in the benefits of the single market without having to become full members of the EU. Full membership was politically controversial within the EFTA states and Delors did not view further enlargement as desirable. The EEA agreement was signed in May 1992, and came into effect in January 1994. It extended the four freedoms of the single market (the freedom of movement of goods, services, capital, and people) to the EFTA states. To allow this, these states had to accept the legislation of the EC, and where necessary incorporate it into their domestic legislation, without having had any voice in negotiating the legislation. This applied not only to the *acquis* (i.e. what had already been accepted), but also to future legislation. Interpretation of the legislation would be by the ECJ, on which the EFTA states had no judges.

These conditions proved unacceptable to Austria, Finland, Norway, and Sweden, who proceeded to negotiate full membership of the EU instead. The extent to which this posed a political risk was evident when the Norwegian people rejected EU membership in a referendum in November 1994.

By 2004, the EEA applied only to Norway, Iceland, and Liechtenstein. It did not cover agriculture (although some agricultural products were allowed free movement within the EEA), tax harmonization, monetary policy, or external trade relations.

Separate agreements were negotiated with Switzerland after a referendum there in December 1992 rejected the terms of the EEA.

At the end of the Cold War, the EC signed technical co-operation agreements with the central and east European countries (CEECs). These were subsequently replaced with 'Europe Agreements'. In addition, agreements were signed with Cyprus, and Malta, who were also applicants. Following the 2004 enlargement, Association Agreements remained with Turkey, Romania, and Bulgaria.

In the Balkans, as part of its Stability Pact for South Eastern Europe, the EU agreed a Memorandum of Understanding (MoU) on Trade Liberalization and Facilitation with Albania, Bosnia and Herzegovina, Croatia, the Federal Republic of Yugoslavia (Serbia and Montenegro), and the Former Yugoslav Republic of Macedonia (FYROM). This was the first stage in what became known as the Stabilization and Association Process (SAP). The next stage would be that once states were considered to have made sufficient progress in political and economic reform, and in building administrative capacity, they would be offered a Stabilization and Association Agreement (SAA) with the EU, to help them to prepare for possible full membership. At the time of writing, SAAs had been agreed with Croatia and FYROM, and one with Albania was under negotiation.

The Euro–Med Agreements

While the governments of France and the Mediterranean member states could see the arguments for enlargement to the east, and even accepted them, they were apprehensive about the effect that such an enlargement would have on the EU. First, they were concerned that an eastern enlargement would shift the balance of power in the EU decisively to the north, especially coming immediately after the accession of Austria, Finland, and Sweden. Second, and related to the first point, they were concerned that the problems of the Mediterranean, which affected them more than did instability in the east, would be relegated to a secondary issue. Instability in North Africa, particularly a civil war in Algeria, was already having an impact on them in the form of refugees, and in threats to their companies' investments in the region. Third, they feared that EU funds that came to them through the Common Agricultural Policy (CAP) and the structural funds would be diverted to support for the central and east European economies.

Their concern that attention would be diverted from the problems of the Mediterranean was recognized by the German government when it held the presidency of the EU in the second half of 1994. Agreement was reached at the Essen meeting of the European Council in December 1994 to launch an initiative on North Africa and the Middle East. This assumed more tangible form during 1995 under the successive French and Spanish presidencies, culminating in a major conference in Barcelona from 23 to 29 November 1995 involving the EU member states, the Maghreb states (Algeria, Morocco, and Tunisia), Israel, Jordan, Lebanon, Syria, Turkey, Cyprus, and Malta. The central and eastern European states were also represented. The conference agreed on a stability pact for the Middle East on the model of the Conference on Security and Co-operation in Europe (CSCE) and the EU agreed to contribute $6 billion in aid and $6 billion in EIB loans to the economic development of the region.

Following on from the Barcelona Conference, the EU developed the concept of a Euro-Mediterranean ('Euro-Med') Partnership. Essential components of the concept were Euro-Med Association Agreements. These were bi-lateral agreements that varied in detail, but had certain common features, including:

- political dialogue;
- respect for human rights and democracy;
- WTO-compatible free trade, to be implemented in stages over twelve years;
- provisions relating to intellectual property, services, public procurement, competition rules, state aids, and monopolies;
- economic co-operation;
- co-operation on social affairs and migration;
- cultural co-operation.

Agreements were eventually concluded with Tunisia, Israel, Morocco, the Palestinian Authority, Egypt, Algeria, and Lebanon.

Garson (1997) argued that the Agreements represented a challenge for both parties, but particularly for the Mediterranean partner states. Compared with the position of Greece, Spain, and Portugal when they opened their markets to free trade with the then EC in the 1970s, most of the new Mediterranean partners of the EU were at a lower stage of economic development in the early twenty-first century. They had inadequate economic and financial structures to attract foreign capital, serious administrative shortcomings, and a lack of educational and training institutions to teach new skills as technology changed. In the medium term they could expect to see negative effects from free trade with the EU. Lowering customs duties would reduce government revenues, requiring higher domestic taxes. Their trade deficits would probably deteriorate because imports would grow faster than exports, and this could trigger devaluations of their currencies. It was also unlikely that there would be any immediate decline in unemployment or poverty. The benefits would only appear in the long term. If foreign direct investment could be attracted, that would give workers in the partner states access to higher levels of knowledge and skills, leading to higher productivity, which would in turn attract further foreign investment. More jobs would be created, and wages would rise.

Despite these warnings about short-term and medium-term risks, the Mediterranean partner states were prepared to accept the terms of the arrangements offered them by the EU. It is instructive to compare these terms overall—not just the economic terms—with those offered to the EU's African, Caribbean, and Pacific (ACP) partner states when the Lomé Conventions were renegotiated in the late 1990s, at about the same time as the Euro-Med Agreements were being negotiated (see below). The similarity of the approach suggests that the analyses of the EU's changing relationship with the ACP states might also have some applicability to the Euro-Med Agreements.

The European Neighbourhood Policy

In 2004, the relations of the EU with neighbouring states were brought together under the European Neighbourhood Policy (ENP). Its objectives are to share the benefits of the 2004 enlargement with neighbouring countries without offering the perspective of membership, and so to prevent the emergence of stark dividing lines between EU and non-EU states; and to build security in the area surrounding the EU. Although the ENP is not a purely economic arrangement, the provision of financial assistance and economic co-operation, including access for the neighbouring states to the EU's internal market, are central to its operation.

The neighbouring countries covered by the ENP are those to the south and to the east. To the south, the ENP incorporates the Euro-Med Agreements and embraces all the states that were already part of that process (see above, p. 499). To the east it covers Armenia, Azerbaijan, Belarus, Georgia, Moldova, and the Ukraine. It does not cover states to the east that already have a prospect of membership—Bulgaria, Romania, Turkey, and the Western Balkan states of Croatia, Serbia and Montenegro, Bosnia-Herzegovina, Albania, and the Former Yugoslav Republic of Macedonia. Nor does it cover Russia, although it has been agreed between the EU and Russia that their mutual relations will be developed in consistency with the ENP, and Russia will benefit from the new European Neighbourhood and Partnership Instrument (ENPI).

From 2007, the ENPI will provide financial support for the ENP, displacing the existing programmes. At the time of writing, the budget framework for 2007–13 was still under negotiation, but the Commission had proposed that there should be a considerable increase in the resources available through the ENPI over the total for existing programmes, from €8.5 billion for 2000–6 to €14.9 billion for 2007–13.

In line with the objective of avoiding stark dividing lines between the EU and its neighbours, it was intended that the ENPI would have a specific focus on cross-border co-operation and intra-regional co-operation. The principles that would be used in the management of the ENPI would be those that had been pioneered in the management of the structural funds for regional development in the EU: multi-annual programming, partnership, and co-financing (Ch. 28, pp. 465–8).

Through the political and economic dialogue with neighbouring states, there will be an emphasis on the development of the rule of law, good governance, respect for human rights—including minority rights—the promotion of good neighbourly relations, and the principles of the market economy and sustainable development. The extent of co-operation with individual neighbouring states, including the extent of their access to the internal market of the EU, will be determined by the extent to which they demonstrated a commitment to those principles.

Relations with the African, Caribbean, and Pacific States

Between 1975 and 2000, trade and aid relations between the EC/EU and a growing number of ACP states were governed by the Lomé Convention. The original ACP states were all former colonies of one or other of the member states of the EU, although as the Convention was regularly updated, other states that had never been colonies of EU members joined (Table 29.1, p. 505). The Lomé Convention was eventually superseded by the Cotonou Agreement in June 2000.

EC–ACP Relations Prior to Lomé

When the Treaty of Rome was signed in 1957, the vast majority of independent countries that are now in the ACP group remained the responsibility of colonial powers. In 1956 France, which had the largest number of colonies, requested that its overseas territories be granted associated status with the proposed EEC. France wanted to protect itself from the economic costs of applying external tariffs to these territories. Following opposition from West Germany and the Netherlands, the French government turned its initial request into a condition for France signing the Treaty of Rome.

The Implementing Convention that was subsequently included in the Treaty applied predominantly to Francophone Africa. The Convention had two main elements: the progressive establishment of a free-trade area between the EC and the associated coun-tries, with the reciprocal reduction of tariffs and quantitative restrictions; and the establishment of a European Development Fund (EDF) for the purpose of granting EC financial aid to the associated countries and territories to promote their social and eco-nomic development (Frey-Wouters 1980: 14).

The Implementing Convention ran for five years before being succeeded in July 1963 by the first Yaoundé Convention, named after the capital of Cameroon, where it was signed. This Convention extended EC relations to the eighteen associated African States and Madagascar (AASM). The provisions of Yaoundé 1 were not significantly different from those of the Implementing Convention. The reciprocal granting of tariff prefer-ences for industrial products and for some tropical agricultural products remained; EC preferences on a number of tropical products were unilaterally reduced or abolished; ag-ricultural products exported by the AASM to the EC were regulated by special trade ar-rangements; and joint institutions at ministerial and parliamentary level were set up to administer the Convention (Frey-Wouters 1980: 14).

Despite concessions to the Dutch and West German governments, which had the ef-fect of widening the coverage of EC policy, the first Yaoundé Convention again pre-dominantly reflected French interests. A. H. Jamal, the former Tanzanian Minister of Communications, described the Convention as providing 'an institutional dependence on the part of some African countries on one particular metropolitan power—France' (Jamal 1979: 134). Although modifications were made to the agreement with the sign-ing of Yaoundé 2 in January 1971, these did not change the essential character of the arrangement.

The EDFs under the Implementing Convention and Yaoundé were described by one commentator as 'basically a device to offload the costs of French colonial mercantilism on the EEC in return for other EEC states receiving access to their markets and sources of supply' (Green 1976: 50). Certainly, neither the Implementing Convention nor the Yaoundé Agreements marked a serious attempt to break with the traditional pattern of relations between Europe and the developing world. Many hoped that the first Lomé agreement would mark a turning point in these relations.

The Lomé Convention

Two factors shaped the particular nature of the first Lomé agreement:

(1) The 1973 enlargement brought Britain into the EC. Britain retained close links with the Commonwealth countries, and this had a major bearing on the successor agreement to Yaoundé 2 being extended to forty-six ACP states.

(2) The negotiations over the Lomé Convention took place in the context of the 1973 oil crisis, during which the OPEC states insisted on linking talks about energy supplies with a review of the whole system of relations between developed and developing countries.

Not only did this crisis alert Europe to the power of solidarity between developing countries, it also underlined the extent of international interdependence; in particular, the dependence of the North on the raw materials of the South. There was a strong call at this time for a move towards a new international economic order, one that would allow less-developed nations greater control over both their own development and international economic arrangements.

The first Lomé Convention came into operation in February 1975 and gave formal recognition for the first time to the inter-linkages between trade and aid. The agreement was received by the ACP states more enthusiastically than its predecessors had been. As one observer put it:

> When Lomé 1 was signed, both sides claimed that it was qualitatively different from anything that had gone before; a contract between equal partners and a step towards a New International Economic Order.
>
> (Stevens 1984: 1)

A key innovation of the new agreement was a system for the Stabilization of Export Earnings (Stabex). Stabex provided financial support for countries experiencing fluctuations in their revenues from the export of many primary commodities, mainly agricultural produce. In addition to Stabex, Lomé removed reciprocity in trade preferences: the ACP states did not have to give preferential access to their markets for EC products in return for the preferential access that they enjoyed to the EC market. Products covered in the EC by the CAP were subject to negotiation, but generally the ACP states were given preferable treatment over third parties. A total of ECU 3 billion of EC aid was provided for the industrialization of ACP economies. The institutions of permanent dialogue were reinforced: a Council of Ministers, a Council of Ambassadors, and a Consultative Assembly (later called the Joint Assembly) were all involved in overseeing the agreements.

The consensus among commentators was that while Lomé was an improvement on what had gone before, it was inadequate in relation to the nature and scale of development problems, and certainly fell short of what the ACP states had hoped for (Cosgrove Twitchett 1981; Stevens 1984). Others were more scathing in their criticism. Galtung (1976: 37) argued that, 'the Convention is economistic, even classical, not only in its formulation but also in its consequences, by emphasising production, processing and marketing/trading without always keeping in mind the purpose of all that, the development of human beings rather than things, systems, structures.' Yet Galtung accepted that not much more could be expected from the EC, which was itself essentially a trading bloc.

Thus the main impact of Lomé 1 was to reinforce the established flow of raw materials in one direction (to Europe) and processed goods in the other (to the ACP). Lomé did require developed states to pay more for their supplies of raw materials, but the cost of this to the ACP states was the reinforcement of the existing international division of labour.

Lomé 2 and Lomé 3

Lomé 2 came into effect in March 1980, ran until 1985, and involved aid worth ECU 4.5 billion Despite criticisms of Lomé 1, the prospect of EDF grants meant the number of ACP signatory states increased. In terms of innovation, Lomé 2 was notable for the introduction of the Sysmin facility. This guaranteed a certain level of income from mineral exports, and thus protected the productive capacity of many ACP states, which were major suppliers of minerals to the EC. For the first time, human rights issues became a controversial feature of the negotiations, with the British and Dutch governments in particular pushing for provisions as part of the overall deal. This move was not well received by ACP states, especially as many European countries continued to trade with and invest in South Africa, where human rights abuses were endemic under the apartheid regime. Thus, in spite of Sysmin and other minor innovations, Lomé 2 was viewed as a disappointing successor to Lomé 1.

Lomé 3 was signed in December 1984 to cover the period from 1985 to 1990, providing ECU 7.4 billion of aid. The trading arrangements remained essentially the same as before, but there was an increased emphasis on private investment in ACP states, and also a shift away from loans and towards grants, for Stabex in particular. Lomé 3 marked a move towards rural development projects to promote food security, and was notable for the inclusion of an agreement by all signatories to work for the eradication of apartheid in South Africa. The amount of aid increased in monetary terms, but it was not clear whether this would mean an increase in real terms. When inflation and population growth were taken into account, the period leading up to Lomé 3 (1976–85) had seen a fall in EC real *per capita* transfers to ACP states of 40 per cent (Hewitt 1989: 291).

Lomé 4

In the period 1980–7, Africa's *per capita* GDP fell by an average of 2.6 per cent and its returns on investment were substantially down (Glaser 1990: 26). This meant that on top of the unfulfilled hopes of various aid schemes, many ACP countries were under intense pressure to repay loans. By 1983, the IMF and the World Bank were implementing stabilization and structural adjustment programmes in response. This meant that the EC response to ACP problems had to be implemented in close co-ordination with these institutions. This situation placed the IMF in the driving seat 'with its own short-run conditions overwhelming those of all the other partners' (Hewitt 1989: 296).

Thus, by the late 1980s, ACP states believed that Lomé seriously neglected their main concerns: the impossibility of servicing debt; the increasing demands of the World Bank and the IMF for changes in economic and social policies; and the ongoing problem of apartheid in South Africa. By the early 1990s, to these concerns were added concerns over the effect of the completion of the single European market and concern over the aid demands of the former Communist countries of Eastern Europe.

Lomé 4 was signed in December 1989 by the EC and sixty-nine ACP states (Table 29.1). It ran for a ten-year period, to 2000, and ECU 12 billion was committed for the first five years with a further ECU 14.6 billion for the remainder of the period.

The new Lomé was governed by the principle of *partnership* between the EC and the ACP states. Article 2 of the Convention stated that co-operation should be based on:

- equality between partners, respect for their sovereignty, mutual interest, and interdependence;
- the right of each state to determine its own political, social, cultural, and economic policy options;

TABLE 29.1

The ACP States

African States

Angola, Benin, Botswana, Burkina Faso, Burundi, Cameroon, Cape Verde, Central African Republic, Chad, Comoros, Congo, Djibouti, Equatorial Guinea, Ethiopia, Gabon, Ghana, Guinea, Guinea Bissau, Ivory Coast, Kenya, Lesotho, Liberia, Madagascar, Malawi, Mali, Mauritania, Mauritius, Mozambique, Namibia, Niger, Nigeria, Rwanda, Sao Tome and Principe, Senegal, Seychelles, Sierra Leone, Somalia, South Africa, Sudan, Swaziland, Tanzania, Togo, Uganda, Zaire, Zambia, Zimbabwe.

Caribbean States

Antigua, Barbados, Barbuda, Bahamas, Belize, Dominica, Dominican Republic, Grenada, Guyana, Haiti, Jamaica, St Christopher and Nevis, St Lucia, St Vincent and Grenadines, Suriname, Trinidad and Tobago.

Pacific States

Fiji, Kiribati, Papua New Guinea, Solomon Islands, Tonga, Tuvalu, Western Samoa, Vanuatu.

* security of relations based on the *acquis* of the system of co-operation (Laffan 1997a: 162).

Partnership aside, the approach of Lomé 4 was essentially similar to its predecessors, albeit with greater emphasis on conditions for recipient states. It continued to address debt problems through the Stabex and Sysmin compensatory schemes, though some changes were made to enhance their effectiveness. To reflect the increased demands on the Stabex scheme in the context of deteriorating prices for agricultural commodities on the world market, Lomé 4 increased allocations to this programme by 62 per cent between 1990 and 1995 (Laffan 1997a: 167).

New environmental protection measures were introduced in Lomé 4, including for example a ban on moving toxic and radioactive waste; more emphasis was placed on the role of the private sector in stimulating development; and the human rights provisions were strengthened by a joint declaration on the elimination of apartheid in South Africa and on the rights of ACP migrant workers and students. However, while human rights provisions were long a feature of Lomé, the EU began to place an increasing emphasis on democracy, the rule of law, and 'good governance'. In 1994, the EU brought a halt to aid negotiations with ten ACP states because of the 'deteriorating political situation in those countries' (Laffan 1997a: 168).

However, the conditions attached to Lomé 4's structural adjustment programme and other forms of assistance led the EC–ACP relationship to look increasingly like the traditional donor-recipient pattern of relations. Although partnership was an innovative feature of Lomé 4, the decline of ACP bargaining power resulting from the fall in commodity prices since the high point of the mid-1970s meant that EU–ACP partnership relations were highly asymmetrical. This was illustrated by the EU's unilateral decisions to suspend aid to states where it deemed political or human rights conditions to be unacceptable.

The Cotonou Agreement

In September 1998 negotiations began over a successor agreement to Lomé 4, which was due to expire in February 2000. These negotiations followed a Commission 'Green Paper' highlighting the ongoing problems of ACP countries (European Commission 1996c). The Green Paper noted that ACP countries' share of the EU market had declined from 6.7 per cent in 1976 to 2.8 per cent in 1994. It argued that this was largely explained by the ACP countries lacking the economic policies and the domestic conditions to take full advantage of the preferences that were available to them under Lomé. The Green Paper went on to say that the preferences were anyway becoming less valuable as a result of the acceleration of the global liberalization of trade.

The main argument put forward by the Commission for a radical change in direction on trade was that the Lomé system of non-reciprocal trade concessions was not compatible with the rules of the WTO. Article 1 of the WTO Charter requires participants not to discriminate between other WTO members in trade concessions. Exceptions are allowed to this rule for less developed countries (LDCs), but the concessions must apply to all LDCs. There were two problems about the compatibility of Lomé with these WTO rules. First, many of the ACP states covered by Lomé were not classified as LDCs by the WTO. Second, there were nine LDCs that were not included in Lomé.

The Green Paper used the banana regime under Lomé as an illustration of this non-compatibility with GATT and WTO rules. Following a complaint from Latin American banana-producers, a GATT disputes panel had ruled that the banana regime was incompatible with GATT rules, and had argued that the whole Lomé arrangement was inconsistent with GATT because of non-reciprocity—which meant that Lomé could not be classified as a free-trade agreement—and because of discrimination against non-member LDCs. As a result, the EU had in 1994 applied for a waiver from the rules for Lomé for the duration of the existing agreement. This had been granted. However, the Commission argued that under the amended rules that governed the WTO, once Lomé 4 expired the waiver would have to be renewed every year. This would introduce an element of uncertainty into the trading relationships of the ACP states, thereby discouraging investment. Also, the banana regime continued to be contested, not just by the Latin American producers, but also by the United States, suggesting that the waivers would be difficult to obtain.

In response to these problems with the existing arrangements, the Commission proposed dividing the ACP states into LDCs, who could choose to continue to receive non-reciprocal trade concessions that would also be offered to the nine LDC states that had previously been excluded, and the non-LDCs, who would be offered Economic Partnership Agreements (EPAs). The EPAs would involve reciprocity, so the ACP states would have to offer free access to EU goods. To be WTO-compatible, they would also have to cover 'substantially all' trade, which was generally interpreted as 90 per cent of products, so agricultural produce that had been excluded from Lomé to protect areas that were adjudged 'sensitive' by EU member states would have to be included. The EU agreed that it would conclude such agreements either with individual states or regional groupings, but indicated a strong preference for Regional Economic Partnership Agreements (REPAs).

The Green Paper also noted that economic developments in many ACP countries had been accompanied by political conflict and major social and humanitarian problems. In other words, EU aid policy had taken insufficient account of the importance of the domestic context in which aid was spent. In negotiating a replacement agreement, the Commission was clear that ACP states would be expected to meet more stringent social, economic, and political conditions than previously. The Commission argued for stronger commitments on democracy, human rights, and 'good governance'.

McQueen (1998) challenged several of the Commission's arguments. First, the figures showing that the ACP states' share of the EU's non-oil imports had declined gave a distorted picture, because there had been a large increase in the EU's non-oil imports from a small number of Asian countries that had rapidly industrialized between the mid-1970s and the mid-1990s. If the picture was looked at from the side of the ACP states, their non-traditional exports to the EU—i.e. exports of goods other than primary products—had increased from negligible levels prior to Lomé 1, to reach 6.9 per cent of their non-oil exports by 1987, and 13.5 per cent by 1994 (McQueen 1998: 425).

Second, the argument that preferential trade agreements were less advantageous because of the general reduction in trade barriers ignored one major benefit of formal relationships such as Lomé. The reason that states wanted to conclude such agreements was to guard against the possibility that when there were economic bad times, discrimination against imports would be introduced in the face of political pressure. Although Lomé did not eliminate entirely the possibility of future trade discrimination by the EU against the ACP states, it made such discrimination much less likely and gave the ACP states a forum for challenging discrimination and mobilizing political support within the EU against any such moves (McQueen 1998: 427).

Third, McQueen (1998: 430) said that the Commission misinterpreted the ruling of the WTO Dispute Panel on the banana regime. The Panel accepted the Commission's argument that discrimination could be justified as part of a general waiver, but found against the EU on a technicality: that the waiver they had negotiated was not worded in such a way as to cover the banana regime.

Fourth, the Commission's statement that in future an annual waiver would need to be negotiated was incorrect. All waivers under the previous GATT system had to be renegotiated for 1 January 1997 as part of the agreement on the setting up of the WTO. After that, though, the annual reviews were a reporting formality. Whatever the outcome of the reviews, the waiver would remain valid for the whole of the period for which it had been agreed (McQueen 1998: 431). Because all waivers were up for renewal, and because other WTO members, including the United States, had waivers that they needed to renew, there was a good prospect that had the EU wanted to pursue renewal, it could have been negotiated.

Gibb (2000: 477–8) took up this last point, arguing that the Commission had presented the requirements of the WTO as an insuperable barrier to continuation of Lomé, but in reality the WTO system was one that the EU had itself been fully involved in installing. An alternative to changing the Lomé principles to make them compatible with the WTO would have been to change the WTO rules to make them compatible with the Lomé principles. Some ACP delegations had suggested that the EU and ACP jointly argue for the acceptance by the WTO of a new category of free-trade agreement, a 'soft' or 'low' agreement, that would not be subject to the same stringent requirements as were implied by existing WTO rules. The EU chose not even to raise this issue during the Millennium Round trade negotiations. The conclusion was that, '[t]he WTO is . . . at the centre of the post-Lomé negotiations because the EU placed it there. And it placed it there because it is in its own best interests to do so' (Gibb 2000: 478).

The successor agreement to Lomé was signed in June 2000, in Cotonou, Benin. This agreement covered a twenty-year period, allowing for a revision every five years. Financial allocations would also be made on a five-yearly basis. Amendments to the agreement would be decided by the ACP–EC Council of Ministers, which would normally meet on an annual basis. The agreement placed emphasis on dialogue between the EU and recipient states. Clarity was given to the partnership principle, so that it would 'encourage the integration of all sectors of society, including the private sector and civil society organisations' (European Commission 2000: Article 2). In the first five-year period, the Agreement provided ECU 13.5 billion for development projects. Other objectives included: the encouragement of equality between men and women at every level—political, social, and economic; and the promotion of sustainable management of the environment and of natural resources. The most significant change from Lomé, though, was the gradual replacement of the system of trade preferences by a series of new economic partnerships based on the progressive and reciprocal removal of trade barriers (European Commission 2000: Chapter 2, Articles 36–8).

Assessments of the new agreement included one by Hurt (2003) that was similar to the critique by Gibb (2000) of the Commission's pre-Cotonou position, although it went further by analysing the aid provisions as well as the trade provisions of the agreement. It drew attention to the similarity of principles underpinning Cotonou to the principles of other institutions of international economic management, including not just the WTO but also the IMF and the World Bank. This similarity was attributed to the dominance of neo-liberal ideas, which served the interests of powerful actors within the developed world.

The current neoliberal hegemony of ideas sits broadly compatibly with the self-interests of political élites and the outward-orientated fraction of the capitalist class within the EU member states.

(Hurt 2003: 174)

This assessment treated the EU as a unified entity that responded to the interests of the dominant political élites and 'the outward-orientated fraction of the capitalist class'. It also appeared to assume that the final agreement reached at Cotonou represented a clear victory for the more radical ideas for reform of Lomé that the Commission had put forward. Using an adaptation of Putnam's two-level game model, Forwood (2001) presented a rather different picture. Against treatments of Cotonou as a radical restructuring of Lomé, Forwood (2001: 424) argued that a closer examination of the negotiations showed 'that the ability of the negotiators to rise to the challenges facing EU–ACP relations was compromised by the complexities of international negotiations'.

Member states of the EU took up different positions on the proposals in the Commission's Green Paper. France wanted to continue with the principles of Lomé to maintain the special relationship with the ACP states. It also opposed adjustments to the relationship that might lead to the ending of agricultural exemptions. Germany wanted to see an end to Lomé, which it considered to be a 'colonial relic'. It was most supportive of the proposals in the Green Paper. Denmark, Sweden, and the Netherlands were primarily concerned to protect the interests of the LDCs. They wanted to see the nine LDCs that were excluded from Lomé brought into the new arrangements. They were also concerned about the Commission's idea of REPAs because they believed that they would benefit the non-LDC members of the ACP group at the expense of the LDCs. Britain shared this suspicion of the idea of REPAs, but like France wanted to maintain a special relationship with the ACP states as a whole (Forwood 2001: 428–9).

The result of these divided views was a compromise mandate for the Commission to take into the negotiations with the ACP states: the continuation of a special relationship would be available, but those ACP states that were unwilling to continue with the relationship would be offered EPAs, either on an individual basis or as REPAs (Forwood 2001: 431).

During the negotiations with the ACP states, the Commission's hand was weakened by the collapse of the WTO trade talks in Seattle in December 1999. This focused attention on the position of developing countries, making it more difficult for the EU to force through any agreement with which the ACP states were unhappy and about which they might complain publicly, thereby damaging the international image of the EU. It also demonstrated that the developing countries still had the ability to throw a spanner in the works of global liberalization (Forwood 2001: 437), particularly in the context of growing public dissatisfaction with the perceived inequities of global trading arrangements. The principal reason, though, that Forwood (2001: 438) invoked for an outcome that is here characterized as one in which 'all the features of Lomé have fundamentally been rolled over into the new Convention', was the historical institutionalist idea of 'path dependence'. In the case of Lomé it was explained thus:

The legacy of 25 years of Lomé was such that negotiators were not able merely to wipe the slate clean and start afresh. This legacy is more than a legal commitment, but also a moral and political obligation of the EU Member States towards the ACP countries.
(**Forwood 2001: 434**)

CONCLUSION

In bringing out the theoretical significance of the material covered in this chapter, it almost goes without saying that the global context is fundamental. This is obvious because the chapter deals with a sector of policy at the interface between the EU and the external environment.

In terms of the supranational–intergovernmental debate, the complex decision-making rules for the common commercial policy might be held to demonstrate the dangers of any oversimplification of the position. The Commission clearly plays an important role, and has a certain autonomy over the conduct of trade negotiations under the articles of the original Treaty dealing with the common commercial policy. The member states have always been influential, though. They have to agree the negotiating mandate within which the Commission works; and they have to secure sufficient domestic support before their representatives dare vote for the ratification of the agreements, which acts as a further constraint on the Commission's room for making deals. This complexity is well captured by the theoretical concept of the multi-level game. Over the newer issues that have arisen within international trade negotiations since the Treaty of Rome, the refusal of the member states to grant the Commission the same formal autonomy as it enjoyed on trade in goods is entirely in line with the retreat from supranationalism that has been seen in other policy sectors since Maastricht.

Multi-level games analysis does not analyse the ideas that underpin the positions of actors, assuming that these can be read off from the interests of the actors. Analyses of the Lomé and Cotonou Agreements have tended to give more emphasis to the role of ideas. This reflects the involvement in these debates of what is essentially a different disciplinary group of scholars, whose academic interests focus on the problems of development, and whose approach to the analysis of EU–ACP relations may have greater sensitivity to effects on ACP states than other scholars. It is important to note, though, that scholars such as Gibb (2000) and Hurt (2003) do not adopt a social constructivist position. Their theoretical frameworks are both neo-Marxian, and they treat ideas not as independent entities, as some social constructivists might, but as reflections of the material interests of the dominant capitalists. With this important proviso, the analysis that they, and McQueen (1998), offered of Cotonou could well provide the basis for a either a social constructivist or a political economy analysis of the EU's wider external economic relations.

On the other hand, Forwood (2001) was working within theoretical frameworks that are more familiar within European studies. The contrast in the analysis produced by this approach, utilizing multi-level games and historical institutionalism, and the analyses utilizing the neo-Marxian frameworks illustrates well the value of a multi-theoretical perspective such as is advocated throughout this book. Which of the two very different conclusions about Cotonou is considered valid is a matter for the judgment of the individual, and readers should turn to the original articles and then to the original Commission (and other EU) documents in order to form their own judgment. The point, though, is that the approach adopted by Forwood (2001) led to empirical findings that challenged those of analysts who came to the subject with different expectations built into their theoretical models.

It should be possible to extend all of the analyses of Cotonou to other bi-lateral trade agreements that the EU has reached, such as the Euro-Med Agreements, or the ENP. The same analyses could also be developed further and applied to other policy sectors. Readers might like to cross-analyse some of the material that is presented in chapter 28 of this book on the EU's internal development (regional and structural) policies, for example. The ideas that McQueen (1998), Gibb (2000), and Hurt (2003) indicate underlay Cotonou might also be detected in the principles that guided the reforms of the structural funds. Similarly, the negotiation of the terms of the most recent enlargement of the EU (Ch. 31) involved the applicant states having to accept conditions that appear to have incorporated some of the same principles of 'post-Fordism' or 'neo-liberalism'.

 KEY POINTS

The Post-War International Economic System

☐ When the EEC was set up in the 1950s world economic relations were governed by the 1944 Bretton Woods agreements.

☐ Trade relations were governed by GATT.

- A key principle of GATT was MFN: that members had to offer to all other member states the terms of trade as favourable as the best terms they offered to any other state.

- The EEC gained exemption from MFN for the internal common market and for its relations with former colonies of EEC members.

- GATT was a weak organization, which found it difficult to enforce its principles and rulings. In 1994 it was superseded by the WTO, which has stronger enforcement procedures. Since then the number of dispute proceedings has increased considerably, many of them directed against the EU.

Trade Relations with the United States

- The EU–US trade relationship is important to both sides, but there are many issues of dispute between the two.

- Tensions in trade relations reflect different cultural attitudes, conflicts of vested interests, and a refusal of the EU to allow the United States to dictate to it.

- To try to reduce the potential damage to EU–US relations, and to world trade, there are several bi-lateral mechanisms to ease tension and promote co-operation, such as the Transatlantic Business Dialogue and the 1995 New Transatlantic Agenda.

Multi-Lateral and Bi-Lateral Free Trade Agreements

- The EU as an organization has competence in multi-lateral trade in goods.

- This competence is exercised by the Commission in conjunction with a committee of representatives of the member states, known as the Article 133 Committee.

- The competence does not extend to trade in services or intellectual products, where the EU shares competence with the member states.

- Shared responsibility for trade negotiations produces a complex pattern of bargaining. Adapting Putnam's idea of international negotiations as a 'two-level game', Collinson has characterized the pattern as a 'three-level game'.

- The complexity of trade negotiations is increased by the number of areas covered: industrial goods, services, intellectual products, and agriculture. Each sector has its own policy networks.

- The thrust of EU trade policy has been in the direction of free trade, despite reservations on the part of some member states, notably France.

- The free-trade orientation has benefited from vigorous leadership by the relevant Commissioner, particularly in the past Sir Leon Brittan, although more recently also by Pascal Lamy.

- The ECJ has made a series of decisions that have helped the Commission to establish its leadership in trade policy.

Agreements with Other European States

- The EC/EU has concluded Association Agreements with other European states, which generally envisage future full membership.

- Special arrangements known as the 'Europe Agreements' were reached with the former communist states of central and eastern Europe.

- The EU has a Stability Pact for South Eastern Europe that facilitates the preparation of Balkan states for eventual membership.

The Euro–Med Agreements

☐ These are agreements with non-European Mediterranean states in North Africa.

☐ They arose out of concern about the stability of that area, which borders the EU.

☐ The agreements involve a phased move to free trade between the North African states and the EU, together with political dialogue and conditions relating to democracy and human rights.

The European Neighbourhood Policy

☐ The ENP aims to share the benefits of the 2004 enlargement with other neighbouring states without offering them the perspective of membership.

☐ It incorporates all the states covered by the Euro–Med agreements, plus Armenia, Azerbaijan, Belarus, Georgia, Moldova, and the Ukraine.

☐ A new financial instrument, the European Neighbourhood and Partnership Instrument (ENPI), will provide financial support from 2007, with an emphasis on support for cross-border development projects.

☐ Political and economic dialogue will encourage respect for the rule of law and human rights, and the development of market economies.

☐ Russia is covered by separate agreements, but will benefit from the ENPI.

Relations with the African, Caribbean, and Pacific States

☐ Prior to 1975 relations between the EEC and the former colonies of the member states were governed by the Implementing Convention and (from 1963) the Yaoundé Conventions, which essentially maintained the relationship of dependence of the developing countries on the European states, but spread the costs within the EEC between the member states, despite most of the dependencies being former French colonies.

☐ Between 1975 and 2000 the relations of the EC/EU with the ACP states were governed by the Lomé Conventions.

☐ The terms of Lomé were more favourable to the ACP states, reflecting the international economic circumstances in which they were negotiated in the 1970s.

☐ By the end of the 1990s, when Lomé was renegotiated, it was clear that its terms were incompatible with the rules of the WTO in many respects. The Commission also argued that the ACP states' share of EU trade was in decline, that the general reduction in trade barriers rendered the special terms less beneficial. All of these arguments were contested by academic writers, including McQueen and Gibb.

☐ A new agreement was signed in 2000 in Cotonou, Benin. The Lomé system of trade preferences was replaced by a series of new economic partnerships based on the progressive and reciprocal removal of trade barriers. There was also a new emphasis on political, social, and environmental issues.

☐ Gibb saw Cotonou as evidence of the dominance of neo-liberal ideas within the EU.

☐ Forwood stressed the limited extent of change from Lomé, and attributed this to the complexity of the negotiating game and the effect of institutionalized 'path dependence'.

B.Y. Hanson, 'Whatever Happened to Fortress Europe? External Trade Policy Liberalization in the European Union', *International Organization*, 52 (1998): 55–85, examines the reasons why the 'threat' of a 'fortress Europe' did not materialize, and the factors behind the liberalization of EU trade policy. S. Meunier and K. Nicolaïdes, 'Who Speaks for Europe? The delegation of Trade Authority in the EU', *Journal of Common Market Studies*, 37 (1999): 477–501, analyses the political factors behind the refusal of the member states to extend full negotiating authority to the Commission in the areas of trade in services and intellectual property, and speculates about the implications of this for the future conduct of the EU's external trade policy. The common commercial policy of the EU is analysed as a multi-level game in S. Collinson, ' "Issue Systems", "Multi-level Games" and the Analysis of the EU's External Commercial and Associated Policies: A Research Agenda', *Journal of European Public Policy*, 6 (1999): 206–24.

On Lomé there is comment and analysis in B. Laffan, *The Finances of the European Union* (Basingstoke and London: Macmillan, 1997). Fuller treatment can be found in M. Lister, *The European Union and the South: Relations with Developing Countries* (London: Routledge, 1997), and M. Lister (ed.), *European Union Development Policy* (Basingstoke and London: Macmillan, 1998).

 **online resource centre**

Visit the Online Resource Centre that accompanies this book for links to more information on the external economic relations of the EU, including the web site of the relevant Directorates-General of the Commission.

CHAPTER 30

Common Foreign and Security Policy

CHAPTER OVERVIEW

External political relations are handled outside of the EC framework, and initially were outside of the treaty framework altogether. They are now governed by the second pillar of the EU, on Common Foreign and Security Policy (CFSP). Although this is officially an intergovernmental pillar, the Commission has come to play an important role, and informally there are some similarities between the way in which the CFSP pillar operates and the way in which the EC pillar operates, even though the formal rules are different. Recently serious attempts have been made to strengthen the security and defence aspects of the CFSP in the face of the threats that face the EU from instability in its neighbouring territories. Explaining the development of close co-operation in areas of 'high policy' poses a challenge for theories of the EU.

> There has been a dramatic increase in the EU's external relations 'output',
> but this has not always matched expectations that the EU will act decisively,
> consistently, and influentially in international relations.
>
> (Karen Smith 2003: 244)

While the trade relations of the EC with the rest of the world are covered by the Treaty establishing the European Community (TEC), and come under the competences of the Commission, the member states have also developed machinery for formulating common positions on political issues of foreign policy. This initially developed outside of the framework of the treaties under the name of European Political Co-operation (EPC). It entered the treaties as Title III of the Single European Act (SEA), although still on an intergovernmental basis. Title V of the Treaty on European Union (TEU) set up a Common Foreign and Security Policy (CFSP) as the second pillar of the EU, and some additions were made to the machinery of the CFSP in the Amsterdam Treaty. In the late 1990s efforts were made to establish a European Security and Defence Policy (ESDP). In this chapter 'political co-operation' will be used as a general term to describe the process, while 'EPC', 'CFSP' and 'ESDP' will be used where the reference is to a specific period in the evolution of the system.

The system of political co-operation has been criticized for not being more effective. It has performed particularly weakly at times of international crisis. At the same time, the level of co-operation between member states that has been achieved on more routine matters of foreign policy is surprisingly high, and higher than would be predicted by realist theories of international relations or by intergovernmentalist theories of European integration. Yet the process of political co-operation did not seem to be driven by the same factors that supranational theories identified as the drivers of integration in the EC. Functional spillover only explained a small part of the progress that was made on political co-operation, and despite a growing role for the Commission, the limits that the rules of political co-operation set on its involvement largely prevented it from playing the role of policy entrepreneur, so that political spillover theories did not provide much explanatory leverage. Indeed, for many years analyses of political co-operation struggled to find a theoretical basis. More recently, though, this theoretical gap has been addressed by social constructivist and historical institutionalist analyses that appear to offer convincing arguments.

European Political Co-operation (EPC)

EPC was suggested by President Pompidou at The Hague summit in 1969, but was seen at the time as little more than a sop to his Gaullist supporters. Few participants or observers thought that it would amount to anything, because it closely resembled the Fouchet Plan, which had already been rejected (Ch. 9, Insight 9.2, p. 132), and because it proposed co-operation in the field of 'high politics' as defined by Hoffmann (1964, 1966), an area where national interests would be expected to get in the way of common action.

The machinery of EPC consisted mainly of regular meetings to co-ordinate national stances to particular areas of the world, or to particular issues. Foreign Ministers met at least twice a year, but in practice much more often. Immediately below the ministerial level, Foreign Office political directors met, on the original plan every three months, but in practice monthly. In addition to the meetings of Foreign Ministers and political directors, other institutional innovations were the COREU (*correspondance Européenne*) telex link, and Working Groups on a range of policy and geographical issues. COREU allowed officials in the Foreign Ministries of member states to communicate with each other as frequently as they wished on a confidential line. By the mid-1970s the Foreign Offices of member states were exchanging an average of 4800 confidential telexes a year in an intensive process of consultation (Smith 2004: 107). By the time that the EPC was superseded by CFSP in the Maastricht Treaty there were more than 20 quasi-permanent Working Groups (Smith 2004: 105). To ease problems in the six-monthly transition between presidencies, from 1976 the rules of procedure that had emerged were codified in a document known as the *coutumier* (the French for 'custom').

Until 1987 EPC had no secretariat to provide administrative back-up. This was provided by whichever member state held the presidency of the Council at the time, imposing additional strain on the state holding the presidency, and also working against proper continuity across changes of presidency. Disappointment at the failure of the EC to respond effectively to the Iranian crisis in 1979 led to a review of EPC—the London Report—that recommended improved procedures for use in a crisis, and the creation of a small permanent secretariat. These recommendations received a guarded response from member states when they appeared, but shortly afterwards the 1981 invasion of Afghanistan by the Soviet Union gave a push to the acceptance of the Report, which was adopted in October 1981, and led directly to the creation in the SEA of a small secretariat, situated in Brussels.

EPC was originally set up as a parallel process to that of economic integration within the EC, but the two became closely linked. The distinction between matters proper to EPC and EC matters was rigidly maintained in the early years of the operation of EPC at the insistence of the French. This reached the heights of absurdity in November 1973, when the Foreign Ministers of the then nine member states met in Copenhagen one morning under the heading of EPC, and then flew to Brussels to meet in the afternoon of the same day as the EC Council of Ministers. The rigid separation finally broke down with the opening of the 'Euro-Arab dialogue' in 1974. This was a structured series of regular meetings between representatives of the EC and representatives of the Arab states, prompted by the oil crisis of 1973–4. The Arab participants in the talks insisted on maintaining a clear linkage between trade and political questions, which forced the EC to fudge the lines of demarcation on its side. Once the artificial distinction had broken down here, it soon became less evident elsewhere in the external relations of the EC.

Once the EPC/EC distinction had been eroded, the Commission, originally excluded from meetings under the machinery of EPC, had to be admitted. One of the most compelling reasons for involving the Commission was that it proved difficult to do anything other than make declarations under EPC without having the use of the normal instruments of foreign policy. As military capabilities were unlikely to be made available to EPC, the obvious 'soft' weapon to use was economic sanctions, together with economic rewards such as loans. These economic instruments fell under the competencies of the EC, and were administered by the Commission. In theory national economic mechanisms could have been used to back up EPC declarations, but this would have been less efficient than using centralized EC mechanisms, and might have worked against EC external economic policies.

After it began to be involved in EPC meetings, the Commission came to play a significant co-ordinating role between EPC and the Council of Ministers. This arose for two reasons: the lack of an EPC secretariat until 1987; and the fact that Foreign Offices tended to send different people to the two different categories of meeting, while the Commission, with a considerably smaller staff upon which to draw, usually sent the same people. Where questions arose that overlapped the two forums, the Commission representatives were the most likely to spot the overlap and to be able to guide a meeting away from making decisions that were incompatible with those already made elsewhere.

Another development was that, for reasons of democratic legitimacy, reports on EPC started to be made to the European Parliament (EP). The reports were originally made only to the Parliament's Political Affairs Committee, but subsequently they came to be made in a full plenary session, usually as part of the same statement on progress in Community affairs that is made by the Foreign Minister of the state holding the Council presidency. Members of the EP were allowed to question the Minister about EPC matters as well as about more strictly Community matters.

Procedurally, then, EPC made big strides in the course of the 1970s, and became intertwined with the institutions and procedures of the EC. These advances were then formalized in the Single European Act in 1985–6. Although EPC was at one time described as an example of 'procedure substituting for policy' (Wallace and Allen 1977), it had several substantive successes. For example, the member states achieved a high degree of unity in the United Nations (UN), voting together on a majority of resolutions in the General Assembly, and developing a reputation for being the most cohesive group there at a time when group-diplomacy was becoming much more common.

Perhaps even more impressively, EPC formulated a common position on the Middle East. This in itself was quite an achievement, given that prior to EPC there had been wide divergences in the extent of sympathy for Israel and for the Arab states in different member states. Reaching an agreed position allowed the EC, through the Euro–Arab dialogue, to pursue its clear interest in improving trade with the Arab OPEC states in the 1970s. In June 1980 this common policy culminated in the Venice Declaration, which went further than the United States was prepared to go in recognizing the right of the Palestinians to a homeland.

The then nine member states were also extremely successful in formulating a common position at the Conference on Security and Co-operation in Europe (CSCE) in Helsinki in 1975, and at the follow-up conferences in Belgrade in 1977, and Madrid in 1982–3. Indeed, the whole CSCE process was an initiative of the EC states. Again the common position adopted by the EC ran somewhat contrary to the position of the United States. The Americans regarded the Helsinki process with some suspicion because they thought it risked legitimating Communist rule in eastern Europe. In January 1995 the CSCE took on more permanent form as the Organization for Security and Co-operation in Europe (OSCE).

Admittedly, there were also failures. It proved difficult to find a joint position on the invasion of Afghanistan by the Soviet Union in December 1979. The British government argued strongly for following the lead of the United States in boycotting the Olympic games in Moscow, while the French in particular were not prepared to do so, and the West German government was unhappy at the way that the United States used the issue to heighten East–West tension. On balance, though, there were more successes than there were failures, and it could at least be argued that these successes helped the procedure to develop as much as vice versa.

The SEA gave EPC a written basis for the first time, but the articles relating to it were not subject to judicial interpretation by the European Court of Justice (ECJ). This represented a compromise between the original position of the German and Italian governments in particular, that the Act should become a basis for a genuine political union, and the reservations of some other member states, particularly Ireland. In Ireland the possible compromising of the state's constitutional neutrality was a tremendously controversial issue.

At the end of the 1980s the issue of extending EPC arose once again in the context of the dramatic political changes in eastern and central Europe. The collapse of Communist rule left a potentially unstable situation in that part of the world. The western states had to prepare contingency plans for responding to any outbreak of violence. In particular, the resurgence of nationalist sentiment held the threat that inter-communal conflict might break out. In this situation there needed to be some sort of regional military force available that could act quickly if the need arose. The Bush Administration in the United States made it clear that it could not be expected to provide this force. Although the Administration did not wish to withdraw US troops completely from western Europe, it needed to cash in the so-called 'peace dividend' from the ending of the cold war to help it tackle the large budgetary deficit that it had inherited from the Reagan Administration. Also, even if the west Europeans could have been persuaded to provide financial support for the US troops, there was no possibility of a US President being able to risk the lives of US troops by intervening in European nationalist conflicts. Yet just how poor were the prospects of a rapid response to regional problems by the member states of the EC was shown clearly by the Gulf crisis that broke out in the autumn of 1990.

The Performance of EPC in the Face of International Crises: The Gulf War and Yugoslavia

When Iraq invaded Kuwait in August 1990, the initial response of the EC was decisive. The invasion was immediately condemned, and economic sanctions were imposed against Iraq. On 21 August the Foreign Ministers meeting under EPC discussed the aggressive actions being taken by the invading Iraqi troops against EC embassies in Kuwait, which included cutting off water and electricity supplies. It was agreed that the embassies would be kept open, but that if any embassy was forced to close, the other EC embassies would act for the citizens of those states (prefiguring a later agreement in the TEU on European citizenship). When Iraqi troops entered the French embassy on 14 September, the EC issued a joint condemnation, and a demand for the release of the hostages.

The Revival of Western European Union (WEU)

WEU was set up in 1954 following the collapse of the Pleven Plan for a European Defence Community (Ch. 7, Insight 7.1, p. 110). By the 1980s it had apparently become moribund, but proposals to revive it as a vehicle for co-ordinating European positions were made by the French government in 1984. Margaret Thatcher had rejected these calls, and made it quite clear that she thought too strong a WEU would undermine the role of NATO. In 1991 the British Foreign Secretary indicated that such a revival would be acceptable to the British government, and he supported the idea that had already been floated by France, Germany, and Italy for it to come under the political guidance of the European Council; although he rejected the Italian suggestion that once the WEU treaty formally expired, the organization should be absorbed into the EC. To facilitate closer co-ordination, in 1992 the WEU secretariat was moved from London to Brussels, where both the European Commission and NATO headquarters were located.

However, the first cracks started to appear in the united front on precisely this issue. The subsequent release of the French hostages by Iraq raised suspicions that the French government had engaged in some sort of unilateral negotiation, perhaps making commitments to Saddam Hussein. This was vigorously denied by the French, but it may have reduced the likelihood that the British and the Dutch, the most Atlanticist of the member states, would agree to subsequent French initiatives designed to avoid the military solution that the United States increasingly favoured. This split came to the fore in January 1991 when the French government submitted to the Foreign Ministers a conciliatory seven-point plan to secure a peaceful Iraqi withdrawal from Kuwait. The British, Dutch, and Germans all found it difficult to accept parts of the plan, which involved organizing an EC—Iraq meeting without the participation of the United States.

The EC had always experienced difficulties in agreeing on military action. Sanctions were a relatively easy matter: although they overlapped EPC and EC competencies, they had been used before, for example against South Africa on apartheid. However, as a civilian power, the EC was not equipped to exercise force, and the issue had to be discussed in the forum of the Western European Union (WEU) (Insight 30.1). The United States in the meantime was able to act decisively in support of the UN in threatening to utilize force. When a UN military force was dispatched to the Gulf, it was under US leadership.

Although the EC states formally backed action through the UN, on 14 January 1991 France broke ranks, and just before the scheduled start of the UN military operation launched an independent peace initiative that had not been discussed with the other member states of the EC. This was clearly in breach of the agreement under EPC to discuss all major foreign policy initiatives with the other states, which had been set out in the London Report of October 1981. The French blamed the British and Dutch for showing such a dedicated and inflexible loyalty to the United States that they were unable to make a joint EC approach.

A second crisis that severely tested the limits of EPC soon followed in Yugoslavia. As in the Gulf, the immediate reaction was positive. When fighting broke out in June

1991 between the federal Yugoslav army and Croat and Slovenian separatist forces, representatives of the EC Troika—consisting of the previous, present, and immediate future presidencies of the Council—flew into the area three times in the first week of hostilities to try to broker a cease-fire, which they did successfully. Peace monitors were then sent to the area to help maintain the cease-fire. Economic sanctions were imposed by the EC on Yugoslavia in November 1991.

The European Council meeting in Luxemburg in June 1991 issued a declaration that implied support for the continued existence of Yugoslavia in some form. However, by the end of the year the pressure of public opinion in Germany had pushed the German government to a position where it insisted on recognition of the independence of Croatia and Slovenia or it would act unilaterally. Both France and Britain, the two countries most likely to have to commit troops if the fighting escalated and required a military response, were opposed, but had to give way in the face of German insistence on recognition.

The recognition went ahead in spite of the fact that the Badinter commission on the future of Yugoslavia, which the EC had itself set up, in its report in January 1992 gave only qualified support to the claims of Croatia to become independent. Badinter did, however, support the claim of Macedonia to be recognized; but the Greek government objected to the recognition of its neighbour under the name of Macedonia, which Greece claimed was tantamount to a territorial claim against its northern region of the same name. It was not until 1993 that Macedonia achieved independence in the eyes of the UN, under the name of the Former Yugoslav Republic of Macedonia (FYROM).

Even this did not satisfy the Greek government, and in February 1994 the EU was faced with the serious embarrassment of the country that then held its presidency unilaterally refusing the Macedonians the right of access to the port of Salonika. When exhortation failed to shift the Greek position, the Commission took the Greek government to the ECJ under the previously unused Article 225 of the Treaty of Rome (EEC). This Article allowed the Commission or any member state to take to Court a member state that was believed to be misusing the claim that its national security interests were threatened in order to act in breach of its obligations under the Treaty. No decision was reached by the ECJ before the issue was resolved, but the Commission's move underlined the seriousness of the divisions within the EC.

Faced with such embarrassing disunity, the EC was probably sensible to try to widen the basis for action at an early stage. The UN was called in to help within four months of the start of the war, and in April 1993 the EC declared that it would in future only take action in support of UN initiatives. When military force was eventually used in Bosnia it was initially under UN auspices, but when air power was needed it was supplied by NATO. The main WEU military contribution was to send warships to the Adriatic in July 1992 to help enforce the UN sanctions. Even then, the use of NATO communications infrastructure proved to be necessary.

When a peace agreement was eventually signed, it was brokered by the United States (the Dayton Agreements). The EU undertook responsibility for the tasks of reconstruction and rehabilitation of refugees. This proved to be a job of formidable complexity, and the EU faced what some felt was unfair criticism from the United States for its slow progress. This all added to a sense of the inadequacy of EPC to provide a response to crises.

The EC's response to these crises lent some support to the view that the differences between the perceptions and national interests of the member states remained too diverse to accommodate within a single foreign policy. However, it also supported the view that some of the problems at least lay in the existence of inadequate machinery for dealing with crises. Two observers of the Gulf crisis defended the latter view in these terms:

The structural problems which arose were of significance in that it was necessary for various institutions to be involved where only one would have sufficed. This created a greater problem with decision-making than existed before, and led to independent national responses and the absence of consensus. A structural vacuum exists in the EC, in the absence of one institution endowed with binding power to create and implement foreign policy. Therefore, as a civilian power asked to go to war, the EC was unable to take a leading role. The only institution in a position to fulfil this role was European Political Cooperation, which ultimately is only a discussion forum and has no powers of application.
(**Poulon and Bourantonis 1992: 28**)

Maastricht: From EPC to CFSP

While it was struggling to deal with crises in the Gulf and former Yugoslavia, the EC was also transforming itself into the EU. The IGC on political union, which began in January 1991, had the future evolution of EPC as a central item on its agenda. The more radical agenda, supported by Delors and by the German government, was to bring EPC into the framework of the EC, with the Commission perhaps not having the sole right of initiative but being centrally involved, and majority voting applying to decisions in the Council of Ministers. Security and defence would be added to the remit of this new mechanism for a common foreign policy. The opposite pole was marked out by the British, who argued against majority voting on issues that were central to the sovereignty of the member states, and were particularly concerned that any moves to establish a common policy for security and defence should not undermine the NATO alliance.

The two voices in this debate drew opposite conclusions from events in the Gulf. Both sides agreed that the failure of the EC to respond effectively to the crisis indicated how far there still was to travel to a common policy. However, whereas Delors told the European Parliament that the ineffective response indicated the urgency of pushing forward to political union (*Debates of the European Parliament*, 23 January 1991, 3–398/139), John Major told the House of Commons that this failure clearly indicated that Europe was not ready for a common policy (*Hansard*, 22. January 1991, col. 162).

The British position had moved, though. Whereas Margaret Thatcher had been opposed to any common European position on security and defence, despite the fact that the Bush administration was pressing for it, Foreign Secretary Douglas Hurd indicated in the Winston Churchill Memorial Lecture in February 1991 that the government was now prepared to back the idea that the WEU should be used as a bridge between the EC and NATO (Hurd 1991).

France and Germany continued throughout the IGC to promote the idea of defence coming under EC rules. It is difficult to believe that this was more than a negotiating ploy for the French: a concession to their German partner that they could be confident would not be adopted because of British opposition. The British government responded to the Franco-German proposals by formally tabling a joint proposal with the Italian government at a meeting of Foreign Ministers in October 1991 stressing the primacy of NATO. France and Germany responded by announcing the expansion of the Franco-German brigade, which had been formed three years earlier, to lay the basis for a European rapid-response force. This upset the British government, because NATO had the previous May established its own rapid-response force under British command, to which the Germans were the second biggest contributors.

Despite this apparent determination to adopt a united front, the French and Germans almost certainly did not expect to succeed at Maastricht in getting the EPC brought into the EC; nor did they. Instead, a three-pillar structure was adopted, with the CFSP and Justice and Home Affairs forming intergovernmental pillars of the new EU alongside the EC pillar. Majority-voting in the second pillar was restricted to the implementation measures needed to carry through decisions of principle that would have to be taken by consensus, and even then the majority voting would only apply if all states agreed to accept it in a particular case. There were some other enhancements of EPC, including moving the old EPC secretariat into the Council secretariat and giving it a larger staff and budget. There was also provision for a review of the structure in 1996. Overall, though, the TEU really represented a victory for the minimalist position on the CFSP.

Common Foreign and Security Policy (CFSP)

Between the agreement of the TEU and its final ratification, Christopher Hill (1993) produced an assessment of political co-operation in which he developed a concept that was to become widely used in the subsequent literature: the 'capability-expectations gap'. Hill (1993: 309) cast doubt on whether the EC should be conceived as an actor in international affairs. It lacked autonomy, and was not distinct from other actors, notably the member states. Many foreign-policy practitioners external to the EC, and some internal practitioners too, had mistaken the EC for an actor. The mistake arose because the EC did have a distinct international 'presence'. To mistake it for an actor, though, was to raise expectations of what it could achieve. It was expected to perform certain functions in the international system, such as acting as a counter-weight to the dominance of the United States. Yet the EC lacked the capability to meet these expectations. It lacked the resources, and the instruments; but also, because it was not an actor, it lacked the ability to reach agreement internally (Hill 1993: 310–15). This was why the capability–expectations gap existed, and Hill (1993: 315) believed that the gap had only been increased by the SEA and the TEU, which suggested advances in the international activity of the EC/EU that it was incapable of making.

Certainly, the start of CFSP did not suggest a great leap forward in either the capabilities or the ambitions of the EU. The first actions undertaken were modest, and were all in areas that built on EPC. Monitors were sent to observe the elections in Russia in December 1993; humanitarian aid for Bosnia was co-ordinated; a new political framework was developed for aid to the West Bank and Gaza. Subsequently observers were sent to monitor the first non-racial elections in South Africa; and the EU played an active role in the preparations for elections in the Palestinian homeland.

A more ambitious proposal, which originated with French Prime Minister Edouard Balladur, came to fruition in March 1995, when fifty-two states from western and eastern Europe signed a Stability Pact binding themselves to be good neighbours, and to respect the rights of minorities. Although there were several flaws in the Pact, especially the exclusion for one reason or another of all the Yugoslav successor states, the pattern was adopted later in the year by the Spanish presidency to develop a regional pact for the Mediterranean, in the face of growing concern in Southern Europe about Islamic fundamentalism in the Arab world and about illegal immigration from there.

On security and defence, the tragedy in former Yugoslavia did have a beneficial effect in bringing France and Britain closer together. The common experience of operating under UN auspices in Bosnia led to increased co-operation on the ground, which spread into the creation of a joint air-force command unit. Nevertheless, when in 1998 a further crisis occurred in the Kosovo province of Serbia, the EU again proved unequal to the task of making a rapid response. It was NATO that undertook a bombing campaign against Serbia to force it to retreat from the persecution of the ethnic Albanians in Kosovo. The United States spearheaded the NATO effort.

The Amsterdam Treaty made some modifications to the CFSP, particularly in agreeing to the appointment of a High Representative who would be the first point of contact for CFSP matters. In November 1999 it was agreed to appoint the then NATO secretary-general, Javier Solana, to this post. The Commission had argued that the post should go to one of the Commissioners, but the heads of government decided to make it a position within the Council framework, thus storing up potential for problems in the co-ordination of the work of the two institutions.

Amendments to the TEU at Amsterdam drew a distinction between, on the one hand, deciding the principles and general guidelines of the CFSP, and common strategies in pursuit of these, and on the other the adoption of joint actions, common positions, and implementing decisions. The first category of decision had to be unanimous; qualified majority could decide the second. Also, a member state could abstain in a vote and make a formal declaration that it would not be bound by the vote. This would allow the EU as a whole to be committed to the decision, but not the individual abstaining state, which would only be obliged not to act in any way that would conflict with the pursuit of the action by the EU.

European Security and Defence Policy (ESDP)

The failure of the EU to act in Kosovo provided the impetus for a move to extend CFSP to security and defence. In December 1998, at a bi-lateral Franco-British summit in Saint-Malo, France, Jacques Chirac and Tony Blair jointly announced their support for a European Security and Defence Policy (ESDP). A year later, the Helsinki European Council announced what was called the 'headline goal' of creating by the end of 2003 a

European Rapid Reaction Force of 50,000 to 60,000 troops, plus naval and air back-up, that could be sustained in the field for up to one year. In March 2000 the institutions of the ESDP began provisional operation: a political and security committee, known by its French acronym COPS; a military committee; and the basis for a joint military command structure.

Heisbourg (2000: 6) pointed to signs that the positions of member states other than Britain and France were drawing closer on the issue of ESDP. In June 1992, the WEU Petersberg Declaration said that member states would allocate armed forces to peace-keeping and humanitarian tasks in Europe: this had committed only the members of WEU, but the 1997 Amsterdam Treaty committed all EU member states to the tasks. Whereas only Britain and France took a full part in the 1991 Gulf War, and Italy supplied combat aircraft, in 1999 both Germany and the Netherlands joined Britain, France, and Italy in the NATO bombing campaign in Kosovo. The member states that were not part of NATO—Austria, Finland, Ireland, and Sweden—all took part in the Kosovo Force (KFOR), although this went beyond being a traditional peace-keeping force. All this progress received a severe setback, though, following the Al-Qaeda terrorist atrocities in the United States on 11 September 2001.

As in previous crises, the EU initially reacted positively and decisively. Within 36 hours declarations in support of the United States had been made by the Commission President, the Commissioner for External Relations, the Special Representative for Foreign Affairs, and the General Affairs Council. The Commission rapidly tabled proposals for a European Arrest Warrant, and agreement on this was reached in December, despite reservations by Italy (Hill 2004: 145–7). Overall, in the 'war against terror', despite the problems of operating across all three pillars of the Maastricht structure, the EU responded with 'an unforeseeable speed, range and flexibility' (Hill 2004: 150). Solidarity was also maintained during the subsequent US campaign in Afghanistan to unseat the Taliban government. The one part of the early response that did not reinforce CFSP was the apparent wish of Britain, France, and Germany to act independently of the EU as a whole. Blair, Chirac, and Schröder met to discuss their responses to September 11 ahead of the Ghent European Council in October 2001, and intended to do so again in London in early November. On the latter occasion, though, the insistent protests of other member states led to a widening of the invitation, with the result that the meeting was also attended by Italy, Spain, and the Netherlands, by the Belgian presidency, and by the High Representative, Javier Solana. Although the instinct of the leaders of the three large states had not been to work through CFSP, the outcome showed that this was difficult for them to do against the wishes of others.

Problems really began, though, with the identification of an 'axis of evil' by President George W. Bush in his 2002 State of the Union speech. Three states were identified as part of this axis: Iraq, Iran, and North Korea. The EU was working diplomatically to bring Iran back into full participation in the international community, and had managed to persuade Tehran to associate itself with the 'war against terror', and not to object to the invasion of Afghanistan. Bush's public condemnation was a setback for these efforts of the EU to build a constructive relationship with Iran. Similarly, the reference to North Korea set alarm bells ringing in Brussels because the EU was following a policy of functional engagement of the North Korean regime in the hope of tempting it out of isolation. Again, the bellicose tone of President Bush did not contribute to the success of this effort. In the case of Iraq, the EU was not following a strategy of its own, but the general view of member states was that the existing UN policy was working: the use of military air patrols to contain Saddam Hussein's reach, together with economic sanctions, and the offer of easing sanctions to lever compliant behaviour.

Of its 'axis of evil' states, it was Iraq that the United States chose to tackle first, and this precipitated a serious split within the EU. In the build-up to the eventual invasion, France and Germany led a small group of states that opposed any military action, while Britain, Spain, and Italy were the leading supporters of a larger group (if the accession states are included) that backed the US action. In March 2003, France publicly declared that it would veto any resolution in support of military action against Iraq that might be presented by the United States and Britain to the UN Security Council. This led to a bitter verbal attack on France by Tony Blair in the House of Commons on 18 March 2003.

As Howorth (2003: 179–80) made clear, the tensions had started to rise before this. Blair's response to the attacks on New York had been to reaffirm Britain's attachment to NATO. When the Spanish presidency attempted to reorient the European Rapid Reaction Force to turn it into a weapon that could be used against terrorism, Blair opposed the change, arguing that the war against terror should be handled through NATO. He subsequently supported a US proposal to the November 2002 NATO summit in Prague for a NATO Response Force to react to terrorist incidents, and in April 2003 he was critical of the French position of rivalry with the United States, which he contrasted with the British position of partnership.

Following the invasion of Iraq by a US-led coalition backed by Britain in March 2003, Franco-British relations were at a very low ebb, and the prospects for ESDP looked poor. Yet Howorth (2003: 187) reported that there were signs at the end of 2003 of both sides trying to improve matters. In August, at a meeting of European states in Rome, a clash was expected over whether ESDP needed its own Planning Headquarters, which France insisted it must have, or whether the EU should develop a permanent planning cell within the Supreme Allied Headquarters Europe (SHAPE) of NATO. But the clash did not happen: the meeting agreed that both developments would be useful, and that they would complement one another. Then in September, Blair agreed in principle that the EU should have the joint planning capacity to conduct operations without the involvement of NATO, a concession that appeared to alarm the United States. So, the signs were that the British wanted to facilitate the relaunch of the ESDP.

There were also three successful international operations under ESDP in the course of 2003 (Allen and Smith 2004: 97). In March, an EU force replaced the NATO force in Macedonia, a move that had been scheduled for 2002 but had been delayed by Greek objections. In the middle of the year, there was a successful EU intervention to restore order in the Republic of Congo. Then, in December the European Council agreed to provide a replacement for the NATO stabilization force in Bosnia. Also, Britain, France, and Germany repaired their damaged relations enough to launch a joint attempt to broker an agreement with Iran on its development of nuclear technology that would be acceptable to the United States; although, as Allen and Smith (2004: 97) pointed out, for the smaller member states this again had overtones of the emergence of a *directoire* of the large states.

Explaining Political Co-operation

Until recently, explanations of political co-operation were rather weakly linked to theory. There were many detailed empirical accounts, some of the best written by practitioners, but although all such accounts are inevitably underpinned by theoretical assumptions, these were rarely made explicit. A lot has been written around the idea of the 'capability-expectations' gap, which was a valid concept but was explicitly not intended as an explanatory theory (Hill 1993: 306), and which therefore did not address the central question of why political co-operation took place at all.

Perhaps the difficulty was that the academic community that initially emerged around political co-operation was dominated by 'realists' who started their analysis from the assumption that national interest was the sole motivating force of national foreign policy. As Glarbo (1999: 634) observed, although realist analyses differed from one another in detail, they all held to the common core proposition 'that the interests of single European nation states will eternally block integration within the high politics realms of foreign, security and defence policy'. Where common policies were devised, this would be explained by the coincidence of converging national interests; more often such common positions were dismissed as trivial. Only with the deployment of social constructivist and other similar perspectives to the understanding of political co-operation has the debate become more theoretically sophisticated.

One early attempt to apply theory systematically to the explanation of political co-operation was Ginsberg (1989). In this book, Roy Ginsberg examined seven theoretical perspectives on EC activity in the field of foreign policy. The first four he termed 'classical perspectives': the national interest perspective, the élite actor perspective, the domestic politics perspective, and the bureaucratic politics perspective. The remaining three he called 'alternative perspectives': integration logic, interdependence logic, and 'self-styled' logic. He argued that the national interest perspective was better at explaining the breakdown of joint action than it was at explaining why joint action sometimes occurred. This judgment anticipated the observation reported above of Glarbo (1999: 634) about realist analyses. The élite-actor perspective, Ginsberg argued, could work either way: élite actors could favour or oppose political co-operation. A domestic-politics perspective offered little theoretical leverage because there was very little input from domestic politics into foreign policy action generally, and especially not into the élite-dominated process of European political co-operation. Bureaucratic politics was neither really accepted nor dismissed by Ginsberg (1989: 17–19). Integration theories he believed provided some explanatory leverage: the creation of EPC was 'in part an example of neofunctionalist spillover' (Ginsberg 1989: 25) because one of the main drivers of the process was the need for a political complement to the economic policies of the EC. Interdependence theories put the focus on the external environment, and saw EPC as an attempt 'to reduce the adverse costs of global interdependence by deliberately coordinating joint policy actions' (Ginsberg 1989: 31). However, while interdependence might be a background condition that could stimulate integration, Ginsberg did not believe that it could explain the why and where of it. His own favoured perspective in the book was the 'self-styled' logic, a synthesis of elements from all of the other perspectives, which took the EC and the member states seriously as actors responding to their environment. This eclectic approach was not, however, taken up by other contributors to the debate, which tended to fall into the same pattern of division as the wider debates about European integration.

Glarbo (1999), whose criticisms of realist attempts to explain political co-operation have already been mentioned, put forward two alternative arguments. The first was that important developments in political co-operation can only be understood as the outcome not just of national interest but also of a growing level of communication between national officials. The second was that, contrary to realist analyses, integration *had* occurred within the field of political co-operation; it was a form of social integration stemming from the communication processes that the institutions of EPC and CFSP had set up.

Prior to the launch of EPC in 1970 there was relatively little routine communication between national foreign policy élites, although some regularized interaction between national élites involved in defence issues had begun through NATO and the WEU. Under these conditions of little cross-national interaction, the national diplomatic actors held national images of the international system and of the foreign policies of other states, including those of their EC partners. They also defined the national interest in a way that was determined by these images and by purely national social interactions. The start of EPC soon began to change that. Perceptions began to change after 1970, when implementation of the Luxemburg Report led to the creation of new structures through which national actors came into institutionalized contact with their counterparts from other member states.

The period between the Luxemburg Report and the Copenhagen Report in 1973 saw the improvisation of institutional developments to put flesh on the Luxemburg Report's skeletal framework of institutions, which was necessary to make EPC work. The whole structure of schedules for meetings of Ministers and the political committee, the setting up of the group of correspondents, the working groups, and the involvement of national permanent representations, ambassadors, etc. was developed incrementally then formalized in the Copenhagen Report. The process did not stop there, though, but continued after the Copenhagen Report. In 1974, in response to divisions between member states over the Middle East and energy policy, the 'Gymnich formula' was devised whereby Foreign Ministers met informally without a fixed agenda and without the involvement of large numbers of officials. The name came from the venue of the first meeting: Schloss Gymnich in Germany. So successful did the formula prove, that the meetings were institutionalized as meetings twice a year.

During the early years of EPC, the focus was almost entirely on two issues: relations with the communist world and with the Middle East. On the first, the member states together devised the idea of the CSCE, which started as a one-off conference in 1975, but through the follow-up conferences became institutionalized as a means of fostering functional links between East and West Europe. The process was never enthusiastically supported by the United States, and eventually was prevented from bearing fruit by the decision of the Reagan Administration to pursue confrontational policies with the Soviet Union that brought about the collapse of the communist system. Nevertheless, CSCE is generally considered to be a success of the EPC, and it generated the Organization for

Security and Co-operation in Europe (OSCE), which was helpful in picking up some of the pieces left after the destruction wrought by the USA. In the Middle East, also, the member states came to define a common position that was distinct from that of the United States. Realists explained CSCE as trivial, and the Middle East as a coincidence of national interests. Glarbo (1999: 643–4) explained them as the emergence of a process of discovering a European identity. From these early endeavours to find a common policy emerged what is often referred to as the 'co-ordination reflex', a habit of co-ordinating responses to the international environment not as a means of achieving national objectives, but as 'the done thing'.

The 'continuous communicative process' (Glarbo 1999: 644) that the EPC set going shifted the perceptions of the actors. They became sensitive to the constraints on the other actors, and tried to accommodate them. A code of conduct emerged whereby actors tried not to surprise their partners with *faits accomplis*. They also came to define the national interest differently, taking account of the emerging *acquis politique*, the cumulation of decisions and policy positions adopted through the EPC process. These developments were recognized by the actors, who were quite prepared to acknowledge in interviews with academics that their national practices had been modified as a result of participation in EPC, and who themselves contributed in surprisingly large numbers to the literature on the process, thereby coming to 'participate in the epistemic community surrounding this field' (Glarbo 1999: 659). In public statements the advantages of EPC were presented in terms of how the process served national interests, but only because this was the language that was expected and understood by the wider public.

In a series of articles, Michael E. Smith (1999, 2000, 2001, 2003, 2004) has developed a theoretical perspective on political co-operation that draws on the insights of social constructivism and historical institutionalism. In this perspective, while the process of political co-operation began as an intergovernmental bargain, once the process was under way it took on a different aspect. It is an analysis that has echoes of neofunctionalism, which also accepted that the spillover process only began after the EC had been set up by intergovernmental agreement. (It should be noted, though, that in the earliest of the articles listed above—Smith 1999: 305—an alternative analysis is suggested, that EPC could be the result of functional spillover 'to augment the expanding economic policies of the EC in the face of its first enlargement'. This echoes the analysis of Ginsberg (1989: 25) as reported above.) There were three linked elements in the transition from intergovernmentalism to a new system that went beyond intergovernmentalism to take on some of the features of supranational governance. In decreasing order of importance these were: the development of transgovernmental relations, the development and codification of EPC rules, and the forging of links with EC actors, especially the Commission (Smith 1999: 309–10).

The initial bargain was part of the deal that allowed President Pompidou to agree to British entry to the EC. In return for lifting the veto that had been imposed by his predecessor—President de Gaulle—Pompidou got agreement to a funding scheme for the common agricultural policy that would benefit France, and to the setting up of a system of political co-operation that resembled the scheme that de Gaulle had advocated in the Fouchet Plan. Initial negotiations within EPC were conducted on the basis of existing national positions, so that in its early years EPC looked like classic intergovernmentalism; but this did not last. The intensive interaction between national representatives that was implicit in the idea of political co-operation constituted a system of transgovernmental relations in which these discrete national positions began to be modified (Smith 2004: 114–22).

Gradually also a system of norms and unwritten rules of behaviour began to emerge (compare the analysis in Glarbo, 1999). The norms emphasized the importance of communication and consultation on foreign policy issues. They also included a firm understanding that discussions were confidential, and that they would proceed on the basis of consensus, not voting nor veto. In addition, reserved domains in areas of particular sensitivity to one or more states were accepted without requiring justification. All of this made it much easier for discussion to take place without any national representation feeling threatened by having entered into the engagement, and facilitated the building of trust between the participants. Out of this trust, and the constant process of discussion, emerged a socialization of participants, which led naturally to the gradual displacement of instrumental rationality by social rationality; the replacement of a bargaining approach by a problem-solving approach (Smith 2004).

The second aspect of the movement of EPC away from intergovernmentalism was the development and codification of EPC rules. This process, which can be described as the 'institutionalization' of EPC, has already been described above (pp. 516–18). The increasingly rich institutional structure provided the forum for intensive interaction between officials from different levels in national Foreign Ministries. The transgovernmental network of diplomats and technical experts was thus extended and deepened. Such intensive interaction could not but influence the attitudes of professional diplomatic actors, and through them the process of defining the national interest (compare here the process described in Chapter 20, pp. 282–7). It fed back into national institutional structures, too. Political co-operation required the creation of new posts to serve it. This led to the expansion of national diplomatic services, and a reorientation of internal structures, sometimes amounting to complete reorganizations (Smith 2000: 619–23).

The third element in the transformation of EPC was the forging of links with EC institutions, especially the Commission. The reasons for involving the Commission and the EP in political co-operation have been outlined above (pp. 516–17). Eventually the role of the Commission in ensuring the consistency of EPC and EC actions was codified in the SEA (Smith 2001: 90). From this point on the involvement of the Commission in political co-operation was not only customary: it was mandatory. The EP was allowed a minor role for reasons of democratic legitimacy, although the ECJ has been kept at arm's length from CFSP.

Can this analysis also be applied to ESDP? Certainly the initiation of the security and defence dimension to CFSP has to be explained in terms of intergovernmental politics. In this case coinciding national interests, one of the realist/intergovernmental explanations for political co-operation, has to be given a dominant role. The experience of the crises in the Gulf, in Bosnia, and in Kosovo all pointed up the weakness of the EU. From the French point of view, awareness of the gap that had opened up between US and European military capabilities, and especially the dependence of the French armed forces on the United States for reconnaissance and for transport of equipment, pushed towards closer collaboration with NATO in the short term because it was obvious that there was no immediate prospect of these vital gaps being filled by France without an unsustainable increase in military expenditure. In the longer term, the gaps might be filled by collaboration between European states, but clearly the co-operation of the British would be essential given that Britain was the other main military power in the EU. From the British point of view, the rapprochement between France and NATO was encouraging, and in the wake of the two Balkan crises the United States began to pressure the Europeans to get their act together so that they could make a bigger contribution to policing their own hinterland.

It is possible, though, that other factors were at work. Howorth (2004) identified an 'epistemic community' that had formed around the issue of defence, although it is questionable whether his usage of the term was accurate, referring as it did to national officials only. Nevertheless, he argued that one of the facilitating factors in the determination of Britain and France to take forward the project of ESDF in 2001 was 'the close-knit epistemic community of senior officials in London and Paris who, from the early 1990s onwards, had gradually developed a common mindset around the necessity and legitimacy of ESDP' (Howorth 2003: 175).

Whatever the contribution of these pre-existing transgovernmental links to the start of the ESDP, once collaboration began, the same process identified by Michael E. Smith for political co-operation generally, and outlined above, could be expected to take place. CFSP had been kept firmly under the control of national Foreign Offices. National Ministries of Defence were not given a role. This changed with the ESDP initiatives. New transgovernmental links started to be built between officials of national Ministries of Defence, and between military personnel. Some links already existed, of course, because of co-operation in NATO and the WEU, although the links were less intense for France, which was outside of the NATO command structure, and for those EU member states that were not members of NATO or WEU.

Because it was in its early stages when events changed everything in September 2001, the ESDP process of socialization was particularly prone to be disrupted. In the summer of 2001 the pre-existing alliance of like-minded officials identified by Howorth (2004) had already been disrupted by a major reshuffle of responsibilities in London. The new officials came into office just before the strategic priorities of the government were re-ordered by the events of 11 September. They were therefore less committed to the ESDP when the political direction changed (Howorth 2003: 177–8). However, by this time the institutional structure of ESDP was already in place, so the process of intensive interaction of officials was going to continue. As Smith (1999) argued, socialization and institutionalization interact with one another. The processes are still new when compared with the parallel CFSP processes for non-military co-operation on foreign policy, and so are particularly vulnerable to being blown off course by events. They operate at a slow pace, beneath the level of current affairs; but once institutionalized, they can be expected to continue, and eventually to have an impact on the way in which national leaders perceive events and respond to them.

It should be noted, though, that the 2004 enlargement brought into membership ten new states that had no prior experience of the socialization processes on which the constructivists pinned their expectations for continuing progress. Not only would they have to be inducted into the process, the central and east European states came with different prior experiences of foreign policy, and with a positive attitude towards the United States that threatened to tilt the balance in favour of the Atlanticists.

CONCLUSION

In the study of political co-operation many of the same theoretical debates have taken place as in the study of the EC proper. The realist/intergovernmentalist voice has been peculiarly muted, though. Although intergovernmentalist assumptions governed much of the early writing on EPC, they have been seriously challenged in recent years by constructivist and institutionalist approaches, and their advocates have largely failed to take up the challenge explicitly.

From the point of view of the multi-theoretical approach adopted in this volume, the most obvious explanatory factor to invoke is the effect of the external environment in prompting political co-operation. It is hardly surprising that the external environment should have an impact on the external relations of the EU, nor that demands for a common external political approach should come from outside of the EU itself. The fact that the EC was the largest trading bloc in the world inevitably meant that other states and groups of states expected to be able to deal with it as a unified political entity. As Delors (*Debates of the European Parliament*, 23 January 1991, 3–398/139) put it:

The EC is now perceived as a major power. Much is expected of it. We must remember this and . . . take the necessary steps to give ourselves the political, legal and financial resources to shoulder our responsibilities.

Hoffmann (1964, 1966) criticized the neofunctionalists for failing to take account of the external environment when analysing European integration, but the need to take account of the global context is now common ground among theorists working with different approaches, so the undeniable influence of this factor does not lend support to the realist/intergovernmentalist argument in particular.

The inability of the EC/EU live up to these external expectations generated the capability–expectations gap that Hill (1993) identified, and this was one of the elements that prompted the transition from EPC to CFSP. Yet at first sight CFSP looks as though it is clearly intergovernmental, and the decision taken at Amsterdam to appoint a High Representative and to locate the post outside of the Commission seems to indicate the reluctance of member states to allow a supranational organization too much influence in this area. Caution on the part of governments about allowing CFSP to run out of their own control reflects Hoffmann's argument about high and low politics (Hoffmann 1964, 1966). Foreign policy, defence, and security are definitely high politics. The decisions made affect matters of life and death if troops are to be committed to back up a policy. This is why the elaborate arrangements have been devised by the EU to allow member states to opt out of specific actions without preventing the others from pursuing them in the name of the EU as a whole. The legitimacy of the whole process would be severely tested if national soldiers of a state where the population did not approve of a particular action were killed in pursuit of that action.

Writers from a realist/intergovernmentalist perspective continue to maintain that there is 'little evidence that a common foreign policy where EC members are willing to yield their foreign policy prerogatives to the Community is emerging' (Wood 1993: 241–2). If the focus is solely on the management of international crises, as is the article quoted, then there is some support for this. If the focus shifts to co-operation in between crises and at a more routine level, though, the constructivist and institutionalist positions appear to have the better of the argument. The failure to engage on the same empirical field resembles the failure of intergovernmentalists and supranational theorists to address the same evidence.

The most rigorous attempt to cut through the claims of the realists/intergovernmentalists and the constructivists/'neofunctionalists' on political co-operation came from Schneider and Seybold (1997), who conducted a statistical analysis of responses by the EPC to external events. The conclusion was that 'the outcomes of the EPC negotiation process are much more varied than predicted either by intergovernmentalism or neofunctionalism' (Schneider and Seybold 1997: 371). The article presented an alternative approach to explaining these outcomes, involving an elaborate model based on games-theoretic assumptions. While nobody has followed up on this particular suggestion for an alternative approach, the conclusions of the statistical analysis do suggest that neither side in the old dichotomy has the 'facts' entirely in its support. However, there is evidence that each makes a contribution in relation to different issues and on different levels of analysis.

KEY POINTS

European Political Co-operation (EPC)

☐ European Political Co-operation (EPC) was set up in 1970. It consisted of regular meetings of Foreign Ministers and of senior Foreign Office officials to try to co-ordinate national foreign policies.

☐ Subsequent institutional innovations included the COREU telex link and working groups of lower-level officials.

☐ EPC was incorporated into the treaties for the first time with the SEA, which also created a small EPC secretariat.

☐ Initially the Commission was excluded from meetings of Foreign Ministers under EPC, but it became increasingly apparent that the linkage between external commercial policy and external political relations was too close for this to work, and gradually the role of the Commission increased.

☐ Reports on EPC started to be made to the EP for reasons of democratic legitimacy.

☐ EPC had several substantive successes to its name: achieving a high degree of unified voting at the United Nations, conducting an effective 'Euro-Arab dialogue', and launching and sustaining the CSCE process.

☐ Failures of EPC occurred in responding to the invasion of Afghanistan by the USSR in December 1979, over the Gulf Crisis in 1990–1, and over successive crises in former Yugoslavia.

Maastricht: From EPC to CFSP

☐ The failures of EPC in the Gulf crisis influenced positions in the IGC on political union in the run-up to Maastricht. The French and Germans argued for EPC to come under EC rules (including majority voting) and to include security and defence issues; the British opposed this, stressing the intergovernmental nature of EPC and the central role of NATO in defence.

- ☐ The TEU made CFSP a separate pillar of the EU from the EC; majority voting was restricted to implementation of agreed measures, and could only be used if all participants agreed.
- ☐ The new arrangements favoured the minimalist position.

Common Foreign and Security Policy (CFSP)

- ☐ Hill (1993) identified a 'capability–expectations gap' in the international activities of the EC, that he expected would only increase when it became the EU.
- ☐ Initial actions under CFSP were modest and built on EPC; subsequently stability pacts for Europe and for the Mediterranean extended the scope of activity.
- ☐ The crisis in Kosovo in 1998 again produced an inadequate response from the EU, and had to be dealt with by the United States acting through NATO.
- ☐ The Amsterdam Treaty (signed 1997) created a High Representative for CFSP, located within the Council Secretariat, not the Commission.
- ☐ Amsterdam also extended majority voting within CFSP a little, and allowed member states to opt out of joint initiatives and actions while not vetoing the others from going ahead.

European Security and Defence Policy

- ☐ The failure of the EU to respond in Kosovo led the British and French governments to take a joint initiative to extend CFSP to security and defence.
- ☐ At the Helsinki European Council (1999) agreement was reached to set up a European Rapid Reaction Force, and new institutions were set up for ESDP.
- ☐ There were signs that member states that had had reservations about ESDP were becoming more supportive.
- ☐ The terrorist attacks in the United States in September 2001 caused a series of setbacks to the progress that had been made on the ESDP. Initial support for the United States began to waver in the light of the Bush Administration's identification of an 'axis of evil'. The invasion of Iraq led to an open rift, especially between Britain, which supported the US action, and France and Germany, which condemned it.
- ☐ Despite the setback to ESDP caused by Iraq, towards the end of 2003 there were signs that both Britain and France wanted to resume progress.

Explaining Political Co-operation

- ☐ Until recently, there was little theoretical analysis of political co-operation.
- ☐ The study was dominated by realists who assumed that political co-operation would never amount to more than trivial actions or would only achieve success where national interests coincided.
- ☐ Social constructivist perspectives emphasize the extent to which social interaction between foreign policy practitioners has led to a changing of their perspectives and the emergence of a common outlook.
- ☐ Historical institutionalist perspectives add to the constructivist analysis the insight that pragmatic institutional developments build in a 'path dependence' for the process, making it difficult to reverse. The evolution of institutional structures and procedural norms is eventually codified into treaties, thereby being transformed from 'soft law' into 'hard law'.

POLICIES

☐ The process that brought about the approximation of general foreign policy positions may now be repeated for security and defence policy.

FURTHER READING

An introduction to the CFSP is provided by F. Cameron, *The Foreign and Security Policy of the European Union: Past, Present and Future* (Sheffield: Sheffield Academic Press, 1999). Given its importance to so many later contributions, and the frequency with which the central idea is misunderstood or mis-used, an article that should certainly be read is C. Hill, 'The Capability–Expectations Gap, or Conceptualising Europe's International Role', *Journal of Common Market Studies*, 31 (1993): 305–28; the analysis can then be followed up by looking at Hill, *The Actors in Europe's Foreign Policy* (London: Routledge, 1996), and 'Closing the Capability–Expectations Gap' in J. Peterson and H. Sjursen (eds.), *A Common Foreign Policy for Europe?: Competing Visions of the CFSP.* (London: Routledge), 18–38. C. Hill also provided one of the better assessments of the impact of the events of 11 September 2001 on the CFSP in 'Renationalizing or regrouping? EU Foreign Policy since 11 September 2001', *Journal of Common Market Studies*, 42: 143–63. The overall record of the CFSP up to the mid-1990s was assessed in M. Holland (ed.), *Common Foreign and Security Policy: The Record and Reforms* (London: Cassell, 1997).

online resource centre

Visit the Online Resource Centre that accompanies this book for links to more information on the Common Foreign and Security Policy, including to the web site of the relevant Directorate-General of the Commission.

Enlargement

CHAPTER OVERVIEW

Starting with six member states originally, the EC/EU has grown through successive enlargements—from six to nine, then ten, twelve, fifteen, and now twenty-five. This chapter analyses the policy on enlargement, looking at each of the main enlargement rounds in turn, and asking why they took place, how they were handled, and what each added to the cumulative set of principles and practices that make up the policy. It also looks at the prospects for future enlargements, and particularly at the position of Turkey. This is a policy area that, more than most, cannot be separated from other policies. Each enlargement has had implications for existing policies and the prospects for successful introduction of future common policies. In that sense it is a fitting final chapter to this section of the book.

> ❝ The enlargement of the European Union is a key political process both for the organization itself and the international relations of Europe in general. ❞
> (Schimmelfennig, F. and Sedelmeier 2002: 500)

The EC/EU has enlarged its membership several times. A procedure has evolved to handle enlargement applications, and this is explained in the first section of this chapter. The second section reviews the enlargement rounds. Each enlargement has raised a variety of questions, although the literature does not investigate these questions evenly. The third section of the chapter looks at one attempt to categorize the questions. Each enlargement also introduced new principles and precedents that would govern future enlargements. The policy on how to handle enlargement has evolved. Also, each enlargement has had an impact both on the new entrants and on the EU.

The Enlargement Procedure

When a potential applicant approaches the EU, the first step is for the European Council to consider whether the application is acceptable in principle. If it is, then the Commission produces an official Opinion on the application. This consists of a report on the economic and political position of the applicant state, and a recommendation on whether to proceed to negotiations immediately, or whether to delay. Usually the recommendation to delay is to give the applicant time to strengthen its claim to be ready for membership. If so, then a plan of action is produced to facilitate this, which will normally involve an association agreement or the strengthening of existing agreements.

If the decision of the European Council is to proceed with the application immediately, it will set a date for the opening of negotiations. The Commission will then convene meetings of various sectoral groups of experts to work out the detail of the EU's negotiating position. Negotiations then commence with the applicant(s). These are handled on a day-to-day basis by the groups of experts, often by correspondence rather than in formal meetings. They are co-ordinated by the Commission, and overseen by the Council of Foreign Ministers.

When agreement has been reached by the expert working groups in all sectors, and have been pronounced acceptable by the Foreign Ministers, the terms are passed to the European Council for formal approval. Assuming that approval is given, an Accession Treaty is drawn up with each applicant state. The Accession Treaty then has to be ratified by the European Parliament on the side of the EU, and by either the national parliament of the applicant state, or by referendum depending on the constitutional procedures of each state.

The Enlargements of the EC/EU

It is not even easy to decide how many enlargements of the EC/EU there have been. Strictly speaking, as each new member state negotiates its terms of entry separately, and signs a separate accession treaty, there have been as many enlargements as member states, minus the original six. Even this, though, would not give an uncontested reckoning, because it could be argued that the reunification of West Germany and East Germany in 1990 also constituted an enlargement, even though it resulted in no increase in the number of member states.

The EC/EU has preferred to negotiate enlargements with groups of states together. This has produced four distinct rounds of enlargement. The first enlargement in 1973 admitted Britain, Denmark, and Ireland. Strictly speaking the second enlargement was in 1981 when Greece became a member, and the third was in 1986 when Portugal and Spain joined. For analytical purposes, though, the second and third enlargements are usually treated as a single 'Mediterranean enlargement', as they were undertaken for similar reasons and involved similar issues. On this reckoning, the third enlargement was that of 1995, which admitted Austria, Finland and Sweden. Because the applicants (including Norway, which rejected membership in a referendum) were the leading members of the European Free Trade Association (EFTA) (Insight 31.1), this is usually referred to as 'the EFTA enlargement'. The fourth enlargement was in 2004, and is often referred to as 'the eastern enlargement' because most of the new entrants were former communist states in central and eastern Europe. This name will be used here, although strictly speaking it is inaccurate because two of the entrants—Cyprus and Malta—were Mediterranean island states.

INSIGHT 31.1

EFTA at the End of the 1980s

By the late 1980s EFTA consisted of seven states of varying size.

Country	Population ('000s)
Sweden	8,640
Austria	7,820
Switzerland	6,790
Finland	5,030
Norway	4,260
Iceland	256
Liechtenstein	30

- The economies of the EFTA states had been linked with those of the EC since the 1970s by a series of bilateral free-trade agreements.
- By the end of the 1980s EFTA was economically closely integrated with the EC.
- The EC did 25 per cent of its trade with EFTA, a higher proportion than with the United States, while the EFTA states sent 56 per cent of their exports to the EC, and bought 60 per cent of their imports from the EC.

Analysing Enlargement Policy

Until recently enlargement was frequently described, but was somewhat under theorized. Much of the literature on enlargement has been very descriptive and where explanations were offered by different writers of specific enlargements, they were not located within a general theoretical framework that would allow for comparative research. A start was made on addressing this lacuna by Schimmelfennig and Sedelmeier (2002) who produced a typology of the academic literature on enlargement, classifying it according to the research focus along four dimensions:

- the enlargement policies of the applicants;
- the enlargement policies of the existing member states;
- the enlargement policies of the EU;
- the impact of enlargement.

Within each dimension the authors identified the central research questions.

(1) A focus on the enlargement policies of the applicants produces the question: Why and under which conditions do non-members seek accession to a regional organization?

(2) A focus on the enlargement policies of the member states produces the research question: Why and under what conditions does a member state favour enlargement to include particular other states?

(3) A focus on the enlargement policies of the EU raises several research questions. Under which conditions does the regional organization admit a new member, or modify its institutional relationship with outside states? When does it offer membership rather than some other form of relationship stopping short of membership? Why does it offer membership to some applicants and not others? Under what conditions are the new members admitted? Which actors' preferences are reflected in the outcomes of the enlargement process?

(4) A focus on the impact of enlargement again generates several research questions. How does enlargement affect the distribution of power within the EU? How does it influence its identity, norms, and goals? How does it affect the effectiveness and efficiency of the EU? What are the implications for the deepening of integration? How does membership change the identity, interests, and behaviour of governmental and societal actors within the new entrants? This last question raises issues related to the Europeanization of member states: (Schimmelfennig and Sedelmeier 2002: 504–8).

Structuring existing studies along these dimensions, Schimmelfennig and Sedelmeier (2002: 523–4) were able to conclude that:

- the bulk of the analytical studies were on the last two enlargements;
- the analyses of the EFTA enlargement focused primarily on their first dimension—questioning why the EFTA states applied for membership;

- the analyses of the eastern enlargement focused primarily on their second and third dimensions—questioning why the applications were accepted, and on what conditions the applicants were offered membership.

The analysis of individual enlargement rounds that follows here organizes the information along the lines of these dimensions of enquiry, but with the following qualifications:

- under item 3, the enlargement policies of the EU, the focus will be specifically on how the way that the EC/EU approached the particular enlargement added to the existing principles and practices to reshape the policy of the EU on enlargement;

- under item 4, the impact of the enlargement, the focus will be primarily on the impact on the EU, because to consider the impact on each of the new member states would be too large and complex a task for a textbook of this nature, particularly as many of the states have not been studied systematically.

Schimmelfennig and Sedelmeier (2002: 508–15) also divided existing studies of enlargement according to whether they emphasized interests or ideas in their analysis. They referred to these as 'rationalist' and 'constructivist' institutionalism (see Chs. 2 and 3). The authors also attempted to embed analysis of the enlargement of the EU within a more general set of theoretical propositions about the enlargement of international organizations. While this is a valid and important step towards comparative analysis, because of the focus of this book on the EU, and of this chapter on the enlargement of the EU, it is not pursued here.

The First Enlargement

In August 1961 Britain, Denmark, and Ireland applied for membership of the EC. In April 1962 Norway also applied. Negotiations went on throughout 1962, until in January 1963 President de Gaulle of France unilaterally announced that France was not prepared to accept British membership. As any member state could veto entry, and as the other applications were dependent on British entry, the enlargement round collapsed. In May 1967 Britain, Denmark, and Ireland applied again, and Norway joined the second application in July. This time negotiations did not even get under way. France blocked agreement on opening negotiations in December 1967. Following the replacement of de Gaulle by Georges Pompidou as French President in 1969, a summit meeting at the Hague agreed on a package of measures to 'relaunch Europe' that included opening negotiations with the applicants, whose 1967 applications remained on the table. On 1 January 1973 Britain, Denmark, and Ireland became members of the EC. Norway negotiated terms of entry, but the Norwegian people rejected membership in a subsequent referendum.

Why did the Applicants Apply?

It can be argued that in answering this question, we need only consider the reasons for the British application. The other applicants were so tightly bound economically to Britain that they could not afford to stay outside the EC if Britain went in. However, it could also be argued that this is an example of a bias to 'big states' in the analysis of the EC. Studies of the possible other reasons for the applications from Ireland, Denmark, and Norway might reveal that economic necessity was only one factor. These studies, though, remain to be done by historians, who now have access to the official archives of the states for the first time.

Not having access until recently to the official papers of the British state did not stop historians debating why Britain, having declined the chance to become a founding member of the EEC in 1955, was already making its first application for membership in 1961. The two main theories are that the application was primarily economic, or alternatively that it was motivated by geo-strategic considerations.

Sluggish economic growth in Britain in the late 1950s was increasingly blamed by economists both inside and outside government on the pattern of trade. Britain at the end of the 1950s still did a high proportion of its trade with the countries of its former Empire, now voluntarily grouped together as the Commonwealth; but the fastest growth in trade was between industrialized countries. This was reflected in the high rates of growth within the newly formed EEC. The success of the EEC surprised British policy makers, and led to efforts in the late 1950s to conclude a free-trade agreement with the six. When this failed, an application for British entry for economic reasons began to be taken seriously. For Moravcsik (1998: 164) such economic reasons were paramount: 'The British membership bid was . . . aimed primarily at the advancement of enduring British commercial interests.'

Political considerations started to point in the same direction, though, when de Gaulle began to dominate the EEC, and became especially influential when he made proposals for political co-operation in the Fouchet Plan. British concern centred on the known hostility of de Gaulle to US hegemony in the capitalist world. Fouchet contained reference to co-operation on defence, but no reference to NATO. Because it was a central doctrine of British defence policy that the United States must be allowed to exercise leadership of the western defence effort through NATO, Fouchet set alarm bells ringing in London. It did the same in Washington. Camps (1964: 336) recorded that the British government came under increasing pressure from the United States to join the EEC so as to act as a counterweight to French influence, and she believed that this was 'a very important—perhaps the controlling—element in Macmillan's decision to apply'. The same perception seems to have been one of the significant factors in de Gaulle's decision to block enlargement throughout the 1960s.

Why did the Existing Member States Accept the Application?

Initially, the EC member states other than France were interested in British membership for predominantly political reasons. They saw Britain as a future counterweight to French domination of the EC. Concern on this issue was particularly strong where political co-operation was involved. As Ludlow (1997) made clear, the negotiations on British accession in the early 1960s were implicitly linked to the parallel negotiations on the Fouchet Plan. When de Gaulle vetoed British entry, the Fouchet negotiations collapsed (Ch. 9, Insight 9.2, p. 132).

The reason why France finally accepted the British application in 1972 was primarily economic. The change of French president cleared the way. More important, though, were changed economic circumstances. The post-war economic boom faltered in the late 1960s. British entry in particular offered the prospect of giving a boost to the EC economies.

France's President Pompidou had to ensure that British entry did not damage French interests. That is why he agreed to a compromise that allowed the EC to move to an 'own resources' system of funding the budget. De Gaulle had blocked such a move in 1965 because he objected to the idea—which became linked to it as part of a package deal—that the budgetary powers of the EP should be increased (Ch. 9, p. 132). Pompidou was prepared to make concessions on this, difficult though it was for him to do so in terms of domestic politics, because the new system would benefit France once Britain was a member. Britain, with a small and relatively efficient agricultural sector, would become a net contributor to a common budget that was dominated by the CAP. France, which had a large agricultural sector and a lot of small farmers who were eligible for financial support, would become a net beneficiary.

What did the Way in which this Enlargement was Handled add to the Policy?

The practice that was established at the time of the first enlargement was that the existing member states would sort out arrangements that suited them before the new members were admitted. The corollary of this was French insistence that accession for the new members could only be on the basis of acceptance of the complete *acquis communautaire* (Preston 1995: 452). This was to ensure that Britain did not try to slip out of the uncomfortable budgetary position into which the French believed that they had manoeuvred it. The implicit understanding that there was a deal in operation here explains the strength of French (and German) resistance to subsequent British demands for a correction of the budgetary imbalance.

What were the Effects of Enlargement?

The impact of the first enlargement on the EC was profound. In terms of bargaining games, not only did the total number of member states increase by fifty per cent: there was another 'big state' among the new members—Britain—which changed the coalition dynamics that had previously been dominated by France and West Germany. In terms of the sense of self-identity of the EC, the admission of two states—Britain and Denmark—that were sceptical of the 'European ideal' made it much more difficult to find a common discourse to conceptualize the mission of the organization.

The Mediterranean Enlargement

As explained above, the second and third enlargements of the EC are often treated as a single 'Mediterranean' enlargement. Greece became a member state in January 1981, and Spain and Portugal in January 1986. In all cases political considerations overrode economic in the decision to enlarge.

Why did the Applicants Apply?

All three of the states concerned had just emerged from periods of dictatorship, and the desire to consolidate democracy and guard against a resurgence of authoritarianism featured strongly in the reasons for the applications and the reasons for their acceptance. It was assumed that EC membership, conditional on democratic government, would help to achieve that.

Why did the Existing Member States Accept the Application?

Ensuring stability on the southern periphery of western Europe was a particular concern of France and West Germany. That stability was threatened from 1974 onwards. In 1974 Turkey invaded Cyprus, leading to a division of the island between Greek and Turkish communities, and precipitating the downfall of the military regime that ruled Greece. Also in 1974 the right-wing dictatorship in Portugal collapsed. In both cases the end of the undemocratic governments was followed by a period of uncertainty about the direction the country would take, with a growing concern that the southern flank of NATO would be weakened.

What did the Way in which this Enlargement was Handled add to the Policy?

The main contribution that the Mediterranean enlargement made to the principles on which future enlargements would be conducted, was the precedent set for the acceptance of applications for geo-strategic and political reasons even where the economic conditions were not ideal. This was relevant to the applications from a range of states in central and eastern Europe following the collapse of communism in 1989. Although the economies of these states were not strong, the need to ensure their political stability was; and the 1975 decision to over-ride the Commission's Opinion on Greece, and later to wave aside doubts about the economic preparedness of Portugal for membership for similar political reasons, created a precedent to do the same for these new applicants.

What were the Effects of Enlargement?

The impact of this enlargement on the EC/EU was in its way as great as that of the first enlargement. Again it changed the bargaining dynamics of the organization. The three new members shifted the orientation of the EC to the south, and ensured that there would be a stronger Mediterranean dimension to policy. In political co-operation, the influence of Spain and Portugal led to a greater emphasis on relations with Latin America. Perhaps most significantly in the short-run, Spain, with the support of the other new entrants, took the lead in demanding larger structural funds, and soon showed itself adept at playing the EC negotiating game to get them.

On the other hand, Greece's membership had some less positive consequences. Its long-standing disputes with Turkey proved an embarrassment on more than one occasion, and spilled over into a hard line on Cyprus. Also, its position on the edge of the Balkans meant that Greece had sensitivities in the region that were difficult for other EU members to understand. These became particularly pertinent in the early 1990s following the break-up of Yugoslavia (see Ch. 30, p. 520).

The EFTA Enlargement

In the early 1990s several member states of EFTA enquired about membership. At first they were offered a form of close association that fell short of full membership. Subsequently, though, they lodged formal applications, and eventually Austria, Finland, and Sweden became members of the EU on 1 January 1995. Norway, not for the first time, rejected membership in a referendum after terms of entry had been agreed.

With this enlargement round, we reach the first to be systematically analysed in the literature. As Schimmelfennig and Sedelmeier (2002: 517) put it, 'the key question pursued is: why did the EFTA countries, after a long period of deliberate nonmembership in the European Community (EC), develop an interest in closer ties with, and membership of, the EC at the beginning of the 1990s?'. It is because of the focus in the literature on this question that the section dealing with it below is much longer than the other sections.

Why did the Applicants Apply?

There are disputes over the answer to this question. There is also a good deal of common ground, however. At the beginning of the 1980s the European economies generally experienced an economic downturn as a result of the 1979 oil crisis. In response to the downturn, the EC launched the '1992 project' to create the single European market. In the course of the 1980s, the member states of EFTA became concerned about the impact on investment in their economies of the EC's decision to create the single internal market. Export-oriented businesses in the EFTA states experienced difficulties in selling to the EU, with the result that increasingly businesses wanted to be inside the single market, and investment began to flow in that direction. Even large national companies of the EFTA states, such as Volvo of Sweden, were locating their investments inside the EC and not in the EFTA countries. This led the EFTA states to enquire about closer links with the EC, despite the unpopularity of the idea of membership inside some of the states concerned.

The other factor that affected the decision was the end of the Cold War. Events in 1989 removed one of the main objections of opponents of membership within the EFTA states. Austria, Finland, and Sweden were all neutral during the Cold War, and there had been doubts about whether membership of an organization that was developing a common foreign and security policy was compatible with neutrality. The end of the Cold War called into question the meaning of neutrality, and effectively dissipated the doubts on that score.

These three factors—the economic downturn, the challenge posed by the EC's 1992 programme, and the end of the Cold War—are common ground between different explanations. The debate is about how these background factors translated into domestic politics in different states.

Sweden is the most studied of the cases from this enlargement. It illustrates well why analysts have considered their main problem to be explaining the reasons for the EFTA states' applications. Sweden was an exemplar of a social-democratic neo-corporatist type of state, and its social-democratic governments had previously rejected membership of the EC on the grounds that the free-market orientation of the organization would jeopardize the Swedish model of capitalism. Yet in 1991 a social-democratic government applied for membership at just the time that the EC was taking a major step in a neo-liberal direction with the single-market programme (Bieler 2002: 576). Why?

Ingebritsen (1998) offered a rational choice explanation for the decision, in the mould of liberal intergovernmentalism. She concentrated on the leading industrial sectors, which in Sweden were export oriented. The largest firms were also transnational, and in the course of the 1980s began to transfer production abroad. Swedish governments were already concerned about the country's lack of competitiveness, and the internal market programme offered a means of injecting more competitiveness into the economy. So the combination of the push factor of the loss of investment and the pull factor of achieving domestic economic objectives through taking on external commitments (hand-tying) made the choice for membership of the internal market rational for the Swedish government. The EEA was abandoned in favour of an application for full membership because it did not satisfy the large Swedish manufacturers and did not stop the outward flow of investment capital. Essentially the same analysis was applied to Finland, where the economy was also dominated by capital-intensive manufacturing exporters.

Fioretos (1997) offered a similar analysis, although this article was not primarily concerned with enlargement, and the reasons for Sweden's application were only used as an illustrative example of a general argument. That argument was primarily directed at the assertion of Moravcsik (1994) that participation in European integration increased the autonomy in domestic politics of the state executive from societal pressures. Essentially Fioretos (1997) argued that globalization had increased the power of corporations in the domestic arena and allowed them to force governments onto paths of policy that they—the corporations—preferred.

European integration does not strengthen the state as much as it is the consequence of a state that has lost its strength.

(Fioretos 1997: 319)

Although the argument was directed against Moravcsik, like Ingebritsen (1998), Fioretos (1997) offered a rationalist analysis that was compatible with liberal intergovernmentalism, and perhaps more so than the author himself recognized.

Liberal intergovernmentalism analyses European integration as an example of a two-level game, in which the first stage is the formation of preferences (Ch. 1, p. 14). At this stage: 'Groups articulate preferences; governments aggregate them' (Moravcsik 1993: 483). This is exactly the relationship theorized by Fioretos (1997). In response to the economic downturn of the 1980s, Swedish firms took advantage of growing globalization to became transnational. This strengthened their hand in domestic bargaining with government because they had a much stronger option to exit the game than previously—i.e. if they did not get their way they could close down production in Sweden and switch it elsewhere. The firms were kept in Sweden in the 1980s by a series of devaluations that kept the krona at a competitive exchange rate with the economies of the EC, which were the main markets for Swedish manufactured products. This strategy could not be pursued indefinitely, though, and increasingly investment capital did leave Sweden for EC locations that offered lower costs of production and lower transport costs because of greater proximity to the market. Weakened in the domestic bargaining game by the greater ease with which capital could relocate, the Swedish social democrats had to pursue membership of the single market, which meant membership of the EC once it became clear that the EEA was an unsatisfactory compromise for Swedish firms.

Bieler (2000, 2002) offered a neo-Gramscian analysis that gave more emphasis to the role of ideas. It also identified a more variegated range of relevant actors. Instead of focusing only on the state and the main industrial employers, this approach divided the economy into transnational and national sectors, and subdivided the latter into nationally-oriented firms that produced mainly for domestic consumption and internationally-oriented firms that produced for export. It also examined the position of organized labour, again dividing this according to the sector that its members worked in.

The importance of the first distinction was primarily useful in allowing Bieler (2000, 2002) to make comparisons between different applicants—in this case Sweden and Austria. There was no disagreement with the analyses of Ingebritsen (1998) and Fioretos (1997) that the transnational sectors were the primary economic actors in Sweden. However, Bieler (2002: 585) emphasized that Swedish membership was pushed most strongly by the Ministry of Finance and the Prime Ministers' Office, and argued that this showed that 'neo-liberal restructuring had become . . . internalized within the Swedish form of state in view of domestic economic recession'. In other words, the Swedish government was looking for a long-term means of solving the country's chronic economic problems, and had accepted the ideological claims of neo-liberalism to provide the only such solution. It was therefore trying to tie its own hands by joining the EC, which would provide an external buttress against resistance to the dismantling of the welfare state and neo-corporatist institutions of Sweden.

Despite the criticisms of 'rationalist political economy approaches' offered by Bieler (2002: 578–9), this conclusion is not incompatible with the approaches of Ingebritsen (1998) and Fioretos (1997). Both accepted that economic restructuring was a motivating element in prompting the Swedish application, although not the dominant element. Bieler (2000, 2002) offered a more distinctive analysis in the comparison of the strategy adopted by industry to achieve membership in Sweden and in Austria, and in the comparison of the roles in the two countries of organized labour.

In Austria the dominant economic sector was not transnational. It consisted of internationally-oriented national firms, which were dependent on exports to the EC but did not have production facilities outside their own country that the larger Swedish firms had acquired during the 1980s. This sector dominated the Austrian Federation of Industrialists. In order to convince the government to apply for membership, the Federation had to overcome political opposition. So it undertook what Bieler (2002: 583) called a 'hegemonic project'. This involved issuing a series of studies that not only advanced a strong version of the neo-liberal economic argument, but also dealt with the constitutional implications of membership and the issue of what it implied for Austria's post-war neutrality. These arguments then fed into internal debates within the two main political parties—the Social Democratic Party and the People's Party. Although they encountered opposition from representatives of the economic sectors that had been sheltered from foreign competition by the state, and from representatives of the public sector, they eventually won over the leadership of both parties, thus setting the course for the application. Organized labour in the two national sectors also divided in its attitude to membership, but again the argument was won by the representatives of the internationally-oriented sector. By the time of the Austrian referendum, a new orthodoxy had emerged around membership, thus ensuring a comfortable 'yes' vote by 66.6 per cent to 33.4 per cent.

In Sweden, Bieler (2002: 586–7) argued that the transnational corporations did not need to build a hegemonic project in favour of membership because they had the option of exit. Instead they brutally spelt out the implications of not joining, notably in a series of advertisements in national newspapers in the run-up to the 1994 general election (Fioretos 1997: 316). Although trade unions in the transnational sector supported membership, they did not do so for the same reasons as their employers. Whereas the employers saw membership as a lever to dismantle the controls that the state exercised over them at the national level, their trade unions saw membership as a means to reassert at the European level a control that had been lost at the national level (Bieler 2002: 591). This difference had implications for the future political struggles over the direction of European integration. It also helps to explain the closeness of the Swedish referendum result: 52.7 per cent Yes to 47.3 per cent No.

Why did the Existing Member States Accept the Application?

The initial response of the EU was to offer the prospective applicants a form of relationship that fell short of full membership. This position was then abandoned, and the applications for full membership accepted. So why the change of attitude?

At the time of the initial approach from the EFTA states, the EC was trying to process the legislation that was needed to make a reality of the internal market. It was also looking to the next stage in the process, which in the view of the President of the Commission (Jacques Delors), the Chancellor of Germany (Helmut Kohl), and the President of France (François Mitterrand) was movement to a monetary union. To prevent another round of enlargement dominating the attention of the organization, and possibly deflecting the course of the spillover from the single market to the single currency, in January 1989 Delors proposed the idea of the European Economic Space (EES), which was later renamed the European Economic Area (EEA). This would give the EFTA states membership of the single market without them becoming full members of the EC. For the governments of the EFTA states, the EEA had the advantage that it might be easier than full membership of the EC to sell to their electorates. The disadvantage was that they would have no voice in the ongoing negotiation of the regulation of the single market. They would be obliged to accept agreements reached in their absence.

The EEA negotiations were successfully concluded in 1991, and a treaty was signed in 1992; but it became increasingly apparent that businesses were simply not prepared to accept that members of the EEA would be full members of the single market. Investment flows did not revert to previous patterns. The EEA suffered a further blow to its credibility when the Swiss people rejected membership of it in a referendum in December 1992. The government of Austria had already applied for full membership of the EC in July 1989, and Finland, Norway, and Sweden did likewise between July 1991 and November 1992.

By this time the prospect had emerged of an eventual eastern enlargement to embrace states that were economically considerably less developed than the existing member states. The EFTA applicants were wealthy, and potential net contributors to a common budget that would come under much greater pressure if the Central and East European countries (CEECs) were eventually accepted. So, the EFTA applications were accepted, and Austria, Finland, and Sweden became members at the start of 1995.

What did the Way in which this Enlargement was Handled add to the Policy?

The main significance of the EFTA enlargement was that it raised for the first time some of the issues concerning the institutional architecture of the EC/EU that were to emerge with more urgency when the eastern enlargement came to the top of the agenda. The weighting of votes in the Council of Ministers was particularly problematical. Britain and Spain raised it as an issue during the negotiations of the accession of Austria, Finland, and Sweden, pointing out that if the existing rules on what constituted a qualified majority (or a blocking minority) were simply extrapolated upwards on enlargement, it would become possible for states representing 41 per cent of the population to be outvoted. This would be compounded with further enlargement because of the number of small states applying, and it would soon be possible for a majority of the population of the EU to be outvoted. Eventually a compromise was reached at a meeting of Foreign Ministers in Ioannina in Greece in March 1995 whereby the blocking minority would be increased in line with the increased number of votes, but if there were twenty-three votes against there would be a delay in proceeding with the measure during which time the Commission would try to find an acceptable compromise amendment to its proposal.

The other institutional issues raised by the EFTA enlargement were the extension of the practice of QMV, and the size of the Commission. It soon became obvious that the increase from twelve to fifteen member states increased the complexity of bargaining and coalition formation more than proportionately to the expansion of the number of actors. The prospect emerged of the organization becoming paralysed if it expanded its membership further without agreeing to remove the national veto. At the same time, the formation of a coherent Commission also became more difficult. Because the larger member states had two Commissioners, a membership of fifteen states meant a Commission of twenty members, and there were simply not sufficient significant portfolios to go round, as Jacques Santer discovered when he tried to accommodate all the national nominees without upsetting anyone by giving them inadequate responsibilities.

So, although compromises were reached on all the institutional issues during this enlargement, an agreement was reached that they would be fundamentally reconsidered before further enlargement.

What were the Effects of Enlargement?

Because the new members were wealthy, were already culturally aligned with the prevailing values of the existing member states, and had been closely associated with the EC prior to their membership, the effects of this enlargement were smaller than those of any other enlargement. One effect of the enlargement was the emergence of a Nordic block within the Council. Since 1995 Denmark has had support from Sweden and Finland for positions on issues such as environmental protection and human rights that it had long defended, and the Nordic states combined to press the membership claims of the Baltic states (Estonia, Latvia, and Lithuania) in the eastern enlargement round. Austria joined the Nordic states in reinforcing the coalition of member states for whom environmental protection was a significant issue. Because the new members were all net contributors to the budget, their presence reinforced the coalition in favour of reform of the budgetary rules.

The 'Eastern' Enlargement

With the collapse of communism in 1989, the EC was faced with a large number of potential new members, all of whom expressed an aspiration to join. The first response was to conclude 'Europe Agreements', association agreements that fell short of envisaging full membership. Then in June 1993 the Copenhagen European Council accepted the legitimacy of the aspirations of the newly independent states to become members, and laid down criteria that they would have to fulfil in order for their applications to be considered. Applications came in rapidly from ten CEECs (Table 31.1). In December 1997 the Luxemburg European Council agreed that negotiations should open with five of these states—the Czech Republic, Estonia, Hungary, Poland, and Slovenia—plus Cyprus (Malta had withdrawn its application), but hold back on the five others. In December 1999 the Helsinki European Council agreed to open negotiations with the remaining five CEECs, plus Malta, which had resubmitted its application. On 1 May 2004 eight CEECs—the Czech Republic, Estonia, Hungary, Latvia, Lithuania, Poland, Slovakia, and Slovenia—plus Cyprus and Malta became members of the EU.

TABLE 31.1

Association Agreements and Accession Applications

State	Date of Association Agreement	Date of Accession Application
Bulgaria	March 1993	December 1995
Cyprus	December 1972	July 1990
Czech Republic	October 1993	January 1996
Estonia	June 1995	November 1995
Hungary	December 1991	March 1994
Latvia	June 1995	October 1995
Lithuania	June 1995	October 1995
Malta	December 1970	July 1990
Poland	December 1991	April 1994
Romania	February 1993	June 1995
Slovakia	October 1993	June 1995
Slovenia	June 1996	June 1996
Turkey	September 1973	April 1987

Source: Europa web site: http://europa.eu.int/scadplus/leg/en/lvb/e40001.htm

Why did the Applicants Apply?

The wish of the former communist states to become members of the EU has hardly been considered problematic. The states that had emerged from Soviet domination wanted to cement their status as Europeans, and to foreclose any possibility of being drawn back into the Russian sphere of influence. From this point of view, membership of NATO was the more important objective, but membership of the EU was also a guarantee, albeit weaker. Membership of the EU was also seen as essential to the future economic success of the former communist states, and it fitted with a widespread desire to reaffirm a European identity. Finally, access to the European single market was seen as essential to the economic future of the CEECs.

In one of the few articles to treat the question as worthy of further investigation, Bieler (2002: 588–9) applied neo-Gramscian concepts to the analysis of why the applications were made. In what was no more than a sketch for future research, Bieler suggested that the decision to apply was taken by what he called 'cadre élites within state institutions'. These élites had taken advantage of the collapse of the previous regimes to take power and to introduce programmes of neo-liberal reconstruction, supported by external forces. When the restructuring programmes precipitated big falls in GDP, the legitimacy of the élites and of their reform programmes were jeopardized. EU membership was pursued as a buttress against resistance and reversion to anti-capitalist politicians and policies. It was sold to the populations of the CEECs as a historical 'return to Europe'. However, the volatility of society and politics in the CEECs ruled out the construction of a pro-EU historical bloc organized around a hegemonic project such as Bieler (2002: 582–5) had identified in Austria. Instead the process in the CEECs was what Gramsci had described as a 'passive revolution', led from above by the state élites. This had implications for the commitment of socio-economic actors to the project

Why did the Existing Member States Accept the Application?

There is a real problem in explaining why the applications were accepted, because the proposed enlargement posed far and away the most serious difficulties of any enlargement to date. These are dealt with below in the section on the effects of enlargement.

Given the difficulties that the decision caused for the EU, the main question that has been considered for the latest enlargement is why the applications were (eventually) accepted. Why was the immediate reaction of the EC to the collapse of communism to offer the Europe Agreements, which did not make a commitment to eventual membership, and why was this approach subsequently abandoned and the applications of the CEECs accepted? Why was it decided in Luxemburg in 1997 to prioritize six of the applications, and then again in Helsinki in 1999 to open negotiations with all the remaining applicants? Why, if the EU was committed to making enlargement happen, were the member states not readily prepared to make sacrifices on trimming back their own entitlements under the structural funds and the CAP?

First it has to be remembered that the collapse of communism came quickly and was not anticipated. The immediate response of the EC to developments focused on the implications of the rapid moves to reunify Germany (Friis 1998: 323). It was clear that Chancellor Kohl was determined to seize this historic opportunity, and even his closest ally, François Mitterrand, was left trailing in his wake. The European Commission had to deal with the prospect of a sudden increase in the territory of the EC, and the adaptation of common policies to the addition of another 17 million people with a GDP per head well below the EC average (see Ch. 28, pp. 479–80). Attention inevitably focused on these issues until they were resolved.

Second, the negotiation of the EFTA enlargement was still at an early stage in 1989. Indeed, the EC was still following a policy of trying to persuade the EFTA applicants to become part of the single market without becoming members of the EC, i.e. the EEA negotiations. As with German reunification, this issue had to be settled before serious attention could be given to the position of the CEECs. Also, it would have been surprising had the CEECs been given a perspective of membership before negotiations had opened on the applications of the prior EFTA applicants. The deal offered in the original Europe Agreements was similar to that on offer to the EFTA states at that stage: membership of the single market without membership of the EC.

Third, the EC was in 1989 about to embark on the process of agreeing to a monetary union. The Delors Report was published April 1989, before Hungary cut the first hole in the iron curtain by throwing open its borders to the west in May. The Madrid European Council in June 1989 agreed to set up an IGC to consider the Treaty changes needed to allow monetary union, and to set a date for the start of stage 1 of the process outlined in the Delors Report. This process may have been accelerated by the events in central and eastern Europe, but essentially it was a separate process that had already begun, and another one that occupied the attention of the member states and the Commission.

The change of policy, marked by the decision at Copenhagen in June 1993, can be explained by reference to the completion of other business, by the persistence of the CEECs in requesting membership, and by geo-strategic considerations.

Between 1990 and 1995 the three pressing issues identified above were all cleared out of the way. Formal reunification of Germany took place on 3 October 1990. The TEU, setting out the timetable and conditions for monetary union, was agreed at the Maastricht European Council in December 1991, and formally signed by Foreign Ministers in February 1992. Terms of entry for Austria, Finland, and Sweden were agreed in the early hours of 1 March 1994. Once these issues were resolved, removing what Friis (1998: 333) described as 'the negative spillover from internal negotiating tables', there was the possibility of contemplating further enlargement.

The persistence of the CEECs in pressing for entry to the EC/EU was strengthened by the acceptance of the EC that the EEA scheme was not going to work for the EFTA applicants. It would have been difficult to convince the CEECs that membership of the single market without membership of the EU would be any more successful or acceptable for them once the argument had been conceded for the EFTA applicants. It would have looked simply as though the EC/EU was prepared to accept prosperous member states and not those most in need of support.

Security considerations became more urgent in the context of growing instability in Russia (Friis and Murphy 1999: 220). The USSR broke apart rapidly between August and December 1991. It formally ceased to exist on 31 December 1991. The Russian state that emerged after many of the former Soviet Republics had proclaimed independence was an insecure place in which nationalist voices received a hearing from the population, and in turn the governments under President Boris Yeltsin came under pressure to talk tough with 'the near abroad'. In these circumstances the concern of the CEECs for security from an aggressive Russia led to increased demands for membership of both the EC and NATO. These two issues became intertwined. The United States was concerned not to expand NATO membership too precipitately for fear of alarming Russia, so it put pressure on the EC to offer membership as a sort of second-order guarantee of independence to the states most affected. There was particular pressure on the EC to offer membership to the three Baltic states—Estonia, Latvia, and Lithuania—because they were too close to Russia to make NATO membership feasible, but they were also too close to Russia for comfort given the rising nationalist sentiment there. Although it was never likely that the EC would accede directly to any such demand from the United States, it had to show that it was prepared to move some way to contributing to the stabilization of the east. Also, as Yugoslavia began to disintegrate on the very doorstep of the EC, concerns about security grew in the member states themselves.

The prevarication on whether to proceed with all twelve applications together or whether to prioritize some of the applicants reflected the different stakes that different member states had in the enlargement. Germany was particularly keen to see early enlargement to take in at least its closest neighbours: Poland, Hungary and the Czech Republic. This was both for security and economic reasons. The security reasons are obvious: reunification rendered Germany once more a central European state itself, and instability in neighbouring states was highly undesirable. The economic motivations reflected the traditional economic links between Germany and its central European neighbours. France, on the other hand, had less of a stake in either consideration, as it had no contiguous land frontier with the central European states, and had fewer economic links. For France and the other Mediterranean member states there was a real risk that eastern enlargement would reduce their influence in the EU, shifting the centre of gravity away from them towards Germany. The French government was therefore more prepared to take a leisurely approach, whereas the German government wanted as few obstacles as possible placed in the way of early accession for its favoured candidates. The European Commission's motivation in proposing to proceed with only some of the applications reflected particularly its concerns about its limited resources. The process of accession is long and complex, and can tie up a lot of the available resources of the Commission. Member states have never been prepared to provide all the extra resources necessary to allow it to perform efficiently the task set for it, and there was no indication that they would do so on this occasion.

Acceptance of the Commission's proposal to limit the number of applicants with which accession negotiations would begin reflected a temporary meeting of minds between Germany and France. The link to NATO enlargement, and the pressure that the EU had come under from the United States to proceed rapidly on a broad front, made it very attractive for France to agree to a more limited start, to show that the EU was not going to be pushed around by the United States.

The change of tactic at Helsinki, to open negotiations with the remaining applicants, reflected a number of changed circumstances. First, the CEECs that had not been placed in the first group had become increasingly restive about their treatment. Second, the pressure from the United States had receded as the security threat posed by Russia appeared also to recede. Third, the change of heart in Malta opened the prospect to France, Spain, Portugal, Italy, and Greece of having another Mediterranean small state in the first group of members to off-set the influx of small and medium-sized CEECs. Of the second six, Malta was the most equipped to catch up with some of the first six applicants and get membership early.

Finally, Bieler (2002: 590) again offered an analysis that approached the question from the neo-Gramscian perspective, and identified the key to the acceptance of the applications as the support given after 1997 by the European Round Table of Industrialists (ERT). Bieler maintained that the ERT was recruited as an ally by the Commission, but was willingly recruited because many of the transnational corporations that made up the membership of the ERT had invested heavily in the CEECs and therefore had an interest in consolidating the conditions for profitable production there.

What did the Way in which this Enlargement was Handled add to the Policy?

For the first time in the history of enlargements, formal criteria were laid down for this round. The Copenhagen criteria were:

- a political criterion—that an applicant must have stable institutions, guaranteeing democracy, the rule of law, human rights, and the protection of minorities;

- an economic criterion—that an applicant must have a functioning market economy and the capacity to cope with competitive pressures within the single market of the EU;

- a criterion relating to the *acquis communautaire*—that an applicant must be able to take on the obligations of membership, including adherence to the aims of political, economic, and monetary union.

Although these were originally criteria for the acceptance of applications, they also came to structure the negotiations on membership. The criteria owed much to the consensus in other international organizations such as the IMF and World Bank on the conditions under which assistance would be given to states requesting it.

What were the Effects of Enlargement?

In order to be ready to take as many as twelve new members, the EU had to deal with some difficult issues requiring reforms of both policies and institutions. Two policy issues were particularly crucial to the prospects for enlargement: agriculture (Ch. 25, pp. 394–6) and the structural funds (Ch. 28, pp. 479–82). In both cases the existing member states that were beneficiaries from the funds proved very reluctant to surrender their benefits to facilitate enlargement. The institutional questions were those that were already apparent at the time of the EFTA enlargement: the weighting of votes under QMV, and the size of the blocking minority; the abandonment of the national veto in more policy sectors; and the size of the Commission (Ch. 18).

Future Enlargement

With the completion of the '10 + 2' enlargement, the EU faced the question of how far it would continue to expand geographically. There was no shortage of prospective applicants. There were two remaining candidatures from former communist states; beyond that the prospect of applications from the Yugoslav successor states; and expressions of interest from successor states of the former Soviet Union and even from several North African states. Above all, there was the pressing issue of Turkish membership.

The two outstanding applications from former East European communist states were from Bulgaria and Romania. Bulgaria was expected to be ready for membership in 2007; Romania was expected to take a little longer to fulfil the necessary conditions.

Most of the successor states to the former Yugoslavia were not expected to be ready to make applications for some time, but in March 2003 Croatia applied for membership, and was granted candidate status in June; then in March 2004 so did the Former Yugoslav Republic of Macedonia. In April 2004 the Commission recommended the opening of negotiations with Croatia, which had made remarkable progress in a short time on both the political and economic fronts. Some commentators expected that Croatia might overtake Romania and perhaps be ready to join together with Bulgaria in 2007. Other of the former Yugoslav territories would obviously take longer, but there was little doubt that their applications would eventually be accepted.

Beyond them lay states that had formerly been part of the Soviet Union itself: Armenia, Azerbaijan, Georgia, Moldova, and Ukraine. After June 2004, the borders of the enlarged EU abutted these states, but there was little prospect that they would be accepted as applicants. In May 2004 Günter Verheugen appeared to rule it out when he said (*Financial Times*, 13 May 2004), 'Membership is not on the agenda for these countries. Full stop.' His statement applied also to North African states such as Morocco and Tunisia that had expressed an interest in eventual membership. Clearly these latter states were not European, which allowed membership to be ruled out. Nothing was so clear about the application from Turkey.

Turkey

Turkey had been an applicant for membership for longer than any of the states that gained entry in 2004. An Association Agreement envisaging eventual membership had been signed in 1963. It had been suspended in 1970 and again in 1980, following military take-overs of power, but reinstated following elections and a return to civilian government in 1973 and again in 1983. In 1987 Turkey lodged its first formal application for membership of the EU. Two years later the EU responded by saying that no further enlargement was envisaged in the foreseeable future. In 1995 a Customs Union Agreement was signed, the first time that such an agreement had not been part of a process of accession. Then in 1997 came the Luxemburg European Council and the decision to move forward with various applications, but excluding Turkey. Two years later, the Helsinki European Council reversed this decision and recognized Turkey as an applicant, although without setting a date for the start of membership negotiations.

Why did Turkey Apply?

There is a standard answer to this question, which links the application for membership of the EC/EU to the attempts of an élite in Turkey, persistently since the early part of the twentieth century, to establish it as a western country.

After the end of the First World War and the collapse of the Ottoman Empire, the modern state of Turkey emerged from a prolonged civil war in which the new nationalists defeated the Sultan. The radicals, led by Mustafa Kemal Atatürk, defeated the more conservative of the nationalist forces and established a republic. The reformists then set about a process of westernizing and modernizing Turkey. This involved legislation to abolish Islamic law and Islamic modes of dress, to institute a new Civil Code modelled on the Swiss example, and to introduce the Roman alphabet (Ahmad 2001: 850; McLaren 2000: 118). When private business interests failed to respond to the reforms by investing in the modernization of the economy, and in the wake of the world economic crisis of 1930, an ideology of 'Kemalism' was developed that involved the state carrying out economic modernization from the top. The armed forces became associated with this process, setting themselves up as the guardians of the secular state. This role was consolidated after the Second World War, as a semi-modernized Turkey stuttered and staggered away from statism towards democracy. The struggles between the classes that benefited from modernization and those that suffered produced political crises that led to military interventions in 1960 and 1970 (Ahmad 2001: 850–1).

In neo-Gramscian terms, the 1959 application for associate membership of the EC, and the post-dictatorship enquiry about full membership, were attempts by the socio-economic classes that benefited from modernization to consolidate that direction for the economy. In constructivist terms it was about strengthening the contested identity of Turkey as a western, European nation rather than as an eastern, Muslim nation. The advocates of Turkish membership at the start of the twenty-first century still played on the risk that the country could be diverted from its secular pro-capitalist course if it was rebuffed by the EU, and they were able to obtain more leverage from this argument in the light of the post-cold war tensions between western capitalism and traditional Islamic forces, and particularly after the Al-Qaeda terrorist attacks of 11 September 2001 in the United States.

How are the Attitudes of the EU towards the Application to be Explained?

The decision in the 1960s to conclude an association agreement with Turkey envisaging eventual membership can be explained in geo-strategic terms. Turkey had just emerged from a period of military rule, and the political scene was volatile. The predominant strategic concern of the period was the Cold War, and Turkey stood on the cusp of the communist world. It was important for the capitalist states to shore up this flank of NATO, and to do that it was important to strengthen the democratic forces that favoured a western and capitalist orientation for the state. The danger was not so much a communist takeover, as that Turkey would lurch into deeper and deeper crises of instability and become an unreliable ally.

Further military intervention in 1970 indicated that this tactic had not worked, and led to the suspension of the association agreement. The restoration of democracy in 1973 reactivated the agreement, but tensions between the neo-fascist right and the extreme left precipitated a further military intervention in 1980. Democracy was restored in 1983, but it was not until 1987 that Turkey was sufficiently stable for a formal application to the EU to be a credible move.

Müftüler-Bac and McLaren (2003) analysed the reasons for the decision of the EU to exclude Turkey from the list of prospective members in 1997, and for the change of position in 1999. They considered this to be a puzzle because nothing significant had changed in Turkey in the intervening period. In solving the problem, they adopted an intergovernmental perspective, arguing that the explanation lay in the changing preferences of the governments of existing member states, which in turn reflected their national interests. Their empirical research consisted largely, although not entirely, of interviews conducted in Ankara with the ambassadors of EU member states to Turkey.

The first finding of the empirical research was that different member states had championed the applications of different candidate states, and that this was for self-interested reasons. Germany had championed the Czech Republic, Hungary, and Poland because stability in those states was essential to German security, but also because of a sense of historical obligation for wrongs committed by previous German regimes. The Nordic states—initially Denmark alone, but with the support of Sweden and Finland once they became members—championed the applications of the Baltic states, with which they had ties of geography and history. France championed Romania because of long-standing cultural links, as a partial counter-balance to the extra influence that the membership of the Central European states would give to Germany. The authors might also have added that France championed Cyprus and Malta for similar reasons.

Turkey not only had no champion among the existing member states: in Greece it had an adversary. Germany also had grave doubts about the acceptability of Turkish entry. The ability of Greece to exercise a veto over moves towards Turkish membership, and the opposition of Germany to any such moves, explained the omission of Turkey from the list of candidates in 1997. By the end of 1999, though, both of these opponents had changed position.

In late 1999 there was a dramatic improvement in relations between Greece and Turkey. Müftüler-Bac and McLaren (2003) offer three explanations for this:

- Theo Pangalos, a long-standing adversary of Turkey, was replaced by the far more pragmatic and accommodating George Papandreou as Greece's Foreign Minister;
- a terrible earthquake in Turkey in August 1999 produced a wave of sympathy among the Greek public, and emergency assistance from the Greek government;
- in trying to gain membership of the European single currency, the Greek government was struggling to cut its budget deficit, and a relaxation of tensions with Turkey offered the prospect of significant savings on defence expenditure;
- Greece was using up a lot of political capital within the EU in causing trouble for the others over Turkey, political capital that it needed to conserve if it was not to lose out in areas such as receipts from the structural funds following the eastern enlargement.

There was also a change in the German position between 1997 and 1999. For the German government of Helmut Kohl, the main objection to Turkish membership, which was often unspoken, was a concern that it was not culturally compatible with the image that the CDU/CSU held of Europe. In other words, Turkey was not Christian. This was also a view held by other Christian Democrat politicians from outside of Germany. The change of position in Germany came about as a result of the replacement of the CDU–CSU government in 1998 with an SPD-Green government under Gerhard Schröder. Müftüler-Bac and McLaren (2003: 23–4) represented the issue for the new government as one of domestic politics: the need to integrate the large Turkish minority more securely into German society. However, it could also be suggested, more cynically, that the change of position was intended to consolidate the ethnic Turkish vote for the left-of-centre coalition.

So complete was the change in the German position that at the June 1999 Cologne European Council, at the end of the German presidency, Schröder formally proposed that the Luxemburg decision on Turkey be reversed. The move proved premature: the change of Greece's position still lay in the months ahead, Italy had just been involved in a diplomatic row with Turkey over its refusal to extradite a Kurdish nationalist leader, and Sweden expressed serious reservations about the human rights situation in Turkey. Nevertheless, the conversion of Germany meant that Turkey now had the advocate that it had lacked in 1997, and a very powerful advocate at that.

As well as marking out clearly the changed position of Germany, the Cologne European Council was also significant because of the adoption of a new approach to enlargement negotiations. Previously the EU had tried to negotiate enlargement with groups of candidates together. At Cologne the 'principle of differentiation' was adopted. Essentially this meant that in future the EU would negotiate with states individually without any target for completion of the negotiations, and the Commission would monitor progress and regularly up-date the member states on when different states might be ready to join. This change of policy was recognition that there was growing discontent in the CEECs that were not in the 'top six' group that had been identified in Luxemburg, discontent that might hinder and even reverse the progress of reform. The Kosovo conflict was then in full crisis as a reminder of the consequences of not moving swiftly to ensure stability. The decision also marked the wish of the Heads of Government to reward Bulgaria and Romania for their support of NATO in Kosovo. Once it has been taken, though, it became more feasible for negotiations with Turkey to begin, and much more difficult to oppose them.

To continue the story beyond where Müftüler-Bac and McLaren (2003) left it: in November 2002 the election of a new government changed the situation in Turkey. The Justice and Development Party (AKP), which now came into office, was an Islamic party, but not a traditionalist or fundamentalist party. It was committed to pursuing the westernization of Turkey, the goal of the secular Republic since Atatürk. This made it difficult for the military, the self-appointed guardians of the legacy of Atatürk, to intervene as they had in the past to overturn the democratic process on the grounds that the principles of the Republic were being betrayed.

Under the premiership of Recep Tayyip Erdogan, the AKP vigorously set about trying to satisfy the political pre-requisites to a successful Turkish bid for membership of the EU. Within the space of little over a year the new government made sufficient change in the political and legal systems to attract a warm commendation from the Commission in its 2003 Report on Turkey's Progress towards Accession. Although a great deal remained to be done, the first steps to removing the blockage had been taken in earnest. The pressure that Erdogan exerted on the Turkish Cypriot government to accept a settlement of the division of the island also helped to win over Greece, and to win Turkey friends in other quarters.

Britain, always sympathetic to Turkey's claims, became a strong advocate of its cause. In the aftermath of a spate of terrorist bombings in Ankara in November 2003, the British Foreign Secretary, Jack Straw, called for Turkish membership 'as soon as possible', and the Europe Minister, Denis MacShane, said, 'Europe is incomplete without Turkey' (Foreign and Commonwealth Office 2004). The dominant reason for British support was geo-strategic. Turkey occupied a geographical position between the EU and the Middle East. It bordered Iran, Iraq, and Syria. It had a majority of Muslims among its population, at a time when the EU was increasingly being accused of a bias against Muslims. A stable and western-oriented Turkey was therefore an important strategic goal for the west, and the best way of ensuring the stability and western orientation of Turkey was to admit it to the EU.

Continuing opposition to Turkey's membership of the EU emerged in particularly France. While chairing the Convention on the Future of Europe, Valéry Giscard d'Estaing publicly expressed the opinion that Turkey's admission would mark 'the end of Europe'. His public remarks expressed what many others said in private. The prospect of France becoming the third largest member state by population was intensely unattractive to French leaders. The prospect was not made more attractive by the strong public support for Turkish membership expressed by the United States. When US President Bush, in Ankara for a NATO summit, called for Turkey to be admitted to the EU, French President Chirac said that he should mind his own business. Nevertheless, Chirac was prepared to go along with the German wish to see negotiations open with Turkey. Erdogan also helped to win the French vote during a diplomatic tour in the summer of 2004 by arriving in Paris with an order from the Turkish state airline for thirty-six Airbus airliners, and an agreement on co-operation on developing nuclear energy.

CONCLUSION

It was surely never envisaged by the founders of the ECSC and the EEC that these organizations of six states would expand over the next half century to a membership of twenty-five, with more applicants waiting to join. The reasons for this expansion have been much debated, both as to why the applications were made and why they were accepted, but they come down to some mix of economic and political considerations. How to handle the negotiations with candidate countries, the actual policy of how to do enlargement, has evolved over time, each enlargement adding to the *acquis*. The effects of the enlargements have been varied, and are difficult to estimate because of the absence of any evidence about how the EC/EU would have developed without the new members. All of these aspects of enlargement have been addressed by different authors, but the coverage is uneven, leaving plenty of room for further research.

While enlargement is not an inevitable consequence of developments internal to the EC/EU, there is evidence of a process of geographical spillover producing pressure on nearby states to co-operate more closely. In particular, as Preston (1997: 137) noted, 'changes in internal trade regimes create demands from external interests for active involvement in policy development'. These pressures were illustrated most clearly with the EFTA enlargement, which gained much of its impetus from the single-market programme. Before that, though, the challenge of the economic success of the EEC was a factor in the first enlargement, as, for Britain at least, were the signs that the economic policies were about to be extended into political co-operation.

Spillover from developments internal to the EC figures more strongly in the explanation for the first and third (EFTA) enlargements than it does for the second (Mediterranean) and fourth (eastern) enlargements. For the Mediterranean and eastern enlargements external developments played a significant role. In both cases the applicants were states emerging from dictatorship and trying to find a new path and a new identity. The economic success of the EC/EU obviously played a part in making membership an attractive option, but the need of pro-capitalist élites to consolidate the western orientation of the Mediterranean states, and the need of the CEECs to cut themselves free as quickly as possible from economic dependence on Russia and to insulate themselves from future political domination from the same direction were more fundamental imperatives.

Just as the reasons for the applications were a mixture of economic and political, so were the reasons why the existing member states were prepared to accept further members. Political reasons predisposed five of the original six to accept a British application; economic pressures finally converted France on this. Political reasons, specifically geo-strategic considerations, were instrumental in persuading the nine member states to over-ride a negative Commission Opinion on Greece and to encourage the applications of Portugal and Spain. Economic considerations seem to have been to the fore again in persuading the twelve member states to accept the EFTA applications. Political, geo-strategic factors were to the fore again in the case of the eastern enlargement, although economic considerations were never far below the surface. Finally, the drive of Turkey to become a member met with both support and resistance on primarily political grounds

The evolution of a policy on how to handle applications is a good illustration of historical institutionalism: of how incrementalism builds into a policy *acquis* through the operation of path dependence. The enlargements have been analysed in these terms by Christopher Preston (1995, 1997). However, too close a focus on the internal dynamics always risks overlooking external influences. In the case of the eastern enlargement, both the Copenhagen criteria for opening negotiations with potential candidates and the conditions imposed by the EU during negotiations strongly resembled the conditionality of both the IMF and the World Bank. This could be pure coincidence; but it could be evidence of a wider ideological orientation underpinning the operating principles of transnational organizations. The question might repay further investigation, but the possibility of raising it shows the advantage of setting the study of the EU in a wider comparative framework.

Obviously the enlargements have all had an impact on the EC/EU. The EFTA enlargement was the least disruptive, and the eastern enlargement promises to be the most disruptive, although it was too early at the time of writing (2004) to be sure of the precise nature of the disruption. Each time new member states have joined they have had to be socialized into the methods of working, the customs and practices of the organization. Some have adapted more quickly and completely than others. Britain, Denmark, and until recently Greece have remained semi-detached on at least some issues, reflecting the tension between different images of the mission and direction of the EC/EU. Three issues in particular have divided the member states: the ultimate political destination of the process of European integration; the relationship of the EU to the United States; and the type of capitalism that would operate at the EU level.

Although it is difficult to disentangle rhetoric from genuine belief, the governments of the six original member states have more easily adopted a discourse of 'ever closer union' as the political purpose of economic co-operation. British politicians in particular have never adopted such a discourse, and have never appeared to accept such a mission for the EU. Both the EFTA and eastern enlargements increased the number of other states for whom this particular approach does not come naturally. The original justification of European integration becomes less and less relevant as the prospect of war between the member states becomes unthinkable. Helmut Kohl was perhaps the last national leader who genuinely thought in such terms. Yet such is the force of path dependence on patterns of thinking that the discourse of ever closer union still recurs, as it did repeatedly during the debates in the Convention on the Future of Europe, much to the irritation of those member states for which this has never been the point of their membership.

The extent to which the EU will try to act independently of the United States is an issue that has rumbled under the surface of debates ever since the formation of the EEC. It came to the fore starkly during the war in Iraq in 2003–4, and divided the continent. France and Germany led a group that not only rejected participation in the war, but also did their best to disrupt the efforts of Britain to work with the United States and the United Nations to find an agreed way forward. Britain, Italy, and Spain led a group that gave support to the United States, a group that, to the irritation of the French President, included most of the eastern applicant states. This issue has become more salient and more divisive with each enlargement.

What type of capitalism will operate at the level of the EU has been one of the most active debates of recent decades, and continues to be contested. Again France leads one group that rejects 'Anglo-Saxon capitalism' or neo-liberalism. Britain leads the other group, which has been much more successful to date. The eastern enlargement, though, will definitely feed into this debate, and in ways that are difficult to predict because of the continuing political volatility within the new member states. The promise of prosperity as a result of membership of the EU is a medium-term promise, even if it is fulfilled, and in the meantime the economies of the new members are undergoing a period of rapid restructuring that had led to disillusionment in several of the new members even before they had fully joined. If this fed into a rejection of open markets, there could be trouble ahead for the neo-liberal project.

Finally, the literature on enlargement has been very uneven. Partly this is because the study of the EU has grown more sophisticated over time. There is nothing to stop analysis of earlier enlargements being revised in the light of later theoretical concepts, but this tends not to happen. The division of the academic world into distinct disciplines means that political scientists try to provide analyses of recent events, while the study of the more distant past is left to historians, who are generally detached from the concerns and concepts of the political scientists, and who focus disproportionately on the official record, which means on the governmental actors (Daddow 2004). An exception is Moravcsik (1998), who examined five major turning points in the history of European integration using the liberal intergovernmentalist approach. These included analysis of the first enlargement. There is scope for the application of other approaches, particularly constructivist and neo-Gramscian approaches, to this enlargement, and for the application of both plus rationalist approaches to the Mediterranean enlargement.

If such research is too lacking in contemporaneity for political scientists, there is still plenty of work to be done on applying theory systematically to the eastern enlargement. For example, because the issue of why the CEECs applied for membership has not been seen as a problem, it has not received much sustained analytical attention. As Schimmelfennig and Sedelmeier (2002: 524) argued, this makes it difficult for comparisons to be drawn with previous enlargements, even with the EFTA enlargement, which has been extensively analysed, but where the analysis has focused particularly on the issue of why the new applicants chose to apply.

There is also room for a more systematic application of theory to the analysis of the Turkish application. Although the claim in Müftüler-Bac and McLaren (2003: 19) that the article 'takes the debate forward by placing this issue within the theoretical perspective of preferences and policy making in the EU' is justified, it might be noted that the approach is not that of liberal intergovernmentalism. There is no analysis of the constellation and role of economic interests within the member states in shaping national preferences, nor, with one exception, do the factors identified as influencing the preferences of member states involve economic considerations. Domestic political and geo-strategic considerations predominate. This does not mean that the analysis is invalid, but it does indicate the possibility for further research both to develop a liberal intergovernmentalist perspective and to apply constructivist and neo-Gramscian perspectives to the reasons for Turkey's application and to the reasons for the rejection and eventual acceptance of the application by the EU.

KEY POINTS

The Enlargements of the EC/EU

☐ It is not easy to count the number of enlargement 'rounds', but four is a reasonable classification.

☐ The four are: the first enlargement of 1973; the Mediterranean enlargement of 1981/6; the EFTA enlargement of 1995; the 'eastern' enlargement of 2004.

Analysing Enlargement Policy

☐ Enlargement policy can be analysed in four dimensions: the enlargement policies of the applicants; the enlargement policies of the existing member states; the enlargement policies of the EU; the impact of enlargement.

☐ The analytical literature on enlargement can be divided into rationalist institutionalist and constructivist institutionalist approaches.

The First Enlargement

☐ Britain, Denmark, and Ireland joined on 1 January 1973; Norway negotiated terms of entry, but the Norwegian people rejected membership in a referendum.

☐ Debate on the reasons for the British application centres around whether economic or geo-strategic reasons predominated. Each played a role.

☐ Five of the original six member states (France being the exception) wanted Britain to become a member for political reasons: so Britain could act as a counter-weight to France. The same reason explains French unwillingness to accept Britain.

☐ Economic considerations explain the French change of position in 1972.

☐ President Pompidou ensured that British entry did not damage French economic interests; in particular, he ensured that the CAP was finalized prior to the opening of negotiations.

☐ The conditions for entry included acceptance of the complete *acquis communautaire*, including the CAP.

☐ Enlargement increased the complexity of bargaining in the EC. It also challenged the sense of identity of the organization that was shared by the original members, because two of the new entrants were sceptical about the European project.

The Mediterranean Enlargement

☐ Greece became a member in 1981. Portugal and Spain joined in 1986.

☐ Geo-strategic considerations predominated in the reasons for the acceptance of the applications. Ensuring stability in the Mediterranean was the prime concern of member states.

☐ The Commission's negative Opinion on Greece's preparedness to join was over-ridden for geo-strategic reasons, setting a precedent for later enlargements.

☐ The Mediterranean enlargement shifted the orientation of the EC to the south, increased the emphasis on relations with Latin America, and led to the emergence of a coalition under Spain's leadership in favour of larger structural funds.

☐ Greek membership created some diplomatic problems with Turkey and with other Balkan states.

The EFTA Enlargement

☐ Austria, Finland, and Sweden became members on 1 January 1995; Norway negotiated terms of entry, but the Norwegian people rejected membership in a referendum.

☐ Reasons for the applications included an economic downturn, the outflow of investment funds to the single market, and the end of the Cold War.

☐ Rationalist explanations stress that governments had little choice in the face of the behaviour of large businesses.

☐ A neo-Gramscian analysis differentiates more than rationalist analyses between the applicants according to their economic structure, recognizes a wider variety of domestic actors, and involves more consideration of the role of ideas.

☐ The EC initially offered membership of the EEA as a compromise because Delors and other influential leaders did not want to deflect the EC from focusing on the single market and the spillover to monetary union.

☐ Full membership was offered when it became apparent that the EEA would not satisfy business interests, and with the prospect of eastern enlargement.

☐ The negotiations raised the issues of weighting of votes in the Council of Ministers, the use of QMV, and the size of the Commission.

☐ The new member states were easily absorbed in the EC/EU.

☐ The main effects of enlargement were the formation of a Nordic bloc, and stronger coalitions in favour of environmental protection and of budgetary reform.

The 'Eastern' Enlargement

☐ On 1 May 2004 Cyprus, the Czech Republic, Estonia, Hungary, Latvia, Lithuania, Malta, Poland, Slovakia, and Slovenia became members.

☐ The former communist CEECs were initially offered association falling short of full membership. The prospect of membership was agreed in 1993; in 1997 it was agreed to open negotiations with six applicants; in 1999 it was agreed to open negotiations with the remaining six.

☐ The CEECs wanted membership for geo-strategic reasons (to protect themselves against future Russian expansionism), for reasons of identity (to 'return to Europe'), and for economic reasons (to access the single market).

☐ The EC's initial reaction is explained by the speed of changes in eastern Europe, and a preoccupation with the EFTA enlargements and with monetary union.

☐ The change of attitude (1993) is explained by the completion of other business, the persistence of the CEECs, and geo-strategic considerations in the face of growing instability in Russia.

☐ The decision to proceed with only six applicants (1997) reflected strong German support for some applicants, French reluctance to rush into a big enlargement, and Commission concerns about its ability to handle a larger set of negotiations.

☐ The decision to open negotiations with six more applicants (1999) is explained by discontent among the remaining CEECs, which threatened to destabilize them; the removal of counter-productive US pressure; and the reactivation of Malta's application.

- [ ] For the first time formal criteria were established for eligibility to negotiate entry. These resembled the conditions imposed on debtors by the IMF and World Bank.

- [ ] Enlargement implied fundamental reform of the CAP, the structural funds, and the existing institutional arrangements of the EU.

Future Enlargement

- [ ] Two applications from CEECs remained outstanding in 2004: Bulgaria and Romania.

- [ ] Negotiations opened with Croatia in 2004, and an application was accepted from Macedonia. Other Yugoslav successor states were expected to apply.

- [ ] Soviet successor states expressed an interest in joining, but were ruled out.

Turkey

- [ ] Turkey has had an association agreement envisaging membership since 1963.

- [ ] It was excluded from the enlargement process in 1997, but offered the prospect of future negotiations in 1999.

- [ ] Its exclusion in 1997 is explained by opposition from Greece and Germany.

- [ ] The shift of the EU's position in 1999 is explained by a dramatic improvement in Greek-Turkish relations in 1999, and a change of government in Germany in 1998.

- [ ] The EU's decision in 1999 to allow states to negotiate entry at their own pace, without having to keep to a 'round' timetable, made it easier for the EU to open negotiations with Turkey, and more difficult for it not to do so.

- [ ] The election of the AKP government in Turkey in 2002 produced rapid progress to meeting the Copenhagen criteria.

- [ ] Geo-strategic factors favoured Turkish membership, but opposition remained strong in 2004, particularly in France.

FURTHER READING

Comprehensive coverage of the first four enlargements is contained in C. Preston, *Enlargement and European Integration in the European Union* (London: Routledge, 1997). It contains sections on the accession process for each new member state and information on other applications. It considers the effects of enlargement on each member state, on the EU's policies and on the structure and processes of the EU. The same author provided one of the early analyses of the enlargement to the east in C. Preston, 'Obstacles to EU Enlargement: The Classical Community Method and the Prospects for a Wider Europe', *Journal of Common Market Studies*, 33 (1995): 451–63. A complete narrative of how those enlargement negotiations developed, with copious quotations from official documentation is provided in G. Avery and F. Cameron, *The Enlargement of the European Union* (Sheffield: Sheffield Academic Press, 1998).

For a full neo-Gramscian analysis the conscientious student will look at A. Bieler, *Globalization and Enlargement of the European Union: Austrian and Swedish Social Forces in the Struggle over Membership* (London: Routledge, 2000), although others may find enough information in Bieler's later article, 'The Struggle over EU Enlargement: A Historical Materialist Analysis of European Integration', *Journal of European Public Policy*, 9 (2002): 575–97. This analysis can be usefully compared with that of C. Ingebritsen, *The Nordic States and European Unity* (Ithaca NY: Cornell University Press, 1998).

 **online resource centre**

Visit the Online Resource Centre that accompanies this book for links to more information on the enlargement of the EU, including the web site of the relevant Directorate-General of the Commission.

References

Adnett, N. (2001). 'Modernizing the European Social Model: Developing the Guidelines'. *Journal of Common Market Studies*, 39: 353–64.

Adshead, M. (2002). *Developing European Regions? Comparative Governance, Policy Networks and European Integration*. Aldershot: Ashgate.

Agnelli, G. (1989). 'The Europe of 1992'. *Foreign Affairs*, 68: 61–70.

Ahearn, R. (2002). 'US–European Union Trade Relations: Issues and Policy Challenges'. *CRS Issue Brief for Congress*. http://fpc.state.gov/documents/organization/9546.pdf

Ahmad, F. (2001). 'Turkey', in J. Krieger, (ed.), *The Oxford Companion to the Politics of the World* (2nd edn). New York: Oxford University Press, 850–1.

Aldcroft, D. H. (1978). *The European Economy, 1914–1970*. London: Croom Helm.

Allen, D. and Smith, M. (1998). 'External Policy Developments'. *Journal of Common Market Studies: The European Union, 1997, Annual Review of Activities*: 69–91.

—— (2004). 'External Policy Developments'. *Journal of Common Market Studies: The European Union, 2003, Annual Review of Activities*: 95–112.

Alter, K. (1996). 'The European Court's Political Power'. *West European Politics*, 19: 458–87.

—— (1998). 'Who Are the "Masters of the Treaty"? European Governments and the European Court of Justice'. *International Organization*, 52: 121–47.

Amoore, L., Dodgson, R., Gills, B.K., Langley, P., Marshall, D., and Watson, I. (1997). 'Overturning "Globalisation": Resisting the Technological, Reclaiming the "Political"'. *New Political Economy*, 2: 179–95.

Anderson, J. (2002). 'Globalization and Europeanization: A Conceptual and Theoretical Overview'. Paper prepared for the conference on 'Germany and Europe: A Europeanized Germany?', ESRC Future Governance Programme, The British Academy, London, 9–10 May.

—— (2003). 'Europeanization in Context: Concept and Theory', in K. Dyson and K. Goetz (eds.), *Germany, Europe and the Politics of Constraint*. Oxford: Oxford University Press, 37–54.

Armstrong, H. (1989). 'Community Regional Policy', in J. Lodge (ed.), *The European Community and the Challenge of the Future* (1st edn). London: Pinter, 167–85.

Armstrong, K. and Bulmer, S. (1998). *The Governance of the Single European Market*. Manchester: Manchester University Press.

Aspinwall, M. (1998). 'Collective Attraction—The New Political Game in Brussels', in J. Greenwood and M. Aspinwall (eds.), *Collective Action in the European Union: Interests and the New Politics of Associability*. London and New York: Routledge, 196–213.

—— and Greenwood, J. (1998). 'Conceptualising Collective Action in the European Union: An Introduction', in J. Greenwood and M. Aspinwall (eds.), *Collective Action in the European Union: Interests and the New Politics of Associability*. London and New York: Routledge, 1–30.

Avery, G. and Cameron, F. (1998). *The Enlargement of the European Union*. Sheffield: Sheffield Academic Press/University Association for Contemporary European Studies.

Bache, I. (1995). 'Additionality and the Politics of EU Regional Policy Making', *Political Economy Research Centre Working Papers*, no. 2. Sheffield: Political Economy Research Centre, University of Sheffield.

—— (1996). EU Regional Policy: *Has the UK Government Succeeded in Playing the* Gatekeeper *Role over the Domestic Impact of the European Regional Development Fund?* PhD thesis, University of Sheffield.

—— (1998). *The Politics of European Union Regional Policy: Multi-Level Governance or Flexible Gatekeeping?* Sheffield: Sheffield Academic Press/University Association for Contemporary European Studies.

—— (1999). 'The Extended Gatekeeper: Central Government and the Implementation of EC Regional Policy in the UK'. *Journal of European Public Policy*, 6: 28–45.

—— (2003). 'Europeanization: A Governance Approach'. Paper given to the European Union Studies Association (EUSA). Eighth Biennial Conference, Nashville, Tennessee, March 27–9. http://aei.pitt.edu/archive/00000554/

—— (2004). 'Multi-Level Governance and EU Regional Policy', in I. Bache and M. Flinders (eds.), *Multi-Level Governance*. Oxford: Oxford University Press, 165–78.

Bache, I. (2006). 'The Europeanization of Higher Education: Markets, Learning or Politics?' *Journal of Common Market Studies.*

——and Bristow G. (2003). 'Devolution and the Core Executive: The Struggle for European Funds'. *British Journal of Politics and International Relations*, 5: 405–27.

——and Flinders, M. (2004). 'Conclusions and Implications', in I. Bache and M. Flinders (eds.), *Multi-Level Governance*. Oxford: Oxford University Press.

——, George, S., and Rhodes, R.A.W. (1996). 'Cohesion Policy and Subnational Authorities in the UK', in L. Hooghe (ed.), *Cohesion Policy and European Integration*. Oxford: Oxford University Press, 294–319.

——and Jones, R. (2000). 'Has EU Regional Policy Empowered the Regions? A Study of Spain and the United Kingdom'. *Regional and Federal Studies*, 10: 1–20.

——and Jordan, A. (2004). 'Britain in Europe and Europe in Britain: The Europeanization of British Politics?' Paper presented at the ESRC/UACES Conference on *The Europeanization of British Politics?*, Sheffield, 16 July. http://www.shef.ac.uk/ebpp/bachejordan16july.pdf (accessed 15.05.05).

——and Marshall, A. (2004). 'Europeanisation and Domestic Change: A Governance Approach to Institutional Adaptation in Britain'. Europeanisation Online Papers No. 5/2004, Queen's University Belfast. http://www.qub.ac.uk/schools/Schoolof PoliticsInternationalStudies/Research/PaperSeries/ EuropeanisationPapers/PublishedPapers/

——and Olsson, J. (2001). 'Legitimacy through Partnership? EU Policy Diffusion in Britain and Sweden'. *Scandinavian Political Studies*, 24: 215–37.

Bachtler, J. and Michie, R. (1994). 'Strengthening Economic and Social Cohesion? The Revision of the Structural Funds'. *Regional Studies*, 28: 789–96.

Bailey, D. and De Propris, L. (2002*a*). 'The 1988 reform of the European Structural Funds: entitlement or empowerment?' *Journal of European Public Policy*, 9: 408–28.

——(2002*b*). 'EU Structural Funds, Regional Capabilities and Enlargement: Towards Multi-Level Governance?' *Journal of European Integration*, 24: 303–24.

Barber, L. (1995). 'The Men Who Run Europe'. *The Financial Times: Weekend FT*, 11/12 March: I–II.

Barysch, K. (2003). 'Germany—The Sick Man of Europe?' *Centre for European Reform Policy Brief*. London: CER.

Beetham, D. and Lord, C. (1998). *Legitimacy and the European Union*. London and New York: Longman.

Benz, A. (2003). 'Compounded Representation in Multi-Level Governance', in B. Kohler-Koch (ed.), *Linking EU and National Governance*. Oxford: Oxford University Press, 82–110.

Beyers, J. (2004). 'Voice and Access - Political Practices of European Interest Associations'. *European Union Politics*, 5: 211–40.

——and Dierickx, G. (1998). 'The Working Groups of the Council of the European Union: Supranational or Intergovernmental Negotiations?' *Journal of Common Market Studies*, 36: 289–317.

Bieler, A. (2000). *Globalization and Enlargement of the European Union: Austrian and Swedish Social Forces in the Struggle over Membership*. London: Routledge.

——(2002). 'The Struggle over EU Enlargement: A Historical Materialist Analysis of European Integration'. *Journal of European Public Policy*, 9: 575–97.

Birch, A. (2001). *Concepts and Theories of Modern Democracy* (2nd edn). London and New York: Routledge.

Blair, A. (2002). 'Adapting to Europe', *Journal of European Public Policy*, 9: 841–56.

Boltho, A. (1982). *The European Economy: Growth and Crisis*. Oxford: Oxford University Press.

Bomberg, E. and Peterson, J. (2000). 'Policy Transfer and Europeanization'. *Europeanisation Online Papers*, No. 2/2000. Queen's University, Belfast. http://www.qub.ac.uk/schools/SchoolofPolitics InternationalStudies/Research/PaperSeries/ EuropeanisationPapers/PublishedPapers/

Borras, S. and Jacobsson, K. (2004). 'The Open Method of Co-ordination and New Governance Patterns in the EU'. *Journal of European Public Policy*, 11: 185–208.

Börzel, T. (1999). 'Why There is no "Southern Problem". On Environmental Leaders and Laggards in the European Union'. *Journal of Common Market Studies*, 7: 141–62.

——(2002). 'Pace-Setting, Foot-Dragging, and Fence-Sitting: Member State Responses to Europeanization'. *Journal of Common Market Studies*, 40: 193–214.

——and Risse, T. (2000). 'When Europe Hits Home: Europeanization and Domestic Change'. European Integration Online Papers (EioP) 4:15. http://eiop.or.at/eiop/texte/2000-015a.htm

Bourne, A. (2003). 'The Impact of European Integration on Regional Power'. *Journal of Common Market Studies*, 41: 597–620.

Bouwen, P. (2002). 'Corporate Lobbying in the European Union: The Logic of Access'. *Journal of European Public Policy*, 9: 365–90.

Bouwen, P. (2004a). 'Exchanging Access Goods for Access: A Comparative Study of Business Lobbying in the European Union Institutions'. *European Journal of Political Research*, 43: 337–69.

—— (2004b). 'The Logic of Access to the European Parliament: Business Lobbying in the Committee on Economic and Monetary Affairs'. *Journal of Common Market Studies*, 42: 473–95.

Bowler, S. and Farrell, D. (1995). 'The Organizing of the European Parliament: Committees, Specialization and Co-ordination'. *British Journal of Political Science*, 25: 219–43.

Branch, A.P. and Øhrgaard, J.C. (1999). 'Trapped in the Supranational–Intergovernmental Dichotomy: A Response to Stone Sweet and Sandholtz'. *Journal of European Public Policy*, 6: 123–43.

Brenton, P. and Manchin, M. (2002). 'Making EU Trade Agreements Work: The Role of Rules Of Origin'. *CEPS Working Document no. 183*. Brussels: Centre for European Policy Studies.

Breslin, S., Hughes, C., Phillips, N. and Rosamond, B. (eds.) (2002). *New Regionalism in the Global Economy: Theories and Cases*. London: Routledge.

Bromley, S. (2001). 'Conclusion: What is the European Union?' in S. Bromley (ed.), *Governing the European Union*. London: Sage, 287–303.

Budden, P. (2002). 'Observations on the Single European Act and the "relaunch of Europe": a less "intergovernmental" reading of the 1985 Intergovernmental Conference'. *Journal of European Public Policy*, 9: 76–97.

Buller J. and Gamble, A. (2002). 'Conceptualising Europeanization', *Public Policy and Administration*, 17: 4–24.

Bulmer, S. (1983). 'Domestic Politics and European Policy-Making'. *Journal of Common Market Studies*, 21: 349–63.

—— (1998). 'New Institutionalism and the Governance of the Single European Market'. *Journal of European Public Policy*, 5: 365–86.

—— and Burch, M. (2000). 'The Europeanisation of British Central Government', in R.A.W. Rhodes (ed.), *Transforming British Government. Volume 1: Changing Institutions*. London: Macmillan, 46–62.

—— and Radaelli, C. (2004). 'The Europeanisation of National Policy?' *Europeanisation Online Papers*, No. 1/2004. Queen's University, Belfast. http://www.qub.ac.uk/schools/SchoolofPolitics InternationalStudies/Research/PaperSeries/ EuropeanisationPapers/PublishedPapers/

Burch, M. and Gomez, R. (2003). 'Europeanization and the English Regions'. Paper presented to the ESRC Seminar Series/UACES Study Group on the Europeanization of British Politics and Policy-Making, Sheffield, 2 May. http://www.shef.ac.uk/ ebpp/meetings.htm#

Burns, C. (2002). 'The European Parliament', in A. Warleigh (ed.), *Understanding European Union Institutions*. London: Routledge, 61–80.

—— (2004). 'Codecision and the European Commission: A Study of Declining Influence?' *Journal of European Public Policy*, 11: 1–18.

Burley, A.-M. and Mattli, W. (1993). 'Europe Before the Court: A Political Theory of Legal Integration'. *International Organization*, 47: 41–76.

Butler, F. (1993). 'The EC's Common Agricultural Policy' in J. Lodge (ed.), *The European Community and the Challenge of the Future* (2nd edn). London: Pinter, 112–30.

Butt Philip, A. (1983). 'Pressure Groups and Policy-Making in the European Community', in J. Lodge (ed.), *Institutions and Policies of the European Community*. London: Pinter, 21–6.

—— (1992). 'British Pressure Groups and the European Community' in S. George (ed.) (1992), *Britain and the European Community: the Politics of Semi-Detachment*. Oxford: Clarendon Press, 149–71.

Calingaert, M. (1999). 'Creating a European Market', in L. Cram, D. Dinan, and N. Nugent (eds.), *Developments in the European Union*. Basingstoke and London: Macmillan, 153–73.

Cameron, D.R. (1992). 'The 1992 Initiative: Causes and Consequences', in A. Sbragia (ed.), *Euro-Politics: Institutions and Policymaking in the 'New' European Community*. Washington DC: Brookings Institution, 23–74.

—— (1997). 'Economic and Monetary Union: Underlying Imperatives and Third-Stage Dilemmas', *Journal of European Public Policy*, 4: 455–85.

Camps, M. (1964). *Britain and the European Community 1955–1963*. London: Oxford University Press.

Camps, M. (1967). *European Unification in the Sixties: From the Veto to the Crisis*. London: Oxford University Press.

Caporaso, J. (1998). 'Regional Integration Theory: Understanding our Past and Anticipating our Future', *Journal of European Public Policy*, 5: 1–16.

—— (1999). 'Toward a Normal Science of Regional Integration', *Journal of European Public Policy*, 6: 160–4.

—— and Keeler, J.T.S. (1995). 'The European Union and Regional Integration Theory', in C. Rhodes and S. Mazey (eds.), *The State of the European Union Vol. 3, Building a European Polity?* Boulder Co. and Harlow, Essex: Lynne Rienner and Longman, 29–62.

Carrubba, C.J. (2003). 'The European Court of Justice, Democracy, and Enlargement'. *European Union Politics*, 4: 75–100.

Cecchini, P. (1988). *The European Challenge 1992: The Benefits of a Single Market*. Aldershot: Gower.

CEPS (1990). *1989 Annual Conference Proceedings*, vol. 1: *The Single Market and Economic and Monetary Union*. Brussels: Centre for European Policy Studies.

Christiansen, T. (1996). 'A Maturing Bureaucracy? The Role of the Commission in the Policy Process', in J. Richardson (ed.), *European Union: Power and Policy-Making*. London: Routledge, 79–95.

——, Jørgensen, K.E. and Wiener, A. (1999). 'The Social Construction of Europe'. *Journal of European Public Policy*, 6: 528–44.

Chryssochoou, D. (2003). 'EU Democracy and the Democratic Deficit', in M. Cini (ed.), *European Union Politics*. Oxford: Oxford University Press, 365–82.

Cichowski, R.A. (1998). 'Integrating the Environment: the European Court and the Construction of Supranational Policy'. *Journal of European Public Policy*, 5: 387–405.

Cini, M. (1996). *The European Commission: Leadership, Organisation and Culture in the EU Administration*. Manchester: Manchester University Press.

——and McGowan, L. (1998). *Competition Policy in the European Union*. Basingstoke and London: Macmillan.

Collinson, S. (1999). '"Issue Systems", "Multi-Level Games" and the Analysis of the EU's External Commercial and Associated Policies: A Research Agenda'. *Journal of European Public Policy*, 6: 206–24.

Coombes, D. (1970). *Politics and Bureaucracy in the European Community*. London: Allen and Unwin.

Corbett, A. (2005). *Universities and the Europe of Knowledge: Ideas, Institutions and Policy Entrepreneurship in European Union Higher Education Policy*. Basingstoke: Palgrave.

Corbett, R. (1993). *The Treaty of Maastricht*. London: Longman.

——, Jacobs, F. and Shackleton, M. (1995). *The European Parliament* (3rd edn). London: Catermill.

——(2003). 'The European Parliament at Fifty: A View from the Inside'. *Journal of Common Market Studies*, 41: 353–73.

Cornish, P. and Edwards, G. (2001). 'Beyond the EU/NATO Dichotomy: The Beginnings of a European Strategic Culture'. *International Affairs*, 77: 587–95.

Cosgrove Twitchett, C. (1981). *A Framework for Development: The EEC and the ACP*. London: Allen and Unwin.

Costa, O. (2003). 'The European Court of Justice and Democratic Control in the European Union'. *Journal of European Public Policy*, 10: 740–61.

Cowles, M., Caporaso, J. and Risse, T. (eds.) (2001). *Transforming Europe: Europeanization and Domestic Change*. Ithaca and London: Cornell University Press.

Cowles, M.G. (1995). 'Setting the Agenda for a New Europe: The ERT and EC 1992'. *Journal of Common Market Studies*, 33: 501–26.

——(2003). 'Non-State Actors and False Dichotomies: Reviewing IR/IPE Approaches to European Integration'. *Journal of European Public Policy*, 10: 102–20.

Cox, R. with Sinclair, T. (1996). *Approaches to World Order*. Cambridge: Cambridge University Press.

Cram, L. (1996). 'Integration Theory and the Study of the European Policy Process', in J. Richardson (ed.), *European Union: Power and Policy-Making*. London: Routledge, 40–58.

——(1997). *Policy Making in the EU: Conceptual Lenses and the Integration Process*. London and New York: Routledge.

——(2001). 'Whither the Commission? Reform, Renewal and the Issue-Attention Cycle'. *Journal of European Public Policy*, 8: 770–86.

Crombez, C. (1996). 'Legislative Procedures in the European Community'. *British Journal of Political Science*, 26: 199–228.

——(1997). 'The Co-Decision Procedure in the European Union'. *Legislative Studies Quarterly*, 22: 97–119.

——(2000). 'Understanding the EU Legislative Process—Codecision: Towards a Bicameral European Union', *European Union Politics* 1: 363–8.

——(2001). 'The Treaty of Amsterdam and the Co-decision Procedure', in G. Schneider and M. Aspinwall (eds.), *The Rules of Integration—Institutionalist Approaches to the Study of Europe*. Manchester: Manchester University Press, 101–22.

CURDS (Centre for Urban and Regional Development Studies) (1997). 'Written Evidence', in House of Lords (1997), *Reducing Disparities within the European Union: The Effectiveness of the Structural and Cohesion Funds, Volume 2—Evidence*. Select Committee on the European Communities, Session 1996–97, 11th Report. London: HMSO, 52–62.

Daddow, O.J. (2004). *Britain and Europe since 1945: Historiographical Perspectives on European Integration*. Manchester: Manchester University Press.

Dang-Nguyen, G., Schneider, V., and Werle, R. (1993). 'Networks in European Policy-Making: Europeification of Telecommunications Policy', in S.S. Andersen and K.A. Eliassen (eds.), *Making Policy in Europe: Europeification of National Policy-Making*. London: Sage, 93–114.

De Bassompierre, G. (1988). *Changing the Guard in Brussels: An Insider's View of the EC Presidency*. New York: Praeger.

De Búrca, G. (1998). 'The Principle of Subsidiarity and the Court of Justice as a Political Actor'. *Journal of Common Market Studies*, 36: 217–315.

De Gucht, K. (2003). 'The European Commission: Countdown to Extinction?'. *European Integration*, 25: 165–8.

Dell, E. (1995). *The Schuman Plan and the British Abdication of Leadership in Europe*. Oxford: Clarendon Press.

Deutsch, K. (1953). *Nationalism and Social Communication: An Inquiry into the Foundations of Nationality*. Cambridge, Mass.: MIT Press.

Deutsch, K.W., Burrell, S.A., Kann, R.A., Lee Jr, M., Lichterman, M., Lindgren, R.E., Loewenheim, F.L., and van Wagenen, R.W. (1957). *Political Community and the North Atlantic Area: International Organization in the Light of Historical Experience*. Princeton: Princeton University Press.

Devuyst, Y. (1999). 'The Community-Method After Amsterdam'. *Journal of Common Market Studies*, 37: 109–20.

Diebold, W., Jr (1959). *The Schuman Plan: A Study in Economic Cooperation, 1950–1959*. New York: Praeger.

Dinan, D. (1994). *Ever Closer Union? An Introduction to the European Community*. London: Macmillan.

——(2004). 'The Road to Enlargement', in M. Cowles and D. Dinan (eds.), *Developments in the European Union*. Basingstoke: Palgrave Macmillan, 7–24.

Duchêne, F. (1994). *Jean Monnet: The First Statesman of Interdependence*. New York & London: W.W. Norton & Company.

Dyson, K. (1994). *Elusive Union: The Process of Economic and Monetary Union in Europe*. Harlow: Longman.

——and Featherstone, K. (1999). *The Road to Maastricht: Negotiating Economic and Monetary Union*. Oxford: Oxford University Press.

Earnshaw, D. and Judge, D. (1995). 'Early Days: The European Parliament, Co-decision and the European Union Legislative Process Post-Maastricht'. *Journal of European Public Policy*, 2: 624–49.

——(1997). 'The Life and Times of the European Union's Cooperation Procedure'. *Journal of Common Market Studies*, 35: 543–64.

Egeberg, M. (2003). 'The European Commission', in M. Cini (ed.), *European Union Politics*. Oxford: Oxford University Press, 131–47.

Eising, R. (2003). 'Interest Groups in the European Union', in M. Cini (ed.), *European Union Politics*. Oxford: Oxford University Press, 192–210.

Eriksen, E. and Fossum, J. (2002). 'Democracy through Strong Publics in the European Union'. *Journal of Common Market Studies*. 40: 401–24.

Etzioni, A. (2004). 'The EU as Test Case of Halfway Supranationality'. *EUSA Review*, 17/1: 1–3.

Eurobarometer (2004*a*). *Eurobarometer Spring 2004: Public Opinion in the European Union, EB61* http://europa.eu.int/comm/public_opinion/archives/eb/eb61_en_pdf

——(2004*b*). *Eurobarometer Autumn 2004: Public Opinion in the European Union, EB62* http://europa.eu.int/comm/public_opinion/archives/eb/eb62_en_pdf

European Commission (1969). 'Memorandum on the Reform of Agriculture in the European Economic Community'. *Bulletin of the European Communities: Supplement*, 3/69. Brussels: European Communities.

——(1970). *Reform of Agriculture (Proposals of the Commission to the Council)*. COM (70)500. Brussels: European Communities.

European Commission (1973). 'Report on the Regional Problems in the Enlarged Community'. Presented to the Council on 4 May. *Bulletin of the European Communities 6, Supplement 8/73*. Brussels: European Communities.

——(1975). 'Preamble' to 'Regulation (EEC) No. 724/75 of 18 March 1975 establishing a European Regional Development Fund'. *Official Journal*, L73, 21/3/75. Brussels: European Commission.

——(1985). *Completing the Internal Market*. COM(85)310. Brussels: European Community.

——(1989). *Guide to the Reform of the Community's Structural Funds*. Brussels/Luxembourg: European Communities.

——(1993*a*). *The Council's Common Position on the Revision of the Structural Fund Regulations*. Communication from the Commission to the European Parliament, SEC (93) final. Brussels: European Communities.

——(1993*b*). *Community Structural Funds 1994–99, Revised Regulations and Comments*. Brussels/Luxembourg, European Communities.

European Commission (1995). *The Agricultural Situation in the European Union*. Brussels and Luxembourg: European Communities.

—— (1996*a*). *First Report on Economic and Social Cohesion*. Brussels and Luxembourg: European Commission.

—— (1996*b*). *Social and Economic Inclusion Through Regional Development: The Community Economic Development Priority in European Structural Funds in Great Britain*. Brussels: European Commission.

—— (1996*c*). *Green Paper on Relations between the European Union and the ACP Countries on the Eve of the 21st Century - Challenges and Options for a new Partnership*. Brussels: European Commission. http://www.euforic.org/greenpap/intro.htm

—— (1997). *Agenda 2000: For a Stronger and Wider Union*. Brussels: European Commission.

—— (1998*a*). 'Proposed Regulations Governing the Reform of the Structural Funds 2000–2006 (preliminary version)'. 18 March. *Inforegio*. http://www.inforegion.org/wbpro/agenda2000/compare/default_en.htm

—— (1998*b*). *Reform of the Structural Funds, Explanatory Memorandum*. Brussels: European Commission. http://europa.eu.int/pol/reg/en/info.htm

—— (1999*a*). *The Amsterdam Treaty: A Comprehensive Guide*. Brussels/Luxembourg: European Communities.

—— (1999*b*). *Agenda 2000: For a Stronger and Wider Europe*. Brussels/Luxembourg: European Communities.

—— (2000). 'Partnership Agreement between the African, Caribbean and Pacific Group of States of the One Part, and the European Community and its Member States, of the Other Part, signed in Cotonou, Benin on 23 June 2000'. http://www.europa.eu.int/rapid/start/cgi/guesten.ksh?p_action.gett.../640|0|RAPID&lg=E

—— (2001). *Communication on Effective Problem Solving in the Internal Market*. COM (2001) 702. http://europa.eu.int/en/comm/dg15home.html

—— (2002). *Action Plan for a Single Market* IP/02/1110, See also the SOLVIT Home Page: http://europa.eu.int/comm/internalmarket/solvit/index_en.htm

—— (2003). *Internal Market Strategy: Priorities 2003–6*. COM (2003) 238. http://europa.eu.int/eur-lex/en/com/cnc/2003/com2003_0238en01.pdf

—— (2004*a*). *First Report on the Implementation of the Internal Market Strategy 2003–2006*. COM (2004) 22 final. http://europa.eu.int/eur-lex/en/com/cnc/2004/com2004_0022en01.pdf

—— (2004*b*). 'A New Partnership for Cohesion: Convergence, Competitiveness, Cooperation'. *Third Report on Economic and Social Cohesion*. Luxembourg: European Communities.

—— (2005). *Second Implementation Report of the Internal Market Strategy 2003–2006*. COM (2005) final. http://europa.eu.int/comm/internal_market/en/update/strategy/2nd-impl-report_en.pdf

European Parliament (1988). *Official Journal of the European Communities. Annex. Debates of the European Parliament*, 1988–9, no. 2–367.

European Union (2005). From the ECSC to the Constitution: Treaty of Maastricht on European Union, Europa: Gateway to the European Union. http://www.europa.eu.int/scadplus/treaties/maastricht_en.htm (accessed 16.08.05)

Eurostat (1980). 'Gross Domestic Product at Market Prices: Regional Indicators', *Basic Statistics of the Community* (various editions). Luxembourg: European Communities.

Evans, A. (1999). *The EU Structural Funds*. Oxford: Oxford University Press.

Faas, T. (2003). 'To Defect or not to Defect? National, Institutional and Party Group Pressures on MEPs and their Consequences for Party Group Cohesion in the European Parliament'. *European Journal of Political Research*, 42: 841–66.

Fairbrass, J. (2006). 'Organized Interests and Interest Politics', in I. Bache and A. Jordan (eds.), *The Europeanization of British Politics?* Basingstoke: Palgrave.

—— and Jordan, A. (2001). 'Protecting Biodiversity in the European Union: National Barriers and European Opportunities?' *Journal of European Public Policy*, 8: 499–518.

Falkner, G. (2000). 'The Council or the Social Partners? EC Social Policy between Diplomacy and Collective Bargaining'. *Journal of European Public Policy*, 7: 705–24.

Farrell, H. and Héritier, A. (2003). 'Formal and Informal Institutions under Codecision: Continuous Constitution-Building in Europe'. *Governance*, 16: 577–600.

Featherstone, K. (1994). 'Jean Monnet and the "Democratic Deficit" in the European Union'. *Journal of Common Market Studies*, 32: 149–70.

—— (2003). 'Introduction: In the Name of "Europe"' in K. Featherstone and C. Radaelli (eds.), *The Politics of Europeanization*. Oxford: Oxford University Press, 3–26.

Fioretos, K.-O. (1997). 'The Anatomy of Autonomy: Interdependence, Domestic Balances of Power, and European Integration'. *Review of International Studies*, 23: 293–320.

Foreign and Commonwealth Office (2004). 'Turkey and the EU'. *Enlargement Update*, Spring 2004. www.europe.gov.uk/enlargement

Forster, A. (1998). 'Britain and the Negotiation of the Maastricht Treaty: A Critique of Liberal Intergovernmentalism'. *Journal of Common Market Studies*, 36: 347–67.

Forsyth, M.G., Keens-Soper, H.M.A. and Savigear, P. (eds.) (1970). *The Theory of International Relations: Selected Texts from Gentili to Treitschke*. London: George Allen and Unwin.

Forwood, G. (2001). 'The Road to Cotonou: Negotiating a Successor to Lomé'. *Journal of Common Market Studies*, 39: 423–42.

Freestone, D. (1983). 'The European Court of Justice', in J. Lodge (ed.), *Institutions and Policies of the European Community*. London: Pinter, 45–53.

Frey-Wouters, E. (1980). *The EC and the Third World: The Lomé Convention and its Impact*. New York: Praeger.

Friis, L. (1998). 'Approaching the "Third Half" of EU Grand Bargaining—The Post-Negotiation Phase of the "Europe Agreement Game"'. *Journal of European Public Policy*, 5: 322–38.

—— and Murphy, A. (1999). 'The European Union and Central and Eastern Europe: Governance and Boundaries'. *Journal of Common Market Studies*, 37: 211–32.

Fuchs, G. (1994). 'Policy-Making in a System of Multi-Level Governance—The Commission of the European Community and the Restructuring of the Telecommunications Sector'. *Journal of European Public Policy*, 1: 177–94.

Galtung, J. (1976). 'The Lomé Convention and Neo-Capitalism'. *African Review*, 6/1: 33–42.

Gamble, A. and Payne, A. (eds.) (1996). *Regionalism and World Order*. Basingstoke and London: Macmillan.

Garrett, G. (1992). 'International Cooperation and Institutional Choice: The European Community's Internal Market'. *International Organization*, 46: 533–60.

—— (1995). 'The Politics of Legal Integration in the European Union'. *International Organization*, 49: 171–81.

——, Keleman, R.D., and Schultz, H. (1998). 'The European Court of Justice, National Governments, and Legal Integration in the European Union'. *International Organization*, 52: 149–76.

—— and Tsebelis, G. (1996). 'An Institutional Critique of Intergovernmentalism'. *International Organization*, 50: 269–99.

—— and Weingast, B. (1993). 'Ideas, Interests and Institutions: Constructing the European Community's Internal Market', in J. Goldstein and R. Keohane (eds.), *Ideas and Foreign Policy*. Ithaca, NY: Cornell University Press, 173–206.

Garson, J.-P. (1997). 'Opening Mediterranean Trade and Migration'. *OECD Observer*, 209: 21–4. www.oecd.org/dataoecd/36/2/1908464.pdf

George, S. (1989). 'Nationalism, Liberalism and the National Interest: Britain, France, and the European Community'. *Strathclyde Papers on Government and Politics* no. 67. Glasgow: University of Strathclyde.

—— (1994). 'Supranational Actors and Domestic Politics: Integration Theory Reconsidered in the Light of the Single European Act and Maastricht'. *Sheffield Papers in International Studies*, no. 22. Sheffield: University of Sheffield.

—— (1996a). *Politics and Policy in the European Community* (3rd edn). Oxford: Oxford University Press.

—— (1996b). 'The European Union: Approaches from International Relations', in H. Kassim and A. Menon (eds.), *The European Union and National Industrial Policy*. London and New York: Routledge, 11–25.

—— (1998). *An Awkward Partner: Britain in the European Community* (3rd edn). Oxford: Oxford University Press.

—— (2004). 'Multi-Level Governance and the European Union', in I. Bache and M. Flinders (eds.), *Multi-Level Governance*. Oxford: Oxford University Press, 107–26.

Gibb, R. (2000). 'Post-Lomé: The European Union and the South'. *Third World Quarterly*, 21: 457–81.

Gillingham, J. (1991a). *Coal, Steel, and the Rebirth of Europe, 1945–1955*. Cambridge: Cambridge University Press.

—— (1991b). 'Jean Monnet and the European Coal and Steel Community: A Preliminary Appraisal' in D. Brinkley and C. Hackett (eds.), *Jean Monnet: The Path to European Unity*. Basingstoke and London: Macmillan, 129–62.

Ginsberg, R.H. (1994). 'The European Union's Common Foreign and Security Policy: An Outsider's Retrospective on the First Year'. *ECSA Newsletter*. Pittsburgh: European Community Studies Association.

—— (1989). *Foreign Policy Actions of the European Community: The Politics of Scale*. Boulder: Lynne Rienner.

Giordano, B. (2004). 'The Future of EU Regional Policy after 2006: Lots More Water to go under the Bridge'. *Regions*, 252: 19–22.

Glarbo, K. (1999). 'Restructuring the CFSP of the EU'. *Journal of European Public Policy*, 6: 634–51.

Glaser, T. (1990). 'EEC/ACP Cooperation: The Historical Perspective'. *The Courier*, 120, March/April.

Goetz, K. (2000). 'European Integration and National Executives: A Cause in Search of an Effect?' *West European Politics*, 23: 211–31.

—— and Hix, S. (eds.) (2000). 'Europeanised Politics? European Integration and National Political Systems'. *West European Politics*, 23: 94–120.

Grant, C. (1994). *Delors: Inside the House that Jacques Built*. London: Nicholas Brealey Publishing.

Grant, W. (1993). 'Pressure Groups and the European Community: An Overview', in S. Mazey and J. Richardson (eds.), *Lobbying in the European Union*. Oxford: Oxford University Press, 27–46.

—— (1995). 'The Limits of Common Agricultural Policy Reform and the Option of Denationalization'. *Journal of European Public Policy*, 2: 1–18.

—— (1997). *The Common Agricultural Policy*. Basingstoke and London: Macmillan.

Green, R.H. (1976). 'The Lomé Convention: Updated Dependence or Departure towards Collective Self-Reliance?' *African Review*, 6: 43–54.

Greenwood, J. (1997). *Representing Interests in the European Union*. Basingstoke and London: Macmillan.

—— (2003). *Interest Representation in the European Union*. Basingstoke: Palgrave Macmillan, 2003.

——, Levy, R., and Stewart, R. (1995). 'The European Union Structural Fund Allocations: "Lobbying to Win" or Recycling the Budget?' *European Urban and Regional Studies*, 2: 317–38.

Grossman, E. (2004). 'Bringing Politics back in: Rethinking the Role of Economic Interest Groups in European Integration'. *Journal of European Public Policy*, 11: 637–54.

Gualini, E. (2003). 'Challenges to Multi-Level Governance: Contradictions and Conflicts in the Europeanization of Italian Regional Policy'. *Journal of European Public Policy*, 10: 616–36.

Haas, E.B. (1958). *The Uniting of Europe: Political, Social and Economic Forces 1950–57*. London: Library of World Affairs.

—— (1968). *The Uniting of Europe: Political, Social and Economic Forces, 1950–1957* (2nd edn). Stanford, Calif.: Stanford University Press,.

—— (1970). 'The Study of Regional Integration: Reflections on the Joy and Anguish of Pretheorizing', *International Organization*, 24: 607–46.

Haas, P. (1992). 'Introduction: Epistemic Communities and International Policy Coordination', *International Organization*, 46: 1–35.

Hall, P. (1990). 'The State and the Market' in P. Hall, J. Hayward, and H. Machin (eds.), *Developments in French Politics*. Basingstoke and London: Macmillan, 171–87.

—— (2003). 'Institutions and the Evolution of European Democracy' in J. Hayward and A. Menon (eds.), *Governing Europe*. Oxford: Oxford University Press, 1–14.

—— and Taylor, R. (1996). 'Political Science and the Three New Institutionalisms'. *Political Studies*, 44: 936–57.

Halstead, J. (1982). *The Development of the European Regional Fund since 1972*. PhD thesis, University of Bath.

Hanf, K. and Soetendorp, B. (eds.) (1998). *Adapting to European Integration: Small States and the European Union*. London: Longman.

Harrison, R. (1974). *Europe in Question*. London: George Allen and Unwin.

Hartley, T.C. (1994). *The Foundations of European Community Law* (3rd edn). Oxford: Clarendon Press.

Hay, C. and Rosamond, B. (2002). 'Globalization, European Integration and the Discursive Construction of Economic Imperatives'. *Journal of European Public Policy*, 9: 147–67.

Hayes-Renshaw, F. and Wallace, H. (1997). *The Council of Ministers*. Basingstoke and London: Macmillan.

—— Lequesne, C. and Mayor Lopez, P. (1989). 'The Permanent Representations of the Member States to the European Communities'. *Journal of Common Market Studies*, 28: 121–37.

Heisbourg, F. (2000) 'Europe's Strategic Ambitions: The Limits of Ambiguity'. *Survival*, 42: 5–15.

Hennessy, P. (1991). 'Public Servant of a New World Order'. *Independent*, 14 October.

Héritier, A., Kerwer, D., Knill, C., Lehmkuhl, D., Teutsch, M., and Douillet, A.-C. (2001). *Differential Europe. The European Union Impact on National Policymaking*. Lanham, MD: Rowman and Littlefield.

Hewitt, A. (1989). 'ACP and the Developing World' in J. Lodge (ed.), *The European Community and the Challenge of the Future* (1st edn). London: Pinter, 285–300.

Hill, C. (1993). 'The Capability-Expectations Gap, or Conceptualising Europe's International Role'. *Journal of Common Market Studies*, 31: 305–28.

—— (1996). *The Actors in Europe's Foreign Policy*. London: Routledge.

—— (1998). 'Closing the Capability-Expectations Gap' in J. Peterson and H. Sjursen (eds.), *A Common Foreign Policy for Europe?: Competing Visions of the CFSP*. London: Routledge, 18–38.

Hill, C. (2004). 'Renationalizing or Regrouping? EU Foreign Policy since 11 September 2001'. *Journal of Common Market Studies*, 42: 143–63.

Hirst, P. and Thompson, G. (1996). *Globalization in Question: The International Economy and the Possibilities of Governance*. Cambridge: Polity Press.

Hix, S. (1994). 'The Study of the European Community: The Challenge to Comparative Politics'. *West European Politics*, 17: 1–30.

—— (1999). *The Political System of the European Union*. Basingstoke and London: Macmillan.

—— (2000). 'How MEPs Vote'. Briefing note 1/00, ESRC 'One Europe or Several?' Programme. http//www.one-europe.ac.uk/pdf/hix-bn3.pdf

—— (2006). Democracy, Parties and Elections. www.lse-students.ac.uk/HIX/working%20Papers/06-Democracy.pdf

—— and Goetz, K. (2000). 'Introduction: European Integration and National Political Systems'. *West European Politics*, 23: 1–26.

—— and Lord, C. (1997). *Political Parties in the European Union*. Basingstoke and London: Macmillan.

Hix, S., Raunio, T. and Scully, R. (2003). 'Fifty Years On: Research on the European Parliament. *Journal of Common Market Studies*, 41: 191–202.

HMSO (1996). *A Partnership of Nations*. London: Her Majesty's Stationery Office.

Hodges, M., and Wallace, W. (eds.) (1981). *Economic Divergence in the European Community*. London: Butterworth.

Hodson, D. and Maher, I. (2001). 'The Open Method as a New Mode of Governance: The Case of Soft Economic Policy Co-ordination'. *Journal of Common Market Studies*, 39: 719–46.

Hoffmann, S. (1964). 'The European Process at Atlantic Crosspurposes'. *Journal of Common Market Studies*, 3: 85–101.

—— (1966). 'Obstinate or Obsolete? The Fate of the Nation State and the Case of Western Europe'. *Daedalus*, 95: 862–915.

—— (1982). 'Reflections on the Nation-State in Western Europe Today'. *Journal of Common Market Studies*, 21: 21–37.

—— (1989). 'The European Community and 1992'. *Foreign Affairs*, 68: 27–47.

Hogg, S. (1989). 'Trying to Market a New Species of EMU'. *Independent*, 4 September.

Holland, S. (1980). *Uncommon Market*. Basingstoke and London: Macmillan.

Hooghe, L. (1996a). 'Introduction: Reconciling EU-Wide Policy and National Diversity' in L. Hooghe (ed.), *Cohesion Policy and European Integration*. Oxford: Oxford University Press, 1–26.

—— (1996b). 'Building a Europe with the Regions: The Changing Role of the European Commission' in L. Hooghe (ed.), *Cohesion Policy and European Integration*. Oxford: Oxford University Press: 89–128.

—— (1998). 'EU Cohesion Policy and Competing Models of Capitalism'. *Journal of Common Market Studies* 36: 457–77.

—— and Marks, G. (2003). 'Unravelling the Central State, But How?' *American Political Science Review*, 97: 233–43.

House of Lords (1997). 'Reducing Disparities within the European Union: The Effectiveness of the Structural and Cohesion Funds, Volume 2—Evidence'. *Select Committee on the European Communities, Session 1996–97, 11th Report*. London: Her Majesty's Stationery Office.

Howell, K. (2003). 'The Europeanization of British Financial Services'. Paper presented to the ESRC Seminar Series/UACES Study Group on the Europeanization of British Politics and Policy-Making, Sheffield, 2 May 2003. http://www.shef.ac.uk/ebpp/meetings.htm

Howorth, J. (2003). 'France, Britain and the Euro-Atlantic Crisis'. *Survival*, 45: 173–92.

Howorth, J. (2004). 'The Role of Discourse, Ideas and Epistemic Communities in the Forging of ESDP'. *West European Politics*, 27: 211–34.

Hu, Y. (1981). *Europe under Stress*. London: Butterworth.

Hurd, D. (1991). 'The Churchill Memorial Lecture. Transcript of speech given by the Foreign Secretary in Luxembourg on Tuesday, 19 February'. London: Foreign and Commonwealth Office, News Department.

Hurt, S.R. (2003). 'Co-operation and Coercion? The Cotonou Agreement between the European Union and ACP States and the end of the Lomé Convention'. *Third World Quarterly*, 24: 161–76.

Hutton, W. (2005). 'My Problem with Europe'. *Observer*, 5 June 18–19.

Ingebritsen, C. (1998). *The Nordic States and European Unity*. Ithaca NY: Cornell University Press.

Jachtenfuchs, M. (2001). 'The Governance Approach to European Integration'. *Journal of Common Market Studies*, 39: 245–64.

—— and Kohler-Koch, B. (2004). 'Governance and Institutional Development', in A. Wiener and T. Diez (eds.), *European Integration Theory*. Oxford: Oxford University Press, 97–115.

Jacobs, F. and Corbett, R. (1990). *The European Parliament*. Harlow: Longman.

Jamal, A.H. (1979). 'Preparing for Lomé Two'. *Third World Quarterly*, 1: 134–40.

Jenkins, R. (1977). 'Europe's Present Challenge and Future Opportunity: The First Jean Monnet Lecture delivered at the European University Institute, Florence, 27 October 1977'. *Bulletin of the European Communities Supplement 10/77*: 6–14.

——(1989). *European Diary, 1977–1981*. London: Collins.

Jordan, A. (2001). 'The European Union: An Evolving System of Multi-Level Governance . . . or Government? *Policy and Politics*, 29/2: 193–208.

——(2006). 'Environmental Protection' in I. Bache and A. Jordan (eds.), *The Europeanisation of British Politics?* Basingstoke: Palgrave, pp. forthcoming.

Judge, D. and Earnshaw, D. (2002). 'The European Parliament and the Commission Crisis: A New Assertiveness?' *Governance*, 15: 345–74.

——and Cowan, N. (1994). 'Ripples or Waves: the European Parliament in the European Community Policy Process'. *Journal of European Public Policy*, 1: 27–52.

Kaelberer, M. (2003). 'Knowledge, Power and Monetary Bargaining: Central Bankers and the Creation of Monetary Union in Europe'. *Journal of European Public Policy*, 10: 365–79.

Kaltenthaler, K. (2002). 'German Interests in European Monetary Integration'. *Journal of Common Market Studies*, 40: 69–87.

Kasack, C. (2004). 'The Legislative Impact of the European Parliament under the Revised Co-decision Procedure - Environmental, Public Health and Consumer Protection Policies'. *European Union Politics*, 5: 241–60.

Kassim, H. (1994). 'Policy Networks, Networks and European Union Policy Making: A Sceptical View'. *West European Politics*, 17: 15–27.

Katz, R. (2000). 'Models of Democracy: Elite Attitudes and the Democratic Deficit in the European Union'. Paper prepared for the Workshop 'Competing Conceptions of Democracy in the Practice of Politics', European Consortium for Political Research Joint Sessions of Workshops, Copenhagen, 14–19 April.

Katzenstein, P. (1996). *The Culture of National Security*. New York: Columbia University Press.

Keohane, R. (1984). *After Hegemony: Co-operation and Discord in the World Political Economy*. Princeton: Princeton University Press.

——(1989). 'Neoliberal Institutionalism: A Perspective on World Politics', in R. Keohane (ed.) *International Institutions and State Power*. Boulder, San Francisco, and Oxford: Westview Press, 1–20.

——and Nye, J.S., Jr (1977). *Power and Interdependence: World Politics in Transition*. Boston: Little, Brown.

Kelleher, J., Batterbury, S., and Stern, E. (1999). *The Thematic Evaluation of the Partnership Principle: Final Synthesis Report*. London: Tavistock Institute.

Kerr, Lord J. (2004). 'Plenary Session: the 2003–2004 Grand Bargain'. Presentation at 'Towards a European Constitution': A Conference Organised by the Federal Trust and the University Association of Contemporary European Studies, Goodenough College, London, 1–2 July.

Kirchner, E.J. (1992). *Decision-Making in the European Community*. Manchester: Manchester University Press.

Knill, C. (2001). *The Europeanization of National Administrations: Patterns of Institutional Change and Persistence*. Cambridge: Cambridge University Press.

——and Lenschow, A. (1998). 'Coping with Europe: The Impact of British and German Administrations on the Implementation of EU Environmental Policy'. *Journal of European Public Policy*, 5: 595–614.

Kohler-Koch, B. (1997). 'Organized Interests in European Integration: The Evolution of a New Type of Governance?', in H. Wallace and A.R. Young (eds.), *Participation and Policy-Making in the European Union*. Oxford: Clarendon Press, 42–68.

Kreher, A. (1997). 'Agencies in the European Community: A Step towards Administrative Integration in Europe'. *Journal of European Public Policy*, 4: 225–45.

Kreppel, A. (2002). *The European Parliament and Supranational Party System: A Study in Institutional Development*. Cambridge: Cambridge University Press.

——(2003). 'Necessary but not Sufficient: Understanding the Impact of Treaty Reform on the Internal Development of the European Parliament'. *Journal of European Public Policy*, 10: 884–911.

Kuper, R. (1998). *The Politics of the European Court of Justice*. London: Kogan Page.

Laffan, B. (1983). 'Policy Implementation in the European Community: The European Social Fund as a Case Study'. *Journal of Common Market Studies*, 21: 389–408.

——(1992). *Integration and Co-operation in Europe*. London and New York: UACES/Routledge.

Laffan, B. (1997a). *The Finances of the European Union*. Basingstoke and London: Macmillan.

——(1997b). 'From Policy Entrepreneur to Policy Manager: The Challenge Facing the European

Commission'. *Journal of European Public Policy*, 4: 422–38.

Laqueur, W. (1972). *Europe Since Hitler*. Harmondsworth: Penguin.

Laurent, P.-H. and Maresceau, M. (eds.) (1998). *The State of the European Union: Vol. 4, Deepening and Widening*. Boulder and London: Lynne Rienner.

Laursen, F. and Vanhoonacker, S. (eds.) (1992). *The Intergovernmental Conference on Political Union*. Maastricht: European Institute of Public Administration/ Nijhoff.

—— (eds.) (1995). *The Ratification of the Maastricht Treaty: Issues, Debates and Future Implications*. Maastricht: European Institute of Public Administration/ Nijhoff.

Lewis, J. (1998). 'Is the "Hard Bargaining" Image of the Council Misleading? The Committee of Permanent Representatives and the Local Elections Directive'. *Journal of Common Market Studies*, 36: 479–504.

—— (2000). 'The Methods of Community in EU Decision-Making and Administrative Rivalry in the Council's Infrastructure'. *Journal of European Public Policy*, 7: 261–89.

—— (2003a). 'Informal Integration and the Supranational Construction of the Council'. *Journal of European Public Policy*, 10: 996–1019.

—— (2003b). 'The Council of the European Union', in M. Cini (ed.), *European Union Politics*. Oxford: Oxford University Press, 148–65.

Lindberg, L. (1963). *The Political Dynamics of European Economic Integration*. Stanford: Stanford University Press; London: Oxford University Press.

—— (1966). 'Integration as a Source of Stress on the European Community System'. *International Organization*, 20: 233–65.

Lodge, J. (1990). 'Ten Years of an Elected Parliament' in J. Lodge (ed.), *The 1989 Election of the European Parliament*. Basingstoke and London: Macmillan: 1–36.

—— (1994). 'The European Parliament and the Authority-Democracy Crisis' in P.-H. Laurent (ed.), *The European Community: To Maastricht and Beyond*. Special Edition of *The Annals of the American Academy of Political and Social Science*, January: 69–83.

Loedel, P.H. (1998). 'Enhancing Europe's International Monetary Power: The Drive Toward a Single Currency' in P.-H. Laurent and M. Maresceau (eds.), *The State of the European Union: Vol. 4, Deepening and Widening*. Boulder and London: Lynne Rienner, 243–61.

Lord, C. (1998). *Democracy in the European Union*. Sheffield: Sheffield Academic Press/University Association for Contemporary European Studies.

—— (2001). 'Democracy and Democratization in the European Union' in S. Bromley (ed.), *Governing the European Union*. London: Sage, 165–90.

——, and Magnette, P. (2004). '*E Pluribus Unum*? Creative Disagreement about Legitimacy in the EU'. *Journal of Common Market Studies*, 42: 183–202.

Lowe, P., Buller, H., and Ward. N. (2002). 'Setting the Next Agenda? British and French Approaches to the Second Pillar of the Common Agricultural Policy'. *Journal of Rural Studies*, 18: 1–17.

Ludlow, P. (Peter) (1982). *The Making of the European Monetary System: A Case Study of the Politics of the European Community*. London: Butterworth.

—— (1991). 'The European Commission' in R. Keohane and S. Hoffmann (eds.), *The New European Community: Decisionmaking and Institutional Change*. Boulder, San Francisco, and Oxford: Westview Press, 85–132.

Ludlow, P. (Piers) (1997). *Dealing with Britain: The Six and the First UK Application to the EEC*. Cambridge: Cambridge University Press.

McAleavey, P. (1992). 'The Politics of European Regional Development Policy: The European Commission's RECHAR Initiative and the Concept of Additionality'. *Strathclyde Papers on Government and Politics*, no. 88. Glasgow: University of Strathclyde.

—— (1993). 'The Politics of the European Regional Development Policy: Additionality in the Scottish Coalfields'. *Regional Politics and Policy*, 3/2: 88–107.

—— (1995a). *Policy Implementation as Incomplete Contracting: The European Regional Development Fund*. Florence: European University Institute, PhD thesis.

—— (1995b). 'European Regional Development Fund Expenditure in the UK: From Additionality to Subtractionality'. *European Urban and Regional Studies*, 2/3: 249–53.

McGowan, L. and Cini, M. (1999). 'Discretion and Politicization in EU Competition Policy: The Case of Merger Control'. *Governance*, 12: 175–200.

—— and Wilks, S. (1995). 'The First Supranational Policy in the European Union: Competition Policy'. *European Journal of Political Research*, 28: 141–69.

McLaren, L. (2000). 'Turkey's Eventual Membership of the EU: Turkish Elite Perspectives on the Issue'. *Journal of Common Market Studies*, 38: 117–29.

McLaughlin, A.M. and Greenwood, J. (1995). 'The Management of Interest Representation in the European Union'. *Journal of Common Market Studies*, 33: 149–65.

REFERENCES

McNamara, K. (2005). 'Economic and Monetary Union', in H. Wallace, W. Wallace, and M. Pollack (eds.), *Policy-Making in the European Union*. Oxford: Oxford University Press, 5th edn, 141–60.

McQueen, M. (1998). 'Lomé Versus Free Trade Agreements: The Dilemma Facing the ACP Countries'. *World Economy*, 21: 421–43.

Mair, P. (2004). 'The Europeanization Dimension'. *Journal of European Public Policy*, 11: 337–48.

Majone, G. (1993). 'The European Community Between Social Policy and Social Regulation'. *Journal of Common Market Studies*, 31: 153–70.

——(1998). 'Europe's "Democratic Deficit": The Question of Standards' *European Law Journal*, 4: 5–28.

——(2002). 'The European Commission: The Limits of Centralization and the Perils of Parliamentarization'. *Governance*, 15: 375–92.

Mancini, G.F. (1991). 'The Making of a Constitution for Europe', in R. Keohane and S. Hoffmann (eds.), *The New European Community: Decisionmaking and Institutional Change*. Boulder, San Francisco, and Oxford: Westview Press, 177–94.

March, J.G., and Olsen, J. (1984). 'The New Institutionalism: Organizational Factors in Political Life'. *American Political Science Review*, 78: 734–49.

——(1989). *Rediscovering Institutions: The Organizational Basis of Politics*. New York and London: Free Press.

——(1996). 'Institutional Perspectives on Political Institutions' *Governance*, 9: 247–64.

Marks, G. (1992). 'Structural Policy in the European Community' in A. Sbragia (ed.), *Euro-Politics: Institutions and Policymaking in the 'New' European Community*. Washington DC: Brookings Institution, 191–224.

——(1993). 'Structural Policy and Multilevel Governance in the EC' in A. Cafruny and G. Rosenthal (eds.), *The State of the European Community, Vol. 2: The Maastricht Debates and Beyond*. Boulder: Lynne Rienner; Harlow: Longman, 391–410.

——(1996a). 'Exploring and Explaining Variation in EU Cohesion Policy' in L. Hooghe (ed.), *Cohesion Policy and European Integration*. Oxford: Oxford University Press, 388–422.

——(1996b). 'An Actor Centred Approach to Multilevel Governance'. Paper presented at the American Political Science Association meeting, San Francisco, August 29-September 1.

Marks, G. and Hooghe, L. (2004). 'Contrasting Visions of Multi-Level Governance', in I. Bache and M. Flinders (eds.), *Multi-Level Governance*. Oxford: Oxford University Press, 15–30.

——, Hooghe, L., and Blank, K. (1996). 'European Integration from the 1980s: State-Centric v Multi-Level Governance'. *Journal of Common Market Studies*, 34: 341–78.

Marsh, D. and Rhodes, R.A.W. (1992). 'Policy Communities and Issue Networks: Beyond Typology' in D. Marsh and R.A.W. Rhodes (eds.), *Policy Networks in British Government*. Oxford: Oxford University Press, 249–268.

Marshall, A. (2005). 'Europeanization at the Urban Level: Local Actors, Institutions and the Dynamics of Multi-Level Interaction'. *Journal of European Public Policy*, 12: 668–86.

Matlary, J.H. (1993). *Towards Understanding Integration: An Analysis of the Role of the State in EC Energy Policy, 1985–1992*. Oslo: University of Oslo, PhD thesis.

——(1997). *Energy Policy in the European Union*. Basingstoke and London: Macmillan.

Mattila, M. (2003). 'Why Bother? Determinants of Turnout in the European Elections'. *Electoral Studies*, 22: 449–68.

Mattli, W. and Slaughter, A.-M. (1998). 'Revisiting the European Court of Justice: A Reply to Garrett'. *International Organization*, 52: 177–209.

Mawson, J., Martins, M., and Gibney, J. (1985). 'The Development of the European Community Regional Policy', in M. Keating and B. Jones, (eds.), *Regions in the European Community*. Oxford: Clarendon Press, 20–59.

Mayne, R. (1991). 'Gray Eminence' in D. Brinkley and C. Hackett (eds.), *Jean Monnet: The Path to European Unity*. Basingstoke and London: Macmillan, 114–28.

Mazey, S. (1992). 'Conception and Evolution of the High Authority's Administrative Services (1952–6): From Supranational Principles to Multinational Practices' in E.V. Heyen (ed.), *Yearbook of European Administrative History 4: Early European Community Administration*. Baden-Baden: Nomos, 31–47.

——and Richardson, J. (1999). 'Interests', in L. Cram, D. Dinan, and N. Nugent (eds.), *Developments in the European Union*. Basingstoke and London: Macmillan, 105–29.

Menon, A. (2003). 'Conclusion: Governing Europe', in J. Hayward and A. Menon (eds.), *Governing Europe*. Oxford: Oxford University Press, 413–22.

——(2004). 'The Foreign and Security Policies of the European Union', in M. Cowles and D. Dinan (eds.), *Developments in the European Union*. Basingstoke: Palgrave Macmillan, 221–36.

Mény, Y. (2003). 'From Popular Dissatisfaction to Populism: Democracy, Constitutionalisation, and

Corruption' in J. Hayward and A. Menon (eds.), *Governing Europe*. Oxford: Oxford University Press, 250–63.

——, Muller, P., and Quermonne, J.-L. (1996). 'Introduction' in Y. Mény, P. Muller, and J.-L. Quermonne (eds.), *Adjusting to Europe: The impact of the European Union on national institutions and policies*. London: Routledge, 1–24.

Metcalfe, L. (1992). 'Can the Commission Manage Europe?' *Australian Journal of Public Administration*, 51: 117–30.

Middlemas, K. (1995). *Orchestrating Europe: The Informal Politics of European Union, 1973–1995*. London: Fontana.

Milward, A.S. (1984). *The Reconstruction of Western Europe, 1945–51*. London: Routledge.

—— (1992). *The European Rescue of the Nation State*. London: Routledge.

Mitrany, D. (1943). *A Working Peace System*. London: Royal Institute of International Affairs.

—— (1966). 'The Prospect of Integration: Federal or Functional'. *Journal of Common Market Studies*, 4: 119–49.

Monar, J. (2001). 'The Dynamics of Justice and Home Affairs: Laboratories, Driving Factors and Costs'. *Journal of Common Market Studies*, 39: 747–64.

—— (2002). 'Justice and Home Affairs'. *Journal of Common Market Studies: The European Union, 2001/2002, Annual Review of Activities*: 121–36.

Monnet, J. (1962). 'A Ferment of Change'. *Journal of Common Market Studies*, 1: 203–11.

Morata, F. and Munoz, X. (1996). 'Vying for European Funds: Territorial Restructuring in Spain', in L. Hooghe (ed.), *Cohesion Policy and European Integration*. Oxford: Oxford University Press, 195–214.

Moravcsik, A. (1991). 'Negotiating the Single European Act'. *International Organization*, 45: 19–56.

—— (1993). 'Preferences and Power in the European Community: A Liberal Intergovernmentalist Approach'. *Journal of Common Market Studies*, 31: 473–524.

—— (1994). *Why the European Community Strengthens the State: Domestic Politics and International Cooperation*. Center for European Studies, Harvard University, Working Paper Series No. 52.

—— (1995). 'Liberal Intergovernmentalism and Integration: A Rejoinder'. *Journal of Common Market Studies*, 33: 611–28.

—— (1998). *The Choice for Europe: Social Purpose and State Power from Messina to Maastricht*. Ithaca: Cornell University Press/London: UCL Press.

—— (2002). 'In Defence of the "Democratic Deficit": Reassessing Legitimacy in the European Union'. *Journal of Common Market Studies*, 40: 603–24.

—— (2003). 'National Interests, State Power, EU Enlargement'. *European Politics and Societies*. 17: 42–57.

—— (2004). 'Plenary session: The 2003–2004 Grand Bargain'. Presentation at 'Towards a European Constitution': A Conference Organised by the Federal Trust and the University Association of Contemporary European Studies, Goodenough College, London, 1–2 July.

—— and Nicolaïdes, K. (1999). 'Explaining the Treaty of Amsterdam: Interests, Influences, Institutions'. *Journal of Common Market Studies*, 37: 59–85.

—— and Vachudova, M. (2002). 'Bargaining Among Unequals: Enlargement and the Future of European Integration'. *EUSA Review*, 15 (4): 1 & 3–5.

Moser, P. (1996). 'The European Parliament as a Conditional Agenda Setter: What Are the Conditions? A Critique of Tsebelis (1994)'. *American Political Science Review* 90: 834–8.

—— (1997). 'A Theory of the Conditional Influence of the European Parliament in the Cooperation Procedure'. *Public Choice* 91: 333–50.

Moxon-Browne, E. (1993). 'Social Europe', in J. Lodge (ed.), *The European Community and the Challenge of the Future*. London: Pinter, 2nd edn, 152–62.

Moyer, H.W. and Josling, T.E. (1990). *Agricultural Policy Reform: Politics and Process in the EC and the USA*. Ames: Iowa State University Press.

Müftüler-Bac, M. and McLaren, L.M. (2003). 'Enlargement Preferences and Policy-Making in the European Union: Impacts on Turkey'. *Journal of European Integration*, 25: 17–30.

Mutimer, D. (1994). 'Theories of Political Integration', in H. Michelmann and P. Soldatos (eds.), *European Integration: Theories and Approaches*. London and Lanham Md.: University Press of America, 13–42.

Nanetti, R. (1996). 'EU Cohesion and Territorial Restructuring in the Member States' in L. Hooghe (ed.), *Cohesion Policy and European Integration*. Oxford: Oxford University Press, 59–88.

NFU (1996). *NFU Briefing: 1996 US Farm Bill*. London: National Farmers' Union.

Nugent, N. (1995). 'The Leadership Capacity of the European Commission'. *Journal of European Public Policy*, 2: 603–23.

—— (1999). *The Government and Politics of the European Union*. Basingstoke and London: Macmillan, 4th edn.

Nugent, N. (2004). 'Previous Enlargement Rounds' in N. Nugent (ed.), *European Union Enlargement*. Basingstoke and New York: Palgrave Macmillan, 10–33.

Nuttall, S. (1994). 'Keynote Article: The EC and Yugoslavia—*Deus ex Machina* or *Machina Sine Deo*?' in N. Nugent (ed.), *The European Union 1993: Annual Review of Activities*. Oxford: Blackwell, 11–24.

OECD (1970). *Economic Outlook* (July): 1–, Table 1.

Olsen, J. (2002). 'The Many Faces of Europeanization'. *Journal of Common Market Studies*, 40: 921–52.

——(2003). 'Europeanization', in M. Cini (ed.), *European Union Politics*. Oxford: Oxford University Press, 333–48.

Payne, A. (2000). 'Globalization and Modes of Regionalist Governance' in J. Pierre (ed.), *Debating Governance*. Oxford: Oxford University Press, 201–18.

Pearce, N. and Paxton, W. (eds.) (2005). *Social Justice: Building a Fairer Britain*. London: Institute for Public Policy Research.

Pech, L. (2003). 'The Solution to the "Democratic Deficit": A New Type of Governance for the European Union?' *Journal of European Integration*, 25: 131–50.

Pelkmans, J. (1994). 'The Significance of EC-1992' in P.-H. Laurent (ed.), *The European Community: To Maastricht and Beyond*. Special Edition of *The Annals of the American Academy of Political and Social Science*, January: 94–111.

——and Winters, L.A. (1988). *Europe's Domestic Market*. London: Routledge.

Peters, B.G. (1992). 'Bureaucratic Politics and the Institutions of the European Community' in A. Sbragia (ed.), *Euro-Politics: Institutions and Policymaking in the 'New' European Community*. Washington DC: Brookings Institution, 75–122.

——(1997). 'The Commission and Implementation in the European Union: Is There an Implementation Deficit and Why?', in N. Nugent (ed.), *At the Heart of the Union: Studies of the European Commission*. Basingstoke and London: Macmillan, 187–202.

——and Pierre, J. (2004). 'Multi-Level Governance and Democracy: A Faustian Bargain?', in I. Bache and M. Flinders (eds.), *Multi-Level Governance*. Oxford: Oxford University Press, 75–89.

Peterson, J. (1991). 'Technology Policy in Europe: Explaining the Framework Programme in Theory and Practice'. *Journal of Common Market Studies*, 31: 473–524.

——(1992). 'The European Technology Community: Policy Networks in a Supranational Setting', in D. Marsh and R.A.W. Rhodes (eds.), *Policy Networks in British Government*. Oxford: Oxford University Press, 226–48.

——(1995a). 'Policy Networks and European Union Policy Making: A Reply to Kassim'. *West European Politics*, 18: 389–407.

——(1995b). 'Decision-making in the European Union: Towards a Framework for Analysis'. *Journal of European Public Policy*, 2: 69–93.

——(1995c). 'European Union Research Policy: The Politics of Expertise' in M. Rhodes and S. Mazey (eds.), *The State of the European Union Vol. 3, Building a European Polity?* Boulder and Essex: Lynne Rienner and Longman, 391–412.

——(1997). 'The European Union: Pooled Sovereignty, Divided Accountability'. *Political Studies*, 45: 559–78.

——(2004). 'Policy Networks', in A. Wiener and T. Diez (eds.), *European Integration Theory*. Oxford: Oxford University Press: 117–136.

——and Bomberg, E. (1993). 'Decision Making in the European Union: A Policy Networks Approach'. Paper prepared for presentation to the annual conference of the UK Political Studies Association, Leicester, 20–22 April.

Phinnemore, D. (2003). 'Towards European Union', in M. Cini (ed.), *European Union Politics*. Oxford: Oxford University Press, 46–64.

Pierre, J. (ed.) (2000). *Debating Governance: Authority, Steering, and Democracy*. Oxford and New York: Oxford University Press.

Pierson, P. (1996). 'The Path to European Integration: A Historical Institutionalist Analysis'. *Comparative Political Studies*, 29: 123–63.

——(1998). 'The Path to European Integration: A Historical Institutionalist Analysis', in W. Sandholtz and A. Stone Sweet (eds.), *European Integration and Supranational Governance*. Oxford: Oxford University Press, 27–58.

Pollack, M. (1995). 'Regional Actors in an Intergovernmental Play: The Making and Implementation of EC Structural Policy', in C. Rhodes and S. Mazey (eds.), *The State of the European Union Vol. 3, Building a European Polity?*. Boulder and Essex: Lynne Rienner and Longman, 361–90.

——(1996). 'The New Institutionalism and EC Governance: The Promise and Limits of Institutional Analysis'. *Governance*, 9: 429–58.

——(1997). 'The Commission as an Agent', in N. Nugent (ed.), *At the Heart of the Union: Studies of the European Commission*. Basingstoke and London: Macmillan, 109–28.

Pollack, M. (2001). 'International Relations Theory and European Integration'. *Journal of Common Market Studies*, 39: 221–44.

——(2003). *The Engines of European Integration: Delegation, Agency and Agenda Setting in the EU*. Oxford: Oxford University Press.

——(2004). 'The New Institutionalisms and European Integration', in A. Wiener and T. Diez (eds.), *European Integration Theory*. Oxford: Oxford University Press, 137–56.

——(2005). 'Theorizing EU Policy-Making', in H. Wallace, W. Wallace, and M. Pollack (eds.), *Policy-Making in the European Union*. Oxford: Oxford University Press, 5th edn, 13–48.

Poulon, C. and Bourantonis, D. (1992). 'Western Europe and the Gulf Crisis: Towards a European Foreign Policy?' *Politics*, 12: 28–34.

——(1984). *The Politics of Implementation: The European Community Regional Development Fund and European Community Regional Aid to the UK 1975–81*. Colchester: University of Essex, PhD Thesis.

——(1995). 'Obstacles to EU Enlargement: The Classical Community Method and the Prospects for a Wider Europe'. *Journal of Common Market Studies*, 33: 451–63.

——(1997). *Enlargement and Integration in the European Union*. London: Routledge.

Putnam, R. (1988). 'Diplomacy and Domestic Politics: The Logic of Two Level Games'. *International Organization*, 42: 427–60.

——(1993). *Making Democracy Work: Civic Traditions in Modern Italy*. Princeton, NJ: Princeton University Press.

Radaelli, C. (2004). 'Europeanisation: Solution or Problem?' Paper presented to the ESRC/UACES Conference on the *Europeanization of British Politics*, Sheffield Town Hall, 16 July.

Ramussen, H. (1986). *On Law and Policy in the European Court of Justice: A Comparative Study in Judicial Politics*. Dordrecht: Martinus Nijhoff.

Reif, K. and Schmitt, H. (1980). 'Nine Second-Order National Elections: A Conceptual Framework for the Analysis of European Election Results'. *European Journal of Political Research*, 8: 3–45.

Rhodes, M. and van Apeldoorn, B. (1997). 'Capitalism versus Capitalism in Western Europe', in M. Rhodes, P. Heywood, and V. Wright (eds.), *Developments in West European Politics*. Basingstoke and London: Macmillan, 171–89.

Rhodes, R.A.W. (1981). *Control and Power in Central–Local Relations*. Aldershot: Gower.

——(1986). *The National World of Local Government*. London: Allen and Unwin.

——(1988). *Beyond Westminster and Whitehall: The Sub-Central Governments of Britain*. London: Unwin Hyman.

——(1995). *The New Governance: Governing without Government*. London: ESRC/RSA.

Rhodes, R.A.W., Bache, I. and George, S. (1996). 'Policy Networks and Policy Making in the European Union: A Critical Appraisal', in L. Hooghe (ed.), *Cohesion Policy and European Integration*. Oxford: Oxford University Press, 367–87.

Richardson, J. (1996a). 'Actor-based Models of National and EU Policy Making', in H. Kassim and A. Menon (eds.), *The European Union and National Industrial Policy*. London and New York: Routledge, 26–51.

Rieger, E. (2005). 'Agricultural Policy', in H. Wallace, W. Wallace, and M. Pollack (eds.), *Policy-Making in the European Union*. Oxford: Oxford University Press, 5th edn, 161–190.

Risse-Kappen, T. (1996). 'Exploring the Nature of the Beast: International Relations Theory and Comparative Policy Analysis Meet the European Union'. *Journal of Common Market Studies*, 34: 53–80.

Risse, T. (2003). 'The Euro Between National and European Identity'. *Journal of European Public Policy*, 10: 487–505.

——(2004). 'Social Constructivism and European Integration', in A. Wiener and T. Diez (eds.), *European Integration Theory*. Oxford: Oxford University Press, 159–176.

Rittberger, B. (2003). 'The Creation and Empowerment of the European Parliament'. *Journal of Common Market Studies*, 41: 203–25.

Rosamond, B. (1999). 'Discourses of Globalization and the Social Construction of European Identities'. *Journal of European Public Policy*, 6: 652–68.

——(2000). *Theories of European Integration*. Basingstoke and London: Macmillan.

——(2003). 'New Theories of European Integration', in M. Cini (ed.), *European Union Politics*. Oxford: Oxford University Press, 109–27.

Rosenthal, G.G. (1975). *The Men Behind the Decisions: Cases in European Policy-Making*. Lexington, Mass.: DC Heath.

Ross, G. (1995). *Jacques Delors and European Integration*. Cambridge: Polity Press.

Sabatier, P. (1988). 'An Advocacy Coalition Framework of Policy Change and the Role of Policy-Oriented Learning Therein'. *Policy Sciences*, 21: 129–68.

——(1998). 'The Advocacy Coalition Framework: Revisions and Relevance for Europe'. *Journal of European Public Policy*, 5: 98–130.

Sandholtz, W. (1993). 'Choosing Union: Monetary Politics and Maastricht'. *International Organization*, 47: 1–39.

——(1998). 'The Emergence of a Supranational Telecommunications Regime' in W. Sandholtz and A. Stone Sweet (eds.), *European Integration and Supranational Governance*. Oxford: Oxford University Press, 134–63.

——and Zysman, J. (1989). '1992: Recasting the European Bargain'. *World Politics*, 42: 95–128.

Scarrow, S. (1997). 'Political Career Paths and the European Parliament'. *Legislative Studies Quarterly*, 22: 253–63.

Scharpf, F. (1989). 'The Joint-Decision Trap: Lessons from German Federalism and European Integration'. *Public Administration*, 66: 239–78.

——(1998). *Governing in Europe: Effective and Democratic?*. Oxford: Oxford University Press.

——(1999a). 'Review Section Symposium—The Choice for Europe: Social Purpose and State Power from Messina to Maastricht. Selecting Cases and Testing Hypotheses'. *Journal of European Public Policy*, 6: 164–8.

——(1999b). *Crisis and Choice in European Social Democracy*. Ithaca: Cornell University Press.

——(2004). 'The European Democratic Deficit: Contested Definitions or Diverse Domains?' *EUSA Review*, 17/1: 5–6.

Scheinman, L. (1967). 'Euratom: Nuclear Integration in Europe'. *International Conciliation*, no. 563.

Schimmelfennig, F. and Sedelmeier, U. (2002). 'Theorizing Enlargement: Research Focus, Hypotheses, and the State of Research'. *Journal of European Public Policy*, 9: 500–28.

Schmidt, V. (2003). 'Democratic Legitimacy in a Regional State'. Paper prepared for presentation at the American Political Science Association National Meetings, Philadelphia, PA, 28–31 August 2003.

——(2004). 'Democratic Challenges for the EU as "Regional State"'. *EUSA Review*, 17/1: 4–5.

Schmitt, H. and Thomassen, J. (eds.) (1999). *Political Representation and Legitimacy in the European Union*. Oxford: Oxford University Press.

Schmitter, P. (1970). 'A Revised Theory of Regional Integration'. *International Organization*, 24: 836–68.

——(2000). *How to Democratize the European Union . . . And Why Bother?* Boulder, Col.: Rowman and Littlefield.

——(2004). 'The European Union is Not Democratic—So What?' *EUSA Review*, 17/1: 3–4.

——and Streeck, W. (1991). 'Organized Interests and the Europe of 1992', in N.J. Ornstein and M. Perlman (eds.), *Political Power and Social Change: The United States Faces a United Europe*. Washington, DC: AEI Press, 46–67.

Schneider, G. and Seybold, C. (1997). 'Twelve Tongues, One Voice: An Evaluation of European Political Cooperation'. *European Journal of Political Research*, 31: 367–96.

Scott, J. (1995). *Development Dilemmas in the European Community: Rethinking Regional Development Policy*. Buckingham and Philadelphia: Open University Press.

——(1998). 'Law, Legitimacy and EC Governance: Prospects for "Partnership"'. *Journal of Common Market Studies*, 36: 175–94.

Scott-Smith, G. (2003). 'Cultural Policy and Citizenship in the European Union: An Answer to the Legitimation Problem?', in A. Cafruny and G. Rosenthal (eds.), *The State of the European Community, Vol. 2: The Maastricht Debates and Beyond*. Boulder: Lynne Rienner; Harlow: Longman, 261–84.

Scully, R.M. (1997a). 'The European Parliament and the Co-decision Procedure: A Reassessment'. *Journal of Legislative Studies*, 3: 58–73.

——(1997b). 'The European Parliament and Co-Decision: A Rejoinder to Tsebelis and Garrett'. *Journal of Legislative Studies*, 3: 93–103.

Seers, D. and Vaitsos, C. (1980). *Integration and Unequal Development: The Experience of the EEC*. Basingstoke and London: Macmillan.

Servan-Schreiber, J.-J. (1968). *The American Challenge*. Harmondsworth: Penguin.

Shackleton, M. and Raunio, T. (2003). 'Codecision since Amsterdam: A Laboratory for Institutional Innovation and Change'. *Journal of European Public Policy*, 10: 171–87.

Sharp, M. (1989). 'The Community and the New Technologies' in J. Lodge (ed.), *The European Community and the Challenge of the Future* (1st edn). London: Pinter, 223–40.

——(1991). 'The Single Market and European Technology Policies' in C. Freeman, M. Sharp, and W. Walker (eds.), *Technology and the Future of Europe: Global Competition and the Environment in the 1990s*. London: Pinter Publishers, 59–76.

——and Shearman, C. (1987). *European Technological Collaboration*. London: Royal Institute of International Affairs/Routledge and Kegan Paul.

Shonfield, A. (1969). *Modern Capitalism: The Changing Balance of Public and Private Power*. Oxford: Oxford University Press.

Smith, A. (1992). 'National Identity and the Idea of European Unity.' *International Affairs*. 68: 55–76.

Smith, G. (1990). *European Court of Justice: Judges or Policy Makers?* London: Bruges Group.

——(2003). 'The Decline of Party', in J. Hayward and A. Menon (eds.), *Governing Europe*. Oxford: Oxford University Press, 179–91.

Smith, J. (James) (2001). 'Cultural Aspects of Europeanization—the case of the Scottish Office'. *Public Administration*, 79: 147–65.

Smith, J. (Julie) (1999). *Europe's Elected Parliament*. Sheffield: Sheffield Academic Press/University Association for Contemporary European Studies.

Smith, K. (2003). 'EU External Relations', in M. Cini (ed.), *European Union Politics*. Oxford: Oxford University Press, 229–45.

Smith, M.E. (1999). 'Rules, Transgovernmentalism, and the Expansion of European Political Cooperation' in W. Sandholtz and A. Stone Sweet (eds.), *European Integration and Supranational Governance*. Oxford: Oxford University Press, 304–33.

——(2000). 'Conforming to Europe: The Domestic Impact of EU Foreign Policy Co-operation'. *Journal of European Public Policy*, 7: 613–31.

——(2001). 'Diplomacy by Decree: The Legalization of EU Foreign Policy'. *Journal of Common Market Studies*, 39: 79–104.

——(2003). 'The Framing of European Foreign and Security Policy: Towards a Post-Modern Policy Framework?' *Journal of European Public Policy*, 10: 556–75.

——(2004) 'Institutionalization, Policy Adaptation and European Foreign Policy Cooperation'. *European Journal of International Relations*, 10: 95–136.

Smith, M.P. (1997). 'The Commission Made Me Do It: The European Commission as a Strategic Asset in Domestic Politics' in N. Nugent (ed.), *At the Heart of the Union: Studies of the European Commission*. Basingstoke and London: Macmillan, 167–86.

——(1998). 'Autonomy by the Rules: The European Commission and the Development of State Aid Policy'. *Journal of Common Market Studies*, 36: 55–78.

Spierenburg, D. and Poidevin, R. (1994). *The History of the High Authority of the European Coal and Steel Community: Supranationality in Action*. London: Weidenfeld.

Stevens, C. (1984). *The EEC and the Third World: A Survey. 4: Renegotiating Lomé*. London: Hodder and Stoughton.

——(2000). 'Trade with Developing Countries: Banana Skins and Turf Wars' in H. Wallace W. Wallace (eds.), *Policy-Making in the European Union*. Oxford: Oxford University Press, 4th edn, 401–26.

Stone Sweet, A. and Sandholtz, W. (1997). 'European Integration and Supranational Governance'. *Journal of European Public Policy*, 4: 297–317.

Strøby Jensen, C. (2000). 'Neofunctionalist Theories and the Development of European Social and Labour Market Policy'. *Journal of Common Market Studies*, 38: 71–92.

Swann, D. (1995). *The Economics of the Common Market: Integration in the European Union*. Harmondsworth: Penguin, 8th edn.

Swift, M. (1978). 'A Regional Policy for Europe'. *Young Fabian Pamphlet 48*. London: Fabian Society.

Taggart, Paul (1998). 'A Touchstone of Dissent: Euroscepticism in Contemporary Western European Party Systems'. *European Journal of Political Research*, 33: 363–88.

Tarrow, S. (2003). 'Contentious Politics in Western Europe and the United States', in J. Hayward and A. Menon (eds.), *Governing Europe*. Oxford: Oxford University Press, 231–49.

Tofarides, M. (2003). *Urban Policy in the European Union: A Multi-Level Gatekeeper System*, Aldershot: Ashgate.

Tranholm-Mikkelsen, J. (1991). 'Neofunctionalism: Obstinate or Obsolete? A Reappraisal in the Light of the New Dynamism of the European Community'. *Millennium*, 20: 1–22.

Tsakaloyannis, P. (1981). 'The Greco-Turkish Dispute in the Light of Enlargement', *Sussex European Papers no. 11: The Mediterranean Challenge VI*. Brighton: University of Sussex.

Tsebelis, G. and Garrett, G. (1996). 'Agenda Setting Power, Power Indices, and Decision Making in the European Union'. *International Review of Law and Economics*, 16: 345–61.

——(2000). 'Legislative Politics in the European Union'. *European Union Politics*, 1: 9–36.

——(2001). 'The Institutional Foundations of Intergovernmentalism and Supranationalism in the European Union', *International Organization*, 55: 357–90.

Tsoukalis, L. (1977*a*). *The Politics and Economics of European Monetary Integration*. London: Allen and Unwin.

——(1977*b*). 'Is the Launching of Economic and Monetary Union a Feasible Proposition?' *Journal of Common Market Studies*, 34: 531–48.

——(1996). 'Economic and Monetary Union: The Primacy of High Politics' in H. Wallace and W. Wallace (eds.), *Policy-Making in the European Union*. Oxford: Oxford University Press, 3rd edn, 279–99.

Urwin, D.W. (1985). *Western Europe since 1945: A Short Political History.* London and New York: Longman, 4th edn.

——(1995). *The Community of Europe : A History of European Integration since 1945.* London and New York: Longman, 2nd edn.

Van Apeldoorn, B., Overbeek, H., and Ryner, M. (2003). 'Theories of European Integration: A Critique', in A. Cafruny and M. Ryner (eds.), *A Ruined Fortress? Neoliberal Hegemony and Transformation in Europe.* Lanham: Rowman and Littlefield, 17–46.

Van der Eijk, C. and Franklin, M. (1996). *Choosing Europe? The European Electorate and National Politics in the Face of Union.* Ann Arbor, Mich.: University of Michigan Press.

Van Schendelen, M.P.C.M. (1996). ' "The Council Decides": Does the Council Decide?' *Journal of Common Market Studies,* 34: 531–48.

Verdun, A. (1999). 'The Role of the Delors Committee in the Creation of EMU: An Epistemic Community?' *Journal of Common Market Studies,* 34: 531–48.

——(2003). 'An American/European Divide in European Integration Studies: Bridging the Gap with International Political Economy'. *Journal of European Public Policy,* 10: 84–101.

Vibert, F. (1994). *The Future Role of the European Commission.* London: European Policy Forum.

Wagstyl, S. (2005). 'The Pull of the West: Why the Benefits Bestowed by Brussels have come early for the EU's Former Communist Countries'. *Financial Times,* 21 February.

Wallace, H. (1973). *National Governments and the European Communities.* London: Chatham House/ PEP.

——(1977*a*). 'National Bulls in the Community China Shop: The Role of National Governments in Community Policy-Making', in H. Wallace, W. Wallace, and C. Webb (eds.), *Policy-Making in the European Communities.* London: John Wiley and Sons, 1st edn, 33–68.

——(1977*b*). 'The Establishment of the Regional Development Fund: Common Policy or Pork Barrel?', in H. Wallace, W. Wallace, and C. Webb (eds.), *Policy-Making in the European Communities.* London: John Wiley and Sons, 1st edn, 137–63.

——(1983*a*). 'Negotiation, Conflict and Compromise: The Elusive Pursuit of Common Policies', H. Wallace, W. Wallace, and C. Webb (eds.), *Policy-Making in the European Communities.* London: John Wiley and Sons Ltd, 2nd edn, 43–80.

——(1983*b*). 'Distributional Politics: Dividing up the Community Cake' H. Wallace, W. Wallace,

and C. Webb (eds.), *Policy Making in the European Communities.* London: John Wiley and Sons Ltd, 2nd edn, 81–113.

——(1986). 'The British Presidency of the European Community's Council of Ministers'. *International Affairs,* 62: 583–99.

——(1997). 'Introduction' in H. Wallace and A.R. Young (eds.), *Participation and Policy-Making in the European Union.* Oxford: Clarendon Press, 1–16.

——(1999). 'Piecing the Integration Jigsaw Together'. *Journal of European Public Policy,* 6: 155–79.

——(2000*a*). 'Europeanisation and Globalisation: Complementary or Contradictory Trends?' *New Political Economy,* 5: 369–82.

——(2000*b*). 'Flexibility: A Tool of Integration or a Restraint on Disintegration?', K. Neunreither and A. Wiener (eds.), *European Integration after Amsterdam: Institutional Dynamics and Prospects for Democracy.* Oxford: Oxford University Press, 175–91.

——(2005). 'An Institutional Anatomy and Five Policy Models', in H. Wallace, W. Wallace, and M. Pollack (eds.), *Policy-Making in the European Union.* Oxford: Oxford University Press, 5th edn, 49–92.

——and Young, A. (2004). 'The Kaleidoscope of European Policy Making: Shifting Patterns of Participation and Influence', in H. Wallace and A.R. Young (eds.), *Participation and Policy Making in the European Union.* Oxford: Clarendon Press, 235–50.

Wallace, W. and Allen, D. (1977). 'Political Co-operation: Procedure as Substitute for Policy' H. Wallace, W. Wallace, and C. Webb (eds.), *Policy Making in the European Communities.* London: John Wiley and Sons, 1st edn, 227–48.

Warleigh, A. (2003) *Democracy in the European Union.* London: Sage.

Warley, T.K. (1992). 'Europe's Agricultural Policy in Transition'. *International Journal,* 47: 112–35.

Watson, R. (1998). 'Sweetening the Bitter Pill of Budget Consolidation'. *European Voice,* 26, March-April: 16.

Weale, A. (1997). 'Democratic Theory and the Constitutional Politics of the European Union'. *Journal of European Public Policy,* 4: 665–9.

——(1999). *Democracy.* London: Macmillan.

Weiler, J.H.H. (1993). 'Journey to an Unknown Destination: A Retrospective and Prospective of the European Court of Justice in the Arena of Political Integration'. *Journal of Common Market Studies,* 31: 417–46.

Wiener, A. and Diez, T. (eds.) (2004). *European Integration Theory*. Oxford: Oxford University Press.

Wendon, B. (1998). 'The Commission as an Image-Venue Entrepreneur in EU Social Policy'. *Journal of European Public Policy*, 5: 339–53.

Wessels, W. (1991). 'The EC Council: The Community's Decision-Making Center', in R. Keohane and S. Hoffmann (eds.), *The New European Community: Decisionmaking and Institutional Change*. Boulder, San Francisco, and Oxford: Westview Press, 133–54.

—— (1996). 'Institutions of the EU system: Models of Explanation', in D. Rometsch, and W. Wessels (eds.), *The European Union and Member States: Towards Institutional Fusion?* Manchester: Manchester University Press, 20–36.

—— and Rometsch, D. (1996). 'Conclusion: European Union and National Institutions', in D. Rometsch, and W. Wessels (eds.), *The European Union and Member States: Towards Institutional Fusion?* Manchester: Manchester University Press, 329–65.

Westlake, M. (1994). *The European Parliament: A Modern Guide*. London: Pinter.

—— (1995). *The Council of the European Union*. London: Catermill.

Wilks, S. and McGowan, L. (1995). 'Disarming the Commission: The Debate over a European Cartel Office'. *Journal of Common Market Studies*, 33: 259–73.

Wincott, D. (1995). 'Institutional Interaction and European Integration: Towards an Everyday Critique of Liberal Intergovernmentalism'. *Journal of Common Market Studies*, 33: 597–609.

—— (2003). 'Beyond Social Regulation? New Instruments and/or a New Agenda for Social Policy at Lisbon?' *Public Administration*, 81: 533–53.

Wise, M. and Croxford, G. (1988). 'The European Regional Development Fund: Community Ideals and National Realities'. *Political Geography Quarterly*, 7: 161–82.

Wishlade, F. (1996). 'EU Cohesion Policy: Facts, Figures, and Issues' in L. Hooghe (ed.), *Cohesion Policy and European Integration*. Oxford: Oxford University Press, 27–58.

Wood, P.C. (1993). 'European Political Cooperation: Lessons from the Gulf War and Yugoslavia', in A. Cafruny and G. Rosenthal (eds.), *The State of the European Community, Vol. 2: The Maastricht Debates and Beyond*. Boulder: Lynne Rienner; Harlow: Longman, 227–44.

Wright, V. (1990). 'The Administrative Machine: Old Problems and New Dilemmas' in P. Hall, J. Hayward, and H. Machin (eds.), *Developments in French Politics*. Basingstoke and London: Macmillan, 114–32.

Young, A.R. (2000). 'The Adaptation of European Foreign Economic Policy'. *Journal of Common Market Studies*, 38: 93–116.

—— (2005), 'The Single Market', in H. Wallace, W. Wallace, and M. Pollack (eds.), *Policy-Making in the European Union*. Oxford: Oxford University Press, 5th edn, 93–112.

Glossary

acquis communautaire Often abbreviated simply to *acquis*, this is a French phrase for which it is difficult to find a precise English translation. A French–English dictionary would define *acquis* as something like 'acquired knowledge' or 'accumulated experience'; but the connotation in this phrase is much more like 'heritage'. The *acquis* is the body of laws, policies, and practices that have accumulated over the lifetime of the European Communities, and now the European Union. Any new member state joining the EU has to accept the *acquis* as part of its terms of entry. The adjective '*communautaire*', when applied to the *acquis* or to other nouns, means more than just 'of the (European) community'. It has connotations of something that is in sympathy with the co-operative spirit that informed the original EC. The term '*communitaire*', which can be found all too frequently in texts on the EU, is simply an incorrect piece of 'Franglais'.

balance of trade The difference between the exports and imports of a state, or other economic unit such as the EU.

Benelux This is an acronym made up of the first parts of the names of the member states: *Bel*gium, the *Net*herlands, and *Lux*embourg. The governments of these three states adopted a **customs union** while in exile in London in 1944, and extended this to an **economic union** on 1 January 1948.

The black box of the state The realist tradition in international relations assumed that relations between states could be understood without analysing the internal politics of the states. It was assumed that each state had a clear and abiding national interest, derived largely from its geographical position in the world and from strategic considerations such

as the need to prevent neighbouring states from being able to dominate the region, and the need to defend any colonies and overseas territories that the state might possess. This national interest was assumed to be stronger than any differences between political parties within the country, so that changes of government would produce little lasting change in foreign policy. Therefore, the state could be treated as though it were a 'black box' into which the analyst need not peer.

Bretton Woods In 1944 a major economic conference was held at Bretton Woods in New Hampshire, USA. Agreement was reached on the basis of a post-war international economic and monetary system. The key principles were free trade and monetary stability. Monetary stability was to be achieved by tying the value of national currencies to the US dollar, which in turn was tied to the value of gold at the rate of $35 per ounce. The **International Monetary Fund (IMF)** was set up to assist in the establishment of the system, and to provide short-term and medium-term loans to states experiencing temporary problems with their balance of payments. The system lasted until 1971, when it collapsed because the United States was forced to devalue the dollar against gold. It was temporarily replaced by the **Smithsonian agreements**.

common market A customs union, but with the addition of free movement of factors of production, including capital and labour (Swann 1995: 12–13).

corporatism/corporatist The terms corporatist and corporatism comes from the Latin verb *corporare*, meaning to form into a body. The process of forming individuals into collective bodies produces corporations, which are artificial persons created by individuals, who authorize the corporation to act on their behalf. Between the wars in Europe the idea of the 'corporate state' emerged, in which representation of the people would not be by geographical constituencies but through vocational corporations of the employers and employees in each trade and industry. It was seen as an alternative 'third way' between capitalism and Communism. In practice corporatism came to be most closely associated with the Fascist regime in Italy after 1928, and was widely imitated by other authoritarian regimes. This association discredited the term in the eyes of the Anglo-Saxon states, but the idea still held some resonance in Roman Catholic social thought, hence its revival, without the formal title of corporatism, in the post-war constitutions of some west European states.

customs union A free trade area, but with a single set of rules on trade with the outside world (Swann 1995: 12–13).

dirigisme A French term that translates literally into English as 'directionism'. It is an economic doctrine that gives a central role to the state in the direction of economic development under capitalism. Typically the state draws up a national economic plan that acts as a framework within which both state-sector and private-sector enterprises can co-ordinate their decisions on investments. The term 'indicative planning' is often used in English to suggest the same system.

economic union A common market with the addition of unified economic and monetary policies (Swann 1995: 12–13).

epistemology The theory of knowledge; about how knowledge is acquired and validated.

European Investment Bank (EIB) The EIB is an EU agency that is charged to provide capital at affordable rates to support projects that contribute to the integration, balanced development, and economic and social cohesion of the member states. It does this by raising funds itself on the capital markets, and then loaning the funds at favourable rates of interest to support projects that further these objectives. It also implements the financial components of agreements under the European development aid policies.

Eurosceptic(ism) Euroscepticism 'expresses the idea of contingent, or qualified opposition, as well as incorporating outright and unqualified opposition to the process of European integration' (Taggart 1998: 366).

free trade area Member states remove all tariff and quota barriers to trade between themselves, but retain independent trade policies with the outside world.

General Agreement on Tariffs and Trade (GATT) The GATT was negotiated in 1947 and started operation on 1 January 1948. It consisted of a standing conference for the negotiation of tariff cuts, and an agreement that all such cuts would be multilateral, not bilateral. This was embodied in the principle of 'most favoured nation treatment' for all signatories of the agreement: any trade concession extended by one member to another had to be extended to all other members. It was originally intended that the GATT would be one part of an overarching International Trade Organization (ITO), but this proposal ran into resistance in the US Congress, and never received ratification. The GATT held eight rounds of multilateral trade negotiations, culminating in the Uruguay Round, which opened in Punte del Este, Uruguay in 1986 and was not completed until 1994. It was this Round that focused attention on the trade-distorting effects of the EU's common agricultural policy. One of the agreements in the Uruguay Round was the creation of a new World Trade Organization (WTO), which began operation on 1 January 1995. Its functions are: to administer WTO trade agreements; to act as a forum for trade negotiations; to handle trade disputes; to monitor national trade policies; to provide technical assistance and training for developing countries; to co-operate with other international organizations (*Source:* WTO Web Site http://www.wto.org/).

International Monetary Fund (IMF) The IMF was set up in 1944 to: promote international monetary co-operation; facilitate the expansion and balanced growth of international trade; to promote stability in exchange rates; to assist in the establishment of a multilateral system of payments in respect of trade between member states; to contribute to the elimination of foreign exchange restrictions; to provide short-term and medium-term loans to states experiencing temporary balance of payments difficulties (*Source:* IMF Web Site http://www.imf.org/external/about.htm).

investment capital Refers to assets that are invested in a country in the form of factories, businesses, etc.

liquid capital Refers to assets that are placed into bank deposits or similar sources from which they may quickly be withdrawn and transferred elsewhere.

neo-corporatism/neo-corporatist In the 1970s academics coined the term 'neo-corporatism' to describe a relationship between the state and organized economic interests that was less formal than **corporatism**, but nevertheless institutionalized patterns of consultation on policy between governments, business, and trade unions in several leading west European states.

ontology Refers to the nature of being; an underlying understanding of the world.

Organization of the Petroleum Exporting Countries (OPEC) OPEC was created at a conference of petroleum exporting states in Baghdad in 1960. The founder members were Iran, Iraq, Kuwait, Saudi Arabia, and Venezuela. They were later joined by eight other Members: Qatar (1961), Indonesia (1962), Libya (1962), the United Arab Emirates (1967), Algeria (1969), Nigeria (1971), Ecuador (1973–92), and Gabon (1975–94). OPEC's objective is to co-ordinate and unify petroleum policies among Member Countries, in order to secure fair and stable prices for petroleum producers; an efficient, economic and regular supply of petroleum to consuming nations; and a fair return on capital to those investing in the industry (*Source:* OPEC Web Site http://www.opec.org/193.81.181.14/xxx1/history.htm).

pareto-optimality The 'best that could be achieved without disadvantaging at least one group' (Allen Schick cited in Louis C. Gawthrop, 1970, p. 32—Web Dictionary of Cybernetics and Systems http://pespmc1.vub.ac.be/ACS/PARETO_OPTIM.html).

pluralism/pluralist In a pluralist system, interest groups lobby the formal institutions to try to get their preferred legislative options. It is a competitive system of seeking influence, but although early pluralist theories suggested that there was a level playing-field of competition, it is now generally accepted that some groups have greater resources than others, and so benefit more from this form of interest representation.

policy entrepreneur A policy actor who seeks to exploit favourable political conditions in order to promote a particular initiative or policy.

principal-agent theory A branch of rational choice theory that investigates the relationship between institutions that delegate tasks and authority (the principals) and the institutions to which they delegate (the agents). The main concern of principal-agent theory is to investigate the degree to which agents can 'cut slack' so as to achieve a degree of freedom from their principals, freedom that they can use to follow their own agenda rather than the agenda of the principals. Principal-agent theory has been widely used in the investigation of the degree of freedom available to Federal Agencies in the United States, and in discussion of the relationship of the European Commission to the governments of the member states.

public procurement Purchases of goods and services by governments or other public agencies for use in the public sector, covering everything from paper clips to major projects of civil engineering such as the construction of highways.

Smithsonian agreements In 1971 the **Bretton Woods** system of international payments, which had been set up at the end of the war collapsed. It was replaced by a new set of agreements that were signed at the Smithsonian Institute in Washington DC in December 1971. Under these arrangements, the dollar was substantially devalued against all other currencies, and the major central banks of all other states agreed to try to hold the value of their currencies in a range of fluctuation of 2¼ per cent either side of the US dollar, a maximum range of fluctuation of 4½ per cent. This attempt to restore fixed exchange rates collapsed in March 1973 in the face of extreme speculative pressure, and the world then entered the era of floating exchange rates that we have today.

stagflation Economists used to believe that there was a trade-off between economic growth and inflation. Policies could either promote economic growth, at the price of higher inflation; or they could focus on restraining inflation at the cost of lower rates of economic growth. Governments made policy choices based on this assumption: some aimed for lower growth in return for low inflation; others preferred high rates of inflation in order to promote high rates of growth. However, following the oil crisis in 1973, the trade-off no longer seemed to work. States began to experience the worst of both worlds: stagnation with inflation, or 'stagflation' as it became known.

subsidiarity Subsidiarity is an ambiguous concept and is taken to mean different things by different political actors. For example, it is interpreted by the British government to mean that action should not be taken at the EU level unless it can be shown that the objectives of the action can be better achieved at that level than at the national level. This interpretation appears to be supported by the wording of Article 5 (formerly 3b) of the TEC. The German government interprets it more generally to mean that decisions should be taken at the lowest level of government at which they can be made effective. This implies a commitment to internal devolution of power within states. This interpretation appears to be supported by the wording of Article 1 (formerly A) of the TEU.

supranational institutions 'Supranational' literally means 'above the national'. A supranational institution is one that has power or influence going beyond that permitted to it by national governments. An international institution, in contrast, is one that results from the co-operation of national governments, and has no power beyond that permitted to it by those governments.

transnational and transgovernmental networks Links across national boundaries between interest groups and individuals outside of government (transnational) or between departments of national government and individuals working for governments (transgovernmental), which are not monitored or controlled by national foreign offices or other core departments of the executive.

variable-geometry Europe The term used to describe 'the idea of a method of differentiated integration which acknowledges that there are irreconcilable differences within the integration structure and therefore allows for a permanent separation between a group of Member States and a number of less developed integration units' (http://europa.eu.int/scadplus/leg/en/cig/g4000v).

World Bank (International Bank for Reconstruction and Development or IBRD) The IBRD was founded in 1944 to give loans to states to aid their economic recovery. It is now one of five closely associated institutions that together constitute the World Bank Group: the IBRD, which provides loans and development assistance to middle-income countries and creditworthy poorer countries; the International Development Association (IDA), which is focused on the poorest countries, providing them with interest-free loans and other services; the International Finance Corporation (IFC), which promotes growth in the developing world by financing private sector investments and providing technical assistance and advice to governments and businesses; the Multilateral Investment Guarantee Agency (MIGA), which helps encourage foreign investment in developing countries by providing guarantees to foreign investors against loss caused by non-commercial risks; the International Centre for Settlement of Investment Disputes (ICSID), which provides conciliation and arbitration facilities for the settlement of investment disputes between foreign investors and their host countries (*Source:* World Bank Group Web Site http://www.worldbank.org/html/extdr/about/wbgis.htm).

Abbreviations and Acronyms

AASM Associated African States and Madagascar

ACP African, Caribbean, and Pacific

AKP Justice and Development Party (Turkey)

APEC Asia Pacific Economic Cooperation

BBC British Broadcasting Corporation

BDI Bundesverband der deutschen Industrie

Benelux Belgium, the Netherlands, and Luxemburg

BkartA Bundeskartellamt (German Cartel Office)

BSE Bovine Spongiform Encephalopathy

CAP Common Agricultural Policy

CBI Confederation of British Industry

CCC Coalfield Communities Campaign

CdP Commissariat du Plan (French Economic Planning Commission)

CDU Christian Democratic Union

CEEC Committee for European Economic Co-operation

CEECs Central and East European Countries

CEEP European Centre of Public Enterprises

CEN European Committee for Standardization

CENLEC European Committee for Standardization of Electrical Products

CEPS Centre for European Policy Studies

CET Common External Tariff

CFDT *Confédération Française Démocratique du Travail*

CFP Common Fisheries Policy

CFSP Common Foreign and Security Policy

CGT Confédération Générale du Travail

CNPF *Conseil National du Patronat Français*

CSFs Community Support Frameworks

CI Community Initiative

CJD Creutzfeldt-Jakob Disease

COPA Committee of Professional Agricultural Organizations of the European Community

CoR Committee of the Regions and Local Authorities

COREPER Committee of Permanent Representatives

COREU *Correspondance Européenne (Telex link)*

COSAC Conference of European Affairs Committees of the Parliaments of the European Union

CSCE Conference on Security and Cooperation in Europe

CP Comparative Politics

CSU Christian Social Union (Germany)

DDR Deutsche Demokratische Republic (East Germany)

DG Directorate General

DTI Department of Trade and Industry (Britain)

EAGGF European Agricultural Guarantee and Guidance Fund

EBRD	European Bank for Reconstruction and Development
EC	European Community
ECB	European Central Bank
ECHO	European Community Humanitarian Aid Office
ECHR	European Court of Human Rights
ECO	European Cartel Office
ECOFIN	Council of Economic and Finance Ministers
ECSC	European Coal and Steel Community
ECJ	European Court of Justice
ECU	European Currency Unit
EDC	European Defence Community
EdF	Electricité de France
EDF	European Development Fund
EEA	European Economic Area
EEC	European Economic Community
EES	European Economic Space
EFTA	European Free Trade Association
EIB	European Investment Bank
EMCF	European Monetary Cooperation Fund
EMF	European Monetary Fund
EMI	European Monetary Institute
EMS	European Monetary System
EMU	Economic and Monetary Union
ENP	European Neighbourhood Policy
ENPI	European Neighbourhood and Partnership Instrument
EP	European Parliament
EPA	European Parliamentary Assembly
EPAs	Economic Partnership Agreements
EPC	(1) European Political Community (till 1952); (2) European Political Co-operation

ERDF	European Regional Development Fund (see also RDF)
ERI	Extraterritorial Income
ERM	Exchange Rate Mechanism
ERP	European Recovery Programme ('Marshall Plan')
ERT	European Round Table of Industrialists
ESC	Economic and Social Committee
ESCB	European System of Central Banks
ESDP	European Security and Defence Policy
ESF	European Social Fund
ESPRIT	European Strategic Programme for Research and Development in Information Technology
ETUC	European Trade Union Confederation
EU	European Union
EUA	European Unit of Account
EUF	European Union of Federalists
EURACOM	European Action for Mining Communities
Euratom	European Atomic Energy Community
EUREKA	European Research Co-ordination Agency
FO	Foreign Office (Britain)
FDP	Free Democrat Party (Germany)
FN	Front National (National Front, France)
FSC	Foreign Sales Corporation
FYROM	Former Yugoslav Republic of Macedonia
GATT	General Agreement on Tariffs and Trade
GdF	*Gaz de France*
GDP	Gross Domestic Product
GM	Genetically Modified
GNP	Gross National Product

HMSO	Her Majesty's Stationery Office
IAR	International Authority for the Ruhr
IBM	International Business Machines
IBRD	International Bank for Reconstruction and Development
ICSID	International Centre for Settlement of Investment Disputes
IDA	International Development Association
IFC	International Finance Corporation
IGC	Intergovernmental Conference
IMF	International Monetary Fund
IMPs	Integrated Mediterranean Programmes
INTUG	Information Technology User Group
IPE	International Political Economy
IR	International Relations
ISPA	Pre-accession Structural Instrument
ITO	International Trade Organization
JHA	Justice and Home Affairs
KFOR	Kosovo Force
LDCs	Less Developed Countries
MAFF	Ministry of Agriculture, Fisheries and Food (Britain)
MCAs	Monetary Compensation Amounts
MEP	Member of the European Parliament
MFN	Most Favoured Nation
MIGA	Multilateral Investment Guarantee Agency
MoU	Memorandum of Understanding
MRP	Mouvement Républicain Populaire (France)
NAFTA	North American Free Trade Association

NAPS	National Action Plans for Employment
NATO	North Atlantic Treaty Organization
NFU	National Farmers' Union (UK)
NUM	National Union of Mineworkers (Britain)
NPD	National Democratic Party (Germany)
NTB	Non-Tariff Barrier
OECD	Organization for Economic Cooperation and Development
OEEC	Organization for European Economic Cooperation
OLAF	European Anti-Fraud Office
OMC	Open Method of Co-ordination
ONP	Open Network Provision
OPEC	Organization of Petroleum Exporting Countries
OSCE	Organization for Security and Cooperation in Europe
PASOK	Panhellenic Socialist Party (Greece)
PCP	Portuguese Communist Party
PHARE	Poland–Hungary: Actions for Economic Reconstruction
PR	Proportional Representation
PS	*Parti Socialiste* (Socialist Party, France)
PSOE	Spanish Socialist Workers Party
PSP	Portuguese Socialist Party
PTT	Post, Telegraph, and Telephone Companies
QMV	Qualified Majority Voting
RDF	Regional Development Fund
Rechar	Community Initiative Programme for the Conversion of Coal Mining Areas
REPAs	Regional Economic Partnership Agreements
RPF	*Rassemblement du Peuple Français* (Gaullist Party, France)

RPR	*Rassemblement pour la République*
SAA	Stabilization and Association Agreement
SAP	Stabilization and Association Process
SAPARD	Special Accession Programme for Agriculture and Rural Development
SARS	Severe Acute Respiratory Syndrome
SDP	Social Democratic Party (Britain)
SEA	Single European Act
SHAPE	Supreme Allied Headquarters Europe
SPD	*Sozialdemokratische Partei Deutschlands* (Social Democratic Party, Germany)
Stabex	System for the Stabilization for Export Earnings
Sysmin	System for the Stabilization of Mineral Export Earnings
TABD	Transatlantic Business Dialogue

TACIS	Technical Assistance for the Commonwealth of Independent States
TEC	Treaty Establishing the European Community
TENS	Trans-European Networks
TEU	Treaty on European Union
UDF	Union pour la Démocratie Française
UKIP	UK Independence Party
UNICE	Union of Industrial and Employers' Confederations of Europe
UN	United Nations
US	United States
USA	United States of America
USSR	Union of Soviet Socialist Republics
VAT	Value Added Tax
WEU	Western European Union
WTO	World Trade Organization

Chronology

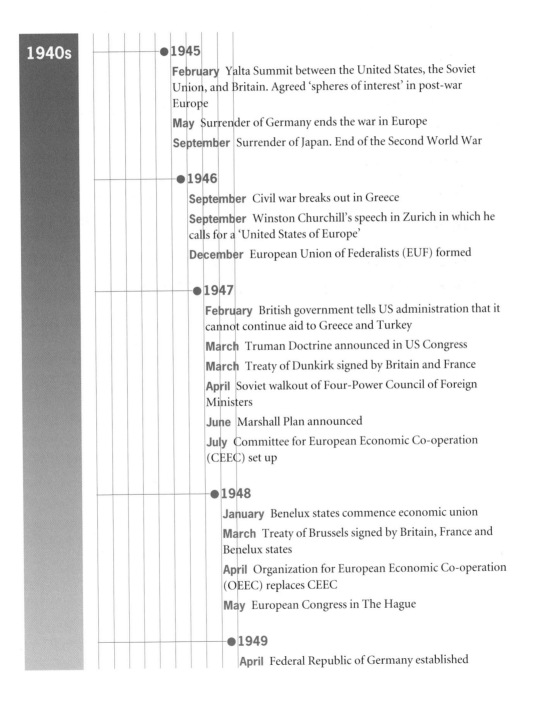

1940s

●1945

February Yalta Summit between the United States, the Soviet Union, and Britain. Agreed 'spheres of interest' in post-war Europe

May Surrender of Germany ends the war in Europe

September Surrender of Japan. End of the Second World War

●1946

September Civil war breaks out in Greece

September Winston Churchill's speech in Zurich in which he calls for a 'United States of Europe'

December European Union of Federalists (EUF) formed

●1947

February British government tells US administration that it cannot continue aid to Greece and Turkey

March Truman Doctrine announced in US Congress

March Treaty of Dunkirk signed by Britain and France

April Soviet walkout of Four-Power Council of Foreign Ministers

June Marshall Plan announced

July Committee for European Economic Co-operation (CEEC) set up

●1948

January Benelux states commence economic union

March Treaty of Brussels signed by Britain, France and Benelux states

April Organization for European Economic Co-operation (OEEC) replaces CEEC

May European Congress in The Hague

●1949

April Federal Republic of Germany established

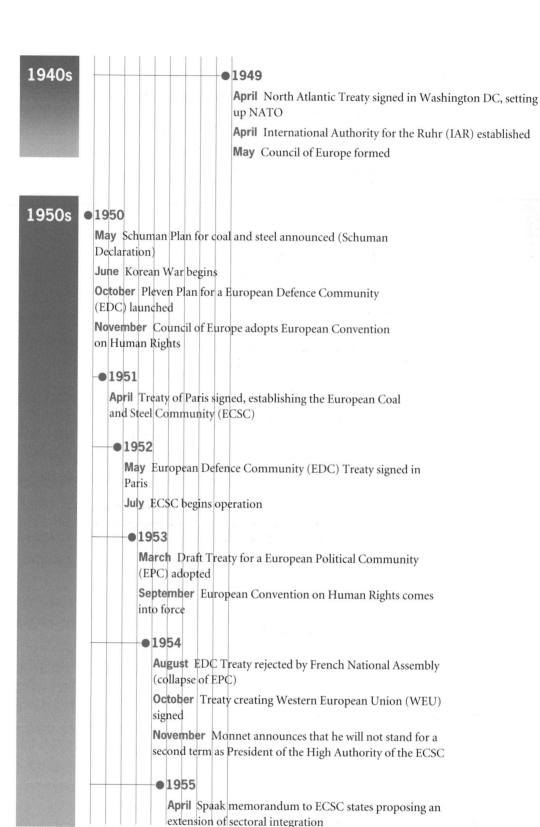

1940s

1949

April North Atlantic Treaty signed in Washington DC, setting up NATO

April International Authority for the Ruhr (IAR) established

May Council of Europe formed

1950s

1950

May Schuman Plan for coal and steel announced (Schuman Declaration)

June Korean War begins

October Pleven Plan for a European Defence Community (EDC) launched

November Council of Europe adopts European Convention on Human Rights

1951

April Treaty of Paris signed, establishing the European Coal and Steel Community (ECSC)

1952

May European Defence Community (EDC) Treaty signed in Paris

July ECSC begins operation

1953

March Draft Treaty for a European Political Community (EPC) adopted

September European Convention on Human Rights comes into force

1954

August EDC Treaty rejected by French National Assembly (collapse of EPC)

October Treaty creating Western European Union (WEU) signed

November Monnet announces that he will not stand for a second term as President of the High Authority of the ECSC

1955

April Spaak memorandum to ECSC states proposing an extension of sectoral integration

1950s

1955

April Beyen memorandum on behalf of the Benelux states proposing a general common market

June Messina conference agrees to set up Spaak Committee to consider future of integration

October Monnet sets up Action Committee for the United States of Europe

1956

March Spaak Report published

May Governments agree Spaak Report

June Start of 'Messina negotiations' based on the Spaak Report

October USSR invades Hungary to put down anti-communist uprising

October Suez crisis: Israel, Britain, and France attack Egypt and occupy Port Said, but forced to withdraw their troops in the face of opposition from the United States

1957

March Completion of 'Messina negotiations'

April Treaties of Rome (establishing the EEC and Euratom) signed

1958

January EEC and Euratom begin operations: Walter Hallstein becomes the first President of the EEC Commission, Louis Armand the first President of the Euratom Commission

July CAP system of common prices agreed at Stresa Conference

1959

January Customs duties within the EEC cut by 10 per cent

1960s

1960

May Acceleration agreement on the common market and agricultural policy between six EC states

December Organization for Economic Co-operation and Development (OECD) supersedes OEEC

1961

February Paris summit agrees to set up committee under Christian Fouchet to review co-operation

1960s

1961

March Fouchet negotiations begin

July Association Agreement signed with Greece

August Britain, Denmark, and Ireland apply for membership of the EC

December Commission convenes first conference on European regional policy

1962

April Norway applies to join the EEC

July CAP system of common prices agreed at Stresa Conference

December Nassau agreement between Macmillan and Kennedy

1963

January De Gaulle announces his veto of British membership

July First Yaoundé Convention comes into effect

September Association Agreement signed with Turkey

1965

April Merger Treaty signed, agreeing to merge the institutions of the ECSC, EEC, and Euratom

July Start of French boycott of the Council of Ministers

1966

January Luxemburg compromise

1967

May Britain, Denmark, and Ireland make a second application for membership of the EC

July Norway makes a second application for membership of the EC

July Sweden applies for EEC membership

July Merger Treaty takes effect: Jean Rey is first Commission President for all three communities (ECSC, EEC, Euratom)

December France blocks agreement on opening negotiations with the applicant states

1968

July Customs Union completed and common external tariff established

1960s

● **1968**

December Commission produces 'Mansholt Plan' for restructuring EC agriculture

● **1969**

December Hague summit: the 'relaunching of Europe'

1970s ● **1970**

June Membership negotiations begin with Britain, Ireland, Denmark, and Norway

July Franco Malfatti becomes President of the European Commission

October Davignon Report on European political cooperation

● **1971**

January Second Yaoundé Convention signed

February Werner Report on economic and monetary union

March Start of first attempt to move to monetary union with the joint floating of European currencies

March Farmers demonstrate in Brussels against Mansholt Plan. Council of Agricultural Ministers agree a modified version of the Plan

August Ending of the convertibility of the US dollar into gold, marks the collapse of the Bretton Woods international monetary system, closely followed by the collapse of the first experiment with European monetary union

December Smithsonian agreements on international monetary regime to replace Bretton Woods

● **1972**

January Completion of membership negotiations with Britain, Ireland, Denmark, and Norway; Accession Treaties signed

March Sicco Mansholt becomes President of the European Commission

March Start of the 'snake in the tunnel' system of EC monetary co-ordination

March European Parliament accepts Commission proposals for creation of EC regional policy

May Irish referendum in favour of EC membership

June British Pound withdrawn from the 'snake in the tunnel'

September Norwegian referendum rejecting EC membership

October Danish referendum in favour of EC membership

1970s

●**1972**

October Paris summit accepts the case for EC regional policy
and requests the Commission to prepare a report on the issue

●**1973**

January François-Xavier Ortoli becomes Commission
President

January First enlargement of EC from six to nine member
states

February Italy forced to leave the 'snake'

May 'Thomson Report' on regional problems presented to the
Council of Ministers

December OPEC oil crisis

●**1974**

January France forced to leave the 'snake'

July Turkish invasion of Cyprus

December Paris summit: agrees to direct elections to the EP,
creation of the European Council, and the creation of the
European Regional Development Fund (ERDF)

●**1975**

January ERDF comes into operation

February First Lomé Convention comes into effect

March First European Council meeting in Dublin

July France rejoins the 'snake'

June British referendum agrees continued membership of EC

June Greek application for membership of EC

August Signing of the 'Final Act' at the Conference on Security
and Cooperation in Europe (CSCE) in Helsinki

●**1976**

January Commission Opinion on Greek application: not very
favourable

April France leaves the 'snake' for the second time

July Opening of Greek accession negotiations

●**1977**

January Roy Jenkins becomes President of the European
Commission

March Portuguese application for membership of the EC

1970s

● 1977

July Spanish application for membership of the EC

October Jenkins lecture at the European University Institute, Florence: calls for a new attempt at monetary union

● 1978

July Bremen European Council agrees to pursue proposal from Schmidt and Giscard for a 'zone of monetary stability in Europe'

October Opening of accession negotiations with Portugal

December Bremen European Council agreed to create the European Monetary System (EMS)

● 1979

February Opening of accession negotiations with Spain

March EMS begins

May Greek Accession Treaty signed

June First direct elections to the European Parliament

June EC makes Venice Declaration recognizing the right of Palestinians to a homeland

November Dublin European Council: Prime Minister Thatcher demands a British budgetary rebate

December USSR invades Afghanistan

1980s

● 1980

March Second Lomé Convention comes into effect

June Venice Declaration of the EC member states on the situation in the Middle East

December Second stage of the EMS scheme postponed indefinitely

● 1981

January Gaston Thorn becomes President of the European Commission

January Greece becomes a member of the EC

October London Report on European Political Co-operation (EPC) published

November Genscher-Colombo Plan calls for a new European Charter to replace the treaties and form a constitution for the European Communities

1980s

● 1982

June EMS currencies realigned. French socialist government agrees to reform its domestic economic policies and to retreat from its attempts to reflate the economy

● 1983

January Stuttgart European Council signs Solemn Declaration on European Union

March Further realignment of EMS currencies

● 1984

February European Parliament approves draft treaty on European Union

March System of quotas for dairy products agreed as part of reform of CAP

June Fontainebleau European Council: British budgetary dispute settled; Dooge Committee on institutional reform set up

June Elections to European Parliament

December Third Lomé Convention signed

● 1985

January Jacques Delors becomes President of the European Commission

February Brussels European Council: mandates Commission to produce a plan or the single European market

June Cockfield White Paper on the freeing of the internal market

June Portuguese and Spanish Accession Treaties signed

June Milan European Council: 1992 programme agreed

December Single European Act agreed in principle by heads of government at Luxemburg European Council

● 1986

January Portugal and Spain join the EC

February Single European Act signed by Foreign Ministers in Luxemburg (nine states) and subsequently the Hague (the remaining three states)

● 1987

April Turkey applies for EC membership

July Single European Act comes into effect

1980s

●1988

February Brussels European Council: agrees to a doubling of the structural funds Legal limit placed on increases in spending on agricultural support

June Hanover European Council: sets up the Delors Committee on monetary union

July Jacques Delors makes a speech to the EP in which he predicts that in ten years time 80 per cent of economic legislation will be directed from Brussels; infuriates British Prime Minister Thatcher

September Margaret Thatcher's Bruges speech

●1989

January Reformed structural funds, with new policy principles agreed during 1988, come into operation

January Start of revived 'social dialogue' between representatives of employers and trade unions

June Delors Report on monetary union. Accepted by heads of government at Madrid European Council

June Elections to European Parliament

July German monetary union

July Austria applies for EC membership

September Start of collapse of communism in Eastern Europe

October Delors lectures to the College of Europe in Bruges

December Fourth Lomé Convention signed

December Strasburg European Council sets up an Inter-governmental Conference (IGC) to consider institutional changes necessary for completing monetary union

1990s

●1990

July Stage 1 of Economic and Monetary Union begins

July Cyprus applies for EC membership

July Malta applies for EC membership

August Iraq invades Kuwait

October Re-unification of Germany; five new Länder become part of the EC

●1991

January Start of IGC on political union

June Start of conflict between federal Yugoslav army and Slovenian separatist forces

1990s

1991

July Sweden applies for EC membership

July Agriculture Commissioner MacSharry introduces his proposals for reform of the CAP

November EC imposes sanctions on Yugoslavia

December Maastricht European Council: agrees principles of Treaty on European Union (TEU), and to set up a Cohesion Fund to assist Greece, Spain, Ireland, and Portugal

1992

January Badinter Commission gives support for recognition of Macedonia and qualified support for Croatian independence

February Maastricht Treaty on European Union signed

March Finland applies for EC membership

May Switzerland applies for EC membership

May MacSharry proposals for reform of CAP agreed by Agriculture Ministers.

June Danish referendum rejects TEU

June WEU Petersberg Declaration commits member states to allocate armed forces to peace keeping and humanitarian tasks in Europe

September French referendum accepts TEU

September British forced to withdraw from exchange rate mechanism of EMS

November Norway applies for EC membership

November Blair House agreement between the EU and the USA on trade in agricultural goods: paves the way for the completion of the Uruguay Round of GATT negotiations

December Swiss referendum rejects membership of the European Economic Area: Swiss government withdraws application for membership of EC

December Edinburgh European Council agrees opt-out for Denmark from single currency

1993

May Second Danish referendum accepts TEU

August The ERM's 'narrow bands' have to be widened to 15 per cent to allow it to survive

November TEU comes into effect

December EU monitors observe Russian elections

1990s

● 1994

January Stage 2 of Economic and Monetary Union begins

January Start of European Economic Area (EEA)

January Reforms of structural funds agreed during 1993 come into effect

February Greek government refuses the Former Yugoslav Republic of Macedonia access to the port of Salonika

April Hungary applies for EU membership

April Poland applies for EU membership

June Austrian referendum in favour of EU membership

June Corfu European Council agrees to extend internal market to energy and telecommunications

June Elections to European Parliament

October Finnish referendum in favour of EU membership

November Swedish referendum in favour of EU membership

November Norwegian referendum rejects EU membership

● 1995

January Austria, Finland, and Sweden become members of the EU

January Jacques Santer becomes President of the European Commission

January World Trade Organization (WTO) begins to operate

January CSCE becomes the Organization for Security and Cooperation in Europe (OSCE)

March A 'Stability Pact' signed by 52 states from western and eastern Europe in an attempt to stabilize the political and security situation in eastern Europe

June Romania applies for EU membership

June Slovak Republic applies for EU membership

October Latvia applies for EU membership

November Estonia applies for EU membership

November Barcelona conference launches the process that leads to the 'Euro–Med' agreements between the EU and North African and other states bordering the Mediterranean

November Agriculture Commissioner Franz Fischler introduces his proposals for further reform of the CAP; they are subsequently incorporated into *Agenda 2000*

December Lithuania applies for EU membership

December Bulgaria applies for EU membership

1990s

● **1995**

December 'New Transatlantic Agenda' agreed between the EU and the USA

December Madrid European Council decides on 'Euro' as the name for the single currency

● **1996**

January Czech Republic applies for EU membership

June Slovenia applies for EU membership

March Intergovernmental Conference to review TEU officially opens in Turin

September Commission requests that member states extend its mandate in international trade negotiations to cover trade in services. This request is refused

December Dublin European Council agrees a 'stability pact' to support monetary union

● **1997**

June Amsterdam European Council: agreement on terms of Treaty of Amsterdam, including to supplement the stability pact with a growth and employment pact. All EU member states commit to the 'Petersberg tasks' as agreed by WEU members in June 1992.

July Publication of Commission's *Agenda 2000* on eastern enlargement and the reform of the CAP and structural funds.

October Treaty of Amsterdam signed

November Special 'jobs summit' held in Luxemburg to work out the principles of the 'co-ordinated strategy for employment' agreed at Amsterdam in June. Effectively the 'Luxemburg process' is the first example of the 'Open Method of Co-ordination' (OMC)

● **1998**

March Opening of accession negotiations with Cyprus, Czech Republic, Estonia, Hungary, Poland, and Slovenia

May Special European Council meeting in Brussels to launch the single currency. Wim Duisenberg chosen to be first President of the European Central Bank

December At the end of a bi-lateral summit at St. Malo in France, French President Chirac and British Prime Minister Blair announce their support for the development of a European Security and Defence Policy (ESDP)

1990s

1999

January The Euro comes into operation, although national notes and coins remain in circulation until 2002

February Negotiations over *Agenda 2000* proposals for agriculture begin.

March Resignation of the Santer Commission

March Berlin European Council agrees on a financial perspective for 2000-6, reform of CAP and structural funds, and to nominate Romano Prodi as the next President of the Commission

May Treaty of Amsterdam enters into force

May Prodi becomes President of the Commission

June Elections to European Parliament

December Helsinki European Council agrees to open accession negotiations with Bulgaria, Latvia, Lithuania, Malta, Romania, and Slovakia, and also recognizes Turkey as an applicant country. Adopts the 'headline goal' of creating a European Rapid Reaction Force by the end of 2003

2000s

2000

March Institutions of ESDP begin provisional operation

March Special European Council held in Lisbon agrees to a new EU strategy on employment, economic reform, and social cohesion, and makes a commitment to turn the EU into 'the most competitive knowledge-based economy in the world' by 2010

June Signing of Cotonou Agreement as successor to Lomé

June Greece gains approval to join single currency

September Danish people vote to reject adoption of the Euro

December Nice European Council agrees the Treaty of Nice and formally proclaims the Charter of Fundamental Rights of the European Union

2001

January Greece joins single currency

June Irish people vote to reject the Treaty of Nice

September Terrorist attacks in New York and Washington DC

September European Council votes to support United States and to develop EU response following September 11 terrorist attacks

2000s

●2001

November In the face of protests from other member states, a planned tri-lateral meeting in London between Blair, Chirac, and Schmidt, to co-ordinate their countries' responses to the September terrorist attacks, has to be widened to include the EU High Representative for the CFSP, the Belgian Presidency of the Council, and the leaders of Italy, Spain, and the Netherlands

December Laeken European Council adopts the Declaration on the Future of the European Union, preparing the ground for a European Constitution

●2002

January Citizens start using Euro notes and coins in the twelve participating member states

February Convention on the Future of Europe begins its deliberations in Brussels, chaired by former French President Giscard d'Estaing

December US President Bush identifies an 'axis of evil' that includes Iraq

●2003

February Treaty of Nice enters into force

March A coalition of states led by the United States and Britain invades Iraq. France and Germany condemn the invasion

March An EU force replaces the NATO stabilization force in Macedonia

April EP assents to the accession of ten new member states

June Agreement in Council of Ministers on final decoupling of agricultural payments from production

June Giscard d'Estaing presents draft EU Constitution to the European Council

September Swedish people vote to reject adoption of the Euro

October Rome IGC convenes to consider draft EU Constitution

November Jean-Claude Trichet replaces Wim Duisenberg as President of the ECB

November Eurozone Heads of Government decide not to impose sanctions on France and Germany for breaching the rules of the stability pact

December Proposals of the Constitutional Convention presented to the European Council

2000s

● **2004**

February Commission outlines its proposals for the operation of the structural funds in the period 2007–13

March Terrorist bombings in Madrid

April Adoption of an Internal Market Strategy to improve transposition of EU agreements into national law

May Ten new member states join the EU

June Elections to European Parliament, marked by a record low turn-out

June European Council nominates Portuguese Prime Minister José Manuel Durao Barroso as the next President of the Commission

October Treaty establishing a Constitution for Europe signed by the Heads of State and Government and the EU Foreign Ministers

November Barroso Commission eventually approved by EP, following resignation of controversial nominee Rocco Buttiglione

November Kok Report on the 'Lisbon Agenda' presented to the Commission

December Heads of government agree to open accession negotiations with Turkey

● **2005**

February Spanish people vote to approve the Constitutional Treaty

April Bulgaria and Romania sign Accession Treaties

May French people vote to reject the Constitutional Treaty

June Dutch people vote to reject the Constitutional Treaty

General Index

European Political Community
(EPC) 106, 108–10, 117, 118,
129
European Political Co-operation
(EPC) 142–3, 145, 153, 161,
196, 279, 373, 515
European Regional Development
Fund (ERDF) 365, 457, 458,
461, 462, 463, 464, 465, 466,
468, 470, 473, 481, 482, 484,
485
European Research
Co-ordination Agency
(EUREKA) 162, 408
European Round Table of
Industrialists (ERT) 154, 162,
164, 336, 369, 371, 411, 421,
423, 424, 552
European Security and Defence
Policy (ESDP) 110, 189, 195,
198, 201, 202–3, 208–9, 250,
254, 255, 258, 515, 523, 524,
525, 529, 530, 533
European single market /
internal market 17, 27, 40,
153–4, 156, 157, 158, 159,
160, 161, 162–3, 163–4, 167,
168, 173, 174–5, 181, 192,
206, 247, 264, 266, 270, 321,
327, 328, 333, 332, 336, 337,
351, 355, 359, 360, 361, 362,
369, 371, 373, 374, 376
European Social Fund (ESF) 235,
364, 458, 465, 466, 470, 481
European Strategic Programme
for Research and
Development in Information
Technology (ESPRIT) 371,
376
European System of Central
Banks (ESCB) 245, 272, 442
European Trade Union
Confederation (ETUC) 337,
365
European Union of Federalists
(EUF) 6–7, 84, 91
European University Institute
149
European Works Councils 336
Europeanization 1, 16, 17, 27, 28,
33, 45, 55, 57, 58–65, 74–5,
75–6, 368
Euroscepticism 75, 206, 213, 217,
261, 586
Eurosclerosis 157, 371
Exchange Rate Mechanism
(ERM) 190, 414, 432–4, 437,
440, 446, 453

F

fascism 6, 83, 98
federal-functionalism *see*
'functional-federalism'
federalism 5, 6–7, 8, 18, 19, 35,
37, 81, 82–4, 90, 91, 92, 103,
106, 109, 110, 117, 155, 160,
205, 207, 422
Federation of German Industry
*see Bundesverband der
Deutschen Industrie* (BDI)
Figaro 181
Financial Instrument of Fisheries
Guidance (FIFG) 458, 460,
481
Finebel 96
Finet, Paul 120, 121, 123
Finland 262, 416, 449, 468, 476,
498, 499, 524, 537, 543–8,
551, 556, 562
Fischler, Frans 395, 396, 497
fisheries *see* Common Fisheries
Policy (CFP) *and* Financial
Instrument of Fisheries
Guidance (FIFG)
flexible integration 111, 177,
180–1, 186, 187, 188, 189
Ford Report 345, 346
Former Yugoslav Republic of
Macedonia (FYRoM) 204,
498, 500, 520, 525, 553, 563
Fouchet, Christian 132
Fouchet negotiations 132, 136
Fouchet Plan 132, 136, 143, 515,
528, 540, 541
France 4, 6, 7, 8, 19, 59, 61, 72,
82, 83–4, 86, 89, 93, 94, 95–7,
98, 101, 104, 107–9, 110,
112–16, 117, 118, 119, 121,
122, 124–5, 126, 129, 132–4,
136, 140, 142, 144, 145, 149,
152, 156, 158, 159, 172, 175,
(176), 178–84, 187, 190,
195–7, 201, 202–4, 207–8,
210, 213, 214, 217, 222, 224,
251, 261, 279, 289, 299, 300,
306, 325, 329, 336, 337, 363,
364, 369, 380, 381, 382, 383,
384, 385, 386, 387, 388, 393,
394, 395, 396, 399, 400, 404,
405, 406, 407, 414–15, 416,
417, 420, 422, 423, 424, 425,
428, 429, 430, 431, 432, 433,
435, 436, 438, 439, 440, 441,
443, 444, 445, 446, 447, 448,

449, 450, 451, 452, 453, 454,
458, 460, 461, 469, 482, 483,
492, 495, 496, 497, 499, 501,
502, 508, 516, 518, 519, 520,
521, 522, 523, 524, 525, 529,
530, 531, 533, 539, 540, 541,
542, 552, 556, 558, 560, 561,
562, 563
Franco, Francisco 150
Frankfurter Allgemeine Zeitung
208
Frattini, Franco 215
fraud 171, 186, 191–2, 199, 273,
274, 303, 359–60, 376
Free Democrat Party (FDP)
(Germany) 139, 153, 383,
385–7, 388, 413, 439
functional-federalism 5, 7–8
functionalism 5, 6, 19, 83, 116

G

Galle Report 345
Galle, Marc 345
gatekeeper/gatekeeping 35, 389,
474, 479, 480, 484, 486
Gaz de France (GdF) 369, 421
General Agreement on Tariffs
and Trade (GATT) 138, 391,
392, 393, 394, 395, 397, 399,
401, 489, 490, 495, 496, 506,
507, 510, 511, 586
genetically modified foods *see*
GM foods
Genscher-Colombo Plan 153,
156
Genscher, Hans Dietrich 153,
413, 445, 446
Georgia 281, 500, 512, 554
Germany (pre-1949) 82, 83, 84,
86, 88, 89, 91, 93, 107
Germany, Democratic Republic
86, 107, 144, 172, 179, 435,
446, 537
Germany, Federal Republic 4, 8,
19, 76, 86, 88, 89, 91, 94,
95–101, 103, 104–5, 107–10,
112–16, 117, 118, 120–5, 126,
129, 130, 132, 139, 142, 144,
145, 149, 151–3, 154, 156,
158, 159, 163, 166, 168–73,
175, 176, 178–84, 186, 187,
190, 196–7, 201, 203–4,
207–8, 211, 213, 214, 238,
251, 261, 279, 289, 299, 301,
317, 325, 329, 336, 367, 368,

Westendorp, Carlos 184
Western European Union
  (WEU) 110, 184, 186, 232,
  519–21, 524, 527, 530
Williamson, David 161, 413
Wilson, Harold 141, 145, 155
Wilson, Woodrow 83
World Bank 138, 489, 504, 508,
  553, 559, 563, 588
World Trade Organisation
  (WTO) 33, 394, 488, 489–90,

491–4, 497, 499, 506–9, 511,
  512
Wulf-Mathies, Monika 193

Y

Yalta Conference (1945)
  85–6
Yanukovich, Viktor 212
Yaoundé Convention 502, 512

Yeltsin, Boris 554
Yugoslavia 98, 195, 204, 373, 498,
  519–21, 523, 532, 543, 551,
  553, 554, 563
Yuschenko, Viktor 212

Z

Zoellick, Robert 497

Author Index

AUTHOR INDEX